"*Fields, Capitals, Habitus* does not just duplicate some forty years later Bourdieu's *Distinction* model on the Australian case. By making this analytical framework travel through time and from one society to another, it puts it to the test, demonstrates its fecundity, and also complements it by integrating new issues (on the relations between ethnicity, Indigeneity and culture in particular). In addition to the formidable empirical knowledge of the social and cultural structures of contemporary Australia that it provides, this intellectual journey makes an essential contribution to the analysis of the role of culture in social life."

Vincent Dubois, *Professor of Sociology, University of Strasbourg, France*

"*Fields, Capitals, Habitus* is the definitive study of how and why Australians make choices about their tastes and practices across a range of cultural areas. Its breadth of reference and its methodological sophistication – especially its fine-grained sensitivity to the specific shape of different cultural fields – make it the outstanding sociological account of Australian culture, and it has important and interesting things to say about the relation between symbolic practices and social power. It is notable for the weight it gives to studying ethnicity and Australian Indigenous culture, something that has never been done with this degree of evidence in previous studies."

John Frow, *Professor of English, University of Sydney, Australia*

FIELDS, CAPITALS, HABITUS

Fields, Capitals, Habitus provides an insightful analysis of the relations between culture and society in contemporary Australia. Presenting the findings of a detailed national survey of Australian cultural tastes and practices, it demonstrates the pivotal significance of the role culture plays at the intersections of a range of social divisions and inequalities: between classes, age cohorts, ethnicities, genders, city and country, and the relations between Indigenous and non-Indigenous Australians.

The book looks first at how social divisions inform the ways in which Australians from different social backgrounds and positions engage with the genres, institutions and particular works of culture and cultural figures across six cultural fields: the visual arts, literature, music, heritage, television and sport. It then examines how Australians' cultural preferences across these fields interact within the Australian 'space of lifestyles'. The close attention paid to class here includes an engagement with the role of 'middlebrow' cultures in Australia and the role played by new forms of Indigenous cultural capital in the emergence of an Indigenous middle class. The spatial distribution of cultural capital and its relations to different types and levels of education are also considered.

The rich survey data is complemented throughout by in-depth qualitative data provided by interviews with survey participants. These are discussed more closely in the final part of the book which explores the gendered, political, personal and community associations of cultural tastes across Australia's Anglo-Celtic, Italian, Lebanese, Chinese and Indian populations. The distinctive ethical issues associated with how Australians relate to Indigenous culture are also examined.

In the light it throws on the formations of cultural capital in a multicultural settler colonial society, *Fields, Capitals, Habitus* makes a landmark contribution to cultural capital research.

Tony Bennett is Research Professor in Social and Cultural Theory at the Institute for Culture and Society at Western Sydney University, and Honorary Professor in the Humanities Research Centre at the Australian National University.

David Carter is Emeritus Professor and formerly Professor of Australian Literature and Cultural History and Director of the Australian Studies Centre at the University of Queensland.

Modesto Gayo is Associate Professor at Universidad Diego Portales, Santiago, Chile.

Michelle Kelly is Research Officer at the Institute for Culture and Society, Western Sydney University.

Greg Noble is Professor of Cultural Research at the Institute for Culture and Society, Western Sydney University.

Culture, Economy and the Social
A new series from CRESC – the ESRC Centre for Research on Socio-cultural Change

The *Culture, Economy and the Social* series is committed to innovative contemporary, comparative and historical work on the relations between social, cultural and economic change. It publishes empirically based research that is theoretically informed, that critically examines the ways in which social, cultural and economic change is framed and made visible, and that is attentive to perspectives that tend to be ignored or side-lined by grand theorising or epochal accounts of social change. The series addresses the diverse manifestations of contemporary capitalism, and considers the various ways in which the 'social', 'the cultural' and 'the economic' are apprehended as tangible sites of value and practice. It is explicitly comparative, publishing books that work across disciplinary perspectives, cross-culturally or across different historical periods.

The series is actively engaged in the analysis of the different theoretical traditions that have contributed to the development of the 'cultural turn' with a view to clarifying where these approaches converge and where they diverge on a particular issue. It is equally concerned to explore the new critical agendas emerging from current critiques of the cultural turn: those associated with the descriptive turn for example. Our commitment to interdisciplinarity thus aims at enriching theoretical and methodological discussion, building awareness of the common ground that has emerged in the past decade and thinking through what is at stake in those approaches that resist integration to a common analytical model.

Editors
Professor Tony Bennett, Social and Cultural Theory, University of Western Sydney; Professor Penny Harvey, Anthropology, Manchester University

Editorial Advisory Board
Andrew Barry, University of Oxford; Michel Callon, École des Mines de Paris; Dipesh Chakrabarty, University of Chicago; Mike Crang, University of Durham; Tim Dant, Lancaster University; Jean-Louis Fabiani, Écoles de Hautes Études en Sciences Sociales; Antoine Hennion, Paris Institute of Technology; Eric Hirsch, Brunel University; John Law, Open University; Randy Martin, New York University; Timothy Mitchell, Columbia University; Rolland Munro, Keele University; Andrew Pickering, University of Exeter; Mary Poovey, New York University; Hugh Willmott, University of Cardiff; Sharon Zukin, Brooklyn College City University New York/Graduate School, City University of New York

For a full list of titles in this series, please visit www.routledge.com/CRESC/book-series/CRESC.

FIELDS, CAPITALS, HABITUS

Australian Culture, Inequalities and Social Divisions

Edited by Tony Bennett, David Carter, Modesto Gayo, Michelle Kelly and Greg Noble

First published 2021
by Routledge
2 Park Square, Milton Park, Abingdon, Oxon OX14 4RN

and by Routledge
52 Vanderbilt Avenue, New York, NY 10017

Routledge is an imprint of the Taylor & Francis Group, an informa business

© 2021 selection and editorial matter, Tony Bennett, David Carter, Modesto Gayo, Michelle Kelly and Greg Noble; individual chapters, the contributors

The right of Tony Bennett, David Carter, Modesto Gayo, Michelle Kelly and Greg Noble to be identified as the authors of the editorial matter, and of the authors for their individual chapters, has been asserted in accordance with sections 77 and 78 of the Copyright, Designs and Patents Act 1988.

All rights reserved. No part of this book may be reprinted or reproduced or utilised in any form or by any electronic, mechanical, or other means, now known or hereafter invented, including photocopying and recording, or in any information storage or retrieval system, without permission in writing from the publishers.

Trademark notice: Product or corporate names may be trademarks or registered trademarks, and are used only for identification and explanation without intent to infringe.

British Library Cataloguing-in-Publication Data
A catalogue record for this book is available from the British Library

Library of Congress Cataloging-in-Publication Data
A catalog record for this book has been requested

ISBN: 978-1-138-39229-8 (hbk)
ISBN: 978-1-138-39230-4 (pbk)
ISBN: 978-0-429-40226-5 (ebk)

Typeset in Bembo
by Wearset Ltd, Boldon, Tyne and Wear

CONTENTS

List of figures   *x*
List of tables   *xii*
Notes on contributors   *xiv*
Acknowledgements   *xviii*
Note on the text   *xxi*
Abbreviations   *xxiii*

Introduction   1
Tony Bennett, David Carter, Modesto Gayo, Michelle Kelly and Greg Noble

PART I
Fields   11

Introduction   11

1 Aesthetic divisions and intensities in the Australian art field   14
  Tony Bennett and Modesto Gayo

2 Book value: reading the Australian literary field   32
  David Carter, Modesto Gayo and Michelle Kelly

3 The mark of time: temporality and the dynamics of distinction in the music field   49
  Tony Bennett, Ben Dibley and Modesto Gayo

4 The elite and the everyday in the Australian heritage field   66
   Emma Waterton and Modesto Gayo

5 Television: the dynamics of a field in transition   83
   Tony Bennett, Modesto Gayo, David Rowe and Graeme Turner

6 Contesting national culture: the sport field   100
   David Rowe and Modesto Gayo

PART II
Class   117

Introduction   117

7 The Australian space of lifestyles   119
   Tony Bennett, Modesto Gayo and Anna Cristina Pertierra

8 Class and cultural capital in Australia   147
   Modesto Gayo and Tony Bennett

9 The middle space of lifestyles and middlebrow cultures   169
   David Carter

PART III
Capitals   185

Introduction   185

10 The persistence of inequality: education, class and cultural capital   188
    Megan Watkins

11 Capital geographies: mapping the spaces of urban cultural capital   208
    Liam Magee and Deborah Stevenson

12 Indigenous cultural tastes and capitals: gendered and class formations   224
    Tony Bennett, Ben Dibley and Michelle Kelly

13 Cultural diversity and the ethnoscapes of taste in Australia   247
    Greg Noble

PART IV
Habitus 265

Introduction 265

14 Engendering culture: accumulating capital in the gendered household 268
Deborah Stevenson

15 Cultural participation and belonging 280
Anna Cristina Pertierra and Graeme Turner

16 The politics of consumption: positioning the nation 293
Greg Noble and David Rowe

17 The ethical and civic dimensions of taste 311
Tim Rowse, Michelle Kelly, Anna Cristina Pertierra and Emma Waterton

Conclusion: 'distinction' after *Distinction* 330
Greg Noble, Tony Bennett, David Carter, Modesto Gayo and Michelle Kelly

Appendix A. Questionnaire design and survey methods 338

Appendix B. Survey questions 340

Appendix C. Methods used in analysing the survey data 347

Appendix D. Occupational class model with examples of occupations 349

Appendix E. Selection of household interviewees 352

Appendix F. Profiles of household interviewees 354

Appendix G. Australian scales 361

Appendix H. International scales 362

Appendix I. Key to Figure 7.2: Australian space of lifestyles (participation) 364

References *368*
Index *384*

FIGURES

1.1	The space of art tastes and practices	19
1.2	The social space of art tastes and practices	21
1.3	Albert Namatjira. Palm Valley. *Circa* 1940	29
2.1	Covering Kate Grenville	37
2.2	The space of literary tastes and practices	38
2.3	The social space of literary tastes and practices	40
3.1	The space of musical tastes and practices	55
3.2	The social space of musical tastes and practices	56
3.3	Gurrumul Yunupingu, Kings Park, Perth, with the West Australian Symphony Orchestra in 2014	59
4.1	Uluru-Kata Tjuta National Park, Sovereign Hill and the Port Arthur Historic Site	70
4.2	The space of heritage tastes and practices	72
4.3	The social space of heritage tastes and practices	73
5.1	The social space of television tastes and practices	90
5.2	Television genres, platforms and channels	91
5.3	Australian TV programmes and personalities	93
5.4	Overseas TV programmes	94
5.5	The Delpechitra family on *Gogglebox Australia*	96
6.1	The space of sport tastes and practices	105
6.2	The social space of sport tastes and practices	106
6.3	Performing sport fandom at a live venue	113
7.1	Australian space of social positions	122
7.2	Australian space of lifestyles (participation)	123
7.3	Australian space of lifestyles (genres)	124
7.4	Australian space of lifestyles (platforms and devices)	126
7.5	Clusters in the Australian space of lifestyles	128

8.1	Class differences calibrated by cultural practices	151
8.2	Correspondence analysis of cultural capital profiles, classes and lifestyle clusters	162
9.1	The middle space of lifestyles (genres)	171
9.2	The middle space of lifestyles (named artists, authors, TV programmes, musical performers, composers, compositions)	173
10.1	Western Sydney University advertisement	198
10.2	University of Sydney parody advertisement	199
10.3	Education, class and the inheritance of cultural capital	206
11.1	Map of Sydney	213
11.2	Distribution of participation in the field of television	214
11.3	Principal component analysis of the Greater Sydney sample	216
11.4	Degrees of participation in cultural fields, Sydney and Australian samples	218
11.5	Relative degrees of participation in cultural fields, Sydney sample	220
17.1	The Commemorative Courtyard at the Australian War Memorial	314

TABLES

1.1	Australian artists, heard of, seen and liked by occupational class and level of education	22
1.2	Relations between most- and least-liked genres	25
2.1	Genres read for interest/pleasure (percentage of occupational class group)	42
3.1	Ratios of genre preferences by frequent participation in musical events	60
6.1	Pearson's correlations of sport practices and taste scales	110
7.1	Comparative degrees of explained field variance across axes 1 and 2	121
7.2	Clusters 1 and 2 (genres and named items)	130
7.3	Clusters 3 and 4 (genres and named items)	136
7.4	Clusters 5 and 6 (genres and named items)	141
8.1	Percentage of social class by socio-demographic characteristics	152
8.2	Class distribution of selected capital assets	154
8.3	Distribution of social classes across clusters	155
8.4	Cultural capital profiles and educational trajectories	159
8.5	Percentages of lifestyle cluster by cultural capital profiles	160
8.6	Percentages of social class by cultural capital profiles	161
10.1	Highest educational qualification by occupation/SES	192
10.2	HE by age group and occupation/SES	193
10.3	University type by occupation/SES	197
10.4	Field of study by occupation/SES	201
10.5	School type by occupation/SES	202
10.6	Father's HE by age group and occupation/SES	204
10.7	Mother's HE by age group and occupation/SES	204
10.8	Partner's highest educational qualification by occupation/SES	205

11.1	Cultural fields and survey participation questions	212
12.1	Regional scales: comparisons of the mean likes of the main, Italian, Lebanese, Chinese, Indian and Indigenous samples	228
12.2	Visual art: Indigenous and main sample comparisons	229
12.3	Heritage: Indigenous and main sample comparisons	230
12.4	Music: Indigenous and main sample comparisons	233
12.5	Literature: Indigenous and main sample comparisons	234
12.6	Television: Indigenous and main sample comparisons	237
12.7	Sport: Indigenous and main sample comparisons	238
12.8	Class differences in Indigenous rates of recognition: Australian items	243
12.9	Class differences in Indigenous rates of recognition: overseas items	243
13.1	Regional scales by item of origin, Australia-born and overseas-born: national sample	252
13.2	Regional scales for ethnic samples, Australia-born and overseas-born	254
13.3	Australian artists known	256
13.4	Visited art galleries	258
13.5	Sachin Tendulkar: percentages of those who have heard of him and like him	260

CONTRIBUTORS

Tony Bennett is Research Professor in Social and Cultural Theory in the Institute for Culture and Society at Western Sydney University. He is a Fellow of the Australian Academy of the Humanities and of the Academy of the Social Sciences in the UK, and has held previous professorial positions at Griffith University, the Open University, and the University of Melbourne. His research spans the fields of cultural studies, cultural sociology and museum studies, and he has served as a director of nationally funded research centres in Australia and the UK. His recent publications include *Making Culture, Changing Society* (2013), *Collecting, Organising, Governing: Anthropology, Museums and Liberal Government* (co-author, 2017) and *Museums, Power, Knowledge* (2018).

David Carter is Emeritus Professor at the University of Queensland and Fellow of the Australian Academy of the Humanities, formerly Professor of Australian Literature and Cultural History and Director of the University's Australian Studies Centre. Books include *Australian Books and Authors in the American Marketplace* (with Roger Osborne, 2018), *Always Almost Modern: Australian Print Culture and Modernity* (2013) and *Dispossession, Dreams and Diversity: Issues in Australian Studies* (2006). He is a contributor to the *Routledge International Handbook of the Sociology of Art and Culture* (2016) and the *Cambridge History of Australia* (2013).

Ben Dibley is a Research Fellow at the Institute for Culture and Society, Western Sydney University, Australia. He has research interests in social and cultural theory, particularly around questions of cultural institutions, colonialism and museums. His essays have appeared in *Australian Humanities Review*, *Cultural Studies Review*, *History and Anthropology*, *International Journal of Cultural Studies*, *Museum and Society*, *New Formations* and *Transformations*. He is co-author of *Collecting, Ordering, Governing: Anthropology and Liberal Government* (2017).

Modesto Gayo is Associate Professor, Escuela de Sociología (School of Sociology), Facultad de Ciencias Sociales e Historia, Universidad Diego Portales (Santiago, Chile). He is co-author of *Culture, Class, Distinction* (2009) and of *Upper Middle Class Social Reproduction: Wealth, Schooling and Residential Choice in Chile* (2019) and single author of *Ideología, moralidades y reproducción social: Una introducción a la sociología de la cultura* (2017) and of *Clase y cultura: Reproducción social, desigualdad y cambio en Chile* (2020).

Michelle Kelly was the Senior Research Officer and Project Manager of the *Australian Cultural Fields: National and Transnational Dynamics* Discovery Project funded by the Australian Research Council (DP140101970). Her research interests include libraries, reading practices and contemporary fiction. She is co-editor of 'Transforming cultures? From *Creative Nation* to *Creative Australia*', a special section of *Media International Australia* (2016), and of *The Politics and Aesthetics of Refusal* (2007). She has published in *Australian Literary Studies, Continuum, Rhizomes, M/C Journal* and several edited collections. She is based at the Institute for Culture and Society, Western Sydney University, Australia.

Liam Magee is an Associate Professor in the Institute for Culture and Society at Western Sydney University. His principal research interests include practices of software (databases, data analytics, coding, gaming), cities and sustainability. His publications include the book *Interwoven Cities* (2015), and contributions to *Urban Sustainability in Theory and Practice* (2015) and *Towards a Semantic Web: Connecting Knowledge in Academic Research* (2011). Together with Ned Rossiter, he co-convenes the Institute's Digital Life Research Program.

Greg Noble is Professor of Cultural Research at the Institute for Culture and Society, Western Sydney University. His research interests centre on the relations between youth, ethnicity, class and gender; migration, multiculturalism and intercultural relations; cultural pedagogies and Bourdieusian theory; and multicultural education. His books include: *Cultural Pedagogies and Human Conduct* (2015), *Disposed to Learn* (2013), *On Being Lebanese in Australia* (2010) and *Bin Laden in the Suburbs* (2004).

Anna Cristina Pertierra is a Senior Lecturer in Cultural and Social Analysis at Western Sydney University. Her research uses ethnography to examine everyday social practice, with a particular interest in media, consumption and material culture, and urban modernities. Previously, she was a Lecturer in Anthropology and an ARC Postdoctoral Fellow in the Centre for Critical and Cultural Studies at the University of Queensland. She has a PhD in Anthropology from University College London and a BA Hons in Social Anthropology from the University of Sydney. Her publications include *Media Anthropology for a Digital World* (2017), *Locating Television: Zones of Consumption* (with Graeme Turner, 2013), the edited volume *Consumer Culture in Latin America* (with John Sinclair, 2012) and *Cuba: The Struggle for Consumption* (2011).

David Rowe is Emeritus Professor of Cultural Research, Institute for Culture and Society, Western Sydney University; Honorary Professor, Faculty of Humanities and Social Sciences, University of Bath; and Research Associate, Centre for International Studies and Diplomacy, SOAS University of London. A Fellow of the Australian Academy of the Humanities and the Academy of the Social Sciences in Australia, his books include *Popular Cultures: Rock Music, Sport and the Politics of Pleasure* (1995), *Sport, Culture and the Media: The Unruly Trinity* (second edition, 2004) and *Global Media Sport: Flows, Forms and Futures* (2011). His work has been translated into seven languages.

Tim Rowse is Emeritus Professor in the Institute for Culture and Society at Western Sydney University and an Editorial Fellow in the National Centre for Biography, Australian National University (ANU). He has taught at Macquarie University, the ANU and Harvard University (where he held the Australian Studies chair in 2003–2004), and he has held research appointments at the University of Sydney, the University of Melbourne, the University of Queensland and the ANU. Since the early 1980s, his research has focused on the relationships between Indigenous and other Australians, in Central Australia and in the national political sphere. In the 1990s, this and other interests led him to write two books about the life and works of Dr H. C. Coombs.

Deborah Stevenson is Professor in the Institute for Culture and Society at Western Sydney University. Her research interests are in arts and cultural policy, cities and urban life, and the role of gender in shaping creative practice and cultural consumption. Her publications include nine authored or edited books with her latest book, *Cultural Policy Beyond the Economy: Work, Value and the Social*, scheduled for publication in 2020. Recent funded projects include a major study of arts practice in Sydney, and an examination of the role of UNESCO in shaping local and national cultural policy.

Graeme Turner is Emeritus Professor in Cultural Studies at the University of Queensland. One of the founding figures in the establishment of media and cultural studies in Australia and internationally, he has published 25 books with international publishers, and his work has been translated into ten languages. A former ARC Federation Fellow (2006–2011), convenor of the ARC Cultural Research Network (2004–2010), a past president of the Australian Academy of the Humanities (2004–2007), he was the chair of the Humanities and Creative Arts Panel for the 2015 Excellence in Research Australia (ERA) exercise. His most recent research has focused on the media, particularly television, in the post-broadcast environment; recent publications include *Re-Inventing the Media* (2015), *Television Histories in Asia* (with Jinna Tay, 2016) and *Locating Television* (with Anna Cristina Pertierra, 2013).

Emma Waterton is Professor in the Geographies of Heritage at Western Sydney University. Her research revolves around: (1) conceptually focused interventions that explore (a) the idea of 'heritage as discourse' and (b) re-theorisations of heritage in relation to emotion and affect; (2) engaging with experimental research methods; and (3) exploring the intersections between heritage and practices of social governance. She is author or editor of 22 books including *Politics, Policy and the Discourses of Heritage in Britain* (2010) and *The Semiotics of Heritage Tourism* (co-authored with Steve Watson; 2014). She has also authored over 90 peer-reviewed articles and book chapters.

Megan Watkins is Professor in the School of Education and Institute for Culture and Society at Western Sydney University. Her research interests lie in the cultural analysis of education and the formation of human subjectivities. In particular, her work engages with issues of pedagogy, embodiment, discipline and affect and the interrelation of these to human agency. Her publications include *Cultural Pedagogies and Human Conduct* (ed.) (2015), *Disposed to Learn: Schooling, Ethnicity and the Scholarly Habitus* (2013) and *Discipline and Learn: Bodies, Pedagogy and Writing* (2012).

ACKNOWLEDGEMENTS

This book is an outcome of the *Australian Cultural Fields: National and Transnational Dynamics* project supported by the Australian government through the Australian Research Council (DP140101970). We therefore express our appreciation of this support.

The grant for this project was awarded to Tony Bennett (Project Director), David Carter, Modesto Gayo, Michelle Kelly (Senior Research Officer and Project Manager), Fred Myers, Greg Noble, David Rowe, Tim Rowse, Deborah Stevenson, Graeme Turner and Emma Waterton. Contributions to this book have also benefitted from the input of researchers who joined the *Australian Cultural Fields* research team later: Ien Ang, Ben Dibley, Liam Magee, Anna Cristina Pertierra and Megan Watkins. The editors are grateful to all of their research colleagues for the positive and productive spirit in which they have engaged with the extended process of writing and revision that has made this book possible.

We also acknowledge the role that the late Michael Volkerling played in the initial conception and early development of the research application for the *Australian Cultural Fields* project. Although Michael's untimely death preceded the submission of the application to the Australian Research Council, its success owed a good deal to the quality and generosity of his contributions.

The editors and authors are also grateful to the Institute for Social Sciences Research (ISSR) at the University of Queensland for its role in administering the survey through which the statistical data for the project was collected. We are especially thankful to Sue York for her role in coordinating the ISSR team that conducted this work, and to Tania Walker, Bernard Baffour, Shane Dinsdale and Joseph Byrne for their contributions as members of that team. We are particularly grateful to the 1461 Australians who gave generously of their time to take part in the survey, and even more so to the 41 members of the survey and an additional volunteer who agreed to be involved in the follow-up programme of interviews conducted by the research team. These interviews would not have been possible without the small army of research assistants who were involved in this stage of the project: Bree Blakeman, Emily Burns, Ben Dibley, Giulia Dal Maso, Ece Kaya, Joanne McNeill, Phillip Mar, Rebecca Olive, Oznur Sahin, Sebastián Martín Valdez and Emily Zong. We also thank Jasbeer Mamalipurath for his help in coding the interview data, Kate Naidu and Jen Sherman for their research assistance in connection with other aspects of the project, and Kristy Davidson and Flora Zhong for their assistance with the SPSS programme.

The *Australian Cultural Fields* project has benefitted enormously from the rich research environment offered by the Institute for Culture and Society at Western Sydney University. We acknowledge in particular the support of Ien Ang and Paul James during their periods as the Institute's Director, of Brett Neilson and Juan Salazar during their terms as its Research Director and of Terry Fairclough as the Institute's Manager. We also record our debt to Simon Chambers, a doctoral student in the Institute, for his excellent assistance in the final stages of preparing the manuscript for this book.

Some of the chapters that follow build on journal articles or book chapters published at earlier stages of the project. These are identified below.

Bennett, T. and Gayo, M. (2016) 'For the love (or not) of art in Australia', in M. Quinn, D. Beech, M. Lehnert, C. Tulloch and S. Wilson (eds) *The Persistence of Taste: Art Museums and Everyday Life After Bourdieu*, London: Routledge, 153–173.

Bennett, T., Dibley, B. and Kelly, M. (2018) 'Marking differences: Indigenous cultural tastes and practices', *Continuum: Journal of Media & Cultural Studies*, 32 (3): 308–321.

Bennett, T., Gayo, M. and Rowe, D. (2018) 'Television in Australia: capitals, tastes, practices and platforms', *Media International Australia*, 167 (1): 126–145.

Carter, D. and Kelly, M. (2017) 'Australian stories: books and reading in the nation', in A. Mannion, M. Weber and K. Day (eds) *Publishing Means Business: Australian Perspectives*, Clayton: Monash University Publishing, 147–181.

Carter, D., Gayo, M. and Kelly, M. (2018) 'Culture, class, distinction: cultural preferences and participation in Australia', *Journal of Australian Studies* (Japan), 31 (March): 42–55.

Dibley, B. and Gayo, M. (2018) 'Favourite sounds: the Australian music field', *Media International Australia*, 167 (1): 146–161.

Gayo, M. and Rowe, D. (2018) 'The Australian sport field: moving and watching', *Media International Australia*, 167 (1): 162–180.

Kelly, M., Gayo, M. and Carter, D. (2018) 'Rare books? The divided field of reading and book culture in contemporary Australia', *Continuum: Journal of Media & Cultural Studies*, 32 (3): 282–295.

Noble, G. and Ang, I. (2018) 'Ethnicity and cultural consumption in Australia', *Continuum: Journal of Media & Cultural Studies*, 32 (3): 296–307.

Rowe, D. (2016) '"Great markers of culture": the Australian sport field', *Media International Australia*, 158 (1): 26–36.

Rowe, D. (2018) 'Competing allegiances, divided loyalties: making sport identities in mobile societies', in D. Hassan and C. Acton (eds) *Sport and Contested Identities: Contemporary Issues and Debates*, London: Routledge, 155–173.

Rowe, D. (2018) 'The sport field in Australia: the market, the state, the nation and the world beyond in Pierre Bourdieu's favourite game', in D. Rowe, G. Turner and E. Waterton (eds) *Making Culture: Commercialisation, Transnationalism, and the State of 'Nationing' in Contemporary Australia*, London: Routledge, 87–100.

Rowe, D. (2019) 'Indigeneity as scandal: mediation and governance of sport', in L. Bamblett, F. Myers and T. Rowse (eds) *The Difference Identity Makes: Indigenous Cultural Capital in Australian Cultural Fields*, Canberra: Aboriginal Studies Press, 222–242.

Rowse, T. and Pertierra, A. C. (2019) 'From white nation to white caution: non-Indigenous reflections on Indigenous difference', *Journal of Australian Studies*, 43 (3): 283–298.

Waterton, E. (2018) 'A history of heritage policy in Australia: from hope to philanthropy', in D. Rowe, G. Turner and E. Waterton (eds) *Making Culture: Commercialisation, Transnationalism, and the State of 'Nationing' in Contemporary Australia*, London: Routledge, 75–86.

Waterton, E. and Gayo, M. (2018) 'For all Australians? An analysis of the heritage field', *Continuum: Journal of Media & Cultural Studies*, 32 (3): 269–281.

Details of other publications arising from the project can be found on its website at: www.westernsydney.edu.au/ACF.

NOTE ON THE TEXT

Fields, Capitals, Habitus is an unusual text, falling somewhere between an edited collection and a book jointly authored by all its contributors. The editors worked to a brief that was developed collectively by the researchers who constituted the initial team for the *Australian Cultural Fields: National and Transnational Dynamics* project or who joined the project later as the research developed.

As all of the chapters are based on data sets produced and analysed through collaborative research processes, there is a cumulative logic to the relations between the chapters and particularly between the different parts of the book: Part III on Capitals builds on Parts I and II, on Fields and Class respectively, just as Part IV on Habitus builds on all three preceding parts.

At the same time, the individual chapters reflect the particular interests and expertise of their authors and are relatively self-contained, so that in most cases they can be read and understood on their own terms if readers are aware of their position within the general architecture of the book and of the ways in which they draw on the methods used in the *Australian Cultural Fields* project.

Guidance on these issues is offered in the concluding section of the Introduction. Readers are therefore advised to consult this to help them navigate the text in the most productive way relevant to their particular interests.

The first-named author for each chapter is the convening author for that chapter, with the other authors identified in alphabetical order.

Percentages at or above 0.5 per cent have been rounded up, or down at 0.4 per cent or below, with a small number of exceptions, including: the percentages for the axes of the figures presenting the findings of the Multiple Correspondence Analyses conducted for the project; percentages below 1 per cent; and where retention of decimal differentiations has been significant for the purposes of the point under discussion.

Aboriginal and Torres Strait Islander peoples are the Indigenous peoples of Australia. The terms 'Indigenous', 'Aboriginal' and 'Torres Strait Islander' are used in this book. The cultures and traditions of Aboriginal and Torres Strait Islander peoples are different in important respects. Furthermore there is significant diversity within each group, with over 250 language groups in the nation.[1] The word 'Indigenous' provides a way of including Aboriginal and Torres Strait Islander persons and communities in a single term for the Australian context. More importantly, it acknowledges the status and rights of Aboriginal and Torres Strait Islander people as Indigenous peoples as defined, for example, in the United Nations Declaration on the Rights of Indigenous Peoples 2007.[2]

Notes

1 https://aiatsis.gov.au.
2 www.ohchr.org.

ABBREVIATIONS

ABC	Australian Broadcasting Corporation
ABS	Australian Bureau of Statistics
ACF	Australian Cultural Fields
ACT	Australian Capital Territory
AEC	Australian Everyday Cultures
AFL	Australian Football League
AIDS	Acquired Immune Deficiency Syndrome
ALP	Australian Labor Party
ANU	Australian National University
ANZSCO	Australia and New Zealand Standard Classification of Occupations
ATAR	Australian Tertiary Admission Rank
BBC	British Broadcasting Corporation
CATI	Computer-Assisted Telephone Interviewing
CBD	Central Business District
CCSE	Cultural Capital and Social Exclusion
CD	Compact Disc
CEO	Chief Executive Officer
COMPAS	Contemporary Patterns of Social Differentiation – The Case of Aalborg
DIY	Do It Yourself
DJ	Disc Jockey
DNA	Deoxyribonuclaeic Acid
DVD	Digital Video Disc
EGP	Erikson-Goldthorpe-Portocarero
FTA	Free-to-Air
GBCS	Great British Class Survey
GFC	Global Financial Crisis

Go8	Group of Eight
GOMA	Gallery of Modern Art
HBO	Home Box Office
HE	Higher Education
HIV	Human Immunodeficiency Virus
ICOMOS	International Council on Monuments and Sites
ICT	Information and Communications Technology
ISCO-08	International Standard Classification of Occupations
IT	Information Technology
LP	Long Play
MCA	Multiple Correspondence Analysis
MCA [S]	Museum of Contemporary Art, Sydney
Mona	Museum of Old and New Art
MP	Member of Parliament
NBA	National Basketball Association
NESB	Non-English Speaking Backgrounds
NGA	National Gallery of Australia
NITV	National Indigenous Television
NPEA	National Program for Excellence in the Arts
NRL	National Rugby League
NS-SEC	National Statistics Socio-economic Classification
NSW	New South Wales
OECD	Organisation for Economic Co-operation and Development
PCA	Principal Components Analysis
PISA	Programme for International Student Assessment
PSB	Public Service Broadcast
PVR	Personal Video Recorder
SBS	Special Broadcasting Service
SES	Socio-economic Status
SOC2010	Standard Occupational Classification 2010
STEM	Science, Technology, Engineering and Mathematics
TAFE	Technical and Further Education
TV	Television
UFC	Ultimate Fight Club
UK	United Kingdom
UNESCO	United Nations Educational, Scientific and Cultural Organization
US	United States
USA	United States of America
VIP	Very Important Person
WSU	Western Sydney University

INTRODUCTION

Tony Bennett, David Carter, Modesto Gayo, Michelle Kelly and Greg Noble

Fields, capitals, habitus: these are undoubtedly the three key concepts of Pierre Bourdieu's sociology, shaping his analyses of cultural, scientific, economic and political fields, and of the relations between them. While drawing on their more general currency, our concerns in this study focus on the roles these concepts have played in Bourdieu's cultural sociology. Even here, there are two main aspects to each of these concepts depending on whether it is their application to the analysis of cultural consumption or that of cultural production that is at issue.

With regard to the former, Bourdieu invoked the concept of *cultural field* to refer to the relationships between the cultural institutions centrally implicated in ordering the distribution and consumption of cultural works, paying particular attention to the interactions between institutions of cultural legitimation, the education system and occupational class divisions to explain how inequalities are reproduced through the differential distribution of cultural capital. *Cultural capital* refers to the assets that people derive from their familiarity with legitimate forms of culture, the educational and associated occupational advantages this confers, and the use of these assets to accumulate social capital (through social connections) and economic capital (through occupational advancement and the higher income levels and opportunities for wealth accumulation this gives rise to). Its unequal distribution across classes and other aspects of social position, and the transmission of the advantages it confers across generations, inscribes cultural capital as a key mechanism within the processes through which inequalities are reproduced through time. *Habitus*, finally, is the set of dispositions – or socialised propensities to think and act in particular ways – that mediates the relations between social position and lifestyle. The habitus provides the principles that organise the relations between the different cultural practices that the members of different social groups and classes engage in across different cultural fields so as to cohere these into more-or-less systematic configurations. We stress the 'more-or-less' here by way of registering the caution that the subsequent literature has enjoined regarding Bourdieu's tendency to interpret class as the aspect of social position that produces unified habitus.

In analysing fields of cultural production, Bourdieu focused on market, state and quasi-state actors (cultural ministries, academies, arts councils, funding bodies, media companies, publishers, galleries, etc.) to examine how the practices of writers, artists and creative workers more generally are conditioned by their struggles over the forms of capital that are specific to different cultural fields. He was equally concerned with how these fields are influenced by the economic and political fields – the fields of power, as he called them (Bourdieu, 1993).[1] Bourdieu invoked the concept of habitus in his analyses of cultural production as a point of mediation between the values that artists and writers, and cultural producers more generally, acquire from their social backgrounds, and the specific inflections given to those values by their trainings and the 'space of possibles' – that is, the structuring of opportunities – open to them within the prevailing organisation of the cultural field in question (Bourdieu, 2017: 49–50).

Our engagements with these three concepts focus mainly on their application in analyses of the social dynamics of cultural consumption based on specially designed surveys or on cultural data collected by cultural ministries, arts agencies or national statistical bureaux. While drawing their inspiration from Bourdieu's work, such studies have also probed its limitations with a view to refining the principles on which it rests so as to make them more generally adaptable to different contexts and changed historical circumstances. These limitations provide the critical points of reference for our engagement with Bourdieu's work and the subsequent analyses it has generated. Three such limitations stand to the fore. The first is that, while by no means guilty of methodological nationalism in his work as a whole, Bourdieu's empirical studies of cultural fields interpreted these as more-or-less hermetically enclosed national fields in ways that are now out of step with, albeit not entirely superseded by, the increasingly transnational character of the production, distribution and consumption of culture. The second limitation concerns Bourdieu's initial interpretation of fields of cultural consumption and the forms of cultural capital they generate as unmarked by the increasingly ethnically heterogeneous populations produced by transnational mobilities.[2] The third concerns the issues posed for the analysis of cultural fields in settler-colonial societies where Indigenous cultures have a significant presence.

We stress, however, the importance of Bourdieu's more general analytical categories and procedures as ones that we have adhered to as a corrective to some of the directions that subsequent engagements with his work have taken, particularly in the sociology of stratification. There are two main issues here. The first concerns a widespread tendency to isolate the analysis of cultural consumption from considerations of cultural production in spite of Bourdieu's insistence on the need to attend closely to the relations between the two.[3] While the former is the centre of our concerns, we draw on the findings relating to the recent dynamics affecting the production and distribution of culture across the visual art, literary, music, heritage, television and sport fields derived from the broader project – *Australian Cultural*

Fields: National and Transnational Dynamics (ACF) – of which the present study is a part. The second issue concerns the influence that a-historical sociological formalisms of the kind represented by the thesis of the 'cultural omnivore' (Gayo, 2016a) have exerted on debates focused on the relations between culture and social stratification. We have, therefore, as part of what is now a widespread counter to this tendency, taken our main methodological bearings from the relational forms of statistical analysis that Bourdieu (1984) used in *Distinction*.

Australia provides a distinctively productive context from which to engage with the issues we have identified. The emergence of a national cultural field came much later in Australia than in the European societies on which Bourdieu's theories are primarily based. Australian culture has also always been closely informed by its relations to changing transnational contexts: initially those of British imperialism; the global cultural ascendancy of the USA throughout most of the twentieth century; and the changing regional coordinates suggested by 'the Asian century' today. Migration to Australia over the post-war period has produced a culturally diverse population (at the 2016 Census, over 50 per cent of Australians were either born overseas or had parents who were) and a greater complexity and intensity of transnational flows of people and goods, with significant consequences for the dynamics of both cultural production and consumption. The increasingly strong cultural presence of Aboriginal and Torres Strait Islander peoples – far outweighing their statistical weight at 2.8 per cent of the population at the 2016 Census – presents a further set of challenges for Bourdieusian approaches to the relations between cultural fields, capitals and habitus.

The significance of these considerations has been recognised in Australian engagements with Bourdieu's work: research on Australian cultural fields has identified a distinctive field of ethnicity (Tabar *et al.*, 2010); ethnically marked forms of cultural capital alongside those of social class (Hage, 1998); distinctive relations between Indigenous visual arts and the international art field (Myers, 2002); the emergence of a distinctive cultural and political field centred on Indigenous/non-Indigenous relations (Bamblett *et al.*, 2019); and the strong influence of American culture on Australian cultural tastes and practices (Bennett *et al.*, 1999). These considerations have an increasingly pressing salience in contemporary Australia in view of the significant transformations that have taken place in the relations between the political field and Australian cultural fields in recent decades. The main direction of travel in this regard can be most conveniently identified by the more notable changes that have taken place since the publication, in 1994, of *Creative Nation* (Department of Communication and the Arts, 1994), Australia's first comprehensive national cultural policy statement. Reflecting the ethos of Paul Keating's Labor government, *Creative Nation* articulated a vision for the development of Australian culture that brought together a range of progressive agendas: a broadened conception of culture going beyond established definitions of the arts; a vision for a multicultural Australia that also accorded increasing significance to Australia's Indigenous cultures; a stronger sense of gender equity as part of a social-democratic framing of cultural access agendas; a recognition of digital and multimedia forms as critical to the future development of the cultural industries; and an enlistment of culture to the cause of a postcolonial (re)formation of nationhood.

Creative Nation also had significant limitations, especially in its susceptibility to neoliberal conceptions of the economy and a related tendency to pay little attention to the significance of the relations between culture and class-based inequalities. Its limitations in this regard were compounded by the succession of conservative Coalition governments which – except for the 2007–2013 Labor governments[4] – dominated the political landscape after Keating's defeat by John Howard in 1996. These governments diluted and, in some cases, reversed the directions that *Creative Nation* had encapsulated: the agendas of multiculturalism were given a new inflection by assimilationist conceptions of cultural diversity; the levels of funding for, and autonomy of, funding bodies like the Australia Council were reduced; the aspirations of Indigenous Australians for Constitutional recognition were repeatedly rebuffed; and market principles were championed against the values of publicness in both the cultural sector (particularly in reduced funding for Australia's main public broadcaster, the Australian Broadcasting Corporation) and the education system where state sector funding declined relative to that for the private schooling sector. The increasing digitisation and globalisation of cultural production, distribution and consumption has also continued unabated. In the pre-Google world of 1994, Mosaic and Netscape were the only Internet providers; the arrival of Netflix in 2015 – as one of the latest moments in this process – has already ignited significant concerns regarding its implications for the Australian screen industries.

These developments were among the backdrop of historical concerns that informed the ACF research project. This set out to explore the forces that have impacted on both the production and consumption of culture across the art, literary, music, heritage, television and sport fields since 1994. We engage with these concerns in this study primarily via the data provided by a 2015 national survey of the different kinds and degrees of cultural participation, tastes and knowledge associated with each of our fields exhibited by the members of both a main sample and boost samples of Aboriginal and Torres Strait Islander, Indian, Chinese, Lebanese and Italian Australians.

We complement and qualify these findings by drawing on the evidence provided by follow-up interviews with selected members of the national survey. The 42 interviewees were chosen to reflect diverse age, gender, class, race/ethnicity, education and income profiles and, while most were drawn from the urban centres of Sydney and Brisbane, some were also from regional areas. These interviews were intended to produce data which connected with the survey data. They were not, however, based solely on elaborations of the survey questions but also examined the ways in which people account for their cultural tastes and practices as a means of positioning themselves in relation to cultural, social and political concerns.

The approaches that were adopted in relation to the conception and design of both the survey and interviews were shaped by recent changes affecting the ways in which the forms of culture associated with our six cultural fields are produced and circulated – questions that are examined in other publications arising from the ACF project (Rowe et al., 2018; Bamblett et al., 2019; Bennett et al., 2020).[5] The field-specific issues identified by these aspects of the project informed our decision to devote Part I of this study – *Fields* – to an in-depth examination of the social distribution of cultural tastes and practices within each of the six cultural fields, considered in the light of the historical forces that have shaped their development. Particular attention is paid in the chapters comprising Part I to the different ways in which indicators of occupational class, education, age and gender interact in shaping the distribution of cultural tastes and practices within the different fields. These chapters also engage with debates focused on the particular aspects of field theory that are most relevant to the field in question: on the role of technological actors, for example, in Chapters 3 and 5 on the music and television fields respectively, and of gender in relation to the sport field in Chapter 6.

Part II – *Class* – moves on from the analysis of specific fields to consider the operation of class relations, considered in their connections to age and gender, across the overarching space of lifestyles and the space of social positions that are produced by bringing the six fields together. We pay particular attention here to the role played by distinctive cultural capital profiles in connecting cultural tastes and practices to distinctive patterns of inheritance which are, in turn, associated with different social trajectories across class relations. Part II also pays particular attention to the middle of the space of lifestyles, drawing on recent developments in the field of 'middlebrow studies' to contribute to a revised understanding of the 'culture of goodwill' Bourdieu attributed to the petite bourgeoisie.

If questions of class provide the organising focus for the concerns of Part II, Part III – *Capitals* – broadens the terms of engagement with cultural capital by looking in closer detail at other aspects of its social articulations which, while closely entangled with questions of class, merit attention in their own right. The chapters in this part look first at the role played by different kinds and levels of education provision in the organisation and reproduction of inequalities, and also at the spatial aspects of cultural capital through a case study focused on Sydney. Part III is also where debates relating to the development of distinctive forms of 'Indigenous cultural capital', as well as the distinctive position of the migrant communities produced by various phases of post-war migration to Australia, are addressed.

Part IV – *Habitus* – brings a specific focus to bear on the role of habitus. These concerns are also present in earlier chapters, particularly in Part I where the ACF household interviews are drawn on to flesh out the ways in which various aspects of social position interact in shaping the cultural tastes and practices of particular individuals. Particular attention is also paid to the class aspects of habitus in Part II, and to the distinctive social forces and pressures shaping the habitus of Indigenous Australians and Australia's Italian, Lebanese, Chinese and Indian communities in Part III. Part IV builds on these earlier discussions to look more closely at four distinctive aspects of habitus: the processes through which the gendering of habitus is effected; the political assumptions and engagements that inform cultural practices and preferences; the role of habitus in mediating the relations between cultural practices and affective relations of belonging; and the ethical and civic aspects of habitus.

The introductions to each of these parts of the book provide a more detailed overview of how the key concepts informing their concerns are approached. In the remainder of this Introduction, we first review the methods used in the ACF project with a view to identifying both the range of issues these methods engage with and those which lie beyond their compass. We also highlight the respects in which our engagements with the relations between fields, capitals and habitus in the contemporary Australian context might contribute most distinctively to broader debates. We then offer some guidance as to how best to read this book in the light of the ways in which it has been written and the relations between its various components, particularly the main text and the Appendices.

Methodological and contextual foci

We have already noted the significance of *Creative Nation* (Department of Communication and the Arts, 1994) as the main point of reference for ACF's engagements with recent changes in the organisation of the cultural fields it selected for study. As it happens, 1994 was also when the survey for the *Australian Everyday Cultures* (AEC) project, reported in Bennett *et al.* (1999), was in the field. Closely modelled on *Distinction* in the design of its questionnaire, this study, along with the limited number of other national cultural capital surveys that have been conducted since *Distinction*, provide points of comparison that will prove helpful in identifying the distinctiveness of the ACF study as well as the limitations of the data it collected.

The range of cultural practices encompassed by the ACF questionnaire was dictated by the need to look at each of our fields in detail and in a manner which, while largely consistent across the fields, would also take account of the properties specific to them – the close interpenetration of the sport field and media, for example. While the questionnaire explored each field in an unprecedented degree of detail, particularly in including a rich set of named cultural items for each field, this meant that other issues of potential interest had to be excluded. These included questions exploring general leisure activities, domestic furnishings, culinary tastes and practices, holiday and tourist practices, and exercises – all aspects of Bourdieu's survey as well as of the AEC questionnaire – while the exploration of media was limited to television (excluding film). It was also decided not to include questions exploring friendship networks which, although not a significant aspect of either of these earlier studies, have been widely used in subsequent sociological studies as a means of exploring the relations between economic, cultural and social capital. This was a significant element of the UK *Cultural Capital and Social Exclusion* (CCSE) project, reported in Bennett *et al.* (2009), the closely related Danish COMPAS project, reported in Prieur *et al.* (2008), and the Serbian project reported in Cvetičanin and Popescu (2011). The ACF survey also differed from these earlier studies by not including questions on political attitudes. These exclusions have their consequences: the ACF data throws no light on the role of social capital in Australia;[6] its focus on six cultural fields at the expense of broader leisure, culinary and domestic practices limits what can be said about the relations between more formalised kinds of cultural practice and everyday cultural activities, with consequences for how far the data can illuminate the varied textures of habitus outside the boundaries imposed by our fields;[7] and excluding questions on exercise has limited what can be said about the embodied aspects of habitus.

The limitations of the main sample also need to be noted. While broadly nationally representative in terms of gender and age, it is somewhat biased towards older age groups as well as towards the more highly educated sections of the population in managerial and professional occupations. This has limited the extent to which it has been possible to explore internal differences in the cultural practices and values of the working-class members of the ACF sample. The same is true of the ACF questionnaire. Cultural capital questionnaires typically accord more space to cultural practices that cleave towards the high end of the cultural spectrum than would be merited by the levels of engagement with them exhibited by general population patterns. This reflects their analytical focus on the forms of advantage associated with such practices in view of the role they play in the relations between the education system and the occupational class structure (Bennett, T., 2011). There are similar shortcomings at the other end of the class spectrum where the ACF sample has not tapped significantly into the upper echelons of the class structure comprising the owners and senior executives of major corporations.[8] This has restricted the extent to which it has been possible to engage with the relations between cultural capital and economic capital beyond a limited range of indicators for the latter.

While taking account of the light that other Australian data throws on these matters, the analyses of the ACF data have focused mainly on the forms of distinction associated with the relations between different sections of the professional and management classes on the one hand and, on the other, the differences between these and the intermediate and working classes. This has also involved paying particular regard to the different gendered compositions of these classes. The significance that Bourdieu accorded to cultural capital as a 'governmental actor' (Bennett, 2017), providing not just a means of explaining specific kinds of social inequality but also a means of acting on them through education and cultural policies in order to counter their reproductive effects, has also been retained. This is evident in the attention accorded to the role played by a variety of state actors in the histories of the six cultural fields and in the significance that is accorded to the role of different levels and kinds of education (public/private; religious/secular; elite/other universities; fields of tertiary study; parental and spousal levels of education) in accounting for the role played by different cultural capital trajectories in processes of class formation.

The more significant departures from both *Distinction* and the AEC study consist in the significance that is accorded to questions of race and ethnicity.[9] With regard to our inclusion of boost samples of Chinese, Indian, Lebanese and Italian Australians, this emphasis is partly in response to the ways in which such questions have been placed on the international agendas of cultural capital research over the intervening period as well as the specific histories of immigration and multiculturalism in Australia. The inclusion of a boost sample for Aboriginal and Torres Strait Islander people, and, for each of the fields, questions engaging specifically with Indigenous cultural practices, was a response to more nationally specific considerations. These concern the respects in which, over the last 20 to 30 years, both Indigenous cultural activism and the increased status accorded Indigenous culture by a range of state and non-state agencies have significantly reconfigured the relations between Indigenous and non-Indigenous Australians. We shall not review here the range of agencies that have been involved in these processes as these questions are addressed in later chapters. The more general issues at stake concern the development of a distinctive set of relations that are quite specific to cultural fields in contemporary settler-colonial societies in which Indigenous cultural practices operate in multiple ways at the interfaces between Indigenous and non-Indigenous populations. These issues are engaged by exploring the ways in which such practices provide a source of cultural capital for particular sections of both Indigenous and non-Indigenous populations while also, for the latter, significantly affecting the relations between the ethical, political and aesthetic aspects of a range of contemporary Australian habitus.

Reading *Fields, Capitals, Habitus*

Although this book bears our names as editors, the research that informs it was based on the collective decisions of the ACF research team who also, through a programme of workshops, helped to shape the brief for this study and the best way of translating that brief into practice. While a division of writing and editorial labour was necessary, the editors and chapter authors have worked together to ensure both that there is an accumulating line of argument that runs throughout the book and that each chapter – while signposting its connections to other chapters – can be read on its own for readers who might wish to dip into and out of particular lines of argument. With these ends in view, we provide more extended discussions of the methods used in the ACF study in the Appendices where they can be consulted as and where methodological issues pertinent to particular chapters arise. Some brief notes on the Appendices, and their relation to the text, are therefore in order.

Appendix A summarises the overall rationale for the design of the ACF questionnaire, describes how and when the ACF survey was administered, the sampling procedures used and the limitations of the main sample that they recruited. The procedures for recruiting the boost samples of Aboriginal and Torres Strait Islander, Italian, Lebanese, Chinese and Indian Australians, and the limitations of these samples, are discussed in Chapters 12 and 13. Appendix B presents a tabular condensation of the cultural field questions included in the ACF questionnaire. Rationales for our selection of the questions relating to the art, literature, music, heritage, television and sport fields are given in the relevant chapters in Part I.

Appendix C discusses the main methods that were used in analysing the ACF survey data. It summarises the principles of Multiple Correspondence Analysis (MCA) that Bourdieu used and which is now regularly used in the literatures that engage with his work. This appendix also summarises how we used MCAs in the analysis of each of the cultural fields discussed in Part I, and in the construction and analysis of the overall space of Australian lifestyles in Part II. A more detailed discussion of the implications of MCA for how to read the figures through which we bring together the relations between cultural tastes and practices and social positions for each of the cultural fields is offered in the second section (Art tastes, practices and social position) of Chapter 1.

The discussions of the relationships between class and cultural practices in Part I are based on an eight-class model of occupational classes. Appendix D describes the procedures used in arriving at these occupational classes. Particularly noteworthy here are the measures through which the Australian and New Zealand Standard Classification of Occupations was converted into the International Standard Classification of Occupations used by the International Labour Organisation in order to permit international comparisons. The consequences of this procedure are discussed in Chapter 8 where our occupational classes are grouped into a three-class model. Appendix D also presents a tabular summary of the kinds of occupations associated with each of the eight occupational classes.

Appendices E through to H present various aspects of the methods used in relation to the ACF household interviews. Appendix E discusses the principles informing the selection of interviewees from those members of the ACF survey who indicated their assent to be included in follow-up interviews. It also summarises the questions that were put to interviewees, and the methods used in the coding and analysis of the interview transcripts. Appendix F provides the pseudonyms a condensed socio-biography for each interviewee. The evidence provided by these interviews is drawn on throughout the study. For reasons of economy, however, only those aspects of their socio-biographies pertinent to the point under discussion are presented in the chapters. Readers wishing to consult more information on these matters should therefore refer to Appendix F. Appendices G and H detail the items that are included in the regional scales that are used in Chapters 12 and 13. Finally, Appendix I provides keys that will facilitate reading the figures presenting the overall space of lifestyles in Chapters 7 and 9.

We note finally that, by the time this book is published, the fortieth anniversary of the original French publication of *Distinction* will have come and gone. In drawing his introduction to that edition to a close, Bourdieu stressed that

> The science of taste and cultural consumption begins with a transgression that is in no way aesthetic: it has to abolish the sacred frontier which makes legitimate culture a separate universe, in order to discover the intelligible relations which unite apparently incommensurable 'choices', such as preferences in music and food, painting and sport, literature and hairstyle.
>
> *(Bourdieu, 2010: xxix)*

Although in what follows we register differences with some of Bourdieu's particular formulations, his commitment to the 'barbarous reintegration of aesthetic consumption into the world of ordinary consumption' (xxix) is one that we share. It is, of course, a breach with the logic of cultural consecration that is a good deal less barbarous now than when first proposed by Bourdieu. But it remains an equally necessary and productive one.

Notes

1 Although not central to our concerns in this study, Bourdieu's conception of the fields of power is susceptible to the criticisms Foucault made of state and capital-centric conceptions of power. Bennett (2010) discusses the respects in which the two positions differ as well as those in which they can be productively aligned with one another.
2 This was not, we stress, because Bourdieu failed to appreciate the significance of ethnicity; his earlier work on the Kabyle and Algeria more generally is sufficient testimony to the contrary (see Goodman and Silverstein, 2009). It was rather, more pragmatically, because the ethos of French republicanism, translated into legislation governing surveys and questionnaires, prohibited the inclusion of questions identifying respondents' ethnicities.
3 See chapter 1 of Purhonen et al. (2019) for an overview of the stress placed on the need to investigate the social relations of cultural production and consumption conjointly by both Bourdieu and in the early take-up of his work by Paul DiMaggio.
4 The development of the policy statement *Creative Australia* (Commonwealth of Australia, 2013) during the closing years of the Labor government was intended to mark a return to, and development of, the signature policies of *Creative Nation*. However, owing to electoral defeat, its proposals were never implemented.
5 The project has also contributed themed sections to *Media International Australia* (Issue 158, February 2016, and Issue 167, May 2018) and to *Continuum: Journal of Media & Cultural Studies* (vol. 32, no. 3, June 2018).
6 See, however, Sheppard and Biddle (2015a) for a summary of the findings of the ANUPoll *Social Class in Australia* which included social capital questions.
7 We anticipated these difficulties and sought to compensate for them by including in our questionnaire a number of cultural practices outside our six fields: going to the cinema, to Bingo, to a casino or to the theatre, going dancing, playing the pokies, cards or computer/video games. These did not, however, prove to have a significant impact on the general patterns of our findings. We also planned to hold focus groups with members of working-class organisations but resource limitations meant we were unable to do so.
8 Anticipating this shortcoming – again a common one – we had planned to conduct a set of elite interviews with senior level executives of a range of private and public enterprises; however, this eventually proved impossible owing to shortages of time and resources.
9 The AEC study accords some attention to these questions, but only in ways that relate to ethnically or racially marked tastes for specific items – the marked Indigenous preference for country and western music, for example. Our inclusion of ethnic boost samples follows the example of the CCSE study.

PART I
Fields

Introduction

The actions of the state and economic agencies comprising what Bourdieu called the fields of power significantly influence the positions that agents take up in relation to one another within the 'space of possibles' which defines the issues at stake in the struggles which characterise particular cultural fields. It will therefore be useful, in setting the scene for the chapters comprising Part I, to identify some of the key changes in the cultural policy and economic settings that have borne consequentially on the current organisation of the art, literary, music, heritage, television and sport fields in Australia.

We have already touched on these questions in the general Introduction where we identified the 1994 *Creative Nation* cultural policy statement as a key point of historical reference for the *Australian Cultural Fields* (ACF) project. It is also important, drawing a slightly longer historical bow, to acknowledge the continuities between the policy trajectories advocated by *Creative Nation* and the earlier directions given to Australian cultural policies under the 1972–1974 Labor government led by Gough Whitlam, which provided the impetus for the establishment of the Australia Council for the Arts as an independent statutory authority in 1975. This was a significant innovation, particularly in the attention the Council accorded to access and equity considerations in the distribution of funding, in operating at arm's length from government and in its initiation of Indigenous and community arts programmes. If this constituted a watershed moment in the development of national arts and cultural policies, it did not eclipse the continuing significance of Australia's State and Territory governments, particularly in the provision and maintenance of cultural infrastructure in the arts and heritage sectors. This is in contrast to broadcasting, where the Federal government is, and has long been, the dominant player in terms of policy and legislation.

The policy agenda highlighted by the continuity between the Whitlam years and *Creative Nation* has been weakened considerably since the late 1990s by a sharper focus on the economic aspects of creative industry development, an erosion of the power of domestic cultural agents in consequence of the increasingly transnational character of cultural and media production, and a winding back of support for access and equity agendas relative to support for elite cultural practices (Meyrick et al., 2018). The principle of arm's length autonomy for art and cultural funding was also weakened in 2015 when the then Arts Minister George Brandis redirected $26 million per annum of Australia Council funding to a programme under his direct ministerial control, the National Program for Excellence in the Arts (NPEA). This detrimentally affected individual artists and small-to-medium arts organisations, and was vigorously protested by the arts community but not the Australia Council itself – a silence widely interpreted as casting doubt on the Council's structural independence as a statutory authority. The establishment of the NPEA harkened back to 1960s Australian arts funding bodies that foregrounded 'excellence' as a singular virtue in contrast to its subsequent melding with other social policy objectives. It was also a move in step with broader trends which have seen the production, management and support of culture in Australia shift from government to market forces. The present context is also more strongly imbricated in transnational processes, ranging from policy settings which place increasing value on the transnational, to developments in technologies and platforms of production, distribution and consumption which present increasing challenges for national cultural and media organisations.

These shifts are among the broader economic and political tendencies that have affected the ways in which the cultural practices associated with ACF's six cultural fields are produced and consumed. In engaging with these, the chapters in Part I do so through the prism of the more particular tendencies specific to each field.

The discussion in Chapter 1 of the close intertwining of the relations between the visual arts and the higher levels of the managerial and professional classes is thus complicated by a consideration of the role played by the development, largely since the 1970s, of Indigenous art as a distinctive sub-sector of the Australian art field. Chapter 2 similarly pays particular regard to changes in the publishing industry which suggest the need for a reassessment of the forms of legitimation that are now in operation in the literary field. These have weakened traditional conceptions of literary value in favour of a flatter and more dispersed regime of value organised around the concepts of book reading and book culture.

In international debates, the music field has long been interpreted as one in which the dilution of earlier hierarchical divisions of tastes has been most pronounced. Chapter 3 on the music field qualifies these accounts. Drawing on Bourdieu's approach to the temporal dynamics of fields, it shows how musical works representing different 'musical times' in the Australian music field are connected to practices of distinction associated with different class fractions. It also shows how the intensity of such distinctions varies with the degree of immersion in musical events. Chapter 4 stresses the significance of the heritage field's closeness to the political field. It pays particular attention to the ways in which this manifests itself in a split between 'public, "elite" or authorised' heritage on the one hand and 'personal, vernacular or everyday' heritage on the other.

Owing to their close imbrication with both market forces and the state, however, television and sport are arguably the fields most directly implicated in the field of power. They are, moreover, deeply intertwined with one other. The point of departure for Chapter 5 is the waning dominance of free-to-air television in the face of new technological actors in the television field: platforms, technologies and distribution mechanisms such as streaming, Netflix, Stan and YouTube. In discussing these developments, Chapter 5 foregrounds the agency of these technological actors in reconfiguring television's interrelation of the symbolic and the material.

Our studies of individual fields are rounded off in Chapter 6 with a turn to classificatory questions exemplified by the complexity of sport's definition as a field. The intersection of sport (as an organised, rule-governed activity) with other physical practices; the varying modes of sports engagement ranging from playing to umpiring to club duties to watching live to consuming via media; its high degree of mediatisation generally – all of these contribute to a field characterised by a high degree of porosity.

It should also be noted that the ordering of the chapters that follow moves progressively from the most sharply divisive field (the art field) to the least (the sport field) in terms of their relations to occupational classes and levels of education. The significance of this hierarchy of fields is taken up in Part II.

1
AESTHETIC DIVISIONS AND INTENSITIES IN THE AUSTRALIAN ART FIELD

Tony Bennett and Modesto Gayo

In his lectures on Manet, Bourdieu distinguishes his approach to the sociology of art from that of T. J. Clark (1984) by stressing the respects in which art fields act as a set of mediating institutions through which the influence of class and other social positions must pass in order to connect consequentially with art practices. To avoid the 'sociological shortcuts' he attributes to Clark's tendency to interpret Manet's work too directly in the light of his immersion 'in the Paris and the streets of Haussmann', Bourdieu interposes the 'intermediary social space' of the field between the artist and the city:

> We do not move without transition from Haussmann to the painting: instead, we have to pass through a social universe, which is the world of the painters, the critics, the artists, etc., and which obeys social laws ... The painter is himself a part of this world and works within its parameters. When he paints ... he is not alone with his work: he has other past and present painters in mind, as well as an audience composed of those for whom he is painting ... In fact what makes a picture are all of these things, which, taken together, form a field.
>
> *(Bourdieu, 2017: 261–262)*

Bourdieu and Darbel (1991) were equally insistent in *The Love of Art* that audience responses to works of art cannot be read off directly from either the work of art or from the audience's social position without taking account of the intermediary social space of the art field. They particularly stressed the role that the positioning of artworks relative to one another within the temporal dynamics of art fields plays in distinguishing the tastes of different class fractions.

This insistence on considering the relations shaping the production and consumption of art as interacting aspects of an overarching art field was lost sight of in engagements with Bourdieu's work in the 1980s and 1990s (Hanquinet and Savage, 2016: 12). The emphasis placed on establishing more routinised connections between culture and stratification tended to abstract these questions from any consideration of the influence of field-specific hierarchies of value. Discerning a return, from the late 1990s, to a sociology of art founded on the relational principles of field analysis, Hanquinet and Savage extol these principles for the potential they afford of a more finely textured approach to the interactions of field-specific aesthetic properties and social dispositions in shaping the social organisations of tastes (see also Hanquinet et al., 2014).

It is with these considerations in mind that we approach our findings regarding the relations between art tastes and practices and social positions through the role played by the contemporary Australian art field in mediating the relations between these. We therefore look first at the distinguishing properties of the Australian art field as a prelude to outlining the rationales for the art field items included in our questionnaire. This paves the way for the presentation of the key connections our survey data demonstrates between different degrees of involvement in the art field, tastes and a range of social positions. We then bring these considerations together with the evidence of our household interviews to explore the distribution of different intensities of aesthetic engagement and the operation of different aesthetic principles among our survey respondents.

There are four main aspects to the argument. First, while qualified and complicated by the force of age and gender, our findings testify to the continuing strength of the relations between family background, level of education and class position in determining both the degree and kinds of involvement in the art field. Second, tastes also manifest the strong influence of education and class. They do so at the most general level in differentiating responses to figurative and non-figurative art forms, albeit that this is complicated by the force of age. Third, the degree of intensity invested in involvement in the visual arts is, more often than not, an inherited disposition strongly connected to family background. Finally, we pay particular attention to the distinctive qualities associated with liking Aboriginal art, particularly the respects in which, even in its abstract forms, it is differentiated from other forms of abstract art in being interpreted as testifying to politically purposive storytelling.

Contemporary dynamics of the Australian art field[1]

In contrast to Britain and France, where national galleries and academies were well established by the mid-nineteenth century, and where national arts and cultural policy organisations were developed in the early post-war years, the emergence of a clearly national art field in Australia came later. Proposals for the establishment of a national gallery go back to the period following Federation in 1901 when Australia's hitherto separate States were brought together under a relatively independent national government. However, these did not acquire any significant political purchase until the 'new nationalism' of the 1970s which also provided the momentum for the establishment of the Australia Council, Australia's first comprehensive arts funding, policy and advocacy body, in 1973. A national gallery was not established until 1982 when what is now the National Gallery of Australia (NGA) opened. Prior to this, the art field was dominated by the major State galleries, particularly the National Gallery of Victoria and the Art Gallery of New South Wales. The connections between such institutions and European art institutions were strong, and artists looked chiefly to Paris and London as the key centres of contemporary artistic practice. Although prefigured by important initiatives in the 1930s, the development of a strongly national school of art criticism and of autonomous arts training schools only gathered significant momentum in the post-war period.

The late 1940s was also when Australia's connections with European art markets and institutions began to decline relative to those of New York, a tendency which has continued and, since the 1990s, been complemented by closer relations with the developing art markets and gallery sectors of Asia, particularly China. While the State galleries remain significant institutions of legitimation within the Australian art field, their influence is now exercised alongside a number of new players. Although the NGA is one of these, its location in Canberra distances it from Australia's main centres of population – especially Sydney, Melbourne and Brisbane – which are also its main centres of arts training and arts production, where the major auction houses connected to international art markets are located and where Australia's most significant arts fairs and biennales are hosted. State capitals are also the primary locations for the new galleries which have been the key drivers of new art practices (contemporary, abstract and video art, installation and performance art) since the 1980s: Sydney's Museum of Contemporary Art (MCA [S]), Queensland's Gallery of Modern Art (GOMA), Melbourne's Australian Centre for the Moving Image, and Hobart's privately funded Museum of Old and New Art (Mona).[2] Nonetheless, alongside the State gallery sector and the Australia Council, the NGA has played a significant role in the legitimation of Aboriginal art. The increasing presence of Aboriginal art practices, and the shift in their framing from the categories of ethnography to their validation as art, has been the most distinctive aspect of the Australian art field over the period since the 1970s. However, for reasons that will become clear later, the category of Aboriginal art suggests a misleading unity for a diverse set of practices shaped by different conditions of production and received and understood in quite different terms.

These are the most salient aspects of the Australian art field that informed our approach to art tastes and practices in our questionnaire. While questions exploring frequency of visitation of art galleries and ownership of art items provide indices of the intensity of participation in the art field, the specific types of art galleries and events included range across State and regional galleries and the NGA, and also encompass newer exhibition contexts (museums of contemporary art, arts festivals and commercial galleries, for example). The genres selected include traditional European genres (Renaissance art), later genres with a broader international currency (modernism, Impressionism, Pop art) and two specifically Australian genres (colonial art, Aboriginal art). We also chose genres with strong figurative associations (landscapes, portraits, still lifes) and, as a counterfoil to these, abstract art. Respondents were asked to identify the two genres they liked most and the two they liked least.

Australian artists were chosen in view of their different positions within the history and current disposition of the Australian art field. John Glover was a nineteenth century colonial artist whose idealised Australian landscapes resonated with the increasing prominence of pastoralists as patrons of the arts (Hoorn, 2007). As an early representative of an 'antipodean perspective', Tom Roberts was a leading figure of the Australian *plein air* movement which was a significant incubator for Australian Impressionism. Albert Namatjira, active from the 1930s through to the late 1950s, was a water-colourist noted for reworking Western landscape traditions from an Aboriginal perspective. Sidney Nolan and Margaret Preston were key representatives of mid-twentieth century Australian modernism. Nolan drew on the folklore of Ned Kelly and the motifs of desert nomadism as a potential source of aesthetic and political renewal, while Preston incorporated Aboriginal art motifs into contemporary domestic settings as a reworking of Australian national identities. Brett Whiteley, one of Australia's best known post-war contemporary artists, was noted for his sensuously stylised nudes and Sydney Harbour landscapes while the work of Imants Tillers, Australian born but of Latvian parentage, explores the themes of migration, displacement and diaspora through a critical engagement with Australian landscape traditions. Ben Quilty is a contemporary arts activist whose work adopts a critical stance on a range of current political issues. Tracey Moffatt is a contemporary Indigenous film and video artist whose work troubles essentialist interpretations of the category of Aboriginal art. Ken Done, finally, is a commercial artist, noted for visually striking depictions of iconic Australian scenes, particularly Sydney Harbour, but with little recognition from the public galleries that are Australia's main institutions of legitimation.

We included Leonardo da Vinci and Rembrandt as foundational figures of European art traditions, and Caravaggio as a later Renaissance artist whose work, 'rediscovered' in recent decades, is less well known and valued for its troubling of Renaissance conventions. Monet and Van Gogh were selected as Impressionists and post-Impressionists with a formative influence on twentieth century modernisms. We included Jackson Pollock as an American modernist whose work has a particular resonance in Australia in view of the controversies occasioned by the purchase of his *Blue Poles* for the future NGA in 1973,[3] and Jeff Koons as an heir to the earlier traditions of American Pop art whose work, like Done's, is commercially successful while also eliciting a greater degree of (somewhat grudging) recognition from official art institutions. Tracey Emin is a controversial contemporary feminist installation artist and Ai Weiwei a contemporary Chinese political artist and activist.

We now explore how preferences for and dislike of these different artists and genres, and participation in different art institutions, interact with each other. We do so by means of the Multiple Correspondence Analysis (MCA) we conducted on our data.

Art tastes, practices and social position

The principles of MCA are reviewed in Appendix C. Here, we focus on how to read the results of the MCA presented in Figure 1.1. Each of the points plotted into this figure represents the statistical mean of the individuals who engage in, or do not engage in, the particular practice concerned or who share the taste in question. Plus signs represent genres that are most liked, activities engaged in, and artists that have been seen and liked; minus signs indicate genres that are least liked, non-engagement in the activities concerned, and artists that have been seen and not liked. Each individual occupies a unique position within this space depending on the overall organisation of their tastes and practices. The points in Figure 1.1 identify the 'centre of gravity', so to speak, for individuals sharing the same tastes or practices. This does not mean that all individuals who like abstract art are located at exactly the point labelled 'Abstract +' towards the bottom centre of the figure. Depending on their other tastes and practices, and thus how they are 'pulled' towards them, the people who like abstract art are scattered around that point in a penumbra which overlaps with the penumbrae surrounding neighbouring points – for liking Pop art, for example. The closer the points, the greater the likelihood of significant degrees of overlap between the individuals who like the genres or artists concerned or participate in adjacent practices. So we can see, towards the far left of the figure, close connections between visiting the NGA, and liking Caravaggio, Bacon and Preston. The further apart the labels are – such as those who like Ai Weiwei (bottom left) and those who like colonial art (top right) – the less likelihood there is of any such overlap.

The differences that Figure 1.1 registers are more significant with regard to the horizontal axis, which accounts for 12.57 per cent of the variation between the tastes and practices that the figure plots compared to the 4.40 per cent accounted for by the vertical axis.[4] We therefore look first at the differences that are laid out across the horizontal axis. The extreme right offers a condensed visual summary of the third of the sample who take little or no part in the Australian art field. There are congregated here those who never go to art galleries or to arts events like biennales, and who do not use the Internet for any of the purposes connected with the visual arts that we asked about (to find out about artists or arts events, to visit the website, read the blog of, or comment on an artist or arts organisation). The positive tastes registered here are mainly for landscapes, colonial art, portraits and still lifes. These are all located in the top part of the figure where some degree of art gallery visiting (once a year) is registered. The genres least liked are Impressionism, modern, Pop art, abstract art and Renaissance art. Aboriginal art is not liked, although the distance separating those who do not like it from those, to the immediate left of the vertical dividing line, who do, is small. No named artists are identified as having been seen and liked; da Vinci, Van Gogh, Monet, Rembrandt, Whiteley, Nolan, Pollock and Namatjira have been seen and not liked.

Looking to the left of the vertical dividing line and to the tastes and practices in the space to the right of an imaginary line running vertically from the liking for Impressionism towards the top centre of the figure and running down to disliking

Aesthetic divisions in the art field   **19**

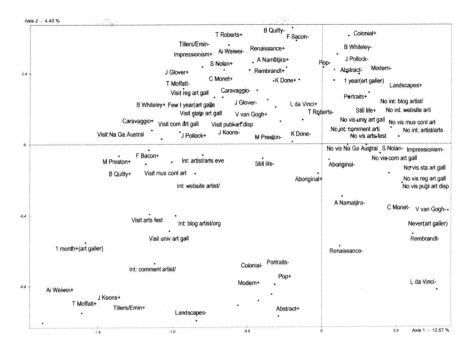

FIGURE 1.1   The space of art tastes and practices.

landscapes at the bottom, we can see, first, indications of greater and more varied forms of participation in the art field. Most of the respondents above the horizontal dividing line visit art galleries periodically, with public art displays, regional and State galleries as the three most popular art venues recruiting 54 per cent, 34 per cent and 37 per cent of the sample respectively. State and regional galleries are, as we have noted, mostly among Australia's oldest galleries, and compared to the exclusively contemporary focus of museums of contemporary art, their activities, like those of the NGA, are balanced more evenly between the maintenance and exhibition of an Australian canon and the promotion of contemporary art practices. In the upper part of this segment of the figure, tastes are mostly identified in relation to specific artists rather than genres except for liking Renaissance art. Artists liked are mainly late nineteenth and twentieth century figures: Roberts, Namatjira, Monet, Nolan and Done, although there also cluster here those who dislike Roberts and Done. Dislikes are mainly for more contemporary figures – Quilty, Ai Weiwei and Koons – but also include twentieth century modernists like Preston and Bacon, and Glover as well as Caravaggio who, for the reasons we have noted, is something of a 'time trickster'. Tastes below the line and to the right, by contrast, are expressed exclusively in relation to genres, with liking Pop, abstract and modern art clustering together along with an aversion to portraits and colonial art. The organising principle of the vertical axis is thus that of more conservative tastes in the upper part of the figure compared to more contemporary tastes in the lower part.

If we look now to the extreme left of the figure, the degree of involvement in the art field increases dramatically just as the forms of involvement multiply: rates of gallery visitation register at once a month (5 per cent of the sample) or more (2 per cent) at the bottom left; the Internet is used for all of the purposes we asked about (to find out about artists or arts events, to visit the website, read the blog of, or comment on an artist or arts organisation); and gallery visitation includes museums of contemporary art (26 per cent), commercial (29 per cent) and university galleries (15 per cent), arts festivals (15 per cent) and the NGA (13 per cent) – a balance tilted towards more recent institutions and more contemporary art practices. These are, moreover, mainly located beneath the horizontal dividing line, as are all the uses of the Internet. Tastes are expressed mainly in relation to named artists and run, in a diagonal line starting with the dislikes for Moffatt, Emin and Tillers registered at the top, through a liking for Glover, Whiteley, Pollock and Caravaggio to, immediately below the horizontal dividing line, Bacon, Preston and Quilty. Likes for Koons, Ai Weiwei, Moffatt, Emin and Tillers congregate in the bottom left of the figure.[5]

Figure 1.2 shows how this distribution of tastes and practices correlates with a range of social characteristics. This figure is constructed in accordance with the same principles as Figure 1.1 with the location of each social position identifying the statistical 'centre of gravity' for the individuals belonging to that position. Level of education maps directly on to the right–left distribution of tastes and practices, running in a more-or-less straight line from lower levels of education on the right to those with tertiary and postgraduate qualifications on the left, but dipping down in the middle where those with partially completed tertiary qualifications, a good many of whom are students, predominate. Those who studied humanities and social science subjects at university occupy the far left of the space; those who studied Science, Technology, Engineering and Mathematics (STEM) or law and business subjects cluster more towards the centre. Occupational class follows a parallel trajectory with routine, semi-routine and lower supervisory and technical workers occupying the lower right quadrant, small employers and own account workers and those working in intermediate occupations nudging more towards the middle of the figure, while the upper left quadrant is occupied mainly by lower managers and professionals, the owners of large enterprises and higher-level managers and, at the extreme left, higher-level professionals.[6] The effects of place of residence are similarly organised, with degree of participation in the art field increasing as we move from rural, remote and small town locations on the upper right through semi-rural and suburban locations towards the centre of the map and inner city areas towards the lower left.

Age dominates the vertical axis: the younger age groups cluster towards the bottom of the figure running up through middle-age groups to the older members of the sample at the top. Gender is distributed mainly along the horizontal axis but with a relatively low degree of differentiation, a pattern that is partly accounted for by the tendency for the selection of prints or paintings at home to be shared decisions as well as for those who go to art galleries to do so as couples.[7] Women do, though, visit galleries more frequently than men at a ratio of roughly 1.3:1; are more likely to own art books, at around the same ratio; and are more likely to

Aesthetic divisions in the art field 21

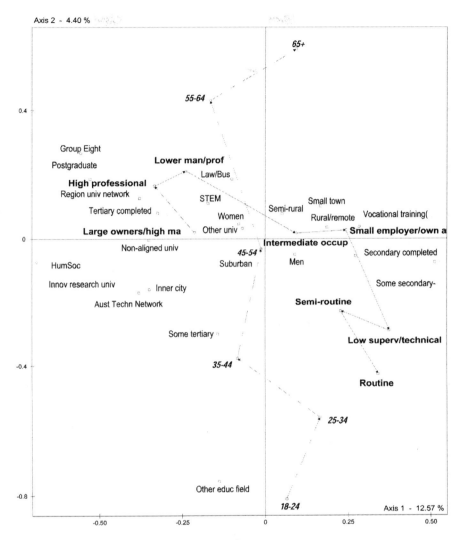

FIGURE 1.2 The social space of art tastes and practices.

dislike landscapes and colonial art at ratios of around 1.6:1 and 1.3:1 respectively. Tastes for artists are mostly similar for men and women. The most significant differences for Australian artists are women's greater preferences for Roberts (at 32 to 24 per cent), Preston (at 16 to 8 per cent) and Done (at 47 to 34 per cent).

Table 1.1 calibrates the effects of class position and level of education in relation to tastes for Australian artists.[8] The main figure in each column is the percentage of that class liking the artist in question; the bracketed figure identifies the percentage of those members of that class liking the artist who have some tertiary education, whether partial, completed or postgraduate. The right-hand column identifies the

TABLE 1.1 Australian artists, heard of, seen and liked by occupational class and level of education

Artists heard of, seen and liked	Large employers/ managers	High professionals	Lower manager/ professionals	Intermediate	Small employers/ own account	Lower supervisory/ technical workers	Semi-routine workers	Routine workers	Lowest/highest class ratios
Done	39 (55)	43 (90)	46 (69)	45 (38)	39 (33)	32 (17)	38 (27)	32 (18)	0.70
Namatjira	53 (62)	53 (83)	57 (70)	65 (45)	53 (40)	34 (16)	36 (28)	37 (29)	0.52
Preston	12 (83)	16 (100)	15 (76)	10 (67)	9 (50)	8 (37)	8 (38)	9 (43)	0.50
Nolan	59 (76)	53 (87)	53 (69)	38 (50)	36 (42)	30 (14)	33 (31)	25 (26)	0.42
Whiteley	38 (75)	39 (88)	35 (72)	22 (52)	25 (49)	21 (17)	19 (33)	16 (13)	0.41
Glover	10 (80)	12 (83)	18 (65)	10 (73)	10 (43)	7 (0)	11 (33)	8 (29)	0.39
Roberts	35 (78)	38 (86)	38 (70)	24 (45)	31 (38)	11 (10)	19 (40)	10 (50)	0.26
Moffatt	6 (66)	7 (100)	7 (93)	4 (100)	3 (66)	2 (0)	4 (33)	8 (29)	0.25
Quilty	16 (50)	16 (92)	19 (66)	13 (62)	13 (61)	4 (60)	6 (20)	11 (40)	0.21

ratio of the class registering the lowest rate of liking for the artist in question relative to the class with the strongest liking for that artist, both represented by shaded areas. The table runs, from top to bottom, from the artist who is least divisive (Done) to the one who is most divisive (Quilty) in terms of the class responses they elicit. The ratio for Done, for example, expresses the rate of liking him among lower supervisory, technical and routine workers at 32 per cent relative to the 46 per cent of lower-level managers and professionals who like him. The lowest rates of liking are all found among the three lowest class positions, particularly routine and lower supervisory and technical workers, both predominantly male in their gendered composition. The highest rates of liking are concentrated in the three highest class positions, except for Namatjira who is most liked by those in intermediate occupations.

The bracketed figures confirm the importance of tertiary education in accounting for the high proportions of the three managerial and professional classes who have heard of, seen and liked all of the artists. However, the proportions of the other classes with tertiary education are also quite high, in some cases (notably routine and semi-routine workers) reflecting the contribution that those who are still at university make to the composition of the classes in question through their part-time or casual employment. More generally, however, given that only those survey respondents who had heard of the named artists could then report having seen and liked them, these figures testify to the significance of tertiary education in distributing a familiarity with those artists across all classes.[9]

To summarise, there are strong connections linking levels of participation in the art field, and familiarity with and liking for the artists named, to ascending class positions and higher levels of education. There is also a significant contrast between preferences for traditional genres and earlier generations of artists, both Australian and international, on the part of middle-aged and older age cohorts, with younger respondents preferring more contemporary institutions, artists and genres.

We now look at the light our household interviews throw on three issues: the role of family in the transmission of particularly intense levels of engagement with the visual arts; the distribution of different aesthetic dispositions across different social positions; and the distinctiveness of responses to both the category and particular examples of Aboriginal art.

Inherited intensities

The close correspondence between degree of participation in the art field and higher class positions and levels of education evident in our survey data is echoed by our interviewees. When asked which galleries they had visited, most interviewees refer to the nearest State or regional gallery, and occasionally the NGA. The few who also identify overseas galleries are usually from higher class positions, university educated and in the upper-age ranges. Eric, a 72-year-old retired advertising executive, makes a point of visiting galleries when overseas on business, citing the Museum of Modern Art and the Whitney Museum of American Art in New York as particular favourites. David, a 78-year-old former manager with a postgraduate qualification, similarly mentions galleries visited in a range of American cities. It is, however, Christine, a 61-year-old Aboriginal woman with an undergraduate degree in a lower-level university management position, who signals the widest range of galleries visited: the Uffizi Gallery in Florence, the National Gallery in London, the Louvre and the Vatican Museums. Giovanni, a 54-year-old vocationally educated middle-level manager of Italian ancestry, has a particular fondness for the Dalí Museums in Paris and Barcelona, and for the Sistine Chapel and Amsterdam's Rijksmuseum. Angela, a vocationally qualified 50-year-old Chinese Australian, visits galleries weekly going beyond State galleries, frequenting Sydney's White Rabbit Gallery, a commercial gallery specialising in contemporary Chinese art, and Sydney's Chinese, Korean and Japanese Cultural Centres.

By contrast, Charles, a 37-year-old Lebanese routine worker with partially completed vocational education, does not visit any galleries, and Naomi, a vocationally qualified 47 year old, does so only rarely. But Craig complicates the picture. A secondary educated 49 year old whose last position was as a forklift driver, Craig is a regular art gallery visitor who relishes abstract art for its challenging qualities and singles out Mona – the so-called 'anti-museum' (Franklin and Papastergiadis, 2017) – for disrupting the snobbishness that he attributes to conventional displays of Australian old masters.

Two other aspects of the interviews are equally striking: the wide range of other involvements in art practice, collecting or sponsorship on the part of those who visit galleries regularly; and the frequency with which such involvement is attributed to a parent or spouse. David, who collects limited edition prints and some originals, tells us his mother was a painter. Christine, who paints and is married to a potter, attributes her interest in art to her parents and is keen to pass it on to her children. Angela also paints, and her husband is an amateur collector. Oliver, a 25 year old with partial tertiary education, attributes his varied tastes in art to his parents – for Australian landscapes to his father and for modern and abstract art to his mother, a postgraduate – who spent 'serious money' in building up their collection. Eric used to buy and sell art semi-professionally, and supported an artist whose work he admired to the tune of $40,000 a year for three years. Finally Gabriel, a 19-year-old university student with a graduate mother and a postgraduate father, speaks knowledgably about a range of contemporary art practices and frequently uses the Internet sites Reddit and Tumblr to access information about the arts.

There is thus a strong tendency for high levels of engagement with the visual arts to be 'inherited intensities'. This is not to say that the aesthetic dispositions that inform such intensities are all of one piece. To the contrary, these differ among those who are deeply immersed in the art field, as well as among those with more modest levels of engagement.

Divided aesthetic dispositions

Genres are notoriously elastic categories, susceptible to different interpretations and evaluations. This is particularly true of art genres given the tension between their more technical, art historical interpretations and — our concern here — their more fluid everyday interpretations. We can best explore these by dividing our genres into two groups: more traditional genres with predominantly figurative associations (landscapes and portraits — two of the most liked genres — Renaissance art, colonial art and still lifes); and modern or more contemporary genres that are often viewed as tending towards abstraction or critical engagements with figurative conventions (Impressionism, plus the three least-liked genres, modern art, Pop art and abstract art).[10] We address the category of Aboriginal art later. Those who like the genres in the first group tend to dislike those associated with the second, and vice versa, as indicated by the ratios in Table 1.2. We calculated these ratios by dividing the percentages of the 'dislikes' for particular genres of those respondents who said they most liked the genre in the first column by the percentage of the dislikes of those who did not include the genres identified in the first column among their most liked genres. To take the first row as an example, 20 per cent of those who included landscapes among their most liked genres identified Impressionism as one of their

TABLE 1.2 Relations between most- and least-liked genres

Genres most liked	Ratios for least-liked genres relative to the rest of the sample
Group 1	
Landscape	Impressionism (1.94:1), modern art (1.7:1), Pop art (1.69:1), abstract art (1.65:1)
Portraits	Impressionism (1.84:1), Aboriginal art (1.59:1), abstract art (1.46:1), modern art (1.12:1), Pop art (1.02:1)
Renaissance art	Modern art (1.76:1), Aboriginal art (1.49:1), Pop art (1.38:1), still lifes (1.15:1), landscapes (1.1:1), abstract art (1.01:1)
Colonial art	Pop art (1.59:1), abstract art (1.38:1), Impressionism (1.29:1), Aboriginal art (1.17:1), modern art (1.10:1)
Still lifes	Renaissance art (1.38:1), Aboriginal art (1.34:1), abstract art (1.22:1), Pop art (1.2:1), modern art (1.19:1), Impressionism (1.13:1)
Group 2	
Abstract art	Landscapes (3.9:1), portraits (2.82:1), colonial art (2.4:1), Aboriginal art (2.01:1), still lifes (1.9:1), Renaissance art (1.59:1)
Pop art	Landscapes (3.37:1), colonial art (2.5:1), Renaissance art (2.1:1), still lifes (1.81:1), portraits (1.45:1), Aboriginal art (1.25:1)
Modern art	Colonial art (3.0:1), landscapes (2.7:1), portraits (2.1:1), Renaissance (1.97:1), still lifes (1.46:1), Aboriginal art (1.12:1)
Aboriginal art	Portraits (1.63:1), landscapes (1.27:1), still lifes (1.25:1), colonial art (1.14:1), Impressionism (1.09:1)
Impressionism	Colonial art (1.55:1), still lifes (1.51:1), landscapes (1.44:1), portraits (1.41:1), Pop art (1.2:1), Aboriginal art (1.1:1), modern art (1.08:1)

least liked genres, while this was true for only 10.3 per cent of the respondents who did not indicate a strong liking for landscapes. The ratio of 1.94 for Impressionism is thus produced by dividing 20 by 10.3.

The most notable aspect of this table is the degree of intensity that is attached to disliking the more traditional and figurative genres on the part of those whose preferences are for more contemporary non-figurative genres: compare the higher ratios registered for the first row in Group 2 to those registered in the first row of Group 1, for example. This reflects the degree to which those who are most involved in the art field register their distinction from those genres with the broadest, and therefore lowest, social currency. The results of a cluster analysis conducted on our data showed that the cluster with the highest rates of art gallery visitation, and with the highest class positions (the higher and lower managerial and professional classes) and levels of education (graduates and postgraduates, with strong associations with the elite Group of Eight universities), is also the cluster whose tastes are characterised by a marked polarity between liking Impressionism, modern, Pop and abstract art, and disliking landscapes, colonial art and still lifes (Bennett and Gayo, 2016: 168).

Similar patterns are evident in our interview data. While there are exceptions, the value placed on landscapes usually stands in contrast to a marked aversion to modern or abstract art. For Aisha, born in Lebanon and now, at 47 years old, a postgraduate-qualified family counsellor, liking landscapes and portraits is accompanied by a sharp dislike of abstract art and Impressionism; she cannot see what these are about, judging that 'they are not for everyone', a view shared by Adrian who finds modern art 'a bit out there somewhere'. For Naomi, abstract art is just 'stupid stuff', not worthy of the respect she accords the technical skills that inform craft art:

> One of the things that I found hilarious was *The Chaser* – that group on TV. They went around and picked up some rubbish off the footpath and walked into the gallery and put it up on a display stand, and only one security guard chased them out. The others just watched them putting junk on a stand. Like, there you go, what does that tell you about art. I think when people have actually got a skill in making something – that it actually looks like something, not just putting bits and pieces to make it look stupid.

While Naomi extends this dislike to surrealism and performance art, dislikes for modern and contemporary art are more usually fleshed out with reference to specific artists. For Lisa, a 42-year-old social science graduate in a lower-level management position, Pollock and Emin are 'self-indulgent ... They're just trying to explore their teenage angst and get paid for it.' For Akela, a 37-year-old vocationally qualified lower manager, Pollock's *Blue Poles* 'just looks like people have splashed paint all over it. I'm like, "Whatever".' Eighteen-year-old Harley, an irregular and somewhat reluctant gallery visitor (he records being obliged to go to Brisbane's GOMA on school visits and occasionally goes there when 'wanting something to do' but not would not go out of his way 'to admire and look at the art'), seems to present a contrary case in his survey preference for both portraits and modern art. But when asked about this he expresses his admiration for the skill of portraitists in their lifelike depictions of 'the person sitting there' while disowning any serious interest in modern art which he appreciates purely for its entertainment value. If he likes Pollock's *Blue Poles* it's because 'just like I could have done that and I could have been rich'.

Dislike of landscapes is usually paired with disliking portraits and/or still lifes, and with liking modern, abstract or Pop art. Jacinta, a tertiary educated 49 year old, contrasts her appreciation of abstract art not to landscapes as such but to those that present 'an idyllic picture of the landscape'. She finds Australian landscapes that capture the harshness and vastness of the land 'much more interesting' than European landscapes, singling out Sidney Nolan's landscapes for the way they 'incorporate human figures in the stories they tell'. Her enthusiasm for Turner's landscapes is more muted on the grounds of her greater preference for 'more abstract art'. Craig, a fan of Andy Warhol and Roy Lichtenstein whose preferences are for modern and Pop art, finds landscapes 'just a bit boring ... You know, might as well look at the photo.' Brenton, a 35-year-old practising artist working across a range of media, is similarly inclined. Expressing a strong commitment to art for art's sake ('I don't go [to galleries] for the small talk ... I go for the art') and relishing its capacity for 'breaking new ground', he prefers the openness of modern and abstract art to what he sees as the closure of landscapes and portraits:

> I don't like being spoon-fed. I like having room to make my own decisions, and to find what I think the artist's intentions are ... And I just like the playfulness of it: the experimentation; the opportunity to break new ground.

This set of oppositions is complicated by Gabriel whose favoured genre is portraits. However, while fond of portraits by the 'old masters', his contemporary preference is for digital portraits which, by emphasising grotesque facial and bodily features, defamiliarise the idealising conventions of portraiture (they are 'a refreshing break from the normal'). Gabriel also dislikes Warhol's work for having 'been pastiched and reused so many times' that it now just 'seems blasé'. Eric similarly complicates the picture by relishing abstract art while also liking landscapes and portraits. But the rationale underlying this combination becomes clearer when he goes on to draw a sharp historical dividing line in his tastes:

> I don't like old/traditional paintings ... No, I've seen enough paintings of [the] Renaissance and I don't want to see any more ... I do not like religious based paintings at all ... I just have no interest whatsoever in seeing another sign of a cross ... No, I find them bleak and uninteresting. So I'd rather go to a museum of contemporary art.

Responses to the category of Aboriginal art are shaped by a distinctive set of considerations. This is partly because of the instability that is built into the category itself, which might be interpreted to refer to traditional forms of Aboriginal art, the more abstract forms of acrylic dot art, contemporary urban Aboriginal art practices, rock art or the kitsch forms of 'Aboriginalia' (Fisher, 2016: 64). The effects of these different interpretations are evident in Table 1.2 where Aboriginal art is disliked along with modern, abstract and Pop art by those who prefer the more traditional figurative genres in Group 1 of landscapes, portraits, Renaissance art, colonial art and still lifes. But the reverse is also true: those who like abstract, Pop and modern art in Group 2 are just as likely to group Aboriginal art with more traditional and figurative genres as ones they dislike. The balance, however, is tilted towards the association of Aboriginal art with abstraction given that, where it is the favoured genre, the genres that are most strongly ranged against it are portraits, landscapes and still lifes.

This association with abstraction is evident in the interviews too, but as an exceptional form of abstraction: abstraction with a readily intelligible referent in view of the ways in which Aboriginal art is typically curated to highlight its connections to country and culture. While Badal, a 42 year old who is currently retraining for a teaching qualification, is attracted to the 'uniqueness of Aboriginal art and the dots', this is distinguished from modern and abstract art ('equivalent to what my daughters would do in kindergarten') because 'there's stories behind it … that art over there is the story they are trying to tell'. Mayra, who dislikes abstract art – 'when I'm thinking of abstract I'm thinking of splotches of colour, or just plain blocks' – similarly likes the 'dynamic colour' of Aboriginal art, 'the movement in it … The stories behind it, the connections that it has.' For Eric, similarly, it is the story that counts: 'loved the story … hated the painting' he says about an Aboriginal painting his wife had bought.

Namatjira is the Aboriginal artist most frequently referred to, usually because of the capacity attributed to his work to mediate the relations between competing values. Eric likes him for not being 'too abstract', arguing against criticisms of his work as 'chocolate-box' art in view of its depiction of 'the beauty of the bush and the country'. For Adrian, Namatjira serves as a counter to his dislike of modern and abstract art because his paintings are 'real … they just feel like he's telling a story in his picture and they're real'. Craig invokes Namatjira's work as a counter to his general antipathy to landscapes in view of how it mediates the relations between Aboriginal and mainstream Australian art:

> He was an Aboriginal guy … But he … didn't paint in the dot style or whatever you want to call it. I mean, he painted in the white man style, but he obviously had talent … And being an Aussie I guess he saw things from his perspective, with the Indigenous perspective and I guess I liked that about his work.

This has been a long-standing aspect of the reception of Namatjira's work, albeit that interpretations of its mediating properties have varied (see Figure 1.3).

Ken Done provides a telling contrast to Namatjira. Both are among the three Australian artists most seen and liked – 40 per cent for Done, and 49 per cent for Namatjira – and, as we saw in Table 1.1, they are the least polarising figures in

FIGURE 1.3 Albert Namatjira. Palm Valley. *Circa* 1940.

Sources: Central Australia/Northern Territory/Australia, Hermannsburg/Northern Territory/Australia; Albert Namatjira (Australia, b.1902, d.1959); *Palm Valley* 1940s; watercolour, 37 × 54.2 cm; Art Gallery of New South Wales; Purchased 1986; © Namatjira Legacy Trust. Licensed by Copyright Agency 2017; Photo: Diana Panuccio, AGNSW; 93.1986.

The first Aboriginal artist to be accorded significant recognition by white Australian art institutions, Namatjira's work was initially viewed as a largely imitative adaptation of the traditions of pastoral modernism that characterised inter-war Australian landscape painting. Interpreted as testifying to a capacity for assimilation into white Australia, his work, when first collected by Australian art galleries, was classified as Australian rather than as Aboriginal (McLean, 2018: 190). His typical scenes – ghost gums, palm-filled gorges, distant mountains in the purple light of dusk, all devoid of any human presence – were also viewed as prophesying a future from which Aboriginal people had been evacuated. Such assimilationist interpretations of the 1950s and 1960s – when reproductions of Namatjira's paintings were a regular feature of suburban households – were often combined with a 'middlebrow' fondness for pastoral modernism. While still influential, such interpretations have since given way, at least in the art world, to transcultural appreciations of Namatjira's work. Far from being empty, his landscapes are imbued with the presence of ancestors whose final resting places give order and shape to nature, thus building 'a new compact between Indigenous and Western worldviews' (McLean, 2016: 85). Indigenous interpretations of Namatjira's work have always appreciated its strategic political value in this regard.

terms of the class distribution of those who had seen and liked their work. Done, however, is far more polarising when dislikes are taken into account: while 30 per cent of those who had heard of Done dislike his work, the equivalent figure for Namatjira is 6 per cent. This disliking of Done was the highest of all the Australian artists we asked about, and most strongly associated with higher class positions: 36 per cent of the professional and managerial classes versus 20 per cent of routine and semi-routine workers. Our interviewees from the former classes either dislike

Done for being too commercial, or accord him grudging respect for his success in the marketplace. Eric brings together both responses:

> I actually know and do like some of Ken Done's work, but not the sort of stuff that you know — that he sells ... He's a really good artist, but he's learnt to paint popular ... he's commercialised his work, so good luck to him.

Done is, then, the Australian artist around whom the art versus commerce polarity — the tension between the 'anti-economy' logic of art versus subservience to capital that characterises Bourdieu's (1993) account of the relations between the restricted and extended fields of cultural production — is most strongly evident.

Conclusion

There is a significant tendency in contemporary art theory to interpret the logics governing contemporary art practice as breaking with those proposed by Bourdieusian art field theory. The category of contemporary art itself, the practices of installation art, the connection between art fairs and the 'experience economy': all of these, it is suggested, cast doubt on Bourdieu's account of the organisation and dynamics of art fields given the centrality he accorded easel painting, his reliance on modernist conceptions of avant-gardes as the driving force of change within art fields and his focus on national art institutions (Jones, 2016; Nagel, 2012; Osborne, 2018). These contentions undoubtedly establish real issues meriting serious attention. At the same time, however, two other aspects of recent developments testify to the continuing pertinence of the principles underlying Bourdieu's analysis of art fields if not their historical particulars. One concerns the continuation, and indeed the strengthening, of the connections between the major art institutions, an increasingly corporatised and global capitalism, and the owning, professional and managerial classes who are its major representatives and beneficiaries (Horowitz, 2011; Stallabrass, 2004). The second concerns the continuing significance of education in drawing the boundary lines between adept consumers in the art field and those who, lacking the means of acquiring the 'cultivated disposition' required for such consumption, are estranged from it. A key factor in the organisation of such distinctions, Bourdieu and Darbel argued, consists in the acquisition of the ability to distinguish different forms and periods of art in terms of their distinctive stylistic characteristics. It follows from this that non-figurative practices tend to be rejected by those who lack such a capacity, given their failure to deliver what they most look for in a work of art: 'an unequivocal meaning, transcending the signifier' (Bourdieu and Darbel, 1991: 40–41).

While we have been careful to shade and qualify the force of such distinctions, their continuing salience is evident. We have already noted that preferences for non-figurative genres are strongest among those occupying the higher class positions and levels of education, and that they are shared by younger arts consumers, also quite strongly immersed in art institutions, but at earlier stages in their educational and occupational careers. In the cluster analysis of our data referred to earlier, the two clusters in which such tastes predominate account for 28 per cent of the sample. These are counterbalanced by two clusters, accounting for 49 per cent of the sample, whose members, chiefly occupying working-class occupations with secondary or vocational qualifications, show zero or very low levels of participation in the art field, and tastes – with the exception of a liking for abstract art on the part of still current students in part-time routine and semi-routine work – that are strongly inclined towards the figurative. One of Bourdieu and Darbel's main conclusions in *The Love of Art* was that the more the education system leaves the task of transmitting skills in the classification and interpretation of works of art to the family, the more it tends 'to sanction and legitimate existing inequalities' (Bourdieu and Darbel, 1991: 66) – a conclusion which holds with equal force in contemporary Australia.

Notes

1 We draw here on earlier discussions in Bennett (2015; 2018) and on Anderson (2011), Grishin (2013) and Van den Bosch (2005).
2 In the 1970s, new art and curatorial practices were largely developed in temporary exhibitions and installations organised mainly outside the State art gallery sector (Mendelssohn et al., 2018: 63–85) which remained largely a conservative force but has since adjusted to accommodate contemporary art practice alongside its longer-term heritage concerns.
3 Prime Minister Gough Whitlam intervened to secure the purchase of *Blue Poles* for the future NGA in the context of controversies concerning whether the gallery should be a gallery of national art or a national gallery of world art that would include Australian art of an equivalent standing. See Thomas (1999) and Van den Bosch (2005) for details.
4 Axes in MCA figures are not labelled since they do not measure single variables that have been determined on an a priori basis prior to the conduct of the MCA. There are rather plotted against the axes the intersections of multiple variables. The determination as to which of this is predominantly related to the horizontal or vertical axes is made in the course of analysing the MCA results.
5 For reasons outlined in Appendix C, Tillers and Emin have had to be grouped together in view of the low responses both elicited.
6 Appendix D gives more detail regarding the composition of these classes.
7 A notable aspect of the household interviews is how frequently, when talking about art, the interviewees would switch from 'I' to 'we' when describing their tastes and practices.
8 Tillers is excluded from this table. Those liking his work are too low in number to provide a basis for meaningful comparisons.
9 The rates of recognition for many of the artists named in our survey are often very low. This is less true for the classic figures of the Renaissance and Western modernism – da Vinci, Rembrandt and Van Gogh – all of whom with rates of recognition above 80 per cent of the sample are more widely recognised than the best-known Australian artist, Ken Done. But recognition rates for more contemporary artists are notably low: 10 per cent or less for Tillers, Ai Weiwei and Emin, for example.
10 The most popular genres were landscapes (52 per cent) followed by Aboriginal art (26 per cent), portraits (24 per cent) and modern art (17 per cent). Impressionism and Renaissance art came in at around 15 per cent each, while abstract art, colonial art, Pop art and still lifes ranged, in order, from 13 per cent down to 7 per cent. Abstract art, Pop art and modern art topped the list of least-liked genres at 40 per cent, 36 per cent and 18 per cent respectively. Dislikes for colonial art, Impressionism and still lifes were bundled closely together at around 15 per cent each, with Aboriginal art, portraits and Renaissance art all clustered at around the 10 per cent mark. Landscapes were the 'least least-liked' at only 7 per cent.

2
BOOK VALUE
Reading the Australian literary field

David Carter, Modesto Gayo and Michelle Kelly

Maria, a schoolteacher who lives in western Sydney, was dismayed to learn her sister-in-law was proposing to throw out a leather-bound set of Encyclopaedia Britannica. Inspired by image-sharing website Pinterest, she enlisted another family member to build a bookshelf out of the encyclopaedias, and this now sits in her primary school classroom. Sean, a high-level manager, was dismantling a bar in his home in order to install bookshelves and create a reading nook. Asked if he discards books after he's read them, Sean replies, 'No, they're like little trophies.'

Maria and Sean are among those interviewed for the *Australian Cultural Fields* (ACF) project, in part about their reading and literary tastes. While the activities cited might not be literary in a narrow sense, they do suggest that both are participants in book culture, the term we use for the wide range of social, domestic and professional engagements with books and reading that attach a distinctive *value* to such engagement: activities such as regular bookstore browsing, book ownership, attending literary festivals or book clubs, investment in reading, or following books in the media or online. Maria loves mystery novels and *The Da Vinci Code* author Dan Brown; she's read all the Harry Potter books and is currently reading Jane Austen's *Emma*. She is passionate about children's reading in her work as a teacher. Sean is a fan of Dorothy L. Sayers and David Malouf; he has met famous writers and attended a talk by Robert Ludlum. He is about to embark on a programme of re-reading 'everything Henry Lawson wrote' (an iconic figure from the late nineteenth century nationalist literary movement in Australia). In their home and workplace, both make manifest the value they ascribe to books and reading. The trophy and the bookshelf join to produce a powerful twinned image of the complex of personal, social and even somatic values attached to books.

In this chapter we first bring Bourdieu's notion of the field of cultural production into dialogue with the literary field in contemporary Australia, noting distinctive aspects of the Australian case in its international context. We then outline the major institutions defining this field, and our choice of survey items for named genres, authors and forms of participation. This account sets the background for our analysis of the distribution of reading tastes and participation as revealed by the ACF survey data and the roles that education, occupation, age and gender play in what is a strikingly unequal distribution of engagement with books and reading. In the final section, interview material is analysed to reveal a range of tastes, practices and socio-demographic factors characteristic of an Australian 'reading class' (Griswold, 2008). This group, we conclude, has distinct and distinguishing educational and professional characteristics, although its tastes range across canonical and popular books, particularly genre fiction, rather than being restricted to high-status literature.

The literary field in contemporary Australia

For Bourdieu, the literary field was exemplary of the field of cultural production, 'obeying its own laws of functioning and transformation' (Bourdieu, 1995: 214) with specific forms of capital at stake in 'a systematic inversion of the fundamental principles of all ordinary economies' (Bourdieu, 1993: 39; Boschetti, 2006). Bourdieu's model is often reduced to a singular polarisation between pure literature and mass-commercial production, then criticised for its incapacity to account for contemporary literary culture. But this is to ignore his emphasis on the dynamics of change, both temporal and structural, driven by ongoing, field-changing struggles between and within avant-garde, bourgeois and petit-bourgeois positions across the literary field.

As such, Bourdieu's model can accommodate major transformations in the structure of the field over time and in different locations – from mid-twentieth century France to twenty-first century Australia – without, of course, predicting their exact nature. At the same time, its logic insists that insofar as the specific forms of capital in play remain the same, the dynamics of the field will be driven by struggles for legitimacy between artistic and other forms of success. Despite major changes, we argue that these dynamics remain central to the field in contemporary Australia even if the legitimating power accorded to the literary and the denigration attached to the commercial have both diminished.

There have been significant impacts in the Australian literary field over the last two decades from digital technologies and changes in the education system, government investment and literary politics, not least the greater prominence of Indigenous authors (Griffiths, 2018). New fractions among writers and readers, however, have emerged less from avant-garde rebellions than from genre communities, especially in fantasy and science fiction (Driscoll et al., 2018), and among digital activists staking new claims to symbolic value against consecrated forms of literary tastemaking (Murray, 2018). Bourdieu (2010: 19) himself observed that certain forms of popular culture were gaining legitimacy, but gave little specific attention to the world of commercial cultural production, assuming its mass qualities rather than its multiplicity and ignoring its capacity to affect conditions at the literary end of the scale (Hesmondhalgh, 2006: 217). Certainly, in twenty-first century Australia – and globally – genre fiction has a greater, field-changing significance with stronger claims on cultural legitimacy than in previous decades. Its success has shifted the meaning of legitimacy itself so that it can now be less about aesthetic form than, say, generic innovation. A niche genre publisher can operate much like a dedicated poetry house, while literary fiction itself can function as a niche sector within the broader fiction industry (Collins, 2010). The unique status of literary art has less power of distinction, as new digital platforms, self-publishing and active genre communities have produced multiple sites of value rather than a single mass market. Even romance fiction has gained in esteem, although, as the ACF survey reveals, it remains the least valued of fiction genres (Carter and Kelly, 2017: 157).

Still, the jostling for position between economic and symbolic capital continues to structure the field across its agents, institutions and consumers (Thompson, 2012; Carter, 2016a). We see this in the ambiguous status of literary festivals and prizes, often the most sought-after rewards yet always liable to be seen as the wrong kind of success (Indyk, 2015); in ambivalent attitudes to the creative writing programmes flourishing in universities, offering new forms of legitimation but still commonly defined against 'autonomous' literary achievement; and in the positions staked out by publishers, often internally, where divisions between commercial and literary fiction remain routine. The tensions between economic and symbolic capital can be intense, especially in the field of fiction, 'the most dispersed genre in terms of its forms of consecration' (Bourdieu, 1993: 51).

In the Australian context, symbolic capital can also involve a form of national cultural capital: the book or author seen to contribute not only to literature but to the national culture. The nation's settler-colonial and immigrant history and its geo-political location gives this dimension a particular valency. While discussions of a national literature emerged in the nineteenth century, and then more urgently in the inter-war and Cold War years, it was only in the post-war decades that a significant local infrastructure developed. Adelaide Writers Week, the first major literary festival, began in 1960; a Literature Board was created within the Australia Council in 1973; university study of Australian literature grew significantly from the 1970s. Local publishers became more active, while resident British firms built strong Australian lists (Carter, 2009).

Australia's is a medium-sized industry and book market within a global industry: small enough to be dominated by imported titles, but large enough to sustain a mix of local and global publishers. It is also protected by parallel importation restrictions (Carter, 2016a).[1] As elsewhere, the Australian market is dominated by the 'big four' – Penguin Random House, HarperCollins, Pan Macmillan and Hachette – but there has been no sudden globalisation of the Australian book trade (Carter and Kelly, 2018). It was in one sense 'born global', as part of the British publishing sphere; and over the last two decades independent firms have played an increasing, not declining, role in local fiction publishing.

The most important effect of digital developments has been an expanded market for writers and readers, especially in genre fiction, an effect confirmed by our interviews with readers. On the production side there has been enormous growth in self-published titles, especially in genre fiction (romance, fantasy). On the consumption side, online retailers comprise around 20 per cent of trade sales (Zwar, 2016: 8), while direct online purchasing from publishers is now common. But there has been no platform revolution in books to match that in television or music. The major houses have launched digital-first imprints with mixed success (Driscoll et al., 2018). Digital publishing has been merged into established operations, while ebooks have stabilised at around 20 per cent of production (Jefferies, 2017: 6). The ACF survey suggests that 62 per cent of people own no ebooks and a further 17 per cent own fewer than ten; but there is also a group of voracious adopters, the 5 per cent who own more than 200 ebooks. Australians also still prefer obtaining books from bookstores: in the year preceding the ACF survey, 65 per cent of respondents had bought from local bookstores compared to 38 per cent through online booksellers and 27 per cent purchasing ebooks.

There now exists a dense institutional structure supporting book culture and literature in Australia. Books are recognised in the Prime Minister's Literary Awards and state-level prizes, writers festivals are expanding, and both independent and multinational publishers are committed to Australian books. While authors' incomes remain low – a classic case of economic capital not matching cultural capital – literature can still carry high prestige. Its autonomy, in Bourdieu's terms, can underwrite its 'disinterested' transference to other discourses around the nation, and despite the academic unfashionability of national paradigms such transferences are confirmed in teaching and criticism both inside and outside the university. Literature can still be invoked in public discourses as *defining* of identity or nation, tradition or the new.

The literary field can be divided into three separate institutional clusters, each with its own forms of legitimating power but also divided internally by competing hierarchies of value: the academic, centred in the universities and secondary education; the state, including funding bodies, libraries and support for awards, writers centres, etc.; and what we might call the public-commercial, including publishers, booksellers, agents, festivals and review forums, whether broadcast, print or online.[2] These three clusters function relationally, with distinct priorities but also overlapping in complementary and conflicting ways. Academics, who perhaps carry the most prestige but the least direct power, engage with other sites in the literary field as reviewers, prize judges or festival speakers, although such engagement typically involves some internal recalibration, even distancing, as institutional boundaries are traversed. Publishers' symbolic capital (Thompson, 2012: 7) can involve engagement with aesthetic forms of legitimation, even as the market is prioritised. Festivals represent a microcosm of the literary field (Weber, 2018) with all three clusters engaged, again in ways both complementary and conflictual.

These institutions of consecration are no doubt less concentrated or autonomous than those in Bourdieu's France, in the sense that literature's authority will often derive from its association with ethical or civic functions. Anti-canonical and anti-elitist gestures are now widespread across the education system, while the most vibrant forms of literary activity such as festivals, reading groups and online discussions occur largely without reference to the academic sphere. Still, as we show, higher education continues to play a critical role in shaping tastes for reading. And while the interests of differently positioned agents will not necessarily match each other or those of government or educational bodies, in the relatively restricted places where such questions matter there is a substantial degree of consensus about where books and authors sit on the scale of literature and which belong to conversations about the nation. How far this consensus is shared by non-professional readers is explored below.

Books and book culture

The ACF survey addressed reading preferences among different genres and selected authors, and respondents' engagement with relevant institutions and events, from bookstore browsing to attending writers festivals to number of ebooks owned. Our focus was specifically on books and book culture – the literary field in Bourdieu's terms – rather than reading habits in general. Respondents were asked to indicate which among 12 kinds of books they read for their own interest or pleasure.[3] The selection covered fiction and non-fiction items, some distinguished primarily by subject matter (Australian history, self-help/lifestyle, biographies), others by their location within the genre system according to the degree of cultural prestige normally attached to them. Thus we surveyed categories such as literary classics and modern novels alongside popular fiction genres such as crime/mystery, sci-fi/fantasy and romance.

We also asked about knowledge of and liking for ten Australian and ten international authors, primarily fiction writers. The Australian authors, mostly contemporary, cover a range of different positions in the literary field. Elizabeth Harrower, David Malouf, Tim Winton, Kate Grenville and two Indigenous authors, Sally Morgan and Kim Scott, have been regularly included in considerations of Australian literature and awarded literary prizes. Some have also had commercial success, especially Winton and Grenville (see Figure 2.1). They sit alongside bestselling authors Bryce Courtenay, whose *The Power of One* (1989) was followed by a series of historical novels and international dramas, and Belinda Alexandra, author of historical romances and family sagas. Thriller and science fiction writer Matthew Reilly and fantasy author Sara Douglass represent more niche tastes in genre fiction, albeit with international success.

Our international selection covers a range of historical and contemporary figures, mostly Anglophone: canonical literary authors such as Virginia Woolf and Margaret Atwood; the postmodern novelist Don DeLillo; esteemed crime writer Ian Rankin; bestseller thriller author Stephen King; respected mainstream novelists Amy Tan and Jodi Picoult; and those who might be considered niche or cult tastes, essayist and novelist Dave Eggers and the widely translated Japanese novelist Haruki Murakami. Last, but by no means least, Jane Austen, whose reputation now covers the range from literary classic to 'women's fiction' to bestselling precursor of modern romance and 'chick lit'.

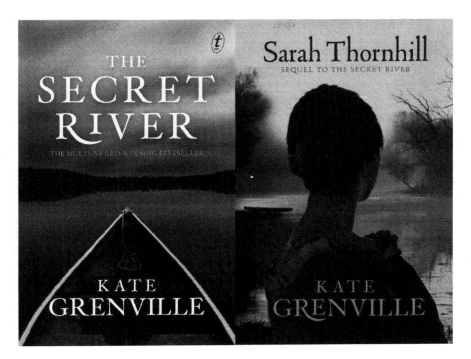

FIGURE 2.1 Covering Kate Grenville.

Source: Covers reproduced with permission of Text Publishing, Melbourne.

Cover images for two of Kate Grenville's novels dealing with early colonisation in New South Wales take different positions within the literary field, reflecting Grenville's 'dual status' as a recognised literary novelist and a commercially successful author of historical fiction. The story of settler–Indigenous conflict central to her prize-winning novel *The Secret River* (2005) is not announced by its cover; instead the aesthetically formal, almost abstract, design seems to invite interpretation. By contrast, its sequel, *Sarah Thornhill* (2011), carries a much more accessible figurative cover, inviting empathy. It seems to present the book as both women's fiction and historical romance.

Figure 2.2, plotting survey responses which correspond to the active socio-demographic variables displayed in Figure 2.3, shows a field starkly split between readers and non-readers, the former partly influenced by hierarchies of legitimacy but also comprising a range of 'interest groups' constituted by invested tastes in certain genres and differing types of involvement in book culture. The top right quadrant reveals a space of significant disengagement from books and book culture. Many of the surveyed book types are not read, and only books about sport register positively. There are fewer than 50 books in the home ('books home'), no ebooks are owned ('ebooks'), no books by Australian authors read ('book read Aus'), nor is there evidence of any discretionary activity relating to book culture. A cluster analysis of the ACF data has suggested that a quarter of respondents have no to very low involvement in the literary field, and a further 14 per cent have limited involvement (Kelly *et al.*, 2018: 7).

38 David Carter *et al.*

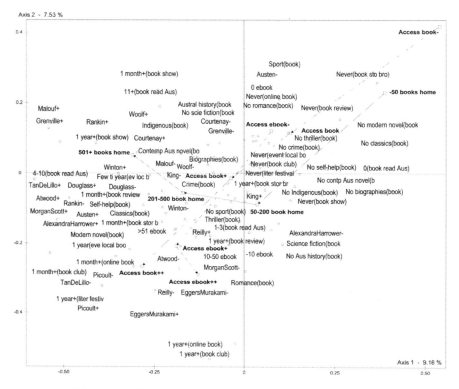

FIGURE 2.2 The space of literary tastes and practices.

The remaining quadrants represent the space of Australian book reading and book culture, although the bottom right quadrant also shows relatively low levels of engagement. Sci-fi/fantasy registers positively here and book ownership increases (50–200), but ebooks remain low (<10). On the border between left and right quadrants, both reading and not reading romance fiction appear, as does liking for King. For the different forms of participation in book culture surveyed, we can observe, first, a series of roughly diagonal lines that link zones of no/low participation in the upper right quadrant to zones of high participation in the lower left. On Figure 2.2 we mark the patterns for obtaining books and ebooks: both range from zero/low in the upper right ('Access book-' and 'Access ebook-') to high levels in the lower left ('Access book++' and 'Access ebook++'). Rates of bookstore browsing ('book sto bro') range similarly, from never to once a month or more; so too do number of ebooks, from 0 to more than 50 in the lower left, albeit with the intermediate ranges (<10; 10–50) lower down. These practices represent the most accessible elements of book culture.

Other participation measures follow a similar diagonal descent from the upper right quadrant except that the highest levels of engagement appear nearer the upper left. This is shown on Figure 2.2 by tracing the line connecting numbers of books in the home: falling then rising and moving leftwards as it plots '50–200', '201–500', then '501+ books' in the upper left. Although the patterns and locations on the chart vary, we can see comparable trajectories – falling diagonally from right to left, then rising towards the upper left – for attending events at local bookstores or similar venues ('ev local book'); reading book reviews or following book shows ('book review', 'book show'); and, lower down but with a similar strong movement up and to the left for the highest levels of engagement, book club participation and following books and authors online or on social media ('book club', 'online book'). The pattern can also be seen in the number of Australian books read, revealing a growing volume of and, perhaps, a more deliberate investment in nationally inflected materials.[4] Together, these lines suggest patterns of increasing participation in more prestigious or specialised forms of book culture and thus of increasing cultural capital.

Arranged around these lines are other patterns relating to book types and named authors. Non-fiction genres, with the exception of self-help/lifestyle books, appear above the horizontal dividing line. Sports books, as indicated, appear among those otherwise disengaged from book culture in the upper right quadrant (the negative indicator for sports books registers lower down but still not far to the left). Australian history, biographies and Indigenous books (fiction or non-fiction) are clustered together in the upper left quadrant, near the centre; but all register negatively in the lower right. The positive indicators for fictional forms are more dispersed, but with clear horizontal and vertical differences: preferences for contemporary Australian novels, modern novels and literary classics sit towards the left, sci-fi/fantasy, thriller/ adventure and romance towards the right and lower. Likes and dislikes for romance fiction are vertically aligned near the vertical dividing line, suggesting that readers to the left have low engagement with the form.

What might appear a straightforward hierarchy of popular and literary genres is complicated by the fiction/non-fiction divide, and further by the responses registered for named authors. There are significant clusters of likes for named authors in both the upper and lower left quadrants, and especially towards the left of these spaces; at the same time, in the 'inner left' there are also many dislikes for authors liked in the outer left (Malouf, Grenville, Woolf, Winton, Douglass). Literary authors such as Malouf, Grenville and Woolf sit alongside Rankin in the upper left, in contrast to Courtenay, say, nearer the centre. But while this pattern suggests a cluster of 'literary' readers, a *wider* range of positive tastes appears in the lower left comprising better known literary figures such as Austen and Atwood alongside a variety of literary, mainstream and niche authors. Certain genre or bestselling authors – Rankin, Douglass, Picoult, even Courtenay – are positioned more to the left than might be expected, near recognised literary figures, while niche or 'cult' authors such as Eggers and Murakami are somewhat isolated at the bottom of the lower left. King and Reilly sit more to the right. In sum, although we see a literary-popular spread from left to right on the chart, there is no singular binary: established literary tastes tend to cluster in the upper left, but these mix with more diverse tastes in the lower left quadrant where Austen appears – as a popular author, perhaps, rather than or as well as a canonised classic.

The significance of these patterns of tastes and participation emerges when mapped against the key socio-demographic variables (Figure 2.3). As revealed in previous studies of reading (Bennett et al., 1999; Wright, 2006; Bennett et al., 2009; Atkinson, 2016; Throsby et al., 2017), gender is a critical dividing line, cutting across the space of participation and non-participation. The mean point for male respondents falls in the upper right and for women in the lower left where the most diverse reading tastes appear, reflecting the diagonal lines of differentiation described above. In the ACF survey, women register a stronger liking for all book types except two, sci-fi/fantasy and sport (Carter and Kelly, 2017: 156–162). Australian history is read by 56 per cent of both genders, but sits higher for men in the ranking of genres (third against fifth), as do all the non-fiction categories except self-help/lifestyle.

Women are also more likely to have read all the named authors except for DeLillo; numbers are very small for both genders but DeLillo does appear to be more a male taste. The survey confirms that romance is read by women significantly more than by men, 42 per cent compared to 7 per cent, but it does not rank highly in women's preferences overall, only ninth among the 12 genres (Carter and

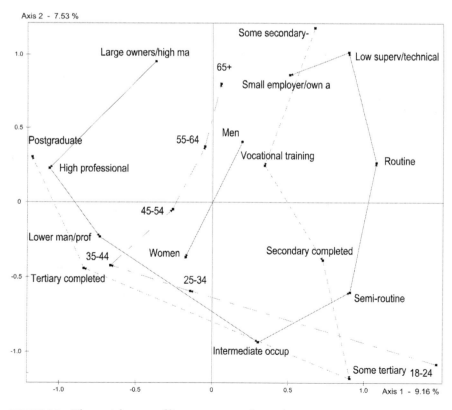

FIGURE 2.3 The social space of literary tastes and practices.

Kelly, 2017: 157). Age also has a clear logic, with 25–54 year olds located in the densest space of books and reading. Older people are oriented more towards non-fiction and established authors and modes of participation. For younger people we see stronger associations with certain contemporary authors (Eggers, Murakami, Reilly), with ebooks and with occasional participation online or through reading groups.[5] The youngest group is set off to the far right in a way that suggests low engagement overall, apart from with sci-fi/fantasy, and again occasional participation in digital forms of book activity.

While gender and age structure configurations of taste and participation, the heavier weighting of the horizontal axis (9.16 per cent against 7.53 per cent for the vertical axis) indicates that education and occupational class are the most significant factors for books and reading. Postgraduate qualifications and higher professional occupations sit close together within the upper left quadrant, where selective, established literary tastes predominate together with high levels of book ownership. (Large owners/high managers also sit in this space but much closer to the zone of low participation.) The more expansive tastes and wide engagement with book-related activities in the lower left are more closely aligned to those in lower professional-managerial occupations and with tertiary qualifications, with intermediate occupations and secondary education to their right. Primary or incomplete secondary education and vocational training are in the space of no/low participation, alongside the routine, lower supervisory/technical and small employer/self-employed categories.

Cumulatively, these patterns strongly confirm that higher education and professional occupations give increased access to, or encourage investment in, the literary field, evidence confirmed by comparing the genre preferences of the different occupational classes (Table 2.1; Carter and Kelly, 2017: 165). Those in professional-managerial occupations register above average positive scores for 10 or more of the 12 kinds of books surveyed; so too those in intermediate occupations. By contrast, large owners/high managers on one side and small employers/self-employed on the other are above average only for four kinds of book (rising slightly to six for lower supervisory and technical workers). These results suggest the existence in Australia of a distinct reading class that is 'educated, affluent ... middle aged and tilted toward women' (Griswold, 2008: 167; Kelly *et al.*, 2018). For Griswold (2008: 160) in the United States, this group represents a significant minority 'with influence disproportionate to their numbers'. We will return to these issues in our conclusion.

Reading and value

In this final section we turn to interviews with survey respondents, concentrating on the 'readers' among them in order to investigate in more detail how those with some level of engagement with the field understand their reading experiences and relation to book culture. Almost all our readers, in this sense, have higher education qualifications and are in professional-managerial occupations, although the majority are in lower rather than higher professional ranks. Even among this group of regular

TABLE 2.1 Genres read for interest/pleasure (percentage of occupational class group)

	1	2	3	4	5	6	7	8	Average
Thriller/adventure	57	65	60	65	51	56	57	55	59
Crime/mystery	50	63	63	67	43	60	52	52	57
Biographies	58	68	61	61	52	58	48	42	56
Australian history	57	60	60	49	59	61	48	55	56
Modern novels	45	57	51	50	42	38	42	28	47
Literary classics	33	58	54	51	34	34	39	22	45
Sci-fi/fantasy	46	48	37	46	30	39	48	46	42
Self-help/lifestyle	37	41	45	42	36	29	44	33	40
Contemporary Australian novels	39	48	46	40	45	29	29	27	40
Indigenous	29	35	38	33	38	35	31	27	34
Sport	29	33	24	28	35	38	24	28	28
Romance	19	15	26	39	23	28	24	20	25
None	8	1	3	0.9	6	5	6	10	4

1 = large owners/high management; 2 = high professional; 3 = lower professional/managerial; 4 = intermediate occupations; 5 = small employer/own account; 6 = low supervisory/technical; 7 = semi-routine; 8 = routine. Average = overall result for each genre across the main sample. Shaded = above average (reversed for 'None', i.e. shaded = *below* average). Bold = highest.

readers, however, there are no spontaneous uses of the word 'literary' and little evidence of the aesthetic disposition, in Bourdieu's sense of the term, valuing 'form over function' (Bourdieu, 2010: 22) – an author's style or symbolism, say, over story or character. Perhaps closest is video editor and performer Brenton, who links tastes for literary authors such as Peter Carey, Edgar Allan Poe and poet Charles Bukowski with 'old occult literature, just for the sake of the weirdness of it all'. Overall, there is little sense that engagement with books and reading is organised primarily in relation to traditional hierarchies of legitimacy, even when canonical status is acknowledged. There is a clear disconnect between most readers' orientations to books and academic or aesthetic orientations. Nonetheless, literary classics have a presence and distinctions of value are recurrent even where 'literature' is absent.

Unsurprisingly, it is the reading experience itself that interviewees highlight, their immersion in character or plots with a twist: a 'really fast paced story', a 'quick read', books that make 'you feel you want to read on'. As Maria puts it, 'I don't mind who I read as long as it gets me in the first few pages.' The idea of reading for enjoyment or escape, of losing oneself in a book, is common, but such expressions conceal diverse responses, including forms of engagement. As Jacinta, a tertiary educated part-time education consultant, comments, 'I want to lose myself in a book [but] not necessarily in an escapist way'; here getting lost is about finding a point of connection, in this case getting 'a sense of the characters'. The value attached to being immersed in a book is often as a form of active engagement in ethical, civic or pedagogical exercises, in 'human nature' or 'historical relevance'.

For Indigenous teacher Kim, reading good paranormal fantasy means 'you learn the people and it's not just a book, it's almost like real people and you get to know the characters'; 'there's always a good message in it too'. (Escapism here also has a political dimension, the genre presented as relief from having 'your history thrown in your face all the time'.) For 34-year-old project training officer Mayra, Jane Harper's crime novel *The Dry* is not only a 'good light read'; the pale-skinned central character stands as a 'metaphor' for not quite fitting into the environment. Diane, a 53-year-old retiree, finds in Anne McCaffrey's sci-fi worlds a 'social conscience', while engineering consultant Holly is interested in Elena Ferrante as one of the few writers able to 'cleverly discuss female relationships'. For Lynne, self-employed with partial secondary education, reading *The Secret River* offers 'new insight into our heritage'.

Jacinta, quoted earlier, alternates reading crime novels 'for their escapist value' with works that are 'much more about human interactions', books that 'stay with you', like Vikram Seth's *Two Lives* or Timothy Conigrave's *Holding the Man*, an account of his and his partner's experience with HIV/AIDS. She is intrigued by her own response to Christos Tsiolkas' challenging novel *The Slap*, which had no characters she could empathise with:

> there was something ugly about the book [but] I wanted to keep on reading it ... I think he did well to construct a book where none of the characters were particularly likeable but there was something engaging about the book.

Although interviewees describe books as 'well written', the interest is less in formal qualities than in the book's capacity to support this kind of ethical or pedagogical extension – one form of 'literary' treatment, after all, even where the work in question is genre fiction or a mainstream bestseller. Other kinds of investment in reading, particularly for literary classics, are presented as 'projects' for the individual: Sean's commitment to reading all of Lawson; 21-year-old Brooke, a tertiary educated recruitment coordinator living with her family in a high income household, 'dedicating' herself to *War and Peace*; others following up on local history after having read Grenville's *The Secret River*. Some are committed *re*-readers. Many would affirm the sentiment expressed by 19-year-old medical science student Gabriel: 'I enjoy being around books.' This sense of belonging with books is also matched by homes full of books, pleasure in their physical form (sometimes alongside a digital device) and a love of bookstores. Households also emerge as key sites of literary engagement and validation, whereas participation in public literary events is much rarer. Engagement with festivals and reading groups remains a minority activity, despite their apparent expansion in recent times.

If these book-friendly responses are predictable enough, what's notable is their ready transference to popular fiction, suggesting in turn how that category needs to be disaggregated. The interviews reveal that some genres are more negotiated than others. Overall, thriller/adventure is the most popular genre, read by 59 per cent of the main sample. Interviewees name particular books and authors such as James Patterson, Stieg Larsson, Wilbur Smith and Dan Brown, but do not engage in much reflection on the genre. This contrasts to accounts of crime/mystery, the second most popular genre at 57 per cent, where interviewees demonstrate an awareness of generic lineages and give detailed accounts of their preferences in terms of content and technique. For Brooke, Agatha Christie's books, showing 'how it all unfolds and how the detective works it out', are preferred over work describing 'the gory details of someone that was murdered'. Sean does not disparage Christie but wants to make the case for Sayers, whose characters 'add more depth'. David, a retired university manager and adjunct professor, describes Rankin as 'the top man' in detective fiction (a shared judgement reflected in Rankin's high position in Figure 2.2); Peter Temple is 'decent', and he reads Peter Robinson in spite of finding him 'a bit inferior obviously'.[6] These calibrated responses reflect the long-standing prestige of crime fiction, making it worth such distinctions for these educated readers.

Perhaps something newer is revealed in the way science fiction and fantasy, in particular, seem to offer the richest fields for such investments; and not just Tolkien or the Harry Potter books, though they are repeatedly mentioned in interviews. Multiple readers detailed at length the virtues of the genre(s) or of particular authors, as in Kim's account of Nalini Singh's paranormal fantasy. For retired high school principal Steven, a fan of quality TV and popular Australian historian Peter FitzSimons, the politics in George R.R. Martin's *Game of Thrones* 'are as real as real politics. You see all the Machiavellian stuff that goes on in there.' Diane likes the 'care of children or community' shown in McCaffrey's novels, while Lynne discovers, in a fantasy novel, how 'humans are actually destroying what is abundant for us and the need to look after our land'. For Mayra, classic sci-fi by Arthur C. Clarke or Philip K. Dick is valued as 'kind of complicated and slightly dark', while Gabriel appreciates the 'almost artistic insanity' in Terry Pratchett, whose books are 'author quality driven rather than genre quality'.

In crime, sci-fi and fantasy, then, we find multiple examples of knowing fans and committed readers who respond to, justify or reframe genre hierarchies and ethical interpretations. At the same time, there is little sense that the intensive or extensive reading of genre fiction is projected *against* more traditional forms of literary consecration, although readers are happy to distance their own preferences from accepted opinion. Of the critically acclaimed Tim Winton, 71-year-old retired engineer Michael remarks: 'I have read one or two of his. I wasn't that impressed ... It's not something I'd say "Oh yeah, I've got to go back and read more of."' Or 38-year-old maths teacher Lauren on literary classics: 'I tried to read the classics and I just can't do it. They're so boring and I think god just get to the point.' Some overtly resist the critical imperative. In the words of 47-year-old former administrative worker/officer Naomi:

And you know, the old what do you think the author meant by this. I'm like, well, I don't really care, I just like what he said. I enjoyed his story. I don't want to pull it apart. I don't think he wrote a story for us to pull it to pieces.

Otherwise, classics are accorded their place, but often through their familiarity rather than their high standing. Indeed, this very familiarity is valued, often in the mode of the 'sentimental canon', a concept developed to describe the attachment to certain books that readers carry from schooling into later life: 'a feel-good moral seriousness in line with the popular-commercial media's idea of literary value' (Dolin *et al.*, 2017: 16). Classics also become familiar through screen adaptations and family exchanges. Several readers describe their enjoyment of Austen, not for the characteristics typically lauded in the academy such as her irony or ethical seriousness, but as 'a little bit of detox', in the words of retired office worker Angela; or for Debra, a former administrator in the wine industry, as 'comfort reading', 'a bit like comfort food'. But Austen's canonical status is also in play. Chinese-born Angela compares Austen to the Chinese classic *Dream of the Red Chamber*, while Mayra links Austen, Woolf and Sylvia Plath in stating that she's not 'really into books specially written for women'. 'Women's writing' can be understood as at once a scholarly and a marketing category.

Accounts of the classics are appreciative but somewhat lukewarm compared to the most declarative statements of allegiance for other kinds of books. Asked about 'literary classics', Diane – who's read *Lord of the Rings* 'twenty or thirty times' – responds 'I mean, I might pick up Thomas Hardy, *The Mayor of Casterbridge* or something. It's in my bookcase.' Holly, who was especially moved by Markus Zusak's *The Book Thief* and has an enduring love for Harry Potter, reflects:

> I was part of a book club for a while so we read things like *Huckleberry Finn*, which was really cool. I think it's just nice sometimes to read about a time so different, and especially with the race element as well.

And in addition to reading *War and Peace*, Brooke read the more modern classics *Brave New World* and *1984* and 'completely loved both of them'. At the same time, there is only slim evidence of investment in the national cultural capital that might be associated with Australian literature, except where history was invoked.

Further, across the interviews, there is little sense of confrontation between different literary tastes, despite the divisions produced by gender and age. While we could chart a sliding scale from 'literary' to 'popular' readers, the majority of those interviewed show relatively diverse portfolios of tastes across the literary field, even if, with only a few exceptions, this diversity is contained within mainstream choices. Nonetheless, most of these choices also represent judgements of quality, whether applied to Tolkien or Dan Brown, Anne McCaffrey or Terry Pratchett; judgements that implicitly exclude other kinds of books. As Mayra puts it, 'If you're going to read something, read something that's good, or something that's engaging.'

Thus Diane remarks it's 'pretty embarrassing' to confess she's been going through the Star Wars books, but she then offers a detailed account of the comparisons she pursues between the books and the movies. Debra's tastes are wide-ranging but judgements are also explicit:

> everything from autobiographical to sci-fi. I like anything from Colleen McCullough or Bryce Courtenay, and then I veer towards Stephen King, Dan Brown, Danielle Steele and Anne Rice. Then to a bit of brain dead literature like Jackie Collins and Sidney Sheldon.

The diversity, however, does not extend to romance as a stand-alone genre, nor do the committed romance readers interviewed mention other kinds of fiction (although Kathleen insists on the diversity of sub-genres within romance fiction itself). Even popular fiction fans draw the line. As Naomi, fan of King, Larsson and the 'romance' *Jane Eyre*, put it: 'Mills & Boon, bleh!'

Our interviews with Australian readers thus suggest that the processes of legitimation that define literature in the most restricted sense play at best only an indirect role in shaping reading tastes and participation in book culture. But they also indicate a body of enthusiastic, committed readers invested in the value of books and reading. As British sociologist Simon Stewart (2010: 126) puts it, wondering why his well-educated, middle-class respondents preferred bestsellers and crime novels above all: 'although the best-sellers are part of popular culture, disconnected from avant-garde movements and academic institutions, they are still books'. Or the earlier UK survey: 'It is reading itself that is legitimate ... rather than particular genres or the stylistic or aesthetic qualities of texts' (Bennett *et al.*, 2009: 105).

The ACF readers interviewed are closer to the public-commercial sphere than the academic, sharing its orientations to the present rather than tradition or its critical opponents, and to celebrity, in the sense of well-known writers, rather than canonicity. They are generally more interested in contemporary books and authors than those that have accumulated prestige over time, although the Harry Potter books suggest that that time can now be very short indeed. But if such readers are only modestly invested in high-status literature, there is little sense of rejecting or resisting established hierarchies. Within the commercial mainstream, they are largely oriented towards its quality end, towards books that are 'prestigious in certain areas of contemporary culture, and ... carry institutionalised cultural capital' (Stewart, 2010: 126). And it is socio-economically privileged readers who are most likely to take on this range of commercially successful genres or authors, without hesitation, but also within limits. The fact that these readers are heavily concentrated in the professional middle classes (from higher professionals to intermediate occupations) and among those with higher education indicates in turn that books and reading still constitute a significant form of cultural capital or a productive means for its accumulation – as well as good entertainment.

Conclusion

Our data does not suggest a social elite exclusively invested in high-status literature, but neither does it 'democratise' reading in Australia. Figure 2.2 does indicate a space of more selective legitimised tastes, and niche tastes appear elsewhere, but the densest space of reading and participation is less exclusive and less elite. While the value of canonical work is recognised, this is not the domain where most readers exercise active engagement with books, even the majority of those from the higher end of the class/educational scale. Moreover, a significant part of the population, almost 40 per cent, is largely uninterested in books and reading (Kelly et al., 2018: 288–289).

Nonetheless, the association of reading and book culture with higher levels of education and professional-managerial occupations is striking, even as we find evidence that such engagement is not tied in an exclusive fashion to literary works. Instead, we find an 'easy' mixing of familiar canonical and popular items, but little evidence of more radical challenges to established hierarchies. This generous reading profile overlaps with more intensive commitments to certain genres, especially fantasy, where readers are invested in distinguishing between different kinds and qualities. 'Popular' genres are distributed right across the field, indicating the necessity of untangling the very different meanings the term conceals. Even where reading is explained simply in terms of immersion or escape, forms of social or ethical engagement and value judgements are commonly implied. Esteem for books and reading per se – not least for books as physical objects and bookstores as unique places – remains strong.

These characteristics, together, enable us to identify a 'reading class', located especially among those in professional and intermediate occupations, with tertiary qualifications, middle aged and predominantly female. If, as Griswold (2008) observes, this group is disproportionately influential, we also note its concentration in the strongly female lower professional-managerial and intermediate occupational groups. Its 'influence', this suggests, comes less directly through economic capital than through its unassuming but committed relation to the cultural capital that literature still represents in contemporary Australia. More precisely, the cultural capital associated with the field is invested to a greater degree in the social value of books and reading than in literary value in any more restricted or formal sense.

Notes

1 These restrictions give local publishers time to produce their own edition of a book for the local market before overseas publishers are allowed to supply copies.
2 While largely determined by commercial institutions such as publishers, booksellers, newspapers, TV and cinema (for adaptations), this sphere also includes public broadcasters. We could also identify a 'professional' sphere – less directly pertinent to the present analysis – comprising professional associations for authors, publishers, booksellers and agents (Driscoll, 2017).
3 Crime/mystery, books by or about Indigenous Australians, science fiction/fantasy, Australian history, self-help/lifestyle, modern novels, romance, books about sport or

sporting personalities, thrillers/adventure, literary classics, contemporary Australian novels, and biographies of historical figures (Carter and Kelly, 2017; Kelly et al., 2018).
4 Data on the number of Australian books read is derived from the question 'how many books by Australian authors have you read for your own interest or pleasure over the past year?'
5 Despite widespread discussion regarding the explosion of book clubs/reading groups, only 9 per cent of ACF survey respondents had ever attended such a group. Overall attendance was strongest among the 25–34-year-old cohort (14 per cent) and higher among the 18–44 year olds than those aged 45 years and over. However, regular attendance (once a week or month) was strongest among older cohorts, with 55–64 year olds the highest at 6 per cent. Women were more likely to participate than men (14 per cent versus 5 per cent), while regular attendees were clustered in the professional-managerial *and* routine occupation groups. Occasional attendance was strongest in higher professional, intermediate and semi-routine occupations.
6 Peter Temple was the first genre fiction author to win the Miles Franklin Award, Australia's most prestigious literary prize, with his crime novel *Truth* in 2010.

3
THE MARK OF TIME
Temporality and the dynamics of distinction in the music field

Tony Bennett, Ben Dibley and Modesto Gayo

In introducing his account of 'the sense of distinction' Bourdieu immediately pluralises that sense in order to explore the variant forms of distinction performed by the dominant class. In bringing the knowledge of and different degrees of liking for named artists, musical works and singers exhibited by different fractions of the dominant class into his analysis, Bourdieu pays particular regard to the different positions that these musical items occupy within the temporalities of the fields to which they belong (Bourdieu, 1984: 261–267). Similarly, when fleshing out these different senses of distinction in his vignettes on the tastes of a 'grand bourgeois', a '"truly classical" university teacher' and a 'young executive who "knows how to live"', he stresses the significance of 'the mark of time' – the opposition between young and old, between senior members of the class and newcomers, and between different generational routes to higher class positions – in explaining how the struggles between variants of dominant tastes are marked by the generationally inflected social trajectories of different class fractions.

    We recall this aspect of *Distinction* by way of marking out the position from which we engage with the debates regarding the relations between musical tastes, practices and social position that have taken place since *Distinction* was published. Music has been a key site for these debates as a field in which traditional value hierarchies have been dramatically diluted. The near-monopoly of legitimacy once held by classical music has been progressively weakened since the 1970s by an increasingly differentiated music industry which has significantly expanded the repertoire of musical forms capable of being annexed to a wide range of practices of social distinction; by changes in cultural policy settings which have supported local popular music alongside (albeit never matching in scale) traditional high musical forms; by educational reforms which have expanded what is instituted as canonical in musical curricula; and by global mutations in the platforms and devices used to consume music, which have increased the volume, diversity and availability of musical forms to listeners.

These are among the developments that have informed the attention accorded to music within the cultural omnivorousness and cultural heterogeneity theses (Savage and Gayo, 2011).[1] The former contends that the middle and upper classes now secure their prestige by knowing about and participating in both high and selected popular cultural forms in contrast to the more singular focus on the latter attributed to those in lower class positions (Peterson and Simkus, 1992; Peterson and Kern, 1996). The cultural heterogenisation or eclecticism thesis contends that cultural hierarchies have given way to an eclectic diversity of practices as individuals' cultural choices are governed by preferences which, having little correspondence to their class position, express a social logic of horizontal differentiation, summarised in the concept of a 'tablature', rather than one of vertical distinctions (Glevarec and Pinet, 2009).

While we shall not engage in detailed analysis or critiques of these positions, they provide useful counterfoils for the presentation of our findings in the respects in which they depart from and, in our assessment, fall short of the procedures Bourdieu used in pluralising the 'sense of distinction'. Unduly reliant on the analysis of musical genres, the omnivore thesis abstracted those genres from any sense of a distinctive historicity of the American music field of the kind which, in *Distinction*, Bourdieu explored through his named musical works. The cultural heterogenisation thesis also relies principally on genre categories and, like the omnivore thesis, makes little use of the forms of qualitative evidence through which different modes of appropriation of shared cultural practices might be explored.

We shall, then, in presenting our survey findings relating to the music field develop a three-pronged approach to engage with the issues at stake here. First, in analysing the results of our Multiple Correspondence Analyses (MCAs) on the music field, we pay particular attention to the light thrown on the historical dynamics of cultural capital formation by the relations between age, education and class, on the one hand, and the temporal coding of our survey items (particularly musical works, composers and performers) on the other. Second, we show how looking at the relations between genre preferences and indicators of varying degrees of participation in different kinds of musical events lends a sharper edge to the relations between musical preferences and practices of distinction than both the omnivore and eclecticism theses allow. We look finally at the evidence of our interviews with survey participants. While many interviewees appear to express eclectic tastes ranging across musical hierarchies, a closer analysis reveals a diversity of 'eclectic taste formations' shaped by different musical times.

In pursuing these arguments we also engage with the 'emerging cultural capital' thesis proposed by Savage and others (Savage, 2015; Savage et al., 2013) in presenting the findings of the Great British Class Survey (GBCS) and echoed by Sheppard and Biddle's (2015a) interpretation of the ANUPoll on social class. While sympathetic to the respects in which this thesis reintroduces questions of time into the analysis of changing cultural capital formations, we have reservations regarding the conclusions the two studies draw in interpreting emerging cultural capital as the basis for a new class. However, for now we merely flag this as an issue that is discussed more fully in Chapters 7 and 8. Our concerns here are rather with the thinness of the evidence that is evoked in support of the emerging capital thesis: for the GBCS it is based on the practices of the well-educated, young and tech-savvy members of the sample as evidenced by their 'engagement with, *inter alia*, video games, social networking, sport and popular music' (Wakeling and Savage, 2015: 317); for the ANUPoll the main practices are 'going to gigs, listening to rock, listening to rap or hip-hop, playing video games, watching sport, and going to the gym, or exercising' (Sheppard and Biddle, 2015a: 44). In both cases these purely generic indicators of emerging cultural capital are opposed to generic markers of traditional cultural capital – listening to classical music, going to operas, visiting art galleries, etc. – as parts of a bi-polar temporal contrast: traditional/emerging. The more detailed evidence furnished by our survey provides the basis for a more nuanced set of historical contrasts.

Before pursuing these lines of argument, we look first at recent changes in the organisation of the Australian music field that are relevant to our concerns, identify the items included in the music field section of the *Australian Cultural Fields* (ACF) questionnaire and explain the reasons for their selection.

The Australian music field: changing national, industry and policy settings

As a medium-sized, lucrative music market, the Australian music industry has been traditionally dominated by the subsidiaries of multinational media corporations, with local content radio quotas for popular music and state subsidy for classical companies. In view of the preponderant influence of the British and US music industries, the presence of a distinctive 'Australian sound' was once hotly contested in critical accounts of local popular music (Stratton, 2007; Turner, 1992) but now attracts little attention, albeit that the effects of changes in the distribution of both local and imported content through globalisation and digitalisation remain pressing concerns.[2] The processes of parallel importing over the 1990s (Rowe, 2001) and more recently the rise of streaming services have been particularly significant in shaping a national market in which a number of new players are now engaged in contests over the distribution of content. Online aggregators like Spotify, YouTube, Google and Apple are now the preferred platforms by which Australians listen to music, especially among the young.[3] Cultural policy directed at the music industry has also been important, particularly as it is implicated in the changing contours of cultural nationalism, discourses of excellence and economic initiatives promoted under the rubric of the creative industries and, more recently, 'music city' policies (Homan, 2018). Here the virtual monopoly that 'the "high" arts' – opera, classical music, music theatre – once had on state support has been eroded since the 1970s, with classical music currently receiving about 60 per cent of the Federal government's funding for music (Homan, 2013: 383).

The Keating Labor government's *Creative Nation* (Department of Communications and the Arts, 1994) was especially significant in this regard, constituting a high point in levels of state support for contemporary music, to a degree redressing the greater levels historically enjoyed by high culture music forms (Homan, 2013: 387). However, a succession of Coalition governments, interrupted by an interval of Labor government (2007–2013), has slowed down or reversed this policy trajectory, most contentiously with the 'Brandis heist' which diverted Australia Council resources to fund various initiatives at the Minister's discretion. Australia's key classical music organisations, including the Australian World Orchestra, Melba Recordings and the country's State opera companies, were among the chief beneficiaries of this policy.[4] In awarding increased funding to these organisations at the expense of more contemporary cultural forms, these allocations were widely seen as being inherently elitist. Moreover, despite coordinated opposition from the arts sector, which saw Brandis' successor, Mitch Fifield, return Australia Council funding, Fifield directed a portion of that allocation to increase support for opera following the recommendations of the *National Opera Review* (Department of Communications and the Arts, 2016). The protection this afforded classical music stands in contrast to the position taken in relation to the contemporary Australian music sector (Caust, 2017; Homan, 2018). This is demonstrated by the lack of traction that Music Australia, the peak body for contemporary music producers, has had with the past two Coalition governments, which have refused to entertain the propositions detailed in its *National Contemporary Music Plan* (2016), including calls for tax offsets for recording studios, the strengthening of quotas for local content and audience development funding (Homan, 2018: 56).

Surveying musical tastes and practices

The ACF questionnaire asked respondents about their participation in, preferences for and familiarity with a wide range of items in the music field. Questions on participation included the number of hours spent listening to music daily; frequency of attending events including live bands in pubs, musicals, opera, orchestral concerts, pop concerts and rock gigs; and the devices used to listen to music (the radio, CD players, computers, mobile devices – phones, iPods, iPads, mp3 players or tablets – record players, minidisks or cassette players, and on live instruments). The items on musical preferences included ten genres: country, classical, light classical, easy listening, jazz, pop rock, hard rock, urban, dance and alternative. We also included ten Australian artists and ten international musical works. The grounds for selecting these included consideration of the different musical times they represented.

Australian musicians

Pioneers of heavy metal AC/DC are an Australian hard rock band formed in 1973 and one of the bestselling bands of all time, selling more than 200 million records (Stratton, 2007). Dan Sultan is an alternative rock singer-songwriter and guitarist who has enjoyed critical acclaim since the 2010s and is a member of The Black Arm Band, a fluid ensemble of Indigenous musicians concerned with issues of

Aboriginal justice (Gillett and Freebody, 2014). Gotye is an alternative pop/dance musician, who came to national prominence with a number of releases over the mid-2000s. Gurrumul Yunupingu was an Indigenous musician from Arnhem Land, northern Australia, who sang in the Yolngu language.[5] He came to national prominence over the late 2000s, winning a string of industry awards and performing alongside pop diva Delta Goodrem and the Sydney Symphony Orchestra. Jimmy Barnes is a key figure in the history of Australian rock. His band, Cold Chisel, exemplified the 'Oz Rock' genre that emerged over the late 1970s and early 1980s and his subsequent solo career has cemented his position as arguably Australia's highest-profile rock singer (Stratton, 2007). Kasey Chambers is a country singer-songwriter who has enjoyed critical acclaim and crossover success with significant commercial album sales. Kate Ceberano is a vocalist renowned for her soul, jazz and pop repertoire. She came to prominence in the mid-1980s with the Melbourne art pop band, The Models. She is best known for her Australian rock classic, 'Pash'. Kylie Minogue is a pop singer-songwriter and actress, who starred in the Australian soap opera, *Neighbours*, in the mid-1980s, before going on to become the highest-selling Australian artist of all time according to the Australian Record Industry Association. Peter Sculthorpe was a composer whose works from the 1960s through to the 1980s epitomised a revisionist cultural nationalism in the Australian music field, in part through their inclusion of Indigenous motifs (Skinner, 2015). The work of jazz singer Vince Jones occupies the borderlines between modern and contemporary jazz, rock and folk, with some connections to classical music.

Overseas works

The Dark Side of the Moon was the watershed album released in 1973 by the UK rock band Pink Floyd. *The Four Seasons* are violin concertos by baroque composer Antonio Vivaldi, popularised in the 1990s by Nigel Kennedy's recording with the English Chamber Orchestra. 'Jolene' was a single released in 1973 by the American country singer, Dolly Parton. Miles Davies' *Kind of Blue* was a landmark album in the history of African-American jazz and in the more broadly based 'birth of the cool' in the late 1950s. 'Vogue' was a single from Madonna's 1990 album, *I'm Breathless*, which popularised the Harlem dance form, 'vogueing'. *The Mikado*, a comic opera by Gilbert and Sullivan first performed at the Savoy Theatre in London in 1885, remains one of the most frequently performed light operas globally. 'Nessun Dorma', an aria from Puccini's opera *Turandot*, exemplifies the processes involved in the popularisation of earlier canonised works through the widespread recognition it achieved after being performed by The Three Tenors for the 1990 World Cup. *Phantom of the Opera* is Andrew Lloyd Webber's long-running musical which first opened in London in 1986. *Rhapsody in Blue* is a 1924 work by the American composer, George Gershwin, which, initially taken seriously by critics, came to appeal mainly to middling taste formations, but has recently once again been accorded higher prestige. *The Piano* by Michael Nyman, a composer with an avant-garde signature, was the soundtrack to Jane Campion's 1993 award-winning arthouse film of the same name.

In turning now to the light that our survey data throws on the social patterns of engagement in, and liking for, these musical practices, genres, works and performers, we shall pay particular attention to the relations between the different positions that they occupy within the temporalities of the music field and the intersections of age, class position and level of education.

Musical times and social positions

It will be useful first to identify the relative popularity of the genres we asked about. Pop rock and easy listening are the two most popular genres, recruiting the support of 41 per cent and 33 per cent of respondents respectively, followed by country and alternative, at 21 per cent and 22 per cent. Hard rock and classical log 17 per cent and 16 per cent respectively, followed by jazz at 14 per cent. Dance and light classical each recruit 10 per cent support, with urban the least popular at 6 per cent. The hierarchies of popularity for the Australian performers run down from Barnes and AC/DC, both at 70 per cent, through Ceberano (64 per cent), Minogue (66 per cent) and Chambers (58 per cent), to Gotye and Gurrumul Yunupingu at 44 per cent and 33 per cent respectively, with Jones (15 per cent), Sultan (12 per cent) and Sculthorpe (6 per cent) 'bringing up the rear'. The most popular international works are *Dark Side of the Moon* (63 per cent), 'Jolene' (62 per cent) and *Phantom of the Opera* (58 per cent), followed, in order, by *The Four Seasons*, *Rhapsody in Blue* and 'Vogue', all in the 40s. *The Mikado* (35 per cent) and 'Nessun Dorma' (28 per cent) come next, with *Kind of Blue* (18 per cent) and *The Piano* (12 per cent) recruiting the least support.

To bring these different preferences together and relate them to the use of musical devices and participation in musical events, we look now at the results of our MCA for the music field (see also Dibley and Gayo, 2018). In doing so we consider how these tastes and practices correlate with social positions by looking at Figures 3.1 and 3.2 together. We discuss these quadrant by quadrant rather than looking at each axis separately. This is the best means of identifying the temporal aspects of the relations between musical tastes, practices and social positions, as it allows us to observe the interplay between class and age. All we need note regarding the axes at this stage is that, in contrast to the art and literary fields, it is age that dominates the most important (horizontal) axis in Figure 3.2, which accounts for the greater degree of variation, while occupational class, level of education and place of residence are more strongly associated with the secondary vertical axis except for the higher levels of education which are inflected across the top of the horizontal axis.[6] Gender differences are laid out diagonally at the centre of the figure and are relatively unmarked, albeit not without consequence in relation to particular genres, artists and works.

Looking first to the lower left quadrant of Figure 3.1, this is characterised principally by low levels of musical participation. Listening to music at less than one hour

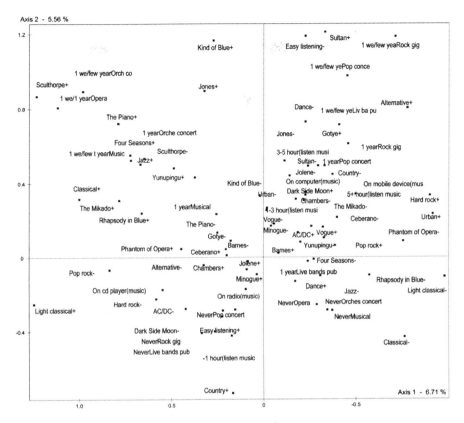

FIGURE 3.1 The space of musical tastes and practices.

a day, is not a significant daily activity, and is largely via the 'legacy technologies' of radio and CD players. Rock gigs, pop concerts and live pub performances register negative levels of participation, marking an age contrast between the older respondents who congregate here and the high levels of involvement in these musical events registered by the younger respondents in the upper right quadrant (Figure 3.2). It is notable that, although not registering as never participating, the older members of the sample in the lower left quadrant do not go regularly to operas, musicals or orchestral concerts. If this marks a difference from the upper left quadrant where high levels of participation in these musical forms are evident, that difference is more strongly marked in the lower right where zero levels of engagement with these musical events predominate. These differences in levels and forms of participation are largely explained by the predominant role that age plays in marking the differences between the lower left and the upper right quadrants, and the role that occupational classes and levels of education play in marking the differences between the lower right and upper left quadrants. In the lower right quadrant, lower class positions and levels of education predominate in contrast to the

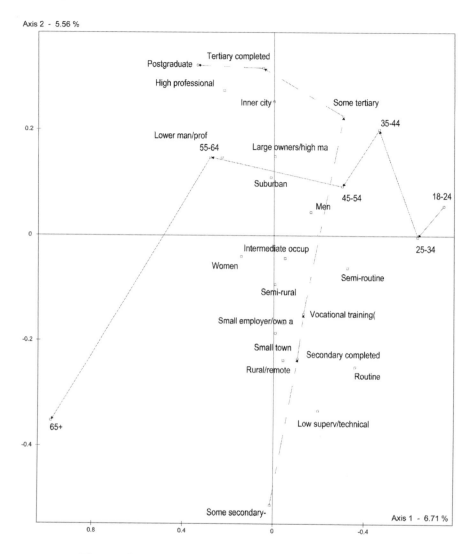

FIGURE 3.2 The social space of musical tastes and practices.

predominance of tertiary education and professional and managerial occupations in the upper left quadrant.

Light classical, easy listening and country are the preferred genres most strongly associated with the lower left quadrant. The location of liking easy listening close to the centre of Figure 3.1 reflects the negligible differences in class preferences that are registered for this genre relative to the greater class differentiation of tastes for light classical music registered by its location at the extreme left of the quadrant. The preference for country music registered at the bottom of the figure reflects its strong association with the members of the sample who did not complete secondary schooling, 47 per cent of whom include this in their preferred genres. However, it also reflects the influence of gender as one of the genres more strongly preferred by women, 25 per cent of whom included this in their most liked genres compared to 19 per cent of men.[7] The same is true for easy listening, the genre most strongly associated with women, 40 per cent of whom like this relative to 27 per cent of men. The genres disliked in the lower left quadrant – alternative, hard rock and pop rock – while chiefly informed by the age contrast with the liking for these expressed by the younger members of the sample in the upper right quadrant also reflect the role of gender. Women are less committed to alternative and hard rock than men – by margins of 7 per cent for the former and 16 per cent for the latter – but more strongly committed to pop rock by a margin of 19 per cent. These genre contrasts are echoed in preferences indicated for Chambers, Minogue and 'Jolene' towards the top right of the lower left quadrant, and the dislike of AC/DC and *Dark Side of the Moon*, in contrast to the more muted enthusiasm for women musicians and their work, and the strong liking for AC/DC and Barnes, towards the lower left of the upper right quadrant.

In the lower right quadrant positive genre tastes are limited to dance, while dislikes are registered mostly for the genres that are liked in the upper left quadrant, notably jazz and classical music, although light classical is also disliked in contrast to its positive evaluation on the left of the lower left quadrant. No positive tastes for specific musical works or performers register here, only dislikes, again for works that recruit support in the upper left quadrant: *Rhapsody in Blue* and *The Four Seasons*.

The key additional points to note in relation to the upper right quadrant are the respects in which levels of daily listening in Figure 3.1 follow the trajectory of age in Figure 3.2, peaking at five hours or more among the youngest members of the sample in the lower part of the quadrant where contemporary popular genres (pop rock, urban and hard rock) predominate. Listening levels drop to between three and five hours higher up the quadrant among the 35–44 year olds, and then to between one and three hours towards the lower left of the quadrant where the over 40s predominate. The most notable aspect of the higher reaches of the quadrant, where both those on the cusp of middle age and with partial tertiary qualifications cluster, is the liking for alternative music and the work of the alternative dance/pop performer Gotye and the Indigenous political rock singer Sultan – a grouping amounting to what we might call an *emerging musical taste* formation.[8]

The musical time that is thus registered here contrasts with the two musical times that are registered in the upper left quadrant of Figure 3.1. The first of these is located at the top of this quadrant where the highest levels of education and occupancy of high professional class positions are connected to a liking for the work of Vince Jones, Miles Davies' *Kind of Blue*, *The Piano* and the work of Sculthorpe. These are all among the least popular works and performers and are all associated with earlier breaks from traditional canonised forms but which have come to function as *established alternatives* to these. The musical time they mark differs from the more *traditional musical time* represented by the liking for *The Four Seasons* just as, in genre terms, the preference for jazz stands in contrast to liking classical music. They also stand in contrast to the more traditional musical time represented by *The Mikado* and the more ambiguous *Rhapsody in Blue*: initially a critical modernist piece, but now predominantly a hybrid light jazz/classical piece. These changes in musical times in the field go hand-in-hand with a movement from high professional to lower professional and both lower and, at the centre of the figure, higher management positions, and towards increasingly older respondents. The rates of liking both jazz and classical music, it should be noted, increase with level of education to peak among postgraduates at 17 per cent and 26 per cent respectively. And, to bring our analysis back to our starting point, these genre preferences stand in marked contrast to those for light classical, easy listening and country music that we find, in the lower left quadrant, among older Australians from lower class positions and with lower levels of education.

We look finally at the positions occupied by the two Indigenous musicians in our survey: Gurrumul Yunupingu and Dan Sultan. Familiarity with Sultan is mostly limited to younger members of the sample in the upper right quadrant where not liking his work, close to the centre of the quadrant, is differentiated from liking it towards the top of the quadrant where those still in tertiary study are concentrated. Liking Gurrumul Yunupingu, by contrast, is distributed around a point in Figure 3.1 close to the centre of the upper left quadrant where 55–64 year olds and lower managers are congregated in Figure 3.2. These contrasts indicate a distribution of preferences for Indigenous musicians across the musical times represented by emerging, established alternative, and more traditional canonised forms. This is confirmed by the position of these items in relation to genre preferences: liking Gurrumul Yunupingu is located close to both jazz and classical, while not liking him is closest to liking pop rock close to the bottom of the upper right quadrant. While men and women like Gurrumul Yunupingu equally at 48 per cent each, liking for him increases with age (from 16 per cent of the youngest age group to 61 per cent for those over 60), occupational class (from 38 per cent of routine workers to 57 per cent of higher-level professionals and managers) and level of education (from 33 per cent of those who completed secondary education to 60 per cent of postgraduates). This pattern of preferences is best explained by the ways in which, in the later stages of his career, the promotion and critical reception of Gurrumul Yunupingu's work located him as a point of fusion between Indigenous musical traditions and spirituality and Western classical music (see Figure 3.3).

Intensities of engagement and genre preferences

To summarise our argument so far, we have identified three distinct musical times associated with emerging, established alternative and traditional high musical tastes and practices. We have further shown how, far from marking a transition to a logic of purely horizontal social differentiation, each of these times functions as an operator within logics of distinction that are connected to different age-inflected articulations of the relations between level of education and class position. A good part

FIGURE 3.3 Gurrumul Yunupingu, Kings Park, Perth, with the West Australian Symphony Orchestra in 2014.

Source: Photograph courtesy of Dr Duncan Barnes, Edith Cowan University.

After an early phase in his career as a guitarist with the Indigenous rock band Yothu Yindi, Gurrumul Yunupingu's career as a solo artist was characterised by a process of progressive canonisation that situated him at a conjunction of Indigenous and Western musical and spiritual traditions. Performing with symphony orchestras in Australia and internationally, he performed before Barack Obama during his presidency and before Queen Elizabeth II at her Diamond Jubilee Concert. Gurrumul Yunupingu's posthumous album, *Djarimirri (Child of the Rainbow)*, released the year after his death in 2017, was promoted by the record company that released it as 'presenting traditional songs and harmonised chants from his traditional Yolngu way of life with dynamic and hypnotic orchestral arrangements in a blend of the highest forms of both his culture and our European culture'. This theme was widely taken up by reviewers. Simon Collins in the *West Australian* (2018) highlighted it by selecting a photograph of Gurrumul Yunupingu in concert with the West Australian Symphony Orchestra. Simon Thomsen (2018), writing for *Business Insider Australia*, stressed the fusion of 'Gurrumul's extraordinary voice with a lush and epic orchestral arrangement'. The *Guardian Australia* team reviewing Australia's best 2018 albums went into greater detail: 'A fully sanctioned blend of traditional Yolngu songs set to string arrangements inspired by minimalist neoclassical composers Philip Glass and Arvo Pärt, *Djarimirri* drew upon the cyclic repetition of both musical traditions, with the pulse of the didgeridoo replaced mostly by cellos' (Valentish *et al.*, 2018).

of this argument has depended on the different musical times associated with different named musical works. However, we have also included the different musical times represented by musical genres, particularly those of alternative, jazz and classical. We now further qualify the cultural heterogeneity or eclecticism thesis by looking at the strong differentiations of genre taste that are evident when these are related to varying intensities of engagement in different sections of the music field as measured by frequency of attending different musical events (Table 3.1).

TABLE 3.1 Ratios of genre preferences by frequent participation in musical events

	Opera	Orchestral concerts	Musicals	Pop concerts	Live bands in pubs	Rock gigs
Classical	3.1:1	3.1:1	1.8:1	0.5:1	0.5:1	0.4:1
Light classical	2.1:1	2.7:1	2:1	0.1:1	0.3:1	0.1:1
Jazz	1.4:1	1.5:1	1.3:1	0.9:1	1.2:1	1.1:1
Alternative	0.7:1	1.1:1	0.5:1	1.5:1	3.1:1	3.8:1
Country	0.9:1	0.8:1	1:1	0.6:1	0.6:1	0.3:1
Easy listening	0.9:1	0.9:1	1.7:1	0.3:1	0.8:1	0.4:1
Pop rock	0.8:1	0.5:1	0.9:1	1.9:1	1:1	1.3:1
Hard rock	0.3:1	0.3:1	0.3:1	0.4:1	1.8:1	3.2:1
Urban	0.6:1	0.9:1	0.5:1	2:1	4:1	1.2:1
Dance	0.6:1	1:1	1.5:1	2:1	1.5:1	1.9:1

The figures for each column in Table 3.1 are ratios indicating the degree to which those who attend the musical events identified at the head of the column a few times a year express a liking for the genres in our survey, relative to those who never attend those events.[9] Opera is an exception here: as overall levels of attending a few times a year are very low, attending once a year has been taken as the benchmark against which to set zero levels of attendance.[10] The figures thus tell us that those who frequent opera and orchestral concerts have much more strongly marked preferences for classical music, light classical and jazz than do non-attendees. By contrast, they have lower preferences for the other genres except for alternative music and dance on the part of concert attendees. The relative preferences of those who frequent musicals exhibit much the same pattern, albeit less sharply, except for the relatively strong preferences shown for dance and easy listening for instance.

The patterns associated with relative frequency of attending live bands in pubs, and pop and hard rock concerts are the reverse of those identified above in many respects: much lower levels of liking for classical and light classical as well as for country and easy listening; much stronger levels of liking for rock genres as well as for urban and dance. It is, however, the ratios relating to jazz and alternative music that are more interesting. The first of these recruits higher levels of support from those who frequent live bands in pubs and rock gigs, but not so marked as the contrast between goers and non-goers to opera, orchestral concerts and musicals. Alternative, by contrast, recruits its highest levels of support from, in ascending order, those who frequently attend pop concerts, live bands in pubs and rock gigs relative to those who never do.

Degree of involvement in different musical cultures, then, clearly qualifies the contention of the eclecticism thesis regarding a flattening out of genre tastes across social positions given the strong role played by age, level of education and class position in differentiating levels of participation in different kinds of musical event.

Qualified eclecticisms

A similar picture emerges from our household interviews. Interviewees frequently express a widely declared openness with regard to musical styles, usually ranging across popular and high genres. For example, when asked about her musical preferences, Lisa, 42 years old and tertiary educated, says: 'It can be anything from '80s trash that I grew up with like Depeche Mode and Prince to classical music or just anything. It's eclectic.' Heath, a vocationally trained commercial printer, also 42, similarly tells us: 'I'll listen to most things. But I'll jump from a Top 10 today in the US, to a Mahler Symphony.' Debra, who is in her late 50s with secondary education, and who is currently undertaking home duties after formerly working in the wine industry, likes 'Bach, Beethoven, everything to the modern, INXS, Human Nature – anything that sort of attracts me; so I'm very diverse with music.'

Nevertheless, there are few such expressions that are not quickly followed by statements on genres or artists disliked. The logics behind these, moreover, are typically informed by the different musical times that characterise the musical taste profiles of the interviewees. It is notable how often, compared to our other fields, temporal registers are invoked by interviewees when asked about their musical tastes. Martin locates the 1930s and 1940s, marked by the music his parents used to listen to, such as Vera Lynn, as the start of his 'musical times'. Maria, who likes 'an eclectic variety of music', expresses that eclecticism across a range of times going back to Cole Porter and running on through Judy Garland, The Beatles, Elvis and Tom Jones to Michael Bublé. But she sets limits: 'I like a broad range but some of the music today doesn't make sense at all so I don't listen to that.' Angela, a regular concert-goer, whose preferences are for classical and light classical as background music ('I don't listen intensely'), also identifies her taste for her favourites with reference to her parents' fondness for Mozart and Beethoven. But she can't accept punk rock which makes her 'really agitated', and, when asked about Jimmy Barnes, says that's just 'noise, not music'. And 66-year-old Steven, while he has updated his listening practices technologically, moving from radio to an iPad, is adamant that 'you wouldn't find me downloading anything from the 1980s on ... It's all back to the seventies and sixties.'

Adrian, in his mid-50s, goes to local gigs regularly and professes a wide range of tastes: 'I love jazz. I love rock. I love blues. Opera; whatever. Yeah. So I like all genres of music.' However, this openness is immediately qualified – 'I like certain styles more than others' – by the limits to the musical times across which his tastes stretch. Identifying his love of jazz as something he inherited from his father, he cites Gershwin's *Rhapsody in Blue* and Louis Armstrong as examples of his fondness for 'jazz that's a bit offbeat'. His taste for rock stretches from The Beatles and The Rolling Stones to Foo Fighters and he also likes Gotye and Vince Jones. But he hates alternative music – interpreted by his interviewer as electronica – with a vengeance: 'I hate that duff duff [music] ... I hate it with a passion.' Similarly, Gabriel, a university student working part time as a sales representative for a surgical tool company, qualifies his expressed openness to all genres by lodging his aesthetic and moral objections to 'a music producer who I hate because ... the music he produces is terrible and he's fairly — even as music producers go — morally sketchy'. Naomi, a 47-year-old vocationally trained administrative officer who identifies as working class, resists the pressures to identify her musical tastes in genre terms or to comply with socially sanctioned taste hierarchies: 'I like a bit of this ... A bit of that. That's me.' When it comes to specific genres, there are likes and dislikes, but exceptions to these in particular instances: 'You could say heavy metal generally, I'm not going to listen to that but there's a couple of songs in that genre that I don't mind.' When quizzed as to why, given that she likes musicals and goes to them often, she dislikes opera in spite of its higher social status, Naomi expresses a general dislike of opera while reserving her preference to make up her mind on a case-by-case basis:

> I don't care if a thousand people say this is the best thing you've got to see. If I don't like it, I'm not going. Yeah I think opera music is horrible. I'm not going there. I've been and I don't like it. Yeah, like with the music, I can like everything from some of Meat Loaf's songs to some of Chopin's music, but it doesn't mean that I'm going to a Chopin show, because I only like one of his songs. I just like what I like and I don't care what other people think or say.

While these examples of qualified eclecticism are widely shared across social positions, there are marked differences in how individuals from different positions speak about their musical preferences and justify their musical engagements. Relations to classical music are widely narrated in passive terms, with interviewees from various social positions describing it as 'relaxing' — echoing the terms in which the pleasures of reading literary classics are often described (see Chapter 2). For lingerie party plan franchisee Lynne, putting 'a bit of classical music on ... just takes you away into another world away from your stresses'. By contrast, Sean, 54 years old in an upper management role, admits to a certain culture pushing when he confesses to forcing classical music 'upon the family every night when we're having dinner, when I'm cooking dinner if I can if the children aren't watching television'. But as the conversation unfolds, it becomes clear that, Sean, who gave classical and popular music as his favourites in the survey, did do only because 'I couldn't put down early seventies and late seventies music'. When finally pinned down, it's 1970s classics that he really likes, allowing for a bit of slippage back into the late 1960s and forward into the early 1980s. Sean is also between musical times in terms of the technologies he uses: he no longer buys CDs, listens to music through streaming services played by Bluetooth through old stereo sets he still has about the house, and largely via playlists of his favourite bands and artists ('they're all old') through to a reluctant extension of his musical times to include a California-based punk/alternative rock band: 'My son likes Blink 182 so I have to listen to that.'

The younger interviewees operate with a different set of musical times in ways that demonstrate the significance of generational shifts. Oliver, a 25-year-old project coordinator in construction, plays the piano, is an amateur composer and likes urban and alternative music most, distinguishing these from generic pop which he avoids by cuing into new music relevant to his tastes via the radio station Triple J which plays 'proper artists' rather than the big record companies that just 'pump out rubbish'. But it's also the newer independent forms of alternative music that he looks to rather than Red Hot Chili Peppers, yesterday's alternative 'but now it's mainstream'. And he accounts for his dislike of classical music as 'just maybe a generation thing'. Harley, 18 years old and an undergraduate, similarly accounts for his relative indifference to classical music as a generational reaction against his mother's musical tastes. While not especially liking classical music but respecting its high status, he tells us that 'it's not something that I really listen to anymore. I grew up listening to a lot of Mozart stuff with Mum claiming it's good for you.' Listening to music exclusively via streaming devices (he owns only two CDs) but, unlike Sean, constructing his own playlists, he identifies the musical times he is most into via his fondness for 'pop punk' exemplified, where Sean's musical times come to an end, with Blink 182. And while interpreting the boundaries of pop punk as relatively fluid, he steers clear of generic pop and country and likes some metal but not death metal ('I cut the line off somewhere'). Finally, Brenton, 35 years old, identifies the core of his musical tastes as 'hard rock' but says that this 'bleeds very far': he has a big collection of classical records that he adores, and he also likes 'the most brutal death metal' but despises ska with all his heart: 'All I can hear is the "*dnt, dnt, dnt, dnt*", and then there'll be some cheesy horn melody "*bre, bre, bre*". It's just so predictable. I can't handle it.'

Conclusion

In his discussion of 'the sense of distinction', mentioned at the start of this chapter, Bourdieu underlines the significance of different musical times in differentiating the tastes of younger executives and engineers from older ones: their liking *Rhapsody in Blue* more, for example, and *Hungarian Rhapsody* and *The Blue Danube* less. He points out that the class significance of such differences is often misinterpreted as an effect of biological or social age, rather than of social trajectories responding to 'a given state of the chances objectively offered to a whole generation by collective history' (Bourdieu, 1984: 295–296). It has been in the same spirit that we have examined the connections between the social logics of distinction associated with the relations between three musical times and the different trajectories associated with different articulations of the relations between age, education and occupational class. We have also, in discussing our interviews, touched on the ways in which the temporalities represented by these musical times mark not simply age differences but generational shifts.

Our purpose in pursuing these lines of analysis has not been to call into question the contention that the role of musical tastes in marking social divisions has changed significantly. The position of classical music as the apex of traditional musical hierarchies has undoubtedly been seriously weakened. The aura that once attached to it through its consumption in special settings divorced from everyday contexts has been undermined by a succession of distribution technologies the latest of which – streaming and its associated formulaic playlists – often reduces it to mere sonic wallpaper. These developments do not, however, gainsay the continuing significance of music in the organisation of more fine-grained but, nonetheless, significant vertical distinctions as opposed to the purely horizontal differentiations of Glevarec and Pinet's 'tablature'. And indeed, when tastes are considered in relation to indices of degree of intensity of involvement in different sections of the music field, such distinctions are often quite sharply drawn.

In relating these questions to different musical times we have shared the interest in the concept of emerging cultural capital advanced by the GBCS study and the ANUPoll on social class. However, our approach has differed from these studies in returning to Bourdieu's theoretical framing of such questions as ones best posed in relation to class fractions, and in our identification of three musical times rather than the bi-polar terms of a traditional/emerging contrast. We have also drawn attention to the limitations of these studies in predicating the existence of emerging cultural capital on evidence limited to the taste for new musical genres and use of new media technologies exhibited by the younger cohorts of their samples. Rather than hypostatising 'musical times' in this way, we return, in Chapter 7, to consider how the three musical times we have identified interact with the different cultural times evident in our other cultural fields as a necessary condition for broader claims about the relations between class and cultural capital.

Notes

1 For a synthesis on the idea of the omnivore see Gayo (2016a).
2 For some key texts on popular music in Australia see Breen (2006), Hayward (1992) and Stratton (2007).
3 The Australia Council for the Arts (2017) reports that 76 per cent of Australians 'used streaming services, or websites', nearly double that recorded in 2013 (40 per cent); while for young people aged 15–24 listening online was nearly universal (96 per cent).
4 The Australian World Orchestra, established in 2011, is an initiative to assemble expatriate Australian musicians who are employed in international orchestras with locally employed classical musicians to play a regular concert series. Melba Recordings is an independent recording company specialising in promoting contemporary Australian classical musicians.
5 Indigenous protocols sometimes proscribe reference to the deceased except in highly formalised terms. In view of his widespread recognition by his first name, however, Gurrumul Yunupingu's family has endorsed the continuing use of this in public discourse, rather than the more formal Dr G. Yunupingu that would otherwise apply.
6 We do not discuss the significance of place of residence here as this is a question explored more systematically on a cross-field basis in Chapter 11.
7 This contrasts with the findings of the Australian Everyday Cultures study where country and western was more strongly liked by men by a margin of 2 per cent: see Bennett et al. (1999: 175).
8 Our inclusion of alternative music in the category of emerging musical tastes is terminologically awkward given that we go on to speak of established alternative musical tastes as a broader category associated with a different musical time. The difficulty arises from the fact that 'alternative music' was one of the genre terms used in the ACF questionnaire prior to the more general analysis conducted for this chapter.

9 The ratios represent the differences between the percentages for frequent and non-attendees rounded up or down to the nearest decimal point.
10 Given this qualification, the respective figures for frequent versus non-attendance for these events is, as percentages of the total sample: rock gigs – 13 versus 66 per cent; orchestral concerts – 7 versus 73 per cent; musicals – 12 versus 54 per cent; opera – 11 versus 87 per cent; live bands in pubs – 21 versus 49 per cent; pop concerts – 7 versus 69 per cent.

4

THE ELITE AND THE EVERYDAY IN THE AUSTRALIAN HERITAGE FIELD

Emma Waterton and Modesto Gayo

This chapter explores contemporary Australian consumption practices in the field of heritage. Previous research highlights two broad categories of heritage that are drawn upon as important markers of social differentiation, determining not only how positions within the field are filled but also how different kinds of capital are distributed across those positions (Merriman, 1991; Smith, 2006; Dicks, 2015). These distinct categories include those labelled public, 'elite' or authorised forms of heritage, and those we might term personal, vernacular or everyday heritage. The first category incorporates places, objects and practices that are considered part of the remit of specific professional or specialised organisations and actors responsible for the management of heritage. Included here are monuments, archaeological ruins, state memorials, national museums and grand homes, as well as that redundant capital of old industrial infrastructures that is nowadays repackaged and re-presented as a form of cultural capital in the present, such as in the conversion of mines into visitor centres, dockyards into tourist waterfronts and industrial estates into creative cultural precincts. This is 'heritage' in its most dominant iteration, and it has been critiqued as speaking to and representing only certain privileged pockets of the population.

Drawing on participant responses to the *Australian Cultural Fields* (ACF) questionnaire, the chapter begins with an exploration of who is invested in this category of heritage. Some places – such as those emblematic of Australian national identity – seem to exhibit an extraordinary and consistent 'pull' when it comes to gathering people to them; that is, they are noticed by a wide range of people who are attuned to an accumulation of symbolic power at the national level. By contrast, other heritage places seem only to service and represent a particular socio-demographic: mature-aged Anglo-Celtic Australians, positioned within the managerial and professional class. A select few places (the heritage of migrant groups, for example) appear almost invisible, but no less remarkable to those who are interested in them.

The consumption of this category of heritage is therefore sharply differentiated by patterns of ethnicity, social class and age.

The chapter then moves on to discuss the project's in-depth household interviews, through which, in addition to further developing our reflections on the first category of heritage, we home in on our second category – personal, vernacular or everyday heritage. Unlike public heritage, this category is not necessarily associated with visiting authorised places of heritage but is instead rooted or significant in everyday life and is upheld by sensibilities that operate on a smaller, private scale. While many participants from a range of social positions spoke of the importance of this sort of heritage, which is constituted in moments of engagement and encounter, and informed by politics, family histories, place of birth and so forth, it is nonetheless also patterned by demographic variables, as we will demonstrate. We limit our focus here to two themes discernible in our data: first, references to family histories/genealogies that operate as part of a wider expression of (often national) identity; and, second, heritage as historical engagement. Before examining our heritage data in more detail we provide an overview of the historical genesis of Australia's heritage field in order to highlight some of its defining features, both nationally and globally.

The genesis of a heritage field in Australia

Heritage in Australia was arguably 'global' before it was 'Australian'. What we mean here is that the development of the Australian heritage field was shaped by an already existing, and relatively stable, set of transnational relationships and assumptions – emerging from a largely Western European context and underpinned by a tendency to elevate the first category of heritage above the second – before a field of a similar kind achieved a distinct shape in Australia. While these global practices have a far longer history, the Australian 'field' is essentially a late nineteenth century development, initiated with the establishment of the country's first national park. Royal National Park in New South Wales (NSW) was the first in the world to be legislated as such on 31 March 1879, commencing a process that would be consolidated thereafter with national parks in each State.[1] This was followed by the creation of Australia's National Trusts, formed first in NSW in 1945 and subsequently in other States in the 1950s, 1960s and 1970s. Membership of the NSW branch grew from approximately 5000 in the mid-1960s to 20,000 by the 1970s (Davison, 2013). The 1960s and 1970s also saw the passing of heritage legislation in various States, the formation of Australia ICOMOS (International Council on Monuments and Sites) in 1976, the establishment of the Register of the National Estate in 1978 and the introduction of the *Australia ICOMOS Charter for Places of Cultural Significance* (Burra Charter) in 1979. This concentrated turn to heritage, both popularly and politically, was primarily motivated by the 'new nationalism' of the Labor Party's Whitlam government, through which the parameters for practice, evaluation and related infrastructures were established (Davison, 1991; Waterton, 2018). These invariably referenced heritage policies and conventions already operating at the global scale, which prioritised an Anglo-European notion of heritage and revolved around archaeological sites and monuments that could point to a nation's longevity; grand homes and groups of buildings that were linked to the socially powerful and their possessions; architecturally significant places and their settings; and great works of art – in other words, a category of heritage we could describe as public, 'elite' or authorised (Smith, 2006).

There have, of course, been challenges to this logic. Class-based campaigns to save old warehouses, workers cottages and industrial buildings from expansive new developments gained considerable momentum, again in the 1960s and 1970s, spearheaded by resident action groups and trade unions pressing for legislation that would acknowledge and protect a more encompassing idea of heritage beyond the iconic (Smith, 2000). At the same time, political activism by Australia's Aboriginal and Torres Strait Islander peoples for the right to identify, manage and control their own heritage – which until then had been considered the preserve of archaeologists – also gained ground, following the 1967 referendum that secured a moral mandate for change in Aboriginal affairs (Attwood and Markus, 2007). Such challenges point to the fact that the historical experiences of Indigenous groups, women, children, different social classes and a variety of ethnic communities had been disproportionately underrepresented, and that, as a consequence, other categories of heritage were in need of recognition. In response, the field saw a broadening of what constitutes heritage, at both national and global levels, alongside an associated desire to 'contemporise' heritage, or allow that which was from the recent past to fall into the category of 'significant', 'valued' and 'meaningful'. This led to the drafting of the Burra Charter in 1979, which was underpinned by efforts to move away from a prioritisation of monuments towards an engagement with meaning and significance.[2] This broadening of heritage also saw the inclusion of industrial sites, festivals and open-air museums, albeit that many of these have been criticised for continuing to trivialise or gloss over aspects of inequality and social conflict.

Despite these interventions, the dynamics of the Australian heritage field are reliant on processes of assessment, listing and ranking that are organised around a nationalising tendency. It is therefore less autonomous than some of the other cultural fields included in this study: the literary, art and music fields, for example. It is implicated in the economic field, for instance, by its intricate links with tourism, visitors and audiences and, perhaps more importantly, it has a clear stake in the political field via its assumed ability to represent the nation (Krause, 2018). With regard to the latter, the Register of the National Estate, established in 1978 (and since replaced by the National Heritage List), was introduced to identify and protect four types of nationally significant heritage: the natural environment; the cultural environment; archaeological or scientific areas; and cultural property, with Aboriginal artefacts and sites assumed to align with the latter two categories. This conceptualisation is clearly reflected in the places that were included on the Register in the decades that followed its inception, such as colonial/pioneer homes, architecturally impressive buildings, historic churches and monuments. Thus, tangible objects detailing a European past became the central focus;

Aboriginal, industrial, working-class, multicultural and women's heritage all remained outside its dominant iterations, leaving nationalism as the key principle of cohesion within the field (Byrne, 2016).

The heritage field represented

The ACF questionnaire included questions about heritage visitation practices, subscriptions and memberships, likes and dislikes, and the use of the Internet to source information about heritage places and events. We asked about a wide range of heritage sites that might have been visited: local, regional or national museums; migration museums; historic buildings or precincts; archaeological sites; Aboriginal heritage sites; military sites or memorials; open-air sites; cultural landscapes; pioneer or settler heritage sites; and sites of industrial heritage. The kinds of heritage included in the survey ranged across family, local and working life heritage through heritage of the respondents' homeland, the heritage of migrant groups and Aboriginal heritage to Australia's national heritage and world heritage. The forms of membership and indicators of more regular engagements we asked about included membership of national and local museums, national parks, local history and archaeology societies, and the National Trust of Australia or similar organisations. We also asked about use of online family history websites and subscription to Foxtel's History Channel.

In addition, so as to elicit indications of the frequency of, and motivations for, participation, we asked if people had heard of, visited and liked a series of ten Australian and ten international heritage places. We included well-known places such as the Australian War Memorial, located in the nation's capital Canberra. It is the main national repository of Australia's military heritage. It also constructs and disseminates a heritage narrative that feeds into a broader set of socio-cultural tools used to author a sense of national identity, one that is tightly enmeshed with the Anzac spirit or Anzac legend.[3] The National Museum of Australia, also located in Canberra, celebrates Australia's social history. Its interpretation covers European settlement as well as making significant overtures towards engaging with, and explicitly narrating, the experiences of Aboriginal peoples, pre- and post-contact. Both are government-supported cultural institutions. Uluru-Kata Tjuta National Park is considered a living cultural landscape for Anangu people, as well as being regularly referred to as the symbolic 'red heart' of the wider Australian nation (see Figure 4.1). It was declared a National Park in 1950 and a World Heritage site in 1987, both of which clearly mark it out as a highly recognisable place of heritage.

Our sample also includes 3 of the 11 places that comprise the Australian Convict Sites serial listing on the World Heritage list: one located in Western Australia (Fremantle Prison), one in Tasmania (Port Arthur) and one in NSW (Cockatoo Island). Inscribed in July 2010, this collective represents the forced migration of convicts to Australia, which is a significant and deeply contested period that has been mythologised in the nation's history. Fremantle Prison is one of the most intact heritage precincts from the convict era whereas the Port Arthur Historic Site is one of the

FIGURE 4.1 Uluṟu-Kata Tjuṯa National Park, Sovereign Hill and the Port Arthur Historic Site.

Source: Photographs courtesy of Emma Waterton.

Uluṟu-Kata Tjuṯa was formally handed back to its Traditional Owners, the Aṉangu, in 1985. It was inscribed on the World Heritage list in 1987 for its natural values and later re-inscribed as a cultural landscape in 1994. It attracts approximately 300,000 visitors a year. Sovereign Hill (bottom right) attracted 546,000 visitors in 2017–2018. Located in Victoria, it is dedicated to the region's gold-mining past, the labour movement and Australian history more broadly. The site is also associated with the Eureka Rebellion of 1854, which is commonly remembered as a historic uprising against British colonial authority and as the birthplace of Australian democracy. Port Arthur (bottom left), located on the Tasman Peninsula, is known primarily for the convict settlement that operated there from 1830–1877. Prior to its establishment as a penal complex, the area belonged to the Pydairrerme peoples. The site contains remnants of the main portion of the nineteenth-century penal and industrial complex, along with historic residences and maritime archaeological resources. In 2017–2018, Port Arthur attracted 368,862 visitors (PAHSMA, 2018). All three places are considered 'iconic' within Australia's repertoire of heritage.

most visited (see Figure 4.1). Port Arthur is also considered an important national memorial following the death of thirty-five people in 1996 at the hands of a gunman. Cockatoo Island is a small sandstone knoll located in the middle of Sydney Harbour and represents a range of significant moments in Sydney's history, including practices of convict management, a reformatory for girls, the development of the Royal Australian Navy, hard labour and shipbuilding.

In addition to the above mainstream places of heritage, a handful of places we might refer to as 'sectional' and/or regional examples of heritage were included.

The Museum of Sydney is a good example of a regional museum in that it focuses on the city's history from European settlement to the present day. Sovereign Hill is an outdoor/open-air museum in Ballarat that showcases the experiences of gold mining in regional Victoria from the 1850s, although there is a relative lack of visibility afforded to the experiences of Chinese and Aboriginal people (see Figure 4.1). Tjapukai Aboriginal Cultural Park is a centre explicitly dedicated to Aboriginal history and culture. Developed in 1987, it communicates Aboriginal and Torres Strait Islander heritage to a range of domestic and international tourists. Finally, we included the Immigration Museum in Melbourne, which opened in 1998 and is located in the Old Customs House. Unlike those places dedicated to colonial or Aboriginal heritage, the Immigration Museum is a regional museum that is committed to documenting the stories of linguistically and culturally diverse migrants to Victoria.

Participants were also asked if they had heard of, visited, liked or disliked a sample of international heritage places. This component of the questionnaire included Gallipoli, which, though overseas, is another example of a place through which abstracted patterns of remembering have become part of the 'general project of developing and maintaining an image that supports [the] collective identity' of Australia (Wertsch, 2008: 68). Like the Australian War Memorial, Gallipoli (and the Gallipoli Campaign of the First World War) provides a clear, though controversial, example of heritage that has gained immense visibility and power due to its associations with the 'birth' of the Australian nation (Waterton and Dittmer, 2016). We also included places representative of well-known classical European heritage, such as Stonehenge (UK), the Vatican Museums (Italy) and the Acropolis of Athens (Greece), as well as those we might refer to as 'non-Western', such as the Taj Mahal (India), the Forbidden City (China), Ankor Wat (Cambodia) and Byblos (Lebanon). Six of these can be considered 'veterans' of the heritage field, gaining World Heritage status in the 1980s; the (slight) exception is Angkor Wat, which was added to the list in 1992. In addition, two places representative of more contemporary history were included: Ellis Island (USA) and Te Papa Tongarewa (the Museum of New Zealand), neither of which have yet been afforded World Heritage status.

Contemporary Australian heritage practices

Responses to our questionnaire are interpreted using two Multiple Correspondence Analysis (MCA) figures to make sense of contemporary Australia's engagements with heritage: the first is concerned with respondents' heritage tastes and practices (Figure 4.2) and the second with their social positions (Figure 4.3). The first point to note in relation to both is that the variance is more-or-less evenly distributed across the left–right (7.58 per cent) and upper–lower (6.56 per cent) axes, both of which play a significant role in the dispersal of individuals across the space. This tells us that class and education, which drive variation across the left–right axis, and age, which does similarly across the upper–lower axis, account for the main differences in the field. Gender, by contrast, plays a less significant role in differentiating heritage practices.

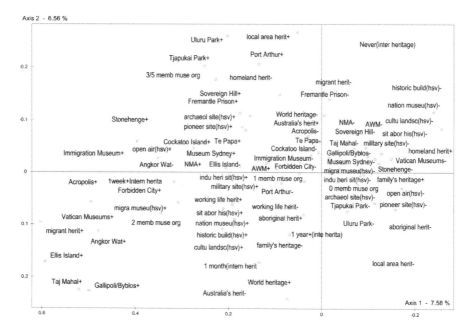

FIGURE 4.2 The space of heritage tastes and practices.

Figure 4.2 plots different patterns of participation arranged around 'scale', 'site' and 'genre' of heritage. By 'scale', we refer to local, national and world heritage, which are evenly spaced along the vertical axis, moving from positive engagement with local heritage in the upper space through to Australia's heritage in the middle of the upper space, to world heritage in the lower space (here, we are referencing those labels with a '+' sign, not a '−' sign). In terms of the horizontal axis, Australia's heritage is immediately adjacent to the vertical axis, with local and world heritage a little to the left. 'Sites' of heritage similarly track from the upper to lower quadrant (though remain exclusively to the left of the space), with archaeological sites, pioneer sites and open-air museums in the upper left and industrial heritage, military memorials, historic buildings/precincts and cultural landscapes in the lower left quadrant. 'Genres' of heritage run from left to right and include migrant, industrial/working life, Aboriginal, family and homeland heritage. We point to these genres as an indication of movement towards a broadened idea of heritage, with homeland and family heritage located to the right (with homeland in the upper and family heritage in the lower quadrant) and migrant, industrial and Aboriginal heritage all in the lower left quadrant.

There are, then, clear differences between the right and left segments of the space. The right contains those respondents who can be described as disengaged or lacking in knowledge about public heritage: they never use the Internet to search for heritage, they do not hold national park or museum memberships/subscriptions and had not visited any heritage places in the previous 12 months. Some positive tastes do register to the right, however, such as a fondness for family history (lower right) and a liking for the heritage of a person's homeland (upper right). The lower right quadrant is also distinguished from the upper right by a strong disliking for Aboriginal heritage and the two sites associated with Aboriginal culture, as well as by age, with the lower quadrant occupied by those aged 18–24 and the upper quadrant, in contrast, by those over 65 (Figure 4.3).

Those to the left of the space display an increasing interest in public heritage. This growing intensity of engagements is mirrored by a simultaneous growth in memberships, subscriptions and Internet use, moving from some (Internet searches once a year; some memberships and subscriptions) to very engaged (Internet searches at least once a week; multiple memberships and subscriptions). Of interest here is the fact that those with a more sustained membership practice are located in

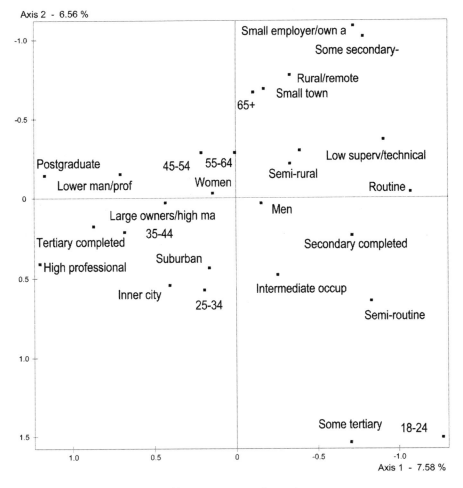

FIGURE 4.3 The social space of heritage tastes and practices.

the upper left while those who use the Internet to engage with heritage are in the lower left quadrant. Demographically, these two spaces are again differentiated by age, with those aged 45–64 located in the upper left and those aged 25–44 in the lower left of the space.

While both domestic and international places dominate the left of the space, there is a clear differentiation between the two: international places are largely positioned in the lower left (except for Stonehenge and Te Papa Tongarewa), whereas positive preferences for a large range of domestic heritage places are found in the top left quadrant. No named domestic sites feature in the lower left quadrant at all, with the exception of a *disliking* for Port Arthur. The different 'sites' of heritage referenced in our questionnaire are also split between the upper and lower quadrants on the left, with historic buildings, national museums, industrial heritage sites and cultural landscapes in the lower quadrant and archaeological sites, settler-colonial sites and open-air museums located in the top, although both quadrants appear to have an appetite for Aboriginal places of heritage (unlike those on the right).

On the whole, then, those occupying the left of the space appear to have an encompassing appetite for heritage, but it is qualified. There are those with an interest in genres of heritage considered mainstream and underpinned by narratives that align with a nationalising tendency, and then there are those with an interest in sites or genres which have only more recently become part of a broadened notion of heritage, such as that of working life/industrial heritage and migrant heritage/museums. As noted earlier, Australian-focused places are situated above the horizontal axis, creating a space we might say is inflected with a nationalist sentiment, whereas the space below that axis is populated by places that are marked by their distinction from national heritage places, such as those invested with a global and/or sectional flavour. Importantly, those with an interest in this sort of heritage also share an explicit dislike for Australian heritage. In other words, it is a space that is notably lacking in national influence.

When read together, Figures 4.2 and 4.3 indicate that age, occupation, place of residence and education all play significant roles in differentiating heritage tastes and practices. Age plays a particularly powerful role. The bottom left quadrant, which is occupied by those with a keen interest in international heritage sites, aligns with those in their mid-20s to mid-40s, whereas the upper left quadrant, which has a concentration of those who have visited and liked a range of domestic heritage places, is defined by those in their mid-40s to mid-60s. The right of the space, occupied by those with an apparent lack of interest in heritage, correlates with those over 65 (upper right), but who like the heritage of their homeland, and those aged 18–24 (lower right), who like their family's heritage. Gender, as noted above, plays a fairly minimal role and is differentiated primarily by the horizontal axis, with women located to the left and men to the right of the space, though both are close to the centre.

Occupation and education are also key to explaining variations in heritage practices. For example, our data suggests that education has a strong bearing on who is actively interested in public heritage, with those who have had the opportunity to undertake tertiary and postgraduate education being most likely to fall in this category. Education likewise affects Internet use, with percentages for those who *do not* use the Internet for heritage purposes steadily declining as education levels move from some secondary (60 per cent) to some tertiary (19 per cent) to postgraduate qualifications (10 per cent). Education also influences the likelihood that respondents will have heard of lesser known international sites, such as The Forbidden City (moving from 75 per cent to 89 per cent alongside an increase in education qualifications), Ellis Island (from 50 per cent to 73 per cent) and Angkor Wat (from 35 per cent to 66 per cent). Highly educated respondents, or those who have completed tertiary education or hold postgraduate degrees, are located on the left of Figure 4.3 (lower and upper respectively), with all others located to the right. Those employed in high-level professional and managerial (higher and lower managerial) roles also congregate to the left, with all other employment classifications situated to the right.

Finally, place of residence has a very strong bearing on heritage practices, with those living in the inner city and suburban locations congregating in the bottom left of the space (and thus aligned with an international appetite) and those living in semi-rural, small towns and rural/remote locations occupying the top right, thereby indicating a move from high levels of involvement to very low levels, as discussed above. A more detailed statistical picture suggests that 47 per cent of those living in the inner city will engage in high levels of heritage activity, while only 6 per cent of those living in a rural or remote context will do so (see Waterton and Gayo, 2018). Likewise, those living in a suburban context exhibit very high levels of participation (35 per cent), particularly in global heritage places, as opposed to those living in small towns (9 per cent).

Other desires for the past: heritage in our household interviews

As the above interpretations illustrate, public, 'elite' and authorised iterations of heritage clearly weigh on what and how we know heritage, flexing and shaping the lenses through which it is understood. But do these 'official' iterations fill *all* the space that is available for knowing, liking and participating in heritage in Australia (Crouch, 2015)? Our household interviews provide a nuanced picture of both authorised notions of heritage and more personal engagements. This picture will be deepened in two ways: first, by providing insight into a demotic deployment of heritage through family histories/genealogies; and, second, by highlighting the role of personal obligation in historical engagements.

Family history, genealogies and the transmission of identity

For many interviewees, heritage is a means of connecting with family, becoming a sort of 'cement' or locus for bringing families together. To borrow from Morgan (2011), it is part of the practice of *doing family*. It is also an important element in related practices of identity-making. As such, heritage cannot be reduced to simple acts of visiting iconic places or seeing officially curated heritage artefacts; rather, it is quite often something that is done *with* or *because* of family. As Christine observes, 'my kids have brought me into [heritage] – you think you share your things with your children, but it is amazing how much they share back'. Likewise, Mayra sees heritage as 'very much about what your family engages with'. For Adrian, this relationship between heritage and family provides a very specific and powerful point of overlap, and has clear links with both Australian and Anglo-Celtic pasts via an identified set of standing stones:

> Well, because my family is involved in a ... stone henge site ... they've got standing stones in [small town in regional NSW] and our family sponsors one of the stones there so – and it means something to me because I understand the heritage of all that sort of – it just means, like, the standing stones did mean something.

We are interested in a specific seam of this sort of engagement, often referred to as 'family history' and which, though recognised as a form of heritage, is seldom captured in official taxonomies used to assess, rank and list it. Once dismissed as 'misty eyed and syrupy', family history has grown in popularity since the 1960s and is today part of a thriving industry, evidenced by the longevity of TV programmes like *Who Do You Think You Are?* and Internet sites such as Ancestry.com and AncestryDNA (Evans, 2011: 49; Barnwell, 2017). As Davison (2000) argues, the rising interest in family history in Australia emerged in the immediate aftermath of agitations for Indigenous, class-based and women-focused heritage in the 1960s, 1970s and 1980s, and sat alongside a broader effort to come to terms with the nation's convict past. Given this, it is unsurprising that our questionnaire revealed 'family history' to be by far the most popular 'genre' of heritage across both our main and boost samples, with 57 per cent of the former and 46 per cent of the latter selecting it as one of the two genres which interests them most. While of similar interest to respondents who identified themselves as belonging to the working (38 per cent) and middle (44 per cent) classes, it has vastly less appeal for those who identify as being part of the upper classes (9 per cent). Education, by contrast, has little bearing on this selection. Interestingly, family history sits in the lower right quadrant of our earlier reported MCA (Figure 4.2), which is characterised by a lack of engagement and a number of dislikes, and is occupied by 18–24 year-olds.

The popularity of 'family history' was nonetheless confirmed by our household interviewees, with just shy of half mentioning their efforts to learn about and engage with it. Some were equally enthusiastic about heritage in all its manifestations; for others, however, this is the *only* form of heritage that holds their attention. In discussing their interests, many interviewees highlight the time and effort (and from this we can infer importance or value) they are willing to put into its pursuit. Others express a deep pride in certain defining features of their genealogies, such as the extent or length of the lineage (i.e. number of generations traced), key individuals identified (particularly well-known historical figures and those associated with wider national narratives) and a sense of 'pedigree'. David, a 78 year old, exemplifies this position:

> I think [my sister and I] are reasonably unique in Australia ... because ... every one of our great grandparents were all born in Australia. And most of our great, great grandparents. So, the last ... in our line that came to Australia was in 1855, so that's 145, no, 161 uninterrupted years of heritage. Yeah, no, most people can't say that.

Diane, a 53 year old, also highlights a sense of her family's continuity as well as her connection to a key moment and place (Gallipoli) in Australia's history:

> Me, personally, my grandfather was in the first battalion that landed on Gallipoli ... so I've grown up with that culture, that heritage of you're an Australian – we're about fourth or fifth generation ourselves. My husband is, too, actually, so that's unusual.

Family trees that can be latched directly on to the retelling of a broader Australian history are particularly prized, such as those with links to the First Fleet, 'free settlers' or convicts (Tranter and Donoghue, 2003: 555–556). This ability to establish a clear connection between one's family and wider national narratives enables some participants to see themselves very clearly in, *and locate themselves as central to*, particular Anglo-Australian national myths. As Donoghue and Tranter (2018) have pointed out, there are class-based distinctions to these national myths and their appeal. Links to free settlers, for instance, tend to appeal to the middle class (such as David and Diane above), whereas convict heritage is more likely to be claimed by working-class Australians. Lynne, a 51 year old who self-identifies as working class, exemplifies this observation in her keenness to connect with Australia's history of convictism:

> Well, I'm very lucky and very blessed. About fifteen years ago, a distant, distant, distant cousin over in Western Australia did a family tree ... And traced our roots back to the First Fleet ... They both came out as convicts. They met out here. They had 15 children, 49 grandchildren, 128 great grandchildren. He put together a family tree – actually, I'm going to go get it. I'm so proud of this [retrieves family tree]. A copy of this is in the National Library ... it's got all the living descendants as a number of the population, one-in-six hundred and forty two natural born Australians are related to my family.

Three points are notable here, all of which dovetail with the work of Barnwell (2017) on convict family histories: first, Lynne's reflections highlight that this interest in convict history is relatively recent (it is not inherited family knowledge but a product of recent research); second, and relatedly, convict history has emerged as an enormous source of pride after enduring a period during which it was seen as a source of shame; finally, it is a narrative that can be easily absorbed into wider national myths, allowing Lynne, in this instance, to connect herself with the National Library of Australia and 'one-in-six hundred and forty two natural born Australians'. Such interest, as Donoghue and Tranter (2018) have recently observed, is often tied to identity claims, particularly given that convicts (alongside bushrangers and gold miners) are a central part of Australia's foundation myths. As they go on to argue: 'Claiming convict heritage taps directly into the foundations myths and collective memory of Australia, and links contemporary citizens with the "chosen" (and in this case "chained") few who helped to establish the modern Australian nation' (Donoghue and Tranter, 2018: 24).

As Evans (2011) has pointed out, the legacies of Australia's settler-colonial policies (of violence, removal and land theft) have meant that the desire to discover one's ancestry is especially strong amongst Aboriginal and Torres Strait Islander peoples. This desire is sometimes underpinned by personal motivations, as in the case of David, identified earlier, who has recently discovered some Indigenous ancestry:

> I've just gradually been piecing stuff together ... when I decided to look at my family, I decided to do it pretty thoroughly ... I wanted to know more than just, you know, names and dates and all that sort of things. I mean, that comes easy.

For others, though, it is more complicated as it can be underpinned by politically pressing motivations such as for the purposes of obtaining proof or confirmation of Aboriginality, as Kim, a 53-year-old Aboriginal woman, observes:

> What I'm hoping to do is put together a living family tree that we can add on and add on and we can print off at stages ... so that we can use that as proof of Aboriginality if we need to ... This way, it's there. *They can see.* It can be added to and added to ... and there'll be a portable hard drive with all the information on that'll be passed on so it's never lost.
>
> *(emphasis added)*

Kim's reference to 'they can see' highlights the continuing need within government policies for Aboriginal and Torres Strait Islander identity to be confirmed, and the anxieties that underpin that process of confirmation. This is because such processes tend to overlook the difficulties posed for those families with relatives who were part of the Stolen Generations or for those whose ancestors hid their identities. In both situations there are significant absences of information that prevent the provisioning of required documentation. References to secrecy or hidden identities are made by both Christine and David in their reflections on family heritage, both of whom intimate that such secret-keeping often 'operated in the service of wider social agendas' (Barnwell, 2018: 453). David's recollections, for example, focus on his great grandfather's side of the family, and particularly his Aunty and Uncle. David recalls his Aunty being 'too Aboriginal' to go to a pool in regional NSW due to the segregation of town amenities until the 1970s, and both his Aunty and Uncle seldom being invited into his grandmother's home for fear that neighbours might see them. While that stigma has undoubtedly lessened since the 1960s and 1970s, it nonetheless remains a potent element of contemporary Australian society, where discrimination, inequality and disadvantage are prevalent. For Christine, this makes the rendering of Aboriginal heritage visible all the more important:

> I think bringing out a lot of Aboriginal heritage now is really important because it was so hidden and so condemned ... Being able to acknowledge that you're Aboriginal or Aboriginal heritage is a big thing because it was such a secret for a long time ... It was a secret from my Dad, my Dad's secret, for a long time. I mean, we knew but you just didn't go and tell people at his age.

Historical engagement as national obligation

Our second theme latches on to the idea of 'heritage as historical engagement', which in many ways emerges from the field's articulation with the wider political field and concomitant assumption about the ability of heritage to represent the nation. Here, we turn to Australia's military past and the historical connections that are established through the Anzac legend, which are used to express a sense of belonging to the nation. This often revolves around feelings of duty or obligation, sentiments that also underpin more general discussions about heritage. Some of our interviewees for example lament that they did not visit heritage sites but they felt they 'probably should' and acknowledged that there exists a suite of individuals and events that 'shouldn't be forgotten' (see Chapter 17). This is a frequent refrain across our interviews, with many participants inferring a feeling of obligation alongside a liking for heritage, but one that was not strong enough to prioritise heritage visiting above other practices. It is a feeling particularly pronounced amongst those who self-identify with the working classes, as both Kathleen and Oliver (respectively) make clear:

> I always planned to but never went and had a look at the first Australian Governor's House. I've never done that sort of stuff. I kept wanting to do it. I never got around to doing it. I lived [in the area] for twenty years.

> I'm saying I'm interested in them but I'm not actually going ... It's strange ... As interesting as it is, I guess you don't apply the time to go and see that stuff, which is a shame.

Particularly salient in our data, but with clear links to the theme of family history discussed earlier, are references to 'military history', whereby a feeling of duty towards a particular genre of heritage emerges either because of a family member who has served in the military or a family member for whom military history is important. Both tap into a socially and politically constructed sense of national identity (Donoghue and Tranter, 2018). Of course, the recounting of family involvement in war does not occur only in the Australian context; individual or personal memories of war have been reproduced and enfolded into wider collective memories of wartime in a variety of national contexts. Nonetheless, military heritage remains a clear and powerful influence for a nation like Australia, which is so defined by its military past (Waterton and Dittmer, 2016). This observation is supported by Donoghue and Tranter's (2018) work, which indicates that 47 per cent of Australians prioritise Anzacs as those who most influence their own identity. It is also evidenced by our own survey, which reveals that military sites and memorials, as places of heritage, are visited more often than any other, with 58 per cent of those surveyed indicating they had visited such places in the past 12 months. While of interest to respondents with an array of educational backgrounds and ages, places of military heritage, unlike family history, speak marginally more clearly to those with a tertiary education and higher income.

Unsurprisingly, the Australian War Memorial figures as a key site of heritage for many interviewees, such as Gabriel:

> Well, in terms of heritage, personal heritage, I would imagine that one of the closest to me or at least to Dad's side of the family would be the Australian War Memorial, the World War One side. I have never seen my Grandad walk out of that without tears in his eyes.

Expressions of obligation extend beyond visiting nationally significant places such as Gallipoli and the Australian War Memorial and are linked with 'performing' a sense of duty at events such as Anzac Day, as Christine makes clear when she states 'I really think that that was so moving for me that every Australian should attempt to go there.' Christine's emotional commitment to remembering is captured by her own willingness (and ability) to travel – or pilgrimage – to Turkey but also by her intense assertion that 'every Australian' should go there. Lynne similarly underscores the importance of performing her Australian identity through/on Anzac Day:

> Every Anzac Day we get them [our children] up and go to the morning service and get them to the march and not let them forget what generations before us did to give them what they've got today. So, heritage – Australian heritage – is very, very important to me.

Others, like Akela, can *feel* the pull of obligation but do not exhibit the same levels of personal commitment. Perhaps Akela is responding to the immense political weight and public funding that has been mobilised over the past few decades, aimed at fostering what Clark refers to as a 'collective attachment to Australia's military past' (2017: 22; see also Chapter 17). Several other interviewees express a strong degree of certainty about the importance of remembering Anzacs (we 'should' or 'must' visit or remember), indicating that they take as given that all Australians will feel the same way. Heath underscores this observation as follows:

> Well, around Anzac Day I spend a lot of time crying because it's so powerful. I feel very thankful for what our soldiers have done for us. *You couldn't be Australian* unless you … you hear the Last Post and you have to well up. There's nothing like it.
>
> *(emphasis added)*

Heath's utterance gels with Clark's observation that there is a continued growth in the number of Australians who actively feel and express 'an intense historical connection through the figure of Anzac' (2017: 21), and supports Donoghue and Tranter's (2018) finding that almost half of all Australians continue to see the Anzac myth as central to the construction of the Australian national identity.

Conclusion

This chapter has examined Australia's heritage field via two entry points: data produced by our questionnaire and by follow-up household interviews. Interpretations emerging from this two-pronged approach were framed with reference to distinct categories of heritage: public, 'elite' or authorised heritage; and private or vernacular heritage. Whilst both are present within policy and professional practice, the former enjoys far greater visibility. Much of the academic literature associated with theoretical and empirical explorations of these categories argues that the first category appeals to the tastes of a certain demographic: the highly educated, occupying higher class positions. Our modelling of the social space of heritage confirms that the practices, tastes and identities bound up with this prominent category of heritage remain structured by class, with the majority of Australians disengaged from it. This indicates that class has a continuing salience in the heritage field, both in terms of what is produced (or prioritised) and by whom it is consumed. Importantly, those who engage with this form of heritage are not a monolithic entity. Though they are largely defined by economic good fortune, there are pronounced differences, or internal differentiations, in terms of their willingness to participate in resource-demanding activities such as international travel. This variation is notably associated with the supplementary categories of age, education and place of residence, all three of which have a bearing on who likes global and sectional heritage whilst also disliking heritage associated with nationalist narratives.

While our interpretations of the questionnaire allowed for an exploration of the field's vulnerabilities to elite pressure, we are also keen to acknowledge that there are moments during which popular sources of heritage exert a certain weight on the field. Our discussion of 'family history', an area of interest that is not especially visible in authorised accounts of heritage, is a particular curiosity. Phrases such as 'disengaged' or 'lacking interest', which we used to discuss the results of the project's questionnaire, suddenly appear less applicable to those located to the right of the social space. Indeed, data from our household interviews revealed family history to be an area of heritage that is open to the tastes and practices of significant sections of the population (all ages, both genders, a range of educational backgrounds and the working and middle classes), the only exception being those occupying the highest class position. Though our explorations of family histories are undoubtedly infused (for some, at least) with the influence of an authorised and national sense of heritage (seen through the prizing of key events and key people), it is nonetheless a popular heritage practice largely orientated towards demotic cultural forms. This is less pronounced for military heritage, which is more often co-opted into authorised forms of heritage by virtue of the role it plays in the construction of narratives of the nation.

Notes

1 The national park only became known as Royal National Park in 1955 in honour of Queen Elizabeth II's visit to Australia (Robin, 2013).
2 The Burra Charter has been periodically updated since 1979 (in 1982, 1988 and 1999), with the current version produced in 2013.
3 'Anzac' refers to the Australian and New Zealand Army Corps. Following Australian and New Zealand engagement in the Dardanelles campaign (at what has come to be known as Gallipoli), the term became a popular way of referring to Australian soldiers and the 'Anzac spirit' they were seen to embody. The Anzac 'legend' remains powerful, though regularly subject to critique. 'Pilgrimages' to the Anzac site in Turkey have become important, especially since the 1980s.

5
TELEVISION
The dynamics of a field in transition

Tony Bennett, Modesto Gayo, David Rowe and Graeme Turner

Television has been dramatically transformed in recent decades, with major structural and technological changes affecting the full range of its activities across production, distribution and consumption. While this trend is evident internationally, it varies significantly in how it plays out in particular national contexts. In Australia, these forces have only taken significant effect relatively recently, and have accelerated notably during the period in which we conducted our research for this project, between 2014 and 2018. As a result, our findings concerning the dynamics of the Australian television field evidence the changing behaviour of an audience rapidly transitioning from a broadcast-only environment via the digitisation of screen viewing into a hybrid broadcast, narrowcast and online environment for the consumption of television. While this transition is inseparably enmeshed within structural changes in the internal economy of the television field in Australia, our primary focus is on the contemporary patterns of Australians' consumption of television.

First, we look more closely at the key changes which characterise the dynamics of the Australian television field. We then review the debates concerning the place of television within field theory that our work engages with: the role of technological actors as active agents in the disposition of field relations, and the role of 'quality television' and of television's personality system in televisual regimes of distinction. This discussion paves the way for outlining the rationale for the items selected for inclusion in the television section of the *Australian Cultural Fields* (ACF) questionnaire. We then present the main findings of our survey and conclude by considering what light these findings and the evidence from our household interviews throw on the rapidly changing dynamics of the Australian television field. The effects of these are most strongly evident in the pronounced significance of age in distinguishing both viewing practices and tastes. Its explanatory power, relative to that of both class and education, is the strongest of all the ACF fields – more so than in the music field, its closest rival in this regard.

A field in transition

It will be useful, first, to highlight some of the key differences between Australian television in 2019, at the time of writing, and 1994 when Australia was still firmly in the 'broadcast era' and free-to-air (FTA) television was the only available option. Television was universally accessible, although with some regional variations for access to the commercial networks which meant that the public broadcasting network, the Australian Broadcasting Corporation (ABC), was the only comprehensively national service. The system was made up of five FTA networks – three commercial and two public service broadcast (PSB) networks. The content that they carried was only available via a set linear schedule. Each network had a distinct identity articulated to the taste preferences of its target demographic (identified principally in terms of social class, gender and age) and legible through its promotional strategies and programme schedules. Notwithstanding the alignment of their network identities to these target demographics, all the commercial broadcasters addressed a mass rather than a niche audience. They were differentiated by their promotion of network-branded personalities, their specific schedules of high-profile, mostly American, content, and aspects of their presentational style and modes of address. Often it was the network personalities – from newsreaders to gameshow hosts to the stars of local soap operas – through whom the networks' identities were expressed and around whom audience loyalties were built.

Weekly ratings were led by Australian news and current affairs (as they are now), followed by American drama series and then by occasional 'event' programming such as sport or locally produced drama miniseries. Pay-TV (subscription and pay-per-view), which commenced in 1995, broadened the range of content available to its subscribers, but induced only minor changes to the commercial FTA networks' identities and strategies. Its subsequent expansion has been limited, never exceeding a 30 per cent share of the available audience. The current situation is markedly different. FTA's share of the television audience is slowly but steadily declining, as are the total numbers watching broadcast television. Australians watched 80 minutes less broadcast television per week in 2017 than in 2016, and one in seven Australians watched no commercial FTA television at all on a normal week day (Turner, 2017). Furthermore, an increasing amount of FTA television consumption – up to 50 per cent – is non-linear, with time-shifting via Personal Video Recorders (PVRs) or catch-up sites now an increasingly important component of industry ratings figures. There is also an increase in out-of-home and mobile device viewing, both of which are associated with preferences for accessing content through video aggregators such as YouTube, social media such as Facebook, or streaming services like Netflix and local providers Stan and Foxtel Now.

These developments have begun to undermine the sense of 'co-presence' and simultaneity – the assumption that a significant part of the nation is watching the same programme at the same time – that underpinned the social and cultural centrality of national FTA TV systems. What was once a relatively simple market, in which only five major providers competed for audiences, has fragmented into a complicated and volatile mix of mass and niche markets within which television must deal with competition from social media platforms, video aggregators, online streaming services and 'the culture of search' (Hillis et al., 2013). Where once the commercial objective was to attract a mass audience, there must now be an alternative or complementary strategy: to locate and service taste fractions while also focusing on the preferred options for attracting a mass audience. For the commercial FTA networks, this latter avenue means reality television and sport, genres which are best watched live, are only available on schedule, generate significant 'water cooler' chatter and carry the potential for creating branded personalities or celebrities as new points of identification for the host network (Meade, 2017).

This last objective has become especially crucial in the digital era. Commercial FTA broadcasters have had to recognise that there is little point in seeking the same levels of channel or network loyalty as in earlier decades through their programmes and personalities. PSB broadcasters have been shielded from this situation to some extent, as they continue to maintain a distinctive identity based on their national cultural remit, which does not explicitly require them to match the ratings of the commercial channels.

The most dramatic disruption of the internal dynamics of Australian television has been the arrival of Netflix in 2015 (Turner, 2018).[1] This was the moment when Australia unequivocally embraced the transition to a multiplatform environment for television consumption. Netflix picked up 15 per cent of the TV market within three months of its introduction, and soon had a larger share (32 per cent) of households than pay-TV (27 per cent) (Roy Morgan, 2017). The effect on the FTA networks has been substantial: for instance, it has greatly reduced their audiences' demand for high-profile new release American drama and comedy, removing one of the traditional pillars of their programming. This kind of content can now be downloaded or streamed on demand, usually with a simultaneous global release, and with multiple episodes or even whole series available online.

All this turmoil, however, does not amount to anything like the 'death of television' in Australia. There are also strong strands of continuity. FTA television remains the dominant mode, accounting for 86 per cent of television viewed (Davidson, 2017). Broadcast television is turning out to be more resilient than some expected. However, the cultural placement and function of television are certainly mutating by degrees as new points of access and modes of consumption develop. This trend means that some of the frameworks within which we might once have connected accounts of television consumption to patterns of class or age or gender have changed, or are in the process of change, as will become apparent when the responses generated by our survey are considered. We turn next, however, to outline how these changes in the Australian television field connect with our concerns regarding the place of television in field theory.

Television and field theory

Although Bourdieu's specific assessments of television have had little impact on television studies, his more general contention that, as a part of the broader journalistic field, television has functioned as a venue where other cultural fields are brought into relation with one another (Bourdieu, 1998: 74) has proved more influential. It has prompted the suggestion that the media – especially television – are sites for the production of 'meta-capital', mediating the relations between different field-specific capitals, assigning them their relative powers and spheres of operation (Couldry, 2003). Television's personality system has similarly been interpreted as part of a broader inter-media field for the production and circulation of 'celebrity capital' (Driessens, 2013), with the consequence that its significance has now to some degree been displaced by the emergence of new forms of 'DIY' celebrity made possible by the Internet (Turner, 2006; Bennett, J., 2011; Kanai, 2015).

This is not to say that television lacks its own internal hierarchies of legitimacy: in Australia these have typically informed the relations between its public broadcasters and the commercial networks as well those between high (current affairs) and low status (reality television) genres – and, of course, gradations of status within genres. Over the last decade or so, however, as Newman and Levine (2012) have shown, the cultural status of television has become more contingent as new kinds of television drama have differentiated themselves from 'ordinary' television, or everyday broadcast network programming. Building on the success of 1990s television drama series such as *Twin Peaks* and *The X-Files*, which 'broke the mould' of formulaic network productions and led to what some have described as a distinctive 'television aesthetic' (Jacobs, 2001), there is now a strong tradition of US cable TV series produced by networks such as Home Box Office (HBO) and Showtime (from *The Sopranos* and *Breaking Bad*, to *Game of Thrones*) which are characterised by their formal complexity and long-running story lines. The same is now true of European series like *The Bridge*. Such programmes underpinned the market for DVD box sets of TV series in the early 2000s, fuelling the practice of binge-viewing, which in turn opened up the space for streaming services which could deliver multiple episodes or whole series at once. Further, media convergence enabled audiences to access this content via a wide range of devices, shifting an increasing proportion of the consumption of television away from the family TV. The cultural status of television has significantly changed as a result: Newman and Levine (2012) convincingly argue that certain kinds of television now rival the cultural legitimacy of cinema. There are, however, quite contradictory tendencies at work. The spread of reality formats across both broadcast and cable might seem to reinforce older formations in which television was a culturally denigrated medium, while the rise of what Jason Mittell (2015) calls 'complex TV' pushes in the other direction. Although a narratively complex and politically progressive series such as Netflix's *Orange is the New Black* may seem to be targeting the niche audiences that would once have been identified in terms of high levels of income and education, streaming services are much cheaper than cable or subscription, and marked by high levels of use on mobile platforms such as cell phones or laptops. This development suggests a market differentiated around age, modest incomes and subcultural lifestyles more than by high levels of income and education.

Television's changing position in the 'field of devices' also gives rise to significant problems of measurement owing to the respects in which the relations between 'the symbolic (content) and material (devices)' of television are now 'diverging and converging in new permutations in "the digital age"' (Livingstone and Local, 2017: 71). Given the degree to which industry measurement tools are strongly geared to devices, difficulties have been created in measuring audience engagement with programme *content* that is usually the primary concern of, for example, PSB (Lowe and Martin, 2014). While Bourdieu's field theory did not afford any place for the agency of technological actors, the attention accorded to the agency of things in actor-network theory has prompted a refocusing of field theory in order to accommodate such concerns (Silva, 2017). Its implications for an inquiry focused on the distribution of the forms of cultural capital associated with television consumption practices centre on the need for an approach that will bring together the relations between the symbolic content and material organisation of viewing preferences, investigating their distribution across a range of socio-demographic indicators.

These were the concerns that informed our decisions about the questions relating to television in the ACF questionnaire. Mindful of the respects in which audience practices were in a state of transition, we sought to explore both tastes and practices related to the still-dominant FTA environment as well as to tap into the implications of the emerging 'field of devices'. With the first of these concerns in view, we explored both channel preferences in the broadcast environment and genre preferences ranging across sport, news and current affairs, reality TV, talk shows, dramas, comedy or sitcoms, lifestyle TV, documentaries, police/detective programmes and arts programmes. The self-reporting of genre preferences has often proved to be notoriously out of line with actual audience figures in relation to genres typically held in relatively low or high esteem, most notably and respectively reality TV and documentaries. To offset this problem, we also asked about familiarity with, and liking (or not liking) particular programmes, divided equally between Australian and overseas (mainly British and American) programmes, and Australian television personalities. The programmes were selected on the basis of being reasonably representative across genres (from reality to drama), broadcasters (PSB, commercial and subscription) and audience segments (including age and gender based). The television personalities were selected on the basis of their prominence across the various channels and association with programming of different types, cultural identities and degrees of prestige.

Australian programmes

Redfern Now is a drama about the lives of urban Indigenous Australians (ABC). *Offspring* and *House Husbands* are light/comedy prime-time drama series broadcast by, respectively, the commercial Ten and Nine Networks. *Offspring* is woman-centred (its main character is a female obstetrician), while *House Husbands*, focused on four 'stay-at-home fathers', is man-centred. *MasterChef Australia* (Ten) is the local franchise of the British competitive reality cooking show. *The Block* (Nine), focused on home renovation, is another competitive reality show, as is *Big Brother Australia* (Nine), the local version of the Dutch format. *Old School* (ABC), a 2014 drama series featuring Bryan Brown and Sam Neill, provided an Anglo-Celtic contrast, for survey purposes, to the Indigenous focus of *Redfern Now*. *Hamish and Andy's Gap Year* (Nine), a youth-oriented comedy travel series, ended as our survey was in the field. *Gardening Australia* (ABC) is a long-running lifestyle show aimed at an older and middle-class audience, while *Australian Story* (ABC) is an established prime-time current affairs show focusing on the life stories of Australians.

International programmes

Mad Men and *The Killing*, from the USA and Denmark respectively, were broadcast by the Special Broadcasting Service (SBS), an Australian PSB network with a multicultural remit. The American fantasy drama *Game of Thrones* was shown on pay-TV (Foxtel). *Midsomer Murders* (ABC) is a long-running, light British crime drama aimed at an older audience. Like *QI*, a British comedy panel show, and *Grand Designs*, a British lifestyle programme dealing with idiosyncratic home-building, it reveals the historical affinity between quirky forms of 'Englishness' and the ABC. The American spy drama *Homeland* (Ten), like *Mad Men*, exemplifies the trend towards imported cable rather than US broadcast network drama. *Big Bang Theory* (Nine) is a CBS 'sitcom', *Under the Dome* (Ten) a US science fiction drama, and *Top Gear* (ABC) a UK entertainment-oriented 'blokey' car show.

Personalities

Eddie McGuire, one of the most controversial figures on Australian commercial television (Heenan and Dunstan, 2013), presents quiz and sport shows on Nine and Foxtel. Julia Zemiro is a French-Australian TV presenter best known for the music game show *RocKwiz* (SBS) and her interview series *Julia Zemiro's Home Delivery* (ABC). Dave Hughes was a panel member of the youth-skewed news and current affairs show *The Project* on Ten, and a host of *Australia's Got Talent* on Seven. Comedian Carrie Bickmore co-hosts Ten's *The Project* and *So You Think You Can Dance Australia*, and won the 2015 Gold Logie Award for Most Popular Personality on Australian Television. Jennifer Byrne is a journalist who worked (1986–1993) on Nine's leading current affairs programme *Sixty Minutes*, and presented the monthly ABC arts programme *The Book Club*. Paul Vautin, a retired rugby league footballer, was the presenter of *The Footy Show* sports variety programme on Nine. Deborah Mailman is an Indigenous actor who has won several Logie Awards, including for her role in *Redfern Now*. The comedian Amanda Keller features in the Ten comic panel show *Talkin' 'Bout Your Generation* (2009–2012), and presented Ten's comedy-oriented domestic lifestyle programme *The Living Room* at the time of the survey. Ray Martin is a veteran news and current affairs journalist known mainly for his work on Nine's current affairs programmes *Sixty Minutes* and *A*

Current Affair, and for hosting *The Midday Show*. Scott Cam presents lifestyle programmes on commercial television, notably *Backyard Blitz* and *The Block* on Nine.

While the survey was designed so as to be intelligible to an FTA audience, it also engaged with the new and more complex media ecology, sketched above, in which the menu of choices available at any one time or in any one region is entangled with production and distribution strategies, marketing and scheduling in a more complex manner than ever before. In asking about the average number of hours of television watched per day, for example, we made it clear that it might be on a range of devices as well as on standard television sets. We also asked which technologies were most used (a television set at home, laptop or desktop computers, mobile devices or game consoles), and explored the relative importance of different ways of watching television (subscription TV, catch-up broadcasting service, PVRs, television apps for mobile devices, video downloads via sites like BitTorrent, video sites like YouTube and streaming services like Apple TV). When various forms of on-demand and catch-up TV and the expanding range of platforms and devices are taken into account, exposure to all of the programmes we asked about extended well beyond the reach of broadcast television. There are, however, limits to the extent to which these survey strategies were able to keep pace with the dynamics of a field in transition. For example, while surveying knowledge of media personalities from programmes or genres which may be outside the consumer's own patterns of viewing may make sense in a mass market, this is much less the case in a narrowcast environment, as our household interviews show.

Genres, platforms, channels

In turning to report our survey findings, we look first at the connections between a range of demographic characteristics (Figure 5.1) and channel preferences and viewing platforms (Figure 5.2). We then look at the social distribution of preferences for particular programmes and personalities (Figures 5.3 and 5.4). The Multiple Correspondence Analyses (MCAs) that we use for these purposes have the advantage of allowing us to see the relations between what Livingstone and Local (2017) call television's 'symbolic (content)' and its 'material (devices)' by bringing both of them together on the same visual plane.

The first point to note in relation to Figure 5.1 is that greater statistical weight and explanatory power attach to the dispersal of the individuals in the survey across the horizontal axis relative to the vertical axis: 5.29 per cent as opposed to 3.95 per cent. This distribution tells us that age, which dominates the horizontal axis running in an arc from older age groups at the bottom left through middle-age groups at the top centre to the younger cohorts at the bottom right, plays the most significant role in differentiating practices in the television field. Gender tastes are differentiated most strongly across the vertical axis – but also with a slight left-to-right trajectory – while occupational class, although running most strongly from higher class positions on the left towards lower ones on the right, is pulled up and down at different points in accordance with the gender and age composition of different classes.

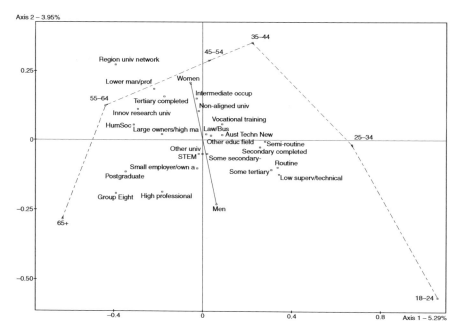

FIGURE 5.1 The social space of television tastes and practices.

Whereas high professionals, owners and senior managers of large enterprises, small employers and own account workers, and lower supervisory and technical workers are all predominantly male, and semi-routine workers marginally so, lower-level managers and professionals and intermediate workers are mainly female.[2]

Bearing these findings in mind, what do the relations between Figures 5.1 and 5.2 tell us? We note, first, in Figure 5.2 the relatively low degree of differentiation of the sample in terms of viewing hours, with those watching varying levels above one hour per day clustered closely towards the middle and top of the space. The location of those watching less than one hour a day towards the bottom of the space is attributable primarily to the youngest members of the sample, 29 per cent of whom reported this level of viewing, a figure dropping to just below or above 20 per cent in the middle-age ranges, and to 6 per cent for those over 65 years. However, other factors are in play here, most notably level of education: those with postgraduate qualifications are, at close to 20 per cent, twice as likely to watch less than one hour's television daily than those with only some secondary schooling, who are far more likely to watch over five hours of television daily. Class plays some role here too, with higher-level professionals and managers scoring the lowest rates of television viewing.

Channel preferences are spread across a diagonal running from the public broadcasters (ABC and SBS) in the lower left quadrant through Channel Seven towards the centre of the upper right quadrant, and Channels Nine and Ten towards, respectively, the top and extreme right of that quadrant.[3] The order of preferences

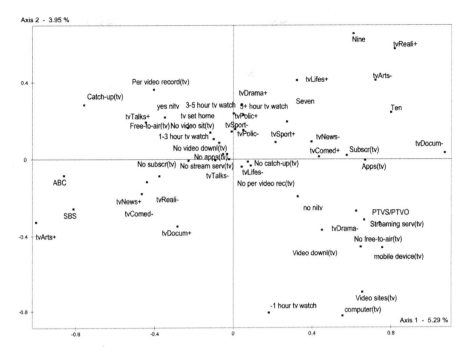

FIGURE 5.2 Television genres, platforms and channels.

for these channels runs from the ABC, the favourite channel for 27 per cent of the sample, through Channels Seven (17 per cent) and Nine (12 per cent), to SBS and Ten at around 6 per cent each. The social affiliations of those who prefer Australia's main public broadcasters are clear: they are strongest among older age groups and those with the highest (tertiary and postgraduate) levels of education, with a notable connection to the elite 'Group of Eight' universities. This lower left quadrant also displays the strongest liking for the most canonical of television genres – arts programmes, news and current affairs, and documentaries, with a predictably strong aversion to reality television and comedy programmes, and relative indifference to sport, police/detective, TV drama and lifestyle programmes.[4] The predominance of FTA viewing here is indicated by the absence of other viewing platforms. This platform preference is less marked for 55–64 year olds and for lower managers and professionals in the upper left quadrant, where a strong preference for FTA viewing on a TV set at home is accompanied by the use of other, longer-established technologies which largely supplement rather than displace broadcast television: catch-up and video-recording devices that enable time-shifted viewing. It is only towards the bottom right of the lower right quadrant, where the youngest members of the sample predominate, that newer devices and platforms (streaming services, mobile devices and so on) are strongly evident.

It is equally notable that, except for disliking television drama, the genres of broadcast television do not figure strongly in the viewing practices of those congregated in the bottom right quadrant. The reverse is true of the top right quadrant, where positive preferences for a range of television genres typically held in low esteem (reality TV, comedy and lifestyle programmes) predominate alongside commercial channel preferences and dislike of arts television and documentaries. The primary social coordinates here are lower class positions, the early-to-middle years of adulthood and, reflecting the articulation of gender divisions across the upper (women) and lower (men) axis, the predominantly female associations of many of the genres preferred here: most notably lifestyle and reality television but also TV drama. The notable exception is sports TV, with both positive and negative relations occurring in this quadrant; the latter at its extreme left edge and the former closer to the middle. Since, overall, women are much less enthusiastic about sports programmes than men, this is, at first sight, a little puzzling.[5] There is, however, a distinctive group of programmes in this part of the space that is strongly favoured by young to middle-aged men, while a cluster of women in this quadrant nominate sport among their preferred TV genres. Both findings help to account for this apparent anomaly. It is, therefore, to the richer texture of tastes that is produced when programme and personality preferences are brought into the picture that we now turn.

Programmes and personalities

We look first at the preferences for Australian television programmes (Figure 5.3). These were widely recognised, especially *MasterChef Australia*, *The Block* and *Big Brother Australia*, all 'heard of' by over 90 per cent of the sample. *Hamish and Andy's Gap Year*, *Australian Story* and *Gardening Australia* all scored in the 80s, with *Offspring* and *House Husbands* rating in the mid-70s. Only *Redfern Now*, at 48 per cent, had been heard of by less than half the sample. The hierarchy of popularity is differently organised, with *Australian Story* the most-liked programme at 60 per cent, followed at some distance by *Gardening Australia* and *Hamish and Andy's Gap Year*, both in the 40s, and then *The Block* at 34 per cent and *Offspring* at 22 per cent. *House Husbands* and *Redfern Now* both scored in the teens, while *Big Brother* was liked most by 10 per cent, with *Old School* bringing up the rear at 4 per cent. The hierarchy of recognition for the television personalities runs from Martin and McGuire, both in the 90s, through Hughes and Keller, in the 70s, and then Cam, Byrne and Bickmore in the 60s, down to Zemiro, Mailman and Vautin, all in the 40s. This hierarchy is replicated in the likes, except for McGuire, who is grouped with Byrne, Cam and Bickmore.

A preference for Australian-produced over imported programmes increases with age, rising constantly from 9 per cent for the 18–24 year olds to peak at 38 per cent for those over 65. However, it is clear from Figure 5.3 that this pattern does not translate into strong preferences for Australian programmes or personalities among the oldest and most highly educated members of the sample congregated in the bottom left quadrant, where high-level professionals and managers are also strongly represented. Only dislikes are registered here: for *The Block* and *Hamish and Andy's Gap Year*, and for all but two (Mailman and Vautin) of the personalities. A much

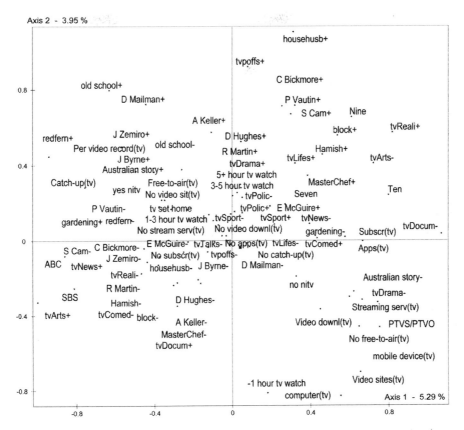

FIGURE 5.3 Australian TV programmes and personalities.

greater degree of engagement with Australian programmes and personalities is evident in the top left quadrant, where *Australian Story* and *Gardening Australia* are both strongly liked, and *Redfern Now* and *Old School* score both likes and dislikes. Liking *Redfern Now*, watching National Indigenous Television (NITV) and liking Deborah Mailman – the Indigenous items in our survey of the television field – are all located in this quadrant, registering the strongest connections with the 55–64 age cohort, lower professionals and managers, the tertiary educated, especially those with humanities and social science qualifications, and women. The TV personalities favoured here are mainly associated with public broadcasters (Zemiro and Byrne) and with the more 'serious' television genres (Byrne [news and current affairs] and Mailman [drama]).

The exception in this regard is Keller, who, however, is close to the border between the top left and top right quadrants. While there is a strong engagement with Australian content in the latter, this preference is registered in relation to comedy dramas/comedies (*House Husbands, Offspring, Hamish and Andy's Gap Year*) and reality shows (*The Block, MasterChef Australia*). The television personalities favoured here are associated primarily with sport (McGuire, Vautin), lifestyle programmes (Cam), comedy (Hughes) and entertainment shows (Bickmore). The connection with the genre preferences that we have already noted are clear, as are the affiliations of these programme, genre and personality preferences with lower levels of education, lower class positions and the late-adulthood to early middle-age cohorts. Engagement with Australian content does not figure at all in the most youthful and most masculine bottom right quadrant, focused mainly on routine, lower supervisory and technical workers, except with respect to disliking *Australian Story*.

If differences in taste regarding Australian content are registered most significantly in the upper part of the space, the same applies to the overseas programmes that we asked about (Figure 5.4). Only two such programmes register, both negatively, in the lower left quadrant: *Top Gear* and *The Big Bang Theory*, which sit alongside an aversion to comedy. If a negative distancing from more popular tastes predominates here, it is only in the top left quadrant that we find engagement with overseas 'quality' television series *Mad Men* and *The Killing*, each registering both positive and negative reactions. The UK shows *Grand Designs* and *QI* also register here, the former articulating socially aspirational values, while the comedy-quiz format of the latter also marks out a distance from more mainstream quiz shows in pivoting on a quest for intellectually oriented demythologisation. *Midsomer Murders* is liked here too, although more towards the south-west of the quadrant most marked by increasing age. The dislikes that are registered here for *Game of Thrones*

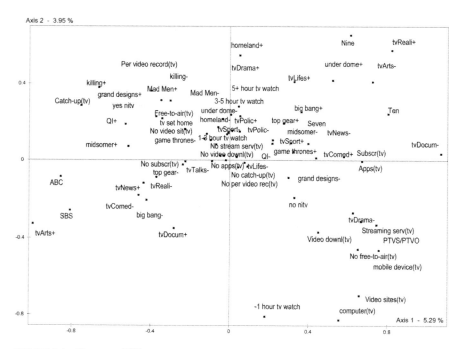

FIGURE 5.4 Overseas TV programmes.

and *Under the Dome* reflect a lower rate of liking for the former on the part of women, while the latter registers a lower degree of interest by those with tertiary and postgraduate qualifications. *Under the Dome*, in contrast, is liked towards the top and right of the upper right quadrant, close to the preferences for reality television and the commercial networks. *Homeland* is liked towards the top left of the quadrant in a strongly marked relation to the 45–54 age cohort. Positive engagement with *Big Bang Theory*, *Top Gear* and *Game of Thrones* is focused towards the lower centre of the quadrant, where sport is one of the most-liked television genres. While *Big Bang Theory* registers no significant gender differences in liking, both *Top Gear* and *Game of Thrones* are markedly popular among men in the late-adult and early middle-age cohorts who largely define this quadrant. A disengagement from broadcast television is evident in the bottom right quadrant, where only one overseas programme registers: a dislike of *Grand Designs*. Our follow-up interviews with survey respondents afford the best means of further amplifying the significance of this finding.

Giving up on FTA TV

As noted earlier, the introduction of the streaming services Netflix and Stan occurred between the administration of our survey and the conduct of the interviews over 2016–2017. The interviews came, therefore, at a point when Australian television was in the midst of its consolidation of the multiplatform environment described earlier in this chapter. Our interviews point to changes in how media content is chosen and consumed. Roughly half of the interviewees whose testimony focuses on television take their content from sources other than broadcast or pay-TV, and their choices are increasingly personalised. There are, of course, important strands of continuity: a significant minority of these interviewees only watch FTA TV, and are enthusiastic network consumers with strong commitments to particular programmes and personalities (Figure 5.5). The majority, however, reveal that there has been a major shift in the cultural status and centrality of FTA TV, particularly for the commercial channels.

Some interviewees say that they are 'over' commercial FTA TV. Naomi, 47 years old, 'has given up on FTA'; Brooke, 21 years old, 'doesn't really watch that much TV anymore. It doesn't really interest me that much.' Eighteen-year-old Harley observes that 'there really isn't much on free to air, to be honest'. Several of the younger interviewees have no access to 'regular TV' at all – that is, to FTA via the TV set in the living room: Rhiannon, also 18, watches Netflix on a laptop or her boyfriend's Xbox, and only sees FTA TV when she visits her parents. Brenton, 35 years old, who doesn't watch any FTA TV, apologises to his interviewer: 'I feel bad, like I'm the worst person you should be interviewing. So, "what do you think of TV?" I don't really watch it.' What might be described as a weariness with FTA TV is thrown into high relief by the competing options provided by streaming services: access to a wider range of new, and what is often regarded as higher quality or more relevant content. The lack of advertising and freedom from the constraints

FIGURE 5.5 The Delpechitra family on *Gogglebox Australia*.

Source: Foxtel (2017) *Gogglebox Australia: Gogglebox Australia: What TV Shows the Gogglebox Stars Really Love* (Season 6), www.foxtel.com.au/whats-on/foxtel-insider/lifestyle/gogglebox-australia/what-shows-gogglebox-stars-really-love.html.

Gogglebox Australia, adapted from the eponymous British programme, is produced by Shine Australia for Foxtel-owned pay-TV channel Lifestyle and FTA Network Ten, being first shown on Lifestyle and on Ten the following day. Ten households, chosen to reflect class, ethnicity, gender, sexuality, age and other forms of diversity, demonstrate how responses to the same televisual text may be shared or divergent, within and between primary social groups positioned in the television field. The show's rapid-fire editing accentuates the drama of receiving and negotiating television which, despite the audience fragmentation demonstrated in this chapter, emphasises the experience of collective viewing on the domestic couch (Brunt, 2017). The Delpechitra family (sons Ethan and Wendel, daughter Vestal, mother Tracey and father Patrick, pictured above) is of Sri Lankan origin. In an online promotional article, Wendel describes commonalities and variations in TV viewing preferences among the family, the latter suggesting relationships to gender and age: 'We love things that keep us guessing. We love surprises on TV. Mum and Vestal hate action/war movies for some reason. They really like slow unfolding shows. Ethan and I love watching action movies that keep going with the story. Dad loves all the current affairs and news shows.' (Tenplay, 2018).

of the schedule or 'appointment viewing' are also important. Those who subscribe to Netflix or Stan most value the capacity to customise their viewing; 'that's what I love about digital TV', says 42-year-old Heath, who, with access to Apple TV, Netflix and Stan, has a virtually inexhaustible range of choices available. The interviews reflect the scale of this transition to streaming services; 14 interviewees (out of a total of 42) report using Netflix, a figure roughly in line with Netflix's share of the national market.

The commercial FTA networks are the big losers here. When asked to nominate their favourite channel, most interviewees decline to do so on the basis that they do not really have a favourite. Diane (53 years old) agrees that her programming selections are 'channel neutral', and a number of others say that they just search around for 'what's on' rather than using a favourite channel as a default. Even those who nominate a favourite still have reservations. Anthony, a 20 year old from a Lebanese background, nominates both Seven and Nine as his preferred channels, before going on to say that 'sometimes I hate them' for the crassness of programming such as *A Current Affair*. He spends two to three hours a day on YouTube, and only one hour a week watching broadcast TV, but notably only when viewing with his parents.

The ABC, and to a lesser extent SBS, generate comparatively high levels of loyalty: ten interviewees nominate the ABC as their favourite channel, with six opting for SBS. Daniel, a 31 year old from a Chinese background, is not unusual in claiming only to watch the ABC and SBS, and a number of interviewees indicate that they make use of the ABC's iView portal for catch-up purposes and as a streaming service. Also, specific ABC programmes such as *QI*, *Grand Designs* and *Rake* are mentioned as examples of the kinds of programme interviewees prefer to watch. On the evidence of these interviews, the ABC seems to have been more successful than the commercial networks in positioning itself across two potentially competing platforms: broadcasting and streaming. This positive response may well have something to do with the fact that the commercial catch-up services carry a higher frequency of advertisements than their broadcasting services.

The second most notable insight to come from the interviews, which reinforces the findings from the survey data, concerns the importance of age as the most active differentiating factor in the contemporary patterns of television consumption. It is more common for the younger (under 29) interviewees to report that they seek their news and entertainment online through social media and online streaming services. In addition, several of the older subjects describe the difference that they themselves observe between their habits of media consumption and those of their children. Giovanni, a 54 year old of Italian background, has Apple TV and Netflix, but says he can't be bothered searching for content on either; his teenage son, in comparison, 'spends all his time Googling things'. Lauren, a 38 year old, only watches TV via her laptop but notes how her two children have 'gravitated towards YouTube': 'they're not watching any kind of commercial television at all, by choice, it's all ... they use iPads and computers'. The use of social media such as Facebook for news is also notable, although, as Rhiannon indicates, while she may use this platform to be alerted to news stories of interest, this practice often means she is redirected to mainstream network sites such as those of Seven and Nine.

The extent to which a generational pattern in consumption practices has become acknowledged or perhaps even normalised among the community is underlined by 21-year-old Brooke, who suggests that her viewing habits might make her a 'strange person for my age'. When asked what she means by this comment, she says that 'not bingeing on TV shows or streaming or watching ahead is probably something a bit atypical. Lots of people my age do that, or get Netflix so they can watch a whole series in a week.' Most of her friends, she says, don't have a TV at all, but rather 'just buy a Netflix subscription and watch on their laptop'. As a generational lifestyle choice, this may reflect the role played by social networks in establishing community or subcultural fashions and expectations for consumption practices, as well as for particular content, through registering 'likes' and other forms of recommendation. Holly, a 29 year old, reflects upon the sense of plenitude that accompanies her consumption of Netflix (in sharp contrast to other subjects' comments that 'there's nothing on' FTA): 'there's been lots of shows that, it's hard to keep up almost because everyone's always saying "You've got to watch this and you've got to watch that."' Social networks are driving consumption here rather than network identities or corporate promotional strategies.

Finally, there is one minor but instructive element emerging from the interviews which was not picked up in the survey responses: the use of streaming, satellite and online platforms by people of Non-English Speaking (NESB) backgrounds. Several of the interviewees report a strong engagement with programming in the language of their country of origin: Aisha, a 47-year-old woman with a strong connection to her identity as a Muslim, is a fan of Turkish soap opera, which she watches online. Thomas, a 49-year-old of Chinese background, reports that his wife watches Vietnamese programming on her phone, while Daniel says that his parents regularly go online to watch Chinese programmes. The online environment opens up this avenue of consumption, allowing these viewers the opportunity to engage with a realm of content that is very much the product of a global, rather than a local, television industry.

Conclusion

Olivier Donnat (2016: 402) has argued that the development of screen culture in France has been governed by two main phases since the introduction of television in the 1960s: first, the move, beginning in the 1980s, towards the ownership of multiple televisions, remote controls, video recording and the multiplication of available content beyond the broadcasting model; and, second, from the turn of the century, the dematerialisation of content, the widespread use of the Internet and the rapid adoption of new screens and mobile devices. One of the chief consequences of this second stage, he contends, is that it has 'destabilised the traditional processes of evaluation and consecration based on judgements by experts' (405). The use of algorithms and crowd sourcing has produced more pronounced horizontal processes of judgement and evaluation, thereby diminishing the power of traditional cultural hierarchies while transforming the dynamics of fame and celebrity.

Our findings point in the same direction, particularly in highlighting the significance of age. In contrast to other fields in our study, the two highest social classes – owners of large enterprises and higher-level managers, and high professionals – are not the most intensively involved in television's most clearly culturally hierarchised practices. The older and tertiary educated members of the strongly feminised class of lower-level managers and professionals, particularly those with humanities and social science degrees, provide the clearest signs of a cultural capital logic in play, connecting television forms with a relatively high degree of legitimacy both to educational achievement and occupational preferment. This pattern also holds for the intermediate class, located towards the centre of the social space and equally strongly feminised in its composition. By contrast, while genre hierarchies have some purchase among the younger cohorts, the forms of judgement and mechanisms of fame associated with quality television and television's personality system seem largely to pass them by. This is not to suggest that the multiplication of viewing platforms, time-shift viewing practices and the role of Internet providers in acting as portals – which, like TV channels, curate content in accordance with their revenue models and target audiences, but unlike channels, do so free from the constraints of scheduling (Lotz, 2017, 2018) – are forces which, in and of themselves, have led to a reconfiguration of television hierarchies and of their aged, classed and gendered social articulations. They have, however, undoubtedly been among the key forces driving the recent dynamics of Australian television as a field in transition.

Notes

1 This change occurred after our survey was conducted, but before the interviews were scheduled, and so its effects are registered only in our interview data.
2 The gender composition of the different occupational classes, expressed in female/male ratios, is as follows: owners/senior managers, 25:75; high professionals, 40:60; lower managers and professionals, 63:37; intermediate, 74:26; small employers/own account, 42:58; lower technical/supervisory, 30:70; semi-routine, 48:52; routine, 42:58.
3 The pattern for NITV is different, running from the upper left to the lower right. However, this was a question about watched/not watched rather than relative channel preferences.
4 In terms of general frequencies, documentaries and current affairs were the most liked genres, at around 36 per cent of the sample each, followed by drama and comedy, both in the mid-20s, and sport and police shows at around 20 per cent each. Reality TV, arts TV and talk shows were the least popular at, respectively, around 1 per cent, 3 per cent and 2 per cent.
5 It is also worth noting that, compared with the AEC study conducted 20 years earlier (Bennett et al., 1999), women are now roughly twice as likely to indicate a preference for sports programmes.

6
CONTESTING NATIONAL CULTURE
The sport field

David Rowe and Modesto Gayo

In 'Program for a sociology of sport', Bourdieu (1988: 155) argues that 'the space of sports is not a self-contained universe. It is inserted into a universe of practices and of consumptions that are themselves structured and constituted in a system.' The sport field is especially permeable for several reasons: the concept of sport is contested and takes many forms, ranging from professional physical contests to more casual forms of bodily movement. Despite its much-touted connection to healthy activity, sport's physical practice, as the *Australian Cultural Fields* (ACF) survey reveals, is heavily outweighed by its spectatorship. Deeply entwined with other domains of consumption, sport is also substantially 'colonised' by another field – the media, especially television (Wenner, 1998). As Bourdieu (2010) also clarifies in *Distinction*, sporting taste, participation and knowledge relate in a range of ways to social variables, and are highly sensitive to their national context, as he notes is the case with rugby union, which he played and often cites in his analysis of distinction (Rowe, 2018). In Australia, the sport field occupies a rather ambivalent position. While it is widely (and, indeed, officially) deemed to characterise 'Australianness', sport is correspondingly the frequent focus of critiques of the national culture as anti-intellectual, masculinist and so on (Rowe, 2016). For example, as feminist critic Erin Riley (2015) has declared, 'You could say, quite accurately, that society has a sexism problem, but sexism is more pronounced in sport.' For Bourdieu (1988: 155), sport is both a 'space of products' and a 'space of dispositions', a field operating as and at a point of intersection between popular and elite forms of cultural capital.

In exploring this space of sport, we first briefly describe and analyse key characteristics of the Australian sport field as indicated in the ACF survey, using a cultural sector interview to provide some field-framing context.[1] The household interviews provide detailed analytical data concerning how cultural preferences and practices are enacted at 'ground level', revealing the ways in which sporting dispositions relate to social variables and to patterns of taste and participation in intersecting cultural fields, notably the media.

The survey data reveals considerable variation in sporting engagement and taste in Australia that questions the nation's official designation as 'a nation of "good sports"' (Sport Australia, 2018a: 43). Sport is conventionally defined as more than just physical exercise. It developed out of folk play as an organised form of physical culture involving a competitive structure within a framework of governance and rules. This degree of organisation, though, is highly variable, ranging from elite professional to grassroots amateur levels. Determining precisely what is a sport, then, is not a simple task. On behalf of the Australian government, Sport Australia (known between 1985 and 2018 as the Australian Sports Commission) 'plays a central leadership role in the development and operation of the Australian sports system, administering and funding innovative sport programs and providing leadership, coordination and support for the sport sector' (Sport Australia, 2018a).[2] The agency advances definitional criteria while making the final determination of what constitutes sport in the country: 'A human activity capable of achieving a result requiring physical exertion and/or physical skill which, by its nature and organisation, is competitive and is generally accepted as being a sport' (Sport Australia, 2018b).

Notably, in a field in which different physical practices may claim to be recognised as sport and to achieve both social status and state funding as a result, Sport Australia arbitrates officially as the 'the final authority for determining if an activity meets the definition of a sport'. James Ferguson, a former Executive Director of the Australian Sports Commission, elaborated on this definitional logic in interview:

> I think sport is a more organised form. If you think of swimming almost everyone in Australia can swim. Lots of people go to the beach. So when they fill in surveys about which sports did you participate in in the last six months, if they've been to the beach they'll say 'yes, I participated in swimming'. That's not actually participating in sport. I mean it's very hard to define precisely what sport is but the general view is that sport involves some sort of a contest … Even if it's a contest against yourself. There's been a big development in informal sport over the last ten or twenty years and those are people who want to participate in a sporting activity rather than just a recreational activity, but who don't want to be in a formal system of competition.
>
> So I think sport probably – it's like a spectrum. It goes from a highly formal level of competition down to a very informal level, but there is still an element of competition in it. If you're running just to get fit you're not involved in a competition. Your aim is simply to get fit. It's not to win anything. I think that's the essential difference.

It is apparent from such deliberations that sport is a 'field of struggles' (Bourdieu and Wacquant, 1992: 101) in which there is contestation over what counts as sport; the placement of individual sports in its institutional hierarchy; and its positioning within characterisations of nation in relation to other cultural forms. Different forms of capital – economic (both public and commercial), social and cultural – are variously at stake in the sport field. For example, in the key Australian sport of cricket, Twenty20, the brief, prime-time, television-friendly form of the game involving newly invented team franchises, competes with the longer established, less commercially attractive but more socially esteemed and culturally prestigious international test matches played over five days. These different forms of cricket are to some degree in competition with each other, as well as with other sports that constitute the Australian sport field, not least in seeking to attract attention and resources from the pivotal media field. The focus of this field is on the performative athletic body in regulated competition with others. Simultaneously, on the fringe of what can be regarded as the sport field, the 'toned', gymnasium-fashioned body may also acquire cultural capital without a strong connection to officially designated sport, even to the Olympic sport of weightlifting or to the proto-sport of bodybuilding. Sport as institutionalised, rationalised, competitive corporeal practice, then, does not command the entire field of physical culture, which is a shifting ensemble of practices of production and consumption. The field is fashioned out of the formal structures that govern it, the public and private organisations that symbolically and materially support it, and the social actors who 'activate' it. In the discussion and data below it is demonstrated that the sport field is shaped by endogenous and exogenous forces and processes that condition its internal hierarchy and capacity to exert influence over the wider domain of physical culture.

Sport in the ACF survey

Far from the common assumption including, as noted, in official self-description (Sport Australia, 2018a) of Australian exceptionalism in the practice and love of sport, 61 per cent of respondents had not played any organised sport in the last year and only 55 per cent had watched sport live at a venue. But sport as culture extends well beyond personal participation in or live attendance at competitive physical practice, with 85 per cent of respondents watching sport live through the media (Gayo and Rowe, 2018). While approximately 80 per cent of respondents had watched either no sport live at a venue or a maximum of two different sports, when live sport viewing through the media is taken into account a similarly large percentage has watched up to six different sports. Therefore, the media drastically increase the boundaries of the field, allowing many people to figure in it as audiences able to watch a wide range of sports across an expansive 'media sports cultural complex' (Rowe, 2004).

In understanding that sport involvement has different layers, it is important to be clear about the very different ways in which people take part in it. In the survey, respondents were asked about practices, tastes and knowledge regarding sports and sportspeople. Before discussing the findings, some brief contextual information about the nominated sports and sports personalities (Australian and international) is required. Ten sports were selected on a range of criteria, including popularity, size, media presence, type (individual or team), participation rates, historical national prominence, and relationship to class and gender. Australian Rules football is played almost exclusively in Australia, and is the largest of its four football codes. Strongest in Victoria, like the other football codes it is developing its women's league structure. Association football (often called soccer in Australia) is the most popular by participation but the least commercially developed football code. Historically stigmatised in Australia as foreign and 'unmanly' (Hallinan and Hughson, 2010), its A-League has little free-to-air television presence, but its national male and female teams, the Socceroos and Matildas, have a high profile. Netball is the most prominent women's sport in Australia, with a large participant base but less TV rights revenue and coverage than the main male-dominated sports. Rugby union and rugby league split in 1907 in Australia along amateur versus professional lines. The latter is popular mainly in New South Wales and Queensland. Rugby union has greater international reach, and is more closely connected to the social elite (as in Bourdieu's France – Rowe, 2018), while rugby league is frequently described as the 'working man's game' (Collins, 2006). Cricket is widely regarded as Australia's truly national sport. Basketball is a popular participation sport, but its professional competition has been financially unstable and overshadowed by the USA's dominant National Basketball Association (NBA). Tennis and golf are prominent individual sports, both skewed upwards in class terms. Swimming is a key Australian Olympic sport, although participation as reported in the survey is less likely to be in organised, competitive sport than swimming for exercise, fitness and recreation.

Ten Australian sportspeople were selected on grounds including fame, esteem, controversy, gender, Indigeneity and ethnicity. More men than women were named, reflecting – though obviously not endorsing – the historically conditioned gender order in Australian sport (Pavlidis and Fullagar, 2014). Don Bradman (1908–2001) is the most revered sporting figure in Australia, a cricketer with the world's best batting record. Liz Ellis is a former Australian netball captain (retired 2008) and TV commentator. Israel Folau, a Tongan-Australian, has played professional Australian Rules football and successfully represented Australia in rugby league and rugby union. Cathy Freeman is a retired Indigenous runner who won the women's 400 metres and lit the cauldron at the Opening Ceremony of the Sydney 2000 Olympics. Lauren Jackson retired from basketball in 2016 after a highly successful career, especially in the USA. Adam Goodes is an Indigenous Australian Rules footballer who retired in 2015 after a long, successful career marred in its latter stages by racially inspired booing (Sygall, 2015). Harry Kewell is a retired soccer player (now manager) who played for a lengthy period in the English Premier League and for the Socceroos. Rod Laver was a leading tennis player, instrumental in tennis going professional in the late 1960s. Greg Norman was one of the best golfers in the world in the late twentieth century and is now in the golf course design business. Ian Thorpe was a highly successful swimmer at the 2000 and 2004 Olympics who came out as a gay man in a television interview in 2014.

In widening the frame of sport engagement, ten international sportspeople were chosen according to criteria relating to sporting image and success, although many would be familiar to people who engage little with sport, having acquired wider celebrity status. As with Australian sportspeople, but even more so given the global 'brand' dominance of sportsmen (Whannel, 2001), there was a preponderance of men on the list. David Beckham is an English soccer player (retired 2013) who played for some of the world's biggest clubs and became a 'celebrity metrosexual' after marrying Victoria Adams of the Spice Girls pop band. Usain Bolt is a (now-retired) Jamaican sprinter who holds both 100- and 200-metre world records, winning these events at three consecutive Olympics. Michael Jordan, the retired African-American basketballer, is globally famous through his pioneering marketing image via Nike corporation. The Argentinean Diego Maradona is renowned for his superlative soccer career, but also for various scandals, including the infamous 'Hand of God' cheating incident at the 1986 World Cup. Rafael Nadal is a leading Spanish tennis player and multiple Grand Slam winner. Michael Phelps is a highly successful US swimmer who has also been associated with some scandal (recreational drug taking). Sachin Tendulkar (retired 2013) is India's most revered cricketer. Serena Williams is an African-American tennis player who has long dominated the women's game, and been embroiled in controversies over sexual racism and on-court conduct. Tiger Woods is an African-American golfer who remains the sport's best-known personality but whose reputation, performance and physical health declined after the 2009 scandal over his serial marital infidelity. Yao Ming is a retired (2011) Chinese basketballer who played in the NBA and was instrumental in enhancing interest in the game in China, symbolising that country's embrace of global sport.

Engagement and taste in the Australian sport field

Figures 6.1 and 6.2 display the ways in which the points in the space are arranged in a manner that enables patterned responses to be discerned according to their proximity and distance.[3] For example, in the upper left quadrant of Figure 6.1, the closeness of liking rugby union player Israel Folau to engagement with that sport suggests an affinity among responses (plus signs indicate engagement as a participant, spectator or club member, or liking of a named sportsperson, and minus signs indicate the reverse); that is, those who like Folau have a higher probability of being participants in rugby union activities than those with relationships to sports such as tennis or netball.

While there are clear outlying points in the space (for example, in the bottom left quadrant, those who play sport annually or like Yao Ming) and major differences in engagement and taste (such as between engagement in golf in the top left quadrant and not watching sport on television in the bottom right), distinctions are generally less pronounced across multiple practices and tastes in the Australian sport field than in some of the other fields addressed in this book, such as art and literature. There is considerable clustering around the middle of the figure, with greater

Contesting national culture **105**

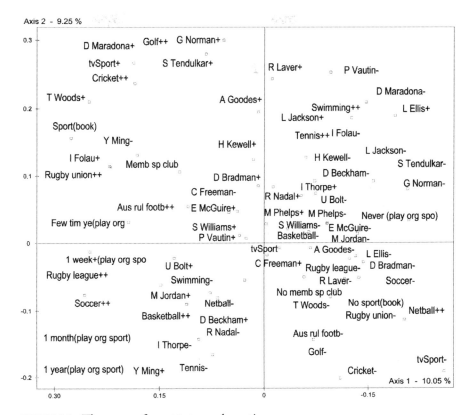

FIGURE 6.1 The space of sport tastes and practices.

Abbreviations and signs in this figure: 'play org': play organised sport; 'Aus rul footb': Australian Rules football; 'no memb sp club': no membership in sport club; 'few tim ye': a few times a year. Regarding frequency, '1 month' indicates at least once a month, as per '1 year' and so on. In relation to symbols and sportsmen/women, '+' indicates liking and '−' neither like nor dislike. In the case of sports, symbols indicate a gradient of involvement in a range of roles (notably playing and volunteering), along with watching sport live at a venue and live through the media. This calculation produces a scale from 0 to 3 for each sport separately: '−' means 0 or non-participation, '+' is 1, meaning that our respondents took part in one out of the three modalities offered, and '++' indicates two or three, the maximum level of participation.

engagement with sport generally near the top of the lower left quadrant. These findings, though, do not incorporate the social relationships that may underpin these practices and tastes. Figure 6.2 provides such information, revealing considerable dispersion according to occupational class, gender and age. For example, men and women are separated principally by the horizontal axis, and to a lesser degree by the vertical one, while there is a considerable distance on the vertical axis between large business owners/higher managers and workers in semi-routine and routine occupations. Notably, the two axes are more or less equally significant in degree of variation (the vertical being 9.25 per cent and the horizontal 10.05 per

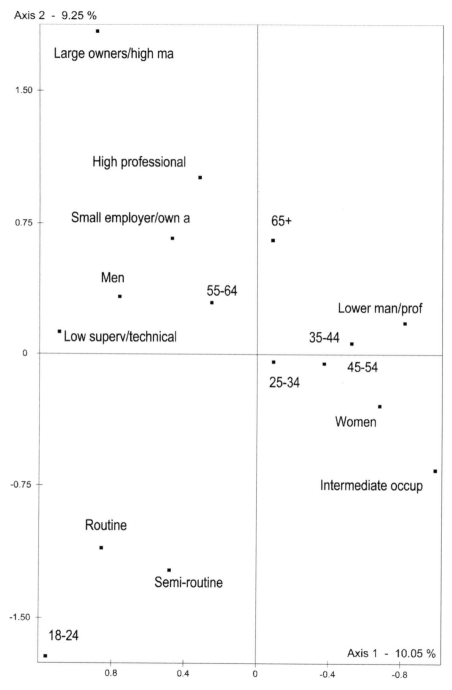

FIGURE 6.2 The social space of sport tastes and practices.

cent), indicating that no single socio-demographic variable is dominant. Nonetheless, there are some striking patterns, including that, apart from 18–24 year olds, all the other age categories are grouped nearer the middle of the figure. The tendency for disliking to be on the right side of the vertical axis and liking to the left is in accord with the evident gendered variation in sport engagement. Gender and class/occupation also intersect in clear ways, with a strong bias towards supervisory/technical work and small employers/owners among males, and towards intermediate and lower managerial/professional work among females. This pattern reflects the gender composition of the relevant class positions (see Chapter 8, Table 8.1).

In returning to Figure 6.1, sport engagement is strongly identified where liking sportspeople was highly evident, with a clear division between those who physically participate in sport and those who only watch it. On the one hand, what we can consider to be the most exclusive sports occupy a prominent or distinctive position; that is, liking golf and cricket is characteristic of the connection between sport-related practices and demographic variables (male, upper class) at the top of the upper left quadrant. Rugby union, followed by Australian Rules football, is especially liked in the lower part of the upper left quadrant where there is a high level of sport club membership. Regular, though not necessarily intense, participation in sport is common in this lower part of the quadrant, while liking many sportsmen, especially Maradona, Tendulkar, Norman and Woods, is notably higher in the upper left quadrant. On the other hand, there is a space in the bottom left quadrant of marked engagement with soccer, rugby league and basketball. Here, participation levels are high (some playing sport every week), and the sportspeople liked include Yao, Jordan and Bolt. In both left quadrants there are also some indicators of dislike of certain sports and/or sportspeople. On the right side of the vertical axis there is a lower level of engagement with sport, as is to be expected given that it contains a higher concentration of women. Relatedly, in the lower right quadrant, the only sportsperson liked is Cathy Freeman and the only sport with which there is significant engagement is the female-dominated sport of netball. In the upper right quadrant there is a wider spread of likes and dislikes, with significant engagement with tennis and swimming, although this is probably more casual and exercise based than competitive. Male-dominated competitive team sports, which are pivotal to the commercial health of the sport and media fields, are not received sympathetically in this (right of the vertical axis) part of the Multiple Correspondence Analysis (MCA) space. This general lack of sport engagement is broadly in accord with a disposition to dislike many sportspeople and/or individual sports.[4]

The three ways of conceiving participation in the sport field we surveyed – volunteering as well as playing and watching – are not only differentiated by what people do, like or know, but also by the social factors associated with the production of this 'triangular' distinction. Those tending to like golf and cricket are older, quite often in their 50s or above, in high managerial or professional occupations and owners of both large and small businesses, and are mostly men. Economic capital, then, is especially important in this field. In accordance with this rationale

(Bourdieu and Wacquant, 1992; Bourdieu 2010), the assemblage of cultural practices, here related to sport, alongside socio-economic and socio-demographic factors, are responsible for the production of distinction. Thus, despite the myth of a national egalitarian ethos as it relates to sport, including claims of common cultural citizenship (Rowe, 2016) and universal access to sports infrastructure, Australian society and cultural taste are shown to be fractured (although imperfectly) along class and other socio-demographic lines. As an illustration, youth and routine/working-class occupations combined go hand-in-hand with a propensity to like soccer, basketball and rugby league in the lower left, which are factors that are good predictors of frequent sport practice (and probably in those same sports). By contrast, a lack of engagement with sport is quite common among middle-aged women in intermediate occupations. Therefore, sport participation helps to define class differences, while at the same time it contributes to the gendered division which, given the strategic celebration of sport as a symbol of quintessential Australianness, allocates to men the prime role of the collective hero in the national narrative. This gendered mythos positions women in a range of subordinate ways, including as hidden, marginalised, 'bit players' or as occasional sporting heroines (especially with regard to Australia's record in the Olympics, where women have historically outperformed men) who are not conventionally viewed as embodying sport as an institution, or routinely constructed as protagonists within its tales of transcendent national identity (Commonwealth of Australia, 2006).

The media are integral to this structurally induced production of distinction in sport and society, selecting from the smorgasbord of sports practice the 'dishes' to be foregrounded and celebrated. These are not random, arbitrary or open choices, being both historically conditioned in socio-cultural terms and reinforced by a persistent imbalance in the quantity and quality of men's and women's sport coverage and remuneration (Australian Sports Commission, 2014). It should, though, be acknowledged that there has been an advance of women's sports leagues in Australia, especially in the four football codes, basketball and netball – albeit from a low base – which has signalled a shift in this media sport landscape.

Emphasising both the strong connection between the sport and media fields, and the association of sport practices and social factors, helps to construct a more comprehensive account of the dynamics of the Australian sport field. In order to capture a fuller range of these relations, several scales were created. First, we created an indicator of sport 'liking' composed as an additive scale of the positive answers to the following question-related variables: liking sport television programmes and sport books, being a member of a sports club and playing sport at least a few times a year. A scale of 'disliking' was also created that was almost the opposite: not liking sports programmes or reading about sport, not ever playing it and not following sport through any media device. As might be anticipated, these scales have a very strong negative correlation with each other of –0.79 (see Table 6.1).[5] Liking and disliking sport was also measured with regard to sportswomen and men. In addition, engagement in the sport field was measured via an indicator of attendance at a sport venue and, finally, there are two indicators associated with the media: the number of sports watched through the media and of media devices used to follow sport.

When the relations between all these variables are appraised, important patterns emerge. Those respondents interested in or liking sport in general have considerable exposure to sport through the media (via different technologies), watch it live at sport venues and display a high propensity to like both sportsmen and women. All these variables positively correlate with each other (see Column 1, Table 6.1). In contrast, the disposition to dislike sport has a negative correlation with most of these variables (Column 2). Surprisingly, perhaps, disliking sport does not have any notable relationship with disliking sportswomen and sportsmen, suggesting that an aversion to sport in general does not automatically transfer to actual sportspeople. Liking sport and taking part in the sport field usually accompany an ethical propensity to acknowledge, prima facie, the merit of competitors. Following this logic, one can be in or outside the sport field, but once inside it there is a general ethos of respect which is likely to be undermined only by serious infractions of sport rules, such as match-fixing or performance-enhancing drug taking, or by criminal off-field conduct such as spousal abuse. The extraordinary response to illicit ball-tampering in the Australian men's cricket team during a 2018 test series in South Africa – including blanket media coverage, claims of a national loss of 'moral compass' and even statements of lament by the Prime Minister (Terry, 2018) – starkly reminds us of the power of the discursive linkage of sport ethics and national identity in Australia.

Therefore, liking sport as a matter of taste does not entail, in any symmetrical or inverse relation, dislike of it as a matter of ethical judgement. Disliking sport means being 'out of the game' as invoked in Bourdieu's (2000: 11) conception of the *illusio*: 'a fundamental belief in the interest of the game and the value of the stakes which is inherent in that membership'. Here, scarcity of knowledge is likely to mean a lack of capacity to assess the 'likeability' of individual athletes. Thus, even though disliking sport overlaps in the social space with an aversion to many sportspeople (Figure 6.1), we should be cautious about regarding them as equivalent. Individuals' propensities (Table 6.1) for disliking sport are consistent with disengagement from it, but are not correlated with a general inclination to dislike sportspeople. Therefore, dislike of and disengagement from sport might be structurally similar in terms of capitals and socio-demographics but they are culturally different, signalling the boundary marking, respectively, of the positions of the 'insider' and the 'outsider'. A 'distaste' for sport and for sportspeople, then, often entails ignoring them altogether. In addition, aversion to sport is concentrated among women in intermediate occupations (to the right side of Figure 6.1). It is also important, though, to understand that disliking sport and sportspeople is evident in a different part of the social space – that is, not all dislikes are for the same reason. For example, there is little trace of recrimination among those in higher class positions regarding the most controversial sportspeople, although there were a few among the named sport personalities who had achieved much notoriety for sport-related misconduct (the principal examples are Maradona and, to a lesser degree, Williams, who are

TABLE 6.1 Pearson's correlations of sport practices and taste scales

	Liking sport	Disliking sport	Exposure through the media	Involvement: watching live at a sport venue	Involvement: watching live through the media	Liking sportsmen and women	Disliking sportsmen and women
Liking sport	1						
Disliking sport	−0.79	1					
Exposure through the media	0.50	−0.60	1				
Involvement: watching live at a sport venue	0.40	−0.39	0.42	1			
Involvement: watching live through the media	0.46	−0.52	0.53	0.49	1		
Liking sportsmen and women	0.36	−0.37	0.38	0.32	0.53	1	
Disliking sportsmen and women	0.002	0.007	0.004	−0.007	−0.01	−0.10	1

For an interpretive elaboration of Pearson's coefficients of correlation, see Note 5. Coefficients that are statistically significant below 0.05 or 5% are in bold.

both international sportspeople). Thus, perhaps winning is prized above all else among the upper-class sport lovers, who are little interested in unethical or questionable conduct on or off the playing field (the main example of the latter among the named personalities being Woods and Phelps). A similar pattern is evident among the younger respondents in routine occupations and lower class social positions. How the game is played, rather than who wins it, then, might be of greater value for those in middle- or intermediate-class locations – what might be called the upholders of a traditional and, in some respects, 'new' petit-bourgeois morality as described by Bourdieu (2010: 339).

For those little interested in the sport 'game' but who become acquainted with sportspeople as part of wider celebrity culture, or who are sensitised to sport's positioning within the field of power, a critical perspective towards sportspeople is more common. It is when those personalities are part of a 'media game' beyond sport (see, for example, the study of Beckham by Cashmore, 2004), that they become more generally controversial, and the 'dislike count' increases. Therefore, some sport-related controversies involving personalities register frequently among those who know at least something about them, and who are in a 'grey area' of partial knowledge and general indifference. They most frequently make judgements beyond strict performance criteria regarding a sports career, and are positioned to develop a disposition that is largely oblivious to sporting success.

The figures, table, discussion and analysis above demonstrate the complexities of the sport field, both internally and in its relationship with the media field. It is, therefore, appropriate to turn to the more detailed ways in which the sport field is constructed, including in terms of governance and classification, and to the techniques of field negotiation exhibited in the household interviews.

Sport field conversations and negotiations

Sport has a prominent place in Australian culture at a range of levels, although its status is widely contested. All who live in the country must negotiate the sport field according to their position within it as it relates to the wider social formation. For example, Aisha, a 47-year-old Lebanese-born Muslim with postgraduate qualifications who does counselling work, never plays organised sport and is not a member of a sports club. She occasionally goes to a venue to watch soccer and views it on television, along with several other sports, although in her survey response she lists sport as one of her least-liked types of television. Aisha has heard of few of the named sportspeople – significantly, she has never heard of Bradman – but likes most of those of whom she has heard. Her engagement with sport is influenced by a number of different factors, including place of birth, gender, religion and family relationships. Although stating 'I'm not interested in sport', Aisha does watch some on television:

> Only when there is a game that I like. I love soccer. I am into soccer. I guess because in my culture sports wasn't a big thing like in Australia. So I grew up

with – and girls don't play sports. So I grew up with this attitude. But my husband likes sport, my kids grew up and sadly, because of our culture I think, we actually conveyed [that to] our kids, so they're not very good at sport. But they follow a few events and matches, so sometimes [it] depends on who is playing, what the game is.

Aisha likes 'any kind of soccer', but the sole team that she actively follows is the national one in expressing patriotism in the sporting sphere: 'Only if Australia is playing I would encourage Australia. That's it.' She likes soccer:

I guess because it was part of my upbringing. In Lebanon soccer, and I think in all Europe, soccer is big and whenever there is a national competition everyone is into it. But it's a boy's thing mainly. Now in Lebanon even the girls are more involved, but in my time no, it's not our thing ... So yeah, so I grew up with soccer being important.

She registers here that sport is male dominated, both in Lebanon and Australia, but that this is changing and, notably, Aisha is drawn to support Australia in international sport contests.

Support for national representative teams is common, even among those who do not much like sport. Kathleen, a 56-year-old Anglo-Australian quality assurance officer who identifies as working class, has a similar orientation to sport to Aisha, although with stronger recognition and liking of the named sportspeople. Kathleen says that 'if I can help it, I don't watch the sports', but immediately commented, 'at the moment, I'm watching the Olympics. It's frustrating me because we're not winning enough gold ... I want gold. I don't like losing. I'm very competitive ... I don't like losing.' She attempts to resolve this contradiction of watching/not liking sport by observing that 'The Olympics is different. It only happens every four years and we have to win. Probably, the main reason I don't watch sport is I'll get cranky and frustrated and I yell.' Like Aisha, sport is a vehicle for patriotism for Kathleen: 'I like to get up on that dais. I love when our national anthem comes up.'

Sport, then, even for someone who doesn't particularly like it (although, like Aisha, Kathleen's initially expressed lack of interest in sport was not entirely borne out at interview), is a ready vehicle for nationalistic sentiment, especially in mediated form (Hobsbawm, 1990; Ward, 2010). It is a key part of the symbolic process of 'nationing' (Rowe et al., 2018). But this articulation of sport and national pride, especially around mediated sport mega-events and associated with more general positive sentiment, is problematised by unethical practices associated with it on and off the field of play. For example, Gabriel, a 19-year-old Australian-born upper-middle-class university student, plays sport a few times a year (rugby, swimming and fencing – his studies prevent him from playing more). While he does not go to live sports venues (like the one presented in Figure 6.3), , he watches the rugby codes and Australian Rules football on television, listens to sports radio and reads

Contesting national culture **113**

FIGURE 6.3 Performing sport fandom at a live venue.
Source: Western Sydney Wanderers fans (AAP Image/Dean Lewins).

There are many forms of participation in the sport field, with crowd attendance at a live venue constituting a spectacular display of sport culture. The spectators shown above support the Western Sydney Wanderers soccer club. They are fans of a code of football that has been historically stigmatised because of its association with the post-Second World War wave of southern European migrants, who encountered a considerable degree of Anglo ethnocentricity in Australia. This club, formed in 2012 and playing in the national A-League competition, is based in the predominantly working-class, culturally and linguistically diverse Greater Western Sydney region. Its fans, drawn from many diasporic communities, have adopted a range of chants, moves and gestures derived from masculinist football fan club cultures across the world, especially from Europe and South America. The carnivalesque behaviour of Wanderers fans has been criticised as unruly, especially in the tabloid media and by local police authorities (Knijnik, 2018). This is an example of a struggle for position and power within the Australian sport field that is deeply imbricated with relations of social class, gender, cultural identity and transnationalism.

the sports press. His sport media consumption is influenced by his family (Gabriel is of Italian and Scottish backgrounds although identifying more with the former, his mother's), with whom he lives, especially by his older brother. Gabriel has heard of and likes most of the named sportspeople, but is 'upset' by sportspeople who are unsatisfactory 'role models'. When asked if there are any sports stars that he doesn't like, he responds by focusing on ethics and the impact of sportspeople's behaviour on younger people, including his two younger siblings:

> None for their sporting ability ... I guess the ones that come into the public eye have – I know that they're meant to be role models for kids who do love sports and then you get the ones who are caught doing something fairly

atrocious. There's the usual steroid scandal but that's kind of not – it's almost – it's pretty pervasive in modern sports, so it's disappointing but almost expected. But then you have the ones who are convicted of domestic violence or statutory rape or mass adultery, or just general violence or assault. These people are meant to be role models, especially for young more impressionable people like my [younger] brother and generally that gets me fairly upset.

Anthony, an Australian-born 20-year-old motor mechanic of Lebanese background with some tertiary education, plays sport every week. His main sporting interest as player and spectator is soccer, which he follows on television. Anthony has heard of few of the named Australian sportspeople (not even Bradman) and only slightly more of the named international sportspeople. He dislikes South American and southern European soccer players like Maradona, Lionel Messi and Cristiano Ronaldo because they are 'show offs' compared to 'the German players' that he favours.

Bianca, an 18-year-old undergraduate student of Aboriginal and other heritages, has been a competitive dancer – there is brief discussion of whether this can be considered 'a sport' at the interview – but is currently too busy to do anything other than study and pursue her (non-sporting) social life. Although she had not heard of several named sportspeople, she notably says 'of course' when Freeman and Goodes were mentioned – a clear identification with Indigenous actors within the Australian sport field. Bianca also sees some sportspeople, such as Indigenous rugby league players Johnathan Thurston and Dane Gagai (who is of Torres Strait Islander and Maori descent), as good role models, in contrast with Jarryd Hayne: 'He's an NRL [National Rugby League] player and he's half Fijian, he moves from like team to team ... Just overall, he doesn't seem like a nice bloke. I don't think he's a good role model in general.' This concern for Bianca extends to celebrity sportspeople, such as Beckham and Bolt, who commercially exploit themselves as 'brands':

> I feel like definitely with sport stars and celebrities that they have their professional life and career, but I also feel like they have a brand and how they facilitate their image to the public. Because I've definitely heard all the time that you yourself are a brand, the way you interact with people and present yourself to people is either going to help the brand or not so much? ... How they're seen as a public figure, that kind of stuff.

This conflict for Bianca between being a 'public figure' and a 'brand' exposes the tension between the heroic, self-sacrificing mythology of sport and its enmeshment with the 'sportainment' industry. Her involvement in competitive dancing also invokes the earlier discussion of what constitutes sport in the Australian sport field, with its complex, shifting arrangement of distinction and associated cultural capital. Angela, a 50-year-old China-born retired office worker with vocational-level education, similarly demonstrates how sport privileges organised, competitive physical culture. She prefers to participate rather than spectate: 'Well, I play badminton ... Yeah and I play table tennis socially.' Angela also swims, but not competitively, and she doesn't 'do organised sport'. She also engages in 'Chinese line dance. They call [it] square dance. It's exercise', which occurs with her community 'once a week in the park, just for fun and that, and it's a social group', emphasising that this is 'not sport, only [a] social club', thereby demonstrating that physical culture is not reducible to sporting practice. Angela's position in the 'space of sports' is not one that is simply 'inserted into a universe of practices and of consumptions that are themselves structured and constituted in a system', as Bourdieu was quoted in the introduction to this chapter. She moves in and out of the Australian sport field in engaging in proto-sporting, exercise-focused and community-oriented practices. Angela's orientation to sport, like that of the other household interview respondents, is one that recognises its symbolic power as a 'great marker of culture' in Australia (Rowe, 2016) while asserting a socially situated disposition towards the body and movement.

Conclusion

This chapter has demonstrated that the Australian sport field is constituted as a 'field of struggles', reflecting, reproducing and contesting the social inequalities and divisions over which a range of claim-makers vie for position. Sport has insinuated itself into everyday popular language, meaning that political agents, state bureaucracies, commercial corporations and the media routinely deploy sport metaphors – not least those relating to the concept of nation – in constructing popularly communicable images of the world. But such discursive practices are only possible because of their deep origins as folk physical culture revised and developed in modernity (first in Britain, Australia's former colonial power) as popular culture that in various ways was commodified and mediatised, and enlisted by the apparatus of the state to signify national identity (Hargreaves, 1986). The sport field's and its sub-fields' scale and character create the conditions for interplay across a range of domains, needing and generating large groups of followers and constructing publics interpellated through the vernacular language of sport.

As has been widely canvassed, rule-governed, competitive physical practice, and the organised gaze upon it, fashion sports hierarchies and establish criteria of distinction at the apex of a now highly commercialised sport system. But beneath and beyond it, availing itself of the sport field's porosity, is the constellation of cultural practices characterised not only by internal struggles for power within and between particular sports, but by alternative, non-institutional modes of corporeal sociality that are resistant to sport's propensity to regulate and keep score (Guttmann, 2004). Thus, what constitutes sport is constantly contested by those who do not accept its foundational attachment to competitiveness or rule-based and performative calculation. Similarly, sport's mythological and ideological uses are confronted by differences of social class, gender, level and type of education, and age. For this reason, the Australian sport field can be said to offer a glimpse of nation, but only insofar as it reveals the tensions and fractures that are inevitable constituents of its sociocultural architecture.

Notes

1 The full project data set included interviews with prominent field agents who have deep knowledge of its coordinates and relations.
2 This change followed the adoption of the *Sport 2030* national plan in 2018.
3 As the variables relating to taste and sport involvement did not easily interrelate, we identified the structuring variables for the space of tastes (sportsmen/women) and sport involvement, which were taken separately for analytical purposes. We then used those socio-economic and socio-demographic variables as active in the production of the social space presented here. This approach allows us to see practices and preferences together.
4 For more details, see Gayo and Rowe (2018).
5 In Table 6.1, we offer as measures of association Pearson's correlation coefficients. This indicator varies from −1 to 1. The figure '0' means that there is no relationship between the variables, '−1' is a perfect negative relationship (the higher one variable, the lower another variable) and '1' indicates a kind of identification or perfect positive covariation. The values in between those extreme points, −1 and 1, have to be seen as mid-points which follow the same rules of interpretation.

PART II
Class

Introduction

In discussing the dynamics of consumption associated with different cultural fields, Bourdieu notes that these are profoundly affected by the degree to which the appropriation of the cultural products associated with them 'presupposes dispositions and competences which are not distributed universally'. Where such products are 'subject to exclusive appropriation, material or symbolic ... they yield a profit in distinction, proportionate to the rarity of the means required to appropriate them' (Bourdieu, 2010: 225). But Bourdieu also notes that when different fields are brought together, then, given that each of these distinguishes in distinctive ways, 'the total field of these fields offers well-nigh inexhaustible possibilities for the pursuit of distinction' (Bourdieu, 2010: 223). It is this last set of concerns that provides the focus for Part II where we examine the intersections between the myriad forms of distinction that are produced when those associated with the different fields discussed in Part I are brought together in an overarching space of lifestyles. In doing so, we pay particular attention to connections between different lifestyles and the class–education nexus as, for most of our fields, the most important statistical marker of practices of distinction.

Chapter 7 makes the shift from field-specific analyses to the construction of an overall space of lifestyles. Looking first at the connections between genre tastes, forms of cultural participation and the use of media platforms and devices across all six fields, the chapter considers how the positions of the fields themselves and the different kinds and degrees of social differentiation that they effect contribute to the distinctive properties of the space of lifestyles. The chapter then goes on to consider the distribution of six clusters across the space of lifestyles, paying particular attention to the ways in which these are distinguished by the varying levels of engagement that they exhibit with forms and practices representing different times within their respective cultural fields: traditional forms of legitimate culture, established alternatives to these, and more contemporary and emerging forms of cultural practice.

Chapter 8 brings these concerns to bear on current debates concerning the relations between cultural temporalities and class formations. For Bourdieu (2010: 122–123), distinctions between and within classes must be understood, first, in terms of the overall volume of capital possessed, producing a 'vertical' scale of difference between high, middle and low volumes of capital, and, second, through capital composition, the relative weight of economic and cultural capital possessed by different fractions within a class, producing 'horizontal' differentiations. Those with relatively high levels of cultural capital but more modest levels of economic capital – such as professionals within cultural institutions or public service positions, academics or teachers – represent the 'dominated fraction of the dominant class'. This is where cultural capital is likely to matter most in confirming a higher class status or compensating for a relative lack of economic capital.

No less significant than capital volume and composition are class trajectories. Class is not a static hierarchy but a dynamic set of relations in which particular class fractions – often old versus new – rise and fall as the kinds of cultural, social and economic capital associated with different occupations or educational qualifications change over time. Chapter 8 focuses initially on class by considering more closely the relations between the occupational class categories that we have used in Part I, underscoring their significance in distinctive configurations of cultural tastes and engagement. Higher professionals and managers and lower professionals and managers, for example, overlap significantly in patterns of cultural preferences and participation, but in ways that also reflect their different capital and gendered compositions. Both categories of professionals and managers manifest higher levels of cultural engagement than the large owners, who sit somewhat closer to those in intermediate occupations and small employers and the self-employed. The chapter then moves on to group the occupational classes into broader class formations. Class trajectories are then examined by considering the relations between the 'cultural capital profiles' of different groups of individuals from across the *Australian Cultural Fields* survey, their current occupational class position and the cultural clusters identified in Chapter 7. This reveals the role of both trajectory and capital composition in shaping cultural orientations.

For those whose cultural capital profiles testify to lower levels of 'inherited' cultural capital, the education system provides the principal means of cultural acquisition, but one that always risks revealing its late and 'scholastic' provenance. This is especially the case for rising fractions within the petite bourgeoisie, a class without long-established cultural resources but with aspirations to cultural insidership: hence what Bourdieu calls *la bonne volonté culturelle* or 'cultural goodwill' of the petite bourgeoisie. The middle of the space of lifestyles, where legitimate and popular tastes meet and comingle in a distinctive set of relations to the intermediate classes, is examined in Chapter 9 in the context of recent scholarship on the 'middlebrow'. In contrast to a good deal of post-Bourdieusian sociology, which has tended to treat the middle of the space of the lifestyles as an 'in-between' space, lacking its own distinguishing properties, the perspectives of 'middlebrow' studies facilitate a return to a more positive assessment of the middle of the space of lifestyles as the location for a socio-cultural formation with its own distinctive modes of consumption.

7

THE AUSTRALIAN SPACE OF LIFESTYLES

Tony Bennett, Modesto Gayo and Anna Cristina Pertierra

In laying out the principles underlying his conception of the relations between the space of social positions and the space of lifestyles, Bourdieu challenged conventional statistical conceptions of the relations between 'dependent' variables (particular cultural tastes or practices) and 'independent' variables (gender, age or level of education, for example). Even the most apparently independent variable 'conceals a whole network of statistical relations which are present, implicitly, in its relationship with any given ... practice' (Bourdieu, 2010: 97). The same goes for the relations between what he presents as primary (class) and secondary (age, gender) variables. Rather than interpreting classes as having a single dimension that is inflected in different directions by such secondary variables, he interprets the latter as introducing divisions and variations into classes that are an integral part of their constitution, urging the need 'to break *linear thinking*, which only recognises the simple ordinal structures of direct determination, and endeavour to reconstruct the networks of interrelated relationships which are present in each of the factors' (Bourdieu, 2010: 101). The three concepts that he proposed for doing so are the space of social positions in which the positioning of class fractions relative to one another is governed by the volume and composition of different kinds of capital; the space of lifestyles comprising the distribution of the cultural practices which make up different lifestyles; and the space of habitus, that is of the generative principles which translate related sets of practices into distinctive lifestyles which derive their coherence from the social positions to which they are most closely related.

In applying these principles in *Distinction*, Bourdieu acknowledges the differences between cultural fields arising from their varying degrees of legitimacy and their placing on a spectrum spanning the sacralised fields of aesthetic consumption and the world of ordinary consumption. However, he does not order the analysis of his survey data specifically with a view to examining field-specific logics governing the relations between practices and social positions. Although the authors of *Culture, Class, Distinction* (Bennett *et al.*, 2009) engage with such questions, they do so by first discussing the relations between cultural practices and social positions at the aggregate level of the relations between the UK space of social positions and space of lifestyles. Only then do they consider how the general properties of these relations are variably refracted in different cultural fields. We have proceeded differently by looking first at the relations between cultural practices, tastes and social positions associated with our fields before proceeding, now, to consider how these interact within an overall space of lifestyles. We have adopted this approach in order to examine how the organisation of the relations between cultural practices and social positions in different fields contributes to the organisation of the overall space of lifestyles and the logics of position-taking that inform its relationship to the space of social positions.

We therefore look first at the relative weighting accorded to level of education, occupational class, gender and age in accounting for the differentiations of cultural tastes and practices across our six cultural fields. We then look at three different aspects of the relations between the overall space of lifestyles and the space of social positions via Multiple Correspondence Analyses (MCAs) focused on the distributions of different kinds and degree of cultural participation, genre tastes and the use of media devices. This prepares the ground for an analysis of the six clusters into which the relations between the lifestyles and social positions of our respondents are most meaningfully grouped. We also draw on our household interviews for the light they throw on both points of connection and key differences between these clusters. Two main lines of argument are pursued. The first concerns the more marked role that practices and tastes linked to the art and literary fields and, albeit to a lesser extent, the music field play in marking distinctions within the professional and managerial classes as well as between those classes and other classes compared to the stronger role that heritage, sport and television play in marking distinctions between the classes occupying the middle of the space of lifestyles and lower class positions. The second concerns the significance of the role played by practices representing different times within the space of lifestyles. Operating at the intersections of age and class, these different times play a significant role in shaping the cultural orientations which differentiate the clusters produced by our cluster analysis.

Field variations relative to the space of social positions

We look first at the explanatory power of the first two axes (horizontal and vertical) accounting for the highest levels of variance or inertia for each of the fields discussed in the preceding chapters. In doing so we also look at the social variables that are most strongly associated with these axes. The first (horizontal) axis is always the stronger of the two and is most typically associated with level of education and occupational class, with the vertical axis being most usually associated with age. There are, however, some exceptions to this. In order to recap these matters, Table 7.1 arranges the fields in the order of their discussion in Chapters 1 to 6.[1] In the art field the horizontal axis, governed by level of education and occupational class, accounts for the greatest degree of variance along this axis of all fields; its power relative to the vertical axis (structured largely by age) is also considerably greater

TABLE 7.1 Comparative degrees of explained field variance across axes 1 and 2

	Horizontal inertia (variance) (%)	Vertical inertia (variance) (%)	Number of active categories and variables	Active variables
Art field	12.57 [Class, Education]	4.40 [Age]	86/42	Practices, tastes
Literary field	9.15 [Class, Education]	7.53 [Age]	22/4	Socio-economic, socio-demographic
Heritage field	7.58 [Class, Education]	6.56 [Age]	27/5	Socio-economic, socio-demographic
Music field	6.71 [Age]	5.56 [Class, Education]	84/37	Practices, tastes
Television field	5.29 [Age, Class, Education]	3.95 [Gender]	118/51	Practices, tastes
Sport field	10.5 [Gender]	9.25 [Class]	16/3	Socio-economic, socio-demographic
Overall space of lifestyles	5.35 [Class, Education, Gender]	2.47 [Age]	533/242	Practices, tastes

than in any other field. The axes for the literary and heritage fields are similarly structured, albeit that the differences between them are less pronounced. In the music field, by contrast, the horizontal axis is organised mainly in terms of age which trumps class position and level of education which are articulated mainly across the vertical axis. In the television field, age, class and level of education interact with one another across the horizontal axis, while the vertical axis is marked by gender. In the sport field, the horizontal axis is structured largely by a sharp gender differentiation while the vertical axis is most strongly associated with class.

When the properties of all these fields are brought together in an overall space of social positions (Figure 7.1), the degree of variance accounted for by the horizontal axis (5.35 per cent) is more than twice that of the vertical axis (2.47 per cent). The variable that is plotted most consistently across the horizontal axis is level of education. While those with only some secondary schooling and those with partially completed tertiary qualifications are located above and below the horizontal axis respectively, reflecting the pull of age which governs the vertical axis, the shift from completed secondary through completed tertiary to postgraduate qualifications runs dead-centre, from right to left, across the horizontal axis. Occupational class positions follow a related trajectory confirming the close interdependency of educational qualification and occupation (Bourdieu, 2010: 97–98). Gender differences, finally, are plotted mainly across a left (women) to right (men) trajectory suggesting a strong degree of alignment with class and education.

In moving now to consider the relations between this space of social positions and the Australian space of lifestyles (Figures 7.2 to 7.4) we pay particular attention to the significance of the relative positioning of field-specific practices within the

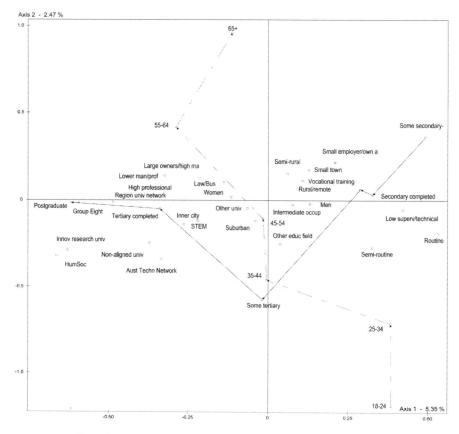

FIGURE 7.1 Australian space of social positions.

space of lifestyles. As the richness of our data precludes the presentation of all of the cultural practices included in our survey within a single figure except at the price of illegible clutter, we look first at the distribution of different degrees and kinds of cultural participation within the space of lifestyles, then at the distribution of genre tastes and, finally, at the use of media devices and platforms. These analyses pave the way for a discussion of the findings of a cluster analysis which adds to these indicators of participation, genre tastes and platforms a consideration of the roles that recognition of, and tastes for, the named items in our survey play within the space of lifestyles. The clusters also allow us to elaborate the significance of the temporalities constituted by the distinction between traditional, established alternative and emerging alternative forms of cultural capital broached in Chapter 3.

Participation, genres, platforms

Figure 7.2 plots the various indicators of the cultural activities participated in by our survey respondents. (For ease of reference, see Appendix I for a key to the items

The Australian space of lifestyles   123

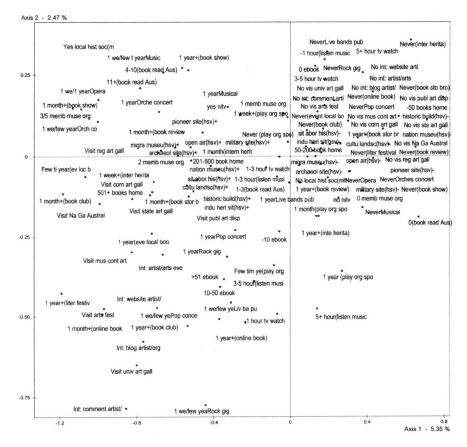

FIGURE 7.2 Australian space of lifestyles (participation).

collated in Figures 7.2 and 7.3.) The extreme left of the space registers exceptionally high levels of participation in institutions and practices associated with the art, literary and music fields. There is a high rate of art gallery visitation, encompassing a wide range of different types of art galleries and arts events. A similar pattern is evident for literary events and institutions, with high rates of book ownership, reading and reading book reviews also registering, while in the music field, opera, orchestral concerts and, to a lesser degree, musicals are frequently attended. Heritage practices, by contrast, do not figure strongly except for membership of museum organisations, and frequent use of the Internet for heritage purposes. No forms of participation in either sport or television register in this part of the space.

Moving towards the centre of the figure, to the 'inner left' so to speak, we can see that – except for visiting public art displays – engagement with art institutions falls out of the picture. But literary institutions remain significant albeit at lower levels than on the 'outer left': reading fewer Australian books, having fewer books at home, and less regular involvement in literary activities, book clubs, and television and radio book

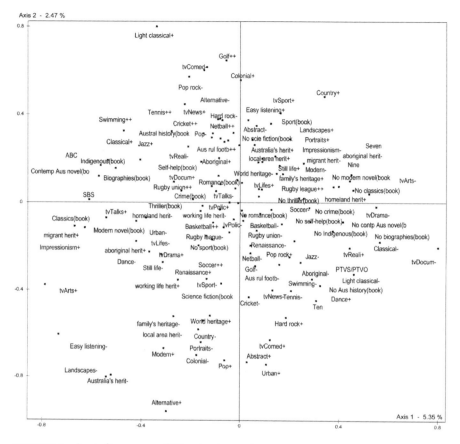

FIGURE 7.3 Australian space of lifestyles (genres).

programmes. Engagement with music remains significant, but is tilted towards more popular music events. It is only in this section of the space, finally, that visitation of a wide range of heritage sites is recorded: pioneer history sites, open-air sites, migration museums, archaeological sites, Aboriginal history sites and the National Museum of Australia all appear here.

The most striking aspects of the two right-hand quadrants are the zero to low rates of participation in the art, literary, music and – to a lesser extent – heritage fields. Television, by contrast, is more popular, particularly among the older respondents in the top right quadrant where heavy daily viewing figures are recorded. Musical involvements are much weaker in this quadrant where low daily listening figures and low levels of engagement with live bands, rock and pop concerts stand in sharp contrast to the high levels of daily listening evident in the lower right quadrant. Playing organised sport also figures prominently here.

Figure 7.3, focusing on genres, presents a broadly similar, albeit more nuanced, picture. The extreme left of the space is dominated by positive tastes in the art, literary and music fields. The literary field predominates here with contemporary Australian novels, literary classics, the modern novel and Indigenous books featuring. Impressionism and classical music register for the art and music fields, while dislikes are registered for landscapes, dance music and easy listening. Television also features with high rates of preference for the Australian Broadcasting Corporation (ABC), Special Broadcasting Service (SBS) and for TV arts programmes. Heritage practices also register here, with migrant and Aboriginal heritage scoring positively while Australian heritage is not favoured, particularly among the younger age groups who congregate towards the bottom of the space. Swimming is the only sport to register here.

A greater range of genres spread more evenly across the six fields comes into play in the centre of the field. Sport plays a significant role in differentiating the 'inner left' and 'inner right' sections of the space. Golf, tennis, cricket, netball, Australian Football League (AFL, better known as Australian Rules football), basketball, rugby union and soccer all figure positively in the 'inner left' where the only sport negatives are disliking rugby league, and not reading sports books or watching sports TV. The 'inner right' reverses this pattern. Television also figures prominently in the relations across these two sections of the space. News programmes, documentaries and drama are liked most in the 'inner left'; comedy, reality and lifestyle television are not liked. Police shows register both positively and negatively. Comedy, lifestyle television, sports TV and talk shows are liked in the 'inner right', but not news programmes. Heritage is also significantly involved in the distinctions that shape the relations between these two sections of the space. A marked preference for Australian, homeland, local area and family heritage, and a dislike of migrant and world heritage characterise the 'inner right'. The 'inner left' mostly reverses this set of heritage preferences. In the case of literature it is the less formally exalted, but still respectable, genres of Australian history, biographies, self-help books, crime, thrillers and science fiction/fantasy that are found here. Only sports books figure in the inner right.

The differences between the upper and lower parts of these sections of the space register the equally telling effects of age in relation to musical tastes. Liking light classical music and jazz in the upper left quadrant is counter-posed to them being disliked in the lower right quadrant; the dislike of alternative and poprock that registers in the upper 'inner left' is in contrast to them being liked in the lower part of the 'inner left'. The liking for easy listening and country music in the upper part of the 'inner right' similarly operates across a diagonal line of differentiation from the dislike of these registered in the far left (easy listening) and 'inner left' (country) of the space. The same principles are at work in relation to art tastes. The liking for modern art and dislike of colonial art and portraits in the lower part of the 'inner left' are mirrored by the dislike of modern art and fondness for colonial art and portraits that is evident, alongside landscapes and still lifes, in the upper part of the 'inner right' of the space. Negative and positive tastes for abstract art are arranged across the upper and lower parts of the 'inner right'.

We can, then, see how, in these two inner sections of the space, sport, heritage and television practices are implicated in a complex set of differentiations among more 'middling' tastes, while in the literary, art and music fields the genres that are in play in the more localised games of distinction that take place here are different from the more traditional high genres we find in the outer left of the space. The extreme right of the space, finally, is dominated by dislikes, most notably for literary genres: the modern novel, literary classics, biographies, Australian history books. Classical and light classical music are also disliked, as are television documentaries, TV dramas, TV arts programmes and Aboriginal heritage. Positive likes are limited to the commercial television channels Nine and Seven, and to reality television shows.

The interplays between age, occupational class and education that these considerations point to is particularly clear in Figure 7.4 which plots the uses of television and music platforms and devices, and Internet usage. The strong association of time-shift, streaming, mobile TV and music devices with the youngest age cohorts is clear in the grouping of these towards the lower centre and right of the space, just as their absence in the upper parts of the space indicates low levels of use by older age cohorts. The use of the Internet in the art and heritage fields, by contrast, is arranged diagonally across a line running from the bottom left to the top right differentiating younger and more highly educated sections of the sample occupying relatively higher class

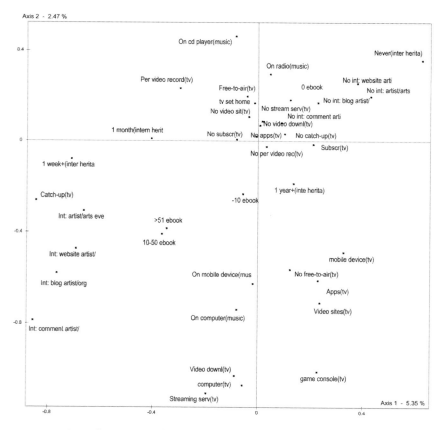

FIGURE 7.4 Australian space of lifestyles (platforms and devices).

positions, in the bottom left, from older, less-well educated (mainly secondary) members of the sample occupying lower class positions in the top right.

In summary, we can identify four main trends from the discussion so far. The first comprises the sharp left–right contrast structured by participation/non-participation in the institutions and practices of the art, literary and music fields and liking/disliking the canonical genres of these fields. While also a part of this picture, the heritage, sport and television fields are more centrally implicated in the distinctions that predominate in the middle sections of the space of lifestyles. This is connected to a tendency – particularly in the heritage field – for practices with strong Australian associations to be preferred in the 'inner right' of the space while more international and cosmopolitan practices characterise the left. There is also evidence, for the art, literary, music and television fields, of a division across the vertical axis between more established and more recent practices with the latter, particularly in the music and television fields, being strongly associated with new platforms and devices. We now consider the further light that our cluster analysis throws on these questions.

Clustering practices, tastes and social positions analysis

Our cluster analysis yielded six clusters (Figure 7.5). Clusters 1 and 2, on the left of the space, are defined principally by higher education and class positions, but are differentiated by age. Clusters 3 and 4 occupy the centre of the space where the 'middling' class positions and levels of education congregate but are, again, divided by age, and the same is true for Clusters 5 and 6 on the right of the space where lower class and education positions predominate. We shall, accordingly, present these clusters in pairs. First, in exploring the relations between the clusters and the MCAs discussed earlier in the chapter, we summarise the socio-demographic characteristics, forms of cultural participation and use of media platforms and devices that are most strongly associated with the two clusters in each pair. We then discuss tabular presentations of the differences in both the generic tastes and the degrees to which the named Australian and overseas cultural items in our survey are recognised and liked across the two clusters. As a means of highlighting the role of different cultural temporalities in distinguishing the clusters from one another, we italicise those art, literary and musical genres and named items which represent established alternative forms of cultural capital and both italicise and bold those which represent emerging forms of cultural capital. In doing so, however, we acknowledge that some cases straddle the boundaries between these categories. We also provide vignettes of household interviewees whose experiences, tastes and interests exemplify characteristics that mark both similarities and differences across each pair of clusters.

Two decisions that have shaped the presentation of our findings need to be noted. First, while all demographic indicators identified by the cluster analysis are included in the discussion of each cluster, for all other items only those accorded a significance level of 4.0 (t-test) or above are included for Clusters 1 and 2. In Clusters 5 and 6, the items with the highest significance levels are overwhelmingly for named items that the survey respondents in these clusters had *not* heard of, with the

128 Tony Bennett et al.

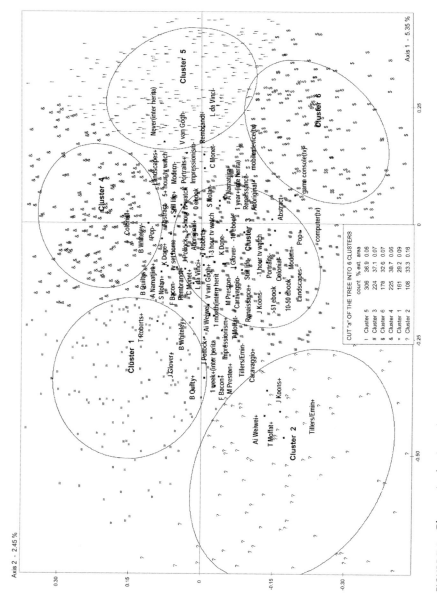

FIGURE 7.5 Clusters in the Australian space of lifestyles.

consequence that positive and negative tastes for genres and named items come lower down the significance hierarchy. In order to paint a picture for these two clusters that has a degree of equivalence to the other clusters – which log no or very few 'not heard of' responses – our second decision was to go below the 4.0 significance level for genre and named item tastes in these clusters. We also do this for Clusters 3 and 4 where likes and dislikes also register at lower levels of significance. The items included on this basis are preceded by an asterisk.

Clusters 1 and 2

Composed primarily of those aged 55 and above, Cluster 1 (11.7 per cent of the sample) leans towards women in its gendered composition and consists mostly of higher- and lower-level professionals and managers, with a bias towards the higher levels. It is also exceedingly well educated: those with tertiary qualifications predominate and the cluster includes a high ratio of postgraduates. Group of Eight universities feature strongly, and favoured areas of study are the Science, Technology, Engineering and Mathematics (STEM) disciplines followed by law and business studies. High levels of participation are evident in the literary, art and music fields, and in heritage practices. Most of the types of heritage sites we identified had been visited in the previous year; membership of/subscription to museum organisations and local history societies is significant. There are no significant involvements with sport or television. Television viewing is exclusively free-to-air (FTA).

Cluster 2 (9 per cent) exhibits similar educational characteristics, the most notable differences being the preponderance of tertiary qualifications in the humanities and social sciences and strong associations with non-aligned universities alongside Group of Eight universities. It is a younger cluster most strongly associated with 35–44 year olds, key years in consolidating career prospects and trajectories for the tertiary educated. Lower manager and professional occupations predominate, but with some higher professionals. Participation levels are high across the art, literary, music and heritage fields, but negligible in relation to both sport, which does not figure at all, and television, where watching National Indigenous Television (NITV) is the only practice that registers. Much the same range of art institutions is engaged with as for Cluster 1, but with a reversed emphasis in that it is museums of contemporary art, art festivals and commercial art galleries that top the list, with State galleries, public art displays, regional galleries and the National Gallery of Australia (NGA) – all more strongly associated with Cluster 1 – following on. Gallery visitation is very frequent at once a month. Participation in literary institutions (bookstores, festivals, shows and clubs) on a monthly basis or a few times a year is the strongest of all the clusters. Book ownership is the highest of all groups at 501 plus. Participation in musical events is widespread, spanning both high (opera, orchestral concerts) and more popular (rock and pop concerts) forms. Visitation of heritage sites is high. Apart from some use of catch-up TV, use of new devices and platforms is limited to the use of the Internet to access arts websites, and literary and heritage sites.

Genre tastes in Cluster 1 are strongly tilted towards the literary field (Table 7.2). In this table, and those that follow, all items are arranged in descending order of their

TABLE 7.2 Clusters 1 and 2 (genres and named items)

	Cluster 1	Cluster 2
Genres like most	Contemporary Australian novel; literary classics; modern novel; Australian history book; ABC; TV news; *Indigenous book*; Biographies; Impressionism; thrillers; light classical; crime novels; swimming; classical music; TV arts.	Literary classics; ***alternative music***; *Indigenous book*; modern novel; contemporary Australian novel; Aboriginal heritage; modern art; TV arts; biographies.
Genres like least	Reality TV; pop music.	Landscapes; Australian heritage; colonial art; easy listening.
Australian items liked	Art: Roberts; Namatjira; Nolan; *Whitely*; Done; **Quilty**; Preston. Literary: *Winton*; Malouf; *Grenville*; ***Morgan***; ***Scott***; Courtenay; Reilly. Music: *Gurrumul Yunupingu*; Ceberano; *Sculthorpe*; Jones. Television: Gardening Australia; Byrne; Redfern; Mailman; Zemiro. Heritage: Port Arthur; National Museum Australia; Sovereign Hill; Uluru; Australian War Memorial; Fremantle Prison; Museum of Sydney. Sport: Laver; Ellis; Jackson.	Art: Preston; ***Tillers***; ***Moffatt***; **Quilty**; *Whitely*; Glover; Nolan; Roberts. Literary: ***Morgan***; ***Scott***; Malouf; *Winton*; *Grenville*; Douglass. Music: ***Sultan***; ***Gotye***; *Gurrumul Yunupingu*; *Sculthorpe*; Jones. Television: Zemiro; Mailman; Redfern Now; Australian Story. Heritage: Sydney Museum; Cockatoo Island; National Museum Australia. Sport: Goodes.

Australian items disliked	The Block; Folau.	Martin; McGuire; Bickmore; Done; Alexandra; Harrower.
International items liked	Art: Monet; Rembrandt; *Pollock*; Caravaggio; van Gogh; Da Vinci; *Bacon*. Literary: *Attwood*; Picoult; Rankin; Woolf. Music: Rhapsody in Blue; Nessun Dorma; Mikado; Phantom of the Opera; Four Seasons. Television: Midsomer Murders; Grand Designs; QI; Killing. Heritage: Stonehenge; Vatican Museum; Acropolis; Ellis Island. Sport: Tendulkar.	Art: Caravaggio; *Bacon*; **Emin**; **Koons**; Pollock; ***Ai Weiwei***; Monet; van Gogh; Rembrandt. Literary: *Attwood*; Austen; ***Eggers***; ***Murakami***; ***DeLillo***; Rankin; Woolf. Music: *Kind of Blue*; Four Seasons; *The Piano*; Nessun Dorma; *Dark Side Moon*; Rhapsody in Blue; Mikado. Television: Mad Men; QI; Killing; Grand Designs; Game of Thrones. Sport: Goodes.
International items disliked	Angkor Wat; Bacon; Maradona; Game of Thrones.	Picoult; Ellis Island.
Items not recognised by field	None	None

significance in defining the cluster. Literary genres dominate the list of positive genre tastes; arts programmes on television, Impressionism, and both classical and light classical music are also present. Swimming is the only sport represented. Dislikes are for the popular genres of reality television and pop music. The generic likes of Cluster 2, by contrast, are distinguished chiefly in being tilted more towards alternative and emerging forms. Dislikes are equally distinctive in being focused on items with strong Australian associations: landscapes, Australian heritage and colonial art.

All of the named items in our survey are broadly recognised in both clusters. The most notable differences concern the greater range of heritage institutions favoured in Cluster 1, and the higher position in the set of preferences of Cluster 2 accorded to emerging forms – Tillers, Moffatt and Quilty in Australian art preferences, for example. Positive tastes for established alternative forms – Gurrumul Yunupingu, Sculthorpe and Jones, for example – are broadly shared across the two clusters.

GLOBAL ENTHUSIASMS, NATIONAL AMBIVALENCES AND GENERATIONAL SHIFTS

Jacinta (49 years old) and Holly (29 years old) exemplify some of the similarities and differences between Clusters 1 and 2 which they respectively most closely represent. Both women are tertiary educated with professional work experience; while Jacinta previously worked in middle management, Holly is an engineering consultant working in the health sector. Both women regularly participate in activities associated with art, literature and heritage.

Jacinta's house and garden, which she shares with her husband and two children, are filled with different kinds of art. Jacinta had decided that her large living room would only have original pieces of art in it. Each artwork she has bought has memories attached to it, and Jacinta sees these original pieces as having a 'vibrancy' to them that is missing from the prints in other parts of her home. Jacinta enjoys abstract art most, and likes the 'earthy colours' that often feature in Indigenous art. She prefers art that captures the harshness of the Australian landscape, and is less interested in paintings that are overly idyllic. Jacinta regularly goes to galleries and museums, most often if there is a special exhibition on show.

Holly is less deeply engaged with the art world, but has periodically visited art galleries in the past, to see major exhibitions such as the Archibald Prize, or to support friends who have curated or exhibited art. Holly likes modern art, especially the work of Mexican painter Frida Kahlo, and also appreciates Indigenous art. She likes to visit art galleries when travelling to other cities and countries. Indeed, many of Holly's interests connect to her love of travel, and her enjoyment of Latin American culture, which was sparked by her being an exchange student in Mexico when at university. Holly admires how Latin Americans respond to music:

people are just having lots and lots of fun and often they come from places that are a lot poorer than Australia, but they're still, when they're listening to music, or when they're dancing, they're having such an amazing time.

While Jacinta describes herself as not having travelled 'all that much' compared to her husband and children, she too has travelled to Latin America and Europe.

This openness to global culture – having a high expectation of international travel, and knowing and enjoying many international genres – marks Clusters 1 and 2 and can be seen across both Holly and Jacinta's tastes. Australian genres, products and personalities are viewed more ambivalently. Holly finds Australian novels less engaging than stories set in other times and places. While she loved reading *The Adventures of Huckleberry Finn* and *The Book Thief* as part of her book club, Holly's response to Tim Winton's work was 'I know it's good, I know it's really well-written and I know I should like it, but I don't really have that much connection to it.'[2]

Jacinta's ambivalence about Australian culture is more explicit. Although interested in aspects of Australian history, she is uneasy with some expressions of Australian nationalism. When visiting the Australian War Memorial, Jacinta appreciated that 'there's a contemplation in the War Memorial, I think there's a sensitivity in the way the collection, the exhibits have been put together. It doesn't glorify I think it shows the brutality of Australia's involvement.' While not disliking settler heritage sites, she argues that, politically, 'the dominance of that as a historical story is very much at the expense of Australia's Aboriginal history and that's what concerns me'. At the same time, Jacinta is uneasy about how being described as middle class or as having 'middle-class tastes' might be conflated with judging or criticising the habits and tastes of 'working-class' Australians.

Although Jacinta is only moderately interested in sports, she thinks about the political impact that sportspeople and their teams can have: she appreciates how the success of Adam Goodes and Cathy Freeman might challenge racism in Australia, for example, and although she makes fun of herself for it, Jacinta doesn't support the Australian cricket team because 'that just props up Australian nationalism'. Holly is much more enthusiastic about sport, to a degree that is unusual in Clusters 1 and 2. She enjoys watching AFL on television and with her friends, and supports both of the Sydney teams. But here, too, Holly is quite cosmopolitan in her tastes, as on her travels through the Americas she greatly enjoyed watching basketball in the United States and soccer in Latin America. Playing and watching different kinds of sport occupies a lot of Holly's social life. She plays in a mixed basketball team with many of her friends, is currently learning to surf and comes from a family of avid golfers.

Comparing Jacinta and Holly's media consumption practices illustrates a generational shift away from FTA television and towards streaming platforms.

> While Jacinta reads books and watches broadcast television regularly, Holly is more engaged with digital platforms. When reading and watching television, Jacinta enjoys the escapism of crime novels and police and detective programmes, although she tries to alternate reading crime novels with other kinds of books that give her deeper insights into the human condition. Holly follows current affairs by watching television programmes like *Q&A*, but prefers using Netflix to watch comedies and sitcoms such as *30 Rock* and *Parks and Recreation*. Holly's music consumption also illustrates a shift towards digital platforms; while driving to and from work, she listens to music by mixing the alternative music radio station Triple J with music podcasts.

Clusters 3 and 4

Cluster 3 (20.2 per cent), dominating the middle of the space of lifestyles, is most strongly characterised by the two middle-age groups, with the 45–54 cohort slightly more represented than the 35–44 year olds. There are no strongly distinguishing occupational class characteristics, and the gender balance is tilted only slightly in favour of women. Although not strongly marked by particular levels of education, there is a bias, among the tertiary educated, towards law and business studies and humanities and social science qualifications as well as towards graduates coming from middle-ranked universities in either the Australian Technology Network or from non-aligned universities.

The most significant levels of engagement are in the art field, albeit at more modest levels than for Clusters 1 and 2. Art galleries are visited once a year, and there are modest levels of Internet engagement with the visual arts. There are similar levels of engagement – significant, but not excessive – with the literary and heritage fields. Bookstores, book reviews and book clubs are most typically engaged with only once a year; only a few Australian authors have been read, and there is regular use of the Internet to access online books, with ownership of ebooks registering in the 10–50 range. Historic buildings, museums and military sites are the most favoured heritage venues, and the Internet is widely used to connect with heritage institutions. Music figures as the fourth-ranked field of engagement, with live pub bands and rock gigs attended a few times a year. Mobile devices are the most favoured platform. Neither television nor sport figure strongly, but there is some use of streaming devices for television viewing.

Cluster 4 (16.6 per cent) is older – mostly over 55 with a marked concentration among the over 65s. Occupations are mainly in lower professional and managerial positions; actual and preferred class identifications are both as middle class. Vocational qualifications followed by incomplete secondary schooling are the educational levels most strongly associated with the cluster. Levels of cultural participation are more modest than for Cluster 3 and tend to be spread across the different fields – a little bit here, a little bit there – rather than focused intensively on any particular field. Art galleries are visited once a year; television is watched between one and three hours a day; music is listened to for less than an hour; only a handful of Australian authors have been read. Practices indicating a more immersive involvement in particular fields do not register. There are no signs of strong engagement with the Internet or with new television or music devices: television is watched FTA at home; music is listened to on the radio or CD players.

Generic likes for Cluster 3 (Table 7.3) are mainly for conventionally esteemed or middling genres: literary classics and light classical music are the two stand-out genres, although the modern novel, science fiction/fantasy, the contemporary Australian novel and self-help books are also liked. Musical likes range across pop and hard rock to alternative music in contrast to a marked aversion to dance music. Rugby union is the most strongly favoured sport. Dislikes focus on the art field: landscapes, colonial art and still lifes. For Cluster 4 the most strongly marked genre tastes are uniformly for genres occupying the middling levels of hierarchies of legitimation: light classical, easy listening, landscapes, colonial art and portraits, for example. There is a distinct set of sports tastes with netball, swimming, golf, tennis, cricket and AFL amounting to the largest range of sports engagement of any of the clusters. Many genre dislikes are age related – hard rock and pop rock, for example. Others reflect a distancing from emerging genres: alternative music, for example, and abstract art whose broader social reception lags behind the renovative role it has played in art practices

Tastes for named items are similarly organised across the two clusters. These are, for Cluster 3, mostly for neither the highest nor the lowest ranked items, with a strong emphasis on more recent but, at the same time, well established alternatives to traditional high culture items: *Dark Side of the Moon*, Madonna's 'Vogue' and *Kind of Blue* in music; Monet, Van Gogh and Whiteley in art alongside more traditional figures like Rembrandt and Roberts. Literary tastes are for the popular writers King and Courtenay. Dislikes fall mainly in two groups: items liked by the older and, on the whole, less well-educated members of Cluster 4: *Midsomer Murders*, Port Arthur, Uluru, *The Mikado*, 'Nessun Dorma', Gurrumul Yunupingu, *Gardening Australia*, *Rhapsody in Blue*, sports figure Norman and TV personalities Martin and Byrne, for example; and writers with higher culture associations, occurring mainly in connection with Clusters 1 and 2: Rankin, Atwood, Morgan, DeLillo, Scott and Woolf. In television, dislikes are registered in relation to both higher (*Mad Men*) and lower (*Big Bang, Big Brother*) programmes.

Specific likes for Cluster 4 are, across all the fields, for middle of the range options. *Phantom of the Opera*, *The Mikado*, 'Nessun Dorma' and Gurrumul Yunupingu are prominent musical likes; the popular writer Courtenay and the classic Austen are the most liked authors; the early to mid-twentieth century Australian artists Roberts, Namatjira and Nolan feature alongside Rembrandt as favoured artists. Preferred television personalities are Martin and Byrne, but also include McGuire. The sports figures who are most liked are mostly long past their glory days – Laver, Norman – and those who are still current – Nadal, Tendulkar and Thorpe – are from the more selective ends of the sports spectrum: tennis, cricket and swimming. Port Arthur and Uluru are the most favoured heritage sites, and figure more strongly in Cluster 4 than in Cluster 3. The higher rate of liking for Australian items in Cluster 4 relative to Cluster 3 is also notable.

136 Tony Bennett et al.

TABLE 7.3 Clusters 3 and 4 (genres and named items)

	Cluster 3	Cluster 4
Genres like most	Literary classics; light classical. ★ Modern novel; Renaissance art; TV comedy; sci-fi/fantasy; contemporary Australian novel; pop rock; self-help; modern art; *alternative music*; Impressionism; *hard rock*; rugby union.	Light classical; landscapes, netball; swimming; golf; cricket; colonial; art; tennis; AFL. ★ Portraits; classical music; easy listening
Genres like least	Dance; landscapes; golf; colonial art; still lifes; working life heritage.	***Hard rock***; pop rock; ***abstract art***. ★ TV comedy; Australian history book; sci-fi/fantasy; ***alternative music***.
Australian items liked	***Gotye***; Hamish and Andy. ★ Hughes; Bickmore; Mailman; Barnes; Courtenay; *Whitely*; Roberts; Offspring; Zemiro; Keller; The Block.	Laver; Namatjira; Martin; Nolan; Norman; Courtenay; Port Arthur; Australian Story; Roberts; Byrne; Gardening Australia; Ceberano; Uluru; Done; Bradman; *Garrumul; Yunupingu*; McGuire; Thorpe. ★ Fremantle Prison; Jackson; Ellis; National Museum Australia; Kewell; Freeman.
Australian items disliked	Reilly; Port Arthur. ★ *Garrumul Yunupingu; Jones*; Gardening Australia; Norman; Thorpe; Martin; Uluru; Big Brother; Morgan; ***Scott; Sultan***; Byrne; Phelps.	*Whiteley*; ***Quilty***; *AC/DC*; Hamish and Andy. ★ Malouf; Australian War Memorial; Redfern Now; *Sculthorpe*; Sovereign Hill.

International items liked	*Dark Side Moon*; Vogue; Monet; van Gogh; da Vinci; King. ★ Under Dome; Picoult; Game of Thrones; *Kind of Blue*; Rembrandt.	Phantom; Midsomer; Rhapsody; Mikado; Rembrandt; Nessun Dorma; Austen; Nadal; Tendulkar. ★ Stonehenge; Monet; Jolene; Vatican Museum.
International items disliked	Nessun Dorma; Midsomer; Mad Men. ★ Rankin; Mikado; *Attwood*; Rhapsody in Blue; Maradona; **Koons**; Homeland; Woods; ***DeLillo***; Big Bang; Caravaggio; Woolf; Four Seasons.	Dark Side Moon; Woolf; Top Gear; King.
Items not recognised	None	Literary: ***Morgan***; ***Scott***; ***DeLillo***.

Asterisked items register a significance level of below 4.0 (t-test).

MODERATE ENTHUSIASMS

Brooke and Leonard – the first leaning more towards Cluster 3 and the latter more towards Cluster 4 – represent different generations: at 86, Leonard was the oldest person we interviewed; Brooke, at 21, was one of the youngest. Despite their age differences, they share a set of orientations towards cultural engagement that might be described as 'moderate'. They do not frequently visit the cultural institutions named in the survey, and do not present themselves as connoisseurs of high culture. But both Brooke and Leonard have enthusiasm for certain cultural pursuits that give great meaning to their lives. Brooke's passion is history. When studying for her degree in commerce, she especially enjoyed English and history subjects, and her interests in these strongly shape her reading tastes. Brooke is a keen reader, though she does not think of herself as a fast reader, so she prefers to read at her own pace rather than join a book club. While she and her mum often share books, Brooke singles out her father's influence as leading to her love of Jane Austen and literary fiction. She has read the *Harry Potter* and *Lord of the Rings* series many times. Brooke loved Bryce Courtenay's *The Power of One* when she read it at school, but singles out Margaret Atwood's *The Handmaid's Tale* as a set book that she particularly disliked.

Brooke sees her enjoyment of period dramas such as *Downton Abbey* and the 1990s BBC adaptation of *Pride and Prejudice* as interwoven with her taste for historical literature. Watching television mostly takes place with her family in the living room, so she will often watch programmes chosen by her parents, and they regularly watch reality shows such as *MasterChef* as well as Australian dramas like *Packed to the Rafters*.

Leonard's particular passion is music. An accomplished violinist, he enjoys listening to the music of André Rieu, and regularly performs music himself, accompanied by his daughter on the piano, at a local aged care home. When his wife was alive, Leonard would play the violin for her on Sunday afternoons, and has found playing music with the church group to be an important part of his social life since her death. He watches television regularly, and enjoys early evening quiz shows in which people can win a cash jackpot. Rather than following specific programmes, he tends to leave the television on Channel 9 or the ABC and wait for something to catch his interest. In addition to watching television most evenings, Leonard reads short Bible passages most nights, in part to ease his loneliness since the loss of his wife.

Both Brooke and Leonard shape their discussions of what they enjoy around their experiences of family – and in Leonard's case, around the absence of his wife. Leonard is more interested in sports as something to be participated in than as something to be watched or followed. His family had often played table tennis at home, and later in life he took up lawn bowls with his wife, and continues to play at the local bowls club where he is a member. He enjoys watching tennis on television, and appreciates the winning qualities of the Williams sisters. While he wants to support Australian players, he finds the behaviour of the rising star Nick Kyrgios to be unsporting.

Brooke reflects upon her tastes as being unusual for someone her age: her lack of interest in bingeing on streamed television, and her love of historical fiction might be seen as 'probably more an older thing'. This suspicion of Brooke's may bear some truth given that Leonard, in keeping with his age, has no engagement with digital technologies.

Clusters 5 and 6

Cluster 5 (25.5 per cent) is strongly working class. Recruiting its members from routine workers, lower supervisory and technical workers, small employers and own account workers – all predominantly male – it is biased towards the middle-age range of 45–54. Levels of education are low, with incomplete secondary education registering most strongly. While some routine workers express middle class as their preferred class identification, a match between working class as both actual and preferred class identity is more common.

The only form of participation to register significantly is watching television for five or more hours a week, exclusively via FTA broadcasts. Art galleries are not visited; there are no books at home, and no engagement with bookstores, book shows or literary festivals. There is no use of the Internet for any purpose connected to the visual arts or book culture. Nor is there any active participation – whether direct or technologically mediated – in the heritage field. There is also little participation in musical events outside the home, whether popular (rock gigs, pop concerts, live bands) or orchestral concerts and opera.

Cluster 6 (17 per cent) is most clearly defined by its youthfulness – it recruits its members chiefly from the 18–34 year olds – and by its bias towards men. It is most closely associated with routine, semi-routine and intermediate workers, and with those who have completed secondary or partial tertiary education. This suggests a cluster comprising mainly young people whose class destinies are likely to diverge as the different trajectories of those who have left school to enter the labour market in lower class positions and those who are in the course of acquiring tertiary qualifications work themselves out. This is supported by the more strongly marked different class identifications (with middle class more evenly matching working class) that are evident in this cluster compared to Cluster 5.

The youthfulness of the cluster is related to its most strongly distinguishing positive characteristic: its active engagement with new devices and platforms. Music is chiefly listened to on mobile devices and computers, while FTA is rejected in favour of practices such as watching on a computer (laptop or desktop), naming a Pay-TV channel or network as a favourite and downloading via sites such as BitTorrent. This is matched by a lack of engagement with many of the cultural activities we asked about, albeit not so marked as for Cluster 5: never watching book shows or reading Australian authors; not visiting the more established galleries (regional, State, the NGA) but going to other types of gallery; not going to opera, musicals and orchestral concerts but attending more popular musical performances, for example.

Turning now to Table 7.4, country and western music, landscapes and alternative music are the three most strongly preferred genres in Cluster 5, followed by a set of heritage interests skewed towards its local and national forms (heritage of working life, Australian, homeland and local area heritage) while sports and reality TV are favoured television genres. Literary genres dominate the dislikes of this cluster. Television documentaries and TV drama are not liked, and the same is true for both migrant and Aboriginal heritage. Soccer, swimming and tennis are also not strongly favoured. Landscapes and Impressionism are the only art genres that register, the former as liked and the latter as disliked. Literary genres are notably unpopular.

Generic likes in Cluster 6 are strongly focused on music – alternative, hard rock, urban, dance and pop – with abstract art, television comedy and science fiction/fantasy also included. Dislikes are most strongly registered in relation to literary genres. But sport also features very strongly: tennis, cricket, netball, swimming, golf and AFL are not liked. Country and western music, local area heritage and colonial art are also not favoured.

In Cluster 5, except for Minogue and Chambers, specific likes are registered only in relation to television channels, personalities, programmes and sportsmen. Specific dislikes focus most strongly on international artists (Rembrandt, da Vinci, Van Gogh, Monet) and Austen: all long-established figures whose names, being in wide circulation, would be more likely to secure a negative response from survey respondents less familiar with more contemporary artists.[3] On television, *Australian Story* and *Gardening Australia* draw negative responses. Except for Thorpe, likes and dislikes for both Australian and international named items in Cluster 6 are focused exclusively on the television and music fields.

The most striking aspect of both clusters, however, is the high rates of non-recognition they record. This is most notably true, in Cluster 5, for authors, 19 of whom are not recognised, with visual artists falling only a couple short of this. Recognition of overseas heritage sites is also markedly low. Lack of familiarity is much less marked in relation to television and sport, and is not registered at all in relation to music. Cluster 6 also shows high rates of non-recognition across the art, literary and heritage fields, albeit mainly in relation to Australian rather than international heritage sites. Fewer television and sports personalities are recognised than is true for Cluster 5.

TABLE 7.4 Clusters 5 and 6 (genres and named items)

	Cluster 5	Cluster 6
Genres like most	Country; landscapes; *alternative music*.	*Abstract art; alternative music*; TV comedy; sci-fi/fantasy; hard rock; urban; dance; pop rock.
	★ TV sport; working life heritage; reality TV; Australian heritage; homeland heritage; sports book; pop rock; local area heritage.	
Genres like least	Literary classics; modern novel; contemporary Australian novel; classical music; biographies.	Australian history books; contemporary Australian novel; country; tennis; No Indigenous books; cricket; netball; local area heritage; swimming; colonial art; literary classics; TV news; golf; classical; AFL; biographies.
	Indigenous book; thriller; TV arts; crime books; soccer; sci-fi/fantasy; migrant heritage; TV documentaries.	
	★Impressionism; light classical; Aboriginal heritage; swimming; tennis; TV drama.	
Australian items liked	Martin; Channel 7.	Big Brother; Hamish and Andy; Gotye.
	★ McGuire; Chambers; Channel 9; Cam; Norman; Vautin; The Block.	
Australian items disliked	Australian War Memorial. Australian Story; Gardening Australia.	Ceberano; Australian Story; Thorpe.
International items liked	Woods; Minogue.	Big Bang; Game of Thrones; Top Gear.
International items disliked	Rembrandt; Da Vinci; van Gogh; Monet; Austen.	Phantom of the Opera; Midsomer

continued

TABLE 7.4 Continued

	Cluster 5	Cluster 6
Items not recognised by field	Art: *Bacon*, Caravaggio; *Pollock*; Monet; Roberts; *Whitely*; **Quilty**; Nolan; Preston; **Koons**; van Gogh; Done; **Tillers**; *Emin*; **Moffatt**; **Ai Weiwei**; Namatjira. Literary: *Winton*; Malouf; *Atwood*; *Grenville*; **DeLillo**; Reilly; Rankin; Picoult; Courtenay; Alexandria; Harrower; Woolf; Austen; **Eggers**; **Murakami**; **Morgan**; **Scott**; King; Douglass. Heritage: Angkor Wat; Ellis Island; Stonehenge; Forbidden City; Acropolis; Museum of Sydney; Te Papa; National Museum of Australia; Immigration Museum; Cockatoo Island;. Television: Zemiro; Mailman; Byrne; Hughes; Bickmore; Keller. Sport: Bolt; Maradona.	Art: Namatjira; Nolan; Rembrandt; Done; Roberts; **Quilty**; *Pollock*; *Bacon*; Monet; Glover. Literary: Courtenay; Woolf; *Grenville*; Malouf; Rankin; **DeLillo**; *Winton*; *Attwood*; Austen; Picoult. Heritage: Port Arthur; Sovereign Hill; Museum of Sydney; Acropolis; NMA; Cockatoo Island; Angkor Wat; Fremantle Prison; Ellis Island. Television: Byrne; Martin; Mailman; Kewell; Zemiro; Vautin; Keller; Chambers; McGuire; Sport: Norman; Tendulkar; Maradona; Laver; Ellis; Jackson; Bradman; Goodes; Nadal.

Asterisked items register a significance level of below 4.0 (t-test).

DIGITAL DIVIDES

Thirty-seven-year-old Charles and 18-year-old Harley illustrate some of the main points of convergence and divergence between Clusters 5 and 6 which they respectively represent. Charles used to work as a truck driver, but for the past several years has been unable to work due to a back injury. Harley works part time in a fish and chip shop, while studying at university.

Both men are interested in music, have broad tastes in television and are moderately engaged with sports including rugby league. Charles used to work as a DJ, and he enjoys listening to music from many genres and in many languages: 'It's relaxing. When I jump in the car, I just listen to it. I always listen to CDs and whatever is playing sometimes on the radio. I just like to play it just to relax.' Harley's musical preferences are more specific and more inclined towards emerging forms: he enjoys pop punk music, and likes to see pop punk bands playing live at a local venue with friends. Harley creates playlists of his preferred songs using the Spotify Premium streaming service, and says he likes most genres of music apart from mainstream pop music and country, but has little real interest in classical music.

Harley's frequent use of digital technologies exemplifies the differences that distinguish Clusters 5 and 6 and echo some broad generational divides. Harley's other favourite pastime shows this digital inclination even more strongly: if he has nothing else on, Harley will play multiplayer video games for around eight hours a day, mostly with a group of friends he knew from school.

With television, too, Harley and Charles demonstrate a differential access to digital options. Charles watches a wide range of Australian and American television programmes on FTA channels; he loves current affairs programmes, and watches comedies and sitcoms such as *Two and a Half Men* and *Seinfeld*. He used to watch the soap opera *Neighbours* as well, and occasionally watches programmes on NITV and SBS. Although he watches videos on YouTube, Charles does not have a pay-TV service, nor does he use streaming platforms to access media (his parents, who live nearby, have a satellite TV service to watch Arabic programming). But Harley finds that there is not a lot on FTA television that interests him, although he does watch *Top Gear* and *The Big Bang Theory*. While his family does not have cable television or Netflix, he often visits his friend to watch the Home Box Office (HBO) series *Game of Thrones*. Harley often watches videos on YouTube, including television series that have been uploaded to the platform.

Before his injury, Charles participated in a number of sports, and although he lives in Sydney he supports the Brisbane Broncos rugby league team. When they play in Sydney, Charles will sometimes go to see them play, and he watches their matches on television at home or at a pub. He admires former Broncos star Darren Lockyer. Harley watches major rugby league matches such as the State of Origin, and supports teams from Brisbane (where he lives),

Queensland or Australia but is not very knowledgeable about individual players. While admiring rugby league player Johnathan Thurston, Harley finds international sports stars like David Beckham, Usain Bolt and Tiger Woods to be 'a bit cocky I guess and overconfident'.

Charles and Harley have little interest in either literature or heritage. Charles does not enjoy reading books, and found reading hard at high school after moving to Australia from Lebanon. But he does write for his own pleasure occasionally, and uses the Notes feature on his smartphone to write personal statements as he works through his feelings about former relationships. Although Harley has been to galleries, museums and heritage sites with school trips, they are not particular interests of his now. His parents are of English descent, but Harley is 'not so interested in the heritage of where I am and my family. It's sometimes interesting, but it's not like I go out of my way to find out.'

Conclusion

Our purpose in this chapter has been to overview the relations between the Australian space of lifestyles and space of social positions. In doing so, we have incorporated clusters within the space of lifestyles as an economical way of presenting the forms of position-taking associated with different cultural practices and their relations to a range of social positions. It should go without saying that these clusters are artefacts of the analytical procedures we have used. It is partly for this reason that, in order to avoid reifying them, we have so far refrained from naming them, preferring to look closely at the clusters before proposing labels for them. Now that we have done so, it will be useful – in view of the issues we address in the next chapter – to christen our clusters. The labels we use for this purpose have been selected with a view to identifying the cultural orientations which most clearly distinguish the clusters. The labels and their rationales are as follows.

Cluster 1: Established High Cultural Orientations as evidenced by strong engagement with the more traditional forms of canonised culture.

Cluster 2: Alternative High Cultural Orientations as evidenced by strong engagement with later cultural forms which have a secured and widely recognised position as alternatives to more traditional forms of high culture, but with significant levels of engagement with emerging cultural practices also in evidence.

Cluster 3: Aspirational Middle Cultural Orientations as evidenced by the stronger participation in both established and alternative forms of high culture on the part of members of this cluster relative to Cluster 4.

Cluster 4: Conventional Middle Cultural Orientations to convey the respects in which the tastes and practices of this cluster are mostly poised between higher and more lowly ranked practices.

Cluster 5: Traditional Popular Cultural Orientations to capture the strong focus on sport and television, the conventionalism of arts and heritage tastes, and the negligible levels of engagement with established and alternative forms of high culture and even more middling ones.

Cluster 6: Contemporary Popular Cultural Orientations to capture the dual focus on both more contemporary forms of popular culture and some emerging cultural forms, and the lack of interest in or knowledge of both more middling and established high cultural practices.

While the principal differences in the social compositions of these clusters clearly consist in the ways in which they articulate relations of age and class, we have fought shy of following the suggestion of the GBCS and the ANUPoll on social class that 'emerging cultural practices' might constitute the basis for a new class. We have already rehearsed some of our reasons for this in Chapter 3: the paucity of the examples of such practices that are cited in support of the concept, and their limitation largely to the music and sport fields; an undue reliance on indicators of negative relations to traditional forms of high culture; and the lack of any evidence that the practices cited are validated by authorities of legitimation in ways that would enable them to function as cultural capital beyond narrow circles of devotees.[4]

It is the over-readiness to convert a particular set of youth/culture connections into a class or quasi-class position, however, that is for us the clincher. While our analysis in this chapter does confirm a connection between emerging cultural practices and youthfulness, this connection is evident, to different degrees, across Clusters 2, 3 and 6, where it appears in conjunction with different occupational classes and levels of education. This last point raises an issue already touched on in Chapter 3 but which merits further emphasis: the respects in which some of our occupational classes bring together people whose class trajectories are likely to diverge owing to their inclusion of significant percentages of students who are in part-time or casual positions. Respondents with incomplete tertiary studies account for 61 per cent of the 18–24 year olds and 34 per cent of the 25–34 year olds who are in part-time or casual work; these account for 70 per cent of all members of the sample employed on this basis. Those classes containing high percentages of these age groups – routine workers (23 per cent), semi-routine workers (40 per cent) and lower managers and professionals (41 per cent) – include many individuals whose class positions will differ from those of their current class compatriots as their educational-occupational trajectories develop. It is with these considerations and qualifications in mind that we move in the next chapter to use the labels we have proposed for our clusters in taking our analysis of the relations between culture and class beyond the categories of occupational class that we have relied on so far. In doing so we take our cluster analysis a step further by examining the relations between the clusters and the role that different cultural capitals play in distinguishing the trajectories of different class fractions.

Notes

1 The figures in Table 7.1 should be interpreted only as indicative of general tendencies given that the number of categories included in the MCAs for the different fields, and the methods used in constructing those MCAs, differ in a number of ways. The variations in the number of categories used are recorded in the third column of the table.

Depending on the needs of the data analysis, the MCAs were constructed either by using cultural practices as the active variables (the preferred alternative) or using socio-economic and socio-demographic variables as the active variables where the production of a space of lifestyles able to incorporate a larger variety of practices and tastes than would otherwise have been obtained was recommended.
2 Although *The Book Thief* was written by Markus Zusak, an Australian author, it is predominantly interpreted in Australia as an international bestseller which, in its main themes, has little connection to specifically Australian concerns.
3 See our earlier discussion of this point in Chapter 1.
4 The examples of emerging culture cited in the GBCS are liking fast food, liking rap music, being indifferent to classical music, being indifferent to heavy metal music, not going for a walk, liking vegetarian restaurants, being indifferent to jazz music, playing sport, taking holidays in Spain and watching live sport (Savage, 2015: 111).

8
CLASS AND CULTURAL CAPITAL IN AUSTRALIA

Modesto Gayo and Tony Bennett

In April 2018 the Australian Broadcasting Corporation (ABC) produced *Class Act*, a series of four podcasts which, while insisting on the reality of class in Australia, also asked why class had more or less disappeared from public discourse over the past 20 years.[1] Historian Stuart McIntyre, a contributor to the series, attributed this to the strong role played by what he called the egalitarianism of manners that permeates the mores of everyday life in Australia. While the political inscriptions and class associations of this egalitarianism have varied historically, McIntyre's purpose was to draw attention to the ways in which it is now most typically mobilised in denial of class, a denial that is frequently given a nationalist inflection in the claim that this ethos distinguishes Australia from status-ridden European societies, particularly the UK. Our project got caught up in this discourse through the interactive online quiz, *What Your Habits Reveal About Your Social Class*, that we produced with the ABC to go alongside its podcast series.[2] The quiz invited respondents to compare the relations between their literary, music and television tastes and their class positions, levels of education, gender and age with those evidenced by our survey data. The premise on which it was based – that class might divide Australians culturally – drew the ire of Australia's radio shock jocks. 2GB's Ben Fordham (20 April 2018) accused the ABC of 'green left propaganda' for trying to impose class on Australians ('We're not into class in this country'), bringing in Scott Cam, a TV personality included in our survey and in the ABC quiz, who protested that he regularly drinks at a bowling club where he, a multi-millionaire business man, and a 'wharfie' regularly drink side-by-side, just mates.

However much it might have been subdued in the 2000s, class did not, of course, entirely disappear from public discourse. There was, indeed, a marked heightening of its presence in the period immediately preceding our 2015 survey. With the Labor opposition being accused by the Coalition government of wanting to reignite the 'class wars' and Labor accusing the government of governing only for the 'top end of town', class was constantly invoked in the everyday vocabulary of political discourse even when its existence was being denied. This was reflected in 2013 in two contrasting public interventions on the topic: a historical overview of class-based inequalities in Australia and their persistence into the present in *Battlers and Billionaires* by Andrew Leigh, at that time a Federal Labor MP, and *The Lucky Country* by Nick Cater, a journalist for *The Australian*, Rupert Murdoch's flagship paper in Australia, and subsequently Director of the Institute for Public Affairs, a right-wing think-tank. Cater's purpose was to chart the rise of a 'new ruling class' in Australia. Drawing selectively on cultural capital theory for this purpose, he argued that the expansion of tertiary education had produced a new ruling political and intellectual class – nowhere more evident, he argued, than at the ABC – thereby promoting Bourdieu's 'dominated fraction of the dominant class' into the dominant class itself. It was equally notable that Cater, in developing this argument, made no reference to any contemporary Australian studies of class.

This was not entirely his fault. The subdued presence that class had in Australian public discourse in the 2000s was matched by its low profile in Australian sociology. The 1990s saw a number of significant engagements with class from a range of different perspectives: the historical work of Bob Connell and Terry Irving (1992), the Australian work (Baxter et al., 1991) that contributed to Erik Olin Wright's (1997) global class project and the first national cultural capital survey conducted outside France (Bennett et al., 1999). However, there has not been any major new sociological study of class in Australia since the 1990s.

The most notable sign of a revived concern with class in Australia was the publication, in 2015, of the findings of the ANUPoll on social class (Sheppard and Biddle, 2015a). Developed in partnership with the ABC, this survey drew on the methods used in the BBC's Great British Class Survey (GBCS). Findings from the BBC survey had begun to appear two years earlier (Savage et al., 2013), occasioning considerable controversy within British sociology.[3] Inasmuch as both projects engage with class by deploying the Bourdieusian categories of economic, social and cultural capital, they provide the most relevant point of contemporary comparison for our own engagements with class. The publication in 2014 of Thomas Piketty's *Capital in the Twenty-First Century* provides another point of contemporary reference. Piketty's work has lent a significant new inflection to debates about the relations between class and inequality in pointing to the re-emergence of the significance of inequalities of wealth relative to those based on income differentials. He has also highlighted the tendency – discernible since the neoliberal ascendency of the 1980s – for inequalities of both kinds to become increasingly polarised between an upper class of 2 to 3 per cent consisting largely of the owners of inherited capital plus new recruits into ascendant class positions represented by the CEOs of large corporations. Piketty also relativises the concerns of cultural capital theory by foregrounding the recentness of the significance accorded to income differences that are associated with different levels and forms of cultural capital. It was, Piketty argues, only during the 30 years or so of post-war welfarism, from the 1950s to the 1980s, that inequalities of income exceeded the significance of inequalities of wealth.

It was only in this period that mechanisms of inheritance and accumulation based on the home–education–occupation–class nexus assumed an importance rivalling the legal and taxation arrangements that secure the transfer of wealth assets across generations.

These three studies, then, provide the chief points of comparison that we shall use in order to highlight the distinctiveness of the approaches we take in this chapter in synthesising our findings in relation to class. We develop these in three main stages. First, we offer a detailed account of the relations between social class and cultural practices evidenced by our survey data. We do so by bringing together the patterns of class structuration associated with our six cultural fields in order to examine how these interact in the overall space of lifestyles reviewed in the previous chapter. We also look at the relations between economic and cultural capital in the composition of different classes. Second, while it is clear from our study, and indeed from the multiple studies that have been conducted in the wake of Bourdieu's *Distinction*, that class remains a key organising force for contemporary forms of sociocultural differentiation, it is by no means the only one.[4] Nor can its actions be properly understood without regard to the ways in which its composition is, so to speak, 'infiltrated' by other aspects of social position: age, education, gender and so on. We accordingly attend to these matters in some detail. In developing the third stage in the analysis of our data, we propose a distinctive methodological innovation by building on the cluster analysis developed in Chapter 7 to consider the light that the relations between our clusters and what we call 'cultural capital profiles' throw on the social trajectories and logics of inheritance of different class fractions. In concluding, we return to some of the comparative and historical questions we have opened up in this introduction by contrasting our methods and findings with those of the GBCS and the ANUPoll on social class.

Class in the overarching space of lifestyles: distinction in Australia

Our analyses of the different cultural fields and of the overall space of lifestyles demonstrate the crucial impact of occupational classes in shaping cultural divisions. In the overall space of lifestyles, occupational class is the variable most strongly associated with axis 1, and therefore the variable with the highest explanatory power in relation to this multidimensional Multiple Correspondence Analysis (MCA) space (see Figure 7.1). Both higher- and lower-level managers and professionals are intensely involved in a wide range of cultural activities (visiting museums, art galleries and heritage sites, high levels of reading and music participation) with a wide range of tastes (appreciating both crime books and literary classics) but with the most strongly marked preferences being for esteemed cultural practices (liking Renaissance and Impressionist paintings, arts television programmes, jazz and classical music). At the other extreme, routine workers exhibit low levels of participation in most of the activities we asked about, with positive tastes clustered around commercial television channels and popular television genres, sports, localised forms of heritage and figurative art genres. These effects of class are not, however, equally important across all of our fields: they are relatively muted in the heritage and, more especially, the sport and television fields.

Thus far the class categories that we have used have been those of the eight occupational classes derived by bringing together aspects of the occupational class codes used in the official statistics of Australia and the UK.[5] We now look at ways of taking these discussions further by considering how this eight-class schema might be compressed into a more limited set of classes, and how the classes produced by this exercise are marked by internal divisions associated with different cultural capital profiles. To this end, Figure 8.1 plots our eight occupational classes into the cloud of individuals. The individual members of each of these classes are grouped into ellipses around their mean points, marked by the class labels, thus demonstrating the extent to which individuals might 'deviate' from the class norm represented by those mean points. We are more interested here, however, in the division of this space into three groups of ellipses. The first comprises the three thicker black ellipses focused mainly on the left of the space and encompassing, as their statistical nuclei, lower managers and professionals, higher professionals, and higher managers and owners. These nuclei are all closer to one another in the space than they are to those for intermediate workers and the owners of small businesses and the self-employed, encompassed by the two lighter grey ellipses towards the centre of the space. And these in turn are closer to one another than they are to the nuclei of the lower supervisory and technical workers, routine and semi-routine workers encompassed by the three thicker black ellipses towards the right of the space.

We shall treat these groupings as the basis for our three-class model, referring to them, respectively, as the professional and managerial class, accounting for 48 per cent of the sample, the intermediate class (21 per cent) and the working class (28 per cent), with 3 per cent either having never worked or who did not include an occupation in their responses to our survey. These classes have been arrived at via a process which assigns a role to culture in their conception and definition in the respect that their differentiation arises principally from their positioning relative to one another across the left–right axis which is arranged principally in terms of degrees of cultural legitimacy and levels and forms of cultural capital. But we can also see the role of age in the composition of these classes in terms of their arrangement relative to the vertical axis, with the working class cleaving more towards the lower regions of the figure where the younger age groups congregate more than the other two classes. We note finally the high degree of overlap between the ellipses for the intermediate class and the professional and managerial class on the one hand, and between the intermediate class and the working class on the other, but also the much lower degree of overlap between the working class and the professional and managerial class.

In order to understand how these classes are 'infiltrated' by other social characteristics, Table 8.1 synthesises a set of cross-tabulations between these classes and a range of socio-demographic indicators. The professional and managerial class, which includes owners of large enterprises, is tilted towards the middle and older age cohorts, with only 4 per cent of its members in the youngest cohort – the

Class and cultural capital in Australia 151

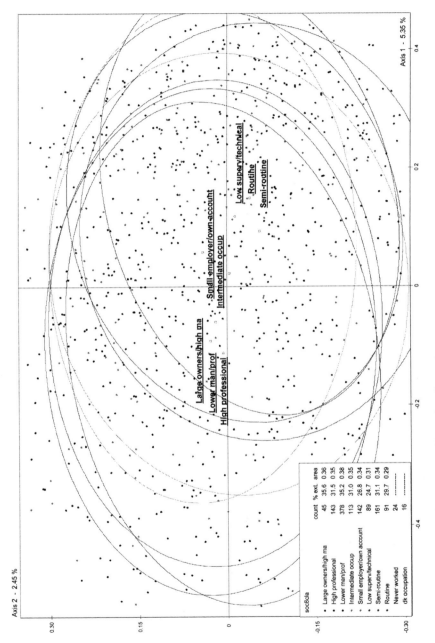

FIGURE 8.1 Class differences calibrated by cultural practices.

TABLE 8.1 Percentage of social class by socio-demographic characteristics

	Professional/managerial class	Intermediate class	Working class
Age			
18–24	4	7	16
25–39	28	27	28
40–59	40	37	32
60+	28	29	23
Education			
Some secondary	7	19	26
Secondary completed	8	21	22
Vocational training	11	21	25
Some tertiary	8	14	12
Tertiary completed	35	18	10
Postgraduate	31	6	5
Sex			
Men	46	44	58
Women	54	56	42
Educational field			
STEM	29	13	8
Humanities/Social Sciences	28	13	11
Law/Business	15	13	7
University			
Group Eight	17	4	4
Australian Technical Network	13	8	2
Non-aligned university	20	6	7
Region university network	6	6	2
Innovative research university	5	2	2
Place of residence			
Inner city	11	4	8
Suburban	51	40	47
Small town	19	25	19
Semi-rural	11	15	14
Rural/remote	8	16	12

One-hundred per cent by column for each socio-demographic variable.

lowest of all three classes. Its members are more highly educated than those of any other class: 35 per cent have completed tertiary education and 31 per cent are postgraduate, and overall 74 percent have had tertiary experience. It is quite a 'feminised' class, largely due to the strong female membership of the lower professional and managerial class. University specialisms are more frequently in the Science, Technology, Engineering and Mathematics (STEM) disciplines and the humanities and social sciences than in law or business studies; Group of Eight and non-aligned universities are the preferred tertiary institutions, followed by those in the Australian Technical Network. The members of this class are mostly city dwellers, congregating mainly in the inner cities (11 per cent) and suburbs (51 per cent) – more so than the other two classes. The distinctiveness of this class thus depends mainly on the high level of education of its members, acquired through Australia's most selective and/or prestigious universities at higher rates than the other classes – all of which are defining steps in their identities, as we will see below when we reflect upon the relations between cultural capital profiles and class trajectories.

The characteristics of the intermediate class are somewhere between those for the two other classes regarding most of the variables. The main exception is its gendered composition: the most strongly female at 56 per cent. Its members are also the least prone to live in suburban or inner city areas, being more likely than the members of the other classes to live in small towns, semi-rural or rural/remote areas. Fifty-six per cent do so against 38 per cent for the professional and managerial class and about 45 per cent for the working class. The strongest levels of educational attainment are those associated with secondary schooling and vocational training; there are notably lower levels of participation in Group of Eight universities, but little difference between fields of university study specialised in. The age composition of the class is similar to that for the professional and managerial class except for its larger recruitment from the 18–24-year-old cohort.

The working class is predominantly male and, of all three classes, has the largest proportion of its members, 16 per cent, within the 18–24-year-old cohort – a good many of these, as we have shown in Chapters 3 and 7, being tertiary students in part-time employment. Levels of education are the lowest of the three classes, with 47 per cent having only secondary schooling; vocational qualifications are the highest for all three classes. The majority of its members live in suburban or inner city areas but at a lower rate (about 55 per cent) than the members of the professional and managerial class (62 per cent).

The classes, then, differ markedly from one another in the other aspects of their social composition as well as in their occupational make-up. We should also note the close correspondence between the classes and the distribution of economic capital as measured by income, the value of businesses and properties owned, and the distribution of total savings, investments and the value of all other assets (excluding first home) across the three-class model (see Table 8.2). Using these measures, it is evident that there are significant differences between the social classes in terms of wealth. High managers and professionals are more likely to have annual household incomes over $100,000 (45 per cent), homes valued at over $600,000 (30 per cent)

TABLE 8.2 Class distribution of selected capital assets

	Professional/ managerial class	Intermediate class	Working class
Total annual household income over $100,000	45	32	18
Value of own business over $100,000	8	17	1
Own home's worth over $600,000	30	19	12
Capital invested (savings, bonds, shares, house contents, vehicles, land, second property) over $100,000	51	43	24

One-hundred per cent by column for each type of economic asset.

and a disproportionate level of capital investment over $100,000 (51 per cent). That only 8 per cent of this class own a business over $100,000 is partly explained by the majority of its members being high-level employees, while the intermediate class – which scores the highest on this indicator – includes the owners of small enterprises and own-account workers. Our survey, it is important to note, recruited relatively few owners of large-scale enterprises valued over $5 million (a little over 1 per cent). Finally, the working class is the least well off, scoring the lowest on all of the economic capital indicators, especially business ownership.

So much, then, by way of identifying the distribution of our three main classes across the space of lifestyles, and outlining the social characteristics which differentiate them along dimensions other than their occupational composition. We look now at the relations between these classes and the clusters discussed in the previous chapter.

Clusters and classes

Let us first recap the principles underlying the six clusters that we used to explore the properties of the space of lifestyles in Chapter 7. These clusters were produced using the individuals' coordinates for the first two axes of the overall space of lifestyles. Employed as a heuristic tool, their identification and 'naming' proved useful in interpreting different cultural orientations within the space of lifestyles as key markers of the processes of cultural differentiation shaping contemporary Australian society. The six clusters offer a range of different cultural orientations encompassing varying degrees of cultural involvement and engagement and the differential distribution of cultural practices across the temporalities of our cultural fields. We now take our analysis a step further by exploring the connections between these clusters and our three-class scheme through Table 8.3. This presents the clusters in the same order as their discussion in Chapter 7.

The distribution of the professional and managerial class across these clusters is distinctive in a number of ways. First, as we would expect from our discussion in

TABLE 8.3 Distribution of social classes across clusters

	Professional/ managerial class	Intermediate class	Working class
Established high cultural orientations (EHCO) (Cluster 1)	17	10	5
Alternative high cultural orientations (AHCO) (Cluster 2)	13	7	5
Aspirational middle cultural orientations (AMCO) (Cluster 3)	23	19	17
Conventional middle cultural orientations (CMCO) (Cluster 4)	20	16	13
Traditional popular cultural orientations (TPCO) (Cluster 5)	16	35	38
Contemporary popular cultural orientations (CPCO) (Cluster 6)	12	14	23
N	571	252	339

One-hundred per cent by column. The names of the clusters are given in the Conclusion to Chapter 7.

previous chapters, its members are the most inclined to exhibit high cultural orientations. Thirty per cent of managers and professionals – representing the most exclusive socio-cultural strata, combining economic and educational success – are involved in the two high culture clusters, the highest ratio for all of the classes. While this degree of difference from other classes is sharpest for the established high cultural orientation of Cluster 1 (17 per cent), this class also registers its distinctiveness, albeit less sharply, in relation to the alternative high culture orientation of Cluster 2 (13 per cent). Membership of the clusters embodying the aspirational (23 per cent) and conventional (20 per cent) middle cultural orientations is also highest among the professional and managerial class, though the degree of differentiation from both of the other classes is considerably less sharp than for the high culture clusters. It is only with the two popular clusters that the professional and managerial classes register lower rates of membership than the other two classes. Only 16 per cent contribute to the traditional popular cultural orientations cluster while just above 12 per cent are within the contemporary popular cultural orientations cluster.

Although most distinguished by their associations with high cultural orientations, then, the cultural practices and tastes of the professional and managerial classes span the relations between the high, middle and popular clusters. The 'middle' clusters concentrate 43 per cent of the class, and these, together with the high clusters, account for 72 per cent of the class. We can also see how a strong temporal dynamic arising from the place that different practices occupy within the temporalities of our fields informs both the high and popular cultural practices of the professional and managerial class. Its involvements in established high and traditional popular cultural orientations are accompanied by significant levels of involvement in alternative high and contemporary popular practices. In all these regards, our results show that there is a considerable diversity of cultural profiles within this class, sufficient reason for caution regarding over-generalising statements about class/culture relations at the higher end of the Australian class spectrum. There is a strong link between social positions (capitals, occupations) and cultural practices, but unless probed carefully this association can hide significant diversities.

The intermediate class is in between the professional and managerial class and the working class on all of the statistical indicators in Table 8.3. On the whole, it exhibits lower levels of cultural participation than those of the professional and managerial class and higher levels than those of the working class. But the balance is tilted towards greater similarities with the working class. Association with traditional popular cultural orientations is almost the same for both classes: 35 per cent for the intermediate class and 38 per cent for the working class. The association of the intermediate class with contemporary popular culture orientations is closer to that of the professional and managerial class at 14 per cent whereas that for aspirational middle cultural orientations is closer to that for the working class at 19 per cent. While association with the two middle clusters accounts for 35 per cent of the intermediate class, this is below the total rate of association with the two popular clusters at 49 per cent – again indicating a stronger pull towards the working class. This suggests that the two middle clusters operate as a diluted form of the two high culture clusters, which recruit the lowest levels of engagement (17 per cent) of the intermediate class.

The tastes and practices of the working class, finally, are strongly congregated in the two popular clusters, accounting for 61 per cent of the class made up of a 38 per cent association with traditional popular culture, and 23 per cent for the contemporary popular culture cluster. Affiliation to the aspirational middle cluster (17 per cent) is higher than that for its conventional counterpart (13 per cent). Association with the two high cultural orientations is notably low: 5 per cent for each of the established high and alternative orientations. Furthermore, if we consider the two sets of high culture clusters relative to the two middle clusters, the working class has the smallest percentage in the first set relative to its participation in all four high and middle clusters: 25 per cent (10 out of 40) compared to 33 per cent (17/52) for the intermediate class and 41 per cent (30/73) for the professional and managerial class.

The shaping up of social differences: class trajectories

In Figure 8.1 we saw that the differences between lower- and higher-level managers and professionals are relatively small, as are those between people in routine and semi-routine occupations, regardless of the level of routinisation or supervision, while the differentiation of those in intermediate occupations from the self-employed and owners of small enterprises is also relatively minor. We also saw that the differences between these groups of occupations were more significant than those within them. Our discussion of the relations between the three main classes we derived from this figure and our clusters has lent further support to this conclusion. In doing so it has confirmed the Bourdieusian thesis of a considerable degree of homology between cultural practices (knowledge, taste, participation) and the accumulation of capitals (economic and cultural). But it has left unanswered the questions we explored earlier regarding the internal fragmentation of these classes along lines which are not reducible to their occupational sub-divisions. It is to these questions that we now turn by revisiting Bourdieu's reflections on social trajectories. These have two dimensions. They refer, in one dimension, to horizontal movements from one form of capital to another – for example, coming from a wealthy family (economic capital) and becoming an intellectual (cultural capital). Our interest here, however, is in the vertical trajectories through which occupants of the same class positions are differentiated from one another by whether they have arrived there through upward or downward trajectories as measured by their different cultural capital profiles, and whether they are, so to speak, 'old settlers' or newcomers to the positions they occupy.

In order to engage with these questions, it was necessary to generate an indicator that would allow us to assess the effects of such movements. We explored a number of possibilities. Our variables on such matters as country of birth, Indigenous identification, ethnicity, place of residence and house owning proved unhelpful in this regard. The variable we finally constructed was arrived at by aggregating (and weighting) university field of specialisation with interviewee's, father's, mother's and partner's levels of education. This produced a continuous variable that was then recoded into an ordered categorical variable with three categories (an approximate third of the cases for each).

The conceptual rationale for this procedure was as follows. Father's and mother's level of education offers a measure of family origin as a key context for the generation of habitus related to different tastes, levels and forms of cultural practice. It also provides an indicator of class, as education and social class are strongly correlated. Taking account of both mother's and father's level of education provides a way of measuring differences between those members of our sample both of whose parents had tertiary education experience against those for whom this was true of just one parent. We also distinguished (with different weights) levels of education: those with incomplete or completed secondary education from those with incomplete or completed tertiary education, and both of these from those with postgraduate qualifications. This takes account of differential levels of achievement at school and university so that we could capture, for example, respondents from high-achieving family educational backgrounds which they had failed to match in their own educational careers. For those who have gone to university, we also took account of field of specialisation (STEM, humanities or social sciences, and law or business studies) as it is clear from our work on the fields that these are differentially associated with higher inclinations towards cultural participation, above all in the most distinctive practices. The last variable in the equation is partner's education, a measure of trajectory indicating whether or not a respondent's partner has a similar, lower or higher level of education.

Bringing all these variables together in a single composite variable allowed us to have a measure of different cultural capital profiles as aggregate indicators of trajectory from family background to current class position. A respondent who is high in every measure is considered someone who has a high cultural capital profile; a low cultural capital profile would be the contrary case. There is an intermediate category for those with more mixed trajectories who have medium cultural capital profiles. Table 8.4 summarises the distribution of the sample across these profiles. We aimed for these to be fairly evenly balanced, each profile accounting for roughly a third of the sample. We stress, therefore, that these measures have to be understood in relative terms; there are not any absolute or objective thresholds distinguishing the high, medium and low cultural capital profiles. That said, Table 8.4 shows that our respondents associated with different cultural capital profiles have very different social trajectories in terms of educational achievement.

With regard to respondents' level of education, the low and high profiles are mirror images of one another: the levels associated with the former are all secondary or vocational, with zero levels of tertiary participation, whereas the latter reverses this pattern except for marginal levels of vocational education. The medium profile shows a much more even distribution across all levels of education. Father's and mother's level of education suggest similar levels of parental influence with regard to the cross-generational transmission of educational advantage. Both parents are congregated in the secondary levels of education for those with low cultural capital profiles, and show similar low figures for tertiary education, but fathers are more prominent in relation to vocational education. There is no pronounced shift towards parents with tertiary levels of education on the part of those with medium profiles where the differences from the low profile are registered chiefly by the large percentage of respondents who do not know the level of their parents' education. The parents of those with high cultural capital profiles shift markedly towards tertiary educational accomplishments at roughly the same rates for mothers and fathers. With regard to field of specialisation, STEM and humanities and social science disciplines make the greatest relative contribution to the high cultural capital profile, followed by law and business studies. Humanities and social sciences contribute most strongly to the medium profile.

We look next (Table 8.5) at the relationships between these profiles and our clusters. These are positive. On the one hand, those with low cultural capital profiles are most strongly associated with the two popular culture clusters, totalling 52 per cent, a point between the levels of association with these two clusters registered by the working (60 per cent) and intermediate (48 per cent) classes in Table 8.3. The association of the low cultural capital profile with the two middle clusters is also significant at 38 per cent, but weak in relation to both the established (7 per cent) and alternative (3 per cent) high culture clusters.

Just as the tastes and practices of the intermediate class cleave more towards those of the working class than towards those of the professional and managerial

TABLE 8.4 Cultural capital profiles and educational trajectories

	Low cultural capital profile N: 379: 32%	Medium cultural capital profile N: 448: 37%	High cultural capital profile N: 376: 31%
Level of education			
Some secondary	27	18	0
Secondary completed	37	10	0
Vocational	35	15	0.3
Some tertiary	0	20	10
Tertiary completed	0	26	46
Postgraduate	0	11	44
Father's education			
Some secondary	47	27	22
Secondary completed	29	15	14
Vocational	15	16	9
Tertiary	8	9	25
Postgraduate	0.8	3	17
Don't know	0	31	14
Mother's education			
Some secondary	47	31	25
Secondary completed	36	19	21
Vocational	6	9	7
Tertiary	8	9	21
Postgraduate	3	3	16
Don't know	0	29	11
Partner's education			
Some secondary	19	13	2
Secondary completed	21	17	5
Vocational	15	13	6
Some tertiary	2	4	3
Tertiary completed	8	6	35
Postgraduate	0	7	31
Don't know	36	42	18
Field of specialisation			
STEM disciplines	0	17	40
Humanities/Social Sciences	0	24	35
Law/Business	0	12	27
Other	0	5	0.5
Don't know	100	43	0

TABLE 8.5 Percentages of lifestyle cluster by cultural capital profiles

	TPCO (5)	CPCO (6)	AMCO (3)	CMCO (4)	EHCO (1)	AHCO (2)
Low cultural capital profile	34	18	22	16	7	3
Medium cultural capital profile	28	20	15	17	11	7
High cultural capital profile	15	11	13	27	17	17
Total N	199	199	243	140	108	1202

One-hundred per cent by row. The brackets numbers identify the clusters referred to in Figure 7.5.

classes, so those with a medium cultural capital profile cleave more towards those with low profiles for both of the popular clusters. They are more divided with regard to the middle clusters: more akin to those with lower cultural capital profiles for the cluster of more conventional cultural orientations, and to those with higher profiles for the aspirational cluster. They cleave more towards the levels of association with the two high culture clusters exhibited by those with high cultural capital profiles: adding the percentages for both types of high culture clusters yields roughly double the figure for the low cultural capital profile (18 per cent compared to 10 per cent). Although falling significantly short of the equivalent figure for those with high cultural capital profiles (34 per cent), this difference underlines the significance of those class environments in which cultural capital is to some degree cultivated, functioning as a gradient that opens or shuts down windows of opportunity for people during their childhood, adolescence and young adulthood.

Our third profile includes those members of our sample whose parents, ideally both mother and father, had high educational qualifications, and who were therefore well equipped to negotiate the barriers of the school system, went on to pursue undergraduate and, in many cases, postgraduate studies at university, and ended up as the partner of someone with a similar history of educational achievement. This is the ideal or most extreme case of our category 'high cultural capital profile'. Only 26 per cent of those with this profile are involved in the two popular culture clusters, similar to the levels registered by the professional and managerial classes (Table 8.3), and around half of those registered by the low and medium cultural capital profiles at 52 and 48 per cent respectively. The high cultural capital profile is also associated with an engagement in 'middle culture', above all in its conventional type, which recruits 27 per cent of these respondents against only 13 per cent inclined to the aspirational middle cultural orientation. Most strikingly, as we could expect, the upper levels of educational accomplishment associated with this high cultural capital profile generate a very strong inclination in favour of high culture. Both the established and alternative high culture orientations recruit 17 per cent support, considerably greater than the levels registered by those with medium and low cultural capital profiles. We can see, then, that affiliation to the high culture clusters constitutes a way of 'being in culture' that is shaped through the interconnections between personal and family histories of educational accomplishment.

We would also expect these different profiles to be strongly associated with class position. Table 8.6 confirms that this is so. The members of the sample with low cultural capital profiles are most likely to be in the working classes (41 per cent). Those with a medium cultural capital profile are more evenly spread across the three classes, albeit most strongly associated with the professional and managerial classes (44 per cent) but not to the same degree as those with high cultural capital profiles (71 per cent). This takes us beyond a static understanding of class positions, allowing us to see how current patterns of occupancy of the different class positions are the product of past histories through which different class dispositions have been accumulated and transmitted across generations. These patterns show that social classes are not only an expression of inequalities today, but an indicator of markedly distinct individual and family trajectories: those who currently occupy different class positions are the products of family histories that did not intersect much in earlier periods – different histories generating symbolic boundaries that are not easily crossed. Our findings demonstrate how far individual trajectories are shaped not just by personal histories but also, and probably above all, by transgenerational mechanisms of class reproduction.

Up to this point in our discussion, we have emphasised the logic of time through the influence of parental background on the formation of class dispositions prior to any occupational achievement. If we consider parents' level of education as an indicator of class belonging, we can see that to a good extent our respondents' class position is a by-product of their parents' social class. Class produced by class through the relations between culture and education: a finding that clearly resonates with the tendencies that Bourdieu identified in the French case.

Internal fragmentation

We look finally at the light our data throws on internal class divisions by bringing our classes, cultural capital profiles and clusters into the same space. The correspondence analysis that generated Figure 8.2 shows a well distributed association between combinations of class position and cultural capital profiles and the six

TABLE 8.6 Percentages of social class by cultural capital profiles

	Professional/managerial class	*Intermediate class*	*Working class*
Low cultural capital	28	27	41
Medium cultural capital	44	21	32
High cultural capital	71	15	11
Total *N*	571	252	339

One-hundred per cent by row.

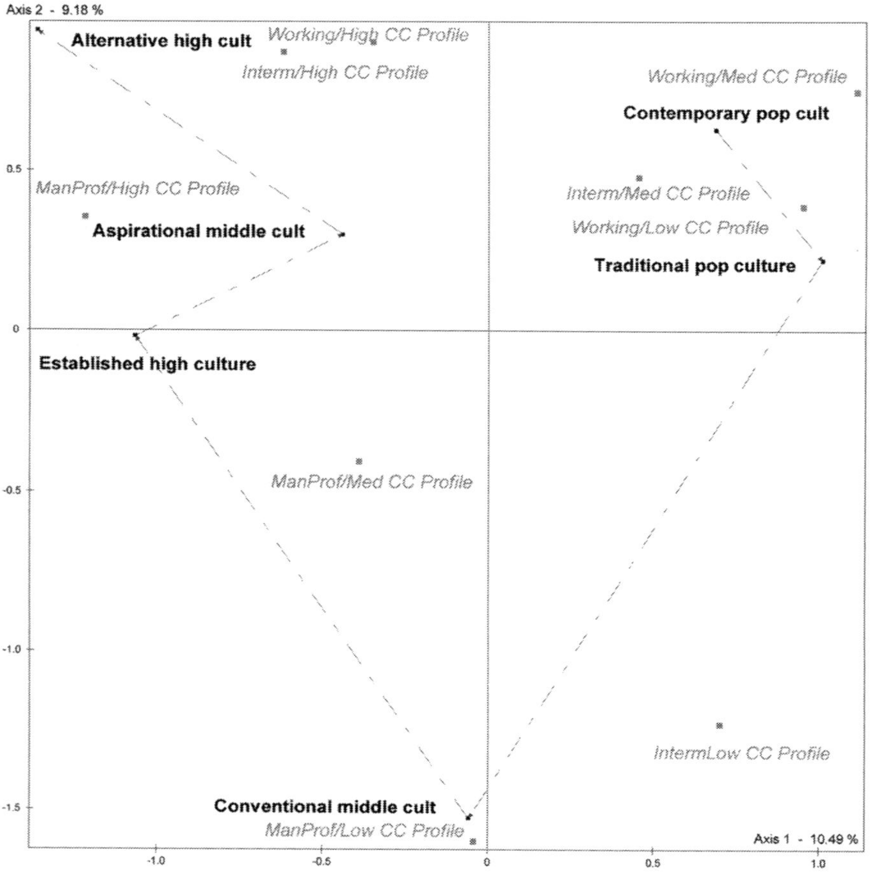

162   Modesto Gayo and Tony Bennett

```
Axis 2 - 9.18 %
                Alternative high cult    Working/High CC Profile
                                         Interm/High CC Profile
                                                                    Working/Med CC Profile
                                                                  Contemporary pop cult
  0.5
        ManProf/High CC Profile                          Interm/Med CC Profile
              Aspirational middle cult                   Working/Low CC Profile
                                                                Traditional pop culture

   0
              Established high culture


                                ManProf/Med CC Profile
 -0.5


 -1.0


                                                                        IntermLow CC Profile
 -1.5          Conventional middle cult
                ManProf/Low CC Profile                                  Axis 1 - 10.49 %
         -1.0         -0.5          0            0.5           1.0
```

FIGURE 8.2 Correspondence analysis of cultural capital profiles, classes and lifestyle clusters.

'CC profile' means cultural capital profile. All the labels with 'culture' in them refer to 'cultural orientations'.

lifestyle clusters. The sections of the working classes with low or medium cultural capital profiles are closest to the two popular culture clusters in the top right of the figure. While there is not much difference between them in this regard, the sections of the working class with low cultural capital profiles cleave more closely towards the traditional popular culture cluster. By contrast, the sections of the intermediate classes with low or medium cultural capital profiles are far apart from one another: while the latter is strongly associated with the two popular culture clusters, the former is located towards the bottom right of the figure where it is closer to the strong association that managers and professionals with low cultural capital profiles have with the cluster of conventional middle cultural orientations.

This suggests a set of tastes that cross different class boundaries different from those proposed by the thesis of the cultural omnivore which focuses on the fondness for both high and popular cultural forms among those in high class positions (Peterson and Kern, 1996). Our findings rather show that shared tastes across classes are more significant in relation to conventional middle cultural forms on the part of those members of the professional and managerial and intermediate classes with low cultural capital profiles. These are questions that are looked at more closely in the next chapter.

We also see significant differences within the professional and managerial class. While all sections of this class are located at a considerable distance from the popular culture clusters, they take up different positions in relation to the other clusters: prone towards the conventional middle cluster where low cultural capital profiles are in play, the sections of the class with medium profiles are most strongly associated with the established high cluster. Members of the professional and managerial class with high cultural capital profiles are most strongly associated with the two high culture clusters, especially the established high culture cluster and the aspirational middle culture. Perhaps the most interesting aspects of the upper left section of the figure, however, are the respects in which it suggests that established forms of high culture are being challenged by the commitment to alternative forms of high culture on the part not only of sections of the professional and managerial classes but also those sections of the working and intermediate classes with high cultural capital profiles. There are, no doubt, variable personal histories behind these combinations of high cultural capital profiles with working and intermediate class positions, including histories of downward mobility, failed social reproduction or lack of occupational achievement on the part of class members with high levels of education. However, recalling that the alternative high culture cluster also includes emerging practices, it is likely that these shared cross-class preferences include the tastes and practices of the younger sections of the three classes, particularly those who are either in part-time routine or semi-routine employment while completing their tertiary studies or in the early stages of their professional or managerial careers. This suggests not a weakening of the relations between culture and inequality in contemporary Australia but their ongoing transformation through the challenge that is presented to established forms of high cultural capital as the rival power of alternative forms of cultural capital operates more effectively among new and impending entrants to higher class positions.

Conclusion

In media presentations of the findings of their ANUPoll, Sheppard and Biddle, while stressing the respects in which their evidence refutes myths of Australian classlessness, nonetheless confirm that 'true to expectations ... Australia does have a flatter social structure than Britain' (Sheppard and Biddle, 2015b: 1). They base this assessment on the fact that while using the same methods as the GBCS, those of latent class analysis, the evidence of the ANUPoll suggested that Australia has only five classes (established working, middle and affluent classes, a mobile middle class and an emergent affluent class) compared to the UK's seven classes (an elite, both an established and a technical middle class, a traditional working class, new affluent workers, emergent service workers and a precariat). They stress the absence, in their findings, of the two most sharply polarised classes – the elite and the precariat – as evidence that 'our social classes are more inclusive than their British counterparts'.[6] The conclusion is incautious in failing to register a significant difference in the methods of the two studies. If a precariat did not show up in the ANU survey, the same was true of the initial GBCS survey where it registered at only 1 per cent alongside the 2 per cent registered by the traditional working class. In this respect, both surveys reflect the limitation of cultural capital surveys that we have already noted in relation to our own survey, and one which Skeggs pithily identifies in her review of the GBCS, noting that members of the working classes have little motivation for engaging with evaluative classification systems given their experience of being constantly assessed as valueless (Skeggs, 2015).[7] It was only a subsequent survey with a controlled sample that, by boosting the membership of these two categories to 15 and 14 per cent respectively, provided the basis for the GBCS seven-class model. By contrast, the original GBCS survey, reflecting the social characteristics of BBC audiences, recruited 22 per cent of its sample from the elite. With a sample of only 1200 and lacking the tilt towards the occupants of higher class positions that would have been produced had it been administered by the ABC, the ANU survey, like our own, was limited in its recruitment of working-class respondents and was too small to recruit significantly from the uppermost echelons of the class structure.

We draw attention to these considerations by way of underscoring how methodological decisions can result in significantly different interpretations of similar data in ways that play into the perpetuation of national mythologies. Silva (2015) touches on this in asking how, given that the questionnaire for the GBCS was derived from that of the earlier *Cultural Capital and Social Exclusion* (CCSE) project, which identified three main classes (a professional-executive class, an intermediate class and a working class), the UK's class structure could have changed so significantly over the intervening seven-year period, from 2003–2004 to 2011, to generate seven classes. While some things had changed as the effects of the UK's post-global financial crisis (GFC) austerity regimes were beginning to be felt by 2011, what had changed most were the methods of data analysis used between the two studies. While following the Bourdieusian tradition in deriving classes from the relations between economic, social and cultural capitals, both the GBCS and the ANU study departed from that tradition in eschewing the relational principles of MCA for those of latent class analysis. The effect, as Bradley (2014) notes in relation to the GBCS, was to effect a misleading alignment between cultural capital theory and the traditional concerns of British stratification theory in interpreting classes as strata laminated on top of one another and thereby converting class into a scale which ranks individuals in terms of their possession of different degrees of economic, social and cultural capital.

It is for these reasons that we have resisted the temptation, born out of engagements with UK stratification theory, to interpret classes as a series of stratification orders arranged gradationally, one on top of the other, at the expense of attending to the more fluid processes through which different classes – and, within classes, class fractions – mark themselves off from one another. This was always a defining feature of Bourdieu's work, reflected in his reluctance to put forward a fully elaborated theory of class, preferring instead to highlight the respects in which cultural capital was connected to economic, social and status divisions between different socio-professional groups. This aspect of Bourdieu's work played a key role in his distinguishing, within a broadly based tripartite class schema, different class fractions reflecting divisions within the major classes that took the form of competitive struggles over the significance to be accorded different kinds of capital, rather than vertical stratification orders. This was the basis for his distinction between the new and the old petite bourgeoisie, for example, or that between professionals and managers, as the dominated fraction of the dominant class, and the bourgeoisie proper. This procedure also allowed the role of other considerations – of gender and age, for example – to be factored into the constitution of such class fractions. These are the processes we have adopted in this chapter by examining a complex set of relations between the different fractions of our three main classes in ways that have taken account of their varying aged and gendered compositions, and the significance of the cultural capital profiles we have identified when considered in their relations to variable cultural orientations as indicators of the social trajectories that illuminate the position-taking of different class fractions.

There is a further methodological issue at stake here, one that has implications for the question of Australian exceptionalism with which we started this chapter. It concerns the manner in which we have derived our main classes from the grouping of the ellipses for our eight occupational classes into three distinct sets. While there are some differences, these classes – the professional and managerial, the intermediate and the working classes – are broadly the same as those arrived at, by using similar methods, in the CCSE study. This finding differs from that produced by an earlier comparison of the CCSE findings with those of the Australian Everyday Cultures (AEC) study discussed in the Introduction. Applying the same methods to the two data sets, this comparison identified not three but four main classes in Australia: manual workers, white-collar workers, employers/managers and professionals. In seeking to explain these differences, the authors of the study in question conjectured that the joint size of the two classes occupying the middle of the space (white-collar workers and employers/managers), accounting for two-thirds of the sample, suggested a weaker social differentiation of the Australian population relative to the UK (Bennett et al., 2013). It was also suggested that the separation of professionals from managers and employers, who were in turn located closer to the working class, might suggest a relatively weaker role in Australia for those forms of cultural capital derived from legitimate culture. It now seems far more likely that these differences derive from the different occupational classificatory schema used in the two studies: Australia and New Zealand Standard Classification of Occupations (ANZSCO) for the AEC study and National Statistics Socio-economic Classification (NS-SEC) for the CCSE study. Our conversion of the ANZSCO codes into categories compatible with the NS-SEC schema via the Standard Occupational Classification 2010 (SOC2010) (see Appendix D) has yielded a much more compatible set of findings.[8]

None of this is to suggest that there are no distinctive aspects to the organisation of class relations in Australia. The scale of income inequalities that is articulated across the relations between classes is not as extreme as in many countries, most notably the USA, but is on a par with the UK, Canada and New Zealand and higher than most north European countries. Inequalities of wealth are significantly less marked than in the USA and behind the levels exhibited by most European countries.[9] There are also significant differences in the status order in Australia and its connections with class relations; the absence of a landed aristocracy has undoubtedly had long-term historical consequences in this regard. These differences do not, however, amount a class structure of a substantially different kind from those in evidence in other advanced economies.

Nor would we wish to place too much emphasis on the differences between the positions we have taken and those adopted by either the GBCS or the ANU class project. For the reasons we indicated at the start of this chapter, these two studies provide the closest comparative points of reference for our work, and if we have underlined the methodological differences between our approaches this should not detract from areas of shared concern. These include the significance accorded to age and its relationship to the positioning of cultural items within the temporalities of cultural fields. More important, perhaps, is the emphasis that the GBCS study and a significant commentary on Piketty's work by Savage (2014) have placed on the changing relations between, on the one hand, the mechanisms of inheritance and accumulation that operate through the home–education–cultural capital–occupation nexus and, on the other, those for the inheritance and accumulation of wealth that operate through the relations between the legal and tax systems. Savage's key point here is that while Piketty's work on wealth inequalities throws crucial light on the changing relations between the top 10 per cent of the population and the rest, it has relatively little to say about the significance and modes of operation of divisions within the remaining 90 per cent of the population. It therefore neither displaces nor rivals the light that Bourdieu's focus on the relations between cultural capital, occupationally linked income differentials and lower levels of wealth differentiation throws on such matters. At the same time, Savage recognises the challenge Piketty's work poses in requiring that the traditional sociological gaze focused on the relations between the middle and working classes needs to be turned upward to explore the mechanisms of social closure, institutional power, symbolic rituals, residential separatism and opulent forms of cultural consumption of the super wealthy and broader elites.[10] In subsequently reflecting on his *Capital in the Twenty-First Century*, where he pays little attention to Bourdieu's work, Piketty stresses the parallels and connections between his work and Bourdieu's.[11] 'The future structure of inequality', as he puts it, 'might bring together extreme forms of domination based simultaneously on property and culture (in brief Marx and Bourdieu reconciled)' (Piketty, 2014: 474).

We make these points by way of noting the need to place our findings in a broader context to provide a more rounded assessment of the dynamics of class and inequality in contemporary Australia. A report published by the Australian Council of Social Service in 2015, the year our survey was in the field, usefully illuminates those aspects of class and inequality that our survey did not reach. With regard to income, while noting that income inequalities, although above the Organisation for Economic Co-operation and Development (OECD) average, were not as extreme as in the USA, the report notes that they had increased significantly over the 25 years to 2010, with real wages increasing by 14 per cent for those in the bottom 10 per cent of income groups compared to 72 per cent for those in the top 10 per cent of income groups, who also benefitted from a doubling of investment income over the 2004–2010 period. With regard to wealth, while Australia had, after Switzerland, the second highest level of median wealth in the world, its distribution had become more unequal, increasing since the GFC by 28 per cent for the top 20 per cent of wealth holders but by only 3 per cent for the bottom 20 per cent. A report by the Evatt Foundation, published in the same year, also found an increasing concentration of wealth in the top 1 per cent of the population (Sheil and Stilwell, 2016). While these are only impressionistic snapshots, the analysis accompanying them is equally important. Both reports argue that if inequalities in the early post-war period in Australia had been held in check by a range of measures: a distinctive system of wage regulation, progressive income taxes, universal access to public education, good social security safety nets – these have all since been considerably weakened through a range of measures – tax concessions for the rich, a greater freeing of labour markets from the fetters of wage regulation, cuts to social security budgets and the increasing privatisation of education. All developments which suggest there is nothing exceptional to the measures through which the dominant classes in Australia pursues their interests. Except, perhaps, in what is, by international standards, one of the most distinctive aspects of the tax regime that has prevailed in Australia since 1978. The absence, over this period, of any inheritance or estate taxes, has played a key role in the accumulation of increasing wealth inequalities and looks set to do so well into the future.

Notes

1 www.abc.net.au/radionational/projects/class-act/.
2 www.abc.net.au/news/2018-04-13/what-your-habits-reveal-about-your-social-class/9610658.
3 See especially Bradley (2014) and the response by Savage *et al.* (2014). See also the papers collected in the special issue of *Sociological Review* 63 (2015).
4 Inspired by *Distinction*, other studies focused on countries beyond France have reinforced his findings: Bennett *et al.* (2009) on the UK, and also Bennett *et al.* (2013) in a comparison between the UK and Australia, Purhonen and Wright (2013) on Finland and also the UK, Ariño (2011) on Spain, Gayo *et al.* (2009; 2013; 2016) on Chile, Rosenlund (2017) on Norway and Gayo *et al.* (2018) comparing more than 20 countries from different areas of the world, as illustrative studies. They all show how influential social class is in the structuration of patterns of cultural practice (knowledge, taste, participation) as always one of the variables with the highest level of explanatory power.

5 See Appendix D for details.
6 Sheppard and Biddle do not infer from this that there is no elite – they put it at 1 per cent – or that precarity is non-existent in Australia.
7 Savage and his co-authors are fully aware of this difficulty and use it in productive and imaginative ways in presenting their findings (Savage, 2015: 11–16).
8 They also reflect that the coding of the AEC data drew more on the class categories of Erik Olin Wright's work – which was influential in Australia at that time – than on Bourdieu's socio-professional categories: see Woodward and Emmison (2015).
9 These assessments regarding the relative rates of income and wealth inequality in Australia are taken from Daley et al. (2019: Figure 2.1).
10 See Friedman and Laurison (2019) for an effective bridging of elite studies and the more usual middle-class focus of cultural capital theory.
11 Where he does draw on Bourdieu, it is only in relation to the significance of elite schooling in mechanisms of reproduction at the highest levels of the class structure (Piketty, 2014: 486).

9
THE MIDDLE SPACE OF LIFESTYLES AND MIDDLEBROW CULTURES

David Carter

This chapter examines what we can term the middle space of lifestyles, that is, the range of cultural preference and practices that falls between and/or combines 'legitimate tastes' and 'popular tastes', in Bourdieu's terms (2010: 8). Even where such terms are questioned, sociological studies of culture and social stratification continue, perhaps inevitably, to be organised around hierarchies of cultural items ranged on a scale from high to low, with analysis focused on the binary relation between 'higher' and 'lower' taste or participation profiles. But such hierarchies also call forth a middle ground, typically less easily defined or socially fixed than the extremes on either side, and relatively neglected in sociological studies despite Bourdieu's leads. The majority of cultural profiles will almost always fall somewhere 'in between', both empirically and as an artefact of survey methodologies, but while an intermediate space might be acknowledged there has been little work analysing the middle range in its own right.

More problematically, sociologists have also called on the language of 'highbrow', 'lowbrow' and 'middlebrow', despite its origins in the polemics of mid-twentieth century culture wars, and, further back, in the pseudoscience of phrenology. The terms always carry the potential to distort interpretations given their 'hidden' histories and the negative connotations they bear, although for the most part they are deployed simply as convenient shorthand for the hierarchies of legitimation existing in a particular time and place, understood in relational rather than essentialist terms. As Bellavance (2016: 326) writes: 'sociological debate focuses on the distinction between highbrow and lowbrow genres because it represents a principle not only of classification, but also, and most importantly, of hierarchisation and legitimisation'. But here, too, the middle, even when named as 'middlebrow', remains largely unexamined (cf. Friedland *et al.*, 2007; Stewart, 2010; Atkinson, 2017). Cultural sociology has been little interested in the middlebrow as concept or cultural formation, tending to use the term loosely with connotations left unstated.

Elsewhere, however, a vibrant field of middlebrow studies can be identified (Carter, 2016b). Although located primarily in literary-cultural and historical studies, it has engaged extensively with Bourdieu's accounts of the field of cultural production and *la culture moyenne* (Bourdieu, 1993; 2010).[1] The notion of capitals has been less explicit, but many studies suggest that the accumulation or exercise of cultural capital is a defining aspect of middlebrow culture (Radway, 1997). The present chapter will draw on this literature, partly to avoid the problems posed by the term's casual use, but more importantly to assist in analysing the cultural tastes revealed in the middle of the space of lifestyles. We return to the data presented in earlier chapters but with a specific focus on the contours and dynamics of this middle space and its relation to key socio-demographic factors. We will define the middlebrow as a particular configuration of tastes and practices within a broader intermediate space: not simply 'in between' or falling short but a cultural formation 'with its own distinctive modes of production, dissemination and consumption' (Driscoll, 2014: 43).

The middle space of lifestyles

Before discussing this scholarly literature further, we return to the overall space of lifestyles examined in Chapter 7, and in particular to the multi-field chart plotting genre preferences (Figure 7.3, reproduced below as Figure 9.1), a significant indicator of the distribution of cultural tastes across the middle space. Here the densest concentration of positive responses falls in the marked middle space on both vertical and horizontal axes, to the immediate right but especially to the left of the vertical dividing line, the 'inner left' as it is termed in Chapter 7. Further right, non-engagement/dislikes are dominant: for Impressionism, Renaissance and abstract art; classical and light classical music; almost all book types; TV arts, drama and documentary; migrant and Aboriginal heritage; and most sports. Likes are restricted to commercial television stations, reality and sports TV, country music, landscapes and portraits, family and homeland heritage, and rugby league. By contrast, the extreme left-hand side, or outer left, is dominated by positive tastes in the art, music and literary fields, especially for the more prestigious or 'learned' genres of classical music, Impressionism, literary classics, modern novels, contemporary Australian novels and Indigenous books; and for Aboriginal and migrant heritage, the Australian Broadcasting Corporation (ABC), Special Broadcasting Service (SBS) and TV arts programmes – selective rather than omnivorous tastes. Dislikes are registered for certain popular or *déclassé* genres including dance music, still lifes and, among younger respondents, easy listening and landscapes.

Between these two spaces lies the crowded and mixed middle space. The line marked on the Multiple Correspondence Analysis (MCA) chart should not be taken as indicating a precise line of demarcation but rather a 'border zone' between the middle space and those either side of it, which can be located here, for example, by the relative positioning of likes and dislikes for key genres. Jazz, for instance, registers positively on the boundary between outer and inner left but negatively on

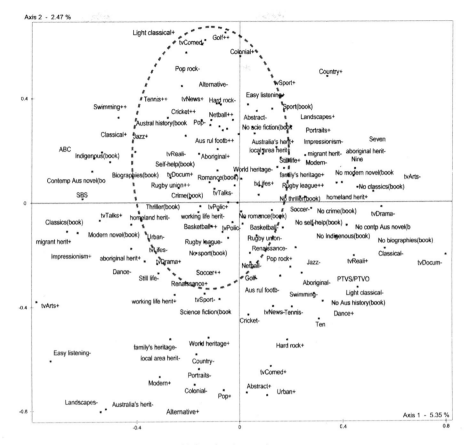

FIGURE 9.1 The middle space of lifestyles (genres).

the right-hand side; this is true for biographies, too, though with less vertical separation. Renaissance art and still lifes also span the middle space, but with likes and dislikes in inverse positions. These divisions suggest a border zone on the left where certain legitimate and 'near legitimate' genres appear: light classical, jazz, biographies, modern novels, and Renaissance art towards the bottom. To anticipate our later discussion, this is where we might locate the middlebrow insofar as it is defined by an orientation towards established cultural forms alongside a mix of respectable and popular tastes appearing nearer the centre: Australian history, crime fiction, self-help/lifestyle books, thrillers and sci-fi/fantasy (lower down); Aboriginal art; and TV news, documentaries and drama.

The left-hand boundary of the middle space might thus be imagined as extending down in the space between likings for light classical and Renaissance art; the right-hand boundary, similarly, as extending down in the space between the likings for colonial art and still lifes. While sport registers significantly across the middle space – except for rugby league, appearing much more to the right – *dislikes* for sports, perhaps surprisingly, are clustered to the immediate right of the vertical divide. The positive items in this border zone are relatively few: still lifes, Australian and local heritage, sports books, lifestyle TV, easy listening and pop/rock. Both the liking and disliking for romance fiction and TV police shows sit close to the vertical dividing line, suggesting limit cases in 'middlebrow' tastes for popular forms.

Between these border zones, the middle space itself is divided internally in terms of the volume of positive engagements and the configuration of preferences. The greater proportion of positive tastes and their concentration in genres with some level of established prestige pulls the 'middle' to the left of the vertical dividing line, while the effect of age pushes it towards the top two-thirds of the chart, separating older preferences for established forms from younger preferences for the contemporary or alternative (cf. Figure 7.1). Positive responses for certain popular genres, such as crime and thriller fiction, appear close to the more prestigious forms on the left of the chart; even romance falls within the middle space. Their positioning supports the arguments of Chapter 2 regarding the increased standing of genre fiction alongside the ongoing prestige of books and reading.

The left-hand bias is even stronger for participation (Figure 7.2), with high levels of engagement in a range of art, literary and classical musical events/institutions in the outer left. In the inner left, participation is concentrated in more accessible or domestic forms such as public art galleries, bookstore browsing and book ownership, conventional 'quality' TV and musicals. Heritage, in particular, reveals strong national and local affiliations in the middle space, where cultural engagement is often conducted within the domestic sphere or, when public, in places accorded national significance. There is a clear separation between Australian and local heritage to the right and Aboriginal heritage to the left of the middle space (Figure 9.1).

A similar distribution is revealed from a different perspective if we focus on named cultural items rather than genres. Figure 9.2 charts the relative positions of likes and dislikes for individual artists, authors, TV programmes, and musical performers, composers and compositions. Again the densest space of likes and dislikes is found in the middle third of the chart, to the left of the vertical dividing line and in its top two-thirds. Here we find a strong concentration of the most established items, if not always those with the highest aesthetic standing; but equally a left–right spread in terms of prestige across items including *The Mikado*, Namatjira, *Midsomer Murders*, *Rhapsody in Blue*, 'Nessun Dorma', Nolan, *Phantom of the Opera*, Courtenay, Austen, Rembrandt, da Vinci – and *Dark Side of the Moon*, lower down. Likes and dislikes are equally present. Indeed, *many* dislikes for authors and artists appear here, for Quilty, Bacon, Malouf, Grenville, Rankin, Ai Weiwei, Preston, Moffatt and Caravaggio, among others. But they appear mostly from the centre to the left of the middle space, indicating that a certain level of cultural capital is necessary for engagement with such figures, whether the response be positive or negative; likes and dislikes were recorded only for those who had heard of the named individuals.

We can also use Figure 9.2 to emphasise the different configurations of the fields represented. Television scarcely appears to the left of centre, although a cluster of respectable Australian and British programmes, such as *Midsomer Murders* or

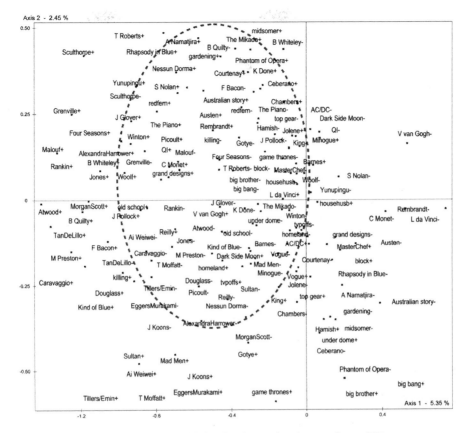

FIGURE 9.2 The middle space of lifestyles (named artists, authors, TV programmes, musical performers, composers, compositions).

Australian Story, registers positively in the inner left, programmes disliked in the lower right. Television preferences are less widely distributed than those for the other fields, although distinctions of quality and specialised tastes are still evident. Literary preferences show an inverse pattern: with very few exceptions – Courtenay and King; Winton and Woolf – likes and dislikes are both located from the centre of the chart to the outer left (where likes predominate). Music is similar, although more strongly 'centred'. Artistic preferences, finally, are the most widely distributed and strongly distinguishing, with a much clearer pattern of more exclusive or specialised tastes on the left, likes for named artists disappearing near the vertical dividing line and a strong pattern of dislikes on the right.

In the middle space we thus find a mélange of esteemed cultural markers and mainstream tastes among 'minor works of the major arts' and 'major works of the minor arts' (Bourdieu, 2010: 8): light classics, crime fiction and *The Mikado*, alongside *Phantom of the Opera* or *Dark Side of the Moon*. But this mixing does not suggest cultural omnivorousness or a radical mixing of elite and popular forms. Rather, the diversity of tastes and participation is contained within the field of the familiar and esteemed, including what we might call the 'popular classics', while its internal organisation largely follows conventional judgements of worth. If the patterns revealed do not suggest any singular hierarchy of tastes, neither do they disturb widely accepted relations of value. Less conventional tastes are found towards the bottom of the chart – for avant-garde artists on the left, modern art, alternative music and world heritage in the middle, and Pop and abstract art, hard rock and urban music towards the right – indicating how, with younger tastes, divisions between old and new or contemporary and classical cut across the high/low binary (Bellavance, 2008; Glevarec and Pinet, 2017).

Such analyses underscore the inadequacy of any simple high(brow)/low(brow) polarity. While there is a relatively clear boundary on the right between popular tastes and no or low engagement, there is a larger 'transition zone' to the left of this, an extensive space of overlaps between high- and middle-status preferences. As suggested, this is where we can locate the middlebrow, while cultural forms requiring rarer forms of symbolic mastery or connoisseurship – from *Kind of Blue* to Caravaggio, from Ai Weiwei to *Mad Men* – are located to the left of the middle space. The inadequacy of the broad notion of 'popular' culture is similarly highlighted. As their relative positions on the MCA charts reveal, there is little in common between tastes for such 'popular' items as Jodi Picoult, *Mad Men*, *Game of Thrones*, hard rock or rugby league.

Further perspectives are provided by the cluster analysis introduced in Chapter 7. While the two middle clusters, Cluster 3 (Aspirational Middle Cultural Orientations) and Cluster 4 (Conventional Middle Cultural Orientations), share certain 'middling' tastes, the *differences* between them are far more striking. The small group of shared preferences (liking light classical music, Courtenay, Roberts, Monet and Rembrandt, plus dislikes for Woolf) contrasts with a much larger number of divided tastes. Landscapes, colonial art, Port Arthur, Uluru, Gurrumul Yunupingu, *Gardening Australia*, 'Nessun Dorma', *Midsomer Murders*, *Rhapsody in Blue* and a range of TV and sporting personalities register positively in Cluster 4 but negatively in Cluster 3. The opposite is the case for TV comedy, hard rock, pop and alternative music, sci-fi/fantasy, Whiteley, *Dark Side of the Moon* and King. Over 80 items appear (as likes or dislikes) in only one cluster, suggesting very different cultural worlds. For Cluster 3, likes are at once 'higher' and more accommodating of contemporary popular forms, celebrities and series such as *Game of Thrones* or *Under the Dome*. Dislikes are concentrated, above all, on 'specialised' literary/artistic tastes (Scott, Rankin, Atwood, Koons, DeLillo, Caravaggio, *The Four Seasons*), alongside sporting celebrities and a few commercial pop culture items (dance music, *Big Brother*). Cluster 4 is more conventional in its likes, more nationally oriented, more engaged with television and less accommodating towards popular-commercial forms. Both likes and dislikes fall within the range of familiar genres/individuals: portraits, colonial art, Nolan and Ken Done, Austen, easy listening, *Phantom of the Opera* and respected heritage sites. AC/DC and *Top Gear* are rejected on one side, abstract art and Malouf on the other.

These relational patterns make it impossible simply to identify the two middle clusters as part of a unified 'middlebrow' culture. Middlebrow scholarship invites us, rather, to attend to the overlaps between high and middle profiles. Although rankings differ, there are significant preferences shared between Cluster 1 (Established High Cultural Orientations) and the middle clusters, especially Cluster 4 (Conventional Middle Cultural Orientations). Thirty items are shared between Clusters 1 and 4, including light classical and classical music, Monet, Namatjira, Rembrandt, Roberts and *Rhapsody in Blue*. At the same time, while tastes split on only nine items, these are almost all high culture items registering positively for Cluster 1 but negatively for Cluster 4 (Malouf, Sculthorpe, Woolf, Whiteley, Quilty), indicating the limits of this shared 'middlebrow' space.[2] The chart representing the relative positions of the clusters (Figure 7.5) also shows that Cluster 4 overlaps significantly with Cluster 1 but not at all with the more contemporary tastes of Cluster 2 (Alternative High Cultural Orientations). How might these patterns be read in the light of scholarship on the middlebrow?

The middlebrow: rhetoric and scholarship

The long-standing notion that culture exists in a hierarchy of high to low gained its distinctively modern sense of crisis towards the end of the nineteenth century in response to the rapid expansion of new forms of commercial entertainment and their publics. The term 'highbrow' emerged in the last quarter of the century, connoting professional expertise, intellectual distinction or cultural refinement. Its pejorative connotations arose in the early twentieth century as the term became attached first to the newly imported concept of 'the intelligentsia' and then, most potently, to artistic modernism. 'Lowbrow' appeared as its necessary opposite, always a loaded term, manifesting the progressive differentiation between 'sacralised' and 'vulgar' forms of culture (Levine, 1998).

'Middlebrow' emerged in the mid-1920s. While largely polemical, the term did articulate major transformations in the cultural field driven by the simultaneous presence of high modernism and mass commercial culture, and by the emergence of new institutions for cultural diffusion aimed at those 'who are hoping that some day they will get used to the stuff they ought to like', or so *Punch* declared of the BBC's new 'middlebrow' audience (*Anonymous*, 1925). New forms, including radio, recordings and fashionable magazines, made restricted tastes accessible to a broader public, with new cultural intermediaries enabling and guiding that access (Rubin, 1992; Doane, 2009). As Q. D. Leavis (1932: 24) put it, 'middlebrow taste has … been organised'.

While such institutions often expressed Arnoldian cultural ideals, 'middlebrow' became a byword for the commercialisation of culture and lack of discrimination taken to be symptomatic of a deeper malaise in modern civilisation. In what amounted to a struggle between competing claims to legitimacy, the brow hierarchy derived much of its potency from its apparent homologies with class divisions. It offered a powerful means for making social distinctions through cultural hierarchies based on the apprehension not just of different tastes but of fundamentally antagonistic values. Most threatening to elites was not the frankly vulgar but the middlebrow's pretensions to quality and good taste, its mixing of values that ought to be kept separate. For while the cultural field seemed increasingly divided, its proper boundaries could also appear increasingly blurred. In Woolf's (1942: 180) memorable words:

> The middlebrow is the man, or woman, of middlebred intelligence who … saunters now on this side of the hedge, now on that, in pursuit of no single object, neither art itself nor life itself, but both mixed indistinguishably, and rather nastily, with money, fame, power, or prestige.

The project of contemporary middlebrow studies is not merely to analyse such rhetoric but to restore the middlebrow to cultural history as a distinctive domain of values, practices and institutions with ongoing manifestations (Driscoll, 2014). A range of authors excluded from the modernist canon have been reclaimed in terms of their 'middlebrow modernity', especially female authors (Humble, 2001; Botshon and Goldsmith, 2003); so too influential commercial magazines, often directed at women or middle-class readers (Hammill, 2007). Institutions such as the Book-of-the-Month Club, and more recently Oprah's Book Club, mass reading events, literary festivals and book prizes, have been analysed through the framework of the middlebrow as accessible, mediatised modes of engagement with legitimate culture (Radway, 1997; Fuller and Rehberg Sedo, 2013; Driscoll, 2014: 45–82).

The history of middlebrow culture in Australia has been addressed in parallel ways, with a particular focus on the 1920s–1960s (Carter, 2013; Kuttainen *et al.*, 2018). Less attention has been paid to more recent manifestations, although again the Australian case seems to parallel what has been seen internationally as a resurgence of middlebrow culture since the 1990s (Carter, 2013: 149–152; Driscoll, 2014), due in part to the relative weakening of distinctions between high and popular culture through the marketisation of legitimate cultural forms and the legitimation of certain popular genres. While Collins (2002: 7) has differentiated the 'popularisation of elite cultural pleasures' from the middlebrow per se, the latter is by no means merely residual. The burgeoning of such phenomena as reading groups, television book shows, screen adaptations, blockbuster exhibitions, 'opera in the park' and literary or movie festivals indicates both old and new forms of middlebrow cultural investment.

Turner and Edmunds (2002) deploy the vocabulary of brows in a sociological analysis of cultural preferences among members of Australia's post-war elite. The baby-boomer professionals interviewed show little interest in high culture forms such as opera, ballet or literary classics and display instead 'distinctly middle to lowbrow tastes' (219). This apparent 'distaste for taste', Turner and Edmunds conclude, indicates both generational and local Australian influences: the predominance of 'mass consumer culture' (225) for this generation and the influence of a 'deeply rooted populist ethos' (235) in Australia. The generational explanation is the more persuasive; a populist ethos may be popular but its sociological significance is easily exaggerated. Indeed, at this general level, the Australian case does not seem exceptional.

On one level, Turner and Edmunds's findings match those of the *Australian Cultural Fields* (ACF) survey, in that it is difficult to identify any 'pure' high cultural elite within the dominant class. Our lower-level professionals and large owners/high managers do indeed express 'a taste for middlebrow culture' (227), while serious engagement with high cultural activity is much rarer. But such a result is already present in *Distinction*, where Bourdieu separates different fractions of the bourgeoisie in terms of capital composition: commercial employers whose tastes are middlebrow in many respects; higher education teachers 'who have very high competence even in less consecrated areas, such as cinema'; and Parisian versus provincial professionals, the latter with 'the most banal preferences of middlebrow taste' (Bourdieu, 2010: 261). The very point of the 'aesthetic disposition' is its rarity. Turner and Edmunds do not consider capital composition or class trajectories; and their use of 'brow' labels implies much clearer distinctions than are helpful for analysis.

Certainly we might now anticipate a looser blending of high and middlebrow interests than in 1960s France, as Friedland *et al.* (2007) have argued for the United States (they define 'middlebrow' as 'the phenomenon of gaining access to high culture only after it has first been mediated by mass culture', 35). But this loosening is not incompatible with a thoroughly hierarchised distribution of cultural capital, as their analysis and the ACF data demonstrate; nor do Turner and Edmunds challenge such a finding. Indeed, their own results suggest a *high* middlebrow profile among their respondents (alongside some 'lowbrow' pleasures): tastes for authors like Orwell or Steinbeck, for Booker Prize winners, for Beethoven, Mozart, *Schindler's List*, *The Kiss of the Spider Woman*, Italian and Asian food, and visiting theatres, museums and art galleries. While all are accessible forms, and while the interviewees seem little interested in distancing themselves from other social groups through their cultural preferences, such a constellation of tastes is still 'distinguishing' as middle class, still present as cultural capital. Further, the ACF data does reveal more exclusive tastes for both established and alternative cultural forms, coinciding with higher levels of education and higher-level professional occupations, partly overlapping with the 'middle' but in quite different configurations.

The breadth of middlebrow scholarship makes it difficult to offer any singular definition of the term. It cannot be defined as an essential quality of artefacts or persons: there is nothing essentially middlebrow about *The Four Seasons*, for example, but the term would describe many occasions for its consumption in contemporary society. At the same time, products and institutions *can* be created expressly for middlebrow tastes. Driscoll usefully offers a grid of recurrent characteristics. While none is exclusive to the middlebrow, their coincidence suggests a distinct middlebrow formation, 'middle-class, reverential towards elite culture, entrepreneurial, mediated, feminized, emotional, recreational and earnest' (Driscoll, 2014: 17–43).

Other scholars have also identified certain modes of consumption as characteristically middlebrow. Radway (1997: 283–284) uses the term 'middlebrow personalism' to describe a mode of appreciation that foregrounds empathetic engagement with books, reaffirming the person but also 'their capacity for identification', for 'connection and communion'. Thus even as it resists elite seriousness whether academic or avant-garde, and even where pleasure is paramount, middlebrow consumers take culture seriously as a form of 'purposeful recreation' involving projects of self-education, 'personal growth and moral redemption' (Driscoll, 2014: 40); a 'discipline of leisure' that encourages the 'taste of reflection' (Doane, 2009: 166–167). Such values can be discovered in a wide range of artefacts, hence the generous spread of middlebrow tastes, but there are always distinctions to be made, against the 'cheap' and sensational, the artificial or obscure.

The modes of appreciation thus described match closely certain of those revealed in the ACF interviews, especially those in the literary field (Chapter 2), but also in the appreciation of landscapes, say, against abstract art, through modes of personal connection (Chapter 1). The individuals presented in Chapter 7 are also revealing, with art field preferences emerging as more 'distinguishing' than the middlebrow literary tastes described. For Jacinta, Holly and Brooke, for example, we can discern a preference for certain accessible instances of legitimate culture, allowing the kinds of engagement described above and sustaining a degree of 'reverence towards elite culture' – within limits.

Class and *la culture moyenne*

Bourdieu's relatively neglected account of *la culture moyenne* can be read productively alongside middlebrow studies despite its very different provenance. Bourdieu's model both identifies and produces a space of lifestyles located in the intermediate, petit-bourgeois position in the class hierarchy. *Distinction* (2010: 8) projects 'three zones of taste which roughly correspond to educational levels and social classes': legitimate, popular and, in between, middlebrow taste (*le gout 'moyen'*). A similar structure is proposed in *Photography: A Middlebrow Art* (Bourdieu, 1990b), with photography positioned alongside cinema and jazz among those cultural forms not yet fully legitimised. While the middlebrow per se is not given extended analysis, practices of photography associated with amateur photographic clubs or with aspirations beyond those of domestic photography define the form's middling status.

Elsewhere, the middlebrow appears in Bourdieu's accounts of artistic production. In its relation to the market, middlebrow culture is scarcely distinguishable from mass culture; but it also resembles art for art's sake in being 'produced by highly professionalised intellectuals and artists [and] characterised by the same valorisation of technique' (Bourdieu, 1993: 127). Thus, even though they prioritise technique for 'effect' rather than as form for its own sake, middlebrow works can present 'formal characteristics predisposing them to enter into legitimate culture' (128). Bourdieu insists that the notion of an 'average' culture is fictitious outside the meanings conferred by specific modes of consumption and intermediation, for the 'same object which is today typically middlebrow – "average" (*moyen*) – may yesterday have figured in the most "refined" constellations of tastes and may be put back there at any moment' (Bourdieu, 2010: 327). If the petite bourgeoisie can 'make "middlebrow" whatever it touches', this is wholly an effect of its position in social space 'determining [its] relation to legitimate culture'.

Bourdieu's model of the field of cultural production organised around the binary of autonomous versus heteronomous spheres has been widely influential, so much so that his extended analysis of cultural consumption in the intermediate space is largely overlooked despite the fact that precisely because of its intermediate position it might best illustrate the dynamic relations between class and the hierarchy of legitimacies. Bourdieu's characterisations of *la culture moyenne* often anticipate those of more recent middlebrow scholarship, and sometimes recall much earlier Anglophone commentaries (Lynes, 1949).

For Bourdieu, the key term defining the petit-bourgeois relation to culture is 'cultural goodwill' (*la bonne volonté culturelle*): its reverence for the legitimacy of the legitimate culture to which it aspires but for which it lacks the cultural capital to possess fully or 'naturally'.

> This middlebrow culture owes some of its charm, in the eyes of the middle classes who are its main consumers, to the references to legitimate culture it contains and which encourage and justify confusion of the two – … accessible works which pass for avant-garde experiments, film 'adaptations' of classic drama and literature, 'popular arrangements' of classical music or 'orchestral versions' of popular tunes … in short, everything that goes to make up 'quality' weeklies and 'quality' shows, which are entirely organised to give the impression of bringing legitimate culture within the reach of all, by combining two normally exclusive characteristics, immediate accessibility and the outward signs of cultural legitimacy.
>
> *(Bourdieu, 2010: 321)*

A range of middle-class registers for the historical middlebrow have been offered, from the lower-middle class in Britain to the professional-managerial class in America. Despite the differences, each analysis identifies a rising class fraction 'whose social position [is] based on its command of cultural and intellectual capital, on a certain acquaintance with the cultural tradition and a measure of specialised knowledge and expertise' (Radway, 1997: 295). For these middle-class consumers, set apart from labour by their educational and professional qualifications, middlebrow institutions repeat the lesson that culture is linked to social and personal distinction and that this can be acquired, not just through inherited cultural capital, but through discerning consumption and (often self-directed) learning.

Bourdieu's account of petit-bourgeois cultural orientations shares this dynamic but also includes established and declining trajectories. His object is not to define middlebrow culture, but rather to map the distribution of petit-bourgeois dispositions, both synchronically, through comparing upper, middle and lower strata, and diachronically, through comparison of older and newer class fractions. Bourdieu identifies differences in this intermediate space according to capital composition. In terms of educational qualifications, for example, he locates primary teachers and certain members of the 'new petite bourgeoisie', such as cultural intermediaries and social service workers, above technicians and junior executives according to cultural capital possessed, followed in turn by the traditional petite bourgeoisie (Bourdieu, 2010: 341). Translated to the occupational categories used in the ACF study, this hierarchy corresponds to lower professional-managerial occupations, overlapping with intermediate and lower supervisory/technical, but above small employer/self-employed. Cultural knowledge and preferences *within* the petit-bourgeois class are thus unevenly distributed according to capital composition, while increasing age tends to 'the most traditional or conservative ethical or aesthetic dispositions' (341) in an opposition linked to rising and declining class fractions.

Adapting Bourdieu's model to contemporary Britain, Atkinson (2017) distinguishes within the dominant class between a culturally well-endowed fraction with relatively modest levels of economic capital (cultural producers/intermediaries, academics, teachers[3]) and another fraction where economic capital is dominant (business executives). In between are those with 'balanced' capital profiles, including the traditional professions, distinguished by capital volume from white-collar workers just below. The intermediate class, in turn, is divided according to capital composition: a cultural fraction, highly feminised in terms of its typical occupations (nurses, counsellors, media workers); an economic fraction (lower managers, proprietors, self-employed); and, in between, technicians and administrators. This breakdown again suggests that the dynamics of the middlebrow are located not simply in the intermediate space but distributed across the cultural fraction of this class and those of the dominant class most dependent on cultural capital. While specific tastes may overlap with those where economic capital is dominant, their configuration differs markedly.

In Figure 7.1, the middle space of lifestyles discussed above corresponds closely to that which extends from the mean point for lower professional-managerial to that for intermediate occupations, embracing large owners/high managers, with high professionals just to the left. Still, there is a significant gap between the lower professional-managerial and intermediate points on the chart, with the latter to the right of the vertical dividing line alongside small employers/self-employed and routine occupations. In terms of education, 'tertiary completed' falls within the middle space, with 'postgraduate' to the left. The right-hand side is less clearly delimited, but some level of post-secondary education appears to be characteristic of the middle space. Women are centrally located; men closer to the less culturally engaged right-hand side. The middle space is also predominantly middle aged, concentrated in the 45–64 age group. This cluster of characteristics – middle aged, predominantly female, well-educated and primarily in lower professional-managerial or intermediate occupations – closely resembles the social locations of the middlebrow identified in recent scholarship and Bourdieu's identification of *la culture moyenne* as distinctively petit-bourgeois. But while Bourdieu asserts a distinct petit-bourgeois habitus, his final insistence is upon the contrasting trajectories that define this space, for its 'system of dispositions takes on as many modalities as there are ways of attaining, staying in or passing through a middle position in the social structure [that] may be steady, rising or declining' (2010: 339; Carter, 2016b: 358–359). The intermediate social space is a structure of 'mobile crossing-points' (Bourdieu, 2010: 344) where all the variables of age, occupation, social origin, educational attainment and cultural capital come into play in a series of 'ordered yet partially disordering' (344) differences and correspondences.

Bringing together these perspectives and the ACF analyses presented above, it is clear that despite compelling homologies between taste profiles and social class positions it makes little sense simply to identify the middlebrow as *the* petit-bourgeois or middle-class habitus. Here Bourdieu's *moyen(ne)* does not translate neatly into 'middlebrow'. To illustrate further, we can draw on the analyses based on the three-class model deployed in Chapter 8, which reveal a high degree of overlap in terms of cultural practices between those in the intermediate class and those on either side, the professional-managerial and working classes (Table 8.3).[4] Indeed, the professional-managerial class is the most strongly represented in the cultural orientations captured in the two *middle* clusters, at 43 per cent, compared to 35 per cent of the intermediate and 30 per cent of the working class. And while almost half the intermediate class are represented in the two popular clusters, a significant minority (17 per cent) figure in the high cultural clusters. Thus, while the intermediate class is closer to the working class in its cultural orientations across all six clusters, it also overlaps significantly with the professional-managerial class, and the differences between classes are smallest in the mid-range.

There are, then, no simple homologies between class position and cultural profiles. Rather, the middle space reveals overlapping and divided cultural orientations and class fractions, in a manner that recalls Lahire's argument that between the 'small intellectual fractions of the dominant classes' and the 'educationally most deprived members of the working classes' – the two groups with the 'most homogenous (least dissonant) cultural practices and preferences' – the 'majority of members of the upper, middle and working classes have in common the heterogeneity of their never perfectly consonant cultural profiles' (2016: 316). The intermediate class is divided internally between a smaller cohort oriented towards established high cultural tastes and a larger cohort oriented towards traditional or contemporary popular cultural forms. Similarly, the professional-managerial class is divided between one fraction, almost 30 per cent, with more consistently high cultural preferences and another *larger* fraction whose cultural orientations fall within the middle range.

These patterns are matched by the analysis of trajectories of class formation based on cultural capital profiles (Table 8.5). A significant percentage of those with high cultural capital profiles (40 per cent) register in the mid-range clusters: a higher percentage, indeed, than for those with medium cultural capital profiles (33 per cent). We should also note that 38 per cent of those with low cultural capital profiles appear in these middle range clusters, especially its aspirational form, in contrast to those with high or medium profiles who figure more strongly in the conventional middle. Nineteen per cent of those with medium cultural capital profiles figure in the high cultural spheres. The middle clusters, in short, contain those with high, medium and low cultural capital profiles, while those with medium cultural capital profiles are divided in their cultural orientations.

The correspondence analysis of class trajectories and lifestyle clusters (Figure 8.2) offers another perspective. Close to the middle of the inner left space, we find the professional-managerial class with medium cultural capital profiles, located between the two middle clusters but in closer proximity to the established high culture cluster. The aspirational middle cluster is located closest to those in working-class and intermediate positions with high cultural capital profiles. The conventional middle cluster, by contrast, appears alongside those in the professional-managerial class with low cultural capital profiles. The professional-managerial class, then, if not its fraction with the highest cultural capital profiles, is that most strongly identified with 'middling' cultural preferences. The positioning of the other class and capital profiles, however, recalls Bourdieu's account of multiple trajectories crossing the middle space rather than a merely complacent acceptance of high cultural or 'high commercial' norms, as is often implied.

Conclusion

These diverse mappings suggest the middle space of lifestyles has an identifiable structure on both horizontal and vertical axes, more clearly distinct in fields where traditional cultural legitimation is most powerful, and strongly determined by level of education, occupational profile and age. Middlebrow tastes will be found across the class spectrum but are most strongly aligned with the lower professional-managerial class, overlapping with higher professionals to one side and intermediate occupations to the other. Lower professional-managerial occupations mean that the middle space is closely aligned with tertiary education, middle age and with women's preferences. Large owners/high managers also fall within this range, but to the right of the lower professionals. Analysis does indicate a 'minority' space of exclusive preferences for established or modernist high cultural items (plus enthusiasms for alternative contemporary forms among younger respondents); but the more extensive cluster of 'high middlebrow' tastes and engagement we have identified will also function symbolically as legitimate culture, with the power of distinction. We can interpret these positions in terms of capital composition: cultural capital matters most for those in professional-managerial occupations where it can confirm social distinctions and/or compensate for a relative lack of economic capital; but also, if occupational status is lower, where it will need to be (l)earned.

The middle space is also divided internally, between older and younger cohorts and different orientations towards established versus avant-garde and mainstream popular versus niche cultural forms. The framework of the middlebrow forces us to disaggregate the popular into a range of very different established, emerging and specialist tastes. It reveals degrees of eclecticism, but little evidence of omnivorous profiles. Rather than the radical collapse of hierarchies of legitimation separating popular and high, we find a modest blending of tastes in the border zone between high and middle cultural profiles. The orientation towards established high culture preferences in the latter is where we find the middlebrow as a distinctive cultural formation: a particular cluster of tastes and practices within a much broader intermediate space, positioned 'above' the *moyen* or merely average, and defined by the distinctions it makes within both high and popular forms. The concept of the middlebrow thus helps foreground the capital dynamics captured in these overlaps and divisions and in their social locations and trajectories. It renders the middle space as something more than residual; rather, as a series of 'ordered yet partially disordering' differences and correspondences.

Notes

1 The translation of Bourdieu's terms remains an issue, one the translator of *Distinction*, Richard Nice, acknowledges by regularly supplying the original French terms, *un art moyen* and *la culture moyenne*, in brackets after the use of 'middlebrow'. The French terms are broader than the English and less historically marked as neologistic; they suggest a 'middle' or 'average', without the pejorative connotations of the English term. See Pollentier, 2012; Carter, 2016b: 357–358.
2 For Clusters 3 and 4, six items are shared and 24 divided (liked in one, disliked in the other); for Clusters 1 and 4, 30 items are shared and nine divided; for Clusters 1 and 3, 16 items are shared and 20 divided. In this sense, Clusters 3 and 4 are least like each other, Clusters 1 and 4 most like each other.
3 'Teachers generally have slightly lower economic capital than other subcategories of the cultural dominant but possess ample cultural capital … In field terms they are positioned outside of (i.e. they do not contribute to the struggles within), even if they are fundamental guardians of (and links in the chains of symbolic power emanating from) the fields of intellectual and cultural power.' (Atkinson, 2017: 18).
4 The 'intermediate class' in the three-class model used in Chapter 8 is not identical to the 'intermediate occupations' defined in the eightfold division of occupational categories (see Appendix D).

PART III
Capitals

Introduction

In this part of *Fields, Capitals, Habitus*, we move from the examination of individual fields in Part I, and the larger consideration of class and the overall space of lifestyles in Part II, to the roles and distribution of cultural capital in specific institutional or social settings. This part of the book is also where we give specific attention to the evidence provided by our boost samples of Australian and Torres Strait Islander people and different migrant communities, and interviews with a selection of their participants, to explore whether and to what degree these testify to the operation of specific forms of cultural capital similar to, or in conflict with, those which have a more general currency among Australians overall.

The use of the term 'capital' is very deliberate in Bourdieu's work, and conceptually rich in its application. It enables the concepts of cultural capital and social capital to be understood precisely in relation to capital in its more familiar economic sense. Like economic capital, they too can be inherited, acquired, accumulated, invested and exchanged. High levels of cultural knowledge and familiarity can be converted into economic advantage, for example, which can then be reinvested in cultural acquisitions or forms of accreditation. Such exchanges will always be more open to some individuals or groups than others and to some forms of cultural capital more than others; and certain forms of cultural capital will be more highly valued in particular fields (Bourdieu, 2010: 119–126). As our previous chapters show, there is no single scale of capital across all fields or for all sections of the population; and yet occupational class and level of education, intersecting with gender, geographical location, family heritage and age, among other factors, continue to define a significant role for forms of cultural capital with the power of social distinction.

'Cultural capital' is perhaps the most widely used of the key concepts in Bourdieu's sociology. Indeed, in recent decades, the term has been extended to a wide range of contexts and new forms of (cultural) capital – national, cosmopolitan, subcultural, multicultural, Indigenous, ethnic, intellectual and emotional capital among them. This multiplication of capitals proves the salience of the concept even as it risks diluting the key dynamics of Bourdieu's arguments in a looser sense of 'cultural resources'. Our analyses reaffirm the importance of Bourdieu's specific uses of the concept and his emphasis on the interrelations between cultural, economic and social capitals in determining class positions and trajectories.

Our analyses also reaffirm Bourdieu's emphasis on the role of education, both formal, within schools, universities and other credentialising institutions, and informal, above all within the home and family, where cultural knowledge or 'insidership' can be acquired as a kind of inheritance. Bourdieu pays particular attention to the relations and differences between these contrasting forms or moments of cultural capital acquisition: early or late, formal or informal, credentialed or auto-didactic (Bourdieu, 2010: 73–81). Inherited cultural capital offers kinds of knowledge and dispositions that are both recognised and rewarded in the education system, not just through disciplinary competence but also in implicit or embodied relations to culture. Such cultural capital can be converted into educational capital in the form of academic qualifications, a 'guaranteed' form of cultural capital in its own right, but one which will often guarantee much more in terms of cultural capital than the disciplinary qualification itself, such as an individual's standing as an educated or cultured person (Bourdieu, 2010: 20). As such, it can also facilitate the acquisition or investment of social capital, through access to networks of influence and recognition. For those with lower levels of 'inherited' cultural capital, as suggested in the introduction to Part II, the education system offers the principal means of its acquisition, but one where the unequal distribution of such capital remains powerful.

Chapter 10 thus examines the role of the education system in the reproduction or reduction of class-based social inequalities, not least in the context of a significant expansion of higher education in Australia. By examining fathers', mothers' and partners' educational levels, it also attends to the issue of class trajectories. Despite the expansion of higher education, the results indicate that educational capital remains very unevenly distributed, with those in managerial and professional occupations across a range of age groups more likely to have higher qualifications, to have attended the more prestigious universities and to be qualified in the more prestigious fields such as medicine and law.

The chapters following shift the focus from the relations between cultural capital and occupational and educational hierarchies to less familiar, but no less critical dimensions of capital distribution in contemporary societies – and especially settler-colonial and immigrant societies like Australia. Taking Greater Sydney as its case study, as a major cultural metropolis, Chapter 11 maps the spatial distribution of cultural capital across the city's different urban and suburban zones. It does so in the context of contemporary arguments over the apparent rise of urban cosmopolitanism in major 'creative cities' globally. Chapter 12 turns to an issue at once national and international in examining Indigenous cultural tastes and capitals, a question that has received little attention in previous studies but one where Australia's history is comparable to other settler-colonial societies. It explores correlations and differences between Indigenous responses and both the main sample and the Italian, Lebanese, Chinese and Indian boost samples, and the critical role that gender, tertiary education and professional-managerial occupations play in differences within the Indigenous cohort. In doing so, it reveals a more complex story than the narrative of cultural deficit common in representations of Indigenous Australians.

The other major issue connecting the Australian case to international comparisons is its history of immigration and status as a 'multicultural nation'. The final chapter in Part III analyses different patterns of cultural participation and consumption between the *Australian Cultural Fields* main sample and the Italian, Lebanese, Chinese and Indian boost samples, as well as comparing results across the ethnic samples. While ethnicity emerges as a major point of distinction in certain instances, these are always crossed by differences between the overseas-born and Australian-born, between older and newer histories of migration, and between different educational and occupational outcomes. These patterns argue against any simple notion of ethnic 'taste cultures' or of a uniform cosmopolitanism.

10

THE PERSISTENCE OF INEQUALITY

Education, class and cultural capital

Megan Watkins

The relationship between education and the reproduction of social inequality has long been a focus of sociological enquiry but it is in the work of Bourdieu where it has perhaps been most assiduously documented. From his early collaborations with Passeron in *The Inheritors* and *Reproduction in Education, Society and Culture* through to his own *The State Nobility*, Bourdieu has shown a close association between levels and forms of educational attainment and social class, proffering the notion of cultural capital to explain why these differences occur. From Bourdieu's perspective, education makes little inroad into the differential distribution of cultural capital. Rather, he saw systems of schooling and higher education (HE) as playing a key role in sanctioning this disparity by giving legitimacy to socially marked forms of knowledge and limiting education's promise of social mobility. With an almost forensic attention to empirical detail, Bourdieu mapped these reproductive tendencies demonstrating that neither the universal availability of schooling nor greater provision of HE has had any appreciable impact in countering this inequality. Instead, he argues, it has simply resulted in a credentialing spiral further disadvantaging those from the dominated classes or alternatively funnelling them into less prestigious institutions and course offerings, upping the stakes to maintain the advantage of the dominant. Data derived from the *Australian Cultural Fields* (ACF) survey confirms these findings and, importantly, allows for an examination of how more recent attempts to improve the representation of students of a low socio-economic status (SES) within Australian HE has similarly had little effect.[1] By plotting the educational attainment of respondents of various age groups and occupational categories, the ACF data documents both the massification of Australian HE and the continued inequities in participation that have accompanied this. Similar inequities are also evident in the representation of different class groupings within Australia's universities, the fields of study that students pursue and the type of schools they attend. Coupled with data on the educational attainment of respondents' fathers, mothers and partners, these findings provide continuing evidence of the strong relation between education, cultural capital and social inequality.

The uptake of cultural capital within the sociology of education

While the notion of cultural capital derives from Bourdieu's work on education, it has wide application as it encapsulates his focus on 'the economy of cultural goods' (Bourdieu, 1984: 1) being representative of the social value attached to all manner of cultural objects and practices. In its three forms as embodied, objectified or institutionalised, it provides a further mechanism beyond the economic for understanding class formation and its reproduction. In the ACF questionnaire, and those that informed Bourdieu's *Distinction*, emphasis is primarily placed on the embodied and objectified forms of cultural capital, markers of taste across various fields that delineate class groupings and which, within education, operate as a hidden curriculum advantaging those who possess them. Rather than detailing how the possession of these forms of capital impact academic performance and how cultivated dispositions within a classed habitus are acquired, much of Bourdieu's work on education was centred around documenting the possession of institutionalised capital, examining the social origins of those attending various schools and HE institutions in France, their fields of study and the recipients of academic prizes such as the prestigious *Concours Général*. In recording this data, often together with that of respondents' fathers and grandfathers, the hereditary nature of cultural capital and the role of education in social reproduction were laid bare. As a result, Bourdieu's notion of cultural capital has been hugely influential within the sociology of education sparking numerous studies investigating its role within various national contexts and different levels and forms of education (Di Maggio, 1982; Lamont and Lareau, 1988; Reay, 1988). How cultural capital is operationalised within these studies differs markedly, a point to which Lamont and Lareau (1988) drew attention quite early in the concept's scholarly application. Di Maggio (1982), in one of the first studies in the USA, focuses on high school students' self-reported involvement in art, music and literature practices, indicative of embodied forms of cultural capital which he demonstrated had a significant impact on student achievement. Sullivan (2001) has conducted a similar more recent study in the UK, where Reay's (1998) examination of the classed nature of the cultural capital that mothers possess and its impact on their children's education is also based. Reay refers to the following as examples of cultural capital that traverse all three of Bourdieu's categories of cultural capital: material resources, educational qualifications, available time, information about the education system, social confidence, educational knowledge and ability to negotiate with teachers. Lareau (1989; 2005) also examines the cultural capital that influences parenting styles and its effects on children's education. She contrasts what she terms the 'concerted cultivation' of middle-class parents with a 'natural growth' approach of working-class parents; cultural capital as embodied practices characteristic of a differing classed habitus.

More recent research around cultural capital and education has similarly utilised varying conceptualisations of the construct. Noble and Davies (2009) focus on students' and parents' engagement in a range of cultural activities as a predictor of participation in HE. Scherger and Savage (2010) examine familial cultural activities together with parental encouragement around pursuits such as reading and playing a musical instrument. Mapped against respondents' educational attainment, they draw conclusions not only about the impact of these embodied forms of cultural capital on academic achievement but also on their transmission through practices of childhood socialisation. Tramonte and Willms (2010) conceive these different aspects of embodied cultural capital as being either 'static' or 'relational'. In their own examination of cultural capital and its impact on educational outcomes, they make a distinction between, on the one hand, children simply participating in high culture activities such as visiting galleries and museums, which they term 'static' and describe as having less impact, and, on the other, forms of 'relational' cultural capital produced through interactions between parent and child, such as reading together and encouraging particular cultural pursuits. Tramonte and Willms (2010: 202) also point out that, while it is possible to transmit certain cultural resources in this way, 'beneficiaries have to activate them' for them to have any effect. Based on their analysis of the Organisation for Economic Co-operation and Development (OECD) Programme for International Student Assessment (PISA) 2000 data, the first large-scale international study to include indicators of cultural capital, they conclude that relational forms of cultural capital are a better indicator that this process has occurred, and have a greater impact on students' academic achievement.

The distribution of institutionalised capital in Australian higher education

In its various manifestations, cultural capital clearly influences educational attainment with some forms proving more potent than others. The significance of such findings, of course, relates to the unequal distribution of this capital, with the dominant classes engaging in practices and possessing the taste that secures both them and their children a clear advantage within the field of education, and following this, their choice of occupation. Such advantage is perhaps best captured through an analysis of the distribution of institutionalised capital which preoccupied Bourdieu in his work on education. Bourdieu viewed various credentials that constitute institutionalised capital, including school diplomas, academic awards and university degrees, as operating as a form of 'social alchemy' or 'performative magic' (Bourdieu, 1997: 50–51) that, once bestowed upon the bearer, provide official recognition that they embody the capital the credential represents. In many respects, these credentials possess something akin to illocutionary force, the term Austin (1962) applied to his account of performative utterances that Bourdieu adopts in *Language and Symbolic Power*. While inflecting Austin's notion with a far greater social valence, what attracted Bourdieu to the idea was not only its focus on the performative but how illocutionary speech acts possess institutional authority, the very qualities that Bourdieu assigns to institutionalised capital. Once in possession of this capital, it has currency beyond the field of education, its symbolic value readily acknowledged within the field of power. Yet, as with any capital, its value fluctuates depending upon availability and competition within the marketplace. Within the education marketplace, the value of academic qualifications, and the institutions that confer them, can vary considerably. The expansion of HE, for example, has led to greater market differentiation and a clear hierarchy of degrees and institutions. The ACF survey data captures these trends but, before examining these, it is important to consider the participation rates of various occupational groupings within Australian HE and the extent to which massification within this field has met its intended goal of increasing the number of those of a low SES attaining a university degree. In Table 10.1 the educational attainment of three broad occupational groupings is shown: those of high managerial/professional, intermediate and routine/manual occupations whose income levels are suggestive of a high, mid and low SES respectively.

Those of a high SES have greater levels of educational attainment with 35 per cent of these respondents having completed tertiary education as their highest educational qualification compared to 19 per cent of a mid SES and only 10 per cent of a low SES, the latter favouring vocational training following schooling as an entrée into a trade as opposed to the professions. These differing levels of educational attainment are even more pronounced when comparing SES and post-graduate qualifications, with 31 per cent of high SES respondents having a postgraduate degree against only 6 per cent of a mid SES and 5 per cent of a low SES. Having a postgraduate qualification, therefore, is a significant discriminator in terms of SES operating as a gatekeeper to the professions and higher managerial occupations from which those of a low SES are generally precluded. Combining all three categories of tertiary education – some tertiary, tertiary completed and post-graduate qualifications – is even more revealing in terms of these class divisions and levels of education, with a significant 74 per cent of those of a high SES possessing these higher levels of educational attainment compared to 39 per cent of a mid SES and 27 per cent of a low SES.

As compelling as these figures are, however, without any breakdown in terms of respondents' age it is difficult to determine the extent to which measures to improve the representation of those of a low SES in Australian HE has had an effect. While there have been various attempts to achieve this goal, beginning with the Whitlam government's abolition of fees in 1974 and the Dawkins' Reforms in 1988 which saw considerable expansion of the HE sector supported by the reintroduction of fees and a student loan scheme, it is with the Bradley Review in 2008 that specific targets were set to achieve greater equity within Australian HE. From this time, universities were compelled to lift their enrolments of low SES students with a target of 20 per cent across the sector by 2020. The Bradley Review also led to the removal of caps on the number of university places resulting in further expansion of the sector. By 2015, when the ACF questionnaire was administered, these measures should already have been bearing fruit and Table 10.2, showing the tertiary

TABLE 10.1 Highest educational qualification by occupation/SES (row %)

Occupational grouping/SES	Primary (or less)	Some secondary	Secondary completed	Incomplete voc. ed.	Completed voc. ed.	Some tertiary	Tertiary completed	Postgrad.
Higher professional/managerial High SES	0	7	8	2	9	8	35	31
Intermediate group Mid SES	4	16	21	2	19	14	19	6
Routine/manual Low SES	2	23	22	2	23	12	10	5

TABLE 10.2 HE by age group and occupation/SES (row %)

Occupational grouping/SES	Some tertiary			Tertiary completed			Postgraduate qualifications					
	18–24	25–39	40–59	60+	18–24	25–39	40–59	60+	18–24	25–39	40–59	60+
Higher professional/managerial High SES	36	9	8	3	41	39	37	26	5	34	33	29
Intermediate group Mid SES	47	12	12	8	5	37	18	6	0	4	11	4
Routine/manual Low SES	29	17	7	4	7	17	10	4	0	7	6	4

educational qualifications by age across the three occupational groupings and SES type, indicates this is in fact the case.

In terms of tertiary completed, the impact of the Bradley Reforms is most evident in the 25–39 age cohort, the group most likely to have entered university and completed their degree in this time. The percentage of low SES respondents achieving this level of education has indeed increased when compared to those in the older cohorts, at 17 per cent (25–39), 10 per cent (40–59) and 4 per cent (60+), but increases are also evident among those of a high and mid SES, with the latter appearing to reap the most benefit from the expansion of HE in Australia. This is even more obvious when considering those 18–24 year olds with some tertiary education, most of whom it is assumed were undertaking a university degree at the time of the survey. Here, those within the mid SES range are most likely, at 47 per cent, to have some tertiary education with those of a low SES at 29 per cent appearing to undertake tertiary study in increasing numbers.

While there is a limited increase in the percentage of high SES respondents with some tertiary education, at 36 per cent, what is most marked is the difference between the 18–24 year olds who have completed their tertiary education, with the high SES respondents more likely to have done so at 41 per cent compared to only 7 per cent for a low SES and even less for those of a mid SES at 5 per cent. Perhaps the higher completion rate of the high SES respondents in this age bracket is a reflection of their greater financial security enabling them to complete their studies at a much faster rate. Such an explanation could also account for the large numbers of mid and low SES 18–24 year olds with some tertiary education taking far longer to complete as they need to juggle both work and study. Whatever the case, Table 10.2 provides clear evidence of the massification of HE in Australia, with tertiary education now far more accessible to those of a lower SES. Clearly, though, it is those of a mid SES who have experienced the greatest gains. In fact, Gale and Parker (2017: 87) report that since participation records commenced following the Dawkins Reforms of the late 1980s, the numbers of low SES undergraduates within Australian HE has remained 'stubbornly low' at around 16–17 per cent, a figure comparable to the percentage of low SES 25–39 year olds who had completed their tertiary study in the ACF sample. Given their 25 per cent share of the Australian population (i.e. as the bottom quartile) this is indeed low, particularly within the context of an expanding HE sector. It also indicates the modest expectations of the Bradley Review, setting a target of only 20 per cent participation by 2020 of low SES students within Australian university undergraduate programmes.

Such poor participation rates of low SES students within HE are not unique to Australia. While the OECD (2017) records rapid improvements in tertiary educational attainment within their member countries, these qualifications are not distributed equally across SES groups within these populations. In the UK, for example, widening participation initiatives have similarly had limited effect, disproportionately benefitting those from wealthier families (Savage, 2015). Such findings are poignant given that this growth in HE is used to challenge Bourdieu's arguments about the unequal distribution of institutionalised capital and his claims the dominated classes are underrepresented in the sector. Goldthorpe, perhaps Bourdieu's harshest critic in this regard, is adamant that theories of cultural reproduction simply do not take adequate account of the massification of HE. In his discussion of education more broadly he claims 'It is simply not the case that children from less advantaged class backgrounds have been excluded from, or have themselves rejected, the education system to anything like the extent that these theories would suggest' (Goldthorpe, 1996: 489), a perspective he continues to pursue (Goldthorpe, 2007). Very early on, however, Bourdieu responded to these critiques. In the appendix to *Reproduction in Education, Society and Culture*, for example, he acknowledges the growth of HE but challenges the view that this represents a 'democratisation' of the system. Instead, he argues, any improvement in the numbers of working class students attending university is still disproportionate to concomitant increases of those from the dominant classes, stressing there is simply no evidence of an 'equalisation of educational opportunities' (Bourdieu and Passeron, 1990: 224). The plateauing of low SES representation within Australian HE at around 16–17 per cent would suggest this is still very much the case within the Australian context, and while the ACF survey data shows increasing numbers of low SES students among its respondents now attending university (as the 29 per cent figure in Table 10.2 for 18–24 year olds with some tertiary education indicates), this is not a measure of completed tertiary education and neither, it appears, is it representative of low SES participation rates at a national level.[2] But, even if these figures were suggestive of improved performance by low SES cohorts, Bourdieu explains that other factors will always counter the possibility of parity of educational opportunity as inequalities within the system will continue unabated:

> Whenever the attempts of the initially most disadvantaged groups to come into possession of the assets previously possessed by groups immediately above them in the social hierarchy or immediately ahead of them in the race are more or less counterbalanced, at all levels, by the efforts of better-placed groups to maintain the scarcity and distinctiveness of their assets.
> *(Bourdieu, 1984: 161)*

One way in which this occurs is through what Bourdieu (1984: 143) terms 'diploma inflation', whereby elites retain their advantage by pursuing postgraduate qualifications. Table 10.1 clearly demonstrates that this is in fact the case among ACF respondents, with Table 10.2 indicating this trend remains unchanged across the age groups most likely to have completed postgraduate study (25–39, 40–59 and 60+). In each case it is those of a high SES who are overwhelmingly in possession of this more valued institutionalised cultural capital, increasing slightly with younger cohorts.

Bourdieu also explains that there are other forms of distinction that operate within the field of education to ensure elites retain their advantage. One example is the type of university attended. As Marginson (2011: 31) points out, 'in the modern age status hierarchies in HE have proven to be highly stable, more permanent than any aristocrat'. Expansion of the sector has simply exacerbated this with various league tables such as Quacquarelli Symonds and *Times Higher Education* now ranking universities on a global scale. At a national level this pecking order is well recognised. In Australia, it is the so-called Group of Eight (Go8) that are considered the most prestigious institutions, including the Universities of Sydney and Melbourne, that attract students with the highest entry examination scores and who are disproportionately of a higher SES. Needless to say, such institutions have difficulties meeting the Bradley Review targets for low SES enrolments, with other less prestigious universities taking up the slack. As Table 10.3 illustrates, this unequal spread of SES groups across Australia HE institutions is also evident among ACF respondents.

Grouped in terms of membership of various networks including the top-ranked Go8, younger technologically focused universities, the mid-ranked innovative research universities, the non-aligned and the lower ranked regional universities, those of a higher SES show a clear preference for the Go8 with twice as many attending these compared to those of a mid and low SES. Popular perceptions of this hierarchy are nicely captured in the comparison of the television advertisement for Western Sydney University (WSU), a young university with high enrolments of low SES and first-in-family students, and a YouTube parody of the advertisement for the prestigious University of Sydney. Captured in a sample of stills in Figure 10.1, the WSU advertisement features the alumnus, Sudanese refugee lawyer Deng Adut, tracing his journey as a kidnapped child soldier rescued by the United Nations, who, despite considerable disadvantage, learns to read at 15, goes on to study law at WSU and becomes a human rights lawyer and advocate for refugees.

As the sample of contrasting stills in Figure 10.2 illustrates, the University of Sydney has a very different student population. The spoof focuses on 'Luke Williams' who, after growing up in Mosman, one of Sydney's affluent eastern suburbs and attending an elite private school, gains entry to a law degree at the University of Sydney before securing a clerkship at his father's law firm only to be struck off and become a real estate agent.

The contrasting imagery of the two advertisements also serves to highlight the differences between the institutions, with WSU keen to portray itself as young, dynamic and egalitarian, carving out a different niche in the market, compared to the University of Sydney parody that foregrounds the wealth and privilege of the Go8, its symbolic capital fully recognised within the social imaginary. Other nations have similar institutional hierarchies within their HE systems such as the Ivy League in the USA and the Russell Group in the UK. In relation to the latter, Savage (2015: 227–229) points out that further forms of distinction are evident, with Oxford and Cambridge at the top of the ladder; the universities of choice of a good number of cabinet ministers of successive Conservative and Labour governments and indicative of the institutional capital required to compete within the field of power. Given this hierarchy, Savage (2015: 245) argues that rather than promoting greater equity, the massification of HE in the UK has resulted in further division within the system whereby 'different universities provide different pathways into the class structure'.

TABLE 10.3 University type by occupation/SES (row %)

Occupational grouping/SES	GO8	Tech.	Non-aligned	Regional	Innovative research	Other	Don't know
Higher professional/managerial High SES	23	18	27	8	6	18	0
Intermediate group Mid SES	11	22	17	14	6	29	1
Routine/manual Low SES	13	9	24	8	5	41	0

FIGURE 10.1 Western Sydney University advertisement.

Source: Western Sydney Advertisement: Finch, VCD and We Collective for Western Sydney University.

Education, class and cultural capital 199

FIGURE 10.2 University of Sydney parody advertisement.
Source: University of Sydney Parody: Old Gregg/YouTube.

The reasons behind the varying SES composition of student cohorts at different universities are manifold. As discussed earlier, with greater stores of cultural capital students of a higher SES tend to excel academically and are more likely to secure places in the more prestigious universities. For low SES students who make the grade, the mismatch between their class habitus and the institution in which they find themselves may result in them dropping out, transferring elsewhere or not opting for a place within the top-tier of universities in the first place. Gale and Parker (2017), for example, found the retention rates of low SES students at Australian universities were lower than for those of a high or mid SES; but perhaps most telling was their finding that dropout rates for low SES students were greater within the Go8 than in lower ranked universities.[3] Numerous studies document similar experiences for low SES students elsewhere (see, for example, Aries and Seider, 2005; Dar and Getz, 2007). In the UK, where it could be argued class divisions are more entrenched than in Australia, much research has focused upon the difficulties of working-class students in HE (Reay *et al.*, 2009; Byrom and Lightfoot, 2013), including many studies that foreground the lack of fit between these students' habitus and the field of HE, their cultural capital being insufficient to allow them to feel at home within these institutional spaces, especially those of elite standing.

Together with these institutional hierarchies, fields of study are also imbued with differing status. Bourdieu examined such differences extensively in his work on education, from the likelihood of the children of parents of different occupational groupings being channelled into particular fields of study in *The Inheritors* to similar analyses conducted almost 20 years later in *The State Nobility*. In his observations in *Reproduction in Education, Society and Culture* on the opportunities afforded the working class from an expanding HE sector, he notes how any improvement in participation is 'offset by a strengthening of the mechanism tending to relegate survivors into certain faculties' (Bourdieu and Passeron, 1990: 230) whereby the dominant classes maintain a monopoly in fields such as medicine, law and engineering. As Table 10.4 indicates, similar trends were evident among the ACF respondents.

Of those studying medicine, 91 per cent were of a high SES, and while the corresponding number for law was not as high, at 65 per cent, again those of a high SES were dominant. Interestingly, those of a low SES had a higher representation within law compared to those of a mid SES who tended to favour fields such as business studies and engineering, although the latter was still dominated by those of a high SES. The preferences for particular fields of study by different SES groupings are obviously a product of a long-term trajectory. As Bourdieu (1996b: 196) shows, parental field of study influences that of their offspring, with childhood socialisation within the family enabling the intergenerational transmission of this cultural capital wherein interest for particular subjects and the ability to excel are actively cultivated within the home. More recent research on the relationship between parents and their children's field of study have yielded similar results with Kraaykamp *et al.* (2013) indicating that the massification of HE has exacerbated this trend. Of course,

TABLE 10.4 Field of study by occupation/SES (%)

Occupational grouping/SES	Science	Med.	Engin.	Soc. sci.	Hum.	Law	Bus. studies	Other	Total
Higher professional/managerial High SES	63	91	72	68	67	65	59	64	66
Intermediate group Mid SES	13	2	20	13	15	6	24	15	15
Routine/manual Low SES	19	7	6	16	14	24	16	15	15

Please note: percentage for never worked not included here.

childhood socialisation extends beyond the home into school, and 'choices' made there similarly have long-term effects with subject choices at secondary school influencing course options at university and then later career prospects. In her UK-based study drawing on longitudinal data to examine the correlation between subjects studied at secondary school and future career, Iannelli (2013) found that curriculum choice at this stage of education was a strong predictor of occupational destination, with the study of more traditional subjects such as English, maths, science and languages reducing the likelihood of entering a more lowly occupation.

Another key aspect of Iannelli's study was what she revealed about the impact of attending certain types of schools on students' later class location, finding that grammar and independent schools provided a strong 'safety net' against a low SES future.[4] The ACF questionnaire also sought information about the types of schools respondents attended, to establish whether or not there were class preferences for the different systems of schooling within Australia, these being state or public schools, Catholic schools, and independent or private schools. While neoliberal policies of school choice, dating back to the mid-1980s, have seen an increase in the number of private schools across Australia, particularly those of various religious denominations (Maddox, 2011), the well-established public system remains strong with 65 per cent of students in state schools compared to 20 per cent in Catholic schools and 15 per cent in various independent schools (Australian Bureau of Statistics, 2017).[5] As Table 10.5 shows, among the ACF respondents this clear preference for state schooling is also evident, although those of a mid or low SES are far more likely to be schooled publicly than those of a high SES. In terms of private education, class preferences are also evident, with those of a high SES, at 17 per cent, far more likely to attend private schools compared to 11 per cent for a mid SES and 6 per cent for the low SES respondents. Greater numbers of respondents of a high SES were also more likely to attend schools within the Catholic system than were the mid and low SES cohorts, further evidence of those of a high SES being more likely to be schooled outside the public system, no doubt viewing these options as offering greater opportunities for their children and increasing the possibility of entry into the more prestigious universities.

TABLE 10.5 School type by occupation/SES (row %)

Occupational grouping/SES	All or mostly state schools	All or mostly Catholic schools	All or mostly private schools
Higher professional/managerial High SES	64	19	17
Intermediate group Mid SES	73	15	11
Routine/manual Low SES	79	15	6

Although not considered within the ACF questionnaire, it is interesting to note that forms of distinction also operate within the public school system in Australia. Much like the grammar schools in the UK, Australia has 'selective schools' within its public education system. These schools have increased in number in recent years, a further symptom of the neoliberal policies of successive governments creating greater differentiation within schooling markets. This is particularly the case in New South Wales (NSW), which now has 47 either fully or partially selective schools compared to four in Victoria, three in Queensland and only one in Western Australia. While ostensibly catering for the most gifted students, Ho and Bonnor (2018) found that the bias towards high SES enrolments in these schools is stark. Fully selective high schools in NSW comprise six of the ten most socio-economically advantaged secondary schools in the state, the others being high-fee private schools, while on average 73 per cent of selective high school students are of a high SES compared to only 2 per cent of a low SES. Given that attendance at these schools almost assures students a place within Australia's elite universities, it is no wonder parents of a high SES actively seek admission for their children by ensuring they are well prepared for these schools' entry examinations through private academic coaching, an example of the concerted cultivation that characterises middle-class parenting (Lareau, 2005).[6]

Education's role in the intergenerational transmission of cultural capital

Various forms of distinction, therefore, are evident across the different levels of education within Australia whereby the dominant classes ensure they maintain their advantage. Even in the face of widening participation within HE, inequalities persist as the differential status of universities and the courses they offer favour those of more substantial means who profit disproportionately from the imperative to obtain the institutionalised capital that the expansion of HE has provoked. The ACF questionnaire not only provides a lens on these trends; it also yielded data on the intergenerational transmission of this capital. By recording the highest educational qualifications of respondents' fathers, mothers and partners, it reveals the way in which this capital is reproduced within families. In combining the responses regarding tertiary education – 'some tertiary', 'tertiary completed' and 'postgraduate qualifications' – we can see that 25 per cent of high SES respondents had fathers who had attained these levels of education as opposed to 18 per cent of a mid SES and 13 per cent of a low SES. Table 10.6, however, unpacks this data in terms of the four age groupings in the sample and is interesting for what it reveals about the impact of the massification of HE on respondents' fathers' levels of education.

As is evident, the younger the respondents, the more educated their fathers, a pattern showing the benefit of the HE reforms of the 1970s and 1980s (those from 2008 are yet to have an effect). Although this trend is apparent across all SES levels and most pronounced for 18–24-year-old respondents, with 50 per cent of those of a high SES having fathers who had attained this level of education against 42 per

TABLE 10.6 Father's HE by age group and occupation/SES (%)

Occupational grouping/SES	Combined some tertiary, completed tertiary and postgraduate qualifications			
	18–24	25–39	40–59	60+
Higher professional/managerial High SES	50	35	24	14
Intermediate group Mid SES	42	30	14	7
Routine/manual Low SES	28	13	5	10

cent of a mid SES and 28 per cent of a low SES, the disparity across SES remains a constant. Interestingly, participation has not resulted in greater equity as there is little change in the proportion of each group in the overall sample; the dominance of those of a higher SES is maintained. Table 10.7 shows this is also the case for respondents' mothers who, while showing slightly higher levels of educational attainment than the fathers, conform to a similar pattern in showing higher levels of education the younger the respondents but with their proportion within the overall sample indicating a continuing disparity between SES groups.

The educational advantage of those of a higher SES is therefore sustained across generations with the institutional capital this attainment represents suggestive of equivalent stores of objectified capital in these respondents' homes coupled with parenting practices that promote the embodied dispositions that ensure their off-spring either replicate or better their own class position, a cycle of social reproduction aided and abetted by the education system. Such processes are reinforced if both parents have equivalent levels of education and, while not confirming this, it is interesting to note the findings in Table 10.8, that high SES respondents are much more likely to have partners with either tertiary or postgraduate

TABLE 10.7 Mother's HE by age group and occupation/SES (%)

Occupational grouping/SES	Combined some tertiary, completed tertiary and postgraduate qualifications			
	18–24	25–39	40–59	60+
Higher professional/managerial High SES	59	37	21	6
Intermediate group Mid SES	45	38	11	3
Routine/manual Low SES	35	22	6	4

TABLE 10.8 Partner's highest educational qualification by occupation/SES (%)

Occupational grouping/SES	Primary or less	Some secondary	Secondary completed	Some voc. ed.	Voc. ed. completed	Some tertiary	Tertiary completed	Postgrad.
Higher professional/managerial High SES	1	12	16	2	13	5	28	23
Intermediate group Mid SES	2	17	21	2	18	5	25	11
Routine/manual Low SES	3	21	32	2	15	3	12	14

qualifications than those of a mid or low SES. The latter, by contrast, are far more likely to have partners with either some secondary or who have completed their secondary education, with these differing levels of educational attainment generally influencing approaches to parenting and the intergenerational transmission of cultural capital.

Conclusion

The focus of this chapter has been to examine the extent to which systems of education are complicit in the reproduction of social inequality and how forms of institutionalised capital are monopolised by those of a high SES. While the various tables of data considered throughout this chapter clearly demonstrate this, highlighting, in particular, the persistence of this inequality across various age groups, the Multiple Correspondence Analysis (MCA) presented below encapsulates the high correlation between class and educational attainment by showing the clustering of these tendencies (Figure 10.3).

Even with the expansion of Australia's HE sector, framed by an intent of widening participation, these forms of social stratification remain intact. As is evident in

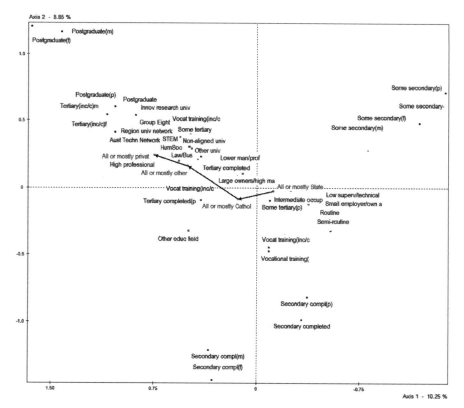

FIGURE 10.3 Education, class and the inheritance of cultural capital.

the top left-hand quadrant, those in higher managerial and professional occupations are not only better educated but dominate enrolments within the Go8 universities and the more prestigious fields of study such as medicine, law and engineering. They are also more likely to attend schools within the private sector compared to those of a mid or low SES, as reflected in the lower right-hand quadrant, improving the likelihood of securing places in these high status institutions and the courses they offer. And we see clearly the force of the mechanisms though which these advantages, and disadvantages, are transmitted across generations and reinforced through partner choices: in the top right quadrant, for example, we see that those with incomplete secondary education are likely to be from families where this is true of both father (f) and mother (m) and of partners (p). Reminiscent of similar analyses of Bourdieu's in *The State Nobility* (Bourdieu, 1996b: 145), the MCA demonstrates how very little has changed. It attests, however, to the ongoing relevance of Bourdieu's work and the importance of an emphasis on notions of cultural capital when interrogating the relationship between class, education and social reproduction.

Notes

1 SES is the favoured term used within the field of education when referring to differences in socio-economic background. Given this, it is used throughout this chapter drawing broad comparisons between high, mid and low SES and the three occupational groupings within the ACF survey data.
2 The mid and low SES numbers here may be inflated because these respondents may be employed in menial jobs while at university and so their nominated occupation may not be reflective of their family's SES. See discussion of this point at the end of Chapter 7.
3 The only exception to this within the Go8 was the Australian National University.
4 Grammar schools are the equivalent of selective schools in the Australian context.
5 The so-called private or independent schools, together with those within the Catholic system, also receive government funding, creating further disparity between the different systems of schooling in Australia.
6 Disproportionate numbers of the students entering these schools are also of Asian backgrounds, the children of skilled migrants now entering Australia in record numbers, further skewing the demographics of these schools (Watkins, 2017).

11
CAPITAL GEOGRAPHIES

Mapping the spaces of urban cultural capital

Liam Magee and Deborah Stevenson

Urban space and the production and consumption of culture are closely entwined. Cities are not only population centres but the locations of significant cultural activity and major, often iconic, cultural infrastructure, much of which is concentrated in the city centre (Stevenson and Magee, 2017). This concentration is particularly marked in a highly urbanised country like Australia, where more than two-thirds of the population live in one of the seven state capitals, and nearly 90 per cent live in cities (Australian Bureau of Statistics, 2019; Trading Economics, 2019). The confluence of physical location and concentration, and their obvious imbalances, give rise to issues of access and equity that are not only class based but have consequences for the relationship between cities and regions, and the city centre and the suburbs (Gibson et al., 2015; Gleeson, 2005). Important, too, are the implications of such imbalances for the acquisition and display of cultural capital, while the extent to which cultural capital is not only expressed but shaped through an engagement with urban space also begs consideration. Such matters are significant if only because of the critical role of urban institutions such as art galleries, opera houses and theatres in the display and consumption of elite cultural forms (Bourdieu, 2010). These institutions play a key part in legitimising and giving meaning to the aesthetic distinctions at the heart of Bourdieu's understanding of cultural capital (Di Maggio, 1983); and not unlike places of worship, they are spatial and symbolic counterpoints to the profanity of everyday urban life, markers of excellence and aesthetic refinement. Indeed, Savage et al. (2018: 140) argue that Bourdieu's understanding of capital materialises in the built environment through the 'monumental urban architecture' of the major cultural institutions that, standing out against their 'everyday urban surrounds', are 'somehow anti-urban' (Savage et al., 2018: 141).

Increasingly though, iconic cultural buildings are enmeshed in what Hanquinet (2016) describes as the aestheticisation of everyday urban life, and Bourdieu's understanding of cultural capital as 'embrac[ing] the urban only to retain a certain distance from it' (Savage et al., 2018: 140) is being called into question as established cultural hierarchies are challenged and the cultural and the urban become increasingly entangled. It is also possible to consume and feel 'ownership' of built cultural infrastructure without partaking of its products and productions – to have a relationship with a cultural space whilst being excluded from its cultural forms on the basis of class and level of education, in particular. An example is the Sydney Opera House, which has come to be a potent sign of urban and national identity and a key element of the symbolic economy of the city. This status operates in parallel to the Opera House's role in (high) cultural production and consumption.

For Savage et al. (2018), cultural capital is now indivisible from the urban because the foundations of the cultural hierarchy of contemporary cultural capital are not only *accidentally* urban (by virtue of population concentration, for instance) but *essentially* so. They argue that the melding of the urban and the cultural directly challenges the Kantian understanding of aesthetics that assumes the separation of art and life that they claim underpins Bourdieu's notion of cultural capital. If urban space is indivisible from contemporary urban culture, then the challenge is to examine this interrelationship in a way that problematises the demarcation of the urban, cultural and social dimensions of everyday life. This task is the starting point for this chapter, which seeks to examine when, and whether, urban space reveals and/or reinforces the acquisition and consumption of forms of cultural capital. Focusing on the *Australian Cultural Fields* (ACF) survey data for the city of Sydney, in particular, the chapter maps the urban dimensions of cultural capital, probing the ways in which the practices and priorities of everyday urban cultural life are embedded at the intersection of culture and forms of 'city-ness'. We also show that underpinning Savage et al.'s (2018) critique of Bourdieu's distinction between art and life that informs their framework of urban cultural capital lie other, more subtle oppositions, and we identify factors that are reshaping capital less uniformly, diffusing it in a polynucleated, multilayered and, in many instances, suburban form.

Urbanising cultural capital

In spite of burgeoning interest in Bourdieu's work highlighting the class dimensions of cultural taste and consumption, this research agenda has been less focused on the complex ways in which 'distinction' is played out spatially. For instance, studies of urban gentrification have assumed the possession of cultural capital by the gentrifying middle class, but have not sufficiently problematised the cultural capital aspects of urban life itself. Other studies have focused on the theories, processes and consequences of attracting the 'creative class' (Florida, 2003) to particular cities and neighbourhoods, or on the use of art and the cultural industries in strategies to revive local economies and animate often declining precincts (Stevenson, 2017). There have also been analyses of the urban aspects of social and cultural inequality that highlight the ways in which cities are implicated in structural inequality and marginalisation, especially those which are based on class, gender, race and ethnicity (Savage et al., 2002). More cultural approaches position the city as a site of empowerment and resistance, often celebrating lived urban rhythms, anonymity and difference. Also emphasised has been the fracturing of cultural hierarchies and the blurring of the boundaries of aesthetic categories of social distinction. In most cases, though, urban space is treated as a container for action rather than itself a cultural form enmeshed in the making and remaking of cultural capital. Savage *et al.* (2018) stand out in that they seek to develop a nuanced account of urban cultural capital. Our own argument borrows certain elements of their analysis, while taking issue with others.

Since the 1980s, the city and its spaces have increasingly become key elements in the acquisition and display of cultural capital, where sites such as art galleries and opera houses, standing above or aside from the profanity of the urban, have now to be considered alongside more contemporary spaces of cultural capital that are enmeshed in the everyday. Savage *et al.* (2018) identify four key markers of this enmeshment. First, they identify the growing importance of elite urban universities that are not only sites of learning, but central elements of place making and marketing and the assertion of urban status. Second, they suggest that physical activity and sport are now routinely 'mobilised' as part of contemporary cultural capital, highlighting the importance of major sporting complexes, as well as the associated teams, cities and events. Like universities, major sporting venues and the hosting of hallmark sporting events often operate as indicators of urban status and branding, as well as of the making of urban cultural capital; these are sites where, through club membership, VIP lounges, sponsorships, brushes with fame and other markers, distinction is developed and displayed. The third marker of the urban underpinnings of contemporary cultural capital is the presence of an urban cosmopolitan elite that is simultaneously local and global. This globally mobile elite references (and consumes) the cultural forms and creative products of major cities around the world. Finally, Savage *et al.* argue that the gentrification of former inner-city warehouse sites and redundant industrial areas is an indicator of the urbanisation of cultural capital. Their point is not that gentrification is new but that this form of gentrification is significant because, traditionally, the spatial display of cultural capital was associated with (suburban) residential neighbourhoods physically removed from the grittiness of the city. It is, they argue, through the claiming of the urban by a cosmopolitan elite, along with the emerging importance of particular forms of urban space, that the contemporary city has become enmeshed in the acquisition and display of cultural capital.

Savage *et al.*'s reconceptualisation of urban cultural capital usefully elaborates the spatiality of culture as more than a relation of exclusion or containment, but it does so in part through the privileging of cityness itself. Although born of a rejection of the dualism they claim underpins Bourdieu's use of the Kantian aesthetic, the notion of the urban at the heart of their reconceptualisation implies a dualism that not only situates the city in opposition to the nation, but geographical and cultural enclaves within the city in opposition to the suburbs. It is along these lines that our analysis develops, not only dissolving the boundaries between urban life and high aesthetic experience but also those between the quintessentially 'urban' (in both its everyday and aesthetic modes) and what are the culturally subordinate categories of the suburban and the non-urban. We also suggest that an additional axis of urban cultural capital is the space of the home. If cultural capital is acquired through the family, then the domestic spaces within which this acquisition occurs and their location must be acknowledged as part of any examination of urban cultural capital.

Cultural participation in Greater Sydney

With a focus on Greater Sydney, we examined a selection of items from the complete set of cultural fields included in the ACF survey using a similar procedure for each field: extracting the variables that relate to participation rather than knowledge and taste; aggregating and normalising the variable scores to produce a single composite measure for each field; and, finally, exploring the spatial distribution of, and correlations between, these field scores. Second, we undertake a Principal Component Analysis (PCA) of the same measures of participation. As introduced and discussed in Chapter 1, Multiple Correspondence Analysis (MCA) has been employed to explore survey categorical variables that measure questions of knowledge, participation and taste. PCA is an equivalent technique for the continuous variables that measure, in most cases, ordered levels of participation (*how often* people attend galleries) rather than either/or questions about knowledge or taste (*whether or not* a respondent has heard of a particular artist). We conclude with two key observations regarding what the results of these analyses might signify in relation to emerging trends in cultural consumption in affluent and international cities such as Sydney, as well as for understandings of the specifically urban dimensions of cultural capital. First, our findings suggest a convergence of sports participation – both playing and watching – with participation in the fields of heritage, literature and the arts, pointing to shifts in the nature of cultural capital that we suggest can in part be explained in terms of urban concentration. Second, higher rates of participation in other cultural fields – music and television – in suburban and peri-urban areas convey a sense of different forms of cultural capital accumulating according to a quite different spatial logic, organised through a complex and less linear set of relationships than that of an implied urban centre and periphery. Where Savage *et al.* (2018) are interested in the spaces of urban cultural capital, we are interested in cultural capital in urban space. The survey included 20 questions relating to participation in the fields of music, heritage, art, literature, television and sport (see Table 11.1).

Within Sydney, participation in the six cultural fields varies in ways that confirm and, in some cases, confound a stereotypical image of the city. That image describes a radiation of economic, political and cultural influence extending from a powerful central business district (CBD), located alongside the iconic cultural landmarks of the Sydney Opera House and Harbour Bridge, to the affluent harbourside and coastal suburbs to the east of the CBD and the population clusters of Parramatta and Penrith, Bankstown and Liverpool to the west and south-west (see Figure 11.1). While Parramatta is the approximate geographic centre of the metropolis, the CBD

TABLE 11.1 Cultural fields and survey participation questions

Cultural field	Participation questions
Music	• How many hours a day do you normally spend listening to music? • Please tell me how often you go to the following events – rock gigs/orchestral concerts/musicals/opera/live bands in pubs/pop concerts
Heritage	• Visits to: local, regional or national museum/historic building or precinct/archaeological site or ruins/site narrating Aboriginal history or heritage/military site or memorial/open air site/migration or immigration museum/cultural landscape/site of pioneer or settler heritage/industrial heritage site • Member of: a local history or archaeology society or club/an online family history website/the National Trust of Australia or a similar Australian organisation (for example, Historic Houses/Association, Australian Conservation Society etc. • A Member or Friend of a national museum/a Member or Friend of a local museum/a Friend of National Parks/the History Channel on subscription TV • Use of the Internet to search for information on heritage places or events
Art	• Frequency of gallery visits • Visited in the past year: the National Gallery of Australia/a state art gallery/a regional art gallery/a university art gallery/a commercial art gallery/a museum of contemporary art/a public art display or installation/an Australian or international arts festival or biennale • Used the Internet in the past year to: research or find out more about an artist or arts event/visit the website of an artist or arts organisation/read a blog or email newsletter by an artist or arts organisation/comment on art or an arts organisation using social media
Literature	• Books read by an Australian author in the past year • Books owned • Ebooks owned • In the past year: visited a book store for browsing/participated in a book club or reading group/attended a literary or writers festival/attended an event in a local book store or similar venue/read book reviews in a newspaper or magazine or online/followed discussions about books or authors online or via social media/watched book shows on TV or listened to book shows on the radio
Television	• Hours spent watching television
Sport	• Frequency of playing sport • Involvement in: Australian Rules football/soccer (Association Football)/netball/rugby league/rugby union/cricket/basketball/tennis/golf/swimming • Watched live: Australian Rules football/soccer (Association Football)/netball/rugby league/rugby union/cricket/basketball/tennis/golf/swimming • Watched via media: Australian Rules football/soccer (Association Football)/netball/rugby league/rugby union/cricket/basketball/tennis/golf/swimming

Capital geographies 213

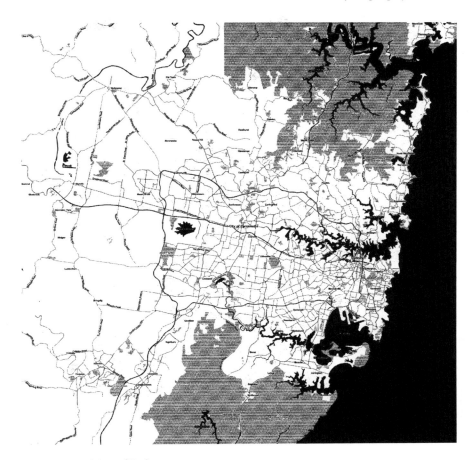

FIGURE 11.1 Map of Sydney.

Source: Map tiles by Stamen Design, under CC BY 3.0. Data by OpenStreetMap, under ODbL.

– 25 kilometres to the east – is the site of the city's major sport stadia, museums, galleries, libraries, performance spaces, film and television studios, and high-profile enclaves of colonial-era architecture. A notable exception, significant given the arguments of Savage *et al.* (2018), is the former Olympic stadium and associated venues located in Homebush to the west of the CBD, which were major built elements of the branding that accompanied the Sydney 2000 Olympic Games but which have been underutilised since and often regarded by locals as being difficult to get to (Kassens-Noor, 2012). The CBD also has the areas of highest population density and, in the surrounding inner-city suburbs, highest per-capita incomes. Many of these suburbs were once working class, and through the ongoing presence of terrace and light industrial architecture, produce today a blended gritty-cum-gentrified aesthetic urban form that attracts both artists and creatives, and the cosmopolitan elite (Pollio *et al.*, 2018).

214 Liam Magee and Deborah Stevenson

Both education levels and incomes decline more or less progressively along Sydney's east–west axis, represented by the Western train line, Parramatta Road, the M4 and M2 motorways and the Parramatta River. Beyond Penrith, the Blue Mountains area contains pockets of comparative affluence and highly educated residents, and is also noted for having a sizeable number of artistic communities and emerging creative industries (Stevenson *et al.*, 2017). Government policy has supported suburban sprawl, medium-density development and the establishment of prominent cultural venues at transport and employment hubs, notably in Homebush, Parramatta and Liverpool. These venues predominantly focus on sport and visual and performing arts, and might be expected to play a role in the spatialisation of the sport and art fields, but with a few notable exceptions (including the Olympic venues) much of this cultural infrastructure is either comparatively new, under development or small when compared with equivalent venues located closer to the city. Consequently it may not yet have a significant effect in boosting participation and building forms of place-based identification.

For each of the cultural fields, we generated maps of Greater Sydney that show participation by postal areas, coded by quintile. We include a sample map for the field of television in Figure 11.2. Postal areas in the top 20 per cent of participation in a given field are coloured black, with lighter shades indicating progressively

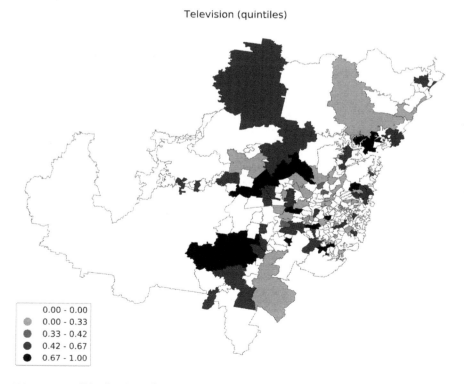

FIGURE 11.2 Distribution of participation in the field of television.

lower levels of participation. The maps provide a partial illustration of correlations between participation in each field and distance from the CBD. For example, higher participation in the field of art appears to correlate moderately with population density (smaller postal areas), but less so with distance from the CBD. This may be due in part to the presence of comparatively high participation along the east–west city axis, particularly in Penrith and the Blue Mountains. With the fields of literature and heritage a similar pattern occurs, although concentrations of participation are not as clearly aligned with the east–west axis. Other fields show different patterns. Participation in music is inversely correlated to proximity to the CBD. The field of television, meanwhile, has higher relative participation in Sydney's middle suburbs, with levels falling away in Penrith and the Blue Mountains. Finally, the field of sport appears to show high participation in inner suburbs, and in peri-urban areas, while skipping over the middle and outer suburbs.

To explore these relationships in greater depth, we correlate the variables of participation with spatial, socio-economic and other demographic variables at both postal area and individual respondent levels. We found reasonably high correlations between each of the fields with the exception of television, which is negatively correlated or uncorrelated with participation in all other fields. This relationship is also true at the individual level, and means that, for our sample, television viewing habits for both postal areas and individuals do not correlate strongly with participation in all other fields of cultural activity. The further individuals are from the CBD, the more likely they are to watch television, with the exception of the far western areas of the metropolis as noted above. Television viewing also correlates, at the area level, with lower socio-economic status, and, at the individual level, with age, lower income and education, and living in areas of lower density. However, lower levels of saving do not correlate. The television watching profile that emerges is that of older people, possibly retirees, living in the outer – though not peri-urban – suburbs, with modest savings and below average incomes.

Correlation results of arts, literature and heritage variables are highly consistent, reinforcing the geographic distributions discussed above. Heritage participation relates least strongly with all other variables measured at area and individual levels, which suggests it is comparatively unanchored to economic and cultural capital, or to spatial location, relative to the art and literary fields. Participation in heritage and the arts is not, in the Greater Sydney sample, related to age or savings, but both of these fields and the literary field correlate to varying degrees with education and population density. In other words, the participation variables for these fields are consistent with arguments that cultural capital is identifiable with a certain urbanism. Living in inner Sydney means individuals are more likely to be highly educated and to visit art galleries, read literature and go to heritage sites.

Participation in sport is, interestingly, quite consistent with participation in the arts, literature and heritage, and many of the same observations hold. Proximity to the CBD is a more important predictor of sports participation, with the location of high-profile sporting venues and infrastructure being one possible explanation, the spaces of Homebush notwithstanding. However, it is also likely that age functions as an intervening variable here: distance from the city relates to age, and older people are less likely, on average, to participate in (and watch, either live or on television) sporting activities.

Participation in music combines features of both television viewing and the other cultural fields. Like television viewing, listening to music or attending music venues do not correlate positively with education or with proximity to the city centre. Music fans are also more likely to live in low socio-economic areas. Yet, unlike television viewing, music participation correlates strongly with youth and income, and also correlates negatively with television viewing itself. The profile that emerges here is one of young people living in the suburbs with disposable incomes and few savings. Given the comparative lack of music venues in the suburbs this result is surprising, but the lack of venues may be compensated for by habits of listening to music while commuting.

A PCA of the Greater Sydney sample (Figure 11.3) also shows the distribution of respondents but adds a more nuanced picture of how individuals align with key variables. The shading of points indicates gender, with dark shading signalling male respondents. The superimposed arrows illustrate positive tendencies of responses to variables: the series of arrows in the lower right quadrant of the graph for example shows individuals with relatively high income, education and occupational standing

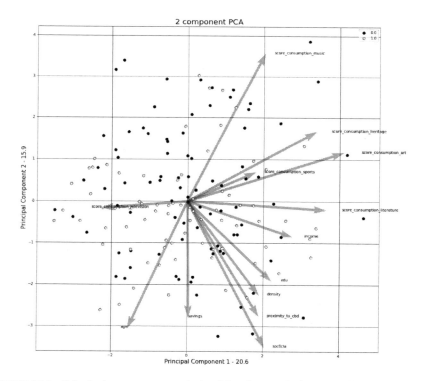

FIGURE 11.3 Principal component analysis of the Greater Sydney sample.

(as measured by an eight-level occupational classification, *soc8cla*), residing in areas with greater population density and proximity to Sydney's CBD. The cluster of points in the upper left quadrant indicates a tendency towards participation in television and music, and away from the associated lines in the bottom left. This group can be interpreted as having a lower occupational class, living further from the city in low density areas and holding lower educational qualifications relative to the rest of the sample. Respondents represented on the right side of the graph participate in heritage, art, literature and sports, and on the whole do not participate in television viewing. In the bottom half of the graph, age, levels of savings and occupational class are closely associated, while living in high density areas close to the CBD is associated with high levels of education and income, and high occupational class categories.

Taken together, the PCA constructs a social space in which music lovers are young and have disposable incomes but no savings; television viewers are older, possess savings but have low incomes; and many (but far from all) consumers of art, literature, heritage and sports are affluent and live relatively close to the city. Gender is relatively evenly dispersed across this constructed space, but women feature more prominently on the lower half of the second component (the vertical axis). Further analysis confirms that women in the Greater Sydney sample consume more television and less music, are slightly skewed upwards in age and skewed upwards with respect to occupational class and education.

These results offer a useful picture of the spatial distribution of cultural participation in Greater Sydney and the spaces of cultural capital. Television is the great outlier here: high participation is a feature of Sydney's middle and outer suburbs, with the exception of cultural enclaves such as the Blue Mountains. Television viewing occurs primarily in the space of the residential home, which is an oft-overlooked site of cultural capital acquisition as well as cultural consumption. It is also the space most closely linked to the intimate and personal. Music, too, is a cultural form often consumed in the home, although mobile technologies mean that it is possible to extend the spatial intimacy of consumption from the home to the city. While on some variables consumers of music present almost an inverse image to that of the television watcher, both groups are more likely to occupy lower positions on the scale of occupational class and live further from the city centre. Consumers of art, literature, heritage and sport, on the other hand, share many characteristics.

Sydney in the national context

To compare Sydney and Australia-wide participation in each field, we aggregated and standardised responses to these questions. Respondents from Sydney participated in each of the fields at levels broadly equivalent to those of the entire Australian sample. Figure 11.4 illustrates both sets of figures: the short and darker bars show figures for Greater Sydney (N = 164), while the lighter and longer bars relate to the Australian sample overall (N = 1202). At both national and city levels, fields

218 Liam Magee and Deborah Stevenson

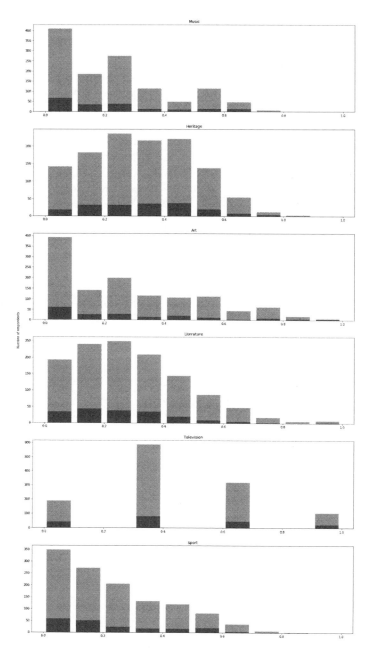

FIGURE 11.4 Degrees of participation in cultural fields, Sydney and Australian samples.

such as music and sport exhibit poor participation relative to more prestigious or niche fields such as heritage and literature. Perhaps surprising given stereotypical images of Australian cultural participation, these results are nonetheless consistent with results from other sources such as the 2006 Australian Bureau of Statistics (ABS) report *Culture and Leisure*, which showed levels of attendance at libraries, museum and art galleries comparable with those for music and sports venues (Australian Bureau of Statistics, 2006). Less surprising is the continued high participation in television, a highly differentiated set of activities, especially as modes of viewing encompass both broadcast television and new media such as YouTube.

In other cases, issues specific to Sydney, such as long-running debates over liquor licensing laws and their influence on the ability of venues to host live music, might be expected to produce lower levels of participation relative to Australia as a whole, certainly relative to Melbourne (another state capital with a comparable population), which has a strong reputation for live music performance (Convery, 2018). Survey responses confirmed this expectation, though with mixed results. In responses to the question 'Please tell me how often you go to the following events – Rock gigs', results for Melbourne and Sydney were very similar: 2.8 per cent of Sydney and 2.7 per cent of Melbourne respondents attended 'about once a month', and distributions of responses were similar for other options. A t-test of both samples confirmed no essential differences. A related question about 'Live bands in pubs', however, produced far more significant differences, with Melbournians registering between 10 and 20 per cent greater participation across all frequencies ('Once a week or more': 2 per cent for Melbourne compared with 1.2 per cent for Sydney, and so on). A t-test showed a statistically significant difference between the two cities on this question ($p < 0.05$). However, Sydney did not differ markedly from Australian responses overall.

These kinds of city-specific effects might be expected to have some impact on the spatial distribution of cultural participation within Sydney itself. They might also point to the ways in which urban cultural capital is shaped differently in different cities. Less opportunity to attend live music events as a whole relative to other state capitals will likely produce less variation across different parts of the city, from inner to peri-urban suburbs. In the case of live music attendance that effect will be relatively muted as it comprises less than 10 per cent of our measure of music participation overall. Nonetheless, the example captures an important point about efforts to measure cultural distinctions in relation to class stratification, spatial distributions and other differences: such distinctions can also be constrained by features that structure specific fields. In this case regulatory conditions, introduced ostensibly to limit violent behaviour in Sydney's night-time economy (Rowe and Lynch, 2012), serve to constrain those distinctions that might otherwise be exhibited in greater measure. Beyond a methodological caution, the point also reflects the role different spatial scales – national and regional as well as intra-urban variations in policy for example – play in the production of cultural capital. Such differences go to the heart of cultural distinction as a form of city branding and positioning, and demonstrate the function of intimate and niche architectural forms (laneways, bars, cafés, cellars and indeed suburban homes), alongside the monumental, in the production of urban cultural capital.

Sydney respondents participated more heavily in television than in other fields. Figure 11.5 shows the relative distributions of participation, with the dark upper band, indicating television, strongly pronounced on the right side of the figure. In comparative terms, the music and sport fields experience low participation, while heritage, art and literature appear more evenly spread. These parallel the national figures, and differ again marginally from Melbourne, which has higher participation in sport, art and literature, and lower television viewing. Considered overall, Melbourne participants' involvement in the field of music was marginally *lower* than Sydney's, though not at statistically significant levels. Differences between the two cities become more marked in response to specific items such as live music attendance which, as noted, may reflect distinct regulatory environments more than cultural preferences. There are also some very well-documented differences between Sydney and Melbourne with respect to people's attendance at live events, while Sydney's significant transport problems means an urban culture of 'staying home' may be more marked than in Melbourne, pointing again to the importance of the domestic.

Together these differences mean that cultural capital is shaped by a variety of spatial forces. As we discussed above, participation in different fields is distributed differentially across the traditional sites of 'high art', the reclaimed spaces of industrial production, the extended beltways of suburbia and the interior places of private homes, vehicles and devices. Alongside these intra-urban variations, inter-urban

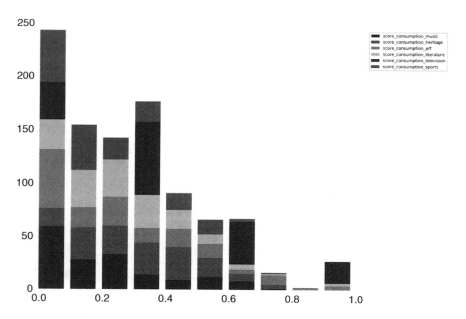

FIGURE 11.5 Relative degrees of participation in cultural fields, Sydney sample.

differences due to policy – as one among many possible historical and geographical influences – also condition the distinctions that operate selectively in the performance of cultural capital.

Urban culture and the suburban 'other'

The exceptional characteristics of music and, in particular, television consumption offer interpretative possibilities beyond what might be read as a homogenising convergence of cultural capital with urban centres. Our analysis supports the idea, advanced by Savage *et al.* (2018), that the contemporary city and its spaces are entangled in the attainment and display of cultural capital: the presence of sporting complexes, high-profile universities, 'elite urban cosmopolitanism' and gentrified former working-class and industrial areas. But we add to this quartet of factors the need to consider the space of the home as also entwined in the acquisition and performance of cultural capital, including in particular the everyday and vernacular. Key to this argument is the role of the family and the household in acquiring cultural capital, but the home is also the site for the consumption of culture, with television being the most obvious form.

We suggest four further developments which we argue now complicate the distinction between the 'city', thought of as the locus of both high modernist culture, and its suburban 'other'. First, the historical emergence of postmodernism in the 1980s served both to describe and, considered very broadly as an argument on aesthetics, to defend and valorise a wider range of cultural media (Harvey, 1989). As Savage *et al.* (2018) argue, it has also lent itself to a specific form of urban spectatorship and experientialism that extends to the cultural dominance in contemporary cities of reflexive and self-conscious 'hipsterism'. In terms of Sydney's urban geography, this development coincides not only with the rise of gentrification and cosmopolitan elites, but also with attempts to spread the effects of such change, in often diverse ways, to suburban areas: medium/high density housing and commercial zones, boutique retail and hospitality precincts, and live music and festival events that take advantage of low land costs. Second, innovation and the concentration of financial capital in media and communications infrastructure mean that much of what once was located in the physical public sphere – the town square, the cinema, the amphitheatre, the library and even the game arcade – can now be consumed through data centres, networks and mobile devices, producing a counter-acting tendency to arguments for the spatial pivoting of cultural capital towards grand architectural monuments. Technological innovation also means that cultural forms once largely consumed in the home can now be consumed in urban public space. In other words, the spatial dimensions of public and private cultural consumption are being reshaped.

Third, the rise of digital media also produced a specific form of avant-gardism in television and music that to some degree upends any previously established hierarchy of fields themselves. The emergence of boutique cable television and various forms of 'art-school' influenced independent music exemplify this inversion, further accentuated by the legitimation of such media through 'high art' forums: orchestral performances of television theme music, gallery exhibitions of comic cells and album covers, and so on. Finally, the arrival and settlement of migrant groups in distinct areas of Sydney at different points in time has led to complex spatial inscriptions of ethic cultural capital. Evidence of spatio-cultural intersections can be found in Sydney's suburban hubs, where cinema chains routinely screen Indian and Chinese alongside Hollywood films, and where, even within specific ethnic groups, class distinctions are exhibited spatially and culturally, along adjoining suburbs on the fringes of Parramatta and Liverpool (Capuano, 2014). Importantly, among such groups, especially first-generation migrants from India and the Middle East, Sydney's central areas are virtually irrelevant in terms of cultural participation beyond occasional apprehension of iconic monuments such as the Opera House.

In spatial terms, this interpretation makes plausible a reorientation towards the city (and specifically its cultural precincts) but also argues for a simultaneous sideways glance towards other emerging places of cultural consumption – not merely as a kind of *demi-monde* inhabited by cultural aspirants, but as zones forming and generating tastes that span the spectrum from high to low and which are very specific features of the image of place. It thus makes sense to talk of the *sub*urbanisation of cultural capital. If, as Savage *et al.* (2018) suggest, the four forces of universities, sporting venues, cosmopolitanism and gentrification can be said to be shaping cultural capital concentrically towards the city centre, we might also point to other forces that in the case of Sydney at least are reshaping this capital less uniformly, dispersing it in effect in a polynucleated and multilayered form. In addition to the digitisation and revalorisation of certain cultural fields and forms, we would also highlight in the case of Sydney and other Australian cities the effects of secondary waves of gentrification that, through the making-residential of industrial space and concomitant rental price rises, steer cultural producers and secondary venues to suburban and peri-urban regions (Ang *et al.*, 2016). Without directly aligning sites of cultural production with those where capital is more directly 'traded', these patterns of internal migration suggest ways in which that capital can operate centrifugally, away from as well as towards urban centres.

The granular distinctions analysed by Bourdieu continue to work in ways that we would argue have become even more fine-grained. As one example, we note the quite specific transversal flows of cultural capital in fields of art and literature between areas of Sydney's Inner West and the Blue Mountains, respectively 5–10 and 50–80 kilometres from the city centre. Other discrete patterns operate among specific cultural enclaves around Sydney's secondary hubs, such as Parramatta, among Indian, Chinese and Lebanese communities for example, where participation has a distinctly local, territorial – and, with respect to class, still an internally discriminating – dimension. Equally, as we noted in relation to live music and liquor licensing, factors impinging upon cultural consumption clearly function at more coarse-grained spatial levels as well. Our analysis of participation in cultural fields here seeks to endorse but also to refine efforts to urbanise, in a theoretical sense, cultural capital. If the form of the city now dominates ways in which culture is consumed, this form needs to be understood – to adopt an urban metaphor – less as a singular monument and more as the sort of intricate and layered laneway streetscape so beloved by the modern urban aesthete.

Conclusion

With a focus on Sydney, the aim of this chapter was to consider cultural capital through an examination of the spatial patterns of consumption. At first glance, our results echo those of Savage *et al.* (2018) and their argument that the contemporary city is a space that nurtures new and emerging forms of cultural capital, where the new spaces for the display of cultural capital are embedded in forms of urbanism that are not markers of distance from the mundane and the culturally profane. Urban cultural capital involves the reinterpretation of existing forms of capital as well as the development of those that are new. So, while the general point holds, understanding urban cultural capital and the intersections of space and culture requires an appreciation of local specificity and the ways in which they are shaped by local histories and demographies. We found, for instance, the coincidence of participation in sport culture with fields traditionally associated with 'high art'. The presence of the 'urban sporting complex' looms large in central and inner west Sydney, along axes of public and private transport that favour residents equally well positioned to attend major universities, galleries and concert halls. Against the narrative of the city acting as a centrifugal force – relentlessly pulling, as it were, cultural capital towards its centre – patterns of participation in fields of music and television indicated other spatial distributions at play. Less dependent upon monumental cultural and civic infrastructure, capital here instead can be imagined as circulating and accumulating through communication and media networks, as well as within spaces of quintessentially suburban and domestic intimacy: the home, the car or the personal space increasingly carved out by headphones and smart devices. As the comparison between Sydney and Melbourne indicates, participation in specific cultural fields exhibits inter-urban as well as intra-urban variation. The 'urban' qualifier to cultural capital shows itself to be as variable, contested and complex as the concept it qualifies.

12
INDIGENOUS CULTURAL TASTES AND CAPITALS

Gendered and class formations

Tony Bennett, Ben Dibley and Michelle Kelly

In an online contribution to the Australian Broadcasting Corporation's (ABC) radio series *Class Act* referred to in Chapter 8, Indigenous woman Timmah Ball, who identifies as middle class ('I was born middle-class and was aware of this privilege as a child'), points to the difficulties that middle-class Indigenous Australians often experience. The messy intersections of class and race in 'a country that belligerently imagines that class doesn't exist', she argues, means that the 'white working class often blame us and other non-white migrants for taking their jobs and benefits, and those of us with class privilege are riddled with our own anxieties as we navigate new freedoms' (Ball, 2018). Many Indigenous academics and intellectuals have made similar points. Rowse identifies academic Marcia Langton and journalist Stan Grant as among those who have taken public issue with stereotypical views of Indigenous Australians as necessarily poor, undereducated and, indeed, as Grant puts it, 'coal black' (Rowse, 2017: loc. 5586).[1] In doing so, he also identifies a range of recent studies, focused on the effects of increased Indigenous participation in higher education since the 1980s, pointing to the emergence of an Indigenous middle class that has been tilted towards women in its gendered composition. These studies do not, however, examine the role of cultural tastes and practices in the processes of Indigenous class formation; nor do they draw on cultural capital theory to frame their concerns.

Xu Daozhi (2018) provides a corrective to this and, drawing on Mary Louise Pratt's concept of 'contact zones' (1992), outlines a useful general framework for engaging with the varied ways in which Indigenous cultural practices operate as a form of capital in the multivalent transactions that take place across and through them between Indigenous and non-Indigenous Australians. In doing so she proposes the concept of 'Indigenous cultural capital' to refer to the 'broad scope of Aboriginal cultural and intellectual manifestations from the historical heritage to more recent developments in Aboriginal stories, songs, paintings, artefacts, social customs, religious beliefs and rituals, which are valued and transmitted in the public domain' (Xu, 2018: 16). Xu Daozhi identifies three applications of this concept that are relevant to our concerns in this study. The first has to do with how engagements with Indigenous culture serve as a capital resource for specific sections of the non-Indigenous populations in settler-colonial societies. These questions are taken up in Chapter 17. The second concerns the role that the political mobilisation of Indigenous culture has played in the struggles of Indigenous populations to move beyond their administrative framing as colonised populations to that of peoples with distinctive rights and identities. Third, while beyond the scope of her own concerns, Xu Daozhi acknowledges the significance of the issues highlighted by Timmah Ball regarding the class ramifications of the different social mobility trajectories resulting from the differential acquisition of Indigenous cultural capital among Indigenous populations. In taking this last set of questions as our point of entry into these debates about Indigenous cultural capital, we also complement it by considering how the more established forms of cultural capital associated with canonised works of both Australian and international culture have operated alongside newly legitimised forms of Indigenous culture in the recent emergence of an Indigenous middle class.

These are questions which have not figured significantly in official statistics addressing the relations between Aboriginal and Torres Strait Islander peoples and the general Australian population. Statistical reports have been mostly governed by what Taylor calls the 'demography of disadvantage', focused on the health, socio-economic, educational and other inequalities experienced by Indigenous Australians relative to the Australian population as a whole (2009: 117). While there are good reasons for a statistical optic focused on 'closing the gap' between Indigenous and non-Indigenous Australians, this has often been at the expense of considering the significance of emerging differences among Indigenous Australians. The 2012 *Review of Higher Education Access and Outcomes for Aboriginal and Torres Strait Islander Peoples* – one of the studies Rowse (2017) cites – is an exception in the light it throws on the influence that Indigenous participation in tertiary education has had on the development of an Indigenous middle class (Behrendt et al., 2012). The *Review* does not, however, engage with the relations between different levels of educational attainment on the part of Indigenous Australians and their cultural tastes and practices. Such data as there is on the latter question – as collected by the National Aboriginal and Torres Strait Islander Social Survey (Australian Bureau of Statistics, 2016), for example – focuses on Indigenous cultural practices that are community specific and centred on specifically Indigenous understandings of the relations between culture and country.

In what follows we aim to complement these studies by looking at what our data tells us about the differences between the tastes of Indigenous and non-Indigenous Australians as registered in relation to their liking for and engagement with the Indigenous, other Australian and overseas items in our survey; and how these aspects of Indigenous cultural tastes and practices are differentiated along gendered and class lines. We pursue these questions initially at an aggregate level by reviewing general patterns of difference between the tastes of the Aboriginal and Torres Strait Islander people recruited by our survey and those evidenced by our main sample and boost samples for Chinese, Lebanese, Indian and Italian Australians. In moving on to take a closer look at these differences on a field-by-field basis, we pay particular attention to the internal differentiations of Indigenous tastes that are most strongly associated with individual fields. We then return to consider the light that these aspects of our findings throw on the broader debates about Indigenous cultural capital discussed above. In concluding, we place these concerns in a longer historical perspective while also outlining the respects in which a proper understanding of the functioning of Indigenous cultural capital requires that it be understood as operating within an Indigenous cultural field that forms a relatively autonomous sub-field within the Australian cultural field.

Before setting out, however, we need to sound a note of caution regarding the limitations of our data. These partly concern the relatively small number of Indigenous cultural items included in our survey: ten items naming specific Indigenous artists, writers, musicians, television programmes and personalities, sportspeople and heritage sites, and a number of Indigenous genres (Aboriginal art, Indigenous writing, etc.). They also concern the composition of the *Australian Cultural Fields* (ACF) Indigenous sample. This consists of 53 Aboriginal and Torres Strait Islander people who were recruited as a boost sample, and a further 28 people from the main sample who identified as Aboriginal or Torres Strait Islander, producing a final sample size of 81.[2] The boost sample was recruited solely from New South Wales (NSW) using computer-assisted telephone interviews and landline random digit dialling to generate telephone numbers within the areas of greatest Aboriginal and Torres Strait Islander population density. This meant that the sample was recruited disproportionately from regional towns. No quotas were applied to the boost sample, nor was it weighted. The overall Aboriginal and Torres Strait Islander sample is consequently far from being a representative national sample. It is biased towards women, towards older age groups and towards individuals with higher levels of education and occupying higher social class positions relative to Aboriginal and Torres Strait Islander peoples as a whole.[3] These qualifications mean that our findings have to be interpreted as exploratory.

Indigenous, national and international tastes

In order to examine aggregate differences in the degree to which the members of the different samples engage with Indigenous, Australian or overseas cultures we produced 'regional scales' for the named items in our survey by grouping them together according to their regional provenance. We divided these scales into two: a set of Australian scales, divided between Indigenous and other Australian items (Appendix G); and a set of international scales, divided between US, UK, European and Asian items (Appendix H). The items in these scales were selected with regard not just to their regional provenance but also to include a balance of popular and 'high culture' tastes, and a balance of items likely to appeal more to women than to men, and vice versa.

In Table 12.1 we compare the mean number of items liked by the members of the Indigenous sample with the means for the main and other samples. The main point to note here is that members of the Indigenous sample like both Indigenous and other Australian items more than the main sample. While lower than that of the Italian sample, Indigenous liking of Australian items is also considerably higher than that shown by the Lebanese, Indian and Chinese samples. Hage's (1998) concept of 'national capital', proposed to account for the disadvantage of Australia's migrant communities in relation to those forms of cultural capital that are closely associated with the dominant forms of Anglo-Celtic Australian culture, is relevant here. We can see something of this in play in the relative lack of engagement with Australian culture evident on the part of the Chinese, Indian and Lebanese samples compared not just to the main sample but also to the longer-standing community of Italian Australians. While Indigenous Australians show stronger levels of engagement with Australian culture, the values invested in this are likely to be complex and nuanced. If it manifests a sense of sharing in the forms of national belonging referenced by Hage's concept of national capital, it likely also reflects a concern to mobilise Indigenous culture in order to contest and transform the dominant currency of national capital.[4] Finally, while Aboriginal and Torres Strait Islander respondents register a stronger liking for US items than other Australians, their rates of liking European and Asian items are lower.

While the differences evident in Table 12.1 are telling, other differences within Indigenous tastes are equally noteworthy. For example, the rates of recognition of Indigenous items, as measured by whether or not respondents had heard of them, and rates of liking them, are both higher for Indigenous women than for Indigenous men at ratios of 1.37:1 and 1.5:1 respectively. The equivalent ratios for other Australian items are 1.15:1 for recognition and 1.21:1 for liking. We note also that Indigenous respondents with tertiary education backgrounds are more likely than those without tertiary experience to recognise and to like Indigenous items by ratios of 1.23:1 and 1.41:1 respectively.

The analysis of aggregate differences between the samples, however, can take us only so far. We need to delve beneath these to see what values might inform the differences between the tastes of Indigenous and other Australians for particular cultural items in different cultural fields. In doing so, in the next three sections, on a field-by-field basis, we also go beyond the items named in our regional scales to include selected aspects of our findings concerning genre preferences and cultural participation. The tables we have compiled for this purpose focus on differences of 5 per cent or more between the Indigenous sample and the main sample, and are limited to comparisons at whole sample levels. The accompanying text also explores differences associated with two sub-sample divisions of roughly equal sizes within the Indigenous group – the male/female, and tertiary/non-tertiary educated divisions. These are overlapping divisions inasmuch as, in the sample, Indigenous women are about twice as likely as Indigenous men to have had experience of

TABLE 12.1 Regional scales: comparisons of the mean likes of the main, Italian, Lebanese, Chinese, Indian and Indigenous samples

Like	Main sample mean	Italian mean [and ratio to main sample]	Lebanese mean [and ratio to main sample]	Chinese mean [and ratio to main sample]	Indian mean [and ratio to main sample]	Indigenous mean [and ratio to main sample]
Indigenous items	3.02	2.83 [0.94]	1.84 [0.61]	1.80 [0.60]	1.89 [0.63]	4.17 [1.38]
Other Australian items	19.91	21.19 [1.06]	15.11 [0.76]	12.90 [0.65]	13.78 [0.69]	20.45 [1.03]
US items	5.40	5.14 [0.95]	4.93 [0.91]	4.05 [0.75]	4.84 [0.90]	6.09 [1.13]
UK items	5.16	5.13 [0.99]	2.87 [0.56]	3.34 [0.65]	3.62 [0.70]	4.65 [0.90]
European items	4.27	5.64 [1.32]	3.13 [0.73]	3.54 [0.83]	2.94 [0.69]	3.46 [0.81]
Asian items	0.73	0.67 [0.87]	0.40 [0.52]	1.34 [1.74]	1.70 [2.20]	0.49 [0.63]

tertiary education.[5] These are also divisions that relate to evidence of a distinctive middle-class formation in the Indigenous sample – issues that we explore through our household interviews with three tertiary educated middle-class women, two in professional class positions and one a student, in tandem with our survey evidence.

The art and heritage fields

Art

The two differences that stand out most in relation to Table 12.2 are the lower rates that are registered for Indigenous liking of half of the ten art genres we asked about and the lower rates of recognition for almost half of the overseas artists. It is notable that the rates of recognition fall behind those of the main sample for Impressionist and modern artists as well as for Caravaggio, a niche taste relative to other Renaissance artists. There are no similar differences in the rates of recognition relating to Australian artists. The strength of the Indigenous sample's positive engagement with Albert Namatjira here is notable, as is the relative dislike of Tom Roberts. There is also a gendered aspect to genre tastes in the art field. The marked preference for Aboriginal art is stronger for Indigenous women (74 per cent) than for Indigenous men (59 per cent), while men show a stronger preference for both Impressionism (8 to 0 per cent) and Renaissance art (12 to 4 per cent). Level of education makes no difference to the levels of liking Aboriginal art. However, the non-tertiary educated are more inclined to like the traditional genres of

TABLE 12.2 Visual art: Indigenous and main sample comparisons (%)

	Indigenous sample	Main sample	Difference
Genres liked most			
Aboriginal art	67	26	(+41)
Landscapes	46	52	(–6)
Modern art	10	17	(–7)
Renaissance art	7	15	(–8)
Portraits	14	24	(–10)
Impressionism	4	16	(–12)
Australian artists seen and liked			
Albert Namatjira	70	49	(+21)
Ken Done	46	40	(+6)
Tom Roberts	20	28	(–8)
Overseas artists heard of			
Vincent Van Gogh	89	95	(–6)
Claude Monet	65	73	(–8)
Francis Bacon	31	42	(–11)
Caravaggio	14	26	(–12)

Renaissance art, landscapes and portraits whereas those with tertiary education are – as is true of the main sample – distinctive in their liking for Impressionism (see Chapter 1).

Heritage

While Indigenous Australians sampled are also (at 42 per cent) more likely than the non-Indigenous Australians surveyed (35 per cent) to visit art galleries once a year or more, this does not translate into higher rates of engagement with particular kinds of art galleries. By contrast, significantly higher rates of engagement with heritage sites – via visiting, Internet access and membership of heritage organisations – are evident (Table 12.3). There is also a distinctive tendency to Indigenous heritage interests. The strong interest in Aboriginal heritage is not matched by an equivalent interest in Australian national heritage or the heritage of migrant groups (although zero interest is expressed in the latter, only 4 per cent of the main sample favour this kind of heritage). The low level of Indigenous interest in world heritage is also notable. Gender plays a key role, with women more involved in heritage practices with strong

TABLE 12.3 Heritage: Indigenous and main sample comparisons (%)

	Indigenous sample	Main sample	Difference
Kinds of heritage most interested in			
Aboriginal heritage	69	18	(+51)
World heritage	11	27	(−16)
Australia's national heritage	21	42	(−21)
Kinds of heritage least interested in			
World heritage	36	17	(+19)
Heritage of migrant groups	43	38	(+5)
Aboriginal heritage	4	14	(−10)
Heritage of local area	10	20	(−10)
Heritage of working life	43	54	(−11)
Visited in past year			
Aboriginal history or heritage site	57	35	(+22)
Cultural landscape	42	31	(+11)
Archaeological site or ruins	25	17	(+8)
Historical building or precinct	52	57	(−5)
Internet search of heritage websites			
Once a week or more	32	19	(+13)
A few times a year	20	28	(−8)
Member, friend, subscriber			
Online family history website	26	13	(+13)
Local museum	19	8	(+11)
National museum	14	5	(+9)
National parks	14	8	(+6)

Indigenous associations. They are 8 per cent more likely than men to include Aboriginal heritage among the kinds of heritage they are most interested in; more than twice as likely to be actively involved in what are identified in Chapter 4 as the vernacular forms of online family history; twice as likely to be a friend or member of a national museum; and a third more likely to be similarly involved in local museums. A little over 22 per cent of Indigenous women are actively engaged with national parks compared to 3 per cent of Indigenous men. The effects of level of education are not so striking. The tertiary educated are marginally more likely to visit local or regional museums, Aboriginal heritage sites and cultural landscapes. They are also more committed to more active forms of heritage engagement such as subscription to online family history websites, and being a friend or member of national, local or regional museums and national parks. There are nonetheless, as our interviews with Christine and Kim show, significant differences in the heritage practices and values of Indigenous women with similar class and education backgrounds.

INDIGENOUS HERITAGE PRACTICES AND VALUES

Christine and Kim are similar in many respects: both are tertiary educated, occupy professional positions, have considerable overseas travel experience and are only eight years apart in age, Kim being the younger at 53 at the time of completing the survey. They differ, however, in their assessments of the relations between their specifically Indigenous heritage interests and their relations to other Australian and overseas heritage sites.

Christine is of mixed descent. She traces her roots in European Christian military organisations back to the Middle Ages and thence, via Scotland and Ireland, to Australia through the transportation of her great great grandfather. Her Aboriginal ancestry had, however, been suppressed – her father, of mixed parentage, had kept his Aboriginality largely under cover – until revealed by genealogical inquires establishing her connections with her people and country in NSW.

Deeply invested in heritage practices generally – she and her husband watch the History Channel regularly – Christine invests most strongly in Aboriginal heritage in view of its personal and familial significance, and its more general significance for Aboriginal people. The comfort she and her family derive from now being able to celebrate their Aboriginal heritage freely is linked to its importance as 'the Aboriginal people's expression of their own self'.

Christine and her husband have also visited a wide range of heritage sites in Europe, Asia and North America. While some of these sites reflect an interest in genealogical itineraries – of her European ancestors, for example — others raise questions about comparative temporalities. Insisting, of the Aboriginal sites she has visited, that 'This is history', Christine continues:

> I get really emotional about it because I really – we've got no idea [of] the ancient stuff here and you go overseas and you see the stuff that's older than the modern Australia and you try and connect these two things together, how ancient Australia was before anybody came.

But Christine engages fully and critically with post-invasion history as both an Aboriginal person, and an Australian. She records her experience of visiting Gallipoli for Anzac Day as having been 'so moving' that she feels 'every Australian should attempt to go there'. Asked whether she has the same appetite for Australian as for other countries' heritage, she replies 'at the end of the day we're very Australian, especially very Australian overseas'. Her sense of Australian culture and heritage, however, has a double register. On the one hand, 'it's sort of like English' – it had stemmed from a culture of 'mate-ism, the ocker, the whole thing all rolled into one' – but this is only in country areas or rural towns like Bathurst or Ballarat. It's different in the cities where 'there's been so many rivers flowing into it that it's so diversified now I don't think you can say "oh that's an Australian culture"'.

Kim, by contrast, evinces no interest in Australian heritage beyond Indigenous heritage sites, and her relationship to these is marked by more community-specific values and sensibilities. These are evident in the discomfort she feels if, when visiting Aboriginal sites, she inadvertently gets too close to areas strongly associated with men's business. And, as a 'salt water' person through her clan affiliations, she avoids river sites. More generally, she is careful not to intrude on Aboriginal sites without appropriate guidance:

> I would feel really uncomfortable trying to seek them out on my own, because if they're places that I'm not supposed to be, that I'm not supposed to be looking for, or looking at, I could have put myself in a world of trouble.

Kim relates to overseas heritage sites in a similar way. The contrast with Christine is most pointed in relation to Stonehenge. Christine finds Stonehenge disappointing compared to Rome's Coliseum and China's Forbidden City. For Kim, however, visiting Stonehenge close to the summer solstice when, as she puts it, its spirituality was approaching maximum intensity, made her feel edgy, unable to breath, 'hyperventilating and everything'. She was nonetheless 'blown away' by the strong cultural connection she felt to the site; not, though, to Stonehenge specifically, but to the Earth: 'So in a sense it didn't matter what country it was, it was the connection through Earth, through stone. It was nature.'

Kim is also deeply involved in genealogical investigations into the ancestry and family histories of her extended kin network. Her postgraduate studies in Indigenous languages had helped her trace her Aboriginal ancestry back to her great great great grandparents, knowledge that proved useful in helping to establish the Aboriginality of her niece – who is 'lily-white and she's got curly blonde hair' – for purposes of enrolment for university study.

The music and literary fields

Music

The main and Indigenous samples share similar participation rates in the music field. However, they differ in the devices used and in the events attended (Table 12.4). The Indigenous sample is more likely to use mobile devices and less likely to attend orchestral concerts and musicals. These items record differences of around 15 per cent. Table 12.4 draws attention to three major differences in taste: country music is significantly more popular with the Indigenous sample; almost half of the Australian musicians are more preferred by this sample; while international pieces are mostly more popular with the main sample. Preferences for Indigenous items are not as strongly marked between the two samples as they are in the art field. While Gurrumul Yunupingu is more popular with the Indigenous sample, the Indigenous alternative rock musician Dan Sultan appeals equally across the two samples. Country and alternative are more popular with Indigenous men by a margin of about a tenth; while Indigenous women are more likely to enjoy classical music (by a margin of 14 per cent) and easy listening (by 22 per cent). The Indigenous women sampled are also more likely than Indigenous men to have heard of

TABLE 12.4 Music: Indigenous and main sample comparisons (%)

	Indigenous sample	Main sample	Difference
Genres liked most			
Country	46	22	(+24)
Easy listening	27	33	(−6)
Alternative	14	21	(−7)
Hard rock	10	17	(−7)
Australian musicians heard and liked			
Gurrumul Yunupingu	47	33	(+14)
Kasey Chambers	68	58	(+10)
Jimmy Barnes	79	70	(+9)
AC/DC	77	70	(+7)
Peter Sculthorpe	3	8	(−5)
Kylie Minogue	56	63	(−7)
Gotye	30	44	(−14)
Overseas music heard and liked			
'Jolene' by Dolly Parton	72	62	(+10)
Phantom of the Opera by Andrew Lloyd Webber	52	58	(−6)
'Vogue' by Madonna	37	43	(−6)
Rhapsody in Blue by George Gershwin	38	44	(−6)
The Mikado by Gilbert and Sullivan	27	35	(−8)
'Nessun Dorma' by Puccini	20	28	(−8)
The Four Seasons by Vivaldi	31	49	(−18)

Yunupingu and Sultan by differences of 20 per cent and 7 per cent respectively, and more likely to like them by margins of 10 and 23 per cent. Indigenous men more frequently express their liking for international and national items, though Australian women musicians are all more likely to be recognised by Indigenous women: Kate Ceberano (by a margin of 19 per cent), Kylie Minogue (6 per cent) and Kasey Chambers (6 per cent).

Level of education registers its most consequential effects in relation to the Indigenous musicians, Sultan and Yunupingu. Around a third of those with a tertiary education have heard of both musicians, compared with around 10 per cent of the non-tertiary educated for Sultan and around 20 per cent for Yunupingu.

Literature

While participation patterns between the two samples are broadly similar in the literary field, members of the Indigenous sample are marginally less engaged in the broader aspects of book culture (Table 12.5). They are around 10 per cent less likely to read book reviews and to watch or listen to television or radio book shows. They are also less likely to obtain ebooks, preferring to purchase print books online or to buy books from local bookshops, department stores or supermarkets, all by margins in the 5–10 per cent range. The major difference in tastes between the two samples, as Table 12.5 shows, is the Indigenous sample's greater liking of books by or about Indigenous Australians. More of the Indigenous sample than of the main sample also like books on Australian history, while the reverse is true for modern novels. This pattern remains largely true for named items, with the Indigenous writers Sally Morgan and Kim Scott and the American horror writer Stephen King more highly liked by Indigenous readers, while the West Australian literary author Tim Winton is less popular. Women in the Indigenous sample are considerably more engaged with Indigenous authors. A quarter more women than men recognise Morgan and a third more like her. The gap is smaller for Scott, about a tenth more women

TABLE 12.5 Literature: Indigenous and main sample comparisons (%)

	Indigenous sample	*Main sample*	*Difference*
Kinds of books liked most			
Books Indigenous Australians	70	34	(+36)
Australian history	63	56	(+7)
Modern novels	36	46	(−10)
Australian authors read and liked			
Sally Morgan	18	12	(+6)
Kim Scott	9	3	(+6)
Tim Winton	19	28	(−9)
Overseas authors read and liked			
Stephen King	56	40	(+16)

recognising and appreciating his work. While men are, on average, 10 per cent more likely to have heard of other Australian authors, women register stronger levels of liking, with an average difference of 25 per cent between genders. This gender difference is more marked for Winton, Belinda Alexandra and Bryce Courtenay. By contrast, except for Haruki Murakami and Ian Rankin, women are around 10 per cent more likely to recognise the international authors in our regional scales. Preferences are generally evenly split between the genders. However, Don DeLillo and Murakami elicit different rates of liking: the former more popular with women, the latter with men, by margins of a half and a third respectively.

Level of education does not significantly affect the literary genre preferences of the Indigenous sample. The exceptions, crime and contemporary Australian novels, are more popular with the tertiary educated while sport books are more popular with those with no tertiary education. However, the two Indigenous authors on the survey are more likely to be recognised and liked by the tertiary educated.

THE WEIGHT OF POLITICS: INDIGENOUS TASTE FOR MUSIC AND LITERATURE

In the household interviews Indigenous interviewees express ambivalence in relation to their preference for the Indigenous music and literature items in the survey, particularly in connection with the ways these items are positioned in relation to identity politics. For example, Bianca, a university undergraduate in her late teens, states she doesn't 'listen to a lot of Indigenous artists' and singles out high profile Indigenous pop singer and actress, Jessica Mauboy, for particular attention. While emphasising Mauboy's talents and acknowledging that not all the musicians she likes are politically engaged, Bianca is nevertheless critical of Mauboy for her lack of activism around Indigenous issues. Bianca takes two points of reference. First, in stating her taste for African-American RnB and hip hop, she contends her preference for this genre is in part because of its capacity to give 'a voice to highlight social issues'. She cites the rap artist, Kendrick Lamar, as a favourite in this regard. Second, Bianca contrasts what she takes as Mauboy's political failings to the more proactive stance of Australian Football League (AFL) player Adam Goodes. Framing her response in terms of politics, not taste, Bianca states: 'I think she's a good actress ... and she's talented; but I don't like her actions politically.' Bianca continues:

> I just feel like even though she stars in some movies about Aboriginal people and stuff she hasn't really done a lot [for Aboriginal communities] which is kind of disappointing. Like even on Australia Day, she went and sung the national anthem and took out the Australian flag on the Harbour Bridge ... but she didn't do anything to recognise Invasion Day or Survival Day which is kind of like, Adam Goodes did something like why wouldn't you. That's what I find a bit disappointing about her.

> Kim's survey responses show she enjoys a number of popular genres as well as books by or about Indigenous Australians, and Australian history. In our interview, however, it is her favourite sub-genre, paranormal romance, which she describes with particularly strong sentiment:
>
>> because of what I taught – imagine if you will, because of my history, because of where I come from and what I teach, you sort of had your history thrown in your face all the time. I had to sort of escape that sort of thing or go crazy. So reading fantasy, paranormal stuff, anything pure escapism, helps.
>
> 'Paranormal romance' was not included in our survey, but it is a genre in which Kim reads avidly and also practices as an unpublished writer. Paranormal romance provides Kim with a leisure and creative release outside the demands of Indigenous history and identity in which she is otherwise deeply invested, both professionally and personally.
>
> Bianca and Kim provide insight into the different ways in which taste for Indigenous cultural items is overlayed by the pressures of the political. In Bianca's case, it is marked by her strong sense that Indigenous public figures ought to be advocates for Indigenous issues; in Kim's case, it is qualified by a desire for a space of private respite from the demands of identity politics.

The television and sport fields

Television

On the whole, the Indigenous Australians surveyed have a greater positive engagement with Australian television content than the members of the main sample (Table 12.6). Indigenous respondents like three out of the ten Australian shows surveyed at notably higher rates, and 37 per cent of the Indigenous sample express a preference for Australian over overseas-produced content, compared to 27 per cent of the main sample. Indigenous engagement with local television is also reflected in the fact that half of the Australian television personalities named in the survey are liked at significantly higher rates by the Indigenous sample. Preferences for overseas shows are more evenly divided, with the Indigenous sample liking three of these more than the main sample and three at lower rates. Indigenous respondents are significantly more likely to have watched National Indigenous Television (NITV) – over three-quarters of the Indigenous sample have done so, compared to just under a half of the main sample. They are, however, less likely to nominate the ABC as their favourite channel, only 9 per cent doing so compared to 27 per cent of the main sample. Gender is an important mediator of Indigenous tastes in television. The Indigenous women surveyed are more likely than the Indigenous men surveyed to like all of the Australian television shows listed in Table 12.6 by a margin of more than 5 per cent.

TABLE 12.6 Television: Indigenous and main sample comparisons (%)

	Indigenous sample	Main sample	Difference
Australian TV shows watched and liked	38	16	(+22)
Redfern Now	30	22	(+8)
Offspring	48	43	(+5)
MasterChef	43	49	(–6)
Gardening Australia			
International TV shows watched and liked	70	55	(+15)
Big Bang Theory	40	30	(+10)
Game of Thrones	48	43	(+5)
Midsomer Murders	7	12	(–5)
Mad Men	33	40	(–7)
QI	32	51	(–19)
Grand Designs			
Australian TV personalities liked			
Ray Martin	69	54	(+15)
Paul Vautin	32	19	(+13)
Deborah Mailman	44	32	(+12)
Amanda Keller	52	43	(+9)
Eddie McGuire	43	34	(+9)
Julia Zemiro	24	31	(–7)
Carrie Bickmore	27	36	(–9)

Although the biggest margin in this respect is for *Gardening Australia* (27 per cent), followed by *Grand Designs* (20 per cent), the Indigenous-focused and produced show *Redfern Now* is also more liked by Indigenous women by a margin of 18 per cent. Indigenous men prefer the international shows *QI*, *Mad Men* and *The Big Bang Theory* by significant margins (all above 23 per cent), and *Game of Thrones* to a lesser degree. Men prefer those personalities who are associated with sport (Paul Vautin by 30 per cent and Eddie McGuire by 7 per cent) and music (Julia Zemiro), while women prefer Indigenous actor Deborah Mailman and Ray Martin, who also has Indigenous heritage through a great great grandmother, by around 20 per cent. Indigenous women are the most avid NITV watchers, but viewing is high for both genders (83 and 71 per cent respectively).

Education is less consequential than gender in determining Indigenous television tastes, particularly for Australian content. The tertiary educated prefer *Offspring* by 10 per cent and those with secondary education prefer *MasterChef* by 9 per cent. The margins for international television are slightly wider, and led by the tertiary educated: *Midsomer Murders* by 16 per cent, and *QI* by 13 per cent. The tertiary educated Indigenous respondents also like Mailman, Zemiro, Amanda Keller and Carrie Bickmore more than the non-tertiary educated (all at 10–14 per cent margins).

Sport

Table 12.7 indicates that the Indigenous Australians surveyed have a greater personal involvement than the general population in several sports; however, it is an involvement that is less often formalised in club membership. The association with rugby league is particularly high, with notably increased rates of media consumption and personal involvement evident in the Indigenous sample. There is a higher level of liking among this group for sports figures who are visible in the international sports arena, in particular those who hail from the USA. The Indigenous sample is also more likely than the main sample to like Australian sportspeople,

TABLE 12.7 Sport: Indigenous and main sample comparisons (%)

	Indigenous sample	Main sample	Difference
Sports club membership			
Membership	26	33	(−7)
Involved in the past year*			
Rugby league	16	4	(+12)
Netball	14	7	(+7)
Basketball	14	8	(+6)
Swimming	21	16	(+5)
AFL	4	10	(−6)
Watched live via media in last year			
Rugby league	67	42	(+25)
Swimming	41	34	(+7)
Tennis	46	52	(−6)
Cricket	42	53	(−11)
AFL	33	49	(−16)
Australian sportspeople liked			
Cathy Freeman	86	75	(+11)
Israel Folau	37	27	(+10)
Adam Goodes	46	36	(+10)
Rod Laver	44	52	(−8)
Overseas sportspeople liked			
Tiger Woods	43	27	(+16)
Michael Jordan	64	49	(+15)
Serena Williams	59	49	(+10)
Michael Phelps	43	37	(+6)
Diego Maradona	27	22	(+5)
Rafael Nadal	54	61	(−7)
Sachin Tendulkar	32	44	(−12)

* 'Involvement' includes playing and non-playing roles, such as coaching, refereeing or committee membership.

albeit that the differences here are less pronounced. No Australian athlete achieves the high margins of differential liking of Tiger Woods and Michael Jordan. In the case of Cathy Freeman, however, this is due to her extremely high level of popularity with both the main and Indigenous samples. The Indigenous men surveyed watch tennis, cricket and AFL at higher rates than Indigenous women, while Indigenous women are more likely to watch swimming and rugby league.[6] Indigenous women are more than three times more likely to be personally involved in netball than men. Within the Indigenous sample, a greater proportion of men than women like Woods, Diego Maradona, and (with lesser margins) Jordan and Serena Williams; but these relations are reversed for the Australian Indigenous athletes Freeman (liked by 91 per cent of Indigenous women compared to 80 per cent of Indigenous men) and Goodes (50 per cent of women and 40 per cent of men).

Indigenous Australians in the sample with tertiary education are more likely than those with secondary or vocational education to watch AFL and cricket live on the media; the non-tertiary group is more likely to watch rugby league. Tertiary education is also related to greater levels of personal involvement in swimming, netball and especially basketball for the Indigenous sample, and to higher rates of preference for Jordan (73 per cent of the tertiary educated compared to 57 per cent of those without tertiary education) and Goodes (54 per cent to 39 per cent), with lesser margins for Freeman and Michael Phelps. The proportions liking Maradona, Woods and Sachin Tendulkar are higher among the secondary/vocational group.

SPORT: FAMILIAL AND POLITICAL AFFILIATIONS

While Bianca and Christine are similarly positioned in terms of class and education, there are differences in the way their sporting interests and pursuits are fostered in the context of family life. The association that sprang to mind for Bianca when asked about sport was dance. While her involvement has waned since starting tertiary study, dance featured prominently in Bianca's childhood. She trained in dance schools since she was 3 years old, and was extensively involved in dance competitions and dance festivals throughout her schooling. Bianca feels 'lucky to have an opportunity with Bangarra [an Aboriginal and Torres Strait Islander performing arts company] and doing workshops with them because our school had a really strong dance culture both for Aboriginal dance and non-Aboriginal'. One of Bianca's parents was 'okay with me doing dance when I was little' but, as she got older, 'thought I should just stick to more solid sports'. Christine, a former skier, describes her children as 'brought up in sport', involved in organised competitive activities like skiing, baseball and other games. She has watched live sports overseas when travelling – major league baseball in the USA, ice hockey in Canada – particularly through the mediation of her children. While age difference no doubt plays a role, the familial nature of Christine's sports engagements contrasts with Bianca's account of her dancing, which she pursued with what she identifies as a degree of independence: while her parents influence her politically, Bianca says, it is not so much the case 'when it comes to those kinds of things like music and sport and art'.

The influence of family is less equivocal for team support, particularly in rugby league. Both women use social media to follow the code. Christine loyally follows a particular National Rugby League (NRL) team and says that in her family 'nobody diverts' from this allegiance. In the past Christine purchased season passes and went to team games 'nearly every week', but this level of engagement has dropped off recently, which Christine attributes to advancing age. Some of her children have married rival supporters; nevertheless her grandsons are fans of her favoured team. Similarly Bianca supports Queensland in the State of Origin, 'probably because my parents do as well', and watches NRL and rugby union especially in family or social settings. She will occasionally go to a live NRL or rugby union match if friends are playing. Shared experiences of sport viewing are clearly important for both women in family and social contexts, as is a communal sense of team support. Indeed, this sense is so strong that both profess allegiance to teams which are outside their own resident state or nation: Bianca, a NSW resident, supports Queensland, and Christine says that while she usually supports Australia at the international level she once championed New Zealand because her favoured NRL club 'had more Kiwis in it than the Kiwi side. We were actually going for the Kiwis … go for your own players'.

Both Christine and Bianca support the Aboriginal athletes we asked about in the survey and the interviews (Christine describes Freeman as a 'pinnacle', and Bianca says she likes Goodes 'for obvious political reasons as well as sporting reasons'). A liking of Indigenous sportspeople was especially pronounced for Bianca, who named Johnathan Thurston as her favourite sport star. On social media Bianca follows 'Johnathan Thurston, Dane Gagai, Cameron Smith and that's who I really bothered to follow. I'm not sure why it's those three, and also I've just noticed they're all Indigenous and they're all NRL players.' Christine also touches on the importance of identity in sport when she invokes a global experience of Indigeneity in describing an unexpected encounter her family had while lost in Canada: 'Instead of turning here we went into an Inuit community and they were having a rodeo and everything like that so it was pretty interesting to get lost and … see that, in culture, Indigenous.'

Christine and especially Bianca expressed support for Indigenous athletes, and both women showed their interest or involvement in physical/movement activities that have an Indigenous component, but this does not seem to be the dominant frame for either of them when it comes to sport viewing and participation. The experience of and opportunities for familial and communal expressions of taste is more pronounced, particularly in terms of sport spectatorship.

The different registers of Indigenous cultural capital

We have, in the preceding sections, identified some features distinguishing Indigenous cultural tastes and practices from those of other Australians. We have also explored the key respects in which Indigenous tastes are differentiated along gender lines and across the tertiary/non-tertiary divide. In turning now to explore the potential broader significance of these findings, we return to the questions we broached at the outset via Xu Daozhi's observations concerning the varied roles played by Indigenous cultural capital in contemporary settler-colonial societies. To date, most attention has been given to the ways in which distinctive Indigenous knowledges and cultural practices may serve as a resource that can promote collective advantages for specific Indigenous communities or benefits for Indigenous individuals in specific contexts. The 2015–2018 Australian Research Council funded project *The Value of Aboriginal Cultural Heritage*, led by David Throsby and Howard Morphy, is an example of the first approach in its concern to examine 'the economic and cultural value of Indigenous cultural capital (i.e. cultural resources in a form of cultural knowledge or other cultural heritage) and identify how such cultural capital creates sustainable development opportunities in remote Indigenous communities in Australia' (Macquarie University, 2015). New Zealand research seeking to identify the respects in which Māori culture can serve as a cultural capital resource for expatriate Māori in London exemplifies the second (Thornley, 2015). Our work in the ACF project on the Deadlys – an arts, culture and community award programme nominated by, voted for and awarded to Aboriginal and Torres Strait Islander individuals and communities – cuts across both approaches in its investigation of the programme's strategic negotiation of individual and collective forms of cultural capital and its expression of Aboriginal and Torres Strait Islander taste and autonomy (Kelly, 2019).

The differences in Indigenous cultural tastes and practices that are evidenced by our survey data also suggest that both collective and more individualised forms of capital are in play. It will be helpful, in regard to the first of these and by way of adding a further dimension to the directions suggested by Xu Daozhi's work, to draw on another of Bourdieu's concepts: that of symbolic capital which, in its most general sense, he defined as an attribute of those cultural practices that bestow a particular honour on those who engage in them. Although not a usage that Bourdieu himself proposed, the concept has since been applied to the value which raced collectives – that is, groups which identify themselves positively in racial terms where race is understood as an identity shaped in response to a history of oppression (Visweswaran, 2010) – derive from those cultural practices which both mark their difference from, while also reaching into, the dominant culture: the Harlem Renaissance, for example (Hutchinson, 1995: 12). In similarly approaching Indigenous cultural tastes and practices as assets rather than liabilities, we follow the Indigenous sociologist Maggie Walter who urges the need to break with the 'five Ds' (2016: 80) – disparity, deprivation, disadvantage, dysfunction and difference – that typically structure statistical data on Indigenous Australians. This is necessary if we are to understand the ways that Indigenous difference may contribute to the well-being and political standing of Indigenous Australians rather than, as Rowse puts it, appearing 'only in negative terms as cultural deficit' (2010: 154).[7]

The issues at stake in the marking of positive political differences are perhaps most strikingly evident in the heritage field where a particularly strong Indigenous engagement with Indigenous heritage is usually accompanied by a more distanced relationship to non-Indigenous Australian heritage (but not always; as we have seen, Christine is an exception). It is not difficult to see, poking through these figures, the themes of cultural survival and the increasingly pointed politics of the 'history wars' as evident in continuing debates over Invasion Day/Australia Day, the 'un-Cooking' of national histories to detach them from the colonial time of foundational narratives centred on the figure of Captain Cook, and the politics of Aboriginal deep time. This is not to suggest that the symbolic significance of Indigenous investments in Indigenous practices is all of one piece. As we have seen in Chapters 1, 3 and 6, the significance of Gurrumul Yunupingu and Albert Namatjira as Indigenous artists whose work occupies the boundaries between Indigenous and Western high cultural traditions is different from the significance invested in the footballer Adam Goodes. At the time our survey was conducted, Goodes became a public symbol of Indigenous resilience – as well as the subject of censure – for performing a war cry after scoring a goal and, in some interpretations, shaking an imaginary spear, a long-standing symbol of Indigenous resistance, at the supporters of the opposing team who had subjected him to racist heckling. The strength of Indigenous liking of African-American sportsmen and women, taken together with Indigenous respondents' greater engagement with American over British and European culture generally, resonates with the strong historical affiliations between American black consciousness movements and Indigenous Australian cultural politics – affiliations that NITV's programming policies consciously nurture (Dibley and Turner, 2018) and that have been well documented in the literary field (Shoemaker, 2004).

Regarding the operation of more individualised forms of cultural capital, our findings need to be placed against the backdrop of debates among Indigenous intellectuals on the need to recognise the significance of the historically recent (largely post-1980s) relations between educational attainment and occupational success in combatting the stereotypical presentations of Indigenous Australians summarised by Walter's five-Ds (Rowse, 2017, ch. 11). Our data throws interesting and, we believe, important new light on these debates in adding cultural tastes and practices to the relations between educational and occupational advancement that Larissa Behrendt and her colleagues have identified. Tables 12.8 and 12.9 provide points of entry into some of the key issues here. Table 12.8 compares the degree to which a specific set of the Australian items from our survey are recognised by those Indigenous respondents who belong to the professional and managerial class with the response rates of those from other class positions. Table 12.9 does the same for a range of overseas items. The items for both tables have been selected for this purpose on the basis of their strong levels of correlation with higher class positions in the main sample as identified in Chapters 1 to 6.

TABLE 12.8 Class differences in Indigenous rates of recognition: Australian items (%)

Indigenous items	Professional and managerial class	Other classes	Other Australian items	Professional and managerial class	Other classes
Redfern Now	81	59	Sculthorpe	13	4
Mailman	61	48	Byrne	68	57
Yunupingu	80	45	Preston	35	18
Moffatt	19	11	Quilty	32	14
Namatjira	90	70	Malouf	32	20
Morgan	55	20	Winton	59	34

TABLE 12.9 Class differences in Indigenous rates of recognition: overseas items (%)

Literary, music, art items	Professional and managerial class	Other classes	TV, sport, heritage items	Professional and managerial class	Other classes
DeLillo	13	5	Mad Men	52	36
Woolf	74	66	The Killing	32	34
The Four Seasons	58	36	Williams	100	98
Kind of Blue	32	24	Tendulkar	71	59
Van Gogh	90	89	Stonehenge	90	84
Monet	81	59	Ellis Island	65	45

Familiarity with these cultural items – all of which have relatively high cultural associations – operates in broadly similar ways in relation to class divisions across the Indigenous and main samples. There are, of course, exceptions (*The Killing*, for example, which is more popular with professionals and managers in the main sample) and it is notable that in some instances (Van Gogh, Stonehenge) the differences are minor. It should be noted that the pattern for genre tastes is also uneven. News and current affairs TV programmes register significant differences between the professional and managerial class and other classes (52 versus 20 per cent) as do classical music (35 versus 14 per cent) and jazz (19 versus 5 per cent). However, tastes for some other genres (liking modern art, for example, or watching golf or tennis on TV) run in a contrary direction in being more preferred by Indigenous Australians occupying lower class positions. When all these qualifications are entered, however, there is strong evidence that class produces similar differences in taste across the Indigenous and main samples.

If we unpack the class statistics for the Indigenous sample in a little more detail, we can also see the crucial significance of education and gender. Thirty-nine per cent of the Indigenous sample belong to the professional and managerial class, and all of these who are in higher-level positions have completed tertiary qualifications. The same is true for 54 per cent of lower managers and professionals. These figures compare with tertiary qualifications having been attained by only 19 per cent of Indigenous respondents in intermediate class positions and by only 13 per cent of those in the working class. We have noted already that women in the Indigenous sample have higher tertiary participation rates than men. They are also disproportionally represented in the higher class positions, accounting for 57 per cent of those in higher management or professional positions, and 75 per cent of those in lower management or professional positions. Confirming a tendency reported by Behrendt et al. (2012), the most common fields of study for Indigenous women with completed tertiary qualifications are the humanities and social sciences (30 per cent). And as a testimony to the historical recentness of this new class formation, only 12 per cent of those with a completed tertiary qualification report similar levels of achievement on the part of their parents, while 41 per cent have partners with tertiary qualifications, a strong testament to the importance of tertiary education to the development of dual-career pathways.[8]

However, it is not only universities but also primary and secondary schooling that have shaped the aspirations that have led both to the development of an Indigenous professional middle class and to a more widely distributed critically reflective Aboriginal consciousness. Bianca says that her primary school emphasised:

> celebrating Indigenous culture, so NAIDOC Day was really big … My high school put a lot of importance on trying to recognise Indigenous culture … Everyone in … Year 10 had to learn about colonisation and [the] Stolen Generations and Eddie Mabo, like that was compulsory and then I looked at other high schools and a lot of other schools don't do that. I think that was definitely a good aspect. Also they always pushed for going to uni, I noticed, my high school was very big on getting an ATAR … A message that was cemented into my head … not just from my family but from my high school is to aim high.[9]

The importance of family is also emphasised by Kim, who stresses the role played by the experience of the forcible removal of generations of Indigenous Australians from their homes as a parental spur to the educational advancement of their children:

> When I was a kid it was, I think mum and dad were afraid of losing us or having us taken away, so we always had to behave. We had to make sure that we always looked clean, we always got top marks at school, we always did as good as or better than everyone else at school.

Positive responses from family and primary and secondary educational institutions in the face of oppression, discrimination and destructive governmental policies have fostered Indigenous educational and occupational achievement, which has in turn shaped the development of specifically Indigenous inflections of cultural capital.

Conclusion

It will be useful, in concluding, to place our concerns in a longer historical perspective by drawing on another concept that has framed the ways in which familiarity with Indigenous cultures served as a capital resource in earlier periods of colonialism. We have in mind Steinmetz's (2007) concept of 'ethnographic capital', referring to the advantages that anthropologists and anthropologically informed administrators acquired in the political fields of colonial administration. While developed by Steinmetz in relation to the indirect forms of rule associated with Germany's overseas territories in the late nineteenth and early twentieth centuries, the same principles have been applied to the uses of anthropology in settler-colonial contexts over the same period, including Australia (Bennett et al., 2017). If the 'ethnographic capital' acquired through knowledge of Indigenous cultures could serve as a capital resource, the processes of colonisation in Australia simultaneously disqualified it as a possible capital resource for Indigenous Australians. British conquest of Australia included frontier wars, followed by policies to manage the lives of Indigenous survivors. These policies aimed to convert people from the status of 'prehistoric primitives' that was attributed to them to the 'more developed' culture of the settler state; they rested on negative valuations of the customs and culture of Indigenous Australians. Their impact on Indigenous social structures and cultural practices varied by region and in timing, but on the whole the system of values, the criteria of legitimation and the institutions shaping the organisation of the Australian cultural field over this period excluded the possibility of Indigenous culture serving as a capital resource for Indigenous Australians. Indigenous commitments to 'country and culture' were maintained in much of Australia as a resource that mattered only within Indigenous peoples' own increasingly beleaguered systems of social reproduction. There were signs of some changes to this situation, particularly in the 1930s, but the most influential forms of Aboriginal political mobilisation in this period reflected an acceptance of the premise of the need for the acceleration of Indigenous acquisition of British culture as the only kind of culture capable of securing collective mobility (McGregor, 2011).

If it is now possible for Indigenous culture to serve as form of capital for both Indigenous and non-Indigenous Australians, this reflects the emergence since the 1960s of a relatively autonomous Indigenous cultural field that occupies a distinctive position within the national cultural field (Rowse, 2017). What defines the Indigenous cultural field are processes that have been developed across a range of institutions giving new salience to the Indigenous/non-Indigenous distinction and to the persons and things marked as Indigenous. It goes beyond the remit of this chapter to trace the key steps in the emergence of this sub-field; nor can we identify the full range of agents whose interactions have promoted a more positive valuation of Indigeneity. Indigenous cultural activists and intellectuals have been the most crucial change agents in this regard. But account must also be taken of the roles of progressive non-Indigenous anthropologists, musicologists, art historians, heritage and literary theorists; the directors of cultural institutions and their staff; arts and cultural policy agencies; the inclusion of Indigenous culture in school and university curricula; the establishment of relatively autonomous state bodies, criteria of assessment and mechanisms for the distribution of state funding to Indigenous writers, artists and musicians. These are among the forces touched on, on a field-by-field basis in the chapters in Part I, which have, despite setbacks and reversals, gained momentum, particularly since the 1970s. Their cumulative effect has been to establish Indigenous culture as a state organised and validated sub-field of the broader Australian cultural field in which Indigenous-specific and Australian inflections of more general Western cultural values have been brought into complex relations of adjudication with one another. The Indigenous responses to our survey suggest that there are class and gender differences in the ways that Indigenous people combine (more or less legitimate) Indigenous and non-Indigenous items in their lifestyles. They also highlight the respects in which the newly legitimised forms of Indigenous culture operate as a differentiating capital resource among Indigenous Australians.

Notes

1 Rowse refers to Langton's 2012 Boyer Lectures broadcast by the ABC and to Grant's memoir (Grant, 2002).
2 The criteria for, and consequences of, determining who shall be counted as Indigenous have varied significantly over the period since Federation. It goes beyond our purpose here to review these issues, but see Rowse (2017). Suffice it to note that we followed current Census procedures in asking survey respondents whether they were of Aboriginal or Torres Strait Islander origin.
3 The female/male composition of the Aboriginal and Torres Strait Islander sample is 56 per cent to 44 per cent. The age distribution is 16 per cent for 18–24 year olds, 10 per cent for 25–39 year olds, 44 per cent for 40–59 year olds and 28 per cent for those aged 60 or older, with the remainder refusing to identify their age. The tertiary/non-tertiary composition of the sample is 45/55 per cent. Thirty-nine per cent of the sample are in lower or higher managerial or professional positions. Our analysis is also offered with the caveat that each of the other boost samples also displays unique differences in socio-demographic composition and is therefore not representative.
4 Hage drew attention to this consideration in arguing that only Indigenous Australians could offer a morally credible alternative to the forms of national capital associated with the field of whiteness (1998: 59).
5 Sixty per cent of female Indigenous respondents had partial or completed tertiary qualifications compared to 26 per cent of male Indigenous respondents.
6 As noted, a significant proportion of the Aboriginal and Torres Strait Islander sample was recruited in NSW, with only a small number of respondents from the States where AFL is particularly popular (Victoria, South Australia and Western Australia; see www.abc.net.au/news/2016-05-06/non-victorian-afl-clubs-are-not-just-making-up-the-numbers/7388444). This may explain the lower rates of AFL viewing and participation recorded by Indigenous respondents to the ACF survey.
7 The role of statistical presentations of Indigenous Australians in this regard, we should add, needs also to be interpreted in the light of earlier racialised methods for the enumeration of Aboriginal and Torres Strait Islander people through anthropometric and related techniques of measurement.
8 Charles Perkins was the first Indigenous Australian to be awarded a degree, in 1966. It is now estimated that more than 30,000 Indigenous Australians have graduated.
9 NAIDOC is an annual week-long observance and celebration of Indigenous culture that takes its name from the National Aboriginal and Islanders Day Observance Committee. ATAR (Australian Tertiary Admission Rank) is the primary criterion for university entrance.

13
CULTURAL DIVERSITY AND THE ETHNOSCAPES OF TASTE IN AUSTRALIA

Greg Noble

It has become a truism of public discourse that migration and multiculturalism have dramatically altered the nature of Australian society and culture. Since Australia commenced a large-scale immigration programme after the Second World War, the country has taken in migrants whose cultural backgrounds diverge increasingly from the British-derived culture dominating Australian society since colonisation in 1788. While initially many of these migrants came from Europe, they hail increasingly from Asia, Africa, South America and the Middle East. Australia is now home to people from more than 300 ancestries. While this diversification is sometimes seen as a threat to the coherence of a national culture, multiculturalism is typically described in official discourse through a language of enrichment which emphasises the economic and cultural benefits ethnic diversity has brought. This sense of enrichment is seen in terms of the 'cultural life' of the nation, but with an 'economic dividend' through forms of consumption (Commonwealth of Australia, 2013). As well as providing much of the labour that has driven economic growth, migration is seen to have led to the expansion of existing markets and the opening of new ones. This portrays multiculturalism as a 'marketing opportunity', worth billions of dollars, and the 'ethnic consumer' as a force in its own right, but also in reshaping 'mainstream' practices (Neilsen Company, 2017). However, neither the extent to which ethnic diversity has transformed patterns of cultural consumption, nor how this diversity is reflected in the distribution of tastes and cultural capital across Australia, is clear.[1]

This chapter draws on survey and interview data from the *Australian Cultural Fields* (ACF) project to consider some of the issues that flow from these changes across diverse fields of cultural practice. As the chapters on these fields in Part I show, it is difficult to draw out the effects of ethnicity from aggregated data, so this chapter focuses on considering a more select set of findings from the data to point to the complex entanglements of migration, ethnicity, culture and taste. As well as having national and Indigenous cohorts, we surveyed four ethnically defined groups – around 50–60 respondents each of Italian, Lebanese, Chinese and Indian heritage – and conducted follow-up interviews with a small number of these participants.

This chapter suggests that, paralleling the developments identified in the previous chapter on Indigenous culture, migration has both reshaped 'mainstream' tastes in Australia and produced niche audiences. While the data confirms a range of similarities and differences between the ethno-specific samples and the main sample, and between the different ethno-specific samples, we argue that the data raises questions about the complex and differentiated ways in which ethnicity and cultural consumption are interrelated in Australia. Unlike conventional market research, and as the generational and demographic differences listed in the samples above indicate, we do not take ethnic categories as given or coherent communities but rather see them as consisting in complex 'ethnoscapes'. Appadurai (1996: 33, 50, 64) used the term 'ethnoscape' to draw attention to the emergent landscapes of people shaped by global flows of things and meanings, as well as people, which have reshaped practices of consumption and produced more 'cosmopolitan' orientations to the world. He also used it to draw attention to the 'perspectival' nature of how we construct the world through grouping people in such categories. We use the term to register the ways that, when we talk about the relation between ethnicity and cultural hierarchies of taste, we are actually talking about a complex set of issues: the transplanting and provisioning of cultural items from elsewhere, the adoption of these items into an increasingly diversified 'mainstream', the dissonance of the migration experience and adaptation to homeland cultures, and the development of transnational relations of consumption.

The chapter argues for the need to disentangle these diverse processes and histories in the composition and recomposition of cultural capital in order to consider the implications of the survey data for understanding the complex logics in migrants' investment in national cultural capital (Hage, 1998) and for engaging with recent claims about the increasingly 'cosmopolitan' nature of cultural tastes. It concludes with a close reading of some interview data to more fully understand the connections between migration, globalisation and cultural consumption in the ways Australians of migrant heritage experience and position themselves in relation to complex forms of cultural capital.

Ethnicity and consumption: adaptation, maintenance and beyond

While the relation between ethnicity and consumption has long been a focus in marketing and commerce (Chattaraman and Lennon, 2008; Lo, 2009), this research has been largely framed in terms of a tension between migrant acculturation and the desire to maintain ethnic identity (Kennedy and Hall, 2006). While consumption is crucial to both migrant acquisition of cultural capital and to the formation of ethnic identity through diaspora markets (Gowricharn, 2017), it is also clear that communal 'self-provisioning' – especially through small businesses – involves processes through which both ethnic identities and related tastes are differentially maintained and adapted (Hamlett *et al.*, 2008). These often also reproduce ethnic stereotypes as a marketing tool for accessing wider audiences.

Ethnicity and migration, however, have been under-scrutinised in sociologies of consumption, and when they are scrutinised they tend to reproduce the binary of cultural maintenance versus adaptation (Vallianatos and Raine, 2008). In Bennett *et al.*'s (1999) Australian study, the discussion of ethnicity is framed in terms of a generational basis to the increasing influence of American culture and the threat this may pose to a sense of a national identity. The later British study by Bennett *et al.* (2009) devotes a chapter to ethnicity but, in addition to using UK categories that do not translate easily to the Australian context, their primary findings are that ethnicity is much less significant than class, education, age and gender in explaining taste, but does connect to weaker national affiliations: yet they also conclude that their data is not as nuanced as they had hoped.

Part of the problem in unpacking the relation between ethnicity and consumption is the difficulty of developing strong data sets across small and diffuse cohorts. Alongside this, both the marketing and sociological literatures have tended to focus on ethnicity as a coherent demographic category deployed to analyse similarities and differences in relation to 'mainstream' consumption and the formation of ethnic-specific markets. Both problematically rely on reductive and static notions of ethnicity and mainstream, as has been shown in relation to the cultural sector (Noble and Ang, 2018). Ethnic identity is not simply transported, but reconstructed through migration (Hamlett *et al.*, 2008). A key consequence is that 'country of origin' is a much less significant factor than a more nuanced sense of 'ethnic orientation' in consumption of both high and popular culture (Trienekens, 2002). As the interview data will show, making sense of preferences has to be explored in terms of the investments in the fashioning of an ethnic identity after migration as well as adapting to a 'national culture'. Moreover, very little research has considered the complexity of ethnic categories, such as the way consumption has been used to negotiate multi-ethnic identities (Harrison *et al.*, 2015). 'Maintenance' and 'acculturation' through consumption are not, therefore, discrete paths but diverse ends of a range of strategic responses to the processes of resettlement.

Given that research has been dominated by the opposition between adaptation and maintenance, there has been much less engagement with a third focus of enquiry: how migration and increasing cultural diversity have changed the ways society as a whole consumes. Most attention in this third area has been given to the take-up of 'ethnic food' in the reshaping of national markets, but there is recognition of the ways migration has also impacted upon various fields, even though it is sometimes construed as a 'problem' (Warren *et al.*, 2002; Australia for Everyone, 2016; Noble and Ang, 2018). Much of the research continues to see the mainstream as 'white' consumers who enjoy the exotic offerings of multiculturalism without a more nuanced understanding of how migration itself reconfigures fields of consumption in Australia (Hage, 1998). However, this issue has been opened up in recent debates around the increasingly 'cosmopolitan' nature of consumption, which suggests a greater 'openness' to cultural diversity than prefigured in Bourdieu's analyses.

Recent analyses argue for emerging forms of 'cosmopolitan' cultural capital (Prieur and Savage, 2013) which challenge assumptions about the coherence of a national culture by pointing to the ways that new forms of consumption are diverging from traditional patterns and aesthetic boundaries. Bourdieu's notion of distinction has retained its centrality in these debates despite these shifts, yet Prieur and Savage (2013) and Coulangeon (2017) have argued that Bourdieu's theorisation of cultural capital needs revision in the wake of the decline of 'highbrow' culture and a recomposition of taste hierarchies. They postulate the emergence of forms of 'cosmopolitan' cultural capital resulting from the globalisation of cultural consumption and a growing 'openness to diversity' and a 'knowing' attitude towards 'exotic' cultures. Yet there are two problems with this literature. First, the use of 'cosmopolitanism' to reference worldliness in contrast to narrow localisms has focused on elites, ignoring the kinds of 'everyday cosmopolitanism' typical of multicultural societies (Kendall *et al.*, 2009). Second, this 'openness' is primarily understood in terms of a 'high' and 'low' distinction: 'ethnic' cultures are positioned as one 'difference' among many, and equated with 'popular' or 'folk' forms to be enjoyed by cultivated consumers (Peterson and Kern, 1996; Ollivier, 2008). As Holt (1997: 112) argues, 'the most powerful expression of cosmopolitan versus local tastes is through perceptions of and desires for the exotic', but he never really unpacks what 'exotic' means in a migrant nation, as we attempt below. Grappling with the cosmopolitan nature of consumption is important precisely because it draws attention to the questions of who is consuming what, and how these new forms of consumption challenge or reproduce dominant hierarchies of taste.

A fourth focus of research has been the transnational dimensions of consumption. Transnationalism is often construed primarily in terms of the international 'content' of particular *items*; while this is important, and we explore it below, we need to see it in relation to the transnational nature of *practices*, the ways global flows reshape relations and processes of consuming (Savage *et al.*, 2010). The studies that have focused on transnationalism as a process rather than a content draw less on Bourdieusian sociologies of cultural fields than anthropological studies on flows of goods and their appropriation across national borders (Emontspool and Woodward, 2018).

This discussion of the literature suggests that while research into the nature of cultural capital has engaged increasingly with questions of migration and ethnicity, it tends to do so in a limited fashion. Singular points of research focus actually work to aggregate and thereby obfuscate complex and diverse processes. As Meuleman and Savage (2013: 254) argue, even 'cosmopolitanism' is too loose a term to cover these several things. We have used the discussion of these four concerns to point out the need to talk about diverse processes of adaptation and maintenance alongside discussion of cosmopolitan and transnational dimensions of consumption. We need a more nuanced approach to interpreting data to separate out those processes. Our data suggests that, while there has been a recomposition of cultural capital in Australia as a consequence of migration and multiculturalism, this actually encompasses a number of different kinds of things: the diversification of goods, the formation of distinct but overlapping ethnoscapes of taste, the cosmopolitanisation of the field and the transnationalisation of consumption. Taken this way, we also need to think about whether 'openness to otherness' best describes the kinds of positions people deploy through consumption.

The samples

As well as having national and Indigenous cohorts, we surveyed four ethnically defined groups – between 55 and 76 respondents each of Italian, Lebanese, Chinese and Indian heritage (both those born in the country of origin and their children) – and conducted follow-up interviews with a small number of these participants. These ethnicities were selected to reflect a range of 'old' and 'new' cohorts of migrants: Italian migration was strong in the 1950s and 1960s; Lebanese migrants (a diverse category constituting both Christians and Muslims) arrived mostly from the 1970s; the Chinese are similarly a diverse category, some of whom have been in Australia for many generations, while others, especially from the Chinese mainland, arrived mostly since the 1980s; and Indians are the most recent cohort, with arrivals high in the 2000s. Ethnic samples were compiled by combining those born in a particular country, those whose parents were born in that country and those who identified as belonging to a particular ethnicity. The survey also recorded the age, gender, occupation, class and education of respondents.

The main sample and the ethnic samples are not, strictly speaking, demographically equivalent: there was a greater percentage of women in the latter, there is some unevenness in age distribution (the Chinese are over-represented in the 18–24 band, Italians over-represented in the 60+ band), in class and education (Indian and Chinese samples included higher proportions of 'large business owners' and tertiary educated while there was a higher proportion of 'small employers' among Italians) and in location (Italian, Chinese and Indian more likely in the inner city; Lebanese, Indian and Chinese more suburban). But these variations in the samples reflect broader variations across Australia's population. Unsurprisingly, the median age for those born in Italy and Lebanon is significantly higher than for those born in India, China or Australia. Perhaps more significantly, those born in China and India are overwhelmingly more likely to have university qualifications and be employed in professional occupations than the other groups. In contrast, however, the Chinese, Lebanese and Indians also have higher levels of unemployment, and Italians, Chinese and Lebanese have lower family incomes (Australian Bureau of Statistics, 2019). The limited research that exists shows that while there is some amelioration of economic and educational inequalities into the second generation, the patterns of disadvantage are largely reproduced (Khoo *et al.*, 2002).

Migrancy, generation and taste in contemporary Australia

An initial analysis of the national and ethnic samples in the survey data provide interesting insights into the ways ethnic diversity plays out in the Australian cultural landscape. These comparisons echo Bennett et al.'s (2009) general finding that ethnicity corresponds with weaker national affiliation, but also indicate that there is variation within ethnic communities around age, class and country of birth. Our survey also showed different types of differences in cultural practices: not just between the ethnic samples and the national sample, but also between those born in Australia and those born overseas (that is, between 'first-generation' migrants and their Australia-born descendants).

We asked respondents about their knowledge, tastes and participation in relation to 130 specific cultural items (programmes, sites, personalities, works and artists of diverse international and Australian provenance) to examine how specific groups relate to cultural referents from different national or world-regional origins.[2] These items from across the six cultural fields included in the study were grouped into six 'scales': Indigenous Australia, non-Indigenous Australia, United Kingdom, United States, Europe and Asia (see Appendices G and H).

While the practicalities of survey design restricted the range of items to represent each scale – particularly those defined as European and Asian – they were chosen to give a broadly recognisable shape to the cultural fields. These scales, when read through the lens of ethnicity, allow new ways of thinking about different patterns of cultural consumption. Table 13.1, for example, presents a simple comparison between respondents born in Australia and those born overseas, grouped together. This simple comparison portrays the significance of *migrancy* in Australian cultural

TABLE 13.1 Regional scales by item of origin, Australia-born and overseas-born: national sample (figures represent means of actual number of items participated with, liked or known)

	Overseas-born, n = 250	Australian-born, n = 952
Indigenous participation	1.7	2
Indigenous taste	2.6	3.1
Indigenous knowledge	4.9	5.6
Other Australian participation	14.6	17
Other Australian taste	17.2	20.6
Other Australian knowledge	34.4	38.6
US participation	5.4	5.3
US taste	5.3	5.3
US knowledge	11.7	12
UK participation	6.3	5.9
UK taste	5.5	5.1
UK knowledge	9.9	10
Europe participation	4.8	4.5
Europe taste	4.7	4.2
Europe knowledge	7.1	6.9
Asia participation	0.4	0.2
Asia taste	0.9	0.7
Asia knowledge	3.4	3.3

consumption patterns rather than ethnicity per se. It captures the challenge of cultural adaptation as an uneven, temporal process of the accumulation of *localised* 'national cultural capital' (Hage, 1998: 53). Across the fields and across the variables of knowledge, taste and participation, overseas-born respondents consistently have a slightly weaker orientation to both Indigenous and non-Indigenous Australian items, for example. At first glance, these differences seem minor, but small differences in small percentages can be relatively very significant. Moreover, the sample of Australian-born includes the children of migrants, and especially those whose ancestries differ markedly from 'white' and Indigenous Australia. These differences suggest that those born in Australia have a small but noticeably stronger attachment to local-national cultural capital. We stress the local dimension of this national capital to designate investment in Indigenous and non-Indigenous Australian items, because some ethnic preferences can also be deemed to be 'nationalist', but in relation to the respondents' homeland. The overseas-born, on the other hand, had a small but stronger orientation to European and Asian items (as non-English speaking background scales), though we note again the complications of aggregating in the category of 'overseas-born' people from the around the world.

In comparison, the local-national inflection of the Australia-born was complemented by slightly less investment in items from these regions. In the other two scales, however, the results are even more complicated: overseas-born respondents have a stronger orientation to American and especially British items – the two most globalised sources of English-speaking cultural content – in terms of taste and participation, but not knowledge. This may mean that while there is an international (rather than cosmopolitan) flavour to dominant forms of cultural capital in Australia, it is selective and unevenly distributed. We might also infer that migrant respondents tend to have more 'cosmopolitan' tastes, but this relies on aggregating the overseas-born. Of course, the overseas-born include people from the UK and New Zealand, historically the two major source countries of Australia's migrants, and the Australia-born includes people of diverse ethnic ancestries, so this initial comparison tells us more about the effects of migrant status than ethnicity as such.

Table 13.2, which separates the four ethnic samples and subdivides them into those born in Australia and those born overseas, suggests several things. First, it shows a significant acquisition of local-national capital compared to the other, overseas scales. Given that these figures are most significant for the Italian sample, the 'oldest' of the four migrant groups, it suggests that the temporality of arrival – or the length of time a migrant cohort has been in Australia – affects the capacity to accumulate this capital. This temporality is accompanied by another: the discrepancy in the accumulation of local-national forms of cultural capital amongst migrants and their Australian-born offspring reflects the expected 'generational' changes in the acquisition of local-national capital. The Australian-born generally also exhibit a significant up-take of what 'matters' here, not just in terms of Australian and Indigenous content, but also in terms of American, British and European content, indicating the internationalised nature of 'local' cultural capital accumulated by the children of migrants. The difference between those born overseas and those born

254 Greg Noble

TABLE 13.2 Regional scales for ethnic samples, Australia-born and overseas-born

	Italian OS-born, n=28	Italian Aus-born, n=48	Lebanese OS-born, n=31	Lebanese Aus-born, n=24	Chinese OS-born, n=41	Chinese Aus-born, n=20	Indian OS-born, n=61	Indian Aus-born, n=3
Indigenous participation	1.8	1.8	0.7	1.3	0.7	1.3	0.9	1.7
Indigenous taste	2.9	2.8	1.4	2.4	1.5	2.4	1.9	2.3
Indigenous knowledge	4.9	5.7	3.5	4.1	3.1	4.1	3.5	4.7
Other Australian participation	16.2	17.8	10.6	13.1	10.3	13	10.8	9.3
Other Australian taste	20.3	21.8	13.2	17.6	12	14.7	13.9	11.3
Other Australian knowledge	35.8	39.7	27	29.5	23.6	30.6	25.7	30.3
US participation	5.3	5.2	3.3	4.1	3.3	4.8	3.2	4
US taste	4.9	5.3	4.3	6.8	3.7	4.9	4.8	5
US knowledge	11.1	12.2	8.2	9.6	8.5	11.3	8.6	9.7
UK participation	5.5	6	2.7	4.1	3.6	4.6	3.6	2.7
UK taste	4.8	5.3	2.5	3.3	3	4.1	3.7	2
UK knowledge	9.3	10	5.6	7	6.3	8.4	6.8	6.7
Europe participation	6	5.6	2.7	3.3	3.4	3.9	2.7	2.7
Europe taste	5.6	5.6	2.9	3.4	3.4	3.8	3	2.7
Europe knowledge	7.8	7.7	5.1	5.4	5.1	5.9	4.7	5.3
Asia participation	0.3	0.3	0.1	0.2	0.9	1	0.9	0.7
Asia taste	0.5	.8	0.2	0.7	1.3	1.5	1.7	1.3
Asia knowledge	2.9	3.1	2.3	2.6	3.6	4.5	3.4	3.3

here is much less significant for the 'oldest' migrant group – the Italians – compared with the Chinese, one of the most recent arrivals, indicating that the 'first generation' of Italians have been here long enough to accumulate their own stocks of national capital, while for the Chinese the generational shift is necessarily of greater significance: period since arrival and generational change are different orders of temporality.[3]

The Lebanese sample presents a more complicated picture. They have been here longer than the two Asian groups (though not as long as the Italians), yet their overall stocks do not differ greatly from the Chinese and Indian samples. Moreover, the difference between the first and the second generation is relatively significant for the Lebanese: more so than the Italians but less than the Chinese. As we noted earlier in the chapter, the Lebanese are the most disadvantaged socio-economically of the groups, suggesting that the class and educational background of the first generation shapes the overall accumulation of new cultural capital and that this is carried through somewhat in the second generation. This interconnection of temporality and class is reflected in other ways.

As we saw in the previous chapter, the 'older' Italian cohort have a greater investment in Indigenous and non-Indigenous Australian content compared to the more recent groups. This pattern, however, is repeated across the American, British and European scales, but much less noticeably and more unevenly, while the generational change is less marked. Again, this reflects the temporal dimensions of cultural capital accumulation and the consequences of participating in the local educational system which valorises such capital. And again, the Lebanese have the lowest stocks in these scales but also have a slightly lower generational change. Returning to the broad demographic profiles of these diasporic groups generally and those sampled in the survey, we can say that the fact that the Lebanese have not accrued as much national cultural capital as the Chinese and Indians suggests there may also be a class dimension to the accumulation of dominant Australian forms of cultural capital by ethnic groups that works in complex relation to the temporalities of settlement.

Lastly, there is also an uneven link between ethnic backgrounds and regional scales. For example, the Chinese and Indian groups have much greater investments in Asian culture, unsurprisingly, but this is also carried through into those born in Australia: indeed, the Australia-born Chinese have a noticeably stronger and deeper investment in Asian cultural items than their migrant (grand)parents. The Italians, similarly, show a much greater investment in European items, which is maintained in the second generation (there is no comparable category for Middle Eastern items).

The broad data, therefore, shows predictable patterns of cultural attachment, the temporality of capital accumulation, the temporality of generational change and the intersection of ethnicity and class around the of distribution of cultural taste, but the degree of unevenness across and within ethnic categories indicates that we should avoid lumping together 'ethnic Australians' or even an ethnically defined cohort to generalise about the relation between ethnicity and consumption. Understanding

256 Greg Noble

knowledge, taste and participation in terms of differentiated ethnoscapes, comprising diverse flows and logics of investment, is crucial to challenge assumptions of a singular national space of cultural consumption and the homogeneity of ethnic groups within that space.

But there is a further point that flows from thinking about using this data for analysing the effects of ethnicity, migrancy, time and generation. The selectivity of the items used is not simply to be understood in terms of the arbitrary nature of such scales and the difficulties of age-based comparisons (Savage et al., 2010: 605; Bennett et al., 1999: 221). It is a reflection of the complexity of contemporary consumption, in which the very nature of the expansion and diversity of the market cannot be easily represented. There is virtually no research which captures the way the marketplace is an enormously more crowded place than it was in Bourdieu's France, or in Australia 50 years ago. The Australian Bureau of Statistics, for example, does not document how migration and globalisation have affected the 'basket of goods' used to calculate the Consumer Price Index; nor does it document the 'size' of the marketplace in terms of numbers and types of goods, although this is now a commonplace understanding both of the consequences of consumer society as a whole and the recent innovations in online consumption. The proliferation of niche markets makes claims about the cosmopolitanisation of taste difficult to measure, but we want to use this as a productive opportunity to reflect upon the possibilities of interpreting complex cultural processes.

The ethnic specificities of consumption

Moving on from the broad comparisons of the survey data, we want to turn to field-specific issues in examining the relationship between ethnicity and 'canonical' culture and its connection with the question of acculturation and national affiliation. We consider data from the most socially exclusive field of art, as we saw in Chapter 7, and those that are much less so, such as sport. Juxtaposing the four ethnic samples and the national sample, we can see significant variations between and within them. Unsurprisingly, the picture of migrant groups and their offspring having relatively lesser amounts (measured in terms of knowledge, taste or participation) of Australian cultural capital is repeated – often more sharply – when we look at ethno-specific cohorts in the art field. As Table 13.3 shows, using just five

TABLE 13.3 Australian artists known (%)

	Sidney Nolan	Tom Roberts	Brett Whiteley	Ben Quilty	Albert Namatjira
Chinese	41	12	34	18	21
Indian	30	8	13	14	19
Italian	70	26	62	22	62
Lebanese	31	11	24	9	29
Main	67	37	53	32	63

artists from a wider list to focus upon significant differences, Australian artists are generally much less well known amongst ethnic groups.

While ethnicity is often construed in terms of weak affiliations to the 'national' culture of the new homeland (Bennett et al., 2009: 247, 250), the exception here is the Italians. While many of this cohort were long-time residents, their responses not only matched the main sample, they registered higher rates of knowledge of Sidney Nolan and Brett Whiteley. The other samples, however, display much less knowledge of these artists, especially the icon of Australian colonial art, Tom Roberts, and a major figure in the contemporary art field, Ben Quilty, who has won several major prizes (including the Archibald) and was Australia's official war artist in Afghanistan. Interestingly, Albert Namatjira remains a relatively well-known figure across the samples (although less so among the Chinese and Indians). Curiously, this is mirrored in the relatively high proportions saying they like Aboriginal art – 38 per cent for Indians and 36 per cent for Lebanese in particular – compared with 26 per cent of the national sample (bearing in mind that taste for 'Aboriginal art', which might include tourist souvenirs, may reflect broader patterns of liking than for fine art figures). This seems to complement the low liking of colonial art: no Italian respondent and only 2 per cent of the Chinese sample, compared with 9 per cent of the main sample.

These findings suggest that, across all ethnic groups, if they engage with Australian art at all, there is a greater predilection towards twentieth century modern Australian art and Aboriginal art, and much less engagement with either nineteenth century colonial art or contemporary Australian art, suggesting a weaker knowledge of or investment in the idea of a national *tradition*. This pattern is most stark in the art field, but echoed in other ways across the fields: ethnic groups have much less of an investment in Australian TV, heritage, music, sport and literature. But such local capital is also shaped by wider traditions.

In a place like Australia, cultural hierarchies are not shaped simply by national affiliations, but also by international connections to canonical items representing the 'West'. Focusing primarily on knowledge, the Italian and Chinese, overall, had greater stocks in Western cultural capital than the other groups, though perhaps for different reasons (proximity to regional provenance for the former, class for the latter): 100 per cent of Italians and 94 per cent of Chinese know da Vinci (compared with 99 per cent of the main sample), while 95 per cent of Italians and 82 per cent of Chinese know Van Gogh, closer to the main sample (95 per cent) than the other groups. But it is uneven: Rembrandt and Monet are known by only about half of the Chinese, much less than the main sample. Significantly fewer Indians have heard of Pollock (22 per cent versus 57 per cent of the main sample), Monet (35 per cent versus 73 per cent) and Rembrandt (35 per cent versus 85 per cent). The Lebanese register similarly less knowledge of artists. In terms of taste for particular genres and periods, Italians and Chinese have much higher rates for Renaissance art (25 per cent and 28 per cent compared to 15 per cent for the main sample). The Chinese (at 16 per cent) like still life almost twice as much as other cohorts, while Indians (at 8 per cent) like portraits much less than all other groups

(23–27 per cent). Both the Indians (8 per cent) and Chinese (8 per cent) like abstract art much less than the Lebanese and Italians (both around 15 per cent) and the main sample (13 per cent). This recounting of diverse findings attests to complex taste patterns that reveal the differentiated intricacies of ethnic groups' engagement with Western artistic traditions, mediated by residency and class.

Reflecting the results above, Lebanese are much less likely to participate in the arts: more than half say they never visit galleries (see Table 13.4). The Chinese, reflecting the class difference noted above in the national statistics, but also consequently faster processes of acculturation, and Italians, perhaps reflecting their greater length of stay in Australia, display patterns of participation comparable to the main sample: indeed, both groups are more likely to visit a few times a year or more. All ethnic groups are more likely than the main sample to have visited the National Gallery of Australia within the last year (ranging from 28 per cent for the Chinese to 16 per cent for the Lebanese, compared with 13 per cent for the main sample). This could be explained by a curiosity about the new homeland common to the migrant experience, but may also reflect a more strategic investment in national capital.

Unsurprisingly, each ethnic cohort indicates strong knowledge, taste and participation for items that reflect their own cultural origins. For example, 43 per cent of Italians say they have heard of Caravaggio (compared with just 25 per cent of the main sample) and 29 per cent say they like his work (versus 15 per cent). Similarly, Ai Weiwei is known by 34 per cent of Chinese, much higher than the main sample (9 per cent).

While we had no artists of Lebanese or Indian background in our list, a comparable preference is found in the data on heritage: there is a huge difference between the percentage of Lebanese who know (98 per cent) and have visited and liked (73 per cent) Byblos compared with the main sample (28 per cent; 0.6 per cent). There is a similar disparity for Indians regarding the Taj Mahal: 100 per cent of the Indian sample know it (not significantly different from the main sample's 96 per cent) but 65 per cent had visited it and like it, compared to 6 per cent for the main sample. (Given that Indian migration to Australia is a recent phenomenon, their Taj Mahal visits may have occurred before their departure.) This echoes the argument in Chapter 4 that, while touristic consumption of overseas destinations is still highly valued amongst elites, the interest in migrant heritage is sharply aggregated by

TABLE 13.4 Visited art galleries (row %)

	Once a month or more frequently	Few times a year	Once a year	Never
Chinese	5	30	48	18
Indian	5	13	41	41
Italian	7	26	28	40
Lebanese	4	18	26	53
Main	7	23	35	35

ethnicity. This data suggests that one of the consequences of multiculturalism is an enhanced stock of global cultural capital across Australian society, based on the diasporic cultural engagements of migrant groups, which complicate long-standing hierarchies of culture. As we suggest above, this expansion and diversification of various fields of consumption point towards the formation of diverse structures of value.

Such variations between ethnic samples and the main sample suggest an ethnic differentiation of cultural tastes in Australia. However, they do not necessarily point to the existence of distinct, ethnically defined 'taste cultures' but rather to an uneven landscape of ethnically inflected taste patterns: what we are suggesting is captured by Appadurai's evocation of the ethnoscape as particular kinds of flows and intensities of investment in consumption rather than bounded entities. When asked how often they participated in cultural activities within their own ethnic community, the majority in each sample say 'a few times a year' or less frequently (or never). Those indicating 'once a month' or more frequently *amongst those who responded* are as follows: Lebanese (40 per cent), Indian (37 per cent), Chinese (28 per cent) and Italian (8 per cent).[4] Length of time in Australia may explain the relatively low levels of communal activity among Italians, while other factors — degree of economic and social marginalisation necessitating the maintenance of diasporic support networks, for example — might explain the high figure for the Lebanese, compared with the Chinese respondents, who, measured in terms of educational attainment and over-representation in professional employment, have greater social and cultural resources to integrate into wider Australian society.

Who and what is cosmopolitan?

This data on ethnic-specific tendencies in relation to Australian, Western and ethnic items reveals complex patterns around national affiliations and the uneven accumulation of national cultural capital. But it also raises the issue of who, or what, is 'cosmopolitan'. So, for example, the cosmopolitan significance of a taste for a non-Australian artist depends on whether the consumer identifies with that ethnic identity, or another, or with an 'openness' to diverse cultures often seen as typical of worldly elites. A Chinese migrant who likes Chinese music is less remarkable than an Anglo-Australian farmer from regional NSW who likes it. Moreover, talking about the cosmopolitanism of tastes has traditionally been defined by the 'highbrow' or the rare — an appreciation of the work of Ai Weiwei, for example, or Chinese Opera — rather than a liking for *If You are the One*, the popular Chinese dating show on Special Broadcasting Service (SBS) TV. But cosmopolitanism can no longer be defined only in terms of rare art forms, even if different forms of cosmopolitanism carry very different kinds/amounts of capital. This is where cosmopolitan as an openness to otherness and an older cosmopolitanism construed in terms of high culture collide. To illustrate this need to take a comparative perspective on cultural tastes, we turn to responses to the Indian cricketer Sachin Tendulkar.

TABLE 13.5 Sachin Tendulkar: percentages of those who have heard of him and like him

	Chinese	Indian	Italian	Lebanese	Main
Heard of him?	36	98	65	33	75
Like him?	21	86	33	15	44

A simple explanation of these varying responses is that Indian-Australians are far more likely to know him and like him than any other group simply because he is an Indian national hero, suggesting a strong homeland-national affiliation. But simple explanations are not enough, especially when we acknowledge, as we do in Chapter 6, that sport as the bearer of key national values is also a key source of social recognition amongst migrant communities. The interesting issue here is that cricket is not a traditional, 'ethnic' cultural pursuit in India but a consequence of British colonialism which is, of course, an early form of globalisation. Tendulkar's career also spans the more recent stages in the globalisation of cricket involving one-day and Twenty20 games, largely dependent on transnational media. So knowledge of and liking for Tendulkar cannot simply be explained in 'ethnic' terms, but as interwoven with the history of colonialism and globalisation. Even if we can see sport in 'cosmopolitan' terms, it would not make sense to talk about Tendulkar's popularity in the main sample as evidence of cosmopolitanism, although it does speak to the effects of globalisation and the ways elite sport has become an international market. However, we might be tempted to see his popularity amongst the other ethnic samples as evidence of an openness to otherness, given that cricket is not an established sport in Italy, China or Lebanon. The high figure for the Italian sample could be explained less in terms of an interest in something 'exotic' than in a measure of the 'acculturation' to a national cultural preoccupation with sport as well as cricket's media visibility, given that Italians began arriving in Australia earliest of the four groups sampled. Given that the Lebanese have been in Australia in greater numbers and earlier than the Chinese, their relative lack of knowledge and interest in Tendulkar represents a weak acculturation, understood both as an ongoing marginalisation from Australia's cultural life and the limited accumulation of national cultural capital.

Our point here is simply to suggest several key issues regarding the significance of an appreciation of the 'exotic'. The first is that we cannot reduce complex processes of taste-formation to simple, ahistorical explanations: a 'taste' for Tendulkar is caught up in histories of colonialism and globalisation which make Indians more similarly placed to white Australians than to the Chinese in this regard. Second, as Coulangeon (2017: 147) argues, 'not all multicultural resources are equivalent. Some are more valued than others.' 'Cultural otherness', he elaborates, 'does not by itself constitute a multicultural capital' but needs to be valued and 'recognised as a capital'. Third, as Coulangeon (2017: 146) also argues, the 'fit' between class and cultural hierarchies needs to be seen in a more relational sense, 'as a dynamic system of positions and oppositions rather than as an immutable set of relations between social positions and cultural repertoires'.

This section has used the ACF data to argue that the effects of migration on Australian cultural fields involve a set of relations of adaptation and maintenance, homeland attachment and strategic investments in accumulating national cultural capital. It has also argued that simple claims about cosmopolitan tastes need to be unpacked, and understood relationally in terms of people's histories. Nevertheless, the diversification of fields reflected in this data can be understood as a particular form of cosmopolitan*isation*.

The cosmopolitanisation of consumption

The analysis above suggests we need to shift the debate away from cosmopolitanism as an attribute of elites and towards Beck's (2006) conceptualisation of cosmopolitanisation as the (often banal) consequences of the international flows of goods and people that reconfigure our experiences of the local and national through the 'globalisation of cultural supply' (Coulangeon, 2017: 147). It also suggests we need to think about varieties of cosmopolitanism and its diverse modes of 'openness' (Høy-Petersen and Woodward, 2018; Ollivier, 2008). In this last section, we consider how the diverse strands discussed – arguments about migration and ethnicity, acculturation and maintenance, openness to diversity and transnational relations of consumption – are woven together in the everyday life of one of our interviewees as she negotiates her positioning in the nation and beyond.

Aisha is a Lebanese Muslim woman who has been in Australia for 25 years. She works as a relationship counsellor, having gained her degree in Lebanon, but she did not gain a local graduate diploma until her kids had grown up and she could return to study and work. She lives in a small house with her husband and two children in south-western Sydney. Though not poor, she is not well endowed in either economic or 'legitimate' cultural capital. But she has varied tastes not reflected through the questionnaire, which articulate her investments in her ethnic origins, her national affiliation and her international connections.

Aisha's favourite programme is *The Project* but she also likes comedies. These tastes are connected strongly to her experience as a Muslim (see Chapters 15 and 16), but she identifies as Lebanese and Australian: 'I belong to both.' She has always striven to be part of Australian life – 'I wanted to make myself grow, I want to learn, I want to be integrated in this society' – so when her youngest child was 3 years old she started attending courses and support groups. But integrating has become harder. She likes current affairs programmes because 'you understand what's happening in the country', but also because 'it opens your mind ... it gives you a wider way of seeing things from different perspectives'. These shows serve both a pragmatic function of national acculturation and what we might call a worldly orientation. Indeed, Aisha returns regularly to the importance of having an 'open mind': she mentions this five times during the interview and it is clearly important to her and a strong motive for her tastes. This also has an educative aspect: she likes the humorous current affairs panel show *Have You Been Paying Attention?* because it focuses on 'what's happening in the world', but she also likes the comedy *Here Come The Habibs* – about a Lebanese-Australian family – 'because it says something as well'. On the other hand, she watches a lot of Arabic programmes via the Internet, but not just programmes from Lebanon: 'I am into the Turkish soapies … because it takes you to a world that you would like to live in, the romantic nice world'.

These diverse elements to her tastes are seen in the collection of nick-nacks she keeps in a cabinet in the front room: under the 'Lebanese section' where the Qur'an sits she has souvenirs from Dubai, Saudi Arabia, the Emirates, Morocco and New Caledonia. Most of these are from the travels of friends and family ('if someone I know visits countries I ask them to bring me a symbol'), as well as from her own limited travelling – but this cabinet is her collection, not the family's. The only regular travel she does is to Lebanon, for family reasons, but she also goes with 'full bags of gifts' of things her family can't get there, and returns with those bags full of things she can't get here.

She also has some examples of art and design from India, Morocco, Turkey and Scandinavia. She especially likes her Indian divider because 'it reflects a culture … it looks nice and different and unique'. She has a particular interest in Indian culture even though she has not been there, as part of her increasing appreciation of ethnic diversity: 'living in Australia and working in the mainstream with white people I more and more appreciate having a culture, appreciate cultures because it gives you a richness and different dimensions to your personality'. She likes the art and heritage of other cultures because 'it opens up your mind about the world basically and different people and different lifestyles'.

Alongside the 'old Arabic singers' she lists from her youth – the Lebanese singer Fairuz and Egyptian stars Abdel Halim, Umm Kulthūm and Hani Shaker – she also listens to French pop music of the time. She acknowledges there is an element of nostalgia to this – 'I don't know if it's because it's related to a happy phase of my life or because songs in those days were much more meaningful and the music was much more enriching.' Her husband introduced her to Phil Collins, and her kids to some English music whose 'soft' and 'meaningful' songs she likes. She usually listens via Internet streaming.

Aisha loves musical performances: she used to go with her sister-in-law, who 'was a very active community worker and she would know about what's happening locally'. As it turns out, a lot does happen locally. She occasionally attends local events, such as Arabic music concerts: 'If they are cultural events like performances, I will go. I recently went to this play, Lebanese play, for this group that came from America [Ajyal].'

Her valuing of open-mindedness is easily categorised as 'cosmopolitan', but it also shows that such cosmopolitanism does not stand as an aesthetic commitment in its own right. It is partly a response to racism in Australian society ('Some of them don't want you to be there') and partly a response to the lack of open-mindedness amongst Lebanese-Australians: 'the problem with our community, sadly, is that many of them, they are not open-minded'. She thus has a strong commitment to a multicultural ideal:

People are more exposed to different things. In many areas of Australia the differences were sort of forced on them ... If I see something outside a Chinese shop I would go and check and probably this Chinese shop reflects a lot of the culture. So without me wanting to, without me making the effort, I am exposed to a different culture and I think it's applicable to everyone. Yes, some people don't like it much due to fear, racism, don't want to change, but I think it's positive. It was positive for a lot of people who are Aussies or not Aussies because it's an exposure of something different and it makes you learn things that you wouldn't learn if those weren't here ... Having a mosque close to you or having a temple close to your house or going somewhere where you're intrigued to know about ... it tells you that there is a different world than mine.

Aisha's preferences do not classify her as a particular 'type' of consumer; even though she may engage in classifying strategies, these exist in tension. She might engage in strategies of 'acculturation', for example, but they sit alongside her desire to maintain a nostalgic relation to homeland items. Her 'nationalist' sympathies (with either Australia or Lebanon) sit alongside her 'international' interests. Many of her tastes are for items 'unaccounted' for in a conventional analysis of mainstream consumption but represent growing, local and ethnically inflected markets that sometimes do and sometimes don't impact on Anglo-Australians' consumption and sometimes do and sometimes don't connect with mainstream institutions (Ang and Noble, 2018). Her practices of consumption are caught up with transnational relations with her homeland, yet her commitment to Lebanese culture is complicated by the fact that it is regional rather than national (Egyptian singers from Egypt, Turkish soapies). It involves a 'making do' with whatever is to hand. Her accumulation of symbols of other cultures might seem superficial and symbolic, given they are not places she has visited, but she sees this as having an educative function to make her a better person.

This account of our interview with Aisha demonstrates a rich life of insightful reflections upon the relations between her practices of consumption and her identity. Aisha, in many ways, exhibits a cosmopolitan openness to otherness, but not as a form of cosmopolitan distinction. Her location in diverse ethnoscapes echoes the complex consequences of 'cosmopolitanisation', and her negotiation of competing attachments to homeland, nation and the wider world.

Conclusion

The findings presented indicate differentiated patterns of cultural taste, knowledge and participation that suggest that we need to think beyond the assumptions of coherent ethnic communities and towards a greater engagement with the entanglement of migration, globalisation and transnationalism captured in the idea of the ethnoscape. Moreover, the dual temporalities of arrival and generation articulate in complex ways with class and education. We have argued that recent claims about the significance of cosmopolitan capital are based on simplistic understandings of the complex dynamics of contemporary practices of consumption. There are multiple dynamics that need to be examined to fully explore the consequences of migration and globalisation for consumption. Cultural capitals in Australia have become increasingly diverse, multicultural, transnational and cosmopolitan, but in complex ways. This complexity points to the need for a stronger examination of the ways that the accumulation of cultural capitals articulates forms of positioning in everyday life that make living and consuming in a place like Australia a meaningful and viable experience.

Notes

1 We use the terms 'ethnic' and 'ethnicity', despite their negative history in Australia, rather than the notion of 'culture', because 'culture' has competing meanings (especially in a project exploring 'cultural fields') and because 'culture', when used in relation to migrant populations, wrongly implies the continuity of a 'way of life'. When we use ethnicity as a demographic category and as a process of identification, such as 'Chinese', we acknowledge the complexity of the terms.
2 The results of the knowledge questions should be interpreted as describing recognition of the item concerned rather than any deeper knowledge.
3 The low number of Australian-born Indians in the sample (three) suggests we cannot grant any significance to the apparent 'loss' of investment in Australian and UK items.
4 This question had a lower response rate, between 55 and 65 per cent, suggesting some reticence in answering.

PART IV
Habitus

Introduction

Taste, as a system of schemes of perception and appreciation, is a crucial part of habitus, yet it is surprising how often discussions of taste focus primarily on cultural capital and field. In Part IV, we use Bourdieu's understanding of habitus to take up particular themes which often slip from view in the analysis of cultural consumption. The chapters examine the gender dimensions of the transmission of taste, the ways taste functions in the accounts people give of their experiences of belonging and the ethical and political positions they take up.

Bourdieu defines habitus as systems of durable dispositions which are structured by social position but also function to generate social practices. He proposes this formulation to avoid the 'dilemma of determinism and freedom' that frames discussions of social action (Bourdieu, 1977: 95), yet scholars have often criticised the way that habitus often retains a reductive and reproductive focus in Bourdieu's work which overstates the unity of class habitus as the 'outward signs expressing social position' (Bourdieu, 1994: 123). We don't intend to revisit these debates but rather work from Bourdieu's characterisation of habitus as the 'indeterminate' but 'regulated improvisations' made possible by 'embodied history, internalized as a second nature' (1990c: 56–57, 77). The interplay of field, capital and habitus produces 'life-styles' but, because social actors move across diverse fields, they acquire complex repertoires of practice and contradictory patterns of taste.

As well as acknowledging the plural nature of the habitus, we also emphasise that it weaves bodily, ethical, aesthetic and cognitive dimensions which anchor the ways we act in the world: habitus is the 'transposable dispositions' which integrate experience via 'a *matrix of perceptions, appreciations, and actions*' which makes possible the generation of social practices (Bourdieu, 1977: 82–83). For Bourdieu, the task is not simply to show the ways in which the habitus involves inhabiting a position, but also to illuminate acts of *position-taking*, which he ascribes to political acts as well as to the appreciation of art.

This balancing of the processual with the structural requires that we see taste as both a system of classification and the generative practices of classification. In the earlier parts of the book we drew on data to foreground the patterns of consumption around class, gender, age, education and so on. In this part, we foreground taste in terms of situated experience. We can't simply read individuals' tastes off maps of social positions for we need to examine the contingencies of the operation of perceptual schema and their role in processes of recognition and differentiation (Bourdieu and Wacquant, 1992: 11). This book attempts to balance an analysis of these maps of position, the forms of capital that circulate across social positions and the ways people mobilise categories of perception and appreciation in their accounts of their tastes.

While Bourdieu focuses on the role of taste in relations of class power, he observes that 'it would be a mistake to seek the explanatory principles of the responses in one factor'; habitus, he suggests, synthesises multiple determinations that arise from 'the material conditions of existence', including 'biological properties that are socially shaped, such as sex or age' (1984: 437–438). Habitus (and the extent to which it is classed, gendered and ethnicised) is, then, the connective but not entirely unified mechanism through which social positions are translated into individual dispositions that simultaneously reflect, reproduce and contradict the social spaces allocated to individuals within structures of power.

Chapter 14 takes up this issue by examining the gendered dimensions of the formation of taste. Bourdieu often invokes the family as the site of primary socialisation of the habitus, but it often seems to stand as a mechanism of class reproduction. This chapter shows that we need to consider more closely the gender relations of the family and especially the deeper investment of women in the accumulation of cultural capital, and how cultural consumption typically involves practices of negotiation and accommodation between partners.

Chapter 15 takes this further, exploring the multiple forms of participation and belonging that are articulated when people talk about tastes. In complementing field-based analyses in previous sections, this chapter suggests that what participation means requires a more textured account of people's lives. Significantly, forms of belonging are sometimes less articulated to a strong sense of class or community than to a sense of family life. This is complicated by the ways that digitisation and transnationalism contribute to an increasingly personalised view of consumption.

Analysing the ways in which taste plays out in participants' understandings of the world and the complex and dynamic positions people inhabit, points to the need to emphasise the practices of position-*taking*. This is the focus in Chapter 16, which demonstrates how discussions of consumption quickly segue into discussions of politics, the nation and cultural diversity. While it points to the role the nation continues to play as a key reference point in political and cultural life in the age of globalisation, it reveals significant degrees of ambivalence in relation to both cultural value and to political institutions.

The final chapter in Part IV foregrounds the ethical dimensions of consumption that Bourdieu rarely explores. Through an analysis of the relationship between our survey participants' responses to 'liking' or 'disliking' Indigenous cultural items and the 'Reconciliation Orthodoxy' promoted by state and civil society organisations, this chapter explores the intimate relations between ethical investment, aesthetic distancing and political commitments in cultural consumption.

14
ENGENDERING CULTURE
Accumulating capital in the gendered household

Deborah Stevenson

The aim of this chapter is to highlight points where the interrelationships between cultural capital, habitus and gender can be detected, including considering whether gender might play a role in the transmission of cultural capital across generations. Where the previous part of the book is focused on cultural capital as the socially valued resources people possess, this chapter shifts attention to the acquisition of cultural capital through the evolution of the habitus. Taking as a point of departure Bourdieu's view that cultural capital is grounded in the habitus (as a set of enduring dispositions) which is acquired at the level of the household through the interplay of education, class and other social factors, the chapter considers what people whose interest in the art field has been classified as 'major' say about the educational and family factors that shaped this interest. In doing so it extends the concept of education to include the informal learning that takes place within the domestic sphere primarily through the emotional work of women. As Chapter 10 argues, cultural capital has both static and relational forms, the latter evidenced in the interactions between family members. Moreover, while 'emotional capital' understood as 'a dynamic resource developed through primary and secondary socialisation and activated and embodied in everyday emotion practice' (Cottingham, 2016: 451) has been linked to the emotional work that women, in particular, do at the interface of home and school, it is also important in the informal education that occurs within the family and which is critical to the acquisition of cultural capital. This informal education can be active as in knowingly exposing children to selected cultural experiences and products to ensure they acquire the cultural knowledge necessary to understand and appreciate them. But it can also be passive as children gain cultural knowledge through incidental exposure and, more commonly, by spending concentrated periods of time in a particular environment or site of socialisation. As part of the emotional work of socialisation, children also learn 'appropriate' emotional responses to cultural forms. This learning is especially pertinent to the arts, where claiming an emotional response or connection to a particular work is common.

Continuing the focus on the household, the chapter also considers what the project interviews reveal about the ways in which cohabiting heterosexual couples negotiate cultural taste and consumption across a number of fields. It is apparent that for many respondents it is accommodation not overt negotiation that is at play. Rather than active discussion and compromise, key here are the tactics of co-presence, including quiet acceptance, that people use to work around another's cultural preferences, with women being more likely than men to be absorbed into the cultural consumption of their partner. For some, the accommodation of/to the cultural taste of another may be at the cost of consuming their own preferred cultural forms; for others, cultural consumption occurs separately although, not uncommonly, in the same space – 'separately-together' so to speak. The result may be a shift in, or expansion of, cultural taste and capital; but a failure to consume does not mean the loss of cultural capital. Grounded in the internalised schemas of the habitus, cultural capital 'endures'; it is not diminished or extinguished through the absence of practice or display.

Gendering cultural capital

It is well established that Bourdieu never paid a great deal of attention to gender and its relevance to the acquisition and expression of cultural capital, although gender relations are implicit throughout much of his work and, undeniably, factors shaping cultural taste and everyday consumption. It is noteworthy, for instance, that in his 2001 book examining the social and economic basis of men's power over women, cultural capital is only mentioned twice: once in an appendix considering gay and lesbian political movements, and again in a discussion of the relationship between cultural capital and the 'economic and cultural autonomy' of women, where he claims the possession of cultural capital is 'not enough in itself to give a woman access to the conditions of real economic and cultural autonomy with respect to men' (Bourdieu, 2001: 107). As Silva (2005: 84) explains, 'In Bourdieusian thinking, and in his research practice, social and cultural origins and values are defined as deriving from the father.' Accordingly, the role of women, both inside and outside the domestic sphere, is essentially 'aesthetic' with women, by extension, being regarded as subordinate to men (Silva, 2005).

Silva further suggests that while there may have been some subtle shifts in Bourdieu's ideas evident across a number of texts written at different times, his thinking on gender relations, the nature of the family and the position of women, remained strikingly constant. Nevertheless, as Huppatz (2012: 8) points out, 'his conceptual toolkit has proven to be adaptable' for the analysis of gender, and there is a robust feminist literature working, and engaging, with his ideas. This literature has focused on such concerns as the relationship between gender and class, education, work and the body (Adkins and Skeggs, 2004). The intersection of work, cultural capital and gender in particular has been probed by many, including

Huppatz (2009) for whom 'gender capital' is a conceptual bridge between class and gender. Huppatz and Goodwin (2013: 297) extend this analysis to propose that occupational choice is framed in terms of 'four different types of gender capital: feminine, masculine, female and male'. Bourdieu's concept of 'embodied cultural capital' (forms of learnt behaviour, including manners, cultural taste and practices of cultural participation) with its grounding in the formation of habitus, has also been rethought to include gender/ed capital. Others have highlighted the need to extend the understanding of capital to encompass the emotional with emotional capital being 'neither gender neutral nor exclusively female' (Cottingham, 2016: 451), but taking different forms depending on gender location and norms, as well as class. There is also an important ongoing debate, outlined by Bennett *et al.* (2009: 215), regarding whether economic, social and cultural capital should each be understood as gendered to 'appreciate better the different kinds of femininities and masculinities associated with them', or whether gender itself is 'an additional axis of inequality: that cuts across all forms of capital'.

Of interest also to those examining gender and capital is the family, which for Bourdieu (1996a) is central to socialisation and the accumulation and intergenerational transmission of cultural capital. It is the primary site where the dispositions and forms of knowledge associated with habitus are learnt. As feminist scholars have pointed out, women, as 'mothers and homemakers, play a crucial role in early development' and in the acquisition of cultural capital because they routinely spend more time caring for children than men do (Reay, 2004: 59). According to Gayo (2016b: 20), the cultural practices of mothers within households 'appear as more significant than fathers', suggesting that cultural transmission within families is particularly related to gender roles, and specifically to children's experiences with their mothers'. The practical and symbolic work that women do within the family and to maintain the family, is clearly relevant with even Bourdieu (1996a: 22) acknowledging (albeit in passing) the 'countless ordinary and continuous exchanges of daily existence' necessary to sustain familial relationships that are performed disproportionately by women. This physical and emotional work involves also imparting the (often class and gender specific) 'feeling rules' deemed appropriate to different social situations (Hochschild, 1979). Moreover, as Reay (2004) explains, women are also often actively involved, and emotionally invested, in the education of children including that which occurs at the interface of home and school. The class dimensions of this involvement have also been highlighted with middle-class women often having the time, means and resources to be more engaged than their working-class counterparts (Gayo, 2016b).

Drawing on the findings of their study of cultural capital and consumption in the UK, Bennett *et al.* (2009: 232) probe whether cultural capital is a resource of households or of individuals, arguing that it is best understood as a 'relational resource operating at the level of the household in dynamic relationships between people living together' – a proposition which serves as a useful touchstone here. The authors are careful not to attribute gender-specific masculine and feminine cultural tastes, or particular kinds of 'emotional or technical capital' because there are women who operate within more masculine spaces of lifestyles and men who draw on, and participate in, cultural practices that are traditionally classified as feminine. By way of example, it is useful to note that in categorising the results of a survey of cultural tastes conducted by the Australian Broadcasting Corporation (ABC) and inspired by the findings of the *Australian Cultural Fields* (ACF) study, men who expressed a strong preference for reading were often classified as women because the literary field came through in the ACF study as strongly associated with the cultural practices of women.[1] But these studies rarely give emphasis to the processes of formation that underlie the accumulation of cultural capital.

Gender and Australian cultural fields

Of the 1202 survey respondents from the main sample, 568 (47 per cent) were men and 634 (52 per cent) were women; 717 respondents were living in a household with a partner, and of these 423 were also living with children. Another 48 respondents indicated that they were sole parents. Alongside divisions between classes and age groupings as explanatory elements in accounting for differences in cultural tastes and practices, gender differences are also evident in the Multiple Correspondence Analyses discussed in Part I of the current volume. The extent of its significance, however, varies greatly across different fields being most pronounced in sport (see Chapter 6) but also marked in fields where practices are more individuated, such as the literature field (see Chapter 2). There are also noteworthy variations within the field of art, with women being more likely than men to visit art galleries and have knowledge of artists.

To gain insights into the question of whether cultural capital is a relational resource of households and/or a resource of individuals that is shaped considerably by the formative experiences of growing up, I draw on the household interviews to consider what people say about their contemporary cultural tastes and practices of consumption, and the factors that they regard as having been pivotal in shaping them. Of particular note, is the role of parents and the effect of childhood cultural experiences and exposures in the formation of those tastes constituted in the habitus. I am also interested in what respondents reveal about the ways in which they negotiate cultural consumption with their domestic partner, including how cohabiting heterosexual couples manage differences in cultural taste and capital. The interviews involved one member of a household only, so it is not possible to consider the 'dynamic' negotiation of cultural taste that might be evident from joint interviews or focus groups with a number of members of the same household. Nevertheless, what respondents say about the people and circumstances (foundational and contemporary) that have influenced their cultural tastes is instructive, as is probing whether gender and gender relations are factors. These issues are examined below with reference, first, to the visual art field, followed by a discussion of cultural consumption at the domestic level that draws on all the household interview data. It should be noted that the analysis here adds to the discussion of inherited intensities undertaken in Chapter 1, by bringing a specifically gendered perspective to bear.

'It's just from when you're kids'

More than half (29/42) of the interviewees were categorised from their survey responses as having either a 'major' or 'minor' interest in visual art, with 15 respondents (9/13 women and 6/16 men) registering a major interest. From a consideration of the transcripts of interviews with these people, three things emerge. First, of the cohort, seven interviewees speak of the important role their parents and grandparents had played when they were growing up in fostering in them an interest in art and several respondents also say that they took their own children to visit galleries because they wanted to share their interest in art with them. Second, a number of people with a major interest in art were now practising artists themselves and/or had parents or grandparents who were. Finally, while there were interviewees who had studied art at secondary or tertiary (TAFE) levels, and some of these continue to produce art, no one in the major interest cohort had studied art at university, although they may have been university educated. This finding is consistent with the literature that suggests artists are often highly educated – for instance, Stevenson *et al.* (2017) found that 70 per cent of respondents to a survey of arts and cultural practice in Greater Western Sydney had a university degree or postgraduate qualification although not necessarily in the creative arts, and a further 20 per cent had a diploma or technical qualification; these survey respondents were also predominantly female.

I turn now to the role of family, and specifically the influence of parents and grandparents, on cultivating an interest in art. Christine (quoted in the subheading above), a 61-year-old Aboriginal woman who identifies as middle class, recalls that as a child she became fascinated by a painting hanging on the wall at her grandmother's house. As she puts it, 'your Gran's got a big landscape there and you've been in trouble and you go in there and you look at it and you think oh it's not so bad'. She goes on to talk about going every year to Sydney with her family to see the Archibald Prize exhibition at the Art Gallery of New South Wales. It was her father who initiated these trips and she sees him as having been particularly instrumental in fostering her interest in art, although she also points out that he was more deeply engaged with classical music than with visual art, and again she traces her own strong interest in classical music to his influence. Similarly, 53-year-old private school educated Diane described being influenced by her grandparents, in particular, who had a liking for colonial art and, along with the poetry of Banjo Paterson and others, would talk to her about it when she was a child. It was her grandparents, she said, who originally owned the 'old prints' currently hanging in her own home. According to Diane, her parents also had an interest in art, and she remembers, in particular, that they were very proud of a Namatjira print they owned when she was growing up and which now belongs to her, although was not on display at the time of the interview. Diane made the following comment about this print:

> It's only a print. But it's a print of one of his famous ones and therefore again as a child I grew up knowing that's a Namatjira picture. He's an Aboriginal artist, et cetera. So, it's just that was what I was exposed to.

Coming through from the interviewees more strongly than having had parents and grandparents who took them to galleries and talked to them about art when they were children, is the importance of having a parent or grandparent who was a practising artist. Three respondents describe growing up surrounded by works of art and the paraphernalia of art making. 'He always painted when I was younger ... He was an oil landscape painter and I remember the smell of the oils in the house and things like that', said Heath, a 42-year-old commercial printer from Brisbane who collects prints, particularly landscapes by the Australian artist Helen Norton. Heath spoke of his father's influence on his cultural taste as follows:

> My father is a painter – well used to be a painter, he is quite elderly now, but we always had artworks at home. A lot of his stuff. I've got some of his paintings still. My sister has got a number of his paintings as well. So, I don't know if it is in the blood or something like that. As an artist myself, I'm hopeless. But I can appreciate a beautiful piece of artwork.

When the interviewers ask Canberra-based Jacinta, aged 49 with a degree in humanities, about the large amount of art she had on the walls of her house and in her garden, she responds that the majority of the works on display had been created by her artist mother who worked in a range of media. Eighteen-year-old Rhiannon also credits her mother, who had done 'photography in school', with nurturing her own interest in art and photography, saying 'she just taught me some of the things when I was younger. I think it started with taking photos of butterflies or something then it just went from there.' Rhiannon also talked about a number of limited edition prints that belonged to her father, suggesting that they may not be, what the interviewers would classify as, 'art' because of their subject matter – 'one of the pictures he has is a sketch of one of the race cars he followed'.

Eight of the interviewees (six women and two men) in the major interest in art cohort, identified themselves as practising artists (although not all were seeking to exhibit and sell work), as well as active consumers of art and attendees of exhibitions. Of these eight, five had studied art at either secondary or tertiary (although not university) levels. One respondent, high school maths teacher Lauren, whose grandmother and uncle are both artists, laments that she had not been exposed to artist-specific curriculum content at high school, suggesting too that she had been disadvantaged by not having attended school in Sydney:

> We were never exposed to artists I suppose was my – we didn't get to study the artists and I often go to work and people there have come from Sydney and their schooling was you studied, and you studied, and I think I would've loved to have done that. That's – so you certainly feel like you've missed that bit.

Lauren further underlines her assessment that there is a link between metropolitan Sydney and the acquisition of the type of capital required to appreciate art, when discussing why it might be that her daughter also 'loves art':

> I always wonder if that's because when we lived in Sydney when she was little, I used to drag her around to all the art things and my son never got the chance to do that so he's kind of like – 'whatever, this is boring'.

Lauren is one of several women who mention that they regularly took their children to art galleries if not now, then when the children were younger. In response to being asked if she thought it was important for children to be exposed to art or taken to galleries, Christine indicates that she did, and that she believes children 'inherit what you're interested in'. She further notes that, in the case of her now-adult daughter, this exposure is a key reason for her current considerable interest in art and habit of attending art galleries both in Australia and overseas. For 58-year-old Debra, visiting galleries as a family had long been important:

> I think, again, it's like a comfort thing for the mind. To wander around an art gallery to see a piece that you really, really love and are attracted to, it's just a wonderful way to spend an afternoon … Yes, it's something I would do say once every couple of months. My husband and I would take the kids and we'd wander around the art gallery or the museum.

She also says that they would go as a family to Canberra every few years and while she prefers to spend time in the art galleries, her husband's preference is for the 'war museums'. Although keen to take her children to galleries, Lauren laments that becoming a mother had not only constrained her own consumption of art, but also put an end to her having the time to paint. As she puts it:

> I loved art, it was certainly a relaxing thing, I used to do lots for a hobby and then once you have kids it's – that's all over, there's no relaxation in it. But – I really enjoy seeing other people's artworks. I like being able to meander around and just look and enjoy and see.

It is worth noting that Lauren's experience is highly consistent with the evidence from the literature examining the constraints faced by women seeking to work in paid and unpaid capacities in the cultural sector, including in fields such as the visual arts and craft, with the demands of balancing family responsibilities being chief among them (Luckman, 2015; Stevenson, 2020).

The influence of family and childhood experiences on cultural taste and, in the examples considered here, the consumption of visual art, is clearly important, and although women as mothers and grandmothers play an important role this influence may be strongest on daughters and granddaughters. In the case of art, the only male respondent who mentions the influence of a parent spoke of his father, and none of the men talk about taking their children to galleries, although 72-year-old retired advertising executive Eric does say that he and his wife regularly took their four grandchildren: 'we decided to try and make the city an experience for them'. What is not clear is whether it was he or his wife who first initiated these outings.

It is possible, though, that his wife's class position and cultural capital could well be higher than his own working-class background because, although now a patron of and investor in the arts (which is, in turn, a source of symbolic capital), Eric speaks of the significant influence of his mother-in-law on his choices of artwork to purchase – 'she had a great eye', he says.

Craig, a 49-year-old former forklift driver, mentions the role played by former and current partners and their mothers in extending his knowledge and appreciation of art. For instance, in response to the question 'where does your interest in art come from do you think? Did it come also from your family?' Craig replies that he has:

> always been interested, but I think I have to thank the women in my life, my girlfriends and their mothers. Particularly [his partner] and her mum and an ex-girlfriend and her mum, who were more knowledgeable and were able to educate me a little bit more. So yeah, I've always been interested but I have, yes, the women in my life to thank for broadening my horizons as well.

It is evident that women play a critical role at the household/family level in the formation and transmission of the cultural capital associated with an appreciation of art. They circulate, although do not necessarily control, cultural capital. Indeed, there may well be a relationship between being a mother and the performance of 'aesthetic' as well as 'emotional' work. The literature on gender and cultural capital highlights the emotional involvement of women in the education of their children, but this education should be understood as both formal and informal and can involve managing exposure to, and transmitting knowledge of, and an emotional vocabulary for appreciating, art. The influence of partners on cultural taste also emerges as important as the examples of Craig and Eric demonstrate, and so the section below considers what the interviewees say about the extent to which their cultural consumption and taste are constrained, shaped or enhanced by their domestic partner.

Negotiation or accommodation

Even though they may have different tastes and possess different levels of cultural capital, cohabiting couples frequently engage in cultural activities together. They watch television together, go to galleries and sporting events together, even listen to audiobooks together, and at least one of our interviewees indicated that he and his partner read at the same time and in the same physical space although the books were different. As reported in Chapter 2, Sean says that he intended 'ripping' out a bar in the lounge room of his home and replacing it with 'two chairs' and 'bookshelves all across there' to create what the interviewer described as a 'reading nook' to share with his wife. It was also not uncommon for both men and women who are currently living with a domestic partner to use the pronouns 'we' and 'our', often unselfconsciously, when describing their cultural tastes and participation, even in response to questions about their individual preferences. For instance: 'We obviously go to things like the Archibald and the Sulman [prizes]. We probably won't go to the nude exhibition – I don't know' (Eric); 'We only watch free to air' (Sean). Giovanni, a 54-year-old sales manager of Italian background, says that there were 'books everywhere' in the house and 'once we've read them' they usually 'end up … in a pile in the garage'. The use of 'we' here is interesting because it could mean that he and his wife routinely read the same books or refer to individual and collective patterns of cultural consumption that, in his mind, are seamless. Although not currently living with his partner, it is nevertheless noteworthy that when discussing films that they had recently seen but not liked, Michael, a retired 71-year-old engineer, says 'our' before quickly correcting himself: 'we almost walked out part-way through. They just weren't our cup of tea, or my cup of tea.' He does not say who had selected the films or made the decision, once there, that they were not for them, although he mentions they were influenced in their choices by the positive 'write ups' the films had received in the media.

Also evident from the interview data are examples of people saying they do or do not do certain things because of the influence of their partner. Patterns of cultural consumption and engagement may be the accommodation of a partner's taste rather than evidence of shared, or even changed, personal taste. The cultural field where this accommodation is perhaps most obvious is sport and, in particular, watching sport on television with women overwhelmingly being the ones who speak of watching (or tolerating the watching of) televised sport to accommodate their partner's taste. Illustrative of common responses are: 'my husband watches football, so we'd watch it every week on TV' (Lisa); 'I watch once or twice rugby with my husband' (Angela); and 'My husband quite likes the cricket. I'll watch the cricket for twenty minutes, half an hour three or four times in a season' (Diane). Where men speak of accommodating their partner's cultural preferences, it is often regarding the choice of television programme. For example, as Robert explains:

> It's mainly my wife who controls the TV controller. So, therefore, there are a few sort of gardening shows and things that, usually when I've finished sort of doing work, if I sit down and sort of watch it I'll, you know, I'll watch that, you know. But it's not that I've set out to sort of watch it. I'm usually just sitting there and wouldn't know what was happening, you know what I mean.

Negotiation and accommodation between couples within households occurs with respect to the cultural products they consume together, but there is often a line between those activities that are undertaken as a couple (together or 'separately-together') and those which are more solitary activities and where the dynamics of lived cultural capital are different. Reading, for instance, is a form of cultural consumption that is primarily connected to personal taste/cultural capital while attendance at art galleries and watching television are more likely to be shared activities. Where there are physical objects connected to individual taste, similar distinctions are often made. In one household with an extensive collection of books, the interviewee is able to indicate which bookshelves contained books belonging to and read solely by him, and which belonged to and were read by other members of the family, including his partner. Discussing several artworks hanging in his house, retired high school principal, Steven, makes an interesting distinction between those works that were 'ours' and those that were his wife's – 'that's my wife'. The key determinant was that joint work was that which 'constantly evokes memories of the things we've done [together]' and it is noteworthy that none of the works were identified as being his alone. When talking about his favourite artists and paintings, David dismisses a particular print on display in his house as being 'my wife's taste', while Sean (asserting, albeit ironically, embodied capital) claims that although he was 'totally in charge of the remote control', his wife was 'in charge of what we actually watch'. Aisha, who 'loves art', says it was she, not her husband, who chose what was hung on the walls of their house because 'it [art] is very special to me. It's putting my personality onto it, so it's very, very special.' Angela, on the other hand, describes the family home as being 'full of paintings, all my husband's paintings. He buys a lot … I just don't think there's the space there for me.'

Adrian says that even though he and his wife have 'been married for 15 years', they do not have to 'see eye to eye on everything in that list there [the ACF survey] … My wife reads three books a day – or a book a day or what[ever] – and she's right into Facebook and Internet and I hate that stuff.' As he further explains:

> But if I don't like – my wife will tend to watch things like *Escape to the Country*, those British type … And all those type shows. If I'm watching it and I'm not enjoying it, I'll watch on a different TV … But I get up early in the morning to go to work so I just fall asleep in front of the TV.

Similarly, Michael says 'My partner reads books all the time. She tends to go to bed and read books; I tend to stay up and watch TV', while according to Angela she and her husband have 'different tastes'. Badal, a man of Fijian-Indian background, 'love[s] watching cinemas', and used to watch films on television and at the cinema with his former wife; his current wife, however, does not share this interest. He explains:

> my second wife is not really into watching telly, she's more into computers, tablets. She gets most of the information from the Internet. So, she'd be sitting beside me, but she'd be surfing the net whereas I'd be watching television. We are together but doing different things.

Consuming culture 'separately-together' is a form of accommodation – sometimes in the same space, as in the example of Badal and his wife, but more often in different spaces in the home at the same time. Even though cultural consumption patterns may change because of the influence of a spouse or cohabiting partner, often they do not. Instead, differences in cultural taste are accommodated. When they do change, this change does not mean that those tastes and preferences that predate a relationship will cease; rather, change involves addition not subtraction. Some people spoke of not being able to participate in their preferred activities because of the influence of their partner, but importantly it was made clear that they still view that cultural activity or form as part of their identity. Aisha poignantly explains the phenomenon as follows:

> I love music basically and I would love to go to concerts, and it would be a pleasure for me to sit there and listen to the music. I love concerts, I love performances. Sadly, because my husband is not into it, I don't attend much now.

She goes on to say that when they 'first got married [her] husband was into Phil Collins ... So, I got to like Phil Collins ... But I don't make an effort to put a song there and listen to it.' Hong Kong-born Thomas describes going to the Museum of Contemporary Art and the Art Gallery of New South Wales in Sydney as being 'for me', and that he would like to go more often 'but unfortunately my partner [is] not interested. So, it's getting less for me to go there.'

This pattern – or at least its traces – was evident from the interviews irrespective of the ethnicity, age, class or gender of the interviewee. Importantly, what it suggests is that rather than being a dynamic negotiation of cultural consumption or representing a change of cultural tastes and the diminution of cultural capital, not consuming does not mean people no longer like, or are interested in, what may have been long held cultural activities and capacities. New forms of cultural consumption may be negotiated, but it could also be a matter of the accommodation of taste that is at play.

Conclusion

Through an examination of what ACF household interviewees said about the childhood influences they regard as having been significant in fostering their interest in the visual arts, this chapter has highlighted the important role played by parents and/or grandparents who themselves were interested in, and engaged with visual art, sometimes as arts practitioners. Women, as mothers and grandmothers, in particular, played a pivotal role in influencing an appreciation of art, although this influence was most marked with respect to daughters. This observation could indicate important ways in which intergenerational gender relations are played out with respect to cultural knowledge that warrant further investigation. It could be, for instance, that men are central to the intergenerational transmission of the particular cultural knowledge associated with sport. Nevertheless, it is well established that women, who as mothers routinely assume the primary role of carer, are deeply and emotionally involved in the formal and informal education and socialisation of children's habitus and the generation of cultural capital in its broadest sense. This role operates, and cultural capital is exchanged and accumulates, in the domestic space as well as the informal learning space at the interface of home and school.

Women also often find themselves adjusting their own patterns of cultural consumption and participation to accommodate caring responsibilities or the cultural tastes and priorities of their partner. This issue of accommodation comes through quite interestingly from the ACF interviews, with both men and women saying that they do and do not do certain things because of the influence of their partner. People accommodate their own tastes to those of their partner and/or accommodate their partner's tastes to their own. Watching sport on television was one area where the accommodation of the interests of another was evident, but it was a theme that applied with respect to a range of cultural activities. Where negotiation implies dynamic interplay, accommodation is more about finding a space – quietly working around or accepting; what I would describe as the tactics of co-presence. People also spoke of cultural participation and consumption occurring 'separately-together'. Those who live together do not necessarily share cultural capital or cultural taste, and the ways in which this difference is accommodated at the level of the household will often involve avoidance, tolerance and parallel consumption. Refracted through the formation of the enduring dispositions of the habitus, cultural capital and cultural taste can be absorbed and transmitted, but not necessarily 'lost' or 'unlearned'. The chapter thus illuminates the potency of cultural capital and the gendered processes by which it is acquired and reproduced.

Note

1 www.abc.net.au/news/2018-04-13/what-your-habits-reveal-about-your-social-class/9610658.

15
CULTURAL PARTICIPATION AND BELONGING

Anna Cristina Pertierra and Graeme Turner

This chapter discusses material generated in the interview component of the *Australian Cultural Fields* (ACF) project to consider how research participants saw their own various forms of cultural participation, and how they expressed their sense of belonging. The stories and examples of cultural participation and belonging shared by respondents during interviews intersect in varying ways with the larger body of survey data discussed in Parts I and II, revealing a more textured and detailed picture of what constitutes cultural participation than could be elicited through the methodology of the questionnaire. Consequently, the interviews enable us to develop a responsively contingent account of individual subjects' self-expressed relation to the cultural fields under examination, opening up the categories of cultural participation and belonging to a more comprehensive and inclusive range of practices and identities.

The methodological benefits of including these interviews in our project do not stem from their subjects being typical or statistically representative: instead they are usefully illustrative of what these cultural fields look like from an individual position. They give us many examples of the ways that participation and belonging can be found 'on the ground' in contemporary Australia – including examples that sit beyond the remit of our questionnaire data. Sometimes, interview respondents themselves complicated or contradicted their own survey responses: the 6 to 12 months that typically passed between the survey and the interviews often meant that people forgot, changed opinions or changed focus in their discussions of cultural practices. At other times, response profiles that had seemed somewhat puzzling became much more comprehensible once a wider picture of the participant's life was explained.

Defining participation: what counts?

What does it mean to participate in a cultural field? And how do people variously understand or identify their own forms of cultural participation? In cultural policy, finding consistent ways to measure cultural participation has important consequences for questions of cultural heritage and arts funding (among other things): sector organisations such as the United Nations Educational, Scientific and Cultural Organization (UNESCO) have developed frameworks for understanding culture that draw explicitly on sociological models to see culture as a cycle in which production and consumption interconnect. Such frameworks acknowledge that cultural participation is difficult to measure, and can take many forms. It can include home-based practices (such as consuming media), going out to attend cultural events and 'identity-building' practices such as participating in community activities, popular culture and amateur cultural groups; such different forms of participation often require different forms of data collection and measurement (Morrone, 2006: UNESCO, 2009).

Depending upon the field, and upon the person being asked, our interview responses revealed a variety of forms that participating in culture can assume. Practical activities, fandom, cultural production or creative expression, forms of consumption, personal projects or preferred leisure pursuits could all constitute participation in ways that were meaningful to the respondents. People can participate in cultural activities with differing levels of intensity, ranging from a casual fleeting interest to a deeply held passion. The ACF questionnaire and interview schedules prompted respondents to reflect upon a range of different activities and preferences that could indicate participation. Just some of the activities that were regularly (but not necessarily consistently) discussed across household interviews included:

- watching television
- playing sport
- following a sports club or code
- being a member of a sports club
- visiting art galleries
- reading books
- buying artwork
- listening to music
- playing music
- making art
- visiting heritage sites
- participating in activities as part of your community.

As we discussed how they engaged in these different cultural practices, interviewees were sometimes hesitant to describe their interests as 'participation'. Furthermore, they did not always see their engagement with a cultural field as connected to a sense of belonging to a community or class. They often explained their motivations for participation as deeply personal, individualised or related to household and family dynamics. Exploring these differences in thinking about participation – and between the various expectations of interviewers and experiences of interviewees

– highlighted how not only researchers, but also respondents, grappled with their notions of what 'counts' as culture. These conversations led us to acknowledge categories of cultural participation and belonging involving a more comprehensive and inclusive range of practices and identities than had been available to us by simply drawing upon the data generated from the questionnaire.

Examples of participation: within and beyond specific cultural fields

The interviews produced much evidence of the richness and power of the experiences provided through participation in those cultural fields that have been traditionally identified with the arts, such as painting and literature. For Debra (58), a former wine industry supervisor who has purchased artworks for herself, attends galleries regularly and has maintained an interest in the visual arts over 30 years, paintings in particular generate unique personal experiences:

> Different things attract you. It could be the peacefulness of a landscape or it could be the heavy colours of say a winter scene … every person can see something different in a painting that attracts them. So, it could be the colour or it could be the style. To me, it's just what catches my eye at the time and it sort of takes you away.

Naomi, a 47-year-old former administrative worker now undertaking home duties, reports that reading books is one of the core shared activities for her family; they all read regularly and voraciously, they discuss what they read and operate something like a domestic circulating library within their household. Interestingly, this occurs without any participation in the public dimensions of literary culture, and without much in the way of explicit consideration of hierarchies of value or critical standing. Naomi says: 'I don't really look at reviews or anything. I just know I like the way this person writes and so I'll go and get their books.' Even more clearly evident from the interviews are the pleasures of the most active mode of participation in these art forms – producing original creative works across various media and platforms or performing as musicians or in other capacities. In relation to the latter, 86-year-old Leonard, a widower still mourning the loss of his wife of 63 years, told us that the opportunity to perform with his violin at a friend's 70th birthday party made him 'feel fantastic'.

While the questionnaire sought information from respondents on their participation in playing sport, it did not seek equivalent information on respondents' active participation in cultural production through other expressive or creative activities. We found that a significant number of the interviewees reported producing their own artworks – paintings, sculptures, musical compositions, videos and photographs. For most of these respondents, the value of their engagement in creative activities is seen as personal. For 19-year-old Gabriel, a medical student who also works part time for a surgical technology company, born in Australia with an Italian background and already collecting his own artworks, the drawing he does himself is not intended for public display; he does it because it is simply 'enjoyable'. For some, creative production can be a fundamental part of their daily lives and of their cultural identity, as it is for Angela, a 50-year-old office worker born in China, who takes pleasure in Chinese ink brush painting. Brenton (35), a musician and video producer, makes no distinction between his personal and professional identities.

The expressive production reported also extends beyond those fields that might be conventionally regarded as artistic or creative. Charles, a 37-year-old former truck driver, for instance, writes 'notes' on his phone that fall between the categories of the personal journal and poetry; while he may not see them as creative productions, they clearly function as important expressive activities. There are many instances where the involvement with sport is the dominant dimension of that individual's cultural participation. However, in at least one case, the line between the pleasures of sport and those of creative expression is blurred. Rehabilitation case manager Akela's (37) responses to the questionnaire provided only a limited sense of significant cultural participation; she herself suggests to the interview team that she 'sounds boring'. The interview corrected that impression. Akela is an enthusiastic gym-goer, where she does something called 'aerial hoop' – a sport (unsurprisingly) not nominated in our survey: 'It's aerial hoop … like circus people do. They suspend from the ceiling and you do all these tricks, I suppose, in a hoop.' That leisure time interest has contributed to her developing a secondary career as a photographer, working exclusively with the pole dancing community. Akela is in demand to take photographs at the competitions run by the relevant associations, and to put them up online or to publish them in the organisations' magazines. Her photography is far from a merely technical activity. In the interview, Akela provides a detailed account of the aesthetics, and of the gendered politics of representation, involved in this area of professional photography. And yet, it would be fair to say, as she acknowledges herself, that pole dancing photography would not readily be included in conventional descriptions of what constitutes creative art. Another apparently 'boring' questionnaire response came from 18-year-old university student Rhiannon, who indicated very little interest in many of our categories of participation. In the interview, however, it turned out that Rhiannon is an enthusiastic photographer, that she and her family have been committed and passionate speedway fans for years and that she has a long record of community service through her engagement with the Rover Scouts organisation and in particular with volunteer work for a charity supporting foster parents.

Such examples remind us that there are many less valorised or established cultural practices in which people engage with commitment and passion, and from which they derive pleasure and satisfaction. The interviews generated quite a list of additional activities – gardening and fishing are two examples that we may well have expected – that were central to our respondents' cultural experiences. An activity that some members of the research team did expect to emerge, and indeed over which there was much discussion during the design of the questionnaire, was that of the gamer, in particular those who participate in multiplayer online games.

(Harley, an 18-year-old business student, reported that he was involved in multi-player gaming for up to eight hours a day.) Less predictable, but interesting for its combination of community building, technical abilities and personal expression, is 71-year-old retiree Michael's hobby of setting up Christmas lights on the exterior of his house, which commenced in 2003:

> After that first foray – I'd worked in a technical role in the industry, I was an engineer – and being familiar with computers, I found you could control Christmas lights with computers. That became a challenge and an interest in retirement and that sort of thing. So it progressed from there, and I spent a long time trying to work out how to synchronise lights with music. Eventually I got that working in 2009 or 2010, and entered the competition; people came and it was great ... . Last year I managed to win the 'Best in [City name]' and 'Best Synchronised'.

Michael's story highlights what falls beyond the purview of a survey of cultural consumption in which an analysis of cultural tastes is articulated to traditional cultural hierarchies. It reminds us that cultural consumption is after all a social practice and that from the perspective of an individual engaged in cultural participation, their activities may not necessarily or even primarily involve the performance of a taste formation. Nor is it necessarily a practice that is only about personal expression, the production of pleasure or even the fashioning of personal or cultural identities; it may also be about the production of communities.

Belonging: identities, communities, families, the nation

The interviews provide many examples of cultural practices that are tightly articulated to the construction of a personal identity; most of the modes of participation recorded in the interviews are to some extent customised. The repertoire of resources available, in all cultural fields but perhaps to a lesser degree in the visual arts, has become much more highly varied in the digital era, and as a consequence the modes of consumption are configured in ways that can defer to logics of personalisation as much as to those of socialisation. Indeed, it is significant that very few of the interviews locate their choices within externally determined and hierarchical structures of value. The vast majority of the interviewees reported on their cultural practices as if they were relatively unconcerned about external arbiters of quality, value or considerations of cultural capital. Where there are such external influences upon their choices and practices, the overwhelming tendency to emerge from all the interviews was the role of the family. Many interviewees reported the influence of a specific family member, mostly but not exclusively their mother, upon their exposure to and interest in particular cultural forms and practices, as we have seen in the previous chapter. Craig, a 49-year-old former forklift driver, attributes the cultivation of his cultural interests to the influence of 'the women in my life'. In relation to their experience of sport, many interviewees locate their fandom or their support for a particular team or sport as a consequence of family loyalties and traditions maintained over time and in some instances over several generations. In such instances, any line we might wish to draw between participation and belonging, something we have done as a heuristic to enable the closer investigation of these categories, becomes blurred.

Much of the scholarly literature within which this project is situated draws upon conceptions of class, variously defined, as a means of organising and understanding the patterns of cultural participation in play. Since Bourdieu's *Distinction*, cultural consumption has long been connected to theories around the power of cultural capital as a means of understanding the politics structuring the choices in consumption that individuals make. In the national context of Australia, there is also a longstanding mythology of egalitarianism which refuses class as a category in principle; historically, an implausibly large proportion of Australians have claimed to be working class, and there is in some contexts a political and social resistance to the claim to be upper class. We do not suggest that this mythology is necessarily motivating the responses we discuss under the category of belonging in this chapter, although we acknowledge that it is a readily available discourse. Notwithstanding the currency of that discourse, earlier studies (Frow *et al.*, 1991; Bennett *et al.*, 1999) have made persuasive cases for the influence of class in Australia as one of the key drivers for the observed patterns of cultural consumption. As we have seen in Part II of this volume, our study has also found a strong association between patterns in consumption and many of the standard markers of class – education, income, occupation. In some fields, however, our research data indicates the importance of other factors: with sport, gender is the most significant factor marking participation, with music, and to an increasing degree with television, it is age. Chapters 7 and 8 of this volume report on the interaction found to occur between such factors – between education, income, occupation, class, gender and age.

Interestingly, in the interviews, class does not emerge as a factor to which respondents explicitly assign much importance as a driver of cultural participation and belonging. In part, this may be because interviewers did not necessarily pursue a class-focused set of discussion topics. But even an implicitly class-based trope that we have encountered routinely in other programmes of interviews about cultural consumption – the apology for an expressed preference for popular or denigrated rather than elite or respected cultural forms – is extremely rare. While Debra does refer to her television choices as a 'guilty pleasure', and a number of others suggest they would spend more time going to museums and galleries if they had the time, this slightly defensive manner of framing their choices is not common. Instead, when asked if she identifies with a particular social class, Lisa, 42, a case manager born in the UK, and a sports fan who reports little interest in most of the art forms surveyed, is more typical: she does not see herself as belonging to a specific class at all, and believes that class is not 'particularly relevant anymore. I think those lines have now become blurred'. Charles, the former truck driver who composes his journal/poetry on his mobile, also refuses a class identity; he prefers to say he is 'just average'. Jacinta, 49, a learning development consultant, is a collector of original art whose mother was a painter and a sculptor, and thus might seem to be firmly located within the high end of the tastes associated with the visual arts; she classifies herself as middle class because of her occupational status. Nonetheless, even though she presented a sophisticated account of the cultural function of class earlier in her interview, Jacinta also rejects the proposition of a connection between taste and class: she does not 'associate working class people with less refined tastes' and agrees with the suggestion that she would not regard taste as 'something you can talk about in class terms'. Aisha, a 47-year-old Muslim woman who works as a counsellor, agrees: 'taste is about personality', she says, while Naomi, 47, who works in administration, says that 'people are just people'.

Class is not entirely invisible, of course. Single mother and schoolteacher, Lauren, 38, aspires to 'become upper class' but identifies the benefits of upward mobility largely in financial terms, the capacity to afford better possessions. University student and speedway fan, Rhiannon, 18, identifies strongly with a class position. In her interview she reveals how uncomfortable it is for someone from her background, a notoriously depressed working-class suburb in Brisbane, within the elite university environment in which she finds herself. Studying law, she continually hears her suburb used as the ready reference point for disadvantage and crime. She also reports what might be described as discrimination against her, because of her upbringing in that suburb, which proceeds from the normatively middle-class perspective of university staff and students.

There are other points of focus for the articulation of belonging which emerged from the interviews. For a small number, their church exercises a major influence over their leisure activities and cultural choices. Leonard reports that most of his cultural activities are associated with his church, including visits to galleries and attendance at concerts. Notably, sport provides more than just the opportunity for physical participation, particularly for men. Playing sport, coaching local teams, volunteering for sporting organisations, embracing a family tradition of support for a particular football team, watching sport either live or on TV – all of these are widespread activities among those interviewed and for some subjects they are the most important element in how they spend their leisure time. The social and community building function of organised sporting clubs is highly visible. For retired school principal, Steven (66), the local golf club is his social hub, 57-year-old part-time accountant/bookkeeper Adrian does volunteering work for his local bowling club, as does Lauren for the local surf club; many others report long-standing family memberships to major sporting clubs (such as the Wests Tigers Rugby League club). Martin, a 59-year-old retiree who emigrated from the UK, talks of the social function of playing sport while a child in the Villawood migrant centre; sport turned out to be a major means for the construction of community for these children, in difficult circumstances.

The most widely reported influence on belonging to emerge from the interviews, however and as noted above, is that of the family. While we recognise the broader social structuring of the personal identification with family, its repeated, often detailed, invocation in these interviews was notable. The influence of parents through early experience of art forms or other cultural pursuits (as outlined in

Chapter 14), the participation in family engagement with particular modes of cultural consumption, the identification with long-standing family practices – from a love of reading to membership of a National Rugby League club – and the continual default to family histories as a means of explaining the origins of personal preferences are all widespread across these interviews. Christine, a 61-year-old education support officer with an Aboriginal background, acquired her love of landscape paintings from her grandmother, while her father interested her in classical music. Angela attributes her interest in classical music to the influence of her parents, and a primary school teacher from an Italian background, Maria, sees her interest in history and heritage coming from her father. Retired retail manager Sean, 54, tells us that his mother was 'big on art and books' and thus led him into those areas of interest. There are many more examples throughout the interviews where participants make explicit connections between their choices and the influence of family members or of habituated family practices.

One of the most revealing demonstrations of the importance interviewees attributed to family lies in their response to questions about heritage. The section of the questionnaire dealing with heritage was dominated by questions about their experience of particular heritage sites – museums, historical sites and monuments – with some questions about specific sites such as the National War Memorial. In the interviews, respondents readily engaged with that dimension of heritage and were often knowledgeable about it. What was most notable, however, was how frequently their first response was to do with the heritage of their own family. Just a little under half of the interviews reported on the interviewee's attempts to learn more about their family's history; this seems a surprisingly large proportion. Many had used a DNA testing facility provided online, and had developed accounts of their family tree through sites such as Ancestry.com. Leonard had gone as far as travelling to the UK to meet representatives of his family from which his side of the family had become estranged several generations earlier. Lynne, a 51-year-old lingerie party plan franchisee, reported that one of her relatives had produced a handsomely presented book on their family's heritage, complete with photos and diagrams of the family tree. Akela, a first-generation Australian from a Laotian background, talks of the importance of the location of the family's history in their suburb, which she describes as a 'living museum'. Her observations prompt the interviewer to remark that 'people's idea of heritage is much broader than the official idea', and that 'people have very personal ideas about heritage'; the evidence of the interviews as a whole would support Akela's view.

A further interesting point that Akela makes, however, is to draw a distinction between heritage and nationality. She approaches this through a discussion of the difficulties her Asian appearance and family heritage presents for her in being seen as 'Australian', despite the fact she has been here since she was 2 years old.

> My friends don't think of me as Akela, the Asian girl. They think of me as Akela. When they describe me, they might put that those elements are in there. I think some of it rubbed off on my older sister as well, because she'll

say, 'Oh my God, you're so Australian'. She'll say. 'I'm still Asian'. I'm like, 'You've got the same accent as me, but whatever'. She got sucked into that for a long time as well, and even as an adult. I just thought 'I'm Australian, I don't care. If people ask me what my nationality is, I have an Australian passport. I have a different heritage, but I'm Australian.'

It is not surprising that there should be significant differences between how this is experienced by Anglo-Australians and how it is experienced by everyone else. Identifying as Australian appears to be unproblematic for those of our respondents who were born here of Anglo parents; they are relatively unreflective about that identity, and only in one or two cases are they critical of it. Jacinta is the primary instance of the latter; her discomfort with a colonialist/nationalist narrative of Australian history leads her to refuse even to support Australian sporting teams. For those not in this category, however, the maintenance of their ethnic, racial or religious identity is challenged by the practical normativity of nationalist and exclusivist constructions of Australian identity.

Among the more familiar ways of talking about this within the public discussion of multiculturalism is to point to a, potentially unresolvable, duality in the structure of belonging. Charles draws upon that discourse when he describes himself as living in a 'lost world', caught between two contexts – Lebanon and Australia – into neither of which he feels that he fits. Aisha talks about this slightly differently, as she outlines the difficulty of negotiating the racialised constructions of cultural difference that create particular difficulties for Muslims in Australia, and specifically for women who wear the hijab:

> I did this course in counselling. I was the only one there. There were three migrants with a hundred blonde blue eyes people. I'm the only one with the hijab. It was always, always hard in the beginning because people don't know who you are. Some of them are afraid. Some of them don't want you to be there. It always takes an effect and I make sure I put an effort to just show people that I am a normal person. I have kids who are giving me a hard time. I have a husband who I fight with. When you start to speak about those little things they realise that she is a normal woman.

Her objective is to dissolve these differences, by demonstrating how she can 'fit in', given a chance. Nonetheless, she notes, 'when something happens, there is an attack or a Muslim who killed someone, yes you feel that you are a stranger in this country'.

Kim, a 53-year-old teacher who is Aboriginal Australian, undertook a Master's degree focused on learning Indigenous languages, and she tells a story of a very different dilemma of national belonging. She describes how difficult it was for her sister to establish proof of Aboriginality in order to enrol in a particular university course. Kim has taken this on as a challenge for her family and outlines what she has done as a consequence:

> What I'm hoping to do is put together a living family tree that we can add on and add on and we can print off at stages, like volume one, volume two, sort of thing so that we can use that as proof of Aboriginality if we need to, and that way it can be added to when people get married, when people have kids, and when people pass on.

In relation to the status of her sense of national belonging, Kim has this to say:

> It's really strange. I mean, I know I'm Australian, but I'm Aboriginal and I think no matter who I am and no matter where I am, I'm always wearing two hats. I mean, even here, I'm always wearing two hats and sometimes it's about which way I'm looking at you; is it this face, or this, you know, whatever side of the face. You know what I mean?

As Kim notes, even within the context of the interview she is present in two capacities: as an Australian citizen and as a member of our Aboriginal and Torres Strait Islander sample. Belonging to the nation, for many Australians, is no simple matter.

By highlighting the relative absence of class as an explicit presence in these conversations, and the preference for respondents to articulate their belonging through such frameworks as personal taste, family, community and heritage or national identity, we cannot assume that class has disappeared. Class may be expressed, reproduced and mediated through the institutional forms of family, community, church, nation – and indeed through the aesthetics of seemingly 'personal' taste, as Bourdieu and many other sociologists have shown. Perhaps of more interest here is the way in which local spaces of socialisation, rooted in family, church and neighbourhood, seem to endure. As Savage *et al.* found when studying several communities in northern England in the early 2000s, the globalised nature of contemporary cultures and economies has by no means diminished the importance of the local: expanding Bourdieu's notion of habitus with a particular reference to spatial dynamics, Savage *et al.* consider how 'residential place continues to matter since people feel some sense of "being at home" in an increasingly turbulent world' (Savage *et al.*, 2005: 10). Seemingly local and traditional institutions endure as spaces of attachment and the expression of local or familial identities. Such obdurate attachment to families and local communities could in our own research be further explored in the face of the substantial changes that our interview participants were experiencing with the rise of globalised digital technologies. In our final section we briefly consider certain aspects of these changes

The digital and the transnational

A running theme across many of the interviews, which has proved a significant insight into how practices of cultural participation and belonging seem to be changing, is their reflection of the influence of a trend that can be found right across the full range of the nation's zones of consumption – from retail shopping to art exhibitions: that is, the individualisation of consumption that comes from the capacity to customise personal choices reflected in the ubiquity of 'playlists', 'menus' and 'favourites' online, and facilitated by what has been called the 'culture of search' (Hillis *et al.*, 2013). The cultural fields into which we have enquired are part of this reconfiguration of the way in which we make our choices from the options and opportunities available to us.

The key influences upon the changing configurations revealed by the interviews are twofold: the role of the digital and of transnationalism. The influence of digital technologies is uneven, of course, but at its most active it has been transformative. For a start, let us just consider the array of consumer technologies retired retail manager Sean reports on having in his household of three persons: four smartphones, six tablets, four tower computers, five laptops, three stereo systems and four TVs. He subscribes to Netflix, he has a Personal Video Recorder and streams music via Spotify. Once, someone in his position would have had a television, a stereo, a landline and a couple of bookshelves. But if this multiplication of options has transformed consumption by massively proliferating the choice of devices, platforms and content, the digital has had an even more significant effect on cultural production. Musician and video producer, Brenton describes how it has changed what he can do:

> I can fit all of my endeavours into one space. I can make a moving image, and I get to edit the video, which I really enjoy doing; and I get to mix the sound, design all the sound, and edit the sound – that's right up my alley; and then use YouTube as the platform … It's great because I've got an instant audience … I can do all that stuff at home with all my own means; hit 'publish', go to bed, sleep; and wake up next morning and 300 people have engaged with it, and they've left comments. There's an audience that I can engage with; they want to talk back and forward, and they can pick it apart and tell me what they like and don't like. It ends up being a more fruitful environment for making art these days.

Such a high degree of personalisation is a direct outcome of the proliferation of platforms and modes of access influencing contemporary modes of consumption and production. The influence of digital practices and digital technologies is pervasive across the data gathered from the interviews, and now needs to be taken into account as one of the most important, albeit highly contingent, drivers for cultural consumption in Australia at the present time.

One of the further ways in which the digital has been transformative is through its provision of access to transnational content. Aisha is a devotee of Turkish soap operas she accesses online, Hong Kong-born Thomas's Vietnamese wife watches programming in her own language online, while Daniel's Chinese-born parents watch programmes streamed from China regularly. The links of belonging enabled by the transnational connections made available online do appear to transform the cultural experience of these individuals. In contrast to Charles' perception of being lost between worlds, the transnational connectivity now available and evident in these interactions seems to invert that relation: these individuals appear to be using this affordance as a means of engaging productively with two worlds at once.

This is not just a matter of new technological capacities, however. There are structural changes in the way national markets now operate and this affects cultural consumption as much as any other economic activity. The globalising trade in cultural commodities, not only in the more obvious areas such as television but also in the visual arts, as well as the manner in which globalising markets have transformed structures and practices in domains as different as literature and sport, has significantly affected how people now participate in cultural consumption and the ways in which they may think of themselves as belonging – to a family, to a community, to a race or ethnicity, to a nation, or to a transnational network. Occasionally, these changes are directly referenced in the interviews, but mostly they are implicit in the overarching strategies of choice and customisation that mark so much of what our interviewees tell us about the manner in which they participate in cultural consumption and how that participation structures their sense of belonging.

Conclusion

While digitisation and transnational connections are clearly significant in shaping cultural participation and belonging in new ways, it is important to note that they still sit alongside existing, long-standing structures and consumption practices in shaping the cultural lives of the Australians interviewed. Much evidence from these interviews underlines the continuing importance of the local, for instance, and the experiences reported demonstrate the continuing relevance of structures of community such as the family, the church or the local sports club. This, notwithstanding their relatively unfashionable status in a world that has become so focused upon engagements online and upon the individual. While the diversity of cultural activities revealed in interviews was remarkably large – and indicated the richness of everyday cultural life for many Australians both within and beyond the remits of our project's specified cultural fields – the drivers for their participation in a range of activities continued to be shaped largely by their commitments to family and local networks of belonging.

In closing, it is worth re-emphasising the breadth and diversity of cultural participation that has been reported by our interviewees. The motivations that propel individual Australians to engage in their chosen cultural activities are various, but notable across the interviews was the enduring capacity for cultural participation to produce and maintain family and community. Also notable was the number of moments in interviews where the practical distinction between the production and consumption of culture disappears; the categories merge through their interaction within particular sets of activities. As a result of the conversations and stories yielded from the interview process, what ends up 'counting' as culture broadens out, both in terms of the forms of participation within our chosen cultural fields, and in terms of learning about the cultural participation beyond those fields. Insights such as these remind us of the value of occasionally returning to the research in which we have engaged, from the perspectives voiced by our interview participants: this enriches our understanding of the varied dynamics of the cultural fields under examination, and of the ways in which our own definitions of such concepts as participation and belonging might best be understood.

16
THE POLITICS OF CONSUMPTION
Positioning the nation

Greg Noble and David Rowe

In *Distinction*, Bourdieu draws out the strong, but mediated, relations between politics and cultural tastes, and the issues through which they are expressed – the right to speak, moral order and class consciousness. While Bourdieu's analysis was framed by an emphasis on French class politics, we adopt a broader sense of the political, focusing less on the political sphere than on the processes through which people position themselves in relation to the state and civil society. Discussions of consumption during the *Australian Cultural Fields* (ACF) interviews drew people to issues around national identity, social cohesion and globalisation, demonstrating the ways in which political subjectivities are mediated through cultural practices. These interviews illustrate the complex forms of position-taking that interviewees undertake and the political dispositions that they reflect. This chapter is particularly concerned with participants' enunciation of the relations between their cultural preferences and ideas of national culture, the array of stances towards the nation that they voice, the challenges to a traditional politics of nation posed by the growing recognition of Indigenous and migrant cultures, and the threats and promises of globalisation.

This chapter uses Bourdieu's account of the relations between habitus and politics to analyse taste not simply as a form of symbolic representation that reproduces relations of inequality, but as practices of positioning which locate people in lived social relations and cultural systems of meaning. It focuses on the ways in which politics and cultural consumption are interwoven, producing complex relations to the nation, cultural diversity and the larger global context within and between different social positions. These accounts demonstrate the centrality of ambivalence – as conflicting and fluctuating stances towards the world – in our relations both to questions of cultural value and the nation.

Positioning habitus: taste, class and politics

As we have seen in the introduction to Part IV of this book, habitus, as the embodied system of durable dispositions, is a key concept capturing the mediation between structure and agency, and between social position and lifestyle. Despite often being characterised as 'deterministic', for Bourdieu habitus is not simply a mechanism of social reproduction. Taste is a generative process of making judgements as well as a system of classification (1984: 170, 467). This task requires not just mapping the 'positions' that people occupy; it must also examine the 'lived experience of agents in order to explicate the categories of perception and appreciation (*dispositions*) that structure action' (Bourdieu and Wacquant, 1992: 11).

Bourdieu emphasises that habitus entails not just embodied capacities, but perceptual schema, typically involving particular categories and oppositions embedded in practices rather than understood as values per se (1984: 468; Lizardo, 2004; Nash, 2005). Beliefs are 'practical' in the sense that they are the means through which we act. Habitus, as each person's ensemble of 'transposable dispositions' acquired through experience, manifests as *'perceptions, appreciations, and actions'* which enable 'infinitely diversified tasks' (Bourdieu, 1977: 82–83). Thus, the task of the researcher is to examine the practices of *position-taking* embedded in these actions, whether they relate to aesthetic and ethical judgements or political opinions (Bourdieu, 1996b: 231–232).

So while Bourdieu was primarily interested in the analysis of taste in terms of class, he cautioned against assuming a direct correspondence between them. Consequently, *political* positioning cannot simply be read off social location. The complex formation of the habitus in its 'material conditions' is full of inconsistencies:

> One of the most determining characteristics of political choices lies in the fact that ... much more than the obscure, deep-rooted choices of the habitus, they involve the more or less explicit and systematic representation an agent has of the social world, of his position within it and of the position he 'ought' to occupy. Political discourse, when it exists as such, is often no more than the more or less euphemised and universalised expression ... of that representation ... between the position really occupied and the political 'positions' adopted, there intervenes a representation of the position which ... may be at odds with the political 'positions' the position seems to entail for an external observer (this is what is sometimes called 'false consciousness').
>
> (Bourdieu, 1984: 453–454)

Habitus is, then, a synthesising but contrary means through which dispositions are transformed into social positions that can both reflect and contradict the social spaces that individuals inhabit. While there is some correspondence between class position and political views such that they can reflect 'maps of power relations', this relationship is highly mediated: similar conditions of existence can 'foster different dispositions, or habitus, among those subject to them and, thus, different aesthetic and ethical outlooks – or lifestyles and political attitudes' (Atkinson, 2017: 3–4). Analysing these spaces of lifestyle and attitude can throw considerable light on the dynamics of political consciousness in variable social contexts. The task, however, is not to point to the overarching correspondence between position and politics, but to explore the ways in which relations between taste and politics play out in people's perceptions of the world as situated practices of position-taking.

'Politics' involves social values that are deeply implicated in operations of power (Leftwich, 2004: 2, 23). For Bourdieu, relations of objective power manifest themselves in relations of symbolic power:

> The categories of perception, the systems of classification, that is, essentially, the words, the names which construct social reality as much as they express it, are the crucial stakes of political struggle, which is a struggle to impose the legitimate principle of vision and division.
>
> *(1990a: 134)*

Both 'the individual struggles of daily life and the collective, organised struggles of political life' involve symbolic struggles 'for the production and imposition of a legitimate vision of the social world'. Bourdieu sees politics in categories of perception that can be played out in the disparaging comments that we might make about others, as well as at the 'properly political' level of institutional organisation (1990a: 135–137). These layers of the political and the competing visions of the world emerge in the responses given by our interviewees. Those discussed here represent a cross-section of social positions, in terms of class, gender, age and ethnicity, as well as taste, but their expression of views represents a complex mediation of politics and social factors.

The taste *for* politics

In the course of the interviews, participants often moved easily from talking about their cultural preferences to unprompted discussions of politics and expressions of political opinion. The blurring of the lines between informational programmes and entertainment – captured as 'infotainment', and often decried – is not new, but rarely has it been analysed in terms of a Bourdieusian analysis of distinction. Several interviewees, however, explained their preferences for certain forms in terms of a taste *for* political content: that is, they found pleasure in items, such as fiction or current affairs programmes, which showcased politics as more than 'hard news' – they saw politics as a source of entertainment. Such shows, which dramatised political contests – often in exaggerated 'tabloid' style (Turner, 2005) – helped cultivate their ways of seeing politics as both entertainment and as a matter of serious deliberation.

Aisha, a 47-year-old relationships counsellor of Lebanese origin (to whom we will return below), likes the TV show *The Project* because, 'it's both comedy and current affairs, which for me it was very attractive and very intelligent … including the comedy in the events makes it lighter'. Craig, a 49-year-old former forklift driver, when asked what kinds of book he preferred, says that he liked those that represent what he called 'unusual politics, revisionist history ... Stuff that shatters our pre-conceived ideas about the past.' While he identifies as working class because of his 'very blue-collar work history', and does not like elitism, Craig's politics are more intellectual than activist. He is critical of corporations 'trying to run everything' and 'stupid free trade agreements', but this political perspective does not translate into political involvement. He has a liking, though, for political content in the items that he consumes. Heath, a 42-year-old printer, when asked what books he likes, similarly nominates the 'political, murder, intrigue' combination of the novels of left-leaning author Richard North Patterson, in accordance with his liking of 'robust discussions' of politics with his conservative father, and his dislike of the politics of fear represented by the right-wing Australian politician Pauline Hanson. For both of these men, politics-as-entertainment aligns with a progressive political position.

In contrast, Lynne, a 51-year-old party plan franchisee, declares herself 'not a political person. Politics I prefer to stick away from.' However, she loves the live debate television programme *Q&A*:

> I get my current affairs through those sort of shows and get more of an objective view rather than what you see on the news and on the commercial TV. Because you're getting the general public, you're getting the political; you're getting professors and doctors giving their point of view. So you're getting a really broad opinion on current affairs and things like that, rather than just what they want to show on the ... five o'clock news. As I said, I love Australian dramas.

Like Heath and Craig, however, there is a pleasure to be derived from the political content of diverse items that is more than informational. For Lynne, who doesn't like politics and does not express strong political opinions, the value of current affairs programmes lies in the promise of entertaining, lively debate which embodies the democratic principle of diverse points of view coming together for the benefit of the 'general public'. It is, perhaps, not accidental that she shifts immediately from expressing her preference for the lively presentation of political points of view on television to her 'love' for 'Australian dramas'.

Politics is much more integral to the life of Steven, a retired school principal, who has a strong commitment to current affairs (his 'morning ritual' involves reading the *Sydney Morning Herald*, and he lists six news and current affairs TV programmes that he watches), his party political affiliation (Labor) and his broader political orientation. He especially enjoys the satirical TV programme *Mad as Hell* because he sees the host, Shaun Micallef, as inhabiting a political position 'on the left', which he describes as 'similar to ours'. However, Steven emphasises that Micallef's humour appeals because of the 'absurdity' of contemporary politics: his deep investment in the political is matched by political cynicism. Significantly, it shapes his other consumption choices: he 'wouldn't subscribe [to] or read [right-wing tabloid] *The Daily Telegraph* because the slant there certainly is opposed to my beliefs and values'. Yet, despite Steven's cynicism, like Lynne he has a commitment to the public debate format of *Q&A* because of its 'opposing viewpoints' and 'challenging ideas': current affairs is not just about 'information getting', he said, because 'you are getting a range of positions as part of the process'. In common with Heath and Lynne, Steven enjoys the Machiavellian intrigue of fantasy shows like *Game of Thrones*, the politics of which are, as we have seen in Chapter 2, 'as real as real politics'. While he does not see himself as 'politically active', Steven is a volunteer for the Labor Party in a Liberal Party-held seat, and has been a teachers' union delegate. He uses his knowledge of current affairs in his local community, such as in his sports clubs, to 'raise issues and raise people's awareness on issues, Aboriginal issues or migrant issues or whatever ... I'll state a stance and give some arguments.' This practice can have consequences, as was evident in his response when asked whether he thinks his tastes are typical of his social group:

> I've thought about that a lot ... I go to the golf and ... at the end we all sit down and have a beer or two and we talk. I feel I'm quite atypical in my views ... which I still struggle with. This is a working-class area ... I go out there and I think I espouse what I believe are working-class values and find that I'm at odds. Most people ... whatever [right-wing broadcaster] Alan Jones has said on the radio this morning, that's the gospel for today and I'll go out and say something quite contrary and find that they're aghast.

He objected to criticism of Indigenous footballer Adam Goodes (see Chapter 6) at his social club, 'challenging them and their attitudes and what they were saying ... I think I was effective in the sense I at least made them think that what they were saying was extraordinarily racist and I called them racist.' Steven, who feels 'almost like a pariah' at the club because he votes Labor, interprets a question about his tastes in terms of a mismatch between his political views and those of his local community, imbricating issues of cultural and political preference with those relating to class, party politics and social values on subjects like Indigenous rights. Moreover, in demonstrating a commitment to political issues and yet scepticism towards the practices of politics, Steven captures a degree of ambivalence in his relations to the political, a theme to which we will return below.

What unites these four participants is a taste for politics as a mode of cultural consumption – even entertainment – though its manifestations diverge. Yet there are significant differences. Steven and Lynne are located in a similar social position, characterised by age and relative affluence, yet have quite different orientations towards politics. In contrast, Craig and Heath, who have similar preferences towards political content in fiction, inhabit quite different social positions. Across these interviews, politics is shown to be strongly but variably mediated through cultural tastes, but what constitutes 'politics' is a disparate set of ideas and diverse layers of 'the political', including the content of fantasy fiction, the format of current affairs shows, party politics, class values and broader social issues. It is a dynamic semantic space where particular kinds of belief and relationship are articulated, with categories of perception not being neatly defined entities, but situated and relational practices of meaning-making. While the comments variously reflect the shifting but persistent connection between social position and habitus, filtered through a range of factors, most interviewees (unlike Steven and Craig) did not have a strong sense of class membership, but negotiated their subjectivities through their cultural tastes. These comments also exhibit complex relations to the nation, globalisation and cultural difference, entailing varying degrees of investment and distance.[1]

The cultural politics of nation

Investigating cultural practices invariably evokes understandings of nation, although the strength and complexion of the nation–culture nexus is highly variable (Stewart, 2013; Bennett et al., 2009). By 'nation' we refer not necessarily to the nation-state, but draw more expansively on notions of the national in various conceptualisations of social relations. Similarly, questions of politics do not necessarily pertain to those directly concerning the nation-state, especially formal political structures and processes within an orthodox framework of law, citizenship and representation. Anthony, a young mechanic of Lebanese background, sees a distinct separation between party politics and the nation. Explaining his preference for sports news, he states, 'Politics I really don't care … Australia is always Australia, if it was the Labor or it was the Liberal it's always Australia'. For others, cultural consumption is used to confirm a sense of national identity through comparison and contrast with signifiers of other nations. Kathleen, a 56-year-old quality control officer, voices a common ambivalence for some Australians in that, while she did not watch much sport, she had been 'glued' to the TV watching the Olympics: 'I like to win. I like to get up on that dais. I love when our national anthem comes up … I love our national anthem' (this complicated negotiation of the relationship between sport and national culture is explored in Chapter 6).

Similarly, echoing findings in Chapter 4, national identification is accomplished through heritage-related travel for Christine, a 61-year-old Aboriginal administrative officer with a university education. Visiting Gallipoli, an overseas war location of deep mythological significance in Australia, although one that is now increasingly open to transnational interpretation (McKay, 2018), resonated deeply with her sense of Australianness. There is no apparent tension between her 'Indigenous' and 'Australian' identities, nor between her nationalism and attitude towards globalisation – the latter, in fact, is seen as enabling rapid communication of the former across space and time through enhanced connectivity:

> at the end of the day we're very Australian, especially very Australian overseas. My daughter's travelled heaps and she's the staunchest … she sits with the Fanatics [supporter group] at the tennis and the cricket. She was actually interviewed on the radio from the tennis and met [tennis player] John

Newcombe and stuff, and dad says 'I heard [interviewee's daughter] on the radio, she's in New York and she was on the ABC'. I went, 'yes, right dad', and she was. It's just the linking of the world now is just so quick.

Reflecting the tensions experienced by migrant Australians explored in Chapter 13, the challenge of competing affiliations is expressed by Thomas, a currently unemployed network engineer born in Hong Kong. He sees support for Australian athletes and teams as a duty for those living in the country: 'normally it's still support Aussie ... [because] you're staying in Australia'. Thomas feels compelled to like and support Australian sportspeople, even when they do something objectionable, as part of a 'migrant compact' from a position of disadvantage. By contrast, Lisa, a 42-year-old British migrant, has sufficient cultural, social and economic capital to remain quite detached from this politics of Australianness. Living in Canberra, she attends the Anzac day ceremony 'most years', but participation in it does not enhance her sense of an Australian identity. She takes a cool, 'cosmopolitan' approach to nation geared towards acquiring knowledge about other cultures:

> I don't think my interests have really changed much. It's just broadened them in terms of, like, we had no knowledge of Aboriginal culture. So we've got more knowledge of that. In terms of interests ... I don't think they are more Australian. I think they're just the same. It's just that we've got access to different things from a different perspective.

Lisa's views indicate, perhaps, a nascent cosmopolitan disposition, sampling difference within a range of national contexts. She was untroubled, unlike some interviewees, by the impact of globalisation on national culture. This disposition, combined with her British origin, affords her a certain confidence in not being pressured to identify with Australia out of political duty, in contrast to Thomas's identification with sport. Possibly, the sport field, and its invitation to support the national team, places specific pressures on social subjects to display their national fealty rather than risk nationalist accusations of 'divided loyalties', lack of integration or, most pejoratively, of being 'un-Australian'. Those of Anglo-Celtic origin can afford to be more relaxed in relation to national identity than those from, for example, south Asia, for whom national sporting affiliation could be 'a very hard question' (quoted in Rowe, 2015: 703).

These comments represent not just competing understandings of the nation, but different stances towards, and degrees of investment in, the nation. As Anderson (2006) has shown, there is no singular national community, only social imaginaries which assume national coherence. The myriad ways in which the national infuses everyday life through both formal and popular rituals (Billig, 1995; Edensor, 2002) underlie the multiple and contradictory stances towards the national exhibited in the interviews. For Bourdieu, the synthesising unity of the habitus is produced when determinations of class and capital intersect with the multiple contingent factors that constitute the materials out of which subjectivity is formed. But in complex, fluid societies – especially a settler-colonial society like Australia, which has been reshaped by large-scale migration – that synthesising unity is harder to identify. For some whose primary socialisation and experience was of a solid, institutionally and spatially reinforced sense of nation, the politics of nation may be reasonably straightforward. But, as in several cases addressed here, experiences of Indigeneity and migration are likely to destabilise the part of the habitus that exhibits an ordered orientation, producing a high degree of ambiguity and ambivalence.

The idea of nation frequently serves as a bridge to a wide-ranging but contradictory political sensibility. Instead of regarding this lack of cohesion as 'false consciousness' (as invoked, ironically, by Bourdieu above), it can be regarded more fruitfully as a negotiation of the tension between acknowledging the social forces bearing upon person formation while also resisting the temptation to reduce people to the status of mere bearers of class taste or to a singular political orientation. Indeed, the idea of belonging may entail specific kinds of contradiction. For example, David, a retired manager, like some interviewees above equates cultural consumption with the exercise of citizenship. He uses public service television current affairs 'to keep up to date' with national politics, 'things like *Sunday Morning [Insiders]* with Barrie Cassidy and those sort of shows that keep you going'. This last comment suggests that maintaining a stake in the nation can be onerous. Significantly, David represents this activity's importance playfully – 'Well, I think as a voter or a citizen you're obliged to be amused by what goes [on] in Canberra' – but does not see himself as politically active. This position is markedly different from a literal sense of national commitment.

As with Steven, David's relationship to nation, glimpsed through the television field, is ambiguous: it is an investment in nation, but marked with irony. He uses the national broadcaster to keep abreast of developments in the political sphere, but undercuts the exercise of informed citizenship via media (Soroka et al., 2013) by likening the 'serious' current affairs genre to comedy. The disposition to the political – 'what goes on in Canberra' – embedded in his habitus is ambivalent in the full sense. In class terms David is affluent and educated, which prima facie would indicate a likely investment in the political. His interest in 'social science subjects', and his professional background in private industry and university management, possibly leads him to be 'a bit of a cynic' regarding the politics of the Australian nation-state. As Adkins (2003) and Razinsky (2017) have argued, ambivalence is crucial to the formation of human subjectivity, particularly for those in 'dominated' positions, but Bourdieu's focus on the congruent and normative relation of habitus to field means that he does not recognise ambivalence as central to social practice. As a strategic response to mediated politics, David's 'amusement' evinces a certain distance found amongst many interviewees which allows people both to believe in, and be disappointed by, the nation's role in cultural life.

Troubling the nation

We have focused so far on three fields – media, sport and heritage – where the nation has a particularly important and conflicted place. But it is worthwhile remembering that cultural policy more broadly has had a deep investment in nation-building. Australia's first national cultural policy, *Creative Nation* (Department of Communications and the Arts, 1994), had at its heart a desire to stake a claim for a shared national culture. Its 2013 successor, *Creative Australia*, was rather less confident about the possibility of such a common culture (Rowe et al., 2018). Nevertheless, 'culture' is frequently both at the centre of projects of national identity, and the source of threats that 'trouble' that identity. 'Nation' is a contested category rather than a coherent normative framework that citizens are socialised into accepting. So, alongside the ambivalence noted above, divergent stances towards nation were expressed ardently by some participants with a more overtly political orientation. Jacinta, a 49-year-old learning consultant, sees 'culture' as inherently political in shaping her taste choices. The interviewer had noted that, while indicating that she 'most liked' Indigenous heritage in the survey, Jacinta also 'least liked' Australian heritage. She elaborates thus:

> On a political level, I've got real concerns about Australia's political history. So it's very difficult to separate the politics and the effect of the last 230 years with the artistic dimensions, that history, so that taints for me that heritage. But I think it also tells a very interesting story as Australia's tried to construct its own identity: the art and the culture that's sprung up or been developed shows and reflects that national identity, the construction of that identity. So I think from a political perspective it's important, it's interesting but … the dominance of that as a historical story is very much at the expense of Australia's Aboriginal history.

This perspective leads Jacinta to a kind of anti-nationalism of taste:

> I generally don't support Australia because I think if Australia wins that just props up Australian nationalism … There's … an arrogance in the Australian cricket team that I don't like, but I do tend to, particularly with cricket, tend to make a decision on what are the wider political ramifications if one team wins or the other, which is probably completely ridiculous. But anyway that [is] the basis I try to side at.

She develops this position in discussing the series of racist incidents involving Indigenous sports stars Adam Goodes and Cathy Freeman:

> As Indigenous sportspeople I think they, through their success, they challenge racism in Australia and so I like that, and I think what happened to Adam Goodes really shows the, really, the sort of racist underbelly that

continues to exist in Australia. I think it's just appalling and [Indian] Sachin Tendulkar, because he's a great cricketer ... but I tend to, particularly with cricket because it's an international game, choose who I'm going to support on a political basis [laughs].

For Jacinta, who feels 'very uneasy' about connecting social class to cultural taste, especially 'associating working-class people with less refined taste', her cultural choices are necessarily political choices which trouble the taken-for-granted status of the nation. Ironically, however, her anti-nationalism represents a deep engagement with the national, as culture embeds a history of colonial oppression which has to be addressed within national life. For others, however, different 'imperial' forces shape and threaten the viability of a national culture in Australia.

Loving or loathing the Other?

Few interviewees were as explicit as Jacinta in voicing a political orientation to their taste. Nevertheless, many articulated similarly complex, ambivalent relations between cultural preference and political orientation. A common position involved what we might call a benign politics of multiculturalism, whereby the national benefits deriving from diversity were framed as cultural richness. Asked if multiculturalism has transformed Australians' or his own cultural pursuits, David (quoted above) responds:

> I think it's transformed Australia since I was young. And living around here is not a bad education in multiculturalism ... The whole thing has always attracted me, I suppose ... as far as I'm concerned Haberfield [a Sydney suburb] and places like that are where I get the best food from. In other words, Italian food, and my wife's the same ... She's always sorry she wasn't born Italian because she loves everything Italian.

Michael, a retired engineer who identifies as 'middle class' but is not interested in 'hobnobbing' with the 'upper class', similarly feels that multiculturalism:

> opened up a much wider range of restaurant types and things. I've been eating out a lot more in the last five years than I ever did previously. Just at our local one here we've got Thai, Chinese, Mexican, Subway, the pub ... and that's just up the road ... Oh, I'm quite comfortable with [multiculturalism].

This position represents less the 'cultural openness' at the heart of debates around cosmopolitan capital (Coulangeon, 2017) than what Hage (1998: 201) calls 'white cosmo-multiculturalism', a form of distinction that he identifies amongst middle-class Australians savouring exotic difference without necessarily involving intercultural interaction. Hage sees whiteness not just in terms of skin colour, but as the accumulated cultural capital necessary to active governmental belonging in the field of national power. This 'multiculturalism without migrants' (1998: 118) is a common positioning for some interviewees, particularly those like Michael and David who inhabit social positions marked by affluence and age. But this seemingly benign view has an edge for migrants. Anthony does not fit the middle-class profile that Hage identifies with 'cosmo-multiculturalism'. Indeed, he sometimes feels like 'an outsider from the Australian community'. And yet, he says:

> I love multiculturalism, for example if I'm going to Ashfield [a Sydney suburb] ... I mean that's good, but you have, for example ... a lot of people from different races clash in society, different levels; rich and poor and lack of education. A lot of people come into Australia but they're not educated ... Some people, they can't merge in ... because Australia is a first world country, it's very advanced and all the rest of the world is rubbish.

The Australian community, Anthony adds, 'absorb everything without even thinking about it. The community now is like we don't know what's the Australian community anymore.' So, Anthony's 'love' of multiculturalism is tinged by an ambivalence deriving from anxiety regarding a perceived loss of community and threat to Australia represented by uneducated migrants: the problem with multiculturalism is for him too many of the 'wrong' kind of migrants. In even greater contrast to a benign middle-class politics of diversity was something approaching a politics of resentment. Kathleen, quoted above, is located in a similar class position to Anthony. Asked about whether she was interested in Indigenous heritage, Kathleen replies:

> I don't really care one way or the other, to tell you the truth ... I've got some friends who got involved with Aboriginals and whatnot. Apart from that, that's not, you know, part of my life, no. I've noticed, yeah, it's more to the forefront nowadays than what it ever was. Again, I think, sometimes, that they get a raw deal. Then again, they need to look after themselves ... I get a bit frustrated that they're given handouts. They don't appreciate anything that they get. My issue was when my kids were growing up, I was a single mother. Again, I had to pay for my kids to go on excursions and shoes and everything else. Then there was an Aboriginal kid that was given everything. I'm thinking, 'I work, I've still got to pay. Why am I paying for something that other people can get for free?'

Here, too, is a kind of ambivalence. While her response initially expresses a degree of indifference — a distancing typical in discussions of taste reflecting a lack of investment — it is clear that Kathleen, an Anglo-Australian woman who identifies as working class but has risen to a low managerial position, declines to recognise the cultural value of artefacts deriving from Indigenous groups. She sees her class identity in terms of being a 'battler' ('I would like to have a house, but that ain't ever going to happen') and is proud of her independence as a working-class woman ('not to have to rely on anyone else'), so this refusal involves a degree of resentment which entangles class, gender and 'race'. This entanglement shapes Kathleen's criticism of what she sees as an 'unfair' politics around Aboriginal welfare as the 'handouts' of national paternalism rather than as an act of social justice.

Recognition and escape: the ambivalent politics of migrant Australia

Recognition was of deep concern to some Australians of migrant or non-Anglo background as part of their accrual of a sense of national belonging. It is illustrated by a response from Aisha, the counsellor we met above, who shares a similar social position to Kathleen, but with quite a different orientation. Aisha, of Lebanese Muslim background, elaborates upon why she likes the current affairs TV show *The Project*. The previous year, one of its hosts, Waleed Aly, became the first Muslim to win the Gold Logie TV award:

> I am going to be now frank and I'm going to be the Muslim woman who is *proud* ... When Waleed Aly received the award, for me it was a big achievement for all Muslims basically, so I became more attracted to it, feeling that this is a person who is giving a good image of Islam. So that sort of belonging and connecting.

Aisha's pride and pleasure is a response to the representation of Muslims in Australia and the cultural validation that the award bestowed. She is critical of the absence of Muslims on TV: 'Not only Muslims. It's mostly white and mostly the programs like *Home and Away* and *Neighbours*, it mostly reflects the white issues. It doesn't reflect the multicultural part of Australia.' But, the ambivalence of this position becomes apparent as recognition gives way to an overwhelming sense of the impossibility of her desire for social justice. Her taste becomes, therefore, defined by a cultural politics of escape:

> I used to be more into news and being involved and trying to make a change, particularly being a Muslim-Australian ... [but] it became a really, really big burden. With one incident, one terrorist incident or one comment from politicians I would feel that ... I am really done, because I got to a point where I felt that whatever I am doing, whatever I do, this thing is too big ... My interest in news and the world became less and less and I went more and more towards comedy. I watch a lot of Turkish soapies where you just chuck your brain down and you watch something romantic and so idealistic and this is where you want to be. Sort of running away from a very, very cruel and ugly reality. Plus, being also an Arabic Muslim, there is always this feeling ... that thousands of our brothers and sisters are suffering in the world and you can't do anything. [she begins to cry]

Aisha's ambivalence, however, is quite different from David's and more akin to that of dominated groups which, together with a fusion of national and global politics, is evident regarding Mayra, a 34-year-old Sri Lankan-born project officer in migrant and refugee issues in the not-for-profit sector. Mayra describes how she met her husband:

> we actually technically met at a protest ... We were both visiting asylum seekers and we'd kind of come into contact in terms of engaging volunteers and how best to deal with people that wanted to visit people in detention ... Do you remember those massive protests against the Iraqi invasion? We're going back a few years. He said, 'I'm going to be here, this time' and so on, and I said, 'I'll be there' ... We didn't really start dating right away, but yeah, we met over our activism and our social justice stuff, yeah. We kind of bonded over that.

Mayra's political disposition, like Aisha's, is ambiguously related to her interests in television, visual art, heritage and literature. She also likes to 'escape' through fiction: 'I was reading romance for a while, that was good and then I'm just like, 'Nah, this is [grimacing]'. Gave up. I think I was in the middle of reading a few romance books. They're okay, it's good escapism.'

Mayra's difficulty with finishing books, even in the light romance genre, is related to her energetic political activism, as if once the weight of being politically 'serious' is released, there is no need to continue. This practice connects with Aisha's account of using 'soapies' and comedy as 'relief' from the burden of being Muslim in Australia. Rather than a contradiction, it suggests that cultural consumption exists in complex economies of commitment and release which mediate individuals' relation to national and international politics. A more multi-faceted and often transnational relation to globalisation is evident than within the touristic ethos of cosmo-multiculturalism. Yet the interviews contain other political stances towards globalisation where the key figure is neither colonialism nor exotic foreignness.

Globalisation, America and the Other

'Americanisation' has long been shorthand for fears and desires regarding the economic and cultural impacts of globalisation in Australia (Bell and Bell, 1998). As Bennett *et al.* (1999: 202, 225) demonstrated many years ago, the increasing influence of American cultural production in the everyday lives of Australians has produced both increasing anxiety about American cultural dominance and the ongoing belief that Australia has a distinct national culture. In the two decades since publication of that book, and despite the continued visibility and significance of American culture, there has also been a more intense globalisation of economic and cultural production, with increasing involvement of European and Asian influences.

Despite the more diversified nature of globalisation, several of our interviewees viewed globalisation as synonymous with Americanisation. Often unequivocal that

American culture has a substantial cultural impact on Australia, they saw it as an inevitable effect of globalisation that for some was regrettable, but for others not necessarily undesirable. Robert, a 66-year-old retired graphic designer who sees himself as passionate about Australian history and environmental issues, displays a 'protective nationalism', complaining that:

> everybody's going through the McDonalds sausage background and coming out the other end exactly the same. I think it's so important to keep [our] diversity and I really love that, you know, that Australian sort of larrikinism and a sense of humour that's disappearing now.

In contrast, Daniel, a 31-year-old of Chinese heritage, sees Australia and other Western countries as especially susceptible to *American*-inflected globalisation: 'I feel a lot of people from different cultural backgrounds are being influenced by American media, American values, whatever that is – yeah, American way of life, yeah.' Daniel feels that American influence in the West is inevitable, based on cultural affinity, but does not see this trend as being of great political significance. Indeed, Hong Kong-born Thomas makes a connection between economic capital and cultural quality in the television field. While watching Australian current affairs for local content, he prefers American programmes on grounds of superior production values. Consequently, their formats were often copied in Australia: 'now some local Australian – they will have – *The Voice* is local but the idea is still from America. *The Voice* is – everything – it may be local here but the first program's still in the US.' He believes that Australian culture is profoundly influenced by America, but adds that:

> I think it's nothing good or bad. It is the market. The population in the US is much larger than Australia so it's easier to make different, good quality programs ... It's just purely because they get huge money background ... It's as simple as that.

Thomas displays a very different orientation to Australianness, though, in the sport and television fields. His close identification with Australia in sport dissipates almost entirely where non-sport television is concerned. Chinese-born Angela, a 50-year-old retired office worker, views globalisation as having a 'huge impact', but predominantly through the instantaneous connectivity of peer-to-peer communication: 'Like the smartphone, what's happen[ed] in China within five minutes or less I sign on here and I can see.'

These Chinese-Australians are generally unperturbed by globalisation, unlike many Anglo-Australians disposed towards modes of Australianness that take on a 'defensive' posture (Clark *et al.*, 2017). For some, the rise of China threatens Australian culture much more than Americanisation. Martin, a 59-year-old retired British-born inventory planner, values the 'mixture of identity' which 'has made a unique identity for Australia'. Yet, he shifts discursively from cultural diversity in sport to the emerging fashion of *feng shui*, which he'd just seen discussed in a current affairs programme:

> They're doing it all in Chatswood [a Sydney suburb]. Now, because there is a big Chinese-committed community there, and to me I thought this country was supposed to be an English-speaking Christian country. I'm not being derogative [*sic*] towards other languages or other ... backgrounds, but the fundamentals of the country is that we're starting to lose that identity, and for Australia to have an identity we've got to get back to bringing the people back together again, because in the end, if we don't do that ... they are going to end up with one hell of a problem.

However, these varying stances towards nation, cosmopolitanism and globalisation – evident in other environments such as Britain (Savage *et al.*, 2010) – do not mean that many interviewees from diverse backgrounds were uninterested in international politics.

The transnational consumption of international politics

Several interviewees of non-Anglo-Celtic migrant background were more interested in international politics and Indigenous history than in national or local politics. This transnational orientation is evident in the case of Anthony. He largely bypasses national television to watch international political and environmental stories on YouTube:

> Every day I sit for two to three hours on YouTube ... When I go to YouTube now recently, channels with Donald Trump and Hilary Clinton and those things, Presidents in America. I used to watch about Malcolm Turnbull and the differences between Labor and Liberal Party, but there's differences like it doesn't affect directly to the Australian community. On YouTube most of the times religion or economy and the environment, for example, solar energy and renewable energy and sustainable energy and China ... for example, *China Uncensored* ... There's a lot of channels of religion ... on Christianity and debates between Islam and Christianity ... I used to watch about Israel, what's happening in Israel and what are the updates, for example solar energy ... interesting, and Australia is trying to do that.

Anthony's interest in politics is broad: he does not mention parliamentary politics but is concerned with diverse socio-political issues around the world that are relevant to the Australian context. Badal, a 42-year-old former production supervisor of Indian-Fijian origin currently retraining as a teacher, similarly abhors a narrow focus on Australian and 'parish pump' news. Living in a culturally and ethnically diverse suburb, he sees Australian TV news on commercial free-to-air networks as too profit oriented and interested predominantly in the Anglo-Australian mainstream, neglecting both international and Indigenous affairs, especially in the area of heritage:

> We are all migrants in Australia, right, even people that came 200 years ago. What is missing is the history before that and it's not available as such. If you can get to hear about it and whatever you hear is misinformation to a large extent, because the news items are presenting one aspect of it. It doesn't present the whole news item. Everything is commercialised, so in the telly they have got 10-second, 30-second, 20-second, you know, what's good to view for the general public. You know, like 40 people died in a bomb in Afghanistan, we have a 10-second coverage for that, but someone got robbed in [south-western Sydney], there was a gun shooting, we have a special of 10 minutes and they talk to every neighbour.

For Badal, every Australian should have a more global orientation and, like Anthony, he does not see globalisation as being in tension with a commitment to Australia – indeed, he sees it as a necessary supplement to it. Commercial media, in this sense, have in his view let their citizenry down. But, he also sees the media as largely responsible for the ignorance of Aboriginal history, which he links to the experiences of recent arrivals trying to cope with the demands of settlement:

> Aboriginal history, the way they were killed and the way they have been removed from the land and had things taken away from them ... Maybe one in 10 people would be able to shed some light about that and the rest don't know, because you go to ... the suburb I live in, we're all foreigners over here. Average time spent in Australia is five years, maybe. So people are still trying to overcome the hardship or whatever they have in the old country, let alone trying to learn about the country itself.

Badal's life experience as a migrant frames this construction of a displaced habitus. His geo-political curiosity ranges from Asia (like Anthony's) to the conditions of Australia's first peoples, and is not satisfied by what he sees as the tabloidised Australian media. He does, however, exempt public service broadcasting and some other media sources from this criticism:

> I just love that program [*Media Watch*] because they're so unbiased. They even criticise ABC ... Most of my sources I trust is ABC, SBS. I think they're good generally, they present information that is well balanced. *60 Minutes* ... Al Jazeera, I watch that once in a while in the daytime ... I think they present reasonably balanced information.

An interest in balance in the media is not in this and most other cases echoed by direct political engagement at the level of, for example, political parties. Thus, while politics is deeply inscribed in the habitus of many interviewees, it is linked in complex ways to the politics of identity, rather than being of a party-political nature.

Conclusion

Politics, broadly understood, is woven into the ways in which participants talked about particular forms of consumption: indeed, many expressed a taste for political content even when they did not declare strong political commitments. A focus on the nation is most evident in the more politically charged fields of television, heritage and sport, where questions of nation, Indigeneity, multiculturalism and globalisation readily came to the fore. These connections reflect Sayer's contention that much of our normative orientation to the world functions at the level of embodied, especially aesthetic and ethical, dispositions. He elaborates,

> we will understand people better if we take their normative dispositions, concerns and rationales seriously, rather than treating these as mere facts about them which can be given a social location in relation to class, gender and 'race', and then left at that, as if they were no different from facts about their age or height.
>
> *(Sayer, 2005: 21)*

The participants' political dispositions revealed in these interview excerpts were highly differentiated in relation to class and other social variables, but the aim of this chapter was not to slot people into broad categories but to reveal how they positioned themselves and their tastes in relation to a political frame. There are no simple or direct across-the-board patterns regarding socio-economic factors, though there are moments when connections across similar social positions are evident. Nevertheless, orientations to the national – sometimes deeply, sometimes lightly inscribed – are central to the ways in which people account for their cultural practices and tastes. This orientation articulates with concerns around globalisation, cultural diversity and Indigenous issues, but rarely in straightforward ways, producing varieties of political ambivalence.

Such ambivalence, however, does not constitute irrational contradictions in people's views of the world, but rather spaces of subjectivity through which they understand and engage with the plural logics of the worlds that they inhabit. A sense of ambivalence is central both to subjectivity generally and to the ways in which we make judgements about the world (Razinsky, 2017). This process suggests that the Bourdieusian focus on position-taking, rather than equating with a single location on a map of socio-cultural positions, allows us to think about the conflicted and fluid ways in which people orient themselves in relation to questions of culture and politics. While there were occasionally unambiguous expressions of nationalism, most participants voiced ambivalent orientations to nation, but with significant differences: a white middle-class Australian ambivalence is very different from that of a migrant or a working-class ambivalence, each representing variable depths of investment in the idea of nation, and differing capacities to identify with it. Ultimately, the participants' comments do not reveal singular 'positions' that imply a simple relationship between class (or ethnic or gender) habitus, taste and national identity, but a diverse range of ways of negotiating the categories through which political subjectivities are expressed.

Note

1 We focus on the politics around nation rather than other political interests, such as feminism or environmentalism, because the latter were rarely invoked in interviews.

17
THE ETHICAL AND CIVIC DIMENSIONS OF TASTE

Tim Rowse, Michelle Kelly, Anna Cristina Pertierra and Emma Waterton

We argue in this chapter that within 'taste' there may be strong ethical commitments, including senses of solidarity – principled, but also strongly felt – with national and sub-national formations, such as those enjoined by the Australian discourse of Reconciliation. To make this argument we engage with a critique of the representation of working class taste in Bourdieu's *Distinction* (Bennett, T., 2011). Bennett questions Bourdieu's reliance on 'aesthetic categories' in his questionnaire. Discussing the items on which Bourdieu drew heavily in demonstrating 'the uniformity of working class taste with regard to its exclusion from legitimate culture' (Bennett, T., 2011: 537), Bennett points to other possible questions that would have revealed 'forms of pleasure and judgment associated with a wider range of cultural practices' than those considered in *Distinction*. A survey instrument better suited to eliciting the 'distinctive forms of pleasure and judgment' of the 'excluded' would pose questions enabling respondents to show how they: 'connect aesthetic evaluations to ethical judgments as a positive value rather than as a failing'; 'express preferences in hedonistic terms, linking aesthetic to bodily pleasures'; and, 'connect cultural choices to forms of collective or group involvement' (Bennett, T., 2011: 538).[1] The analysis of data elicited by such questions, Bennett suggests, would be more likely to substantiate 'subordinate systems of cultural capital production and circulation'. Such analysis, Bennett speculates, might discern 'autonomous systems of judgment' by distilling 'principles' implicit in these ethical judgements, hedonistic effusions and senses of connection to others. Such 'systems' could be significant, he further suggests, 'irrespective of their exchange value in the relations between the schooling system, the institutions of legitimate culture, and the occupational class structure' (Bennett, T., 2011: 538).

This chapter does not seek to illuminate Australian working-class tastes. Rather, we illustrate some dimensions of 'liking' cultural items that seem to be widespread among contemporary Australians: ethical judgements, hedonistic effusions and senses of connection to others, including the (dis)connections evoked by what we call the Reconciliation Orthodoxy. The *Australian Cultural Fields* (ACF) household interview data illustrates contemporary Australians' readiness to present their cultural consumption in terms that are ethical and/or hedonistic and that evince certain senses of belonging to some kind of community. First, we show interviewees liking or disliking heritage in terms of feelings of various kinds: spiritual connection, national belonging, moral obligation. Second, we note the moralisation of sport and the alternative of refusing to allow athleticism to stand for any value higher than itself. Third, we witness some interviewees' sense of taking their pleasures within a field of more or less authorised tastes. Our fourth section suggests something noteworthy in the ways people talk about watching television: sensitive to the different ways TV inflects what is 'real', they assert a kind of curatorial prerogative. Having evoked the interviewee as a choosing customer, relishing personal autonomy, we then return, in our fifth and final section, to a quality of response that is also evident in our first section on 'heritage' – a sense of obligation to imagined moral communities of some kind. In this section, picking up on the analysis of the place of Indigenous cultural capital in Chapter 12, we see Reconciliation discourse as regulating orientations towards 'Indigenous' persons and artefacts, and we point to survey evidence about what kinds of contemporary Australians are more likely to be susceptible to this appeal.

Heritage: feeling, belonging and obligation

Interviews about the consumption of heritage, where individuals recall being physically within a site or surrounded by artefacts, elicited intensity of feeling, as Kim, a 53-year-old Indigenous Australian teacher, recalls of her visit to Stonehenge:

> The closer I got to Stonehenge, the more edgy I got and when I got there I actually felt quite ill. I had to go and sit down, and I was on a bus full of, I think it was about twenty-three, twenty-four of us, and they ended up all around me and I could hardly breathe. I was hyperventilating and everything. The further I got away from it the better I felt. Then I found out it was like just a few days before solstice and it was at its strongest time and I knew none of that while I was there, and I'm thinking, idiot. No wonder I'd had such a strong connection to it because culturally those sort of things would affect me.

The anticipation of the impact of some heritage sites is invoked by Sean, a 54-year-old manager, to account for his avoidance of Holocaust sites:

> I've been to some Holocaust places which are fascinating. I don't think that I could bring myself to go to Auschwitz or any of those but I've been to some memorials in Germany. I quite like them. I just don't think I could go to that. I think it'd be too – you'd be overcome with too much grief.

Setting limits to his response, Sean's account expresses respect for Holocaust memory.

As Chapter 4 has shown, Australia has sacralised the nation through sites of memory such as the Australian War Memorial (Canberra) (Figure 17.1) and the Anzac Commemorative Site and Lone Pine Memorial at Gallipoli (Turkey). As Christine recounts: 'we went to Gallipoli for Anzac Day. See that's a big thing. I really think that that was so moving for me that every Australian should attempt to go there.' Heath says that visiting the Australian War Memorial is 'another thing' on his 'bucket list' (he lives in Brisbane): 'Must do it. All my kids have gone, you know they all do it with school, which I think is great. That is a perfect thing to take kids in early high school.' Some spoke of heritage consumption as civic duty. Lynne says that 'Australian heritage … is very, very important to me', so that her family holiday to Thailand:

> wasn't just all about beaches and swimming. We took [our children] to Kanchanaburi [War Cemetery, the main prisoner of war cemetery for victims of Japanese imprisonment while building the Burma Railway] … and went to the war museums over there.

However, respect for Australian military sacrifice may be tinged with ambivalence, as Brenton illustrates when asked about the Australian War Memorial:

> Yeah. I don't know. It's just war. I'm not engaged with it. I don't want to be engaged with it. I find it all gross and disgusting, and I don't know how to celebrate it. I'm grateful that people put their lives on the line to make the society that we live in now. Yes, fantastic, but me worshipping a dead person isn't going to do anything, and I don't want to celebrate war to encourage more people to join armies, and encourage more people to think that violence and bombing people is the solution to our problems of the world. I try to keep my mouth shut about it, though, because no-one likes the guy going, 'Oh well, you signed up for it. Go over there and die. You know what you signed up for'. But at the same time, I guess you need it. I find it very complicated: ethically, very complicated.

His final words – 'I hope I got that across without sounding like a total arse' – imply awareness that his 'taste' is a position within a socially regulated field of positions. Similarly, Mayra acknowledges that a site which for some elicits dutiful attendance and respectful presence may be, for others, an object of moral disgust:

> I hate the War Memorial. I had to go there on a school trip and I think I went back there with my husband from Canberra. He wanted to visit and I said, 'Do we have to go?' I think I remember distinctly there was – was it the Kokoda trail that they put up all the pictures of the guys who've been through it and that all die? It was just like, 'That was someone's kid'. It was horrible. It's horrible. I don't know – see that's – why do we have things? But I guess we need to have them.

FIGURE 17.1 The Commemorative Courtyard at the Australian War Memorial.

Source: Photograph courtesy of Emma Waterton.

According to the Australian War Memorial Act of 1980, the functions of the Australian War Memorial are 'to maintain and develop the national memorial', to 'develop and maintain ... a national collection of historical material', 'exhibit ... historical material from the memorial collection' and 'conduct, arrange for and assist in research into matters pertaining to Australian military history'. Collectively, these functions draw a range of people to the site, from tourists to researchers to family members of deceased servicemen and servicewomen. Commenced in 1927 and completed in 1942, the Memorial's iconic sandstone building consists of a Roll of Honour housed within cloistered arches as well as the domed Hall of Memory (which incorporates the Tomb of the Unknown Australian Soldier), the Flame of Remembrance and the Pool of Reflection, all of which form the 'shrine' component of the complex. The complex also includes a sculpture garden, several galleries including Anzac Hall and the Hall of Valour, a Discovery Zone and other educational spaces, a research centre and a parade ground. In 2018, the Australian government committed $498 million to an ambitious and controversial redevelopment project that will see the introduction of new elements, some areas of the Memorial refurbished and others demolished and replaced.

Brenton and Mayra's comments point to a common ethical disposition: whether military memorials are experienced positively or negatively, interviewees expressed *obligation* ('I guess you need it'; 'I guess we need to have them') – a shared obligation to remember sacrifice. However, for Oliver, the Australian War Memorial is more of a technical achievement than a stimulus to explicitly ethical self-positioning:

> Definitely the history of it and obviously there's a high level of respect for that but also the way it's presented is absolutely fantastic with the planes and all of the tanks and everything like that, it's just unbelievable and I went on a guided tour there at school again and the knowledge that the gentleman had of everything was just amazing so every question was answered and you can see everything. You can see the battlefield scenes that they create and I think when you go to that big hall there they put the show on every hour or something like that, they do all the noises. It was really interesting.

To consume heritage could be presented by the interviewee as intellectual, not just emotional, openness. Heritage is important to Angela, a Chinese Australian, because it increases respect for difference: 'Trying to understanding the community I live in, it's worthwhile to know the past and to understand the future a little bit better. Also the rapid change make you more appreciate what happen before.' Angela continues that she is:

> quite interested in family trees and because my background, my great granddad came over during the gold rush. So since I was very little parents used to talk about it. They talk about Aborigine and I was always had an idea there's a different culture out there, not just Chinese. There are many different culture out there.

Interviewees readily articulated responses to heritage sites in which senses of identity and obligation were experienced as feelings – positive or negative – about meaningful places. In these responses we see interviewees connecting themselves to communities of feeling and to imagined ethical formations.

Sports stars as role models?

Some interviewees implicitly or explicitly mobilise ethical criteria for 'liking' or 'disliking' named sportspeople, and often these are vehement judgements. Several interviewees referred censoriously to Tiger Woods, for: mistreating his wife, 'all of this shenanigan in his life', petulance, bad manners on the golf course, unwillingness to give children his autograph, cockiness and overconfidence. The Australian tennis player Nick Kyrgios was likewise censured for being a 'doofus', for thinking 'the world owes him everything', for losing his temper on court, for having a 'bad attitude', for not being tough enough to accept what happens, for not being a 'sportsman'. These judgements enact a widely held assumption that the public has the right to judge sportspeople as (good or bad) role models. When asked what makes a 'good sporting role model', Christine replies: 'In any sort of chosen profession it's the ethics of it all. I mean being a role model is good sportsmanship and trying your hardest and accepting that you got beaten by a better person but still striving.'

Sports stars are said to 'represent' their sport – a signifier central to the commercial sponsorship of clubs, teams and individuals. Rugby league player Johnathan Thurston is said to be a great 'ambassador' and a 'very giving character'. Lauren says:

> if they're good sportsmen and they have good morals even if they stuff up but say they're sorry I think you can like them. I just don't like the cheating, lying, sleaziness of sport ... they should represent the sport. That's what they get paid to do.

One interviewee gives Don Bradman as an example of a great role model; another says Australian Football League (AFL) footballer Adam Goodes is 'a good role model for young Aboriginal – well for anybody really'. One interviewee asserts that sportspeople are models 'especially for young more impressionable people like my brother'. Aisha, a 47-year-old Lebanese-Australian Muslim and qualified counsellor, explains that she watches rugby league because the Canterbury Bankstown player Hazem El Masri is 'a good model for kids'. The ability to speak well is among the qualities expected of an athlete 'role model'. Giovanni says that Wally Lewis (former rugby union and rugby league player) is 'a very good statesman for the game. I think he's well-spoken and I think he says the right things. He shows that not all rugby league players are uneducated bums.'

However, some interviewees dispute that sportspeople should be assessed as 'role models'. Sean tells us that he refused to adopt what he sees as a media-driven expectation:

> I think there's too much emphasis on sports stars to be more than they are. Like football players are all stupid and they're expected to be icons to children and it's kind of fine it you get paid all that money but it's also a lot on them ... Some of them they're just football players. A bit different with cricket players and a bit different-ish with rugby union players but I think there's too much – poor Eddie McGuire's 98 per cent on television, obviously entire life and then he says one stupid thing and he's ... If he was only on TV this much and he said it – everything that comes out of his mouth – I felt very sorry for him. It was a bit of a stupid thing to say but he said it. But anyway, your whole life's in front – so that's why. There's been too much scrutiny.[2]

When the interviewer prompts, 'the football stars may be a bit masculine sometimes', Sean responds: 'Yes. Well they're just – they've got to behave. But I think there's too much emphasis on them being for everyone. Everyone needs a piece of them.'

When the 'team' is 'Australia', performance is a spectacle of nationhood, and the invitation to spectator patriotism may be accepted or refused. Explaining why he does not watch the Olympics, Robert tells us that he is:

> a very community minded person. I think that there's, you know, I see that we spend so much money on sport. There's a huge amount of money, you know, to develop sport to get people to win the Olympics so that, you know, the Australian flag's higher than anything else.

Because sport is a mass media spectacle, respondents' commentary may be more on the mediation than on the sport. Martin, a 59-year-old British-born retiree, described as 'hype' the dramatisation of not only sport but society itself:

> A lot of people blame the actual fans, but I blame the media, because of the hype that they bring into it. It's country against country and yes, you can be passionate about a sport, but you don't have to go to the extent that some of them go to. I think a lot of those, again, is brought by the hype that's generated within the media. It's like a lot of the things today, the rapes, the killings, the abductions, they did a statistic and analysis of crime. Crime back in the sixties and seventies no different than it is today. The only difference is the media and the hype. People are scared to allow their kids to even walk to school.

Another way to drain sport of its moral significance is to highlight technical excellence. In the following exchange the interviewer encourages Badal to distance himself from ethical consideration of Ultimate Fight Club (UFC).

> BADAL: I just like the violence.
> INTERVIEWER: You do?
> BADAL: Yeah.
> INTERVIEWER: I laugh because my granny likes it. She's been known to leap up and yell at the telly, something like 'hit him with a chair' or something.
> BADAL: No, it's pretty good the UFC. It's very technical. As much as there's a lot of violence, but it's quite technical and they're world-class athletes.

The sport field seems to be open to reflective choice about how 'value' can be invoked. Although athletes symbolise moral values (and the mass mediation and commercialisation of sport makes persons and organisations into 'brands'), athleticism itself remains a value – technique as excellence – that some interviewees insist is ultimate in this domain of culture. Consumers choose to frame their tastes as emotionally and/or ethically saturated or as strictly technical or formal. Even when explicitly eschewing feeling and ethical judgement, they acknowledge the possibility of responses – by others or by themselves at other times – that evaluate and emote.

Self-positioning in a field of authorised judgements

Interviews with people about what they like and do not like, and why, do not give researchers direct access to habitus; interviews generate data about how people represent – to interlocutors such as interviewers who are strangers – their disposition towards what they engage with. Interviewees sometimes positioned themselves dialogically within an imagined field of authorised tastes and values. We heard a claim to self-permission when Debra tells us that she has 'a little guilty pleasure' watching *Married at First Sight*:

> INTERVIEWER: That's okay, guilty pleasures are allowed. So you like lighter entertainment for TV?
>
> DEBRA: I enjoy movies very much. Another guilty pleasure, I've watched an American soap ever since I was a teenager. It's whatever attracts my attention at the time. But reality TV like *Survivor* and things like that, I must admit I'm not a fan of.

Here, the interviewer and interviewee collaborate in acknowledging that there is a hierarchy of more worthy and less worthy pastimes. However, they playfully permit rebellion against it, in the name of the individual liberty to do the less socially approved thing. Interviewees' talk sometimes implies negotiation. Craig brought the imagined hierarchy of taste into view by denouncing it: he praises what he saw as Tasmania's Mona's 'equal' presentation of artworks, discouraging 'elitism':

> They were all presented equally, you know, as if all the artists were equally of merit or worth presenting with each other, and I just thought that was really good. No elitism, you know. That's what I liked about it.

Christine argues that if personal autonomy were respected there could be no basis for taste hierarchies:

> What you might enjoy somebody else might think it's rubbish but then you've got to respect their difference of opinion and their different eye and their different feelings because to me everything comes back to feelings, how you feel about something. How it resonates with you. It doesn't matter if it doesn't resonate with anybody else.

For Martin, every relationship of viewer to art object is personal, and all tastes are entitled to respect:

> I suppose my interpretation of art is no different to people. We all have the same problems. We all have the same likes, dislikes. It doesn't matter what culture you go into, everybody has the same. They all have the same problem

with their kids. They all like to have a house. They all like to have money. They all like to have cars and everything, it doesn't matter where you go in the world. Art is no different.

This ethical commitment to taste equality is part of a feeling that class distinctions are (or should be) unimportant because 'Everyone's just people', as Naomi insists when we asked her whether her taste had anything to do with her class. As Naomi explains:

> I don't actually think a lot about different classes either. To me, people are just people. Like, I've known some extremely wealthy people who get around – they've had a farm, they have dirty feet, dirty thongs [casual footwear], dirty old Range Rover, and they're extremely wealthy. Then you get some people who want to you know, dress up nice and think they look good and they're struggling with their money. So, I don't know. To me in a way, class is irrelevant. Everyone's just people. Different.

Elsewhere in the interview, Naomi asserts the primacy of her personal judgement: 'I just like what I like. I don't care if a thousand people say this is the best thing you've got to see. If I don't like it, I'm not going.'

While some people expressed visceral distaste for violence or the morbid on screen, in print (crime thrillers 'too dark and graphic') and in music ('death metal'), others exercised their playful prerogative to enjoy what they sense others abhor. Thus, Naomi distinguishes herself from the interviewer:

> INTERVIEWER: I haven't been able to sit through a whole episode of *Vikings*. Horrible usually happens about ten minutes in, and somebody gets their eye gouged out.
> NAOMI: Yeah. That's what we like.

These admissions of a liking for violence are self-consciously transgressive and/or playful: they display the interviewee as a 'knowing', genre-savvy consumer, confidently refusing the (dis)taste offered by the interviewer.

In presenting themselves as autonomous in their choice of pleasures, interviewees sometimes invited support for their claiming of relief from distasteful realities. Heath says that after giving up on TV news ('with all the bad things that have been happening in the world') he had returned to it: 'because my partner always wants to watch the news. So, while it's on, I've started to take an interest again. But, sometimes it's not bad to be ignorant and naïve to current affairs. You can live a lot happier.'

As we saw in the previous chapter, Aisha also reasons her need to evade the serious engagement demanded by current affairs TV, and the subsequent 'escape' into comedy, in terms of 'being a Muslim Australian and the stresses of the world'. She tells us that the 'burden' of having to constantly demonstrate that 'Muslims are good' got to the point where she felt that she can't change 'political agendas'. So in 'running away from a very, very cruel and ugly reality' she lost her appetite for current affairs and became more interested in soapies and comedy, 'where you can just chuck your brain down'. Jacinta explains why she likes police and detective programmes:

> Oh I don't know, they're escapist, you don't have to work very hard following the plot and if they develop the characters well, particularly if there's some quirkiness to the characters, those interactions can be quite entertaining. I don't know, there's a grittiness to them which can be quite, you know, it doesn't, strips back the sort of, I'm not so keen on shows that are flowery or have pretentious characters. So I think there's an honesty to the shows but primarily because there is [sic] escapist and you can just, you don't have to work hard watching them basically and I enjoy reading crime novels, again for their escapist value.

Repeatedly characterising this choice as 'escapist', Jacinta is claiming the autonomy to choose when and where to be (un)serious. She goes on to say that her leisure time reading is valuable because:

> it gives you an insight into communities that I wouldn't have any contact with in a point in history which says more about the characters, it goes beyond just the individual characters and gives you an insight into that historical period.

Television and the curators of realities

By presenting her likes in terms of genres, Jacinta demonstrates that consumers, at least when in dialogue with us, have the capacity to objectify their own consumption. Perhaps television's programme flow has heightened consumers' awareness of genre and thus of the capacity to choose which of their emotional/ethical dispositions is to be exercised in a night's viewing. Because broadcast television offers an array of genres, it has been an especially effective tutor in such popular formalisms – 'genre-savviness'. Interviewees demonstrate that one can adopt more than one posture towards the truthfulness of television's representations. When Lisa reasons about genres of television, her sense of value refers to the potential of a genre to be truthful:

> I like the police dramas just because it's – I like the methodical side of it. I just like the fact that if something happens they show you how they work it out and then it ends. I just like that, but I just like reading that genre. So a lot of the books I read have adapted to the TV so I just like watching them. Documentaries I like just because you learn something and because it's not – it makes up for the mindless nonsense that I watch. You're learning something.

While dramatic fiction and documentaries can be 'real' in these ways, 'reality TV' was widely rejected. The questionnaire asked people to name (from a list) the TV genre that they liked least. 'Reality TV' appeared in 667 responses (55 per cent of sample), almost twice as many as the second least popular: sport (340, or 28 per cent). As Kathleen said of 'reality TV', it 'may be real life, but it's not really real life, because they're not really on their own. They're not really doing the things themselves, they are actually filming it and there's other people helping them.' Naomi indicates that she likes fantasy drama such as *Game of Thrones* but dismisses 'the bullshit drama that goes with' *Big Brother* and unnamed cooking shows. She describes *Big Brother* as 'disgusting' and 'grotesque', and says of cooking shows that it's:

> nice watching people cook, but then they've gone down the path of, well this one's got a nasty mouth, and this one's got a stupid laugh, so let's tee them up and see the drama that erupts, and that will get more viewers.

When asked by the interviewer whether it is the 'fakeness' that annoys her, she adds: 'I can't stand that. That's childish.' Naomi's implicit message is 'don't take me for a fool' – an assertion of autonomy.

David likes to cook and to watch TV shows about cooking, but he is also repelled by gratuitous dramatisation:

> I was more interested in what they were doing in the cooking I suppose than I was in the competitive aspect of it. But as soon as people start to have these things build up into some drama, well, that leaves me for dead. I don't think there's anything dramatic about this. But as an interest it's – it's something worthwhile pursuing.

Oliver distinguishes between *Grand Designs* and *The Block*:

> *Grand Designs* is about building and the architecture and all that but *The Block*'s all about drama and couples having little tiffs but they don't actually show you how to do anything. So if they say if you get to a certain stage in the building it's really important when you waterproof or when you tile to do this, they don't actually show you it. So it's not educational for me and I feel as though it's just all about more about the drama and the building's something that happens on the side and it's – I think a lot of its rehearsed and setup and it doesn't appeal to me at all. I think that show could actually be really good if they actually taught some people how to do something.

Lisa finds 'reality TV' 'false', although she freely admits that she knows of it only through the advertisements for it:

> I think people are aware that they're being filmed so they don't behave in a way that they normally would behave. So I don't think it gives an accurate

reflection of society and if it does then I weep for society because they seem to pick brainless idiots who just – I don't know. It's just that whole culture of being famous for being famous. I just don't like it. That line between the documentary and reality TV, it's just – I just don't like them.

I don't like the way they play on people's emotions. Like, they make everything a big drama and play on stuff and try and pull out the nastier aspects of – and you see it. I mean, I don't watch them so I'm just assuming that that's what they do but when you see it on the adverts it's all very dramatic.

This rejection of 'drama' as spurious, a veil over realities, harks back to the interviewees reported earlier who refuse the mediation of sport as a moral spectacle. These TV viewers are practised curators of generic realities, disdainful of artifice in some genres ('reality TV'), enjoying and justifying artifice in others ('police drama', *Vikings*). Television gives them an array of windows on to the world, via different genres, and they are adept at reasoning their selection of realities.

The interviews quoted above illustrate that when speaking about visiting heritage sites, watching sport and choosing what to watch on TV, interviewees often presented themselves as emotionally and ethically responsive. As well, they demonstrated how easily they could choose to be *not* emotionally and/or ethically invested, emphasising their detached appreciation of technique and form, their willing pleasure in artifice. Similarly, the interviewees' awareness of a socially authorised scale of legitimate culture was often demonstrated by their explicit repudiation of it, asserting the right to be themselves. Perhaps the common thread here is the interviewees' assumption of the autonomy of the person – as customer, as ethical reasoner, as knowing subject. We do not claim that these interviewees are autonomous in the sense of not being determined by their social position. Rather, their autonomy is a cultural norm typified by (but not limited to) television's address to the customer/citizen; it is further secured as a premise of the interview itself (which cannot proceed without the opening ritual of signing a consent form).

'Liking' the Indigenous

Autonomy can be exhibited in an interview as a performance of knowing when to be normative – about what is good, what is real, what matters – and knowing when to be playful, wilful, pleasing no one but oneself. However, there are some spaces of lifestyle that are so saturated with civic normativity (the obligations of belonging to a national community or to an ethnic or religious minority) that interviewees position themselves with care. That is, there are some tastes and ways of talking about tastes in which respondents 'connect cultural choices to forms of collective or group involvement' (Bennett, T., 2011: 538), and such involvements may be significant to respondents as felt obligations and commitments. As we have begun to explore in Chapter 12, 'liking' Indigenous people and things has this kind of meaning in contemporary Australia.

Tastes in 'Indigenous Australia' were revealed in two ways in the ACF research: responses to our questionnaire's 'Indigenous items'; and interviews. The ACF questionnaire asked people: if they had ever watched National Indigenous Television; if they liked or disliked Aboriginal heritage and Aboriginal art; whether they liked to read books by or about Indigenous Australians; whether they knew of and (dis)liked: Deborah Mailman (actor); *Redfern Now* (TV drama); Sally Morgan and Kim Scott (writers); Gurrumul Yunupingu and Dan Sultan (musicians); Cathy Freeman and Adam Goodes (athletes); Albert Namatjira and Tracey Moffatt (visual artists). As well, we asked interviewees a version of the following question:

> From our research, we think that Indigenous Australians have become more visible in Australian society in all sorts of ways in the last 20 years. Can you think of any ways that this has made a difference to the sorts of cultural pursuits we've been discussing today?

The resulting harvest of quantitative and qualitative data revealed the careful ways that (mostly non-Indigenous) people are now speaking of Indigenous people and things.

Liking or not liking Indigenous taste items has become especially loaded with ethical significance. How a person situates him or herself in relation to Indigenous persons and artefacts signifies a relationship – sometimes difficult, but inescapable – to the national project of 'Reconciliation'. Ways of talking about such tastes can be illustrated by considering ACF's interviews with 31 non-Indigenous Australians in 2015–2017 – including these statements by Holly and Craig. Holly says: 'I guess it seems important to me to learn about Indigenous culture and heritage because they were here long before my ancestors were here and I think that's important.' Craig similarly comments: 'So I think yeah, Aboriginal culture being more prevalent, I think it's for the better. The more we know, the more in touch we are with our Indigenous heritage the better really.' Holly, 29 years old, has tertiary education and a professional job, living in Sydney. Craig, 49 years old, has secondary education and previously had a routine job but had been a full-time carer for his mother in Canberra until her recent passing. Notwithstanding their socio-economic differences, Holly and Craig share sentiments about Indigenous Australia. While neither of them claim to have a deep involvement in Aboriginal communities, or to be active champions of Indigenous cultural production, both Craig and Holly are explicitly supportive of Indigenous cultural sites and products as an acknowledged and, perhaps, esteemed part of Australia's culture. They agree that Aboriginal/Indigenous culture has become more prominent in Australia in recent decades, and that this was a positive development of relevance to all Australians.

Their sentiments are encouraged by a state-managed civic programme that has become so influential since 1991 as to be a source of social regulation (Sayer, 2005: 47). We find it helpful that Sayer develops the concept 'habitus' by highlighting the possibility that habitus includes normative orientation. That is, Sayer urges us to recognise 'the close relationships between dispositions and conscious deliberation, the powers of agency and mundane reflexivity' and thus to address 'actors' normative orientations, emotions and commitments' (50–51). For Sayer, 'normative orientation' is intrinsic to human agency. He highlights agents' capacity for 'internal conversation' (29–30). Emotions have weight in Sayer's formulation of 'habitus', not as 'the antithesis of reason, but as responses to and commentaries on our situations' (36). Sayer points to the susceptibility of habitus to discourse – including historically entrenched racial and national discourses. These observations lead Sayer to present 'commitment' and 'identity' as integral to habitus:

> The causes, practices, or other people that matter most to actors are not merely things which they happen to like or prefer but things in terms of which their identities are formed and to which they are committed, sometimes to the extent that they will pursue them against their self-interest.
>
> *(39)*

The 'ethical disposition' of any habitus 'is more socially regulated and momentous than matters of aesthetic taste' (47). 'Moral behaviour and evaluation', he suggests, 'may vary independently of divisions such as those of class, "race", gender, or age' (49).

So it may be, but in the case that we are dealing with – 'liking' Indigenous taste items – there is evidence from the questionnaire of an association with certain social variables. Indigenous items in the ACF questionnaire are slightly more likely to be known and liked by women than by men; such persons are more likely to be in the age range 35–65 than in younger age groups. Those with high levels of formal education and tertiary training in the humanities and social sciences are more likely than the less educated and those whose tertiary qualifications are in Science, Technology, Engineering and Medicine (STEM), business and law to know and like Indigenous items. Those knowing and liking Indigenous taste items are more likely to be born (and/or their parents to be born) within the English-speaking regions of Australia, England and New Zealand than to be migrants from non-Anglophone parts of the world. Their incomes and occupations are at the higher end of the scale. Reviewing a number of studies, Walter (2012) notes the consistent finding that older, white male respondents are more likely to express negative attitudes about government support for Aboriginal people and towards Aboriginal people themselves. Her analysis of the 2007 Australian Survey of Social Attitudes (AuSSA) data confirms this pattern.

> In line with previous studies, for non-Indigenous Australians, being female, residing in an urban location, being a professional and being of Euro-Australian background and especially holding a bachelor degree or higher level of education are statistically associated with more positive attitudes towards Aboriginal issues in general.
>
> *(Walter, 2012: 26)*

ACF quantitative data is also broadly consistent with Bulbeck's (2004) South Australian survey data.

The normative frame of contemporary representations of Indigenous persons and things is what we call the Reconciliation Orthodoxy.[3] The preamble to the Council for Aboriginal Reconciliation Act 1991 affirms that:

> (a) Australia was occupied by Aborigines and Torres Strait Islanders who had settled for thousands of years, before British settlement at Sydney Cove on 26 January 1788; and (b) many Aborigines and Torres Strait Islanders suffered dispossession and dispersal from their traditional lands by the British Crown; and (c) to date, there has been no formal process of reconciliation between Aborigines and Torres Strait Islanders and other Australians.[4]

The Act, including this preamble, was unanimously endorsed by the Parliament of Australia on 2 September 1991. Although subsequent parliamentary debate showed partisan disagreement on the priorities and content of the Reconciliation agenda (Pratt, 2005), these three points are orthodoxy. Reconciliation – a continuing commitment of government, a civic ideal – has helped secure the distinction between 'Aboriginal and Torres Strait Islander people and other Australians' (henceforth the 'Indigenous/non-Indigenous binary') as shared conceptual ground for thinking about Australian nationhood as an unfinished *ethical* project.

Like any dichotomy, the Indigenous/non-Indigenous binary has analytic limitations. Jupp, a leading historian and theorist of Australian 'multiculturalism', has pointed out that 'to divide Australians in this simplistic way devalues the significance of a wide variety of cultures' in that it 'suggests that an English-speaking, thoroughly Australian Aborigine living in Blacktown is in some way more legitimately distinctive than a Macedonian living in Thomastown or a Vietnamese living in Cabramatta'. However, Jupp then concedes that 'some form of reconciliation with Australia inevitably will have to be made and … Australian identity has only slowly confronted the lie of its foundation – *terra nullius*' (1994: 88). That is, Jupp points to the unique civic pertinence and moral force that the Indigenous/non-Indigenous binary was acquiring in the 1990s. In the same year as Jupp published his views, the Keating government published *Creative Nation*, a cultural policy statement affirming that:

> As never before we now recognise the magnificent heritage of the oldest civilisation on earth – the civilisation of Aboriginal and Torres Strait Islander people. In literature, art, music, theatre and dance, the indigenous culture of Australia informs and enriches the contemporary one. The culture and identity of Aboriginal and Torres Strait Islander Australians has [sic] become an essential element of Australian identity, a vital expression of who we all are.
> *(Department of Communications and the Arts, 1994: 6)*

The Indigenous/non-Indigenous binary has become salient whenever 'Australia' is what people are talking and thinking about. In such conversations, each Australian is interpellated as either an Indigenous Australian or not. The resulting 'Reconciliation Orthodoxy' is a discursive structure or national imaginary consisting of three points of agreement, each point accommodates a variety of opinion (in italics).

- That in Australian society there are two kinds of people: 'Indigenous' and 'non-Indigenous'. (*Australians disagree about who is truly 'Indigenous'*.)
- That the relationship between Indigenous and non-Indigenous is a problem of nationhood, requiring Australians' ongoing attention. (*Australians debate how to describe the 'problem' and the 'solutions'*.)
- That giving such attention includes affirming the Indigenous as valued. (*Australians disagree about the terms of positive valuation, but to say that the Indigenous has no value at all is now widely censured*.)

When answering questions that nominated Indigenous items, our survey respondents were more or less consciously taking a position within a field in which 'the Indigenous' is distinguished as presumptively good. As with the presence of ambivalence on positioning seen in the previous chapter, the interviews with non-Indigenous respondents reveal that the 'habitus' mobilised in such position-taking is often hesitant, reflexive and conscious that the ground of belonging to an imaginable Australian community has been shifting as the responsibility attached to being non-Indigenous has become more salient within civic identity. Lauren presented the field of possible orientations as polarised between extremes, and placed herself in the reasonable middle:

> I think there's an undergrowth of people that are ... who almost put [Indigenous culture] on a pedestal that it's this wonderful thing and I don't think that's good either ... and I think there's still the element that are racist, are horribly racist and won't change, and I think if most people are somewhere in between that's great and I think more people are in between than going that way. It's nice to see that shift.

Indigenous culture and Indigenous people are sometimes mentioned cautiously, as Heath illustrates when asked about how Australia should approach issues of Aboriginal history:

> Delicately usually. I don't know, I don't give it a lot of thought. I think over the time, they've probably had a hard go, but then you make your own life in the face of adversity. You've got to dig out your own and make it good – I don't have that big of an opinion about it. I think everyone deserves a go, no matter.

Caution was also evident in the response of Lisa when we suggested that she was 'quite reserved in making a judgement or taking a side' in her comments on the public debate about Sydney Swans' Adam Goodes' response to being called an 'ape' by a supporter of the opposing team. Lisa replies:

I just don't think it's as simple as just — I just don't think it's as simple — I just don't think, or I'd like to think that people would not just be really horrible to someone because of their race or ethnicity.

Interviewing Robert, we asked: 'in the survey you said that you weren't particularly enthusiastic about Aboriginal art or I think the other one was Pop art'. He responds:

Okay. Yeah. Yeah, did I say that? Yeah. Probably, I mean, as I say, if art's valid, you know — and I think I can appreciate, you know, anything bad, or I probably don't. I didn't like — as far as Aboriginal art's concerned it's kind of like a respect for Indigenous people I think ... I don't understand the culture and I'd say therefore I don't, you know, I can't relate to it all that much. I've got the greatest respect for it but, yeah ...

Some present scenarios of enlightenment that they had observed or experienced. Sean, who grew up in rural Queensland before moving to Brisbane, remarks that 'the city is more multicultural and tolerant. So even at Caboolture it's full of racist, narrow-minded people and the further north you go the worse it gets.' Former high school principal Steven expresses dismay that the term 'invasion' was still rejected by many as a way to refer to colonisation. He then tells of how an Aboriginal guest teacher had confronted students' prejudice by explaining his own life history:

Well, this kid, in one session I saw — he wouldn't have changed the boy in terms — but he certainly brought an awareness in this fellow and to the others in the class that there were things about that existence that were not right — part of how we see ourselves as Australians and how we see that we've got a long, long way to go. It won't happen in my lifetime but at least I can see things starting to move, but it will be a long time before we ever right the wrongs of what we've done.

Thus Steven depicted the field of opinion as changing, with ignorance giving way to awareness.

Contrasting the present with the remembered past was a motif of several interviews, including stories about changing awareness of Indigenous presence. Asked whether 'Indigenous Australians are becoming more high profile', Brooke says:

The school I work at give about ten scholarships a year to bring Indigenous students in and have the opportunity, when they're not living locally, to be able to come to the school. In my grade, I didn't have any Indigenous students, but that's something they're engaging in more and more. I'd say yes, but it's still baby steps probably.

Heath recalls:

> When I was at school we were only taught ... Australian history was all about the First Fleet and Captain Cook and that sort of thing. We didn't learn too much about before that in Australia. Surely they're teaching it now though.

Michael reports:

> I've seen a lot of emphasis recently on the development of the Aboriginal art and its popularisation, and I guess until fairly recently, I didn't have great respect for the Aboriginal art, I figured it was all just primitive and stuff; it's either developing or it was an aspect that I never appreciated, but they've got a totally different approach on some of this, and I guess other cultures.

Most interviewees who situated themselves within these changing times did so neutrally or approvingly, welcoming the revised terms in which Australian society and its Indigenous minority can be talked about. Others were wary in ways that suggested that they were still negotiating their relationship with a pro-Indigenous norm. We asked Gabriel if he had 'any interest in Indigenous heritage'. 'Not as much as I probably should', he replies:

> I have to say that other than the art gallery which I've been to and a few trips on school I haven't intentionally gone out and sought Indigenous heritage sites which I think I should probably at one point remedy because I find history interesting. Kind of it's an oversight [on] my part.

Oliver had said in his survey response that 'colonial art' and 'Aboriginal art' were his 'least liked' in a list of ten kinds of art. We asked him to explain.

> I don't know what to say. It doesn't appeal to me I guess is probably the only way I'd put it. I think it's – obviously it's important, don't get me wrong, but I think it's nothing that – it doesn't really – I don't know. Just nothing that interests me really. It's ... I don't feel it's – obviously it's relevant to me being an Australian but I think it's a different culture so it's obviously important to them but it's not something that I'd really look into or [be] interested in.

Conclusion

Drawing mostly on interview data, our chapter has illustrated forms of pleasure and judgement that correspond to what *Distinction* failed to examine. That is, our interviews elicited ways of talking about consumption: that 'connect aesthetic evaluations to ethical judgments as a positive value rather than as a failing'; that 'express preferences in hedonistic terms, linking aesthetic to bodily pleasures'; and that 'connect cultural choices to forms of collective or group involvement' (Bennett,

T., 2011: 538). We remain agnostic on whether the aspects of habitus illustrated in the first four sections of this chapter contribute to 'exclusion from legitimate culture'. We can say little about the class location of these ways of talking about what one likes because such ways of 'liking' as our interviewees evince in interviews are not visible in the ACF questionnaire. Thus we make no claim about their social distribution, and their 'exchange value' 'in the relations between the schooling system, the institutions of legitimate culture, and the occupational class structure' (Bennett, T., 2011: 538) remains beyond our knowledge. However, we believe that the data illustrates the possibility of habitus being profoundly informed by socially regulated senses of identity, belonging and obligation – as Sayer has argued in his reflection on the concept 'habitus'. In the fifth section we turned to a particularly powerful governmental discourse about Australian nationhood, which we described as the Reconciliation Orthodoxy. The Reconciliation Orthodoxy evokes Australia as a nation engaged in self-transformation, and this discourse has established the terms of a new form of 'collective or group involvement' in which liking Indigenous things signifies a re-positioning of self in relation to the nation's imagined community. In socially locating the take-up of this way of judging and feeling we are better served by our questionnaire: data shows the profile of non-Indigenous Australians who not only recognise the Indigenous as a distinct order of Australian experience but also affirm its worth to the nation and to the self as an Australian. By small but noticeable percentages they tend to be female, humanities and social sciences educated, older. We suggest that liking Indigenous things has become a significant form of cultural capital. Our interview data suggests that individuals vary in their negotiation of a relationship to the emerging 'legitimacy' of Indigeneity.

Notes

1 As Sayer has pointed out, Bourdieu remarked that 'aesthetic choices belong to a set of ethical choices which constitutes a lifestyle' when contrasting 'ascetic' and 'luxury' embodiments of cultural capital (Bourdieu, 1984: 283).
2 Eddie McGuire is an Australian AFL sports club president and sports commentator who was widely criticised for a 2013 racist statement about footballer Adam Goodes.
3 For an exploration of non-Indigenous interviewees' talk about Indigenous matters, see Rowse and Pertierra (2019).
4 Council for Aboriginal Reconciliation Act 1991, No. 127, 1991.

CONCLUSION

'Distinction' after *Distinction*

Greg Noble, Tony Bennett, David Carter, Modesto Gayo and Michelle Kelly

It has been 40 years since *Distinction* was published: the world has changed enormously over the intervening period, yet Bourdieu's work continues to hold its place as a major contribution to social theory generally as well as to cultural sociology in particular. Many works since then have testified to *Distinction*'s continuing capacity to inspire rich empirical work that has been methodologically and theoretically innovative in refining Bourdieu's approach to accommodate the changes that have taken place over that period.

Often criticised for developing an analysis which only applied to a particular place in a particular time, Bourdieu was insistent that theoretical frameworks should be malleable. As he argued, his terms 'are not to be conceptualized so much as ideas, ... but as a method ... a manner of asking questions' (Bourdieu, 1985, quoted in Mahar, 1990: 33). In other words, the concepts of field, capitals and habitus were designed to be adapted in the course of empirical inquiries conducted in changing historical circumstances (Bourdieu and Wacquant, 1992: 96).

Fields, Capitals, Habitus has attempted to continue this process of theoretical and methodological adaptation by being constantly aware of the specific challenges posed by applying these concepts in studying Australia in the twenty-first century. It will be useful then, in concluding, to identify some of the more distinctive ways in which we tailored these concepts in applying them in the Australian context. In doing so we shall focus mainly on those aspects of the processes of distinction that are most specific to contemporary Australia, on the different logics that are in play in the varied forms of cultural capital we have identified and on the ways in which the mobilisation of cultural capital as a governmental actor in Australia have differed from the political career that Bourdieu had envisaged for it.

'Distinction' in the Antipodes

Our emphasis on the particularities of distinction in Australia has meant that we have avoided universalising notions of class and culture in order to situate these categories in their national and historical manifestations. This has involved thinking about distinction in terms of a settler-colonial society, under constant refashioning through migration, and subject to all of the dynamic economic, technological, social and cultural transformations associated with globalisation. As we argued in the Introduction, Australia's first national cultural policy, *Creative Nation*, was illustrative of the ways in which Australian governments have tried to manage the conflicts between the key logics at the heart of these relations between nation and culture.

In contrast to the France of *Distinction*, for example, settler-colonial relations are fundamental to the existence of Australia as a nation-state and are thus central to the constitution of the regimes of cultural value that circulate within it. This was not simply a story of the transplanting of British culture in a distant land, but a history of cultural, political and economic struggle to accomplish that transplanting, and of resistance to it. The place of Aboriginal and Torres Strait Islander cultures in Australia's history is therefore a complex one. One of the great indictments of modern Australia is that the increasing interest in Indigenous culture since the mid-twentieth century has not fundamentally changed the economic and social disadvantage of most of the Indigenous population. Yet, as several chapters in this book highlight, there is a very significant engagement with Indigenous culture which has become not only an economic asset as part of the touristic economy, but part of a cultural hierarchy which is itself premised on colonial subjugation. So while 'legitimate culture' in Australia is still fundamentally shaped by British and European cultural dominance, it has also accommodated, as a form of distinction, a revaluing of Indigenous cultures. And yet this accommodation has taken place alongside the role those cultures play as a resistant identity politics for many of those of Indigenous heritage.

Again, unlike Bourdieu's France, distinction in Australia has also been dramatically reshaped by its status as a migrant nation, particularly in response to the increasing cultural diversity produced by successive histories of migration since the Second World War. This is often told as a story of ethnic enclaves, on the one hand, and the growing cosmopolitanism of a multicultural society, on the other, but of course the consequences are much more complex. Ongoing anxieties around cultural diversity have produced an ambivalent politics of multiculturalism even as the Australian 'mainstream' has been reshaped by the growth of the 'multicultural marketplace'. This has produced a much more diversified cultural sector, a proliferation of subcultural fields rather than a dramatic transformation of cultural hierarchies, suggesting a banal cosmopolitanisation of Australian cultural consumption rather than the emergence of cosmopolitan capitals as a cultural dominant.

The migratory flows of people have been intimately connected to the intensification of transnational economic and cultural flows referred to rather broadly as globalisation. At stake here are diverse cultural practices which often transcend the limits of the nation-state. These processes are sometimes seen as dismantling national cultures, but in reality the relations between transnational and national identities and forms of consumption are complex and multi-layered. So while the findings reported in this book have generally shown the continuing salience of the nation in the regulation of cultural fields, it is not without qualification. What the flows of people and things do demonstrate, however, is the increasingly diversified nature of cultural consumption, particularly in terms of the role of new technologies in enabling new practices and mediating new identities and relations. This is most clearly seen in the analysis of the media field, but it is a presence across all the fields encompassed by this study.

These key dimensions of our findings are not simply the reconfiguration of Bourdieusian theory to meet the Australian context; they also suggest that practices of consumption and patterns of taste are fundamentally reshaped in an age defined by global flows of people, goods and meanings. A key issue for us in addressing these concerns has thus been to define what is distinctive about the operation of capital logics in a settler-colonial society with a culturally diverse population increasingly immersed in transnational relations.

Capital logics

Our findings have confirmed the continued salience of the relations between class and culture, but with degrees of complexity that build upon Bourdieu's initial focus in several key ways. Central to the Australian mythos is the perception that Australia is a 'classless' society. This, of course, is not true. Australia may historically have had a 'flatter' classed landscape than, say, the UK, with arguably less of a sense of class distinction marked by highly stratified patterns of cultural consumption. However, our findings demonstrate a mismatch between Australia's egalitarian ethos and patterns of increasing inequalities of income and wealth that are strongly aligned with international tendencies. In developing more complex measures of class, acknowledging the importance of inherited family assets alongside conventional measures of occupation, income and education, our findings also show that the role of cultural capital in the reproduction of inequalities is not significantly different in kind from other developed societies.

None of this is to suggest that class operates in isolation from other social forces. As Chapters 7 and 8 demonstrate, there is substantial variation in the social logics that structure the relations between cultural practices across cultural fields. While class as a broad measure is central to the organisation of these relations in most of the fields, some are more sensitive to the consequences of educational levels than occupational categories in and of themselves. Our findings also show that the effects of occupation and education are mediated by relations of age and gender, again with varying degrees of significance across the fields. Our cluster analyses show how giving greater attention to the relations between these factors within specific fields yields a more nuanced account of relations between different regimes of cultural value in a society like Australia. The hierarchies that structure cultural consumption in Australia are not evenly spread across diverse areas of cultural life, raising the question as to what constitutes 'legitimate' culture in contemporary Australia: while some fields continue to show strong state and social support for traditional cultural items, this is by no means as solid as it may once have been. We have also qualified the high–low binaries that characterise over-polarised accounts of cultural fields in the attention we have paid to the middle of the space of lifestyles, preferring the light that middlebrow studies have thrown on these questions to the more radical dissolution of taste hierarchies proposed by the eclecticism thesis. The attention paid to the increasing valorisation of Indigenous cultures and the proliferation of ethnoscapes resulting from migration has also testified to a more dispersed set of cultural orientations distributed across diverse populations.

A number of chapters have also taken up Bourdieu's discussion of social trajectories (beyond a simple focus on social position) in an attempt to build a stronger sense of temporality into how we understand the formation and transmission of cultural capital. While we have not undertaken any systematic comparisons between our data and similar evidence for earlier periods, we have captured several temporal dimensions to the operation of our capital logics. Age-generation differences, for example, can register the effects of significant historical changes (the consequences of different circumstances of educational credentialing for Indigenous Australians identified in Chapter 12, for example), cultural changes (the differences in cultural formations between young people and their parents) and biographical changes (young people are likely to have different cultural capital trajectories from their parents). For those of migrant backgrounds and their children, this last consideration is particularly acute as the experience of adaptation has its own specificities, while for the 'second generation' their parents' adaptation affects their own accumulation of cultural capital. More than this, however, we have pointed, where we can, to particular processes of taste formation in order to emphasise the specific practices through which distinctive dispositions are acquired and developed.

This greater processual emphasis is most clearly seen in chapters which focus on the role of family in fostering patterns of participation, belonging and taste. Bourdieu frequently referred to the family as the primary site of socialisation, but rarely explored how it operates in the transmission of cultural capital. Several chapters have drawn attention to the interactional nature of the acquisition of cultural capital. Chapter 14, echoing a term introduced in Chapter 1, examined the 'inherited intensities' of taste through interviewees' accounts of the ways in which their cultural interests were cultivated during the course of their upbringing. This chapter also points to the gendered dimension of these practices and how this entails relations of negotiation and accommodation between partners. The emphasis on intensities reminds us that taste is not simply about attachment to particular values and categories, but entails varying degrees of investment in them. This insight is paralleled by other chapters in Part IV which focus on the function of taste in relation to the ethical and political aspects of habitus that emerge when people talk about their likes and dislikes. In combining the extensive richness of the *Australian Cultural Fields* (ACF) survey data with the intensive richness of the interviews, we have sought to capture both the social positions people inhabit and their relations to the position-taking they undertake in defining regimes of cultural and political value. But, of course, for Bourdieu as for us, the processes at play in producing the varied capital logics in which contemporary forms of cultural capital are enmeshed are not of interest purely for their own sake. They matter, rather, because of the political and policy challenges that they pose.

Acting on capitals

For Bourdieu, as we noted in the Introduction, the concept of cultural capital offered not just an account of social and cultural inequalities but a means for acting on them in order to reduce them. However, his position on how this might be done was marked by a number of limitations and equivocations (Ahearne, 2010). As we saw in Chapter 10, while viewing a broadened access to higher education as a means of securing the more equitable distribution of cultural capital, he was critical of extending higher education opportunities in the context of stratified higher education systems which perpetuated the discriminatory effects of cultural capital through the differential value of the degrees awarded by universities of different standings. He was also unsympathetic to attempts to valorise subordinate cultural practices through access and equity policies that sought to ennoble them by lending them state support. Appearances to the contrary, Bourdieu was something of a Kantian when it came to questions of cultural value. While critical of the forms of purity he associated with bourgeois appropriations of the Kantian aesthetic disposition, he subscribed to a historicised version of Kantianism (Bennett, 2005). Interpreting those cultural practices that had innovated and extended the repertoire of possibilities in their field as part of an accumulating 'historical universal', he called on the French government to 'universalise access to the universal' by extending education in the arts through state schooling (Bourdieu, 2002: 67; Ahearne, 2011). He was, as a consequence, opposed to valorising working-class cultural practices, viewing this as a form of populism that worked to entrap subordinate classes in their oppression (Bourdieu, 2000: 76). His position on these questions has led to qualified take-ups of his work by working-class activists (Mckenzie, 2016). Further, Bourdieu did not effectively engage with political and policy issues posed by extensions of the concept of cultural capital to questions of ethnic and racial diversity.

There are also a number of more general historical considerations which need to be taken into account in assessing both the political limitations and potential of cultural capital. The first concerns the respects in which, while breaking with it, the conceptual framework of cultural capital also initially resonated with aspects of the problem of eugenics. The immediate post-war period in France witnessed a revival of eugenic conceptions of the inheritance of innate abilities in processes of social mobility. The displacement of biological by sociological conceptions of inheritance was initially urged in the work of Augustus Girard who argued that the aptitudes associated with higher occupational and social positions constituted forms of intellectual capital transmitted via associative mating (Desrosières, 1985; Thévenot, 1990). Bourdieu's intervention into the problem space of eugenics was thus distinguished not by the introduction of a social dimension, for this had been done, but rather by introducing a cultural dimension into earlier sociological accounts in the stress he placed on the role of cultural aptitudes in the reproduction of social positions. At the same time, what Desrosières (1998: 109) called Bourdieu's 'statistical grammar' was remarkably similar in its formal structure to that developed in earlier eugenic traditions, particularly Francis Galton's examination of the mechanisms shaping the inheritance of what he called the artistic faculty (Galton, 1889; Bennett, 2017).

The second historical consideration concerns the relatively late emergence, in twentieth-century France, of a concern with culture as a political matter at the level of the state. Dubois (1999) has shown how, right up to the Vichy period, issues concerning the social management of culture took place largely outside the bureaucratic field of the state. It was only in the 1960s, after the establishment in 1959 of a Ministry of Culture, that culture became unequivocally a state matter. This was, then, a distinctive historical moment which brought questions concerning access to and participation in the fine arts together with questions of cultural democracy more generally; it did so in the context of an expanding higher education provision that was invested with the distinctive values of French republicanism which universalised the right to full participation in both art and culture; and during a period when earlier problematics of inheritance were given a socio-cultural inflection. This was the context in which, through Bourdieu's empirical studies initiated in the 1960s, cultural capital began its career as an aspiring governmental actor (Robbins, 2005). This moment in its career was marked by a distinctive statistical grammar that brought together questions of inheritance, social position, and cultural knowledge, tastes and practices in ways which endowed cultural capital with a range of capacities which made it a plausible lever for state action directed towards the levelling out of social inequalities as a means of qualifying all French citizens for full participation in universal culture. As such, the concept resonated more with Weberian conceptions of how governmental action might ameliorate the relations between class and life chances than it did with Marxist conceptions of working-class action as the best means for achieving social equality.

Like all social science concepts, then, the concept of cultural capital was marked by the discursive, social and intellectual terrain on which it was initially developed. At the same time, its political currency has been adapted and modified in the light of the changed historical circumstances and national contexts in which it has been applied. While there is no doubt that the concept has had an active, albeit chequered, career in Australia, this has not been in the ideal forms that Bourdieu envisaged. Widely invoked in the expansions of publicly funded higher education from the late 1960s through to the late 1980s, it also informed the introduction of the Higher Education Contribution Scheme, but in a more individualised form as a repayment of student loans made by those who benefit from their higher education in career and financial terms. The social returns this delivers are in the form of a reduced tax burden on the general population rather than in any general transformation of the set of relations between class position, home background, the education system and occupational destiny. And the influence that cultural capital has had on arts and cultural policies in Australia – quite apart from never being susceptible to Bourdieu's historicised universalism – has always been limited: none at all on those of Coalition governments, and only marginally on the cultural policies of the Australian Labor Party (ALP). We have already noted the limitations of the 1994 *Creative Nation* cultural policy statement in this regard (see p. 4), and these track through to *Renewing Creative Australia*, the arts and cultural policy statement put out by the ALP in 2019. While commendable in its support for Indigenous culture and cultural diversity, and in committing to restoring arts education in view of its role in the creative economy, the statement had nothing to say about the potential for cultural policies to engage with the more general connections between cultural consumption, education and the role of the inheritance of cultural capital in the reproduction of inequalities.

The point at issue here is not to exaggerate what a policy focus on cultural capital might accomplish. Although Bourdieu was often criticised for his overly theoretical style and for, in his later years, distancing himself from policy practicalities, a part of his purpose was to retain a more critical role for the concept in underscoring the extent to which even its more modest purely meritocratic aspirations were unrealisable within the economic-political system of the Fifth Republic. We have already noted the relative inability of the concept to provide an effective political or policy response to the rampantly increasing inequalities of wealth that have prevailed since the 1980s. It also needs to be recognised that it is not the only governmental actor engaged with the relations between the inheritance of differential capabilities and inequality; more general conceptions of human capital have informed a legion of policy interventions aimed at mitigating the effects of disadvantaged home backgrounds on the development of linguistic and cognitive skills (Marks, 2014). The value of cultural capital theory – together with Bourdieu's notions of field and habitus – consists in the light it throws on the mechanisms through which such differential capabilities are compounded and translated into a set of more fine-grained distinctions between levels and types of education, educational venues, occupational destinies and class positions. Nor is any purpose served by prioritising such discriminations over those that are the effects of Indigeneity or ethnicity. It is rather, we have argued, their intersections that need to be attended to in the complex ways in which cultural practices articulate with class divisions among Aboriginal and Torres Strait Islander peoples and Australia's diverse ethnic populations as well as between those populations and other Australians.

Despite our desire not to overstate the practical possibilities of cultural capital in addressing inequalities, this is not to suggest that the currency of cultural capital discourse cannot have a role in addressing the myth of a classless society, so central to the Australian experience: but that perhaps is for another time.

This book has suggested that Bourdieu's *Distinction* rightly continues to hold a central place in the socio-cultural analysis of taste not because its conceptual framework — and especially its core concepts of field, capital and habitus — should be slavishly applied, immune to critique and revision, but because, as a method of 'asking questions', it continues to offer valuable tools for exploring the complex relations between culture, consumption and power in an increasingly globalised and complex world.

APPENDIX A

Questionnaire design and survey methods

The *Australian Cultural Fields* (ACF) questionnaire was modelled on the French study pioneered by Pierre Bourdieu (1984). While there have been many subsequent studies that have explored the cultural tastes and practices of particular social groups or educational cohorts, or focused on particular cultural fields, there have been only a few national surveys encompassing a wide range of cultural fields. Such surveys have been conducted in Australia (Bennett *et al.*, 1999), Britain (Bennett *et al.*, 2009), Denmark (Prieur *et al.*, 2008) and Serbia (Cvetičanin and Popescu, 2011). In building on these earlier studies, the ACF survey sought to address the distinctive socio-cultural coordinates of a settler-colonial society with an Indigenous population asserting an increasingly strong cultural presence, and a large and growing multicultural population with a rapidly changing composition from mainly southern European sources of migration towards east and southern Asia. The key innovations in questionnaire design are that, by opting for an in-depth inquiry into patterns of consumption in the art, literary, sport, television, heritage and music fields – but excluding other areas: film and culinary practices, for example – we were able to go beyond questions relating to tastes for the main genres and patterns of participation most strongly associated with those fields, to ask our respondents whether they recognised, engaged with and, if so, liked or disliked an extensive repertoire of named cultural items. These were further differentiated according to whether they were international or Australian in provenance, ensuring that the international items were spread across Europe and America with some items from Asia. The Australian items identified for each field also included examples of Indigenous culture available to 'mainstream Australia'.

The questions focused on the six cultural fields were followed by detailed explorations of the socio-demographic characteristics of the respondents. These included age, gender, occupation, class position and identification, level of education, field of study and university attended for those with tertiary education, occupations of partners, levels of education for partners and parents, ethnicity and ethnic identification, country of birth, Indigenous identification, level of income, capital holdings, housing and place of residence.

The questionnaire, piloted in a survey of 29 respondents in November 2014, was revised and then administered over the period May–July 2015 to a main sample of 1202 Australian residents supplemented by an additional 259 respondents recruited via 'boost' samples of Aboriginal and Torres Strait Islander, Italian, Lebanese, Chinese and Indian Australians, yielding a total of 1461 respondents. The main sample was recruited using Computer-Assisted Telephone Interviewing (CATI) techniques administered by the Institute for Social Science Research at the University of Queensland. A response rate of 5.18 per cent was achieved for the main sample and of 1.46 per cent for the boost samples. Quotas were applied during the screening process for the main sample to ensure that a representative population by age and gender was recruited. These target quota sizes were developed using proportional allocations based on population estimates from the Australian Bureau of Statistics (ABS) data (cat. no. 3101.0). Achieved quota sizes closely matched the target quotas for gender and most age groups. However, the 25–39 year olds were under-represented while 40–59 year olds were over-represented, as were the over 60s (but only marginally so). These age differences were partly a reflection of budget limitations which enforced an exclusive reliance on landlines rather than mobile phones. The data set used for the analysis was weighted in accordance with the target quota sizes for gender, age and State of residence. It should also be noted that, as has been the case with most cultural capital surveys, the main sample recruited disproportionately from those with tertiary educational qualifications. Thirty-eight per cent of the men in the main sample had attained Bachelor degrees or above, and 45 per cent of the women. Comparable figures reported by the ABS for 2017 were 28 per cent and 35 per cent. See 'Education and Work, Australia, May 2017', ABS Catalogue No. 6227.0.

Details of achieved quota sizes for the boost samples and other variations relating to the administration of these samples that bear on their analysis are discussed in Chapters 12 and 13. Fuller discussion of these matters and of the survey overall are available in Walker et al. (2015).

APPENDIX B
Survey questions

TABLE B.1 Overview of survey questions relating to cultural fields

Television field	Sport field	Music field
Two liked most and two liked least among:	*Participated in past year (playing or non-playing role e.g. coach, medical support) (yes/no):* *Watched live at sports venue past year (yes/no):* *Watch live through the media (yes/no):*	*Two liked most and two liked least among:*

Genre

Television field	Sport field	Music field
Sport	Australian Rules football	Country
News and current affairs	Soccer (Association Football)	Classical
Drama	Netball	Light classical
Reality TV	Rugby league	Easy listening
Talk shows	Rugby union	Jazz
Comedy or sitcoms	Cricket	Pop rock
Lifestyle	Basketball	Hard rock
Documentaries	Tennis	Urban
Police/detective	Golf	Dance
Arts programmes	Swimming	Alternative

Named items (national)

Programmes
Heard of, not heard of, watched and liked/not liked, not watched:

Redfern Now
Offspring
House Husbands
MasterChef Australia
The Block
Big Brother Australia
Old School
Hamish and Andy's Gap Year
Gardening Australia
Australian Story

Television personalities
Heard of, not heard of, like/not like, do not especially like/dislike:

Eddie McGuire
Julia Zemiro
Dave Hughes
Carrie Bickmore
Jennifer Byrne
Paul Vautin
Deborah Mailman
Amanda Keller
Ray Martin
Scott Cam

Sportspeople
Heard of, not heard of, like/not like, do not especially like/dislike:

Don Bradman
Liz Ellis
Israel Folau
Cathy Freeman
Lauren Jackson
Adam Goodes
Harry Kewell
Rod Laver
Greg Norman
Ian Thorpe

Musicians/musical acts
Heard of, not heard of, listened to and liked/not liked, not listened to:

Peter Sculthorpe
Jimmy Barnes
Dan Sultan
Gurrumul Yunupingu
Kate Ceberano
AC/DC
Vince Jones
Kylie Minogue
Kasey Chambers
Gotye

continued

TABLE B.1 Continued

Named items (international)

Programmes

Heard of, not heard of, watched and liked/not liked, not watched:

Mad Men
The Killing
QI
Game of Thrones
Midsomer Murders
Homeland
Grand Designs
The Big Bang Theory
Under the Dome
Top Gear

Sportspeople

Heard of, not heard of, like/not like, do not especially like/dislike:

David Beckham
Usain Bolt
Michael Jordan
Diego Maradona
Rafael Nadal
Michael Phelps
Sachin Tendulkar
Serena Williams
Tiger Woods
Yao Ming

Musical pieces

Heard of, not heard of, listened to and liked/not liked, not listened to:

The Four Seasons by Vivaldi
The Piano by Michael Nyman
Kind of Blue by Miles Davis
'Nessun Dorma' by Puccini
Rhapsody in Blue by George Gershwin
The Phantom of the Opera by Andrew Lloyd Webber
'Vogue' by Madonna
The Dark Side of the Moon by Pink Floyd
The Mikado by Gilbert and Sullivan
'Jolene' by Dolly Parton

Technology/media used

Apparatus

Technology used most among:

Television set
Laptop
Desktop
Mobile device (e.g. tablet, phone)
Game console (e.g. Xbox)

Media used to follow sport

(yes/no):

Newspapers
Magazines
Radio
Television
Computer (desktop or laptop)
Tablet
Mobile phone
Game console (e.g. Xbox)

Apparatus

Used most among:

Radio
CD player
Computer (desktop, laptop)
Mobile device (phone, iPod, iPad, mp3 player, tablet)
Record player (vinyl records, LPs)
MiniDisk or cassette player
Live instruments

Platform

Two used most over past year among:
Free-to-air broadcast TV
Subscription TV (e.g. Foxtel)
Catch-up broadcasting services (e.g. iView)
Personal video recorders for time-shifting
TV apps for mobile devices (phone, tablet)
Video downloads (e.g. BitTorrent)
Video sites (e.g. YouTube)
Streaming services (e.g. Apple TV)

Field specific
Daily level television viewing
Watched National Indigenous Television (NITV) (yes/no)
Favourite TV channel/network (open-ended)
Preference for Australian/overseas produced programmes

Frequency of playing organised sport
Sports club membership

Daily level music listening

Music event attendance
Frequency of attendance at:
Rock gigs
Orchestral concerts
Musicals
Opera
Live bands in pubs
Pop concerts

continued

TABLE B.1 Continued

Heritage field	Art field	Literary field

Genre

Two which interest most and two which interest least among:	*Two liked most and two liked least among:*	*Read for own interest or pleasure in the past year (yes/no):*
Your family's heritage	Renaissance art	Crime or mystery
Heritage of your local area	Colonial art	Books by/about Indigenous Australians
Heritage of working life	Aboriginal art	Science fiction or fantasy
Heritage of your homeland	Landscapes	Australian history
Heritage of migrant groups	Impressionism	Self-help or lifestyle
Aboriginal heritage	Still life	Modern novels
Australia's national heritage	Modern art	Romance
World heritage	Abstract art	Sport or sports personalities
	Portraits	Thriller or adventure
	Pop art	Literary classics
		Contemporary Australian novels
		Biographies of historical figures

Named items (national)

	Artists	*Writers*
Locations*	*Heard of, not heard of, seen and liked/not liked, not seen:*	*Heard of, not heard of, read and liked/not liked, not read:*
Heard of, not heard of, visited and liked/not liked, not visited:		
Museum of Sydney	Sidney Nolan	Matthew Reilly
Sovereign Hill	Tom Roberts	Kate Grenville
National Museum of Australia	Margaret Preston	Tim Winton
Fremantle Prison	Brett Whiteley	Sally Morgan
Cockatoo Island	Tracey Moffatt	Sara Douglass

Tjapukai Aboriginal Cultural Park
Uluru-Kata Tjuta National Park
Immigration Museum
Port Arthur Historic Site
Australian War Memorial

Imants Tillers
Ken Done
John Glover
Albert Namatjira
Ben Quilty

Kim Scott
Belinda Alexandra
Elizabeth Harrower
David Malouf
Bryce Courtenay

Named items (international)

Locations*
Heard of, not heard of, visited and liked/not liked, not visited:

Stonehenge
Gallipoli
Ellis Island
The Acropolis
The Forbidden City
Angkor Wat
Taj Mahal
Byblos
The Vatican Museums
Museum of New Zealand (Te Papa Tongarewa)

Artists
Heard of, not heard of, seen and liked/not liked, not seen:

Francis Bacon
Tracey Emin
Jackson Pollock
Vincent van Gogh
Caravaggio
Ai Weiwei
Claude Monet
Rembrandt
Leonardo da Vinci
Jeff Koons

Writers
Heard of, not heard of, read and liked/not liked, not read:

Amy Tan
Don DeLillo
Dave Eggers
Stephen King
Ian Rankin
Jane Austen
Virginia Woolf
Jodi Picoult
Haruki Murakami
Margaret Atwood

Technology/media used

Frequency of Internet to search for information on heritage places/events such as visiting museum collections and exhibitions online, investigating family histories, reading about heritage events online

Internet use for researching arts/artists; visiting website of artist/arts organisation; reading blogs or email newsletter by an artist or arts organisation; commenting on art/arts organisation using social media

*Number of ebooks owned
(also see digital items in 'Field specific' below)*

continued

TABLE B.1 Continued

Field specific

Affiliations
Member of/subscriber to (yes/no):

Local history/archaeology society/club
Online family history website
National Trust of Australia or similar Australian organisation (e.g. Historic Houses Association, Australian Conservation Society)
National museum member/friend
Local museum member/friend
National Parks friend
History Channel subscriber (TV)

Heritage sites visited in past year (yes/no):

A local, regional or national museum
A historical building or precinct (e.g. The Rocks, Chinatown, Burra)
An archaeological site or ruins
A site narrating Aboriginal history or heritage
A military site or memorial
An open air site
A migration or immigration museum
A cultural landscape (e.g. Kakadu)
A site of pioneer or settler heritage
An industrial heritage site

Frequency of gallery attendance
Ownership of art books; original paintings/drawings; limited edition prints (yes/no)
Locations visited in the past year (yes/no):

The National Gallery of Australia
A State art gallery
A regional gallery
A university art gallery
A commercial art gallery
A museum of contemporary art
A public art display or installation
An Australian or international arts festival or biennale

Number of books by Australian authors read in past year
Number of books in the home
Methods used to obtain books in past year (yes/no):

Local bookshop purchase
Department store/supermarket purchase
Discount/second-hand bookstore purchase
Purchase print books via online bookseller (e.g. Amazon, Abebooks)
Ebook purchase
Borrow from library
Borrow from friends/reading group
Download free ebooks

Participation in book culture
Frequency of:

Visiting bookstore for browsing
Participating in book club/reading group
Attending a literary/writers festival
Attending event at local bookstore/similar (e.g. book launch, author reading)
Reading book reviews in newspaper/magazine or online
Following discussions about books/authors online or via social media
Watching book shows on TV/listening to book shows on radio

* Geographical locators, such as the name of the relevant town/State/country, were provided for each heritage location.

APPENDIX C

Methods used in analysing the survey data

We have, for the greater part, followed the tradition inaugurated by Bourdieu by using Multiple Correspondence Analysis (MCA) as the primary method for analysing our survey data. However, we have also complemented MCA with the techniques of cluster analysis and, in a distinctive innovation, incorporated the clusters produced by this analysis within the overall space of lifestyles produced by our MCAs. Our purpose in this appendix is therefore to outline these two techniques of statistical analysis, our reasons for bringing them together and the consequences of doing so.

We look first at the principles of MCA which inform the overall analytical logic of the study. Chapters 1 to 8, focused on the analysis of our cultural fields, the overall space of lifestyles produced by bringing these together and the relations between class and cultural capital, make extensive use of this technique. MCA also informs the concerns of Chapters 9 and 10, focused on middlebrow cultures and on education and culture respectively. Following the rationale proposed by Bourdieu, particularly in *Distinction* (1984), MCA produces the space of lifestyles as a matrix of multiple interrelations between the cultural items included in the questionnaire. We shall not review the basic principles of this method here as these have been amply reviewed elsewhere (see especially Le Roux and Rouanet, 2004). We focus rather on those specific aspects of our use of the method which merit attention.

In implementing the procedures of MCA, we have generally used cultural tastes and practices as active variables: that is, those from which the space of lifestyles is generated. However, even though we always followed this procedure, in some fields we needed to produce the final space by including socio-demographic variables among those used to construct the space. We did so only in those fields where this yielded specific benefits (the sport, heritage and literary fields). We have also, in a few cases, adapted the results in order to place outlier modalities closer to adjacent ones than is statistically warranted in order to avoid large empty spaces in the figures showing the findings. This is true only of the following: in the art field: 'Tillers/Emin+' and 'T Moffatt+'; and in the sport field: '1 year (play org sport)', 'Y Ming+' and 'Golf++'.

As our primary method, we have used MCA largely independently of other statistical procedures in our analysis of the relations between cultural knowledges, tastes and participation on the one hand, and capitals and socio-demographics on the other. However, once our MCAs were completed, we then complemented them by using cluster analysis to highlight and amplify those aspects of their findings most salient to our purposes. We did this originally for publications focused on each of our six cultural fields,[1] and, subsequently, specifically for this book, for our overall space of lifestyles informing the concerns of Chapters 7, 8 and 9.

We had two aims in view in bringing these two methods together. The first was to have a means of strengthening the visual presentation of our findings in the figures produced by our MCAs by performing a cluster analysis to generate groups of individuals distinguished from one another by their relative positioning in relation to the variables distributed across axes 1 and 2 of the MCAs. This provided a basis for further statistical analyses testing the association between the clusters and all the variables in our data set. Our second aim was to provide a means for the generation of typologies of orientations to cultural practice. In particular, the analysis of the overall space of lifestyles (Chapter 7) produced a classification of cultural orientations which aimed to make it easier to understand the complexity and variety of individuals' approaches to culture. The cultural orientations this yielded were also used as new variables in the analysis of the relation between class and culture (Chapter 8). In summary, the synthesis of MCA and cluster analysis that we have undertaken proved essential in guiding our interpretations and allowing us to see phenomena that would not have been detected had we relied solely on the original observed variables.

Note

1 See the papers collected in the ACF-themed sections of *Continuum* (vol. 32, no. 3, June 2018), and *Media International Australia* (Issue 167, May 2018). Although we have not included the results of field-specific cluster analyses in this book, they have informed our interpretations of the results for every field.

APPENDIX D

Occupational class model with examples of occupations

The construction of the eight-class model has been a crucial methodological building block for our study, serving as the basis for our analyses of the different fields, and as the bedrock for the four- and three-class models used in later chapters. It was constructed using the classificatory rules of the National Statistics Socio-economic Classification (NS-SEC) based upon the Standard Occupational Classification of 2010 (SOC2010), which was originally based on the so-called 'Goldthorpe or EGP Schema'.[1] This classification offers eight 'analytic classes', and two other analytic and increasingly simplified classifications of five and three classes, nested in the original or most disaggregated typology. Finding and using the appropriate SOC2010 codes was therefore a key moment in the construction of the eight-class model. However, as the survey was conducted in Australia where the codifications for occupations are provided by the Australian and New Zealand Standard Classification of Occupations (version 1.2), or ANZSCO, this required the implementation of a number of conversion procedures. The ABS offered the information needed to make a conversion between ANZSCO and the International Standard Classification of Occupations of the International Labour Organization, that was agreed between the end of 2007 and the start of 2008, and became known as 'ISCO-08'. In parallel, the Office for National Statistics of the UK provided a 'mapping' of equivalences between the SOC2010 and the ISCO-08. With this information at hand, we followed a sequence of conversions from the original ANZSCO codes to those from ISCO-08, and then migrated from this latter to SOC2010 codes. In summary, we converted the ANZSCO classification into the NS-SEC/SOC2010 one via the ISCO-08 typology. Where exact matches could not be obtained, we based our decisions on the codes of the general group in which a particular occupation was nested. This means that our occupational classes are created from an internationally agreed classification system that is supported by relevant institutions and studies at the level of governments, international organisations and universities. Table D.1 provides examples of

TABLE D.1 Examples of occupations in each class

Classes, identified by NS-SEC name	Examples of occupations in each class
1 *Large owner/high managers*: large employers and higher managerial and administrative occupations (Large employers account for 11, or 0.9%, of our sample.)	Chief executive or managing director, corporate general manager, local government legislator, manufacturer/production manager, supply and distribution manager, finance manager, human resource manager, defence force senior officer
2 *High professional*: higher professional occupations	Chemist, botanist, medical laboratory scientist, historian, interpreter, computer network and systems engineer, ICT business analyst, dentist, general practitioner, ophthalmologist
3 *Lower managers/professionals*: lower managerial, administrative and professional occupations	Agricultural consultant, forester, web developer, optometrist, midwifery and nursing professionals, middle school teacher, archivist, gallery or museum curator, copywriter, ICT customer support officer
4 *Intermediate occupations*	Private tutors and teachers, ambulance officer, fashion designer, illustrator, private investigator, agricultural technician, social security assessor, human resources clerk, data entry operator, call or contact centre team leader
5 *Small employers/own account workers*	Aquaculture farmer, flower grower, hotel or motel owner-manager, cafe or restaurant owner-manager, antique dealer, hair or beauty salon owner-manager, beef cattle farmer, mixed crop and livestock farmer, forestry worker, roof tiler
6 *Lower supervisory/technical occupations*	Gunsmith, metal fitters and machinists, saw maker and repairer, toolmaker, automotive electrician, aircraft maintenance engineer, lift mechanic, chemical plant operator, power generation plant operator, wool classer
7 *Semi-routine occupations*	Production clerk, purchasing officer, metal polisher, fitter, metal machinist (first class), vehicle painter, clothing patternmaker, dental technician, sales assistant
8 *Routine occupations*	Blacksmith, plumber, gasfitter, visual arts and crafts workers, truck driver, aircraft refueller, bulldozer operator, garden labourer, bar useful or busser, hospitality worker

the resulting allocation of occupations to class categories. The independence of these procedures means that our analyses of the relations between class and culture do not rest on any kind of statistical tautology, but bring together two quite different types of information that are independent from each other in their nature and in the procedures followed to build them up as usable data.

In providing the examples of occupations in the second column of Table D.1 we followed the simplified method suggested by NS-SEC for working with SOC2010. This method effects a direct translation of occupational codes to classes, without taking into account employment status and size of organisation. Even though we used SOC2010 codes, we provide ANZSCO names for occupations in order to offer the original information in our survey. Taking the eight-class schema as a baseline typology, the four-class model brings together classes 1 and 2 (higher managerial, administrative and professional occupations) as class 1; converts class 3 (lower managers and professionals) into its second class; combines classes 4 and 5 (intermediate occupations, small employers and own account workers) into its class 3; and integrates classes 6, 7 and 8 ((lower supervisory and technical occupations, semi-routine and routine workers) into the fourth class. Taking the four-class model as its point of departure, the three-class model combines classes 1 and 2 (higher and lower managerial, administrative and professional occupations) into its first class and retains the two other classes without any change.

Note

1 See www.ons.gov.uk/ons/guid-method/classifications/current-standard-classifications/soc2010.

APPENDIX E
Selection of household interviewees

After the survey was completed, follow-up interviews with 42 participants were undertaken. Selection of those interviewed was based on accessing participants who reflected the issues and circumstances the project was examining, rather than statistically representative cohorts. Consequently, interviewees were selected to capture a range of people across age, gender, class, education and income levels. Fifteen of the participants came from the survey's boost samples. Because of the difficulty of finding young Indigenous participants, we included an interview with one person in this category who had not completed the survey. While most interviewees were drawn from Sydney and Brisbane and their fringe areas, there was a selection from regional centres. Brief profiles of the interviewees are provided in Appendix F. These profiles offer basic socio-demographic information for each interviewee: in the text, more details will be found specific to the context, but sometimes authors will focus on one to two features as relevant. Interviews were conducted in participants' homes or a venue of their choice by pairs of researchers from the project team, or sometimes involving research assistants. Note that there was often a long delay between the survey and interview, during which time the participant may have aged a year. We decided, however, to identify their age at the time of the survey only, when we collected their broader demographic data.

While these interviews were intended to furnish data which connected with the survey data, they were not simply elaborations of the survey questions. A schedule of typical questions was drafted, but interviewers were encouraged to pursue issues that came up during discussion. Consequently, the focus varied across the interviews, depending on the fields that were of the greatest interest to the individual, and participants were encouraged to describe their tastes, activities and interests in more nuanced and expansive ways than was permitted in the survey. We also asked interviewers to observe whether there were particular household items (if the interview was conducted in the home) that could be the basis of discussion: examples of artwork, the presence of books, display cabinets, technologies, markers of ethnicity and so on.

Questions invited reflection on participants' likes and dislikes; their use of technologies; their preferences for Australian or overseas content; their involvement in events and organisations across the fields; and their engagement with items from a cultural background other than their own. A set of more contemplative questions asked participants to reflect on how their educational background, or family members, might have influenced their cultural tastes; how their cultural interests might relate to feeling a sense of national or ethnic belonging; and how their cultural practices have been affected by multiculturalism, the increasing visibility of Indigenous Australians, globalisation and new technologies.

The interviews were coded according to themes that were generated through an initial analysis; summaries of key aspects of each interview, including observational notes, and profiles of the interviewees were developed to aid use of the data. The analyses of the interviews looked for:

- patterns of taste, activities and interests across key demographic categories (such as class, gender, age and ethnicity);
- elements of taste and participation beyond the survey's focus;
- points of comparison and contrast across interviewees;
- lines of continuity and contradiction within interviewees' accounts of their tastes; and
- articulation of identities, positions, judgements, attitudes, values and beliefs, relating to senses of national belonging, multiculturalism, Indigenous Australia, technological change and globalisation.

Presentations of the findings were discussed at a series of writing workshops to further elucidate themes and issues across the interviews and connections with survey data analysis, and to highlight continuities and contrasts across the individual chapters.

APPENDIX F
Profiles of household interviewees

Adrian was born in Australia, and is 57 years old. He lives in Sydney's inner west with his partner. He attended a state school and completed tertiary education in accounting at a College of Advanced Education. His partner had also completed tertiary-level education, as had his father, and his mother was secondary-level educated. He is an accountant by training but also undertakes part-time work as a bookkeeper and labourer and does not identify in class terms.

Aisha was born in Lebanon, and is 47 years old. She lives in western Sydney with her partner and children. She attended a state school and completed tertiary education in Lebanon before migrating. In Australia, she completed diploma and certificate courses at several institutions. Her partner has tertiary-level education. Her father completed vocational training and her mother has primary-level education. She works part time as a counsellor and identifies as middle class.

Akela was born in Laos, and is 37 years old. She is not married and lives in the Australian Capital Territory (ACT). She attended a state school and completed vocational training. Her father has a secondary level of education and her mother a primary level of education. She works full time as a rehabilitation case manager and identifies as middle class.

Angela was born in China, and is 50 years old. She lives in Sydney's inner west with her partner and two children. She attended a state school and completed vocational training. Her partner has postgraduate qualifications and both her parents also completed postgraduate-level education. She is retired but was previously employed in office work and bookkeeping and identifies as middle class.

Anthony was born in Australia but raised in Lebanon where his parents are from, and is 20 years old. He lives in south-western Sydney with his grandparents.

He attended a Catholic school and began tertiary education in Lebanon, where he also learned to be a mechanic, but is currently unemployed. Both his parents completed tertiary-level education. He identifies as working class.

Badal was born in Fiji, of Indian ancestry, and is 42 years old. He lives in western Sydney with his partner and children. He attended a state school, and completed a degree in science from a university in rural NSW. He is currently completing a Master's degree, retraining as a teacher. His partner also is a graduate. His father undertook some tertiary-level education while his mother had some vocational training. He has worked as a production supervisor in the food manufacturing industry but is not employed at the moment. He identifies as working class.

Bianca is 18 years old and identifies as Aboriginal, as well as having other, non-Aboriginal ancestries. She lives in the inner city of Sydney, NSW. She went to a private Catholic school and is currently studying at a Sydney university (degree unknown). She is the one interviewee who had not completed the initial survey.

Brenton was born in Australia, and is 35 years old. He is divorced and lives in Newcastle. He attended a state school and has a secondary level of education. He does not know the educational qualifications of his parents. He is not employed at the moment but has been engaged in various creative activities. He did not identify in class terms.

Brooke was born in Australia, and is 21 years old. She lives on the upper north shore of Sydney with her parents. She attended a denominational private school, and completed tertiary education in business studies at a Sydney university. Her father has postgraduate qualifications and her mother completed tertiary education. She works full time as a recruitment coordinator and is currently employed in the private school system. She identifies as upper middle class.

Callum was born in Australia, and is 22 years old. He lives on the Central Coast of NSW. He attended a state school, and completed tertiary education in information technology at a university in NSW. His parents completed vocational training. He worked as a fast-food delivery driver on a casual basis at the time of the survey, but had been employed in an IT position in a small business by the time of interview. He identifies as working class.

Charles was born in Lebanon, and is 37 years old. He is a divorcee and lives in western Sydney. He attended Catholic school, completed some vocational training and previously worked as a truck driver but at the time of interview he had been unable to work for several years due to an ongoing injury. As a consequence, he moved between his own flat and staying with his parents. Both his parents completed tertiary-level education. He identifies as working class.

Christine was born in Australia, of Aboriginal and other mixed ancestry, and is 61 years old. She lives in western Sydney with her partner. She attended a state school and studied education at a Sydney university. Her partner has some vocational training. Her mother completed some secondary education but her father's education is unknown. She works full time as an education support officer in a medical school. A supervisor/professional, she identifies as middle class.

Craig was born in Australia, and is 49 years old. He lives in Canberra, ACT, with his partner. He attended a state school, and completed secondary education. His partner has tertiary-level education and his parents were secondary-level educated. A former storeman and forklift truck driver, he had been a full-time carer for his mother until her recent passing. He identifies as working class.

Daniel was born in Australia, of Chinese ancestry, and is 31 years old. He is unmarried and lives in the inner west of Sydney with his parents. He attended a state school and studied science at a Sydney university. Both his parents completed secondary education. He works full time as an analyst with a sports betting company and identifies as middle class.

David was born in Australia, and is 78 years old. He lives in a middle-class suburb in Sydney's north-west with his partner. He attended a state school and studied engineering at a Sydney university, later doing a PhD in management. His partner has vocational training, while both his parents had primary education. He is a retired manager and also worked within universities. He identifies as middle class. While he claims some Aboriginal ancestry, he only discovered this very late in life.

Debra was born in Australia, and is 58 years old. She lives in outer north-western Sydney with her partner and children. She attended a state school, and completed secondary education. Her partner is a postgraduate and both her parents are secondary-level educated. She previously worked as a supervisor in the wine industry but is currently undertaking home duties. She identifies as middle class.

Diane was born in Australia, and is 53 years old. She lives in the wealthy Southern Highlands of NSW with her partner. She attended a private non-denominational school, and completed secondary-level education. Her partner is tertiary educated and so are her parents. She is retired but had been part of the administrative staff at a local high school. She identifies as upper middle class.

Eric was born in Australia, and is 72 years old. He lives in Sydney's central business district with his partner. He attended a state school and completed some secondary education. His partner also completed secondary-level education, as did his parents. He is a retired executive of an advertising agency who has been actively involved in many organisations and charity work since retirement and identifies as middle class.

Gabriel was born in Australia, of Italian ancestry, and is 19 years old. He lives in Sydney's inner west with his parents. He attended a denominational school, and is studying medical science at university. His father and mother both completed tertiary-level education. He works part time as a surgical company representative and identifies as upper middle class.

Giovanni was born in Australia, of Italian ancestry, and is 54 years old. He lives in Sydney's west with his partner and children. He attended a state school and completed vocational training. His partner has tertiary-level education and both his parents completed vocational training. He works full time as a sales manager and identifies as working class.

Harley was born in Australia, and is 18 years old. He lives near Brisbane, Queensland, with his parents. He attended a state school, and is undertaking a degree in business studies from a Queensland university. His father and mother both completed tertiary education. He also works as a cook in a fish and chip shop on a casual basis. He identifies as middle class.

Heath was born in Australia, and is 42 years old. He lives near Ipswich, in the south-west of the Brisbane metropolitan area, with his partner and children. He attended a state school, and completed vocational training. His partner is secondary-level educated. His father had vocational training and his mother completed secondary education. He works as a printer and identifies as middle class.

Holly was born in Australia, and is 29 years old. She lives in a wealthy, harbourside suburb of Sydney with her partner. She attended a Catholic school and completed a degree in engineering from a Sydney university. Her partner is a postgraduate. Her father has postgraduate qualifications and her mother completed tertiary education. She works full time as a consultant in the health sector, having previously worked in the transport industry and identifies as upper middle class.

Jacinta was born in Australia, and is 49 years old. She lives near Canberra, ACT, with her partner and children. She attended a state school and completed tertiary education in humanities at a Sydney university. Her partner is a graduate and so are her parents. She works as an educational consultant on a casual basis. She identifies as middle class.

Kathleen was born in Australia, and is 56 years old. She is divorced and lives in western Sydney with her brother. She attended a state school, and completed secondary-level education. She does not know her parents' educational qualifications. She works full time as a quality assurance officer and identifies as working class.

Kim was born in Australia, of Aboriginal ancestry, and is 53 years old. She lives in inner western Sydney with her partner and children. She attended a state school and studied humanities at a Sydney university, and has postgraduate qualifications. Her partner has some vocational training. Her father had completed vocational training but she doesn't know her mother's educational qualifications. She works full time in TAFE teaching Aboriginal studies. Kim identifies as middle class.

Lauren was born in Australia, and is 38 years old. She is divorced and lives on the north coast of NSW with her children. She attended a state school, and completed a tertiary degree in education from a university in NSW. Her father has secondary-level education and her mother vocational training. She works full time as a maths teacher at high school. She identifies as middle class.

Leonard was born in Australia, and is 86 years old. He is a widower and lives near Ryde, in Sydney, by himself. He attended a state school and completed vocational training. His partner also had completed vocational training. His father too had vocational training and his mother a secondary-level education. He is a retired printer and identifies as working class.

Lisa was born in England, and is 42 years old. She lives in Canberra, ACT, with her partner and two children. She attended a state school, and completed tertiary education in social sciences at a UK university. Her partner has postgraduate qualifications and both her parents completed secondary education. She works full time as a case manager and doesn't identify in class terms.

Lynne was born in Australia, and is 51 years old. She lives in Sydney's inner west with her partner and children. She attended a Catholic school, and completed some secondary education. Her partner completed vocational training and so did her father. Her mother is secondary-level educated. She works full time as a lingerie party plan franchisee and identifies as working class.

Maria was born in Australia, of Italian migrants (she declined to give her age). She is unmarried and lives in western Sydney with her parents. She attended a state school and completed tertiary study in education at a Sydney university. Both her parents completed primary-level education. She works full time as a primary school teacher and identifies as upper middle class.

Martin was born in England, and is 59 years old. He is married but lives in outer western Sydney by himself. He attended a state school, and completed business studies at TAFE. His partner has secondary-level education and both his parents also completed secondary education. He is a retired national inventory planner for an electrical goods company and identifies as middle class.

Mayra was born in Sri Lanka, and is 34 years old. She lives in western Sydney with her partner and children. She attended a state school and studied medicine at a Sydney university, followed by a postgraduate diploma. Her partner has a postgraduate qualification, as do both of her parents. She works part time as a project training officer in a not-for-profit organisation and owns a small business with her partner. She identifies as middle class.

Michael was born in Australia, and is 71 years old. He is a widower and lives in a middle-class area of south-western Brisbane. He attended a state school, and completed tertiary education in engineering at a Queensland university. His partner had also completed tertiary-level education. His father completed vocational training but his mother's education level is unknown. He is a retired professional engineer and identifies as middle class.

Naomi was born in Australia, and is 47 years old. She lives near Redland, Queensland, with her partner and children. She attended a state school, and completed vocational training. Her partner is tertiary-level educated while both her parents attained secondary-level education. She is not working at the moment but is undertaking home duties. She had previously been employed in administrative work. She identifies as working class.

Oliver was born in Australia, and is 25 years old. He lives in an outer suburb of Canberra, ACT, with unrelated others. He attended a Catholic school, and undertook some study in metalwork at a university in NSW. His mother has postgraduate qualifications but his father's education is unknown to him. He works as a project coordinator for a construction company and identifies as working class.

Rhiannon was born in Australia, and is 18 years old. She lives in Brisbane, Queensland, with her parents. She attended a state school, and is undertaking a degree in education from a Queensland university. Her father has a secondary level of education and her mother vocational training. She works in junk mail delivery on a casual basis. She identifies as working class.

Rishika was born in Fiji, and is 64 years old. She is a widow and lives in western Sydney. She attended a Catholic school and completed secondary-level education. Her partner had completed secondary-level education and was a telecommunications technician. Both her parents are primary-level educated. She works full time as bank teller and identifies as working class.

Robert was born in Australia, and is 66 years old. He lives on the Central Coast of NSW with his partner and children. He attended a Catholic school, and completed vocational training. His partner completed secondary-level education, as did his parents. He is retired but used to work as a graphic designer. He identifies as working class.

Sean was born in Australia, and is 54 years old. He lives in a middle-class area north of Brisbane with his partner and children. He attended a state school and completed business studies at TAFE. His partner is also a graduate and both his parents have secondary-level education. He is currently semi-retired but worked as a manager and identifies as upper middle class.

Steven was born in Australia, and is 66 years old. He lives in Sydney's outer west with his partner. He attended a state school, and completed a teaching degree and a Master's degree in social sciences at a university in Western Australia. His partner has secondary-level education. His father has secondary-level education and his mother is primary-level educated. He is a retired high school principal and identifies as middle class, but lives in a working class area and says he has working class values.

Thomas was born in China (Hong Kong), and is 49 years old. He lives in southern Sydney with his partner and two children. He attended a state school and studied computer science at university. His partner has completed secondary education and both his parents completed tertiary education. He doesn't have a paid job at the moment but is undertaking home duties/childcare. He identifies as working class.

APPENDIX G

Australian scales

Indigenous items

Television: *Redfern Now*, Deborah Mailman
Sport: Cathy Freeman, Adam Goodes
Music: Dan Sultan, Gurrumul Yunupingu
Heritage: Tjapukai Aboriginal Cultural Park, Uluru-Kata Tjuta National Park
Visual arts: Tracey Moffatt, Albert Namatjira
Literature: Sally Morgan, Kim Scott

Other Australian items

Television: *Offspring, House Husbands, MasterChef Australia, The Block, Big Brother Australia, Old School, Hamish and Andy's Gap Year, Gardening Australia, Australian Story*, Eddie McGuire, Julia Zemiro, Dave Hughes, Carrie Bickmore, Jennifer Byrne, Paul Vautin, Amanda Keller, Ray Martin, Scott Cam
Sport: Don Bradman, Liz Ellis, Israel Folau, Lauren Jackson, Harry Kewell, Rod Laver, Greg Norman, Ian Thorpe
Music: Peter Sculthorpe, Jimmy Barnes, Kate Ceberano, AC/DC, Vince Jones, Kylie Minogue, Kasey Chambers, Gotye
Heritage: Museum of Sydney in New South Wales; Sovereign Hill in Ballarat, Victoria; National Museum of Australia in Canberra; Fremantle Prison in Western Australia; Cockatoo Island in Sydney, New South Wales; Immigration Museum in Melbourne, Victoria; Port Arthur Historic Site in Tasmania; Australian War Memorial in Canberra; Gallipoli, Turkey
Visual art: Sidney Nolan, Tom Roberts, Margaret Preston, Brett Whiteley, Imants Tillers, Ken Done, John Glover, Ben Quilty
Literature: Matthew Reilly, Kate Grenville, Tim Winton, Sara Douglass, Belinda Alexandra, Elizabeth Harrower, David Malouf, Bryce Courtenay

APPENDIX H
International scales

US items

Television: Mad Men, Homeland, The Big Bang Theory, Under the Dome
Sport: Michael Jordan, Michael Phelps, Serena Williams, Tiger Woods
Music: Kind of Blue by Miles Davis, Rhapsody in Blue by George Gershwin, 'Vogue' by Madonna, 'Jolene' by Dolly Parton
Heritage: Ellis Island in New York
Visual arts: Jackson Pollock, Jeff Koons
Literature: Amy Tan, Don DeLillo, Dave Eggers, Stephen King, Jodi Picoult

UK items

Television: QI, Midsomer Murders, Grand Designs, Top Gear
Sport: David Beckham
Music: The Piano by Michael Nyman, The Phantom of the Opera by Andrew Lloyd Webber, The Dark Side of the Moon by Pink Floyd, The Mikado by Gilbert and Sullivan
Heritage: Stonehenge
Visual arts: Francis Bacon, Tracey Emin
Literature: Ian Rankin, Jane Austen, Virginia Woolf

European items

Sport: Rafael Nadal
Music: The Four Seasons by Vivaldi, 'Nessun Dorma' by Puccini
Heritage: Acropolis of Athens, Greece; Vatican Museums in Rome, Italy
Visual arts: Vincent van Gogh, Caravaggio, Claude Monet, Rembrandt, Leonardo da Vinci

Asian items

Sport: Sachin Tendulkar, Yao Ming
Visual arts: Ai Weiwei
Heritage: the Forbidden City in Beijing, China; Angkor Wat, Cambodia; the Taj Mahal in Agra, India
Literature: Haruki Murakami

APPENDIX I

Key to Figure 7.2: Australian space of lifestyles (participation)

Yes Local hist soc(m)
Is a member of a local history/archaeology society/club

4–10 (book read Aus)
Has read 4 to 10 books by Australian authors in the past year

1 we/few t year Music
Has attended musicals between a few times a year and once a week

1 year+(book show)
Has listened to or watched a book show once or more in the past year

11+(book read Aus)
Has read 11 or more books by Australian authors in the past year

1 we/1 year Opera
Has attended opera between once a year and once a week in the past year

3/5 memb muse org
Is a member of 3 to 5 different types of heritage organisations

1 year Orche concert
Has attended orchestral concerts about once a year

1 year Musical
Has attended musicals about once a year

1 memb muse org
Is a member of one type of heritage organisation

1 month+(book show)
Has listened to or watched a book show about once a month or more frequently in the past year

1 we/few year Orch co
Has attended orchestral concerts between a few times a year and once a week

1 month+(book review)
Has read book reviews about once a month or more frequently in the past year

Visit reg art gall
Has visited a regional art gallery in the past year

1 month(intern herit)
Uses the Internet to find heritage information about once a month

1 week+(play org spo)
Plays organised sport once a week or more

Never (play org spo)
Never plays organised sport

yes nitv
Has watched programmes on NITV

NeverLive bands pub
Never attends live bands in pubs

5+ hour tv watch
Watches TV for 5 hours or more each day

Never(inter herita)
Never uses the Internet to find heritage information

−1 hour(listen music)
Listens to music less than 1 hour each day

0 ebook
Personally owns 0 ebooks

NeverRock gig
Never attends rock gigs

Never(online book)
Has not followed online discussions about books/authors in the past year

Never(book sto bro)
Has not visited a book store for browsing in the past year

3–5 hour tv watch
Watches TV for between 3 and 5 hours each day

NeverPop concert
Never attends pop concerts

No vis publ art disp
Has not visited a public art display or installation in the past year

No vis univ art gall
Has not visited a university art gallery in the past year

No vis mus cont art
Has not visited a museum of contemporary art in the past year

−50 books home
Has less than 50 books in the home

Never(book review)
Has not read book reviews in the past year

No vis arts fest
Has not visited an Australian or international arts festival or biennale in the past year

No vis sta art gall
Has not visited a State art gallery in the past year

Never(liter festival)
Has not attended a literary or writers festival in the past year

1 year+(book stor br)
Has visited a book store for browsing at least once in the past year

Never(event local bo)
Has not attended an event in a book store or similar venue in the past year

Never(book club)
Has not participated in a book club or reading group in the past year

No vis Na Ga Austral
Has not visited the National Gallery of Australia in the past year

No vis com art gall
Has not visited a commercial art gallery in the past year

Few ti year(ev loc b)
Has attended an event in a book store or similar venue a few times in the past year

2 memb muse org
Is a member of 2 different types of heritage organisations

1–3 hour tv watch
Watches TV for between 1 and 3 hours each day

1 month+(book club)
Has participated in a book club or reading group once a month or more frequently in the past year

1 week+(inter herita)
Uses the Internet to find heritage information at least once a week

201–500 book home
Has between 201 and 500 books in the home

1–3 hour(listen musi)
Listens to music for between 1 and 3 hours each day

Visit Na Ga Austral
Has visited the National Gallery of Australia in the past year

Visit State art gall
Has visited a State art gallery in the past year

501+ books home
Has over 500 books in the home

Visit publ art disp
Has visited a public art display or installation in the past year

1–3(book read Aus)
Has read 1 to 3 books by Australian authors in the past year

Visit com art gall
Has visited a commercial art gallery in the past year

1 month+(book stor b)
Has visited a book store for browsing once a month or more frequently in the past year

1 yearLive bands pub
Attends live bands in pubs about once a year

1 year(eve local boo)
Has attended an event in a book store or similar venue about once in the past year

1 yearPop concert
Attends pop concerts about once a year

–10 ebook
Personally owns fewer than 10 ebooks

Visit mus cont art
Has visited a museum of contemporary art in the past year

>51 ebook
Personally owns at least 51 ebooks

1 yearRock gig
Attends rock gigs about once a year

Few tim ye(play org sp)
Plays organised sport a few times a year

1 year+(liter festiv)
Has attended a literary or writers festival once a year or more frequently in the past year

10–50 ebook
Personally owns 10 to 50 ebooks

3–5 hour(listen musi)
Listens to music for between 3 and 5 hours each day

Visit arts fest
Has visited an Australian or international arts festival or biennale in the past 2 years

1 we/few yeLiv ba pu
Attends live bands in pubs a few times a year or more up to once a week

–1 hour tv watch
Watches TV for less than 1 hour each day

1 month+(online book)
Has followed online discussions about books/authors at least once a month in the past year

1 we/few yePop conce
Attends pop concerts a few times a year or more up to once a week

1 year+(online book)
Has followed online discussions about books/authors at least once in the past year

Visit univ art gall
Has visited a university art gallery in the past year

1 year+(book club)
Has participated in a book club or reading group at least once in the past year

1 we/fe yeaRock gig
Attends rock gigs a few times a year or more up to once a week

50–200 book home
Has 50 to 200 books in the home

No vis reg art gall
Has not visited a regional art gallery in the past year

NeverOpera
Never attends opera

No local hist soc(mh)
Is not a member of a local history/archaeology society/club

NeverOrches concert
Never attends orchestral concerts

1 year+(book review)
Has read book reviews once or more in the past year

Never(book show)
Has not listened to or watched a book show in the past year

0 memb muse org
Is not a member of any heritage organisations

No nitv
Has not watched programmes on NITV

1 month(play org spo)
Plays organised sport about once a month

0(book read Aus)
Has read 0 books by Australian authors in the past year

1 year+(inte herita)
Uses the Internet to find heritage information at least once a year

NeverMusical
Never attends musicals

1 year (play org spo)
Plays organised sport about once a year

5+ hour (listen music)
Listens to music 5 hours or more each day

REFERENCES

Adkins, L. (2003) 'Reflexivity: freedom or habit of gender?' *Theory, Culture & Society*, 20 (6): 21–42.

Adkins, L. and Skeggs, B. (eds) (2004) *Feminism After Bourdieu*, Oxford: Blackwell.

Ahearne, J. (2010) *Intellectuals, Culture and Public Policy in France: Approaches from the Left*, Liverpool: Liverpool University Press.

Ahearne, J. (2011) 'Designs on the popular: framings of general, universal and common culture in French educational policy', *International Journal of Cultural Policy*, 17 (4): 421–437.

Anderson, B. (2006) *Imagined Communities: Reflections on the Origin and Spread of Nationalism*, London: Verso.

Anderson, J. (ed.) (2011) *The Cambridge Companion to Australian Art*, Melbourne: Cambridge University Press.

Ang, I. and Noble, G. (2018) 'Making multiculture: Australia and the ambivalent politics of diversity', in D. Rowe, G. Turner and E. Waterton (eds) *Making Culture: Commercialisation, Transnationalism, and the State of 'Nationing' in Contemporary Australia*, London: Routledge, 140–153.

Ang, I., Rowe, D., Magee, L., Wong, A., Swist, T., Rouillard, D. and Pollio, A. (2016) *Mapping Culture: Venues and Infrastructure in the City of Sydney LGA*, an independent report to the City of Sydney Council.

Anonymous (1925, 23 December) 'Charivaria', *Punch*, 673.

Appadurai, A. (1996) *Modernity at Large: Cultural Dimensions of Globalization*, Minneapolis, MN: University of Minnesota Press.

Aries, E. and Seider, M. (2005) 'The interactive relationship between class identity and the college experience: the case of lower income students', *Qualitative Sociology*, 28 (4): 419–443.

Ariño, A. (2011) *Prácticas culturales en España: Desde los años sesenta hasta la actualidad*, Barcelona: Ariel.

Atkinson, W. (2016) 'The structure of literary taste: class, gender and reading in the UK', *Cultural Sociology*, 10 (2): 247–266.

Atkinson, W. (2017) *Class in the New Millennium: The Structure, Homologies and Experience of the British Social Space*, London: Routledge.

References

Attwood, B. and Markus, A. (2007) *The 1967 Referendum: Race, Power and the Australian Constitution*, Canberra: Aboriginal Studies Press.

Austin, J. L. (1962) *How to Do Things with Words*, Oxford: Oxford University Press.

Australia Council for the Arts (2017) *Connecting Australians: National Arts Participation Survey: June 2017*. Retrieved from www.australiacouncil.gov.au.

Australia for Everyone (2016) *Pop Go the Migrants*. Retrieved from www.australiaforeveryone.com.au.

Australian Bureau of Statistics (2006) 'Culture and leisure', in *Measuring Australia's Progress* (No. 1370.0), 56–59. Retrieved from www.ausstats.abs.gov.au.

Australian Bureau of Statistics (2016) *2014–15 National Aboriginal and Torres Strait Islander Social Survey (NATSISS): Household Survey Questionnaire* (No. 4714.0). Retrieved from www.ausstats.abs.gov.au.

Australian Bureau of Statistics (2017) *Schools, Australia: Highlights* (No. 4221.0). Retrieved from www.abs.gov.au.

Australian Bureau of Statistics (2019) *Regional Population Growth, Australia, 2017–18* (No. 3218.0). Retrieved from www.abs.gov.au.

Australian Council of Social Service (2015) *Inequality in Australia: A Nation Divided*. Retrieved from www.acoss.org.au.

Australian Sports Commission (2014) *Towards a Level Playing Field: Sport and Gender in Australian Media*. Retrieved from www.dca.org.au.

Ball, T. (2018, 12 April) 'Why does Indigenous success make some white Australians uncomfortable?' *ABC News*. Retrieved from www.abc.net.au/news.

Bamblett, L., Myers, F. and Rowse, T. (eds) (2019) *The Difference Identity Makes: Indigenous Cultural Capital in Australian Cultural Fields*, Canberra: Aboriginal Studies Press.

Barnwell, A. (2017) 'Convict shame to convict chic: intergenerational memory and family histories', *Memory Studies*, 12 (4): 398–411.

Barnwell, A. (2018) 'Hidden heirlooms: keeping family secrets across generations', *Journal of Sociology*, 54 (3): 446–460.

Baxter, J., Emmison, M., Western, J. and Western, M. (eds) (1991) *Class Analysis and Contemporary Australia*, Melbourne: Macmillan.

Beck, U. (2006) *The Cosmopolitan Vision*, Cambridge: Polity Press.

Behrendt, L., Larkin, S., Griew, R. and Kelly, P. (2012) *Review of Higher Education Access and Outcomes for Aboriginal and Torres Strait Islander People: Final Report*, Canberra: Australian Government.

Bell, P. and Bell, R. (eds) (1998) *Americanization and Australia*, Sydney: University of New South Wales Press.

Bellavance, G. (2008) 'Where's high? Who's low? What's new? Classification and stratification inside cultural "repertoire"', *Poetics*, 36 (2–3): 189–216.

Bellavance, G. (2016) 'The multiplicity of highbrow culture: taste boundaries among the new upper middle class', in L. Hanquinet and M. Savage (eds) *Routledge International Handbook of the Sociology of Art and Culture*, London: Routledge, 324–336.

Bennett, J. (2011) 'Architectures of participation: fame, television and web 2.0', in J. Bennett and N. Strange (eds) *Television as Digital Media*, Durham, NC: Duke University Press, 332–357.

Bennett, T. (2005) 'The historical universal: the role of cultural value in the historical sociology of Pierre Bourdieu', *British Journal of Sociology*, 56 (1): 141–164.

Bennett, T. (2010) 'Culture, power, knowledge: between Foucault and Bourdieu', in E. Silva and A. Warde (eds) *Cultural Analysis and Bourdieu's Legacy: Settling Accounts and Developing Alternatives*, London: Routledge, 102–116.

Bennett, T. (2011) 'Culture, class, necessity: a political critique of Bourdieu', *Poetics*, 39 (6): 530–546.
Bennett, T. (2015) 'Adjusting field theory: the dynamics of settler-colonial art fields', in L. Hanquinet and M. Savage (eds) *Routledge International Handbook of the Sociology of Art and Culture*, London: Routledge, 247–261.
Bennett, T. (2017) 'Capitalising culture: the political career of a governmental actor', in L. Adkins, C. Brosnan and S. Threadgold (eds) *Bourdieusian Prospects*, London: Routledge, 91–111.
Bennett, T. (2018) 'Beyond nation, beyond art? The "rules of art" in contemporary Australia', in D. Rowe, G. Turner and E. Waterton (eds) *Making Culture: Commercialisation, Transnationalism, and the State of 'Nationing' in Contemporary Australia*, London: Routledge, 28–39.
Bennett, T. and Gayo, M. (2016) 'For the love (or not) of art in Australia', in M. Quinn, D. Beech, M. Lehnert, C. Tulloch and S. Wilson (eds) *The Persistence of Taste: Art Museums and Everyday Life After Bourdieu*, London: Routledge, 153–173.
Bennett, T., Emmison, M. and Frow, J. (1999) *Accounting for Tastes: Australian Everyday Cultures*, Cambridge: Cambridge University Press.
Bennett, T., Savage, M., Silva, E., Warde, A., Gayo-Cal, M. and Wright, D. (2009) *Culture, Class, Distinction*, London: Routledge.
Bennett, T., Bustamante, M. and Frow, J. (2013) 'The Australian space of lifestyles in comparative perspective', *Journal of Sociology*, 49 (2–3): 224–255.
Bennett, T., Cameron, F., Dias, N., Dibley, B., Harrison, R., Jacknis, I. and McCarthy, C. (2017) *Collecting, Ordering, Governing: Anthropology, Museums, and Liberal Government*, Durham, NC: Duke University Press.
Bennett, T., Stevenson, D., Myers, F. and Winikoff, T. (eds) (2020) *The Australian Art Field: Practices, Policies, Institutions*, New York: Routledge.
Billig, M. (1995) *Banal Nationalism*, London: Sage.
Boschetti, A. (2006) 'Bourdieu's work on literature: contexts, stakes and perspectives', *Theory, Culture & Society*, 23 (6): 135–155.
Botshon, L. and Goldsmith, M. (eds) (2003) *Middlebrow Moderns: Popular American Women Writers of the 1920s*, Boston, MA: Northeastern University Press.
Bourdieu, P. (1977) *Outline of a Theory of Practice*, New York: Cambridge University Press.
Bourdieu, P. (1984) *Distinction: A Social Critique of the Judgement of Taste*, London: Routledge.
Bourdieu, P. (1988) 'Program for a sociology of sport', *Sociology of Sport Journal*, 5 (2): 153–161.
Bourdieu, P. (1990a) *In Other Words: Essay Towards a Reflexive Sociology*, Stanford, CA: Stanford University Press.
Bourdieu, P. (1990b) *Photography: A Middlebrow Art*, Stanford, CA: Stanford University Press.
Bourdieu, P. (1990c) *The Logic of Practice*, Stanford, CA: Stanford University Press.
Bourdieu, P. (1993) *The Field of Cultural Production: Essays on Art and Literature*, New York: Columbia University Press.
Bourdieu, P. (1994) *Language and Symbolic Power*, Cambridge: Polity Press.
Bourdieu, P. (1995) *The Rules of Art: Genesis and Structure of the Literary Field*, Stanford, CA: Stanford University Press.
Bourdieu, P. (1996a) 'On the family as a realized category', *Theory, Culture & Society*, 13 (3): 19–26.
Bourdieu, P. (1996b) *The State Nobility: Elite Schools in the Field of Power*, Cambridge: Polity Press.

Bourdieu, P. (1997) 'The forms of capital', in A. H. Halsey, H. Lauder, P. Brown and A. Sturt Wells (eds) *Education: Culture, Economy and Society*, Oxford: Oxford University Press, 46–58.

Bourdieu, P. (1998) *On Television and Journalism*, London: Pluto Press.

Bourdieu, P. (2000) *Pascalian Meditations*, Stanford, CA: Stanford University Press.

Bourdieu, P. (2001) *Masculine Domination*, Stanford, CA: Stanford University Press.

Bourdieu, P. (2002) 'Inequality at school as the key to cultural inequality', in J. Ahearne (ed.) *French Cultural Policy Debates: A Reader*, London and New York: Routledge, 62–69.

Bourdieu, P. (2010) *Distinction: A Social Critique of the Judgement of Taste*, Routledge Classics, London: Routledge.

Bourdieu, P. (2017) *Manet: A Symbolic Revolution*, Cambridge: Polity Press.

Bourdieu, P. and Darbel, A. (1991) *The Love of Art: European Art Museums and their Public*, Cambridge: Polity Press.

Bourdieu, P. and Passeron, J.-C. (1979) *The Inheritors: French Students and their Relation to Culture*, Chicago, IL: University of Chicago Press.

Bourdieu, P. and Passeron, J.-C. (1990) *Reproduction in Education, Society and Culture*, London: Sage.

Bourdieu, P. and Wacquant, L. J. D. (1992) *An Invitation to Reflexive Sociology*, Cambridge: Polity Press.

Bradley, H. (2014) 'Class descriptors or class relations? Thoughts towards a critique of Savage et al.', *Sociology*, 48 (3): 429–436.

Breen, M. (2006) *Rock Dogs: Politics and the Australian Music Industry*, Lanham, MD: University Press of America.

Brunt, R. (2017) 'Constructing "ordinary people" on British television: notes on the politics of representation', in R. Sanz Sabido (ed.) *Representing Communities: Discourse and Contexts*, London: Palgrave Macmillan, 217–235.

Bulbeck, C. (2004) 'The "white worrier" in South Australia: attitudes to multiculturalism, immigration and reconciliation', *Journal of Sociology*, 40 (4): 341–361.

Byrne, D. (2016) 'The need for a transnational approach to the material heritage of migration: the China–Australia corridor', *Journal of Social Archaeology*, 16 (3): 61–85.

Byrom, T. and Lightfoot, N. (2013) 'Interrupted trajectories: the impact of academic failure on the social mobility of working-class students', *British Journal of Sociology of Education*, 34 (5–6): 812–828.

Capuano, G. (2014) *The Story of Culturally Diverse Communities: Indians in Parramatta*. Retrieved from https://blog.id.com.au.

Carter, D. (2009) 'Publishing, patronage and cultural politics: institutional changes in the field of Australian literature from 1950', in P. Pierce (ed.) *The Cambridge History of Australian Literature*, Cambridge: Cambridge University Press, 360–390.

Carter, D. (2013) *Always Almost Modern: Australian Print Cultures and Modernity*, Melbourne: Australian Scholarly Publishing.

Carter, D. (2016a) 'The literary field and contemporary trade-book publishing in Australia: literary and genre fiction', *Media International Australia*, 158 (1): 48–57.

Carter, D. (2016b) 'Middlebrow book culture', in L. Hanquinet and M. Savage (eds) *Routledge International Handbook of the Sociology of Art and Culture*, London: Routledge, 351–366.

Carter, D. and Kelly, M. (2017) 'Australian stories: books and reading in the nation', in A. Mannion, M. Weber and K. Day (eds) *Publishing Means Business: Australian Perspectives*, Melbourne: Monash University Publishing, 147–181.

Carter, D. and Kelly, M. (2018) 'The book trade and the arts ecology: transnationalism and digitization in the Australian literary field', in D. Rowe, G. Turner and E. Waterton (eds)

Making Culture: Commercialisation, Transnationalism, and the State of 'Nationing' in Contemporary Australia, London: Routledge, 15–27.
Cashmore, E. (2004) *Beckham*, Cambridge: Polity Press.
Cater, N. (2013) *The Lucky Culture and the Rise of an Australian Ruling Class*, Sydney: HarperCollins.
Caust, J. (2017, 27 September) 'Does opera deserve its privileged status within arts funding?' *The Conversation*. Retrieved from https://theconversation.com.
Chattaraman, V. and Lennon, S. (2008) 'Ethnic identity, consumption of cultural apparel, and self-perceptions of ethnic consumers', *Journal of Fashion Marketing and Management*, 12 (4): 518–531.
Clark, A. (2017) 'The place of Anzac in Australian historical consciousness', *Australian Historical Studies*, 48 (1): 19–34.
Clark, A., Rees, A. and Simmonds, A. (eds) (2017) *Transnationalism, Nationalism and Australian History*, Singapore: Palgrave Macmillan.
Clark, T. J. (1984) *The Painting of Modern Life: Paris in the Art of Manet and His Followers*, Princeton, NJ: Princeton University Press.
Collins, J. (ed.) (2002) *High Pop: Making Culture into Popular Entertainment*, Oxford: Blackwell.
Collins, J. (2010) *Bring on the Books for Everybody: How Literary Culture Became Popular Culture*, Durham, NC: Duke University Press.
Collins, S. (2018, 20 January) 'Gurrumul film is raw beauty', *West Australian*. Retrieved from https://thewest.com.au.
Collins, T. (2006) *Rugby's Great Split: Class, Culture and the Origins of Rugby League Football*, London: Routledge.
Commonwealth of Australia (2006) *About Time! Women in Sport and Recreation in Australia*, Canberra: Senate Environment, Communications, Information Technology and the Arts References Committee.
Commonwealth of Australia (2013) *Creative Australia: National Cultural Policy*, Canberra: Australian Government.
Connell, R. W. and Irving, T. H. (1992) *Class Structure in Australian History: Poverty and Progress*, Melbourne: Longman Cheshire.
Convery, S. (2018, 15 November) 'Live music "crisis": report urges NSW to lift unnecessary restrictions on venues', *Guardian*. Retrieved from www.theguardian.com.
Cottingham, M. (2016) 'Theorizing emotional capital', *Theory and Society*, 45 (5): 451–470.
Coulangeon, P. (2017) 'Cultural openness as an emerging form of cultural capital in contemporary France', *Cultural Sociology*, 11 (2): 145–164.
Couldry, N. (2003) 'Media meta-capital: extending the range of Bourdieu's field theory', *Theory and Society*, 32 (5–6): 653–677.
Crouch, D. (2015) 'Affect, heritage, feeling', in E. Waterton and S. Watson (eds) *The Palgrave Handbook of Contemporary Heritage Research*, Basingstoke: Palgrave Macmillan, 177–190.
Cvetičanin, P. and Popescu, M. (2011) 'The art of making classes in Serbia: another particular case of the possible', *Poetics*, 39 (6): 444–468.
Daley, J., Duckett, S., Goss, P., Terrill, M., Wood, D., Wood, T. and Coates, B. (2019) *Commonwealth Orange Book 2018: Policy Priorities for the Federal Government*, Carlton: Grattan Institute.
Dar, Y. and Getz, S. (2007) 'Learning ability, socioeconomic status and student placement for undergraduate studies in Israel', *Higher Education*, 54 (1): 41–60.
Davidson, D. (2017, 24 February) 'Seven, Ten, Nine red ink the signal for television reform', *Australian*. Retrieved from www.theaustralian.com.au.

Davison, G. (1991) 'A brief history of the Australian heritage movement', in G. Davison and C. McCoville (eds) *A Heritage Handbook*, Sydney: Allen & Unwin, 14–27.

Davison, G. (2000) *The Use and Abuse of Australian History*, Sydney: Allen & Unwin.

Davison, G. (2013) 'My heritage trail', in A. Clark and P. Ashton (eds) *Australian History Now*, Sydney: NewSouth Publishing, 181–182.

Department of Communications and the Arts (1994) *Creative Nation: Commonwealth Cultural Policy*, Canberra.

Department of Communications and the Arts (2016) *National Opera Review*. Retrieved from www.arts.gov.au.

Desrosières, A. (1985) 'Histoire de formes: statistiques et sciences social avant 1940', *Revue française de sociologie*, 26 (2): 277–310.

Desrosières, A. (1998) *The Politics of Large Numbers: A History of Statistical Reasoning*, Cambridge, MA: Harvard University Press.

Di Maggio, P. (1982) 'Cultural capital and social success: the impact of status culture participation on the grades of high school students', *American Sociological Review*, 47 (2): 189–201.

Di Maggio, P. (1983) 'Cultural entrepreneurship in nineteenth-century Boston: the creation of an organizational base for high culture in America', in J. Storey (ed.) *Cultural Theory and Popular Culture: A Reader*, London: Prentice Hall, 488–508.

Dibley, B. and Gayo, M. (2018) 'Favourite sounds: the Australian music field', *Media International Australia*, 167 (1): 146–161.

Dibley, B. and Turner, G. (2018) 'Indigeneity, cosmopolitanism and the nation: the project of NITV', in D. Rowe, G. Turner and E. Waterton (eds) *Making Culture: Commercialisation, Transnationalism, and the State of 'Nationing' in Contemporary Australia*, London: Routledge, 129–139.

Dicks, B. (2015) 'Heritage and social class', in E. Waterton and S. Watson (eds) *The Palgrave Handbook of Contemporary Heritage Research*, Basingstoke: Palgrave Macmillan, 366–381.

Doane, R. (2009) 'Bourdieu, cultural intermediaries and *Good Housekeeeping*'s George Marek', *Journal of Consumer Culture*, 9 (2): 155–186.

Dolin, T., Jones, J. and Dowsett, P. (eds) (2017) *Required Reading: Literature in Australian Schools Since 1945*, Melbourne: Monash University Publishing.

Donnat, O. (2016) 'The rising power of screens: changing cultural practices in France, from 1973 to 2008', in L. Hanquinet and M. Savage (eds) *Routledge International Handbook of the Sociology of Art and Culture*, London: Routledge, 396–408.

Donoghue, J. and Tranter, B. (2018) *Exploring Australian National Identity: Heroes, Memory and Politics*, Bingley: Emerald Publishing.

Driessens, O. (2013) 'Celebrity capital: redefining celebrity using field theory', *Theory and Society*, 42 (5): 543–560.

Driscoll, B. (2014) *The New Literary Middlebrow: Tastemakers and Reading in the Twenty-First Century*, Basingstoke: Palgrave Macmillan.

Driscoll, B. (2017) 'Contemporary Australian literary culture', *Oxford Research Encyclopedia of Literature*. Retrieved from https://oxfordre.com/literature.

Driscoll, B., Fletcher, L., Wilkins, K. and Carter, D. (2018) 'The publishing ecosystems of contemporary Australian genre fiction', *Creative Industries Journal*, 11 (2): 203–221.

Dubois, V. (1999) *La politique culturelle: Genèse d'une catégorie d'intervention publique*, Paris: Éditions Belin.

Edensor, T. (2002) *National Identity, Popular Culture and Everyday Life*, Oxford: Berg.

Emontspool, J. and Woodward, I. (2018) *Cosmopolitanism, Markets, and Consumption: A Critical Global Perspective*, London: Palgrave Macmillan.

Evans, T. (2011) 'Secrets and lies: the radical potential of family history', *History Workshop Journal*, 71 (1): 49–73.

Fisher, L. (2016) *Aboriginal Art and Australian Society: Hope and Disenchantment*, London: Anthem Press.
Florida, R. (2003) *The Rise of the Creative Class: And How it's Transforming Work, Leisure, Community and Everyday Life*, North Melbourne: Pluto Press.
Foxtel (2017) *Gogglebox Australia: What TV Shows the Gogglebox Stars Really Love* (Season 6). Retrieved from www.foxtel.com.au.
Franklin, A. and Papastergiadis, N. (2017) 'Engaging with the anti-museum? Visitors to the Museum of Old and New Art', *Journal of Sociology*, 53 (3): 670–686.
Friedland, L., Shah, D. V., Lee, N.-J., Rademacher, M. A., Atkinson, L. and Hove, T. (2007) 'Capital, consumption, communication, and citizenship: the social positioning of taste and civic culture in the United States', *Annals*, 611 (1): 31–50.
Friedman, S. and Laurison, D. (2019) *The Class Ceiling: Why it Pays to be Privileged*, Bristol: Policy Press.
Frow, J., Emmison, M. and Turner, G. (1991) 'Youth attitudes to the arts', *Culture and Policy*, 2 (2–3): 77–110.
Fuller, D. and Rehberg Sedo, D. (2013) *Reading Beyond the Book: The Social Practices of Contemporary Literary Culture*, New York: Routledge.
Gale, T. and Parker, S. (2017) 'Retaining students in Australian higher education: cultural capital, field distinction', *European Educational Research Journal*, 16 (1): 80–96.
Galton, F. (1889) *Natural Inheritance*, London: Macmillan.
Gayo, M. (2016a) 'A critique of the omnivore: from the origin of the idea of omnivorousness to the Latin American experience', in L. Hanquinet and M. Savage (eds) *Routledge International Handbook of the Sociology of Art and Culture*, London: Routledge, 90–103.
Gayo, M. (2016b) 'Cultural capital reproduction in the UK', in D. Rowe and R. Dobson (eds) *The Occasional Papers, Institute for Culture and Society*, 7 (2).
Gayo, M. and Rowe, D. (2018) 'The Australian sport field: moving and watching', *Media International Australia*, 167 (1): 162–180.
Gayo, M., Teitelboim, B. and Méndez, M. L. (2009) 'Patrones culturales de uso del tiempo libre en Chile: una aproximación desde la teoría bourdieuana', *Universum*, 24 (2): 42–72.
Gayo, M., Teitelboim, B. and Méndez, M. L. (2013) 'Exclusividad y fragmentación: los perfiles culturales de la clase media en Chile', *Universum*, 28 (1): 97–128.
Gayo, M., Méndez, M. L. and Teitelboim, B. (2016) 'La terciarización en Chile: desigualdad cultural y estructura ocupacional', *Revista CEPAL*, 119 (Agosto): 187–207.
Gayo, M., Joye, D. and Lemel, Y. (2018) 'Testing the universalism of Bourdieu's homology: structuring patterns of lifestyle across 26 countries', *Center for Research in Economics and Statistics Working Papers*, 4.
Gibson, R., Ashton, P. and Gibson, C. (eds) (2015) *By-Roads and Hidden Treasures: Mapping Cultural Assets in Regional Australia*, Perth: University of Western Australia Press.
Gillett, S. and Freebody, C. (2014) '"I know that face": Murundak: Songs of Freedom and the Black Arm Band', *Cultural Studies Review*, 20 (2): 115–140.
Gleeson, B. (2005) 'Landscapes apart: museums and Australian suburbia', *Queensland Review*, 12 (1): 11–16.
Glevarec, H. and Pinet, M. (2009) 'La "tablature" des goûts musicaux: un modèle de structuration des préférences et des jugements', *Revue française de sociologie*, 3 (50): 599–640.
Glevarec, H. and Pinet, M. (2017) 'Is cultural eclecticism axiological and a new mark of distinction? Cultural diversification and social differentiation of tastes in France', *Cultural Sociology*, 11 (2): 188–216.
Goldthorpe, J. (1996) 'Class analysis and the reorientation of class theory: the case of persisting differentials in educational attainment', *British Journal of Sociology*, 47 (3): 481–505.

Goldthorpe, J. (2007) 'Cultural capital: some critical comments', *Sociologica*, 2: 1–23.
Goodman, J. E. and Silverstein, P. A. (eds) (2009) *Bourdieu in Algeria: Colonial Politics, Ethnographic Practices, Theoretical Developments*, Lincoln, NE, and London: University of Nebraska Press.
Gowricharn, R. (2017) 'Practices in taste maintenance: the case of Indian diaspora markets', *Journal of Consumer Culture*, 19 (3): 398–416.
Grant, S. (2002) *The Tears of Strangers: A Memoir*, Sydney: HarperCollins.
Griffiths, M. R. (2018) 'Indigenous literature in postwar Australia', *Oxford Research Encyclopedia of Literature*. Retrieved from http://literature.oxfordre.com.
Grishin, S. (2013) *Australian Art: A History*, Melbourne: Megunyah Press.
Griswold, W. (2008) *Regionalism and the Reading Class*, Chicago, IL: University of Chicago Press.
Guttmann, A. (2004) *From Ritual to Record: The Nature of Modern Sports*, New York: Columbia University Press.
Hage, G. (1998) *White Nation: Fantasies of White Supremacy in a Multicultural Society*, Annandale: Pluto Press.
Hallinan, C. and Hughson, J. (eds) (2010) *The Containment of Soccer in Australia: Fencing Off the World Game*, London: Routledge.
Hamlett, J., Bailey, A. R., Alexander, A. and Shaw, G. (2008) 'Ethnicity and consumption: South Asian food shopping patterns in Britain, 1947–75', *Journal of Consumer Culture*, 8 (1): 91–116.
Hammill, F. (2007) *Women, Celebrity and Literary Culture Between the Wars*, Austin, TX: University of Texas Press.
Hanquinet, L. (2016) 'Place and cultural capital: art museum visitors across space', *Museum & Society*, 14 (1): 86–81.
Hanquinet, L. and Savage, M. (2016) 'Contemporary challenges for the future sociology of art and culture: an introductory essay', in L. Hanquinet and M. Savage (eds) *Routledge International Handbook of the Sociology of Art and Culture*, London: Routledge, 1–18.
Hanquinet, L., Roose, H. and Savage, M. (2014) 'The eyes of the beholder: aesthetic preferences and the remaking of cultural capital', *Sociology*, 48 (1): 111–132.
Hargreaves, J. (1986) *Sport, Power and Culture: A Social and Historical Analysis of Popular Sports in Britain*, Cambridge: Polity Press.
Harrison, R., Thomas, K. and Cross, S. (2015) 'Negotiating cultural ambiguity: the role of markets and consumption in multiracial identity development', *Consumption Markets and Culture*, 18 (4): 301–332.
Harvey, D. (1989) *The Condition of Postmodernity: An Enquiry into the Origins of Cultural Change*, Oxford: Basil Blackwell.
Hayward, P. (ed.) (1992) *From Pop to Punk to Postmodernism: Popular Music and Australian Culture from the 1960s to the 1990s*, Sydney: Allen & Unwin.
Heenan, T. and Dunstan, D. (2013, 31 May) 'Eddie McGuire, Adam Goodes and "apes": a landmark moment in Australian race relations', *The Conversation*. Retrieved from http://theconversation.com.
Hesmondhalgh, D. (2006) 'Bourdieu, the media and cultural production', *Media, Culture and Society*, 28 (2): 211–231.
Hillis, J., Jarrett, K. and Petit, M. (2013) *Google and the Culture of Search*, New York: Routledge.
Ho, C. and Bonnor, C. (2018) *Institutionalised Separation: The Impact of Selective Schools Discussion Paper*, Sydney: Centre for Policy Development.
Hobsbawm, E. J. (1990) *Nations and Nationalism Since 1870: Programme, Myth, Reality*, Cambridge: Cambridge University Press.

Hochschild, A. (1979) 'Emotion work, feeling rules, and social structure', *American Journal of Sociology*, 85 (3): 551–575.

Holt, D. (1997) 'Distinctions in America? Recovering Bourdieu's theory of taste from its critics', *Poetics*, 25 (2–3): 93–120.

Homan, S. (2013) 'From Coombs to Crean: popular music and cultural policy in Australia', *International Journal of Cultural Policy*, 19 (3): 382–398.

Homan, S. (2018) 'The "music nation": popular music and Australian cultural policy', in D. Rowe, G. Turner and E. Waterton (eds) *Making Culture: Commercialisation, Transnationalism, and the State of 'Nationing' in Contemporary Australia*, London: Routledge, 51–63.

Hoorn, J. (2007) *Australian Pastoral: The Making of a White Landscape*, Fremantle: Fremantle Press.

Horowitz, N. (2011) *Art of the Deal: Contemporary Art in a Global Financial Market*, Princeton, NJ, and Oxford: Princeton University Press.

Høy-Petersen, N. and Woodward, I. (2018) 'Working with difference: cognitive schemas, ethical cosmopolitanism, and negotiating cultural diversity', *International Sociology*, 33 (6): 655–673.

Humble, N. (2001) *The Feminine Middlebrow Novel, 1920s to 1950s: Class, Domesticity, and Bohemianism*, Oxford: Oxford University Press.

Huppatz, K. (2009) 'Reworking Bourdieu's "capital": feminine and female capitals in the field of paid caring work', *Sociology*, 43 (1): 45–66.

Huppatz, K. (2012) *Gender Capital at Work: Intersections of Femininity, Masculinity, Class and Occupation*, Basingstoke: Palgrave Macmillan.

Huppatz, K. and Goodwin, S. (2013) 'Masculinised jobs, feminised jobs and men's "gender capital" experiences: understanding occupational segregation in Australia', *Journal of Sociology*, 49 (2–3): 291–308.

Hutchinson, G. (1995) *The Harlem Renaissance in Black and White*, Cambridge, MA: Belknap Press of Harvard University Press.

Iannelli, C. (2013) 'The role of the school curriculum in social mobility', *British Journal of Sociology of Education*, 34 (5–6): 907–928.

Indyk, I. (2015) 'The cult of the middlebrow', *Sydney Review of Books*. Retrieved from https://sydneyreviewofbooks.com.

Jacobs, J. (2001) 'Issues of judgement and value in television studies', *International Journal of Cultural Studies*, 4 (4): 428–447.

Jefferies, B. (2017) 'The market down under', in *Think Australian 2017*, Melbourne: Thorpe-Bowker, 4–6.

Jones, C. A. (2016) *The Global Work of Art: World's Fairs, Biennials, and the Aesthetics of Experience*, Chicago, IL, and London: University of Chicago Press.

Jupp, J. (1994) 'Identity', in R. Nile (ed.) *Australian Civilisation*, Melbourne: Oxford University Press, 78–94.

Kanai, A. (2015) 'Jennifer Lawrence, remixed: approaching celebrity through DIY digital culture', *Celebrity Studies*, 6 (3): 322–340.

Kassens-Noor, E. (2012) *Planning Olympic Legacies: Transport Dreams and Urban Realities*, London: Routledge.

Kelly, M. (2019) '"When we win, our culture wins": community ascription and autonomy at the Deadlys', in L. Bamblett, F. Myers and T. Rowse (eds) *The Difference Identity Makes: Indigenous Cultural Capital in Australian Cultural Fields*, Canberra: Aboriginal Studies Press, 38–61.

Kelly, M., Gayo, M. and Carter, D. (2018) 'Rare books? The divided field of reading and book culture in contemporary Australia', *Continuum: Journal of Media & Cultural Studies*, 32 (3): 282–295.

Kendall, G., Skrbis, Z. and Woodward, I. (2009) *The Sociology of Cosmopolitanism: Globalization, Identity, Culture and Government*, Basingstoke: Palgrave Macmillan.

Kennedy, W. and Hall, J. (2006) 'Diversity, ethnicity and consumption', *International Journal of Diversity in Organisations, Communities and Nations*, 5 (3): 71–80.

Khoo, S., McDonald, P., Giorgas, D. and Birrell, B. (2002) *Second Generation Australians*, Canberra: Department of Immigration, Multicultural and Indigenous Affairs.

Knijnik, J. (2018) 'Imagining a multicultural community in an everyday football carnival: chants, identity and social resistance on Western Sydney terraces', *International Review for the Sociology of Sport*, 53 (4): 471–489.

Kraaykamp, G., Tolsma, J. and Wolbers, M. H. J. (2013) 'Educational expansion and field of study: trends in the intergenerational transmission of educational inequality in the Netherlands', *British Journal of Sociology of Education*, 34 (5–6): 888–906.

Krause, M. (2018) 'How fields vary', *British Journal of Sociology*, 69 (1): 3–22.

Kuttainen, V., Liebich, S. and Galletly, S. (2018) *The Transported Imagination: Australian Interwar Magazines and the Geographical Imaginaries of Colonial Modernity*, Amherst, NY: Cambria.

Lahire, B. (2016) 'Cultural dissonances: the social in the singular', in L. Hanquinet and M. Savage (eds) *Routledge International Handbook of the Sociology of Art and Culture*, London: Routledge, 312–323.

Lamont, M. and Lareau, A. (1988) 'Cultural capital: allusions, gaps and glissandos in recent theoretical developments', *Sociological Theory*, 6 (2): 153–168.

Lareau, A. (1989) *Home Advantage: Social Class and Parental Intervention in Elementary Education*, New York: Falmer Press.

Lareau, A. (2005) *Unequal Childhoods: Class, Race and Family Life*, London: Routledge.

Le Roux, B. and Rouanet, H. (2004) *Geometric Data Analysis: From Correspondence Analysis to Structured Data Analysis*, Dordrecht: Kluwer.

Leavis, Q. D. (1932) *Fiction and the Reading Public*, London: Chatto & Windus.

Leftwich, A. (2004) 'Thinking politically', in A. Leftwich (ed.) *What is Politics?* Cambridge: Polity Press, 1–22.

Leigh, A. (2013) *Battlers and Billionaires: The Story of Inequality in Australia*, Collingwood: Redback.

Levine, L. (1988) *Highbrow/Lowbrow: The Emergence of Cultural Hierarchy in America*, Cambridge, MA: Harvard University Press.

Livingstone, S. and Local, C. (2017) 'Measurement matters: difficulties in defining and measuring children's television viewing in a changing media landscape', *Media International Australia*, 163 (1): 67–76.

Lizardo, O. (2004) 'The cognitive origins of Bourdieu's habitus', *Journal for the Theory of Social Behaviour*, 34 (4): 375–448.

Lo, L. (2009) 'The role of ethnicity in the geography of consumption', *Urban Geography*, 30 (4): 391–415.

Lotz, A. D. (2017) *Portals: A Treatise on Internet-Distributed Television*, Ann Arbor, MI: Maize Books.

Lotz, A. D. (2018) *We Now Disrupt this Broadcast: How Cable Transformed Television and the Internet Revolutionized It All*, Cambridge, MA: MIT Press.

Lowe, G. F. and Martin, F. (eds) (2014) *The Value of Public Service Media*, Gothenburg: Nordicom.

Luckman, S. (2015) 'Women's micro-entrepreneurial homeworking', *Australian Feminist Studies*, 30 (84): 146–160.

Lynes, R. (1949, February) 'Highbrow, lowbrow, middlebrow', *Harper's Magazine*, 19–28.

McGregor, R. (2011) *Indifferent Inclusion: Aboriginal People and the Australian Nation*, Canberra: Aboriginal Studies Press.

McKay, J. (2018) *Transnational Tourism Experiences at Gallipoli*, Singapore: Springer.

Mckenzie, L. (2016) 'Narrative, ethnography, and class inequality: taking Bourdieu into a British council estate', in C. Burke, J. Thatcher, N. Ingram and J. Abrahams (eds) *Bourdieu: The Next Generation*, London and New York: Routledge, 25–36.

McLean, I. (2016) *Rattling Spears: A History of Indigenous Australian Art*, London: Reaktion Books.

McLean, I. (2018) 'Modernism and the art of Namatjira', in E. Harney and R. B. Phillips (eds) *Mapping Modernisms: Art, Indigeneity, Colonialism*, Durham, NC: Duke University Press, 187–208.

Macquarie University (2015) 'The value of Aboriginal cultural heritage', Macquarie University Department of Economics. Retrieved from www.businessandeconomics.mq.edu.au.

Maddox, M. (2011) 'Are religious schools socially inclusive or exclusive? An Australian conundrum', *International Journal of Cultural Policy*, 12 (2): 170–186.

Mahar, C. (1990) 'Pierre Bourdieu: the intellectual project', in R. Harker, C. Mahar and C. Wilkes (eds) *An Introduction to the Work of Pierre Bourdieu*, Basingstoke: Macmillan, 26–57.

Marginson, S. (2011) 'Equity, status and freedom: a note on higher education', *Cambridge Journal of Education*, 41 (1): 23–36.

Marks, G. N. (2014) *Education, Social Background and Cognitive Ability: The Decline of the Social*, London and New York: Routledge.

Meade, A. (2017, 12 February) 'Australia's TV channels plunge into the battle for the water-cooler', *Guardian*. Retrieved from www.theguardian.com.

Mendelssohn, J., De Lorenzo, C., Inglis, A. and Speck, C. (2018) *Australian Art Exhibitions: Opening Our Eyes*, Melbourne: Thames & Hudson.

Merriman, N. (1991) *Beyond the Glass Case: The Past, the Heritage and the Public in Britain*, Leicester: Leicester University Press.

Meuleman, R. and Savage, M. (2013) 'A field analysis of cosmopolitan taste', *Cultural Sociology*, 7 (2): 230–256.

Meyrick, J., Phiddian, R. and Barnett, T. (2018) *What Matters: Talking Value in Australian Culture*, Clayton: Monash University Publishing.

Mittell, J. (2015) *Complex TV: The Poetics of Contemporary Television Storytelling*, New York: New York University Press.

Morgan, D. (2011) *Rethinking Family Practices*, Basingstoke: Palgrave Macmillan.

Morrone, A. (2006) *Guidelines for Measuring Cultural Participation*, Montreal: UNESCO Institute for Statistics.

Murray, S. (2018) *The Digital Literary Sphere: Reading, Writing, and Selling Books in the Internet Era*, Baltimore, MD: Johns Hopkins University Press.

Myers, F. (2002) *Painting Culture: The Making of an Aboriginal High Art*, Durham, NC: Duke University Press.

Nagel, A. (2012) *Medieval Modern: Art Out of Time*, London: Thames & Hudson.

Nash, R. (2005) 'The cognitive habitus: its place in a realist account of inequality/difference', *British Journal of Sociology of Education*, 26 (5): 599–612.

National Contemporary Music Plan: Music Australia and Australia's Contemporary Music Industry (2016) Erskineville, NSW: Music Australia. NSW. Retrieved from https://musicaustralia.org.au/wp-content/uploads/2016/03/National-Contemporary-Music-Plan-Sept-2016-final.pdf.

Neilsen Company (2017) *Culturally Diverse and Expanding Their Footprint: The Ethnic-Australian Consumer Report*. Retrieved from www.nielsen.com.

Newman, M. and Levine, E. (2012) *Legitimating Television: Media Convergence and Cultural Status*, New York: Routledge.

Noble, G. and Ang, I. (2018) 'Ethnicity and cultural consumption in Australia', *Continuum: Journal of Media & Cultural Studies*, 32 (3): 296–307.

Noble, J. and Davies, P. (2009) 'Cultural capital as an explanation of variation in participation in higher education', *British Journal of Sociology of Education*, 30 (5): 591–605.
OECD (2017) *Education at a Glance 2017: OECD Indicators*, Paris: OECD Publishing.
Ollivier, M. (2008) 'Modes of openness to cultural diversity', *Poetics*, 36 (2–3): 120–147.
Osborne, P. (2018) *The Postconceptual Condition: Critical Essays*, London: Verso.
Pavlidis, A. and Fullagar, S. (2014) *Sport, Gender and Power: The Rise of Roller Derby*, London: Routledge.
Peterson, R. and Kern, R. (1996) 'Changing highbrow taste: from snob to omnivore', *American Sociological Review*, 61 (1): 900–907.
Peterson, R. and Simkus, A. (1992) 'How musical tastes mark occupational status groups', in M. Lamont and M. Fournier (eds) *Cultivating Differences: Symbolic Boundaries and the Making of Inequality*, Chicago, IL and London: University of Chicago Press, 152–186.
Piketty, T. (2014) *Capital in the Twenty-First Century*, Cambridge, MA: Belknap Press of Harvard University Press.
Pollentier, C. (2012) 'Configuring middleness: Bourdieu, *l'art moyen* and the broadbrow', in E. Brown and M. Grover (eds) *Middlebrow Literary Cultures: The Battle of the Brows, 1920–1960*, Basingstoke: Palgrave Macmillan, 37–51.
Pollio, A., Ang, I., Rowe, D., Stevenson, D. and Magee, L. (2018) *Cultural Creation and Production in the Inner West LGA: A Case-Study Needs Analysis*, an independent report to Inner West Council.
Port Arthur Historic Site Management Authority (PAHSMA) (2018) *Annual Report 2017–2018*, Port Arthur, Tasmania. Retrieved from https://portarthur.org.au/wp-content/uploads/2018/11/PAHSMA_Ann_Report_2017-18-as-published.pdf.
Pratt, A. (2005) *Practising Reconciliation? The Politics of Reconciliation in the Australian Parliament, 1991–2000*, Canberra: Parliament of Australia Department of Parliamentary Services.
Pratt, M. L. (1992) *Imperial Eyes: Travel Writing and Transculturation*, London and New York: Routledge.
Prieur, A. and Savage, M. (2013) 'Emerging forms of cultural capital', *European Societies*, 15 (2): 246–267.
Prieur, A., Rosenlund, L. and Skjott-Larsen, J. (2008) 'Cultural capital today: a case study from Denmark', *Poetics*, 36 (1): 45–71.
Purhonen, S. and Wright, D. (2013) 'Methodological issues in national-comparative research on cultural tastes: the case of cultural capital in the UK and Finland', *Cultural Sociology*, 7 (2): 257–273.
Purhonen, S., Heikkilä, R., Hazir, I. K., Lauronen, T., Fernández Rodríguez, C. J. and Gronow, R. (2019) *Enter Culture, Exit Arts? The Transformation of Cultural Hierarchies in European Newspaper Culture Sections, 1960–2010*, London: Routledge.
Radway, J. (1997) *A Feeling for Books: The Book-Of-The-Month Club, Literary Taste, and Middle-Class Desire*, Chapel Hill, NC: University of North Carolina Press.
Razinsky, H. (2017) *Ambivalence: A Philosophical Exploration*, London: Rowman & Littlefield.
Reay, D. (1998) 'Cultural reproduction: mothers' involvement in their children's primary schooling', in M. Grenfell and D. James (eds) *Bourdieu and Education: Acts of Practical Theory*, London: Falmer Press, 55–71.
Reay, D. (2004) 'Gendering Bourdieu's concepts of capitals? Emotional capital, women and social class', in L. Adkins and B. Skeggs (eds) *Feminism After Bourdieu*, Oxford: Blackwell, 57–74.
Reay, D., Crozier, G. and Clayton, J. (2009) 'Strangers in paradise? Working class students in elite universities', *Sociology*, 43 (6): 1103–1121.
Riley, E. (2015, 10 March) 'Sexism in sport excludes women from one of Australia's most important cultural products', *Guardian*. Retrieved from www.theguardian.com.

Robbins, D. (2005) 'The origins, early development and status of Bourdieu's concept of "cultural capital"', *British Journal of Sociology*, 56 (1): 13–30.

Robin, L. (2013) 'Being first: why the Americans needed it, and why Royal National Park didn't stand in their way', *Australian Zoologist*, 36 (3): 321–331.

Rosenlund, L. (2017) 'Class conditions and urban differentiation: applying *Distinction*'s methodology to the community', *Bulletin de Méthodologie Sociologique*, 135 (1): 5–31.

Rowe, D. (2001) 'Globalisation, regionalisation and Australianisation in music: lessons from the parallel importing debate', in T. Bennett and D. Carter (eds) *Culture in Australia: Policies, Publics and Programs*, Melbourne: Cambridge University Press, 46–65.

Rowe, D. (2004) *Sport, Culture and the Media: The Unruly Trinity*, New York: McGraw-Hill Education.

Rowe, D. (2015) 'The mediated nation and the transnational football fan', *Soccer & Society*, 16 (5–6): 693–709.

Rowe, D. (2016) '"Great markers of culture": the Australian sport field', *Media International Australia*, 158 (1): 26–36.

Rowe, D. (2018) 'The sport field in Australia: the market, the state, the nation and the world beyond in Pierre Bourdieu's favourite game', in D. Rowe, G. Turner and E. Waterton (eds) *Making Culture: Commercialisation, Transnationalism, and the State of 'Nationing' in Contemporary Australia*, London: Routledge, 87–100.

Rowe, D. and Lynch, R. (2012) 'Work and play in the city: some reflections on the nighttime leisure economy of Sydney', *Annals of Leisure Research*, 15 (2): 132–147.

Rowe, D., Turner, G. and Waterton, E. (eds) (2018) *Making Culture: Commercialisation, Transnationalism, and the State of 'Nationing' in Contemporary Australia*, London: Routledge.

Rowse, T. (2010) 'Re-figuring "Indigenous culture"', in J. Altman and M. Hinkson (eds) *Culture Crisis: Anthropology and Politics in Aboriginal Australia*, Sydney: University of New South Wales Press, 153–178.

Rowse, T. (2017) *Indigenous and Other Australians Since 1901*, Sydney: New South Books.

Rowse, T. and Pertierra, A. C. (2019) 'From white nation to white caution: non-Indigenous reflections on Indigenous difference', *Journal of Australian Studies*, 43 (3): 283–298.

Roy Morgan (2017, 28 September) *Netflix Hits New High in Australia: 7.6 Million*. Retrieved from www.roymorgan.com.

Rubin, J. S. (1992) *The Making of Middlebrow Culture*, Chapel Hill, NC: University of North Carolina Press.

Savage, M. (2014) 'Picketty's challenge for sociology', *British Journal of Sociology*, 65 (4): 591–606.

Savage, M. (2015) *Social Class in the 21st Century*, London: Pelican.

Savage, M. and Gayo, M. (2011) 'Unravelling the omnivore: a field analysis of contemporary musical taste', *Poetics*, 39 (5): 337–357.

Savage, M., Warde, A. and Ward, K. (2002) *Urban Sociology, Capitalism and Modernity*, Basingstoke: Palgrave Macmillan.

Savage, M., Longhurst, B. and Bagnall, G. (2005) *Globalization and Belonging*, London: Sage.

Savage, M., Wright, D. and Gayo-Cal, M. (2010) 'Cosmopolitan nationalism and the cultural reach of the white British', *Nations and Nationalism*, 16 (4): 598–615.

Savage, M., Devine, F., Cunningham, N., Taylor, M., Li, Y., Hjellbrekke, J., Le Roux, B., Friedman, S. and Miles, A. (2013) 'A new model of social class? Findings from the BBC's Great British Class Survey experiment', *Sociology*, 47 (2): 219–250.

Savage, M., Devine, F., Cunningham, N., Friedman, S., Laurison, D., Miles, A., Snee, H. and Taylor, M. (2014) 'On social class, anno 2014', *Sociology*, 48 (3): 1–20.

Savage, M., Hanquinet, L., Cunningham, N. and Hjellbrekke, J. (2018) 'Emerging cultural capital in the city: profiling London and Brussels', *International Journal of Urban and Regional Research*, 42 (1): 138–149.

Sayer, A. (2005) *The Moral Significance of Class*, Cambridge: Cambridge University Press.

Scherger, S. and Savage, M. (2010) 'Cultural transmission, educational attainment and social mobility', *Sociological Review*, 58 (3): 406–428.

Sheil, C. and Stilwell, F. (2016) *The Wealth of the Nation: Current Data on the Distribution of Wealth in Australia*, University of Sydney: Evatt Foundation.

Sheppard, J. and Biddle, N. (2015a) 'Social class in Australia: beyond the "working" and "middle" classes', *ANUpoll*: Report no. 19.

Sheppard, J. and Biddle, N. (2015b, 28 October) 'Is Australian as egalitarian as we think it is?' *The Conversation*. Retrieved from https://theconversation.com/au.

Shoemaker, A. (2004) *Black Words, White Page: Aboriginal Literature 1929–1988*, Canberra: ANU E Press.

Silva, E. (2005) 'Gender, home and family in cultural capital theory', *British Journal of Sociology*, 51 (1): 83–103.

Silva, E. (2015) 'Class in contemporary Britain: comparing the Cultural Capital and Social Exclusion (CCSE) project and the Great British Class Survey (GBCS)', *Sociological Review*, 63 (2): 373–392.

Silva, E. (2017) 'Objects and materials: with, against and beyond Bourdieu', in L. Adkins, C. Brosnan and S. Threadgold (eds) *Bourdieusian Prospects*, London: Routledge, 112–131.

Skeggs, B. (2015) 'Introduction: stratification or exploitation, domination, dispossession and devaluation?' *Sociological Review*, 63 (2): 205–222.

Skinner, G. (2015) *Peter Sculthorpe: The Making of an Australian Composer*, Sydney: University of New South Wales Press.

Smith, L. (2000) 'Doing archaeology: cultural heritage management and its role in identifying the link between archaeological practice and theory', *International Journal of Heritage Studies*, 6 (4): 309–316.

Smith, L. (2006) *Uses of Heritage*, London: Routledge.

Soroka, S., Andrew, B., Aalberg, T., Iyengar, S., Curran, J., Coen, S., Hayashi, K., Jones, P., Mazzoleni, G., Woong Rhee, J., Rowe, D. and Tiffen, R. (2013) 'Auntie knows best? Public broadcasters and current affairs knowledge', *British Journal of Political Science*, 43 (4): 719–739.

Sport Australia (2018a) *What is Sport Australia*. Retrieved from www.sportaus.gov.au/sportaus/about.

Sport Australia (2018b) *Recognition of National Sporting Organisations*. Retrieved from www.sportaus.gov.au/recognition_of_national_sporting_organisations.

Stallabrass, J. (2004) *Art Incorporated: The Story of Contemporary Art*, Oxford: Oxford University Press.

Steinmetz, G. (2007) *The Devil's Handwriting: Precoloniality and the German Colonial State in Qingdao, Samoa, and Southwest Africa*, Chicago, IL: University of Chicago Press.

Stevenson, D. (2017) *Cities of Culture: A Global Perspective*, London: Routledge.

Stevenson, D. (2020) 'The unfashionable cultural worker: considering the demography and practice of artists in Greater Western Sydney', *International Journal of Cultural Policy*, 26 (1): 61–80.

Stevenson, D. and Magee, L. (2017) 'Art and space: creative infrastructure and cultural capital in Sydney, Australia', *Journal of Sociology*, 53 (4): 839–861.

Stevenson, D., Rowe, D., Caust, J. and Cmielewski, C. (2017) *Recalibrating Culture: Production, Consumption, Policy*, Sydney: Western Sydney University.

Stewart, S. (2010) *Culture and the Middle Classes*, London: Routledge.

Stewart, S. (2013) *A Sociology of Culture, Taste and Value*, Basingstoke: Palgrave Macmillan.
Stratton, J. (2007) *Australian Rock: Essays on Popular Music*, Perth: API Network Books.
Sullivan, A. (2001) 'Cultural capital and educational attainment', *Sociology*, 35 (4): 893–912.
Sygall, D. (2015, 30 July) 'Why booing Sydney Swans star Adam Goodes is racist', *Age*. Retrieved from www.theage.com.au.
Tabar, P., Noble, G. and Poynting, S. (2010) *On Being Lebanese: Identity, Racism and the Ethnic Field*, Beirut: Lebanese American University Press.
Taylor, J. (2009) 'Indigenous demography and public policy in Australia: population or peoples?' *Journal of Population Research*, 26 (2): 115–130.
Tenplay (2018) *The Delpechitra Family*. Retrieved from https://tenplay.com.au.
Terry, P. (2018, 26 March) 'The day Australian cricket lost its integrity and a country reacted with shock and anger', *The Conversation*. Retrieved from https://theconversation.com.
Thévenot, L. (1990) 'La politique des statistiques: les origins sociales des enquêtes de mobilité sociale', *Annales: Histoire, Sciences Sociales*, 45 (6): 1275–1300.
Thomas, N. (1999) *Possessions: Indigenous Art/Colonial Culture*, London: Thames & Hudson.
Thompson, J. B. (2012) *Merchants of Culture: The Publishing Business in the Twenty-First Century*, New York: Plume.
Thomsen, S. (2018, 27 March) 'The late Aboriginal artist Gurrumul's final album is coming and the first track is mind blowingly brilliant', *Business Insider Australia*.
Thornley, D. (2015) 'Mobilising Māori identity: cultural capital and expatriate "portable personhood"', *Palgrave Communications*, 1: 15008.
Throsby, D., Zwar, J. and Morgan, C. (2017) *Australian Book Readers: Survey Method and Results*, Sydney: Macquarie University.
Trading Economics (2019) *Australia: Urban Population (% of Total)*. Retrieved from https://tradingeconomics.com.
Tramonte, L. and Willms, J. D. (2010) 'Cultural capital and its effects on education outcomes', *Economics of Education Review*, 29 (2): 200–213.
Tranter, B. and Donoghue, J. (2003) 'Convict ancestry: a neglected aspect of Australian identity', *Nations and Nationalism*, 9 (4): 555–577.
Trienekens, S. (2002) '"Colourful" distinction: the role of ethnicity and ethnic orientation in cultural consumption', *Poetics*, 30 (4): 281–298.
Turner, A. (2017, 29 March) 'Decline in broadcast TV viewing accelerates as Aussies tune out', *Sydney Morning Herald*. Retrieved from www.smh.com.au.
Turner, B. and Edmunds, J. (2002) 'The distaste of taste: Bourdieu, cultural capital and the Australian postwar elite', *Journal of Consumer Culture*, 2 (2): 219–240.
Turner, G. (1992) 'Australian popular music and its contexts', in P. Hayward (ed.) *From Punk Rock to Postmodernism: Popular Music and Australian Culture from the 1960s to the 1990s*, Sydney: Allen & Unwin, 11–24.
Turner, G. (2005) *Ending the Affair: The Decline of Television Current Affairs in Australia*, Sydney: University of New South Wales Press.
Turner, G. (2006) 'The mass production of celebrity: celetoids, reality TV and the "demotic turn"', *International Journal of Cultural Studies*, 9 (2): 153–166.
Turner, G. (2018) 'Netflix and the reconfiguration of the Australian television market', *Media Industries*, 5 (2).
UNESCO (2009) *The 2009 UNESCO Framework for Cultural Statistics*, Montreal: UNESCO Institute for Statistics.
Valentish, J., Stafford, A., Jolly, N., Welsh, C. and Hennessy, K. (2018, 27 December) 'From Camp Cope to Gurrumul Yunupingu: the best Australian albums of 2018', *Guardian*. Retrieved from www.theguardian.com/au.

Vallianatos, H. and Raine, K. (2008) 'Consuming food and constructing identities among Arabic and South Asian immigrant women', *Food, Culture & Society*, 11 (3): 355–373.

Van den Bosch, A. (2005) *The Australian Art World: Aesthetics in a Global Market*, Sydney: Allen & Unwin.

Visweswaran, K. (2010) *Un/common Cultures: Racism and the Rearticulation of Cultural Difference*, Durham, NC: Duke University Press.

Wakeling, P. and Savage, M. (2015) 'Entry to elite positions and the stratification of higher education in Britain', *Sociological Review*, 63 (2): 290–320.

Walker, T., Baffour, B., Dinsdale, S. and Byrne, S. (2016) *Australian Cultural Fields Survey 2015: Technical Report*, Brisbane: Institute for Social Science Research, University of Queensland.

Walter, M. (2012) 'Keeping our distance: non-Indigenous/Aboriginal relations in Australian society', in E. Pietsch and H. Aarons (eds) *Australia: Identity, Fear and Governance in the 21st Century*, Canberra: ANU E Press, 15–31.

Walter, M. (2016) 'Data politics and indigenous representation in Australian statistics', in T. Kukutai and J. Naylor (eds) *Indigenous Data Sovereignty: Toward an Agenda*, Canberra: Centre for Aboriginal Economic Policy Research, 79–98.

Ward, T. (2010) *Sport in Australian National Identity: Kicking Goals*, London: Routledge.

Warren, J., with Harper, A. and Whittington, J. (2002) *Sheilas, Wogs & Poofters: An Incomplete Biography of Johnny Warren and Soccer in Australia*, Sydney: Random House.

Waterton, E. (2018) 'A history of heritage policy in Australia', in D. Rowe, G. Turner and E. Waterton (eds) *Making Culture: Commercialisation, Transnationalism, and the State of 'Nationing' in Contemporary Australia*, London: Routledge, 75–86.

Waterton, E. and Dittmer, J. (2016) 'Transnational war memories in Australia's heritage field', *Media International Australia*, 158 (1): 58–68.

Waterton, E. and Gayo, M. (2018) 'For all Australians? An analysis of the heritage field', *Continuum: Journal of Media & Cultural Studies*, 32 (3): 269–281.

Watkins, M. (2017) 'We are all Asian here: multiculturalism, selective schooling and responses to Asian success', *Journal of Ethnic and Migration Studies*, 43 (14): 2300–2315.

Weber, M. (2018) *Literary Festivals and Contemporary Book Culture*, London: Palgrave Macmillan.

Wenner, L. (ed.) (1998) *MediaSport*, London: Routledge.

Wertsch, J. (2008) 'Blank spots in collective memory: a case study of Russia' *Annals of the American Academy of Political and Social Science*, 617 (1): 58–71.

Whannel, G. (2001) *Media Sport Stars: Masculinities and Moralities*, London: Routledge.

Woodward, I. and Emmison, M. (2015) 'The intellectual reception of Bourdieu in Australian social sciences and humanities', in P. Coulangeon and J. Duval (eds) *The Routledge Companion to Bourdieu's 'Distinction'*, Abingdon: Routledge, 43–60.

Woolf, V. (1942) 'Middlebrow', in *The Death of the Moth and Other Essays*, London: Hogarth Press, 176–186.

Wright, D. (2006) 'Cultural capital and the literary field', *Cultural Trends*, 15 (2–3): 123–139.

Wright, E. O. (1997) *Class Counts: Comparative Studies in Class Analysis*, Cambridge and Paris: Cambridge University Press/Éditions de la Maison des Sciences de l'Homme.

Xu, D. (2018) *Indigenous Cultural Capital: Postcolonial Narratives in Australian Children's Literature*, Oxford: Peter Lang.

Zwar, J. (2016) *Disruption and Innovation in the Australian Book Industry: Case Studies of Trade and Education Publishers*, Sydney: Macquarie University.

INDEX

Page numbers in **bold** denote tables, those in *italics* denote figures.

ABC (Australian Broadcasting Corporation) 4, 84, 97, 125, 126, 147, 148, 170
Aboriginal art 15, 16, 17, 18, 25, 27–29, 31n10, 171, 229, 257, 323, 327, 328
Aboriginal culture *see* Indigenous culture
Aboriginal deep time 242
Aboriginal heritage 68, 69, 71, 72, 73, 74, 78–79, 124, 125, 126, 140, 170, 172, 230, 231, 308, 323
Aboriginal and Torres Strait Islander peoples *see* Indigenous Australians
abstract art 18, 19, 25, 26, 27, 28, 31n10, 31, 135, 140, 170, 178, 258
AC/DC 52, 54, 57, 174
acculturation 248, 249, 256, 260, 261, 263
Acropolis (Athens) 71
actor-network theory 87
Adelaide Writers Week 34
Adkins, Lisa 300
affluent class: established 163; emergent 164
AFL *see* Australian Rules football
age 5, 119, 120, 121, 127, 145, 149, 150, 165, 166, 180, 185, 332, 333; and art tastes and practices 15, 20, 23; and book reading and book culture *40*, 41, 48n5; and heritage tastes and practices 71, 73, 74, 81; intermediate workers/class **152**, 152; and middle space of lifestyles 172, 182; and musical tastes and practices 54, 55, 56, 57, 58, 60, 63, 121, 125, 285; professional/managerial class 150; and sport tastes and practices 105, *106*, 107, 115; and Sydney cultural participation 215–216; and television tastes and practices 83, 89, 90, 91, 92, 94, 95, 97, 98, 121, 285; and tertiary education *19*, 194

agency 87; normative orientation as intrinsic to 324; and structure 294
Ai Weiwei 17, 19, 20, 31n9, 172, 174, 258
Alexandra, Belinda 36, 235
alternative high cultural orientations (AHCO) 144, **155**, 155, 156, **160**, 163, 175
alternative music 54, 57, 59, 60, 64n8, 125, 135, 140, 174, 233
ambivalence, cultural/political 266, 293, 297, 300, 302–303, 304–305, 309
Americanisation 305–306
Ancestry.com 76
AncestryDNA 76
Anderson, Benedict 299
Angkor Wat (Cambodia) 71, 75
ANUPoll 50, 51, 145, 148, 163–164, 166
Anzac Day 80, 81
Anzac spirit or Anzac legend 69, 79, 80–81, 82n3
Appadurai, Arjun 248, 259
Apple 51; Apple TV 89, 96
appreciation and habitus 265–266, 294
archaeological sites 68, 72, 74, 124, **230**
archaeology societies 69

art fairs 30
art field 12, 14–31, 120, 178, 209;
  contemporary dynamics of 15–17; non-recognition of items in 140, **142**; tastes and practices 18–31, 120–121, 123, 124, 129, **130**, **131**, 132, 135, *218*, 219, 268, 269, 282; and age 15, 20, 21, 23; and educational level 15, 20, 21, **22**, 23, 24, 26, 30–31, 229–230; and ethnicity 256–258; and family background 15, 24, 272–275; and gender 15, 20–21, 271; genre preferences 24–30, 125, 127, 140, 170, 171, 229–230; Indigenous Australians 229–230; and Internet use 18, 20, 126, 129, 134, 139; middle space of 170, 171, 172, 173, 174, 175; and occupational class 12, 15, 20, 21, **22**, 23, 26, 29, 30–31, 149; and place of residence 20; social space of 15, 20–23; space of 18–20, *19*; Sydney 211, **212**, 214, 215, *218*, 219, 220, 222; *see also names of individual artists and genres*
art galleries 15, 16, 19, 29, 208, 210
Art Gallery of New South Wales 16
art gallery visits 18, 19, 20, 23–24, 26, 123, 129, 132, 134, 140, 149, 172, 177, 190, 211, 215, 219, 230, 258, 271, 272, 273, 274, 285, 286
arts television 91, 92, 125, 126, 142, 149
aspirational middle cultural orientations (AMCO) 144, **155**, 155, 156, **160**, 163, 174, 182
assimilation 4, 29
association football *see* soccer
Atkinson, Will 180, 294–295
Atwood, Margaret 36, 39, 135, 174
Austen, Jane 36, 39, 45, 140, 172, 174
Austin, J.L. 190
Australia Council for the Arts 4, 11, 16, 34, 52
Australia Day 235, 242
Australia ICOMOS Charter for Places of Cultural Significance see Burra Charter
Australia and New Zealand Standard Classification of Occupations (ANZSCO) 165–166, 349, 351
The Australian (newspaper) 148
Australian Bureau of Statistics (ABS) 219, 225, 256, 349
Australian Centre for the Moving Image, Melbourne 16
Australian Council of Social Service 167
Australian Cultural Fields (ACF) project 2–3, 4–5, 11; Australian scales 362; household interviewees 352–360; international scales 362–363; methods used in analysing survey data 347–348; questionnaire design and survey methods 338–339; methodological and contextual foci 6–8; occupational class model with examples of occupations 349, **350**, 351; survey questions **340–346**
Australian Everyday Cultures (AEC) project 6, 10n9, 165
Australian Labor Party (ALP) *see* Labor party/government
Australian Research Council 241
Australian Rules football (AFL) 103, 107, 125, 135, 140, **238**, 239
Australian Sports Commission *see* Sport Australia
Australian Story (TV programme) 88, 92, 93, 94, 140, 173
Australian Survey of Social Attitudes (AuSSA) 324
Australian War Memorial 69, 71, 80, 133, 313–315, *314*
Australian World Orchestra 52, 64n4
Australianness 100, 108, 298–299, 306
Australia's Got Talent (TV programme) 88
authorised judgements, self-positioning in a field of 318–320
authors/author preferences 36, 39, 44, 172, 176, 234–235; *see also names of individual authors*
autonomy 318, 319, 322

Backyard Blitz (TV programme) 89
Bacon, Francis 18, 19, 20, 172, **229**
Ball, Timmah 224, 225
Barnes, Jimmy 43, 54, 57
basketball 103, 104, 107, 108, 125, **238**, 239
Battlers and Billionaires (Leigh) 148
Baxter, Janeen 148
BBC (British Broadcasting Corporation) 148, 164
Beck, Ulrich 261
Beckham, David 104, 111, 114
Behrendt, Larissa 242, 244
Bellavance, Guy 169
belonging 6, 266, 280, 284–291, 300, 329; and class 285–286; community 286, 289, 291; and family 286–288, 289, 291; national 227, 287–289, 304; and residential place 289; and transnationalism 290–291
Bennett, Tony 6, 148, 249, 252, 270, 305, 311, 322, 328
Bickmore, Carrie 88, 92, 94, 237

Biddle, Nicholas 50, 51, 148, 163–164
The Big Bang Theory (TV programme) 88, 94, 95, 135, 237
Big Brother Australia (TV programme) 88, 92, 135, 174
biographies 38, **42**, 125, 126, 171
BitTorrent 89
The Black Arm Band 52–53
The Block (TV programme) 88, 89, 92, 93
Blue Poles (Pollock) 17, 26, 27, 31n3
Bolt, Usain 104, 107, 114
Bonnor, Chris 203
The Book Club (TV programme) 88
book clubs/reading groups 32, 35, 39, 41, 43, 48n5, 124, 129, 134, 176
book ownership 32, 35, 38–39, 123, 129, 172
book reading and book culture 12, 32, 36–48, 123–124, 129, **130**, **131**, 134, 135, 139, 140, *218*, 219, 276, 277, 282; and age *40*, 41, 48n5; author preferences 36, 39, 44, 172; cultural capital 39; and educational level 36, *40*, 41, 46, 47, 235; and gender *40*, 40, 48n5, 234–235; genre preferences 38, 39, 40–41, **42**, 44, 47, 125, 126, 140, 170, 171, 172, 234, 235; Indigenous Australians 234–236; middle space of 170, 171, 172, 173, 174, 175; non-fiction 39, 40, 41; and occupational class *40*, 41, **42**, 46, 47, 48n5, 149; reading experiences and relation to 41–47; sentimental canon 45; social space of *40*, 40–41; space of 37–39, *38*; Sydney 211, **212**, 215, 217, 218, 219, 220, 222; *see also* literary field; *and names of individual authors and genres*
book reviews 39, 123, 134, 234
Book-of-the Month Club 176
bookstore browsing 32, 35, 38, 39, 129, 139, 172, 234
Bourdieu, Pierre 1–2, 10n2, 12, 64, 87, 108, 111, 118, 148, 161, 169, 173, 210, 250, 329n1; art 14–15, 30, 31; cultural capital 7, 165, 166, 185–186, 190–191, 208, 209, 334; education 188, 189, 194–195, 200; family 270, 333; fields of power 10n1, 11; habitus 265–266, 293, 294, 299, 300; institutionalised cultural capital 190–191; *la culture moyenne* concept 170, 178–182; literary field 32, 33, 34, 42; music 49, 63; sport 100, 101, 109; symbolic capital 241; symbolic power 295; television 85–86; *Distinction* 3, 6, 9, 49, 50, 63, 100, 117, 119, 177, 178, 189, 293, 311, 330, 337; *The*
Inheritors 188, 200; *Language and Symbolic Power* 190; *The Love of Art* 14, 31; *Photography: A Middlebrow Art* 178; *Reproduction in Education, Society and Culture* 188, 195, 200; *The State Nobility* 188, 200, 207
bourgeoisie 165, 177; *see also* petite bourgeoisie
Bradley, Harriet 164
Bradley Review 191, 194, 196
Bradman, Don 103, 316
Brandis, George 12, 52
Breaking Bad (TV programme) 86
The Bridge (TV programme) 86
Britain *see* United Kingdom (UK)
broadcasting 11; public service 84, 85, 86, 87; *see also* radio; television
*also*built environment 208, 209, 219–220
Bulbeck, Chilla 325
Burra Charter 67, 68, 82n2
Byblos (Lebanon) 71, 258
Byrne, Jennifer 88, 92, 93, 135, **243**

Cam, Scott 89, 92, 94, 147
Canada 166
capital 118, 119, 170, 185, 299, 337; celebrity 86; composition 177, 180, 182; educational 186; emotional 268, 270; ethnographic 245; gender/ed 270; human 336; inherited 148, 148; meta-capital 86; social 1, 7, 102, 118, 148, 164, 185, 186, 270; symbolic 34, 35, 241; *see also* cultural capital; economic capital
capital logics 332–334
Capital in the Twenty-First Century (Piketty) 148
Caravaggio, Michelangelo Mersi da 17, 18, 19, 20, 172, 174, 229, 258
Carter, David 176, 181
Cashmore, Ellis 111
Cater, Nick 148
Catholic schools 202
Ceberano, Kate 53, 54, 234
celebrity capital 86
Chambers, Kasey 53, 54, 57, 234
childhood cultural experiences 271, 272–275, 278
Chinese Australians 4, 5, 7, 187, 222, 226, 227, **228**, 248, 251, **254**, 255, 306–307; art field tastes and practices 257, 258; intra-community cultural activities 259; and Sachin Tendulkar 260
Christie, Agatha 44
church 138, 286, 289, 291; *see also* religion

citizenship 78, 108, 289, 298, 300, 301
civic dimension of consumption 322, 323–324
Clark, Anna 81
Clark, T.J. 14
class 2, 3, 7, 14, 76, 77, 109, 111, 115, 119, 121, 127, 145, 147–168, 167, 299, 310, 332, 336; and belonging 285–286; and brow hierarchy 175–176; and cultural capital profiles 161–163, 181–182; dominant 148, 165, 180; and educational level 188, 206, 285; and family educational background 157–161; and inequality 148, 209; and *la culture moyenne* 178–182; and national cultural capital accumulation 255; political discourse of 147–148; and political views 294–295; and space of lifestyles 149–154; and taste 294; trans-generational mechanisms 161; *see also* middle class; occupational class; petite bourgeoisie; working class
Class Act (podcasts) 147, 224
class consciousness 293
class fractions 118, 119, 149, 165, 180, 181
class wars 147
classical music 49, 51, 52, 57, 58, 59, 60, 62, 63–64, 125, 126, 132, 149, 170, 175, 243; *see also* light classical music
Cockatoo Island 69, 70
Cold Chisel 53
Collins, Jim 176
Collins, Simon 59
colonial art 16, 19, 21, 25, 26, 28, 31n10, 125, 132, 135, 171, 257
colonialism 245, 260
colonisation 37, 245, 247, 327
comedy TV programmes 87, 88, 91, 93, 94, 99n4, 125, 140
commercialisation of culture 175
communications infrastructure 221
community belonging 286, 289, 291
COMPAS project 6
competitiveness, sport field 101, 102, 115
Conigrave, Timothy 43
Connell, R.W. 148
contemporary art 16, 17, 19, 20, 24, 26, 30, 129, 140, 257
contemporary popular cultural orientations (CPCO) 145, **155**, 155, 156, 181
conventional middle cultural orientations (CMCO) 144, **155**, 155, 156, **160**, 162, 163, 174, 175, 182
convict heritage 69–70, 77–78
Cook, Captain James 242

corporate capitalism 30
cosmo-multiculturalism 302–303
cosmopolitan cultural capital 250
cosmopolitan elite 210, 221
cosmopolitanisation 251, 256, 261–263, 307, 331
cosmopolitanism 186, 187, 221, 222, 248, 249, 250, 253, 259–261, 264, 299, 331
Cottingham, Marci 268, 270
Coulangeon, Philippe 250, 260, 261
Council for Aboriginal Reconciliation Act (1991) 325
country music 10n9, 54, 56–57, 58, 60, 125, 140, 170, 233
country of origin 98, 249, 251
Courtenay, Bryce 36, 39, 135, 172, 173, 174, 235
Creative Australia 10n4, 301
creative class 209
Creative Nation 3–4, 6, 10n4, 11, 51–52, 301, 325, 331, 336
creative writing programmes 34
cricket 102, 103, 104, 107, 109, 125, 140, 239, 259–260, 301, 302
crime/mystery fiction 36, **42**, 44, 125, 149, 171, 173, 235
crowd sourcing 98
cultural adaptation 249–251, 253, 261
cultural capital 1, 2, 3, 5, 7, 8, 87, 102, 118, 127, 145, 149, 157, 164, 177, 182, 285, 311, 330, 333, 334–336; Bourdieu 7, 165, 166, 185–186, 190–191, 208, 209, 334; cosmopolitan 250; and education 148, 158, **159**, 160–161; embodied 189–190, 270; emerging 50–51, 64, 127; and family 266, 268, 270, 271, 272–275; and gender 266, 268, 269–271, 274–279; global 259; Indigenous *see* Indigenous cultural capital; and inequality 332; inherited 118, 179, 186, 335, 336; institutionalised 189, 190–203, 206; intergenerational transmission of 200, 203–206; and literary field 34, 39, 46, 47; and middlebrow culture 170, 177, 179, 180; national 34, 45, 227, 248, 253, 255, 259, 261; objectified 189, 204; relational 190; suburbanisation of 222; uptake within sociology of education 189–190; urban *see* urban cultural capital; women and 266, 268, 269, 270, 271, 274–275, 278–279
cultural capital profiles 149, 165; and class 161–163, 181–182; and educational trajectories 158, **159**, 160–161

388 Index

Cultural Capital and Social Exclusion (CCSE) project 6, 10n9, 164, 165
cultural consumption 1, 2, 12; globalisation of 4, 250
cultural diversity 4, 249, 266, 293, 331
cultural fields 1, 2, 3; *see also* art field; literary field; music field; sport field; television
cultural goodwill 118, 179
cultural heterogeneity/eclecticism thesis 50, 59
cultural industries 4, 209
cultural intermediaries 175, 180
cultural landscapes 69, 72, 74, **230**, 231
cultural maintenance 249–251, 261
cultural omnivore thesis 3, 50, 64n1, 163, 170, 173, 183
cultural orientations 144–145, 154–156, 158, 160, 162, 163, 165, 174–175, 181–182
cultural participation, defining 280–282
cultural policy 3, 4, 11–12, 51–52, 280–281, 301, 325, 331, 336
cultural production/distribution 1, 2–3, 12; active participation in 282–283; commercial 33; globalisation of 4
Culture and Leisure report 219
A Current Affair (TV programme) 88
current affairs programmes 86, 88–89, 91, 99n4, 243, 295, 296
Cvetičanin, Predrag 6

da Vinci, Leonardo 17, 18, 31n9, 140, 172, 257
dance music 54, 57, 60, 125, 135, 140, 174
Darbel, Alain 14, 31
Dark Side of the Moon (Pink Floyd) 53, 54, 57, 135, 172, 173, 174
Davis, Miles, *Kind of Blue* 53, 54, 57, 135, 174, **243**
Davies, Peter 190
Dawkins Reforms 191, 194
Deadlys award programme 241
DeLillo, Don 36, 40, 135, 174, 235, **243**
Desrosières, Alain 335
Di Maggio, Paul 189
digital technologies 3–4, 221–222, 266, 289–291; and literary field 33, 34–35
Distinction (Bourdieu) 3, 6, 9, 49, 50, 63, 100, 117, 119, 177, 178, 189, 293, 311, 330, 337
'DIY' celebrity 86
documentaries 87, 91, 92, 99n4, 125, 126, 170, 240
Dolin, Tim 45

dominant class 148, 165, 180
Done, Ken 17, 19, 21, **22**, 23, 28–29, 31n9, **229**
Donnat, Olivier 98
Donoghue, Jed 77, 78, 80, 81
Douglass, Sara 36, 39
drama television 86, 87, 88, 91, 94–95, 99n4, 125, 140, 170, 171
Driscoll, Beth 170, 176, 177, 178
The Dry (Harper) 43
Dubois, Vincent 335

easy listening music 54, 56, 57, 58, 60, 125, 135, 170, 174
ebooks 35, 38, 41, 134, 234
eclecticism 50, 59, 183, 333; in musical tastes 50, 61–63
economic capital 1, 7, 34, 35, 102, 107, 118, 148, 149, 157, 164, 175, 180, 186, 270; intermediate class 154; professional/managerial class 153–154, 182; working class 154
economic field 2, 68
Edmunds, June 176–177
education 1, 4, 5, 7, 33, 118, 186, 336; and class 188, 206, 285; informal 268, 270, 275, 278; and intergenerational transmission of cultural capital 203–206; and social inequality 188, 189, 206
educational capital 186
educational levels 120, 121, 126, 129, 134, 139, 149, 177, 180, 182, 185, 188, 332, 336; and art tastes and practices 15, 20, 21, **22**, 23, 24, 26, 30–31, 229–230; and book reading and book culture 36, *40*, 41, 46, 47, 235; and cultural capital profiles 158, **159**, 160–161; and heritage practices 71, 73, 74–75, 81, 231; Indigenous Australians 225, 227, 229–230, 231, 234, 237, 239; intermediate class **152**, 153, **204**, **205**; and musical tastes and practices 54, 55–56, 57–58, 60, 63, 121, 234; and occupational class **152**, 152, 153, 186, **192**, **193**, **204**, **205**, 207, 242–244; parental *see* parental educational level; of partners 158, **159**, **204**, **205**, 206, 207; professional/managerial class 152, 153, 186, **204**, **205**, 243–244; routine/manual workers **192**, **204**, **205**; and socio-economic status (SES) 188, 191, **192**, **193**, 194–196, **197**, 200, **201**, 202–203, **204**, **205**; and sport tastes and practices 115, 239; Sydney 214, 215, 216; and television tastes and practices 90, 91, 94,

95, 98–99, 121, 237; *see also* postgraduate education; tertiary education
egalitarianism 147, 285, 332
Eggers, Dave 36, 39, 41
elite class 164; cosmopolitan elite 210, 221
Ellis Island (USA) 71, 75, **243**
Ellis, Liz 103
embodied cultural capital 189–190, 270

emerging cultural capital 50–51, 64, 127
emerging cultural practices 145
Emin, Tracey 17, 20, 26, 31n9
emotional capital 106, 268–269, 270
equity 11, 12; gender 11
escapism 43, 236, 304–305, 319–320
established high cultural orientations (EHCO) 144, **155**, 155, **160**, 163, 174, 181
ethical dimension of consumption 267, 311–329, 334; heritage 312–315; Indigenous people/cultural items 322–328, 329; sport 109, 112, 113–114, 312, 315–317; television 320–322
ethnic diversity 251–252
ethnic identity 248–249
ethnicity and cultural consumption and participation 3, 7–8, 10n2, 187, 247–264; art field 256–258; Australian-born respondents 252, 253, **254**; heritage 258–259; intra-community cultural activities 259; overseas-born respondents 252, 253, **254**, 255; sport 259–260
ethnographic capital 245
ethnoscapes 248, 251, 256, 259, 263, 333
eugenics 334–335
Eureka Rebellion (1854) 70
Evatt Foundation 167

Facebook 84, 97
false consciousness 294, 300
family 284–285, 333; and art tastes and practices 15, 24, 272–275; and belonging 286–288, 289, 291; and cultural capital 266, 268, 270, 271, 272–275
family educational background: and class belonging 157–161; and transmission of cultural capital 203–204
family heritage/history 72, 73, 74, 75–79, 81–82, 125, 231, 287–288
fantasy fiction 33, 35, 36, 38, 39, 40, **42**, 44, 47, 125, 140, 171, 174
fathers, level of education 157, 158, **159**, 160, 203–204
feeling, and heritage consumption 312–315
Ferguson, James 101

Ferrante, Elena 43
field (s) 1, 336, 337; economic 2, 68; political 2, 3, 13, 68, 79; of power 2, 10n1, 11; *see also* cultural fields
fields of university study **152**, 153, 157, 158, **159**, 200, 207; Indigenous women 244; intermediate class **152**, 153, **201**; professional/managerial class **152**, 153, **201**; routine/manual workers **201**; working class **152**
Fifield, Mitch 52
Folau, Israel 103, 104, **238**
football *see* Australian Rules football; soccer
The Footy Show (TV programme) 88
Forbidden City (China) 71, 75
Fordham, Ben 147
Foucault, Michel 10n1
The Four Seasons (Vivaldi) 53, 54, 57, 174, 177, **243**
Foxtel Now 84
France 15, 33, 35, 98, 103, 177, 189, 334, 335
Freeman, Cathy 103, 107, **238**, 239, 240, 301, 323
Fremantle Prison 69
Friedland, Lewis 177
friendship networks 6

Gagai, Dane 114, 240
Gale, Trevor 194, 200
Gallery of Modern Art (GOMA), Queensland 16
Gallipoli 71, 77, 80, 313
Galton, Francis 335
Game of Thrones (book) 40
Game of Thrones (TV programme) 86, 88, 94, 95, 174, 237, 297
Gardening Australia (TV programme) 88, 92, 93, 135, 140, 174, 237
Gayo, Modesto 270
gender 5, 119, 120, 134, 149, 165, 185, 187, 209, 332, 333; and art tastes and practices 15, 20–21, 271; and book reading and book culture 40, 48n5, 234–235; and cultural capital accumulation 266, 268, 269–271, 274–279; equity 3; and heritage practices 71, 73, 230–231; intermediate class **152**, 153; and musical tastes and practices 54, 56, 57, 233–234; and professional/managerial class **152**, 244; and sport tastes and practices 105, *106*, 107, 108, 115, 121, 239, 285; and Sydney cultural participation 217; and television tastes and practices 89, 92, 236–237

gender capital 270
generational shifts 176–177, 333; and cultural capital accumulation 255; and musical tastes and practices 62–63; and television tastes and practices 97–98, 133–134
genre preferences: and age 172; art field 24–30, 125, 127, 170, 171, 172, 229–230; book reading and book culture 38, 39, 40–41, **42**, 44, 47, 125, 126, 140, 170, 171, 172, 234, 235; clusters 129, **130**, 131, 135, **136**, 140, **141**; middle space of 170–172; music field 50, 54, 56–60, 61–62, 125, 126, 127, 140, 170–171, 172, 233, 243; television 91–92, 94, 99n4, 125, 126, 140, 170, 171, 172
gentrification 209, 210, 221, 222
Gershwin, George, *Rhapsody in Blue* 53, 54, 57, 58, 135, 172, 174, 175
Gilbert and Sullivan, *The Mikado* 53, 54, 58, 135, 172, 173
Girard, Augustus 335
globalisation 4, 34, 51, 248, 250, 256, 260, 261, 263, 264, 266, 291, 293, 298, 299, 305–309, 331, 332, 353
Glover, John 17, 19, 20, **22**
Gogglebox Australia (TV programme) 96
Goldthorpe, John 195
Goldthorpe or EGP schema 349
golf 103, 104, 107, 125, 140, 235
Goodes, Adam 103, 235, **238**, 239, 240, 297, 301–302, 316, 323, 326, 329n2
Goodwin, Susan 270
Google 51
Gotye 53, 54, 57
Grand Designs (TV programme) 88, 94, 97, 237
grandparents 272, 273, 278
Grant, Stan 224
Great British Class Survey (GBCS) 50, 51, 145, 148, 164, 166
Grenville, Kate 36, 37, 39, 43, 172
Group of Eight (Go8) universities 153, 196, 200, 207
Gurrumul Yunupingu 53, 54, 58, 59, 59, 132, 135, 174, 233, 234, 242, **243**, 323

habitus 1–2, 5–6, 7, 119, 181, 265–267, 298, 299, 300, 310, 329, 334, 336, 337; commitment and identity as integral to 324, 329; and cultural capital 268, 270; definition of 265; and normative orientation 323–324; and politics 293, 294; spatial dynamics of 289

Hachette 34
Hage, Ghassan 227, 302–303
Hamish and Andy's Gap Year (TV programme) 88, 92, 93
Hanquinet, Laurie 15, 208
Hanson, Pauline 296
hard rock music 54, 57, 60, 135, 140, 174
Harlem Renaissance 241
Harper, Jane 43
HarperCollins 34
Harrower, Elizabeth 36
Hayne, Jarryd 114
heritage field 12–13, 66–71, 120, 121; contemporisation of 68; genesis of 67–69; non-recognition of sites 140, **142**; personal, vernacular or everyday 66, 67, 73, 81; public, 'elite' or authorised forms 66, 67, 68, 72, 73, 75, 81
heritage tastes and practices 71–82, 123, 124, 125, 127, 129, **130**, 132, 134, 139, 140, 149, *218*, 219, 287–288; and age 71, *73*, 74, 81; and class positions *73*, 74, 75, 76, 77, 81, 149, 150; and educational level 71, *73*, 74–75, 81, 231; and ethnicity 258–259; feeling, belonging and obligation 312–315; and gender 71, *73*, 230–231; as historical engagement 79–81; Indigenous Australians 230–232, 242; Internet searches 72, *73*, 74, 75, 123, 126, 129, 134, 230; middle space of 170, 172, 174; and place of residence 74, 75, 81; social space of *73*, 73–75, 81; space of *72*, 72–73; Sydney 211, **212**, 215, 217, 218, 219, 220
high cultural orientations 144, 145, 155, 156, 158, 160, 163, 175, 177, 181, 182, 183
high culture forms 50, 51, 52, 135, 169, 175, 176, 177, 190, 222, 223, 250, 259
highbrow culture 169, 175, 250, 259
higher education *see* tertiary education
Higher Education Contribution Scheme 335
historic buildings/precincts 72, 74, 134, **230**
history books, reading of 39, 40, **42**, 125, 126, 234
History Channel 69
Ho, Christina 203
Holding the Man (Conigrave) 43
Holocaust sites 312
Holt, Douglas 250
home, space of 221

Home Box Office (HBO) 86
home—education—occupation—class nexus 149, 166
homeland heritage 69, 72, 73, 125, 140, 170
Homeland (TV programme) 88
households, and cultural capital accumulation 268–279
House Husbands (TV programme) 87, 92, 93
Howard, John 4
Hughes, David 88, 92, 94
humanities and social sciences specialisation 93, **152**, 153, 157, 158, 244, 324
Huppatz, Kate 269, 270

Iannelli, Cristina 202
identity 76–79; class 285–286; ethnic 248–249; as integral to habitus 324, 329; national 81, 109, 112, 115, 293, 298, 299, 301, 332; personal 284; transnational 332
immigration 8, 187, 247
Impressionism 16, 17, 18, 25–26, 31n10, 125, 132, 140, 149, 170, 229
income 153, **154**, 285; inequality 148, 166, 332; Sydney 214, 215
Indian Australians 4, 5, 7, 187, 222, 226, 227, **228**, 248, 251, **254**, 255; art field tastes and practices 257–258; heritage tastes and practices 258; intra-community cultural activities 259; and Sachin Tendulkar 260
Indigenous art (s) 11, 12; *see also* Aboriginal art
Indigenous Australians 3, 4, 8, 68, 78; Constitutional recognition of 4; cultural tastes and practices *see* Indigenous cultural tastes and practices; educational attainment and occupational success 242–244; inequalities experienced by 225; middle class 224, 225, 244; participation in tertiary education 224, 225, 243–244; and politics of resentment 303–304
Indigenous authors/literature 33, 36, 39, **42**, 125, 170, 234–235, 323
Indigenous cultural capital 224–225, 226, 241–244
Indigenous cultural tastes and practices 225–226, 226–240, 241; art 229–230; book reading and book culture 234–236; and educational levels 225, 227, 229–230, 231, 234, 237, 239; gender differences 227, 229, 230–231, 233–234, 234–235, 236–237, 239; heritage 230–232, 242; Indigenous items, rates of recognition and likes 227, **243**; music 233–234, 235; and occupational class 242–243; overseas items, rates of recognition **243**; and politics 235–236, 239–240, 242; sport 238–240; television 236–237, 243
Indigenous culture 2, 8, 186–187, 331, 333; ethical dimension of liking/not liking items of 322–328, 329; as form of capital for Indigenous/non-Indigenous Australians 225, 245–246; political mobilisation of 225; recognition of 293
Indigenous heritage *see* Aboriginal heritage
Indigenous musicians 52–53, 58, 233–234, 323
Indigenous/non-Indigenous binary 325–326
industrial heritage 68, 69, 72, 74
inequality 1, 148, 166, 167, 293, 336; and class 148, 209; and cultural capital 332; and culture 163; and education 188, 189, 206; income 148, 166, 332; and Indigenous Australians 225; structural 209; urban aspects of 209; wealth 148, 166, 167, 332, 336
infotainment 295
inheritance 148, 149, 166, 332, 334–335
inherited cultural capital 118, 179, 186, 335, 336
The Inheritors (Bourdieu and Passeron) 188, 200
institutionalised cultural capital 189, 190–203, 206
intermediate class 164, 165, 180; age composition **152**, 152; cultural capital profiles **161**, 162, 163, 181; cultural orientations 156, 158; economic capital 154; educational levels **152**, 153, **192**, **193**, **204**, **205**; fields of university study **152**, 153, **201**; gender composition **152**, 153; place of residence **152**, 153; preferred tertiary institution **152**, 153; school type **202**; university type **197**
intermediate occupations 139, 150, 156–157, 180, **350**
International Council on Monuments and Sites (ICOMOS) 67
International Labour Organization 349
international politics 307–308
International Standard Classification of Occupations (ISCO-08) 9, 349

Internet 86, 99; and art field 18, 20, 126, 129, 134, 139; heritage searches 72, 73, 74, 75, 123, 126, 129, 134, 230
Invasion Day 235, 242
Irving, T.H. 148
Italian Australians 4, 5, 7, 153, 187, 226, **228**, 248, 251, **254**, 255; art field tastes and practices 257, 258; intra-community cultural activities 259; and Sachin Tendulkar 260
Ivy League universities 196

Jackson, Lauren 103
jazz 54, 57, 58, 59, 60, 125, 149, 170–171, 243
'Jolene' (Dolly Parton) 53, 54, 57
Jones, Vince 53, 54, 57, 132
Jordan, Michael 104, 107, **238**, 239

Kantianism 210, 334
Keating, Paul 3, 51
Keller, Amanda 88, 92, 237
Kelly, Ned 17
Kewell, Harry 103
The Killing (TV programme) 88, 94, **243**
Kind of Blue (Miles Davis) 53, 54, 57, 135, 174, **243**
King, Stephen 36, 38, 39, 135, 173, 174
Koons, Jeff 17, 19, 20, 174
Kraaykamp, Gerbert 200
Kyrgios, Nick 315

la culture moyenne concept 170, 178–182
Labor party/government 3, 4, 11, 51–52, 67, 336
Lahire, Bernard 181
Lamar, Kendrick 235
Lamont, Michèle 189
landscape art 17, 21, 25, 26, 27, 31n10, 125, 132, 135, 140, 170, 174, 178, **229**, 230
Langton, Marcia 224
Language and Symbolic Power (Bourdieu) 190
Lareau, Annette 189
large owners/high managers 118, 180, **350**; and book reading and book culture 41; and middlebrow culture 177, 182
Laver, Rod 103, 135, **238**
law or business studies specialism **152**, 153, 157, 158, **159**, 186, 200, 207, 324
Lawson, Henry 32
Leavis, Q.D. 175
Lebanese Australians 4, 5, 7, 187, 222, 226, 227, **228**, 248, 251, **254**, 255, 261–263; art field tastes and practices 257, 258; heritage tastes and practices 259; intra-community cultural activities 259; and Sachin Tendulkar 260

legitimate culture 1, 9, 117, 165, 169, 171, 176, 178, 179, 182, 331, 333
Leigh, Andrew 148
Levine, Elana 86
Lewis, Wally 316
Lichtenstein, Roy 27
lifestyle books 39, 40, **42**, 171
lifestyle TV programmes 88, 89, 92, 94, 125, 172
lifestyles, space of 295; and class 149–154; middle space 169, 170–175, 180–182, 333; and space of social positions 117, 119–146; clusters in 127–145; cultural participation 122–124, *123*, 129, 134–135, 139; genre tastes *124*, 124–126, 129, **130**, 131, 135, **136**; platforms and devices *126*, 126–127, 129
light classical music 54, 56, 57, 58, 60, 125, 132, 135, 170, 171, 174, 175
literary festivals and prizes 32, 34, 35, 43, 129, 139, 176
literary fiction/classics 34, 39, **42**, 42, 45, 126, 135, 149, 170
literary field 32–36, 120, 121, 124, 125, 127, 129, 178; academic sphere 35, 46; and cultural capital 34, 39, 46, 47; digital developments 33, 34–35; economic capital 34, 35; genre communities 33, 34; genre fiction 33, 34–35; and globalisation 291; and national cultural capital 34, 45; non-recognition **137**, 140, **142**; public-commercial sphere 35, 46; state 35; symbolic capital 34, 35; *see also* book reading and book culture
Literature Board 34
The Living Room (TV programme) 88
Lloyd Webber, Andrew, *Phantom of the Opera* 53, 54, 135, 172, 173, 174
local heritage 72, 149, 172, **230**
The Love of Art (Bourdieu and Darbel) 14, 31
lowbrow culture 175, 176, 177
The Lucky Culture (Cater) 148

McCaffrey, Anne 43, 44, 45
McGuire, Eddie 88, 92, 94, 135, 237, 316, 329n2
McIntyre, Stuart 147
McLean, Ian 29
Mad as Hell (TV programme) 296

Mad Men (TV programme) 88, 94, 135, 174, **243**
Madonna 53, 135
magazines 175, 176
Mailman, Deborah 88, 92, 93, 237, **243**, 323
Malouf, David 36, 39, 172, 174, 175, **243**
managerial class *see* large owners/high managers; professional/ managerial class
manual workers *see* routine/manual workers
M ori culture 241
Maradona, Diego 104, 107, 109, 111, **238**, 239
Marginson, Simon 195
Martin, George R.R. 44
Martin, Ray 88–89, 92, 135, 237
mass commercial/consumer culture 175, 176, 178
MasterChef Australia (TV programme) 87–88, 92, 93, 237
Mauboy, Jessica 235
media: platforms and devices *126*, 126–127, 129, 139; and sport field 100, 102, 108–109, 111; *see also* radio; social media; television
medicine 186, 200, 207
Melba Recordings 52, 64n4
Melbourne 219, 220
Meuleman, Roza 250
Micallef, Shaun 296
The Midday Show (TV programme) 89
middle class 77, 111, 139, 163, 164, 166, 177; Indigenous 224, 225, 244
middle space of lifestyles 169, 170–175, 180–182, 333
middlebrow culture 5, 118, 169, 175–183, 333; *la culture moyenne* concept 170, 178–182; studies of 170, 175–179
Midsomer Murders (TV programme) 88, 94, 135, 172, 174, 237
migrant culture, recognition of 293, 304–305
migrant heritage/museums 69, 72, 74, 124, 125, 170, 230, 258–259
migration 163, 247, 248, 249, 250, 256, 261, 264, 300, 331, 333; *see also* immigration
The Mikado (Gilbert and Sullivan) 53, 54, 58, 135, 172, 173
military heritage 69, 71, 72, 79–81, 134, 313–135, *314*
Minogue, Kylie 53, 54, 57, 234
Mittell, Jason 86
mobile middle class 163–164

The Models (pop band) 53
modern art 16, 18, 19, 25, 26, 27, 28, 31n10, 125, 174, 229, 257
modernism 16–17, 29, 31n9, 175
Moffatt, Tracey 17, 20, **22**, 132, 172, **243**, 323
Monet, Claude 17, 18, 135, 140, 174, 175, **229**, **243**, 257
Morgan, Sally 36, 135, 234, **243**, 323
Morphy, Howard 241
mothers' level of education 157, 158, **159**, 160, 204
multiculturalism 4, 8, 247, 249, 250, 259, 264, 302–303, 309, 331
multiplayer online games 283–284
Multiple Correspondence Analysis (MCA) 9, 17, 50, 71, 89, 120, 149, 170, 206, 211, 347–348
Murakami, Haruki 36, 39, 41, 235
Museum of Contemporary Art (MCA), Sydney 16
Museum of Old and New Art (Mona), Hobart 16
Museum of Sydney 71
museums 69, 71, 72, 74, **230**; visits to 124, 134, 149, 231
Music Australia 52
music field 12, 49–52, 120, 221; and cultural policy 51–52; funding 51, 52; music industry 51; national market 51; regulatory conditions 219, 220
music field, tastes and practices 52–65, 121, 123, 124, 125, 129, **130**, **131**, 134, 135, 139, 140, 143, 282; and age 54, 55, 56, 57, 58, 60, 63, 121, 125, 285; and educational level 54, 55–56, 57–58, 60, 63, 121, 234; and gender 54, 56, 57, 233–234; generational shifts 62–63; genre preferences 50, 54, 56–60, 61–62, 125, 126, 127, 140, 170–171, 172, 233, 243; Indigenous Australians 233–234, 235; intensities of engagement 58–60, 64; middle space of 170–171, 172, 173, 174, 175; and occupational class 54, 55–56, 57–58, 60, 63, 121, 149; participation in musical events 50; and place of residence 54; qualified eclecticism 50, 61–63; social space of 54, 55–58, *56*; space of 54, 55; Sydney 211, **212**, 215, 216, 217, 219, 220, 222, 223; temporal aspects of 12, 50, 54–59, 61; *see also names of individual genres, composers and musicians*
music streaming 51, 64
Muslims 288, 304

Nadal, Rafael 104, 135, **238**
Namatjira, Albert 17, 18, 19, **22**, 23, 28–29, 135, 172, 175, 229, 242, **243**, **256**, 257, 323; *Palm Valley* 29, *29*
nation 266, 293, 309, 331, 332; as contested category 301–302; cultural politics of 298–300
National Aboriginal and Torres Strait Islander Social Survey 225
national belonging 227, 287–289, 304
National Contemporary Music Plan 52
national cultural capital 34, 45, 227, 248, 253, 256, 259, 261
national culture 34, 100, 247, 250, 293, 299, 301, 302, 305, 332
National Gallery of Australia (NGA) 16, 129, 258
National Gallery of Victoria 16
national heritage 68, 69, 72, 74, 230
National Heritage List 68
national identity 81, 109, 112, 115, 293, 298, 299, 301, 310, 332
National Indigenous Television (NITV) 93, 129, 242
National Museum of Australia 69, 124
National Opera Review 52
national parks 67, 69, **230**
National Program for Excellence in the Arts (NPEA) 12
National Statistics Socio-economic Classification (NS-SEC) 165, 166, 349, 351
National Trusts 67, 69
nationalism 2, 68, 69, 133, 288, 298–299, 301; cultural 51; new 15–16, 67
neoliberalism 4, 148, 202, 203
'Nessun Dorma' (Puccini) 53, 54, 135, 172, 174
netball 103, 107, 108, 125, 135, 140, **238**, 239
Netflix 4, 13, 84, 85, 86, 95, 96
New Zealand 166, 241
Newman, Michael 86
news programmes 84, 87, 88, 91, 125, 171, 243
NITV (National Indigenous Television) 93, 129, 242
Noble, John 190
Nolan, Sidney 17, 18, 19, **22**, 27, 135, 172, 174, **256**, 257
non-English speakers, television tastes and practices 98
Norman, Greg 103, 107, 135
normativity 322, 323–324
Nyman, Michael, *The Piano* 53–54, 57

objectified cultural capital 189, 204
obligation 322, 329; and heritage consumption 313, 315
occupational class 1, 5, 7, 9, 118, 120, 121, 126, 129, 134, 145, 149–154, *151*, 185, 285, 332, 349, **350**, 353; and art tastes and practices 12, 15, 20, 21, **22**, 23, 26, 29, 30–31; and book reading and book culture *40*, 41, **42**, 46, 47, 48n5; and educational level **152**, 152, 153, 186, **192**, **193**, **204**, **205**, 207, 242–244; and field of university study **201**; and heritage tastes and practices 73, 74, 75, 149, 150; and musical tastes and practices 54, 55–56, 57–58, 60, 63, 121; and sport tastes and practices 105, *106*, 107, 108, 109, 111, 150; and Sydney cultural participation 217; and television tastes and practices 89–90, 91, 94, 98–99, 121, 149, 150; and university type **197**
Office for National Statistics (UK) 349
Offspring (TV programme) 87, 92, 93, **237**
Old School (TV programme) 88, 92, 93
open-air museums 72, 74, 124
openness 249, 250, 251, 259, 302
opera 51, 52, 53, 60, 62, 123, 129, 176
opera houses 208, 209, 210, 211
Oprah's Book Club 176
Orange is the New Black (TV programme) 86
Organisation for Economic Co-operation and Development (OECD) 167, 190, 194

Pan Macmillan 34
parental educational level: and class belonging 157–161; and transmission of cultural capital 203–204
parental influences 271, 272–274, 278, 286–287
parenting styles 189, 190
Parker, Stephen 194, 200
partners: level of education 158, **159**, 204, **205**, 206, 207; negotiation and accommodation of cultural tastes 269, 271, 275–278, 279
Parton, Dolly, 'Jolene' 53, 54, 57
Passeron, Jean-Claude 188, 195, 200
Patterson, Richard North 296
Penguin Random House 34
Personal Video Recorders (PVRs) 84
petite bourgeoisie 33, 111, 118, 165, 179, 180
Phantom of the Opera (Lloyd Webber) 53, 54, 135, 172, 173, 174
Phelps, Michael 104, 111, **238**, 239

photography 178, 283
Photography: A Middlebrow Art (Bourdieu) 178
The Piano (Nyman) 53–54, 57
Picoult, Jodi 36, 39, 174
Piketty, Thomas 148, 166
Pink Floyd, *Dark Side of the Moon* 53, 54, 57, 135, 172, 173, 174
pioneer history sites 72, 124
place of residence: and art tastes and practices 20; and belonging 289; and heritage tastes and practices 74, 75, 81; intermediate class **152**, 153; and musical tastes and practices 54; professional/managerial class **152**, 153; working class **152**, 153
pleasure 311, 312
plein air movement 17
policy *see* cultural policy
political field 2, 3, 13, 68, 79
politics 266, 293–310, 334; and Indigenous cultural tastes and practices 235–236, 239–240, 242; and Indigenous culture 225; international 307–308; of migrant Australia 304–305; of multiculturalism 302–303; of nation 298–300; of resentment 303–304; and social position 294, 295; and taste 295; taste for 295–298
Pollock, Jackson 17, 18, 20, 257; *Blue Poles* 17, 26, 27, 31n3
Pop art 16, 18, 19, 25, 26, 27, 28, 31n10
pop rock music 54, 57, 60, 125, 129, 132, 135, 140, 174
Popescu, Mihaela 6
popular culture 33, 46, 50, 115, 174, 176, 249, 281
popular culture orientations 144–145, 155, 156, 158, 160, 162, 181
Port Arthur Historic Site 69–70, *70*, 74, 135, 174
portraiture 17, 19, 25, 26, 27, 28, 125, **229**, 230, 257–258
position-taking 266, 293, 294, 295, 309, 334
post-Impressionism 17
postgraduate education 20, 21, 24, 26, 41, 58, 75, 90, 91, 95, 121, 129, **152**, 153, 157, 159, 160, 180, 272; and socio-economic status (SES) 191, **193**, 195, 203, 204–205
postmodernism 221
power 294–295; fields of 2, 10n1, 11; symbolic 66, 115, 295
Pratchett, Terry 44, 45

Pratt, Mary Louise 224
precariat 164
Preston, Margaret 17, 18, 20, 21, **22**, 172, **243**
Prieur, Annick 6, 250
Principal Component Analysis (PCA) 211, 216–217
professional-executive class 164
professional/managerial class 7, 12, 118, 129, 134, 145, 149, 150, 165, 180, 187, **350**; age 150, **152**; art tastes and practices 20, **22**, 23, 26, 29, 30, 120, 149; book reading and book culture 41, 42, 46, 47, 120, 149; cultural capital profiles **161**, 161, 162, 163, 182; cultural orientations 154–156; economic capital 153–154, 182; educational level 152, 153, 186, **192**, **193**, **204**, **205**, 207, 243–244; fields of university study 152, 153, **201**; gender composition 152, 244; heritage practices 66, 75, 149; Indigenous Australians 242–244; and middlebrow culture 176, 177, 182; music tastes and practices 56, 57, 58, 120, 149; place of residence **152**, 153; preferred tertiary institutions 152, 153; school type **202**; sport tastes and practices **106**, 107; television tastes and practices 90, 91, 92, 93, 98; university type **197**
Programme for International Student Assessment (PISA) 190
The Project (TV programme) 88, 295–296
Public funding 4, 11, 12, 16, 245, 281; literary field 35; music field 51, 52, 62; sport field 101; and private schools 207n5
public service broadcasting (PSB) 84, 85, 86, 87
publishing industry 12, 34–35
Puccini, Giacomo, 'Nessun Dorma' 53, 54, 135, 172, 174
Punch (magazine) 175

Q&A (TV programme) 296, 297
QI (TV programme) 88, 94, 97, 237
Quacquarelli Symonds 196
Quilty, Ben 17, 19, 20, **22**, 23, 132, 172, 175, **243**, **256**, 257

race 7–8, 209
racism 301–302
radio 51–52, 55, 61, 63, 112, 123–124, 134–135, 145, 175, 234
Radway, Janice 178, 179
Rankin, Ian 36, 39, 44, 135, 172, 174, 235

Razinsky, Hili 300
reading *see* book reading and book culture
reading class 33, 41, 47
reading groups/book clubs 32, 35, 39, 41, 43, 48n5, 124, 129, 134, 176
reality television 86, 87, 91, 92, 93, 132, 140
Reay, Diane 189, 270
recognition, of Indigenous and migrant cultures 293, 304–305
Reconciliation, discourse of 311, 312, 323
Reconciliation Orthodoxy 267, 312, 325, 326, 329
Redfern Now (TV programme) 87, 88, 93, 237, **243**, 323
Register of the National Estate 68
Reilly, Matthew 36, 39, 41, 173

religion 111, 225, 288, 307, 322, 206, 289, 291; art 27; schools 202
Rembrandt 17, 18, 31n9, 135, 140, 172, 174, 175, 257
Renaissance art 16, 18, 25, 28, 31n10, 31n9, 149, 170, 171, 229, 230, 257
Renewing Creative Australia 336
Reproduction in Education, Society and Culture (Bourdieu and Passeron) 188, 195, 200
resentment, politics of 303–304
residential place *see* place of residence
Review of Higher Education Access and Outcomes for Aboriginal and Torres Strait Islander Peoples 225
Rhapsody in Blue (Gershwin) 53, 54, 57, 58, 135, 172, 174, 175
Riley, Erin 100
Roberts, Tom 17, 19, 21, **22**, 135, 164, 175, 229, 256, 257
Rockwiz (TV programme) 88
role models, sportspeople as 113–114, 315–317
romance fiction 34, 35, 36, 38, 39, 40, **42**, 46, 172
routine/manual workers 23, 139, 145, 150, 156, 163, 180, **350**; art tastes and practices 20, **22**, 29, 31; book reading and book culture 41; educational level **192**, **193**, **204**, **205**; fields of university study **201**; music tastes and practices 58; school type **202**; sport tastes and practices 105, *106*, 108, 111, 149; television tastes and practices 90, 94, 149; university type **197**
Rowse, Tim 224, 225, 242
Royal National Park, New South Wales 67

rugby league 103, 107, 108, 125, 170, 171, 174, 238, 239, 240
rugby union 100, 103, 104, 107, 125, 135
Russell Group of universities 196

Sarah Thornhill (Grenville) 37
Savage, Mike 15, 50, 51, 166, 190, 196, 208–209, 210, 213, 221, 222, 223, 250, 289
savings 153, **154**, 215, 216, 217
Sayer, Andrew 309, 323–324, 329
Sayers, Dorothy L. 44
Scherger, Simone 190
school choice 202–203, 207
science fiction 33, 36, 38, 39, 40, **42**, 44, 125, 135, 140, 171, 174
Scott, Kim 36, 135, 174, 234–235, 323
Sculthorpe, Peter 53, 54, 57, 132, 175, **243**
The Secret River (Grenville) 37, 43
self-employed 41, 118, 150, 157, 180
self-help books 39, 40, **42**, 135, 171
self-publishing 34, 35
Seth, Vikram 43
settler-colonial society 2, 8, 78, 300, 331
Sheil, Christopher 167
Sheppard, Jill 50, 51, 148, 163–164
Silva, Elizabeth 164, 269
Sixty Minutes (TV programme) 88
Skeggs, Beverley 164
The Slap (Tsiolkas) 43
Smith, Cameron 240
So You Think You Can Dance (TV programme) 88
soccer 103, 104, 107, 108, 111–112, 113, 125, 140
social capital 1, 7, 102, 118, 148, 164, 185, 186, 270
social class *see* class
social cohesion 293; *see also* Facebook; YouTube
social position 1, 2, 5, 298, 334, 335; and art tastes and practices 14, 15, 18–23; and heritage tastes and practices 67, 72, 73, 73–75; and music tastes and practices 49, 54–58, 60, 62; and politics 294, 295; and sport tastes and practices 105, *106*, 107–108, 111; and television tastes and practices 89–92, *90*; *see also* age; class; educational level; ethnicity; gender; lifestyles, space of, and space of social positions
social stratification 2, 3
socialisation 190, 202, 266, 268, 270, 278, 289, 333

socio-economic status (SES): and educational level 188, 191, **192**, **193**, 194–196, **197**, 200, **201**, 202–203, 204, **205**; and field of university study 200, **201**, 202; and school choice 202–203, 207; and Sydney cultural participation 215; and tertiary education 188, 191, **192**, **193**, 194–196, **197**, 200, **201**, 203, 204, **205**, 207

sociology of education, notion of cultural capital and 189–190

The Sopranos (TV programme) 86

Sovereign Hill 70, *70*, 71

Special Broadcasting Service (SBS) 97, 125, 170

Sport Australia 101

sport field 13, 100–102, 120; competitive aspect of 101, 102, 115; conversations and negotiations 111–115; definition of 101, 115; and globalisation 291; informal level 101; non-recognition 140, **142**; racism in 301–302; sexism in 100; and urban status 210, 222

sport tastes and practices 100–101, 104–115, 124, 125, 129, **130**, **131**, 132, 133, 135, 140, 143–144, *218*, 219, 271, 283, 286; accommodation of partner's taste 276; and age 105, *106*, 107, 115, *218*, 219; and class positions 105, *106*, 107, 108, 109, 111, 115, 121, 150; and educational level 115, 239; ethical aspects of sport and 109, 112, 113–114, 312, 315–317; and ethnicity 258–259; and family 284–285; and gender 105, *106*, 107, 108, 115, 121, 239, 285; Indigenous Australians 238–240; and liking/disliking sport 108–109, **110**, 111, 171–172; and media 100, 102, 108–109, 111; middle space of 170, 171–172, 174; and national identity 109, 112, 115, 299; physical participation 101, 102, 107; social space of 105–108, *106*, 111; space of 104–105, *105*; spectatorship 100, 102, 107, 109, **110**; sportspeople, liking/disliking 107, 108, 109, **110**, 111, 113–114; Sydney 211, **212**, 214, 215–216, *218*, 219, 220, 223; *see also names of individual sports and sportspeople*

sports books 39, 40, **42**, 108, 125, 172, 235

sports TV 88, 91, 92, 100, 108, 125, 140

sportspeople 103–104, 107, 108, 109, **110**, 111, 238–239; as role models 113–114, 315–317

Spotify 51, 143, 290

Stan 13, 84, 95, 96

Standard Occupational Classification 2010 (SOC2010) 166, 349, 351

state 2, 35, 335

The State Nobility (Bourdieu) 188, 200, 207

Steinmetz, George 245

STEM (Science, Technology, Engineering and Mathematics) specialisation 20, **152**, 153, 157, 158, **159**, 324

Stewart, Simon 46

still lifes 17, 25, 26, 27, 31n10, 125, 135, 171, 172, 257

Stilwell, Frank 167

Stolen Generations 78, 244, 312

Stonehenge (UK) 71, 74, **243**, 312

stratification theory 164–165

streaming 13; music 51, 64; television 84, 85, 86, 95, 97, 126, 134

structure and agency 294

subjectivity 299, 300, 309

suburbs 210, 211, 213, 220, 221–222

Sullivan, Alice 189

Sultan, Dan 52–53, 54, 57, 58, 233, 234, 323

swimming 103, 104, 107, 125, 132, 135, 140, **238**, 239

Sydney: educational levels 214, 215, 216; incomes 214, 215; suburbs 213, 221, 222

Sydney, cultural participation in 209, 211–217, 221, 222, 223; and age 215–216; art 211, **212**, 214, 215, 217, *218*, 220, 222; book reading and book culture (literature) 211, **212**, 215, 217, *218*, 220, 222; and educational levels 215, 216; and gender 217; heritage 211, **212**, 215, 217, *218*, 219, 220; music 211, **212**, 215, 216, 217, *218*, 219, 220, 222, 223; in the national context 217, *218*, 219–221; and occupational class 217; and socio-economic status (SES) 215; sport 211, **212**, 214, 215, 217, *218*, 219, 220, 223; television 211, **212**, *214*, 214–215, 217, *218*, 219, 220, 223

Sydney Opera House 209, 211, 222

symbolic capital 34, 35, 241

symbolic power 66, 115, 295

Taj Mahal (India) 71, 258

talk shows 87, 125

Talkin' 'Bout Your Generation (TV programme) 88

Tan, Amy 36

taste: for politics 295–298; and politics 295

tax system 166, 167

Taylor, John 225
Te Papa Tongarewa (Museum of New Zealand) 71, 74
technical/lower supervisory workers 20, **22**, 23, 41, 90, 94, *106*, 107, 139, 150, 180, **350**
television 13, 120, 221; catch-up services 84, 89, 97; changing dynamics of the field 83, 84–85; commercial FTA networks 84, 85, 86, 96–97; and the curators of realities 312, 320–322; and field theory 83, 85–87; free-to-air (FTA) 84, 85, 95–98, 129, 135; and globalisation 291; non-recognition 140, **142**; Pay-TV 84, 85; personalities 85, 86, 88–89, 99; public service broadcasting (PSB) 84, 85, 86, 87; streaming services 84, 85, 86, 95, 97, 126, 134
television tastes and practices 83, 124, 129, **130**, **131**, 132, 134–135, 139, 143, *218*, 219; accommodation of partner's taste 276; and age 83, 89, 90, 91, 92, 94, 95, 97, 98, 121, 285; channel preferences 90–91; and educational level 90, 91, 94, 95, 98–99, 121, 237; ethical dimension of 320–322; and gender 89, 92, 236–237; generational patterns in 97–98, 133–134; genre preferences 91–92, 94, 99n4, 125, 126, 140, 170, 171, 172; Indigenous Australians 236–237, 243; middle space of 170, 171, 172–173, 174; Non-English Speaking (NESB) backgrounds 98; and occupational class 89–90, 91, 94, 98–99, 121, 149, 150; out-of-home and mobile device viewing 84; personality preferences 92–94, 135, 236, 237; programme preferences 92, 93, 94–95; social space of 89–92, *90*; Sydney 211, **212**, 214, 214–215, 217, 218, 219, 223; viewing hours 90; *see also names of individual programmes and genres*
temporalities 122, 127, 154, 155–156, 166, 263, 333; music field 12, 50, 54–59, 61; of national cultural capital accumulation 253, 255
Tendulkar, Sachin 104, 107, 135, **238**, 239, **243**, 259–260, 302
tennis 103, 104, 107, 125, 135, 140
tertiary education 121, 127, 129, 139, 148, 157, 158, 180, 187, 335–336; age cohorts **193**, 194; and art tastes and practices 20, 21, 23, 26, 230; and book reading and book culture 41; Bradley Review 191, 194, 196; Dawkins Reforms 191, 194; distribution of institutionalised capital in 190–203; fields of study *see* fields of university study; and heritage tastes and practices 75; Indigenous participation in 224, 225, 243–244; intermediate class **152**, 153; massification of 188, 194, 195, 196, 200, 203; and musical tastes and practices 56, 58, 234; parental 157, 158, **159**, 160, 203–204; professional/managerial class **152**, 153, 243–244; and socio-economic status (SES) 188, 191, **192**, **193**, 194–196, **197**, 200, **201**, 203, 204, 207; and sport tastes and practices 239; and television tastes and practices 90, 91, 95, 98–99; working class **152**, 153; *see also* universities
Thomsen, Simon 59
Thorpe, Ian 103, 135, 140
thriller/adventure stories 36, 39, **42**, 44, 171
Throsby, David 241
Thurston, Johnathan 114, 240, 316
Tillers, Imants 17, 20, 31n9, 132
Tjapukai Aboriginal Cultural Park 71
Top Gear (TV programme) 88, 94, 95, 174
Torres Strait Islanders *see* Indigenous Australians
traditional popular cultural orientations (TPCO) 144–145, **155**, 155, 156, **160**, 181
Tramonte, Lucia 190
transnationalism 2, 3, 12, 250, 251, 263, 264, 266, 307–308, 331–332; and belonging 290–291
Tranter, Bruce 77, 78, 80, 81
Tsiolkas, Christos 43
Turner, Bryan 176–177
Twin Peaks (TV programme) 86
Two Lives (Seth) 43

Ultimate Fight Club (UFC) 317
Uluru-Kata Tjuta National Park 69, 135, 174
Under the Dome (TV programme) 88, 95
UNESCO (United Nations Educational, Scientific and Cultural Organization) 281
United Kingdom (UK) 147, 164, 166, 180, 189, 194, 196, 200; *see also* Great British Class Survey (GBCS)
United States (USA) 3, 166, 167, 177, 189, 196

universities 195–196, **197**, 207; drop-out and retention rates 200; preferred 153, 196; rankings 196; urban 210, 222
University of Melbourne 196
University of Sydney 196
urban cultural capital 208–211; *see also* Melbourne; Sydney
urban music 54, 57, **60**, 140, 174

The Value of Aboriginal Cultural Heritage project 241
Van Gogh, Vincent 17, 18, 31n10, 135, 140, **229**, **243**, 257
Vatican Museums (Italy) 71
Vautin, Paul 88, 92, 94, 237
Vivaldi, Antonio, *The Four Seasons* 53, 54, 57, 174, 177, **243**
vocational education 24, 31, 41, 134, **152**, 153, 158, **159**, 191, 239
'Vogue' (Madonna) 53, 135

Wacquant, Loïc . 101, 108, 266, 294

Wakeling, Paul 51
Walter, Maggie 241, 324
Warhol, Andy 27
wealth 153–154; inequality 148, 166, 167, 332, 336
Western Sydney University (WSU) 196
What Your Habits Reveal About Your Social Class (online quiz) 147
Whiteley, Brett 17, 18, 20, **22**, 135, 174, 175, **256**, 257
whiteness 302–303
Whitlam, Gough 11, 31n3, 67, 191
Who Do You Think You Are? (TV programme) 76
Williams, Serena 104, 109, 111, *38*, 239, **243**
Willms, J. Douglas 190

Winton, Tim 36, 39, 44, 234, 235, **243**
women: accommodation of partner's cultural tastes 276, 278, 279; art field tastes and practices 20–21, 271; and book reading and book culture 48n5, 234–235; and cultural capital accumulation 266, 268, 269, 270, 271, 274–275, 278–279; emotional work 268, 270; heritage tastes and practices 73, 230–231; Indigenous 229, 230–231, 233–234, 234–235, 236–237, 239, 243–244; musical tastes and practices *56*, 233–234; and sport *106*, 107, 108, 239; Sydney cultural participation 217; television tastes and practices 92, 236–237
Woods, Tiger 104, 107, 111, **238**, 239, 315
Woolf, Virginia 36, 39, 45, 135, 174, 175, 176
working class 7, 31, 77, 79, 139, 150, 163, 164, 165, 166, 181, 285, 311, 334; age composition **152**, 153; cultural capital profiles **161**, 161, 162, 163; cultural orientations 156, 158; economic capital 154; educational levels **152**, 153; fields of university study **152**; gender composition **152**; place of residence **152**, 153; and tertiary education **152**, 153, 195
world heritage 69, 71, 72, 125, 174, 230
Wright, Erik Olin 148

The X-Files (TV programme) 86
Xu Daozhi 224–225, 241

Yao Ming 104, 107
YouTube 13, 51, 84, 89, 219, 307
Yunupingu *see* Gurrumul Yunupingu

Zemiro, Julia 88, 92, 93, 237

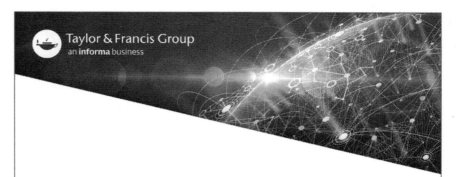